The Handbook Series

SCHOOLS ABROAD
OF INTEREST
TO AMERICANS

SCHOOLS ABROAD
OF INTEREST
TO AMERICANS

1985-86
6th Edition

PORTER SARGENT PUBLISHERS
11 Beacon Street
Boston, Massachusetts 02108

Copyright © 1985 by J. Kathryn Sargent

MANUFACTURED IN THE UNITED STATES OF AMERICA

LIBRARY OF CONGRESS CATALOG CARD NUMBER 67-18844

ISBN 0-87558-111-0

384202<del>4</del>

TABLE OF CONTENTS

   Austria — Belgium — Bulgaria — Czechoslovakia — Denmark
— Finland — France — Germany — Greece — Hungary —
Iceland — Ireland — Italy — Luxembourg — The Netherlands
— Norway — Poland — Portugal — Romania — Spain —
Sweden — Switzerland — United Kingdom (England, North-
ern Ireland, Scotland) — U.S.S.R. — Yugoslavia

TABLE OF CONTENTS

TABLE OF CONTENTS

PAGE LISTING OF COUNTRIES

SCHOOLS ABROAD OF INTEREST TO AMERICANS
PORTER SARGENT PUBLISHERS, INC.

Coordinator-Manager/Art Director   Jennie B. Fonzo

Senior Editor   Ann A. Himebaugh

Coordinating Editor   Peter M. Casey

Editor/Paste-up Artist   Karen E. O'Brien

Editor   Ken Seiger

PREFACE

Completely revised and updated, this 6th edition of *Schools Abroad* has been compiled from current data solicited by this office through hundreds of letters of inquiry as well as with assistance from international educational associations, consultants and agencies of the United States and foreign governments. The book's primary purpose is to objectively describe some 975 elementary and secondary schools in 132 countries of interest to young Americans and others seeking pre-college programs of study abroad.

In Section II we present — at no cost or obligation to the schools — the information parents and advisors want and ought to know. All schools described in this section have indicated either a history of enrolling American students or a willingness to consider American applications. The statistics are printed as supplied by the schools. The accuracy and completeness of a school description depend greatly on the thoroughness of the school's response. In preparing the descriptive text, all suggestions are carefully reviewed, but our editorial staff reserves the right to determine what information is pertinent and significant in keeping with our long tradition of impartial reporting of facts.

This book does not seek to evaluate differences among schools, although careful study of school descriptions may reveal varying approaches and attitudes. From an aggregate of information, we select those aspects which seem to most effectively characterize a school in the limited space available. Final selection of a school or program should come only after careful thought and planning — involving direct contact with prospective schools — as well as advice from reputable educational consultants and associations. Selecting a program solely on the basis of the school's own literature is unwise and may have unfortunate consequences.

A number of schools authorize Illustrated Announcements in Section I of the book. Through these individualized statements, schools are able to stress features they consider most significant in describing their programs and aims. All those concerned with international independent education welcome the opportunity to read these distinctive statements and a school thereby not only furthers recruitment, but public relations in general. However, a school's purchase of space in the autonomous Illustrated Announcements section does not affect the length or content of its free listing in Section II.

Section III is intended to be a representative sampling of post-secondary, specialized and summer opportunities available abroad. It includes some at college or university level, as well as others sponsored by private schools or travel organizations in the U.S.

Section IV, Additional Schools Abroad, lists schools for which limited information was available at time of publication. Information on schools received too late for inclusion in this 6th edition will appear in a future revised volume.

The editors wish to thank the hundreds of school officials in all parts of the world who supplied information to make this edition possible. We are also indebted to the many educational associations — in the U.S. and abroad — whose assistance in one form or another contributed to the completion of this book.

INTERNATIONAL SCHOOLS FOR INTERNATIONAL STUDENTS

by

W. Gray Mattern, B.A., M.A. (Hon.), D. Litt.

One of the well-recognized phenomena of the second half of the current century is the growth of transnational enterprise. It existed prior to the Second World War, of course, but it was spotty, largely confined to certain kinds of endeavor, and for the most part a peculiarly British sort of activity, an extension of the old outreach of an island people that for the better part of four hundred years planted the flag around the globe and almost always found a way to turn a shilling while they were at it.

Other nations — the Dutch, the Portuguese, the Spanish, the French, the Germans, even the Italians, amongst the Europeans — all had their day at it, but none lasted so long or made such a success out of it as did the British. Certainly none turned so gracefully from empire-builders and decorous exploiters into scrupulous international businessmen, using the old contacts and the long familiarity with the far-flung outposts of the crown.

But it was the Americans in the immediate post-war era, eyes newly opened from campaigns abroad, self-confident in the aftermath of victory, with a pocketful of new technology and industrial know-how, and — perhaps most important of all — uniquely prosperous while the rest of the developed world licked its wounds and wondered who had won after all — it was the Americans who set forth and in the matter of a decade made transnational business the biggest business in the world, with American capital and American expertise in commanding

Reprinted with permission from the 1984-1985 *Vincent/Curtis Educational Register,* Boston, Massachusetts.

lead. The giants at home became even more awesomely giant-like abroad; it seemed, for a while, as if no one else would ever come close. And whereas when Englishmen went abroad on their affairs of gain they took with them their clothes and their games and their customs but never their children (at least when they stopped being babes-in-arms), the American retinue was frequently less materially and culturally encumbered but almost always included the young. However, whilst father and mother too might be prepared to eat strange food, live in strange dwelling-places with funny furniture, take up new recreations and even new moral attitudes, they were determined that their children not lose out on what they would have had back in Bakersfield or Tulsa or Columbus. So they recreated, as near as they could, the schools of Bakersfield and Tulsa and Columbus in Tokyo and Tehran, Madrid and Makati, Cairo and Cali — and an awful lot of other places, too, where kudu and zebu replaced the deer and the antelope, and a "discouraging word" was in any case incomprehensible. By the end of the second decade after the war, there was practically nowhere on the globe that an American family might be assigned to live, by government or industry, where a fairly respectable U.S.-style education, at least through Grade 8, was not available.

But the Americans were not, after all, to have the goldmine to themselves forever. Almost imperceptibly at first, but then with increasing pace and vigour, other nationalities entered the competition for a share of the booming international trade and industrial development — the British, the Germans, the French, the Dutch, the Israelis, the Japanese, in major numbers, others with lesser delegations. And now, perhaps emulating the Americans in their family practice as they were doing in commerce, they more and more brought their families with them. Where there were sufficient concentrations of their own countrymen, they might sooner or later establish schools in their own national pattern, but at least to begin with, the tendency was to enroll their children in the expatriate of the community, which in most cases meant the American school (the British being the notable exception, setting up their own educational arrangements almost when there were only two or three families gathered together).

The results were interesting and highly significant. One, of course, was to broaden the base of financial support for many existing schools, permitting them to evolve from being essentially expedient support facilities for an itinerant, highly mobile, relatively homogeneous population, to a much more institutional mode of operation. They could move from temporary rented premises into permanent purpose-built facilities. They could hire staff who were not primarily junketeers paying for their travels by teaching along the way, but qualified and experienced men and women who had chosen to work in overseas schools because of the unique challenges of this discrete branch of the profession. And they could set up detailed Board policy manuals and long-range Planning Committees, organize international sports tournaments and arts festivals, establish sophisticated associations to provide a wide variety of support services to the member institutions and in-service training for teachers, and gradually encrust themselves with school songs and school colours and yearbooks and alumni associations and even, if the climate was suitable, grow ivy on the walls. They could, in short, claim to have come of age.

But another result of the broadening of the base of patronage was and continues to be much less obvious, though in the long run of potentially far greater significance. It was all very well, in the days when the American Community School of X had a student population 90% of whom were U.S. nationals, to offer a curriculum imported intact from Bakersfield or Tulsa or Columbus, complete with American teachers and American textbooks, American tests and grading systems, and American goals and results. After all, that was where the students had come from and where they would return — if they did not go on to another school of the same ilk. The statements of purpose often read — and some still do — "to keep children abreast of what their contemporaries are learning at home" (and of course everybody knew where that was) "and to prepare them to re-enter the schooling system at the appropriate level." But when "home" began to mean more and more different places and "the school system" to which clients intended returning their sons and daughters came in 57 varieties, the pressures mounted for some sort of reflection of this state of affairs in the academic programme.

The responses — they still go on — have been far from uniform. In some cases, to be sure, school boards and administrations simply dug in their heels and refused to make any significant changes, with predictable and usually not very happy results. But in other instances, the decision to retain the American format was not simply quixotic: the point has been made — and not entirely without justification either — that a good American-style school has more flexibility and offers greater opportunity for the exercise of individual choice and the pursuit of individual patterns of study and achievement than does any other style of academic institution. And surely it is true that the local autonomy characteristic of U.S.-style education, in matters of courses, requirements, standards and assessment procedures, can, theoretically, provide the base for almost any kind of curriculum a school might desire to offer. Indeed, it is the case that some of the best adaptations to the needs and desires of a highly heterogeneous student population are to be found in institutions which have evolved from those indistinguishable from U.S. domestic counterparts. In such cases, they have found new curricular patterns both reflecting the differing backgrounds, needs and goals of the children enrolled, and at the same time creating out of these differences a fresh synthesis, a truly international ingredient unique to these schools.

There have been other kinds of responses as well. Some schools have added another curriculum — most commonly that of the British General Certificate of Education, with examinations at Ordinary and Advanced Level set externally by one of the U.K. university boards. There is no attempt to blend the two programmes; they simply run side by side within the one institution, and students must choose one or the other at the appropriate entry point and then stick with the results thereafter. There is certainly no synsthesis, nor is any individual eclecticism permitted. In other instance, a curriculum based in a different language and cultural/educational tradition has been offered, creating two distinct divisions within the school, frequently with the result that the only truly international experience for students is that which takes place on the playing fields or in the unstructured social encounter. In a few cases, chiefly those of quite large institutions with major external resources, three or more curricula are available, organized to run side by side but on separate tracks, or with some little blending and intermingling along the way, as may be possible and expedient. Parallel to these developments, there have arisen, too, other types of schools catering to the mobile expatriate populations generated by international trade and government activity, often deriving from some particular set of historical circumstances — e.g., the schools operated by the European Economic Community for the dependents of its employees, essentially, in each case, nine schools under one roof; the similar type of schools organized by NATO; the schools established by the French Mission Laique, essentially French lycees with "international" sections; the United World Colleges, with their clear commitment to an international mix of students and global perspective as an essential outcome of the instructional programme. Another unique model is that of the Lycee International in St. Germain, on the outskirts of Paris. Starting life as the school providing for dependents of those serving at SHAPE, it has continued, after that organization moved northwards, and is now a French lycee under the auspices of the Ministry of Education, but including eight national sections — American, Dutch, German, British, Italian, Danish, Swedish, and Portuguese — in each of which students receive instruction in their own language, literature and history, while the rest of the curriculum is conducted, in French, as in any other state school.

Of all the attempts to respond creatively to the increasing heterogeneity of the expatriate population requiring schooling, one stands out as perhaps most significant world-wide, because of its impact on a large and annually increasing number of schools and their senior students. Not single curriculum or combination of curricula could, it has always been clear, adequately provide for the educational needs of children from such a bewildering variety of backgrounds; any particular solution was at best a compromise for some. But the problem became most critically acute as students approached the end of their secondary years and faced the necessity of presenting their credentials for university entry. An American curriculum, even with a solid Advanced Placement program, was fine for those wishing to enter U.S. colleges, but it did not much impress most universities in the U.K., left the German universities decidedly chilly, and was totally incomprehensible to the Korean, Nigerian and Argentinian admissions authorities. Much the same could be said for the French baccalaureate, the Spanish bachillerato, the German abitur, and indeed any examination system providing credentials peculiar to a particular national educational scheme. British GCE's probably had (and have) the widest acceptability beyond the bounds of their own country of origin, but they were very far from being universally recognized and understood.

But to cope with this unsatisfactory state of affairs there arrived on the scene in 1968 an entirely new curriculum and examination scheme, called the International Baccalaureate. It was a two-year final program of instruction for secondary schools (originally designed for the twelfth and thirteenth years, but now taught by many institutions at the eleventh and twelfth years), and while it maintained the breadth of study characteristic of U.S.-style education, it included the rigour and depth associated with British A-Level studies. There was also a strong required component of language, and a mandatory course basic to all of the disciplines, called "Theory of Knowledge." The IB seemed, thus, to bring together all of the ingredients which many of those who had been struggling for years with the problem of acceptability of credentials had been hoping to find.

Of course, university authorities around the world did not all at once leap to recognize the validity of the IB diploma — and until there was at least a significant measure of acceptance, schools were chary of committing themselves and their students. It was a classical "chicken-and-egg" problem, but slowly at first and then with increasing rapidity, schools adopted the program, and colleges and national educational systems have accorded their recognition. The struggle goes on, to be sure, and it is probably unlikely that the IB will ever become the one perfect final curriculum for all schools serving expatriate population or universally accepted by all institutions and systems of higher education. But it has certainly caught on with remarkable vigor and is clearly a better solution to the problem than any other currently available.

It seems likely, too, that the success of the IB will give renewed impetus to the attempts of international schools to find creative answers to all of the challenges inherent in operating such institutions, at all levels of the curriculum. And it is time. For these schools have now reached a level of maturity, possess the resources, and have accumulated a body of experience which should provide the opportunity to take the lead in demonstrating, for all schools everywhere, that communication and understanding amongst people of every conceivable kind of diversity is not only possible, but provides one of the few remaining avenues, perhaps even the last and only one — to a viable future for the planet.

WALTER GRAY MATTERN, JR. is the Executive Secretary of the European Council of International Schools. He was born in Tarrytown, N.Y., and received a B.A. from Yale University in 1946. He attended the Yale Graduate School of Education from 1948 to 1949, and holds honorary degrees form Wesleyan University and Western New England College. Mr. Mattern began his career in education in 1946 as an English teacher at the Taft School, and has served as headmaster at the Irving School in Tarrytown and the Wilbraham School in Massachusetts. A member of the Headmaster's Association, he is married and has four children.

EDUCATIONAL SYSTEMS
OF OTHER NATIONS

WHAT KINDS OF SCHOOLS ARE AVAILABLE?

Variety is one of the basic characteristics of independent schools abroad. Countless variables exist from country to country and from school to school. Nevertheless, to aid in gaining an overall perspective, most schools may be classified in one of three general groups.

The first group consists of privately operated American-sponsored schools, often referred to as "community schools." They have been founded by members of English-speaking business and diplomatic communities abroad in response to the need for an English-language school program for their children. Many such schools are missionary founded and sponsored; some are sponsored by corporations; others are operated by individuals of diverse backgrounds.

The American community school constitutes the nearest overseas parallel to schools in the United States. The curricula, teaching methods and materials are American, as are the majority of faculty and students. The basic objective of the academic program is to facilitate transfer back to schools in the U.S. and to prepare for the U.S. College Boards. Most of these schools offer courses in the language and culture of the host country and encourage enrollment from a variety of nationalities.

The second group of schools is variously referred to as binational, multinational or international and includes many American schools. They offer curricula adapted from more than one country's system of education and often enroll highly cosmopolitan students. Frequently instruction is in more than one language. Some schools offer a program leading to the International Baccalaureate, the first international university entrance examination.

Most of these schools, however, provide different national sections or divisions (e.g. English-speaking, French-speaking, German-speaking) which fulfill curricula and college preparation requirements of specific countries. Private schools in Switzerland probably best exemplify this kind of school, although schools of a multinational nature are located in many other parts of the world. American and foreign-sponsored international schools may include as many as 20 to 30 nationalities among their students and often have at least a half dozen countries represented on the faculty.

The third category of schools are those native to the host country. Here is the greatest opportunity to totally enter into another culture. There are, of course, many inherent obstacles to enrolling in an entirely native program, but the potential rewards are great. *Schools Abroad* contains a number of these schools throughout the world which indicate a desire to accept American students.

While a comprehensive comparison of differing national systems is beyond the scope of *Schools Abroad,* we provide the following capsules of educational systems of a few key countries represented in this volume.

Familiarization with the British system of education should help in understanding the concept of education elsewhere in Europe. The British influence, especially on the secondary level, is present in many other parts of the world.

UNITED KINGDOM

Although the two countries share a common heritage and language, the school systems of Great Britain and the U.S. differ widely. In England, independent secondary schools are called "Public Schools" and are usually boarding programs. A "Preparatory School" prepares for Public School, not for college or university. The school year is divided into three terms running from mid-September to mid-July, with a month's holiday in both winter and spring.

Grade Levels. An essential difference in the structures of the two systems is the concept of grade levels. A four-year secondary program, found almost universally in the U.S., does not exist as such in England. Boys and girls in English schools do not progress automatically from grade to grade (the term "grade" is not part of the English school vocabulary). Nor do pupils accumulate "credits" for having covered work at a certain grade level. Depending entirely on ability, a student may be placed in one of several basic "forms" and in different "sets" for mathematics and languages. Once ability has been demonstrated, a pupil may be promoted during the year, sometimes more than once. There is no automatic promotion at year's end.

Examinations. Required for admission to most Public Schools is successful passage of the Common Entrance Examinations (C.E.E.), taken before age 14. After two to three years in a Public School, the student may begin taking the General Certificate of Education (G.C.E.), the British equivalent of a national examination.

The G.C.E. is divided into two stages or levels, Ordinary ('O') and Advanced ('A') Levels. Ordinary Level is taken two or three years after the student enters Public School (ages 15-16), and covers usually six to eight subjects (with a maximum of twelve) spread over several terms. Once the 'O' Levels are behind him, the student moves into the Sixth Form to begin in-depth study and specialization. Most work during the next two years is concentrated on a continuous course in two or three subjects, probably in the same general field. At the end of this period (ages 17-18) the student takes the second stage of the G.C.E., the Advanced Level examinations, in his chosen subjects only.

If a student elects to go on to university, he usually stays another term or two and takes University Scholarship Exams. Six 'O''s and two 'A''s are generally required for university entrance, but even further study may be necessary as competition for admission increases.

There is no graduation ceremony at a British school. A student remains as long as necessary and then "leaves." The British sometimes use the term "leaver" to designate a graduate.

Age and Grade Equivalencies. Passage of the British G.C.E. 'O' Level roughly corresponds to graduation from an American secondary school. By age 15 or 16, the average British student has covered the same ground as a 17- or 18-year-old in the U.S. However, British children begin school at age 5 and have a slightly longer school year calendar. The American student who has graduated from a secondary school before going to England is usually fitted into a second-year Sixth Form with his own age group. Successful results in the G.C.E. 'A' Levels are regarded as the equivalent of having completed at least the first year of an American college course.

College Preparation and Entry. Only about one-third of the students who "leave" a British Public School go on to university. Several factors account for this. Until recently the concept of a liberal arts college was unknown in Britain. Many young people choose higher education only if a degree is required for an intended career such as law or medicine. Many firms and industries actually prefer to take students directly from school to conduct their own training.

The examination and selection procedures in British schools tend to screen university candidates rather thoroughly. Despite the "New Universities" founded in recent years and a growing number of colleges of technology, commerce, business studies and the creative arts, competition for entrance is even keener than in the U.S. because there are comparatively fewer places available.

FRANCE

French secondary schools provide a seven-year course of study leading to the State Baccalaureate examination. The youngest class, called *sixième,* is roughly equivalent to sixth or seventh grade in the U.S. and is composed of 11- and 12-year-olds. The *cinquième, quatrième, troisième, deuxième* and *première* follow. During the *première* (the sixth secondary year, equivalent to twelfth grade in the U.S.), students 16 or older may prepare for the first part of the Baccalaureate. The seventh secondary year, or *année philosophie,* is open to French students who have passed the first Baccalaureate exam or to foreign students of similar level. At the end of this final year, equivalent to the first year of college in the U.S., the second part of the Baccalaureate is required for admission to a French university.

NETHERLANDS

Secondary schools in the Netherlands which prepare for university entrance are grouped as higher institutions. These are the *gymnasia* or higher burgher schools *(hogere burger-schools)* for ages 12 to 18, which provide a broad and rigorous general education to enable a student to specialize in a major discipline immediately upon entering a university. Completion of the Dutch secondary curriculum corresponds approximately to passage of the British G.C.E., Ordinary or Advanced levels.

EDUCATIONAL ASSOCIATION MEMBERSHIP

Following are several educational associations for which school membership or affiliation is reported in the description of individual schools.

ASSOCIATION OF INTERNATIONAL COLLEGES AND UNIVERSITIES
William J. Petrek, President
  27, Place de l'Universite, 13625 Aix-en-Provence, France. Tel. (42) 23.39.35

An affiliate of the American Council on Education, the Association was founded in 1971 at Deree-Pierce Colleges in Athens, Greece. It provides a unified source of information regarding independent institutions in and around Europe offering a liberal arts or technical education.

EUROPEAN COUNCIL OF INTERNATIONAL SCHOOLS
Dr. W.G. Mattern, Executive Secretary
  18 Lavant St., Petersfield, Hampshire GU32 3EW, England

Founded in 1965, ECIS provides a variety of services to its member schools in Europe and over 400 associate member schools worldwide. It conducts professional conferences as well as specialized in-service courses, evaluates and accredits international schools, assists schools with staffing, offers placement assistance to teaching candidates and provides comprehensive consultative services. ECIS publishes the *Directory,* an annually revised descriptive guide to member institutions, and the semi-annual *International Schools Journal.*

THE INTERNATIONAL BACCALAUREATE OFFICE
Roger M. Peel, Director-General
  Route des Morillons, 15, 1218 Le Grand
  Saconnex, Geneva, Switzerland
  U.S. Office: 200 Madison Avenue, New York, NY 10016. Tel. 212-696-4464.
  H. Gilbert Nicol, Executive Director

The International Baccalaureate Office was established in Geneva in 1965 as a foundation under Swiss law and maintains a non-governmental status in official relations with UNESCO. The IB program involves two years of intensive preparation, corresponding to the American grade 12 and one postgraduate year. Students who pass the test are awarded a Diploma which is recognized for admission to universities in most countries. The IB is comparable to the British G.C.E. Advanced Level, the French Baccalaureate, and other national school leaving examination systems.

INTERNATIONAL SCHOOLS ASSOCIATION
CIC Case 20, CH-1211 Geneva 20, Switzerland. Tel. 33.67.17

A professional association, ISA provides advisory and consultative services to its international and internationally-minded member schools, as well as to other organizations in the field of education, such as UNESCO. The Association promotes innovations in international education, conducts conferences and workshops and publishes various educational materials.

INTERNATIONAL SCHOOLS SERVICES
C. William Schultheis, President
P.O. Box 5910, 13 Roszel Rd., Princeton, NJ 08540

An independent, nonprofit organization founded in 1955, ISS provides educational services to elementary and secondary schools abroad which enroll the children of personnel engaged in international programs of industry, commerce, technology and diplomacy. Recruitment of teachers and administrators, ordering of books and school supplies, financial management, retirement program services and liaison services between schools and individuals in the U.S. are among the many programs offered by ISS to nearly 300 American and international schools in all parts of the world, most of which are represented in this guide.

NATIONAL ASSOCIATION OF INDEPENDENT SCHOOLS
John C. Esty, Jr., President
18 Tremont St., Boston, MA 02108. Tel. 617-723-6900

The National Association of Independent Schools is a voluntary membership organization composed of more than 900 independent elementary and secondary schools in the United States and other countries, as well as 65 member associations. A nonprofit organization incorporated in 1962, NAIS provides a wide range of services to trustees, administrators and faculty. The Association maintains an affiliate membership classification of over 90 schools located outside the United States which have been in continuous operation for five years or more.

OFFICE OF OVERSEAS SCHOOLS
Ernest N. Mannino, Director
Room 234, SA-6, U.S. Department of State, Washington, DC 20520

Information is available on 160 independent elementary and secondary schools abroad which receive some assistance from the U.S. Department of State. These schools demonstrate American educational philosophy and prepare students to enter schools, colleges and universities in the United States.

The accreditation of schools serving American children abroad is provided through a cooperative agreement of the regional associations. American-type schools in Europe, Africa, the Near East, South Asia, Puerto Rico and the Virgin Islands are accredited by the Middle States Association of Colleges and Schools; the New England Association of Schools and Colleges accredits schools in Europe; schools in Latin America are accredited by the Southern Association of Colleges and Schools; and the Western Association of Schools and Colleges accredits American and international schools in East Asia. Schools for American dependents abroad which are sponsored by the U.S. Department of Defense are accredited by the North Central Association of Colleges and Schools.

MIDDLE STATES ASSOCIATION OF COLLEGES AND SCHOOLS
Cecile G. Betit, Secretary of the Association
  3624 Market St., Philadelphia, PA 19104

NEW ENGLAND ASSOCIATION OF SCHOOLS AND COLLEGES
Richard J. Bradley, Executive Director
  The Sanborn House, 15 High St., Winchester, MA 01890

NORTH CENTRAL ASSOCIATION OF COLLEGES AND SCHOOLS
Dr. John W. Vaughn, Executive Director
  Commission on Schools, P.O. Box 18, Boulder, CO 80306

SOUTHERN ASSOCIATION OF COLLEGES AND SCHOOLS
Bob E. Childers, Executive Director
  795 Peachtree St., N.E., Atlanta, GA 30365

WESTERN ASSOCIATION OF SCHOOLS AND COLLEGES
Don E. Halverson, Executive Director
  1614 Rollins Rd., Burlingame, CA 94010. Tel. 415-697-7711

AFRICA AND THE MEDITERRANEAN

ASSOCIATION OF INTERNATIONAL SCHOOLS IN AFRICA
Charles A. Kite, Executive Secretary
  The International School of Kenya, P.O. Box 14103, Nairobi, Kenya

MEDITERRANEAN ASSOCIATION OF INTERNATIONAL SCHOOLS
Elaine Amdurer, Executive Secretary
  American School of Mallorca, Calle Oratorio 9, Portals Nous, Mallorca, Spain

ASIA

EAST ASIA REGIONAL COUNCIL OF OVERSEAS SCHOOLS
Barbara Leister, Executive Secretary
c/o Singapore American School, 60 Kings Rd., Singapore 1026, Republic of Singapore

NEAR EAST SOUTH ASIA COUNCIL OF OVERSEAS SCHOOLS
Stanley Haas, Executive Director
The American College of Greece, P.O. Box 60018, 153-10 Aghia Paraskevi, Attikis, Greece

CANADA

CANADIAN ASSOCIATION OF INDEPENDENT SCHOOLS
Allison Roach, Executive Secretary
Branksome Hall, 10 Elm St., Toronto, Ontario M4W 1N4, Canada

LATIN AMERICA

ASSOCIATION OF AMERICAN SCHOOLS IN THE REPUBLIC OF MEXICO
Albert Argenziano, President
The American School Foundation of Guadalajara, Apartado Postal 6-1074, Guadalajara, Jalisco 44640, Mexico

ASSOCIATION OF AMERICAN SCHOOLS OF CENTRAL AMERICA
Keith Miller, Director
Lincoln School, P.O. Box 1919, San Jose, Costa Rica

ASSOCIATION OF AMERICAN SCHOOLS IN SOUTH AMERICA
James W. Morris, Executive Director
AASSA Regional Development Center, FIU, Bay Vista Campus, Biscayne Blvd. at 151st St., No. Miami, FL 33181

ASSOCIATION OF COLOMBIAN-CARIBBEAN AMERICAN SCHOOLS
Roger Krakusin, President
Apartado Aereo 2899, Cartagena, Colombia

INTERNATIONAL EDUCATIONAL CONSULTANTS

CONSULTANTS ON EUROPEAN SCHOOLS
Ilse Nelson
12 East 93rd St., New York, NY 10128. Tel. 212-369-7560

Established in 1954. Member of Independent Educational Counselors Association. Advice given on American and foreign schools in Europe — elementary, high school, pre-college; summer schools, camps, trips, language schools. Educational Adviser to the United Nations staff and missions.

EDUCATIONAL COUNSELING FOR SCHOOLS U.S.A & ABROAD
Emily S. Lewis
150 East 72nd St., New York, NY 10021. Tel. 212-861-7325

Member of Independent Educational Counselors Association. Mrs. Lewis has over 25 years of educational experience. She specializes in both American day and boarding schools and in schools abroad from the pre-school level through college.

EDUCATIONAL COUNSELING SERVICE, INC.
John Oliver Rich.
Birnam Wood Farm, Box 517, Clarcona, FL 32710. Tel. 305-886-3117

A founding member of Independent Educational Counselors Association. Mr. Rich, who has held teaching and administrative positions in European and American preparatory schools and colleges, offers parents and students guidance towards schools and programs in Europe.

THE GABBITAS-THRING EDUCATIONAL TRUST
J. Murrell, M.A., Senior Managing Governor
Broughton House, 6, 7, & 8, Sackville St., Piccadilly, London W1X 2BR, England. Tel. 01-734-0161

This organization offers advisory services regarding all aspects of independent education in Great Britain up to, but not including, university level.

OVERSEAS SCHOOLS SERVICES
446 Louise St., Farmville, VA 23901. Tel. 804-392-6445

OSS is a private, non-profit, educational consultant and staff recruitment service founded in 1972 by Yvonne E. Phillips (S.R.N., Q.N., S.C.M., H.V.) and her husband, Donald K. Phillips (A.B., M.A., Ed.D., Columbia). Four types of consultant recruitment services are offered: 1) to overseas Boards of Directors: conduct of the "search" for a new Headmaster or a new Superintendent; 2) to overseas Headmasters & Superintendents: recruitment, evaluation, short-listing of teaching and supervisory candidates; 3) to overseas parents: guidance, counsel, evaluation of educational problems; and 4) to international business firms: assistance to Personnel Divisions in the evaluation of individual and family suitability for overseas assignment.

THE TRUMAN & KNIGHTLEY EDUCATIONAL TRUST
Dr. M.A. Hooker, Chief Executive Governor
76-78 Notting Hill Gate, London W11 3LJ, England. Tel. 01-727-1242
Telex: 268141 (refer TK)

British educational agents and consultants, and publishers of *Schools,* an annual comprehensive directory of all independent schools in Great Britain.

OTHER SOURCES OF INFORMATION ON INTERNATIONAL EDUCATION

AMERICAN FIELD SERVICE INTERNATIONAL SCHOLARSHIPS
313 East 43rd Street, New York, NY 10017

Active in 65 nations with over 4500 students involved in its programs each year, AFS provides scholarships for students between the ages of 16 and 18 to live for a year or summer with selected families of different cultures, to attend school, and to participate fully in a new community.

THE AMERICAN-SCANDINAVIAN FOUNDATION
Lynn Carter, Director and Secretary
127 East 73rd Street, New York, NY 10021

Among its programs, the Foundation provides information, scholarships and grants on study programs and teacher exchange in Scandinavia. Publications: *Travel, Study, and Research in Sweden, Scandinavian Review,* a quarterly and *Scan,* a newsletter published eight times a year.

ASSOCIATION FOR THE ADVANCEMENT OF INTERNATIONAL EDUCATION
Gordon E. Parsons, Executive Director
Room 200, Norman Hall, College of Education, University of Florida, Gainesville, FL 32611

AAIE fosters international education through its School-To-School Projects, providing professional services and resource personnel to overseas schools, and through publications and yearly conferences.

BRITISH AMERICAN EDUCATIONAL FOUNDATION
Mrs. Frederick Van Pelt Bryan, Executive Director
351 East 74th St., New York, NY 10021. Tel. 212-772-3890

The BAEF offers qualified American secondary school graduates the opportunity to spend a year at an independent boarding school in the United Kingdom. Scholarships are awarded on the basis of financial need.

COUNCIL ON INTERNATIONAL EDUCATION EXCHANGE
205 East 42nd St., New York, NY 10017. Tel. 212-661-0310

Founded in 1947 as the Council on Student Travel, CIEE is a private, nonprofit membership organization of 168 colleges, universities, secondary schools and youth-serving agencies. Among the services it offers to institutions and individuals are International Student Identity Card, intra-European and transatlantic transportation arrangements, and information on work, study and travel opportunities abroad. The Council publishes *Work, Study, Travel Abroad: the Whole World Handbook, Where to Stay USA,* and *Volunteer! A Comprehensive Guide to Voluntary Service in the U.S. and Abroad.*

THE ENGLISH SPEAKING UNION
John D. Walker, Executive Director
16 East 69th St., New York, NY 10021

Under two exchange programs, boys and girls from participating private schools in the United States and Great Britain spend an academic year in a school in the opposite country. The program is designed primarily to provide the opportunity for American students to spend a postgraduate year in a British school. However, students may apply to spend their junior or senior year in a British school. Preference is given to applicants for a senior or postgraduate year.

FRIENDS WORLD COMMITTEE FOR CONSULTATION
Section of the Americas, 1506 Race St., Philadelphia, PA 19102. Tel. 215-241-7250

Publishes the Handbook of the Religious Society of Friends, which lists Friends schools throughout the world.

THE GOVERNING BODIES ASSOCIATION (GBA)
LT. Col. C.J.M. Hamilton, O.B.E., Secretary
The Flat, The Lambdens, Beenham, Reading, Bershier RG7 5JY, England. Tel. 0734 302677

INDEPENDENT EDUCATIONAL COUNSELORS ASSOCIATION
William B. Peirce, Assistant to the President
Cove Rd., P.O. Box 125, Forestdale, MA 02644
Tel. 617-477-1756

IECA is a nonprofit association founded in 1976, whose members provide parents with objective information concerning a wide range of educational opportunities for young people, including school placement abroad. The membership is pledged to accept fees only from parents who are their sole clients.

INDEPENDENT SCHOOLS INFORMATION SERVICE
Tim Devlin, Director
56 Buckingham Gate, London SW1E 6AG, England. Tel. 01 630 8793/4
U.S. Office: William Cobbett, Esq., Choate Rosemary Hall, Wallingford, CT 06492

ISIS provides information on more than 1300 elementary and secondary schools in the United Kingdom and Ireland. It is the official information center founded in 1972 by the leading associations of independent schools in England. Parents may contact ISIS International at the London address above for assistance with school placement of children living outside the United Kingdom.

INSTITUTE OF INTERNATIONAL EDUCATION
809 United Nations Plaza, New York, NY 10017

Founded in 1919, the Institute of International Education is a private, nonprofit organization which develops and administers programs of educational exchange for colleges, universities, foundations, private organizations, governments and corporations in the United States and abroad. IIE's services include free information and counseling, student hospitality programs, a research and reference library, conferences/seminars, an overseas application information service, and publications including *U.S. College-Sponsored Programs Abroad,* and *Teaching Abroad.*

NATIONAL COUNCIL OF INDEPENDENT SCHOOLS
Sarah M. Booth, Acting Executive Director
P.O. Box 279, Woden ACT 2606, Australia. Tel. (062) 823477

SWISS FEDERATION OF PRIVATE SCHOOLS
Lisette Butikofer, Director
40, rue des Vollandes, P.O. Box 171, CH-1211 Geneva 6, Switzerland

U.S. DEPARTMENT OF DEFENSE — OFFICE OF DEPENDENTS SCHOOLS
Room 152, Hoffman Building #1, 2461 Eisenhower Ave., Alexandria, VA 22331

THE UNITED STATES — UNITED KINGDOM EDUCATIONAL COMMISSION (THE FULBRIGHT COMMISSION)

Anne Collins, Chairman; Margaret McDonald, Student Adviser
6 Porter St., London W1M 2HR, England

The Commission was established in 1948 by the American and British governments to promote educational and cultural exchange between the two countries. A wide range of reference sources are available through the Student Adviser's Office.

HOW TO READ THE SCHOOL DESCRIPTIONS

Following the concept utilized in the annual *Handbook of Private Schools,* the editors have employed a standardized, abbreviated format which presents numerous statistics in a concise manner. Although the appeal of volume is international, the intent has been to provide information in a form understandable to the American reader.

To this end, certain liberties in terminology have been taken in the interest of clarity. In listings for schools which do not follow U.S. programs, grade spans are given as *equivalencies* of grade spans found in the U.S. Other Americanizations appear throughout the text with the use of terms such as 'Graduates' ('Leavers' is the common designation in British schools), 'College Prep,' 'Boarding,' 'Day,' 'Tuition' — which may have different meanings in a foreign setting.

For further clarification of the terminology used in *Schools Abroad* consult the Keys to Abbreviations, Examinations and Associations as well as the Glossary. Brief notes on systems of education in selected countries may be found in the Introduction.

1. **MODEL SCHOOL DESCRIPTION**
   Bdg Coed Ages 10-18; Day Coed 6-18. Gr N-12.

2. 1427 Lausanne (Vaud), Switzerland. Tel. (091) 9 29 31.

3. George L. Carson, BA, Dartmouth, EdM, Harvard, Head.

4. Col Prep Gen Acad. Tests SAT GCE IB. Curr—Intl USA. LI—Eng. A—Fr Eng Math. CF—Fr Ger Span Photog Drama Arts. SI—Tut Rem Reading.

5. Enr 220. B 90/110; G 110/10. Elem 50, Sec 170. US—150. Grad '84—25. Col—20.

6. Fac 45. Full 40/Part 5. M 39; F 6. US 10. Switzerland.

7. Tui Bdg 22,000 (+3000) SwF; Day 2700-9230 (+1500) SwF. Schol.

8. Summer Session. Acad Enrich. Tui Bdg 1000 SwF/mo; Day 500 SwF/mo. 8 wks.

9. Est 1956. Inc 1960 nonprofit. Sem (Sept-Je). ECIS ISS.

10. Bldgs 5. Dorms 4. Lib 10,000 vols. Courts 2. Field.

11.   With enrollment drawn chiefly from Switzerland and the United States, this school prepares students for the American College Boards as well as the British G.C.E. and International Baccalaureate. The study of French is required of all pupils from grade 5. The broad curriculum offers a variety of liberal arts electives and advanced placement courses.

   The active extracurricular and sports program is similar to that found in American secondary schools, and includes joint activities with students from surrounding Swiss schools. There are frequent excursions to cultural events and vacation-study trips to various parts of Europe.

12.   **See Also Page 67**

1. SCHOOL NAME AND SUMMARY.
   Boarding and/or day, sex and age range of students are designated. U.S. grade span or equivalent follows.

2. ADDRESS AND TELEPHONE.
   City or town (province, county, canton or *departement* follows in parentheses where applicable), street and/or mailing address and telephone number. In some cases a U.S. mailing address is reported on the next line.

3. ACADEMIC HEAD OF SCHOOL.
   The individual's title and educational credentials are given. This is the official who administers the academic program.

4. CURRICULUM, EXAMINATIONS FOR WHICH STUDENTS ARE PREPARED AND COURSE OFFERINGS.
   The basic curriculum is indicated as College Preparatory, General Academic, Business or Vocational.

   Examinations and college admissions tests for which graduates are prepared are cited next. For a Key to Examinations, see page 48.

   The country(ies) whose educational curricula a school follows are denoted after the heading '**Curr.**' '**Nat**' indicates a native or national curriculum.

   Classroom languages of instruction are given after the designation '**LI.**'

Standard courses are assumed, with English, mathematics and science offerings not reported unless of an advanced or unusual nature. '**A**' indicates advanced level or honors courses; '**CF**' denotes curriculum features, i.e., language offerings and other courses of special interest; '**SI**' calls attention to offerings in specialized instruction (tutoring or remedial courses).

5. ENROLLMENT AND GRADUATE RECORD.
   The total number of students enrolled is reported with the following breakdown: number of boys boarding/day; girls boarding/day. Elementary, secondary and postgraduate divisions. Number of U.S. students enrolled.

   Total number of graduates from a recent class follows. Where information is available, the number entering college or university is cited.

6. FACULTY.
   Faculty figures are detailed as follows: Total number. Number of full/part-time. Number of men, women. Number of U.S. teachers on faculty. Other countries predominantly represented on teaching staff are indicated.

7. TUITION AND SCHOLARSHIP AID.
   When both boarding and day divisions are maintained, both tuitions are given. Fees are reported in either U.S. dollars or native currency (abbreviations of foreign monetary units appear in each country's geographical description preceding the school listings). Grouped tuition figures (e.g. $3000-4500) give the fee span from the lowest to highest grades. Extra expenses are indicated in parentheses. Because of fluctuating international equivalency rates, parents are urged to contact the schools directly regarding fees. Scholarship aid, if available, is designated by **Schol.**

8. SUMMER SESSION.
   The type, orientation, tuition and duration are given for schools with summer programs.

9. ESTABLISHMENT, CALENDAR AND ASSOCIATION MEMBERSHIP.
   The establishment date, organizational structure (incorporated, nonprofit, proprietary, etc.) and religious affiliation or control are cited. The school calendar (semester, trimester) and months of operation follow.

Each school's American educational association membership is listed from reports issued by the associations. For a Key to Associations, see page 48.

10. SCHOOL PLANT.
A brief listing of school facilities is reported when available.

11. PARAGRAPH DESCRIPTIONS.
The comments are provided to amplify or supplement data reported in the statistics. They are written by the Sargent Staff according to the publisher's Editorial Policy, based upon questionnaires and supplementary literature received from school officials. Material is not presented when it does not serve to objectively define a school. Frequently information is provided on a school's curriculum, setting, location and history.

12. PAGE CROSS-REFERENCES TO ILLUSTRATED AN-NOUNCMENTS.
Many schools supply their own appraisals of ideals and objectives in paid advertisements in the "Illustrated Announcements" section. Page cross-references are appended to each of their paragraph descriptions.

KEY TO ABBREVIATIONS

A	Accelerated or Advanced Study
Acad	Academic
Accred	Accredited
Adm	Admissions
Admin	Administrator
Am, Amer	America, American
Anthro	Anthropology
Archaeol	Archaeology
Astron	Astronomy
B	Boys
Bdg	Boarding
Bio, Biol	Biology
Bldgs	Buildings
Bus	Business
Calc	Calculus
Can	Canada, Canadian
Cantab	A graduate of Cambridge Univ.
CF	Curriculum Feature
Chem	Chemistry
Chrmn	Chairman
Coed	Coeducational
Col	College
Comm	Commercial
Comp	Computer
Coord	Coordinator
crse(s)	course(s)
Crt(s)	Court(s)
Curr	Curriculum
Dev	Developmental
Dip, Dipl	Diploma
Dir	Director
Ec, Econ	Economics
Ed, Educ	Education
EFL	English as a Foreign Language
Elem	Elementary
Eng	England, English
Enr	Enrollment
Enrich	Enrichment
Environ	Environmental
ESL	English as a Second Language

Est	Established
Eur	European
Exec	Executive
F	Females
Fac	Faculty
Fr	France, French
G	Girls
Gen	General
Geog	Geography
Geol	Geology
Ger	Germany, German
Govt	Government
Gr	Grades
Grad	Graduates
Head	Headmaster, Headmistress
Hist	History
Indus	Industrial
Intl	International
Ital	Italy, Italian
JC	Junior College
K	Kindergarten
Lab(s)	Laboratory(s)
Lang	Language
Lat	Latin
LI	Language of Instruction
Lib	Library
Lit	Literature
M	Men
Man	Manual
Mech	Mechanical
Mex	Mexico, Mexican
Mod	Modern
mo(s)	month(s)
N	Nursery
Nat	Native, National
Nor	Norway, Norwegian
Oxon	Graduate of Oxford Univ.
PG	Post Graduate
Philos	Philosophy
Photog	Photography
Pol	Political

Port	Portugal, Portuguese
Prep	Preparatory
Pres	President
Prgm	Program(s)
Prin	Principal
Psych	Psychology
Quar	Quarter
Read	Reading
Rec	Recreational
Rem	Remedial
Relig	Religion
Rom Lang	Romance Languages
Russ	Russia, Russian
Scan	Scandinavia, Scandinavian
Sch	School
Schol	Scholarship
Sci	Science
Sec	Secondary
Sem	Semester
SI	Specialized Instruction
Soc	Social, Sociology
Span	Spain, Spanish
Steno	Stenography
Stud	Study
Supt	Superintendent
Swed	Sweden, Swedish
Switz	Switzerland, Swiss
Tech	Technical
Tel	Telephone
Theol	Theology
TOEFL	Test of English as a Foreign Language
Tri	Trimester
Trig	Trigonometry
Trng	Training
Tui	Tuition
Tut	Tutorial
Typ	Typing
UK	United Kingdom
var	variable
Voc	Vocational
wk(s)	week(s)
yr(s)	year(s)

GLOSSARY

B.E.P.C. Brevet Etudes Premier Cycle, an academic diploma in France awarded to students of about age 14 or 15

Bachillerato Completion of secondary level in Spanish-speaking Latin American countries

Gymnasium A secondary school in northern European countries which prepares for university

Lycee A secondary school in France which prepares for university

Premario Required language instruction in Portuguese.

Preparatory School A school in Great Britain which prepares for Public School

Public School An independent secondary school in Great Britain, usually a boarding school

KEY TO ASSOCIATIONS

AASCA	Association of American Schools of Central America
AASSA	Association of American Schools of South America
ACCAS	Association of Colombo-Caribbean American Schools
AICU	Association of International Colleges & Universities
AISA	Association of International Schools in Africa
A/OS	Overseas American Sponsored Elementary and Secondary Schools Assisted by the U.S. Department of State
CAIS	Canadian Association of Independent Schools
EARCOS	East Asia Regional Council of Overseas Schools
ECIS	European Council of International Schools
ISA	International Schools Association
ISS	International Schools Services
MSA	Middle States Association of Colleges and Schools
MAIS	Mediterranean Association of International Schools
NAIS	National Association of Independent Schools
NEASC	New England Association of Schools and Colleges
NE/SA	Near East South Asia Council of Overseas Schools
SACS	Southern Association of Colleges and Schools
WASC	Western Association of Colleges and Schools

KEY TO EXAMINATIONS

Consult the Introduction for additional information

C.E.E.

The **Common Entrance Examination** is required for admission to most Public Schools in Great Britain and is usually taken before age 14.

C.E.E.B.

College Entrance Examination Board tests are taken by students applying to college in the United States. Commonly referred to as "College Boards," they include the Scholastic Aptitude Test (SAT) and Achievement Tests in various subjects. The abbreviation **CEEB** in school descriptions indicates that a school offers preparation for College Boards.

French Baccalaureate

The national examination in France, the **Baccalaureate** is divided into two parts: the first portion usually taken after age 16, and the second after age 17 or 18.

G.C.E.

The **General Cerfiticate of Education** is the British equivalent of a national examination. Ordinary (O) Level is taken usually at age 15 to 16 and Advanced (A) Level at age 17 or 18. Scholarship (S) Level exams are frequently taken by university candidates following additional study.

International Baccalaureate

After two years of preparation, usually at the age of 17 or 18, students sit for the **IB,** which is recognized at most universities throughout the world as an acceptable entrance examination. See introduction for further explanation.

I.

ILLUSTRATED

ANNOUNCEMENTS

INDEX TO ANNOUNCEMENTS

INDEX TO ANNOUNCEMENTS

INDEX TO ANNOUNCEMENTS

INDEX TO ANNOUNCEMENTS

SALZBURG INTERNATIONAL PREPARATORY SCHOOL

Salzburg International Preparatory School is a coeducational boarding school located in one of the most beautiful cities of the world. The school offers an American college preparatory high school curriculum for grades 8 to 12 as well as a post graduate course. The curriculum lays emphasis on the traditional major subjects that are the necessary basis for successful university studies. All classes are taught in English and the American system of grades, tests and teaching techniques is used. Advanced Placement courses are available in Social Studies, Science, Mathematics, and Foreign Language. College Board, Achievement Tests, and Advanced Placement examinations are held on campus.

In addition to the academic major subjects, the school offers a wide range of electives in subjects such as competitive sports, computer programming, photography, skiing, tennis, riding, music and drama. The academic program is augmented by an extensive series of field trips and excursions to places such as Munich, Vienna, Paris, Rome, Florence, Zurich, Moscow and London.

During the summer months, the Salzburg International Preparatory School offers a summer language program. German, Russian and ESL courses lasting from two to eight weeks are offered during July and August. These courses are aimed at high school age students as well as adults.

The school currently has 165 students enrolled. Most students are housed in double rooms. The school is set in a picturesque park area 10 minutes from the historic center of Salzburg.

For catalog and information please write:

Admissions Director
Salzburg International Preparatory School
Moosstrasse 106
A-5020 Salzburg
AUSTRIA
Tel. (662) 44485, 46511
Telex 633065

SALZBURG INTERNATIONAL LANGUAGE CENTER

The Salzburg International Language Center offers intensive summer courses in German, Russian and English. These courses are designed primarily for American and European high school age students, and are organized under the auspices of the Salzburg International Preparatory School. Classrooms, language labs, library facilities and supervised dormitories are housed on the SIPS campus in a suburb of Salzburg.

The German program lays emphasis on intensive program practice, i.e. letting the students actually speak German as much as possible as well as providing a solid foundation in German grammar. Classroom construction is enriched by language lab sessions and by joined activities with the Center's German speaking students. German language books and periodicals as well as numerous German video movies are available in the campus' library.

The Language Center offers two intensive introductory Russian courses as well as ESL courses during the months of July and August. Russian is offered at an introductory level only, English as a Second Language is offered at all levels.

Students who are under 17 years of age are housed in a separate dormitory tract, and are supervised by full time professional counselors who coordinate numerous recreational, cultural and sporting activities.

The language courses are enriched by numerous excursions through the surrounding Alpine area and by trips to cities such as Vienna, Munich and Venice.

For catalog and information please write:

**Admissions Director
Salzburg International Language Center
Moosstrasse 106
A-5020 Salzburg
AUSTRIA
Tel. (662) 44485, 46511
Telex 633065**

BREITENEICH COURSES

A-3580 Horn
Schloss Breiteneich
AUSTRIA

Walter H. Sallagar,
Director

Breiteneich offers a unique musical and cultural course of study in its four-week summer program. The program which is open to all ages specializes in wind instruments.

WIND CHAMBER MUSIC. This course specializes in the Viennese style of interpretation. It deals with a wide range of chamber music selected through long professional experience.

MUSIC OF THE MEDIAEVAL & RENAISSANCE. This course is designed for well advanced players and singers. It opens possibilities for coaching ensembles with emphasis on recorders, shawms, sackbuts, crumhorns and gambas. Special attention is given to style and interpretation.

INSTRUMENT MAKING. Breiteneich has several workshops with modern and historic tools and machines. The course is an introduction to woodwind making and combines enough theory and practice for the production of satisfying instruments.

RENAISSANCE COURTLY DANCING. Dancers receive information and melodic line of each dance studied. A final performance is staged in an historic setting using costumes and live music. Costume making for dancers.

Breiteneich conducts Term I from July 14-28, and Term II is held from July 28-August 11. The program is situated near Horn in Lower Austria, surrounded by beautiful landscape. Course work is complemented by concerts, jogging, yoga and swimming. Living accommodations are available.

SEA PINES ABROAD
A-5324 Faistenau bei Salzburg
AUSTRIA

Eva-Maria Rowley, *Director*

Located in a rural ski-resort village near Salzburg, Sea Pines Abroad is a co-educational American boarding school which offer its students a sound academic program, the enrichment of supervised travel to many fascinating places, a close and cordial relationship with the people and culture of Austria, and a warm friendly atmosphere. It accepts students from grades 9 through 12 and prepares them carefully in the fundamental subjects needed as a foundation for success in college. Its enrollment is limited to 60 students of proven academic ability. All courses are taught in English and the faculty is American. During the school year, the students visit Venice, Munich, Vienna and other cultural centers of Italy or France. Five ski lifts are within walking distance of our front door and many more are only a short drive away. We invite you to send for our catalog.

SUMMER CAMPS AND SUMMER SCHOOLS

Over 1100 summer academic, travel, pioneering, camping and recreational programs are described in this comprehensive *Guide to Summer Camps and Summer Schools.* Listings are arranged by type, specialty and individual features. Data includes location, enrollment, director's winter address, fees, length of session and other pertinent data.

Special programs for the handicapped and maladjusted, as well as for those with learning disabilities are included. The geographic range covers recreational programs in the U.S. and Canada, and travel programs throughout the U.S., Canada, Mexico and abroad.

Published biennially, the *Guide* is a comparative reference for all types of summer opportunities. The *Guide* is designed for the counselor or parent concerned with meeting the specific needs of boys and girls.

Write for brochure and order form.

PORTER SARGENT PUBLISHERS, INC.
11 Beacon Street, Boston, MA 02108

ST. JOHN'S INTERNATIONAL SCHOOL
Drève Richelle 146-1410 Waterloo
BELGIUM

Sr. Barbara Hughes, FCJ, *Superintendent*

St. John's is a private, coeducational, Catholic-ecumenical school offering a total environment of warmth and dedication that lets every student know he really counts as an individual. The elementary day school (Grades K-8) was established originally in Brussels in 1964, and moved to Waterloo in 1969. The high school was established in 1971, and began accepting boarding students in 1978. It is fully accredited by the Middle States Association.

The nursery school was opened in 1979. The elementary school is fully accredited by the Middle States Association and the European Council for International Schools.

The school is located in a residential area on its own grounds a short distance from the historic battlefields of Waterloo. It is easily accessible from Brussels by a fast autoroute.

St. John's stresses contemporary education familiar to students from schools in the United States and other English-speaking countries. General instruction is in English, with French as a second language. An American course of study is basic, with Advanced Placement courses available. However, a flexible curriculum includes preparation for the British G.C.E., 'O' level, and the International Baccalaureate. Approximately 60% of the students are American, but students from 35 other countries contribute to the varied ethnic and religious environment.

Advanced courses are offered in mathematics, the sciences, English, History, French and art. Independent Study is available, and the school has a Chapter of the National Honor Society. Religion classes are held twice weekly, and full-time college and personal counseling services are provided. Supplemental instruction may be arranged for children whose needs cannot be met completely in the classroom.

In addition to academics, St. John's offers a year-round, well-balanced interscholastic athletic program for both elementary and high school levels. Teams include cross-country, volleyball, basketball, softball, baseball, soccer, swimming, tennis and cycling. Varsity and Junior Varsity teams are open to grades 9-12.

Among extra-curricular activities are interest clubs such as Art, Publications, Archery, Photography, Chess and Drama. During the spring and fall, kayaking trips in the Ardennes and sailing trips to Holland are organized; and cultural trips to France, Italy and Germany. Many trips are taken during school vacations to other cities and countries. During mid-winter, ski trips are organized and students may take several hours of ski instruction each day.

COPENHAGEN INTERNATIONAL JUNIOR SCHOOL
Stenosgade 4
DK-1616 Copenhagen V, DENMARK

Inez Venning, B.A., M.A., *Principal*

Founded in 1973, Copenhagen International Junior School provides a coeducational day program for children in kindergarten through grade 9. The structured curriculum aims to develop basic educational skills as well as study habits which will serve children throughout their school careers.

Students in kindergarten through grade 6 are taught in self-contained classrooms which are highly individualized. Danish is taught in all classes, and pupils elect French or German beginning in grade 5. The departmentalized program in grades 7 to 9 includes mathematics, language arts, science, social studies, French or German, music, art and physical education. English as a Second Language is conducted on a small group basis in all grades. Instrumental music, a variety of sports, student council and school publications are among the extra-curricular activities. Students also enjoy the many cultural and historical opportunities in Copenhagen.

CIJS strives to help children of all lands to maintain a sense of their roots and at the same time to develop an international awareness that is open-minded and judicious. This principle of unity with respect for diversity is one of the strengths of international education and one which the school especially seeks to foster.

For information on admissions contact the Principal's Office.

ROUDYBUSH FOREIGN SERVICE SCHOOL

Place des Arcades
SAUVETERRE DE ROUERGUE
(AVEYRON) FRANCE

Franklin Roudybush, A.B., M.A., Ph.D., *Director*

Founded seventy-five years ago, the Roudybush Foreign Service School (formerly Crawford's) opened a European school to continue its specialty of preparing men for the foreign service.

Here a program, for boys 16 or over, offers six months of study on the continent before entering college. Courses are offered in both French and English so that students can do their work in either or both languages.

Men over 20 are prepared for the foreign service examinations and take courses in a local university. Portuguese and Spanish, in conjunction with diplomatic and commercial courses, are now offered in a beautiful villa, in Moledo do Minho in Portugal on the Spanish frontier for both secondary and college age students.

Emphasis is placed on drawing and painting, especially still life, antiques, portraits and composition. The country lends itself to interesting landscapes.

Students and their families may enjoy residence and courses in arts and painting at Sauveterre, Aveyron, France, adjacent to the Pyrenees and the Mediterranean.

At the Summer School, which begins June 15, advantage is taken of the school's location in the country, with golf, fishing, hunting, tennis, and rowing. Popular extra-curricular activities, and again social contacts with French families intensify the language program.

PARIS AMERICAN ACADEMY

Richard Roy, *Director*

Live and study in the most exciting school in the world — the city of Paris. The Paris American Academy enrolls students from 16 years of age who are interested in studying the French language and culture. Founded in 1965 by its director, Mr. Roy, PAA also features university-credit courses in painting, sculpture, ceramics, photography, drawing, printmaking, and art history. The School of Fashion of PAA consists of practical courses in fashion design, illustration, textiles, draping and marketing. Guest designers frequently present seminars and lectures. The Paris American Academy has established a warm rapport with the world of fine arts and welcomes people sensitive to the joys of learning. Listed below are the study programs available —

- ACADEMIC YEAR — Oct 15 — May 20
- SPRING TERM — Feb 3 — May 20
- SUMMER IN FRANCE — July 1 — Aug 4
- JANUARY INTERIM — Jan 3 — Jan 29
- FASHION WORKSHOPS — June — Sept — Jan
- INTERIOR DESIGN/ ARCHITECTURE — Jan & June

To apply to these programs contact —

PARIS AMERICAN ACADEMY
9, Rue Des Ursulines
75005 Paris
FRANCE

ODENWALDSCHULE

GERMANY

Dr. Wolfgang Harder, *Director*

The ODENWALDSCHULE, founded in 1910 as a part of the "Progressive Education Movement" of that time, is a German boarding school of international reputation.

Although times and conditions have changed, the basic philosophy still is:

* that man is not only mind but body and soul as well
* that learning by doing is an indispensable concept
* that learning together should be completed by living together and working together
* that free and courageous citizens can only be educated in a community which is friendly and open and which expects responsibility of every member.

The school is rather small: 270 boarders, ranging from about 9 to about 20 years of age, 2/3rds of them boys, live in 35 family-type groups together with their teachers in 14 different houses.

All "normal" and some unusual academic subjects are taught, but the younger students (grades 5-10) also have to complete a serious handicraft-training (which is optional in grades 11-13).

The German "Abitur," a certificate of general education normally recognized in the U.S. as something between the high school diploma and a B.A., which is the standard requirement for entering a European university, can be achieved within the last three years (grades 11-13), assuming sufficient knowledge of German.

The Odenwaldschule is situated in a beautiful mountainous forest district about 20 miles north of Heidelberg.

Inquiries should be addressed to:

Odenwaldschule Ober Hambach, 6148 Heppenheim 4, Germany

AMERICAN COMMUNITY SCHOOLS

"Heywood", Portsmouth Rd.
Cobham, Surrey KT11 1BL
ENGLAND

The American Community Schools were founded in 1967 to serve the needs of the international business families in Greater London. Because of the mobile nature of these families, the Schools' curriculum is designed to facilitate transitions from one American or international school to another.

Two distinct and geographically separate campuses are operated: Uxbridge, Middlesex, located on an 11-acre site northwest of London; and Cobham, Surrey situated on a 128-acre country estate southwest of London. Both programs are nonsectarian, coeducational day schools with lower, middle and high school divisions offering coordinated college preparatory curricula from pre-kindergarten through grade twelve. While each campus has its own special character, both follow the principles and practices of American education. The Schools are traditional in outlook and observe high standards of scholarship which are reflected in a curriculum that is basic, rigorous and academic. High standards of discipline create a school where students exhibit responsible behavior and have respect for the rights and property of others.

Academics are organized around language, literature, mathematics, natural science, social studies, physical education, and the visual and performing arts. These subjects are basic and constitute the foundation on which subsequent education rests. A carefully selected teaching staff takes an active role in the development of a student's values, ethics, and moral sensitivity. School related activities are designed to stimulate creative and imaginative powers. Extensive extracurricular sports and non-sports teams, clubs and activities are provided.

Confidence in our program was expressed by the New England Association of Schools and Colleges and the European Council of International Schools in May of 1982 when the School received accreditation.

THE AMERICAN SCHOOL IN LONDON

2-8 Loudoun Road
LONDON, NW8, ENGLAND
Telephone: (01) 722 0101

Founded in 1951, The American School in London is an independent, non-profit trust administered by a Board of Trustees composed of distinguished members of the educational, business and professional communities. The school offers a full, high quality, American curriculum from Kindergarten to grade twelve including a wide range of extracurricular, music, art, drama and sports activities.

Dedicated to the promotion of scholarship, international understanding and responsible citizenship, the school is open to all who can profit from its programs, regardless of nationality, race or creed.

The school's modern building complex located in St. John's Wood provides its 1400 students with extensive facilities including seventy-eight classrooms, six science laboratories, two theaters, a double gymnasium, four art studios, five music rooms, a large woodworking/ ceramics area and two libraries containing 35,000 volumes and large audio-visual department. The building is divided into three distinct sections — lower, middle and upper schools — each with a separate faculty and administration.

In 1977, after rigorous self-study and evaluation by a team of American educators, ASL earned American accreditation from the Middle States Association of Colleges and Secondary Schools.

The school continues to present a demanding academic program which enables graduates to gain admission to colleges and universities of the first rank in the United States.

THE HAMPSTEAD INTERNATIONAL SCHOOL — LONDON

(Grades PK-8)

The Hampstead International School is the only American-oriented international elementary school in Central London. Small classes, a home-like atmosphere, and a dedicated and highly trained staff of British and American teachers enable children to settle in without difficulty. With its completely individualized program, the School meets the needs of children wherever they fall on the ability spectrum. A rigorous academic program drawing on the resources of the whole of London and enriched by the presence of children from around the world, makes a stay at the Hampstead International School a broadening and unforgettable experience.

For information write to:
Mrs. Edna Murphy, Principal
The Hampstead International School
16 Netherhall Gardens
London NW 3, England

STOVER SCHOOL

Newton Abbot, Devon
ENGLAND

Mrs. W. Lumel, *Head Mistress*

The Stover School overlooks the southeastern slopes of Dartmoor and is beautifully located within five miles of a seaside resort. Operating on a boarding and day basis, the school accepts girls between the ages of 11 and 18. The British-oriented curriculum prepares students for the Ordinary, Advanced and Scholarship levels of the General Certificate of Education, Certificate of Secondary Education and University Entrance. The comprehensive academic program is complemented by athletic opportunities in lacrosse, hockey, netball, tennis and swimming. In addition, girls enjoy a wide variety of extracurricular actitivies.

Information on admissions may be obtained from the Head Mistress, Tel. Newton Abbot 4505.

BROWN & BROWN AND TUTORS, OXFORD

OXFORD, ENGLAND

Mrs. C. H. Brown, M.A. (Oxon), *Principal*

Brown & Brown is a tutorial establishment preparing pupils for University and Polytechnic Entrance in the United Kingdom and the U.S. by private tuition. The course of study leads to the General Certificate of Education and the Oxford and Cambridge Entrance Examinations. Pupils are also prepared for Advanced Placement examinations. The establishment is a member of the Association of Tutors Incorporated, the Independent Schools Association and holds associate membership in the European Council of International Schools.

The tutorial system is based on that of the University, where students work under the supervision of one or more tutors. It is expected that a piece of written work, based on a recommended reading-list, is prepared for each tutorial. Weekly meetings are held with each student to review his reports. The tutors are usually engaged in doctoral research at the University. Suitable accommodations in central Oxford are arranged for all pupils. Tuition is individual, with flexible terms usually of 10 to 13 weeks in duration. Short vacations courses, in which students may design their own programmes are also arranged.

Prospectuses are available from The Secretary, 20 Warnborough Road, Oxford. Telephone: (STD. 0865) 56311. Telex: 83147 BBTO/ORG.

BATTISBOROUGH SCHOOL

ENGLAND
Simon Gray, B.A., M.Phil. (Cantab),
Headmaster

Battisborough was founded in 1955 by a master from Gordonstoun School, whose founder, the late Dr. Kurt Hahn, was a governor for many years.

The School has a maximum of 65 boys and girls between the ages of 13 and 18 and aims to develop the strengths and potential of each student both as an individual and as a member of the community. All students live within the school campus.

Students are taught to GCE O Level and A Level (since 1985) in the usual range of subjects, but the organization of the school permits some flexibility on the age at which the GCE is taken and allows for weaker candidates to take the CSE in addition. The American SAT and TOEFL exams and the Cambridge English exams may also be taken.

The size of the school, very small teaching groups, a weekly reporting system between the student's personal tutor, teachers and headmaster; the development of organised personal study habits combine to make Battisborough particularly suitable for those who dislike larger institutions or are transferring from another country's educational system.

In addition to some regular sporting activity during the week each student chooses a major weekend activity from canoeing, climbing, wind-surfing and the expedition club and follows an appropriate programme which includes elements of other activities. As individuals become more proficient they are expected to assist in instructing others. This develops into a form of service, which with the Cliff Rescue, conservation and First Aid Work emphasises the individual's duty to be of help to others. Such use of the outdoors helps to instill self-discipline and personal motivation; qualities which further assist a student's academic progress and all-round education.

For families resident overseas, we are able to arrange end of term traveling; half-term programmes and an escort service from the London airports. Parents are always welcome at the school.

BATTISBOROUGH SCHOOL
Devon PL8 1JX Holbeton
Tel: Holbeton (075 530) 223
Telex: 45639 Comput G

MILLFIELD SCHOOL
STREET, SOMERSET, ENGLAND
Telephone: Street 42291
Headmaster:
C.R.M. Atkinson, B.A. (Durham), B.A. (Queen's), M.Ed., D.L.C.

JUNIOR AND PREPARATORY SCHOOL:
EDGARLEY HALL, GLASTONBURY
Telephone: Glastonbury 32446
Headmaster: T.M. Taylor, M.A., Dip.Ed., M.I. Biol.

Millfield is a co-educational Boarding/Day school, with over 1,000 pupils and 165 members of staff. These numbers allow relatively small classes and greater timetable flexibility and subject choice (for instance 39 subjects at G.C.E. 'A' level and 49 subjects at 'O' level are annually taken); and there is ample opportunity to take part in some 40 extra-curricular activities.

Whilst appropriate educational treatment is provided both for those who are gifted in any sphere and for those who, perhaps because of dyslexia or because they are slow learners and unacademic, find 'O' and 'A' levels difficult paths to follow, the majority fit happily in between these two extremes and clear their academic hurdles in step with their contemporaries.

It may help parents to know that about 100 pupils annually gain entry to Universities and an average of 20 are successful Oxbridge applicants. And, in recent years 20 or more pupils have gained international recognition each year in a variety of sports.

Traditional discipline exists alongside both traditional teaching methods and the use of closed-circuit television and other modern aids. The work of both the Remedial English and the Foreigners' English Departments is internationally recognised.

A significant number of bursaries is available, on a competitive basis, for those who show both attainment and high potential in academic, sporting or artistic fields. Formal academic and/or music scholarship examinations may be taken annually in spring.

Millfield Junior School, Edgarley Hall, prepares boys and girls aged 8 to 13 for Common Entrance Examination for entry to Millfield and other public schools. The teaching methods and tutor-to-pupil ratio and facilities are very similar to those at Millfield. There are approximately 400 pupils and 60 members of staff. Scholarship examinations are held in spring.

Prospectus, and further details concerning applications for admission available from the Tutor for Admissions at the Senior School or from the Headmaster at the Junior School.

MARYMOUNT SCHOOL
on the outskirts of London

- Day and boarding school for girls

- Grades 7-12, 12-18 years

- American College Preparatory Curriculum

- International Baccalaureate Programme

- Excellent university entrance rate

- Many nationalities and religions represented

- Associate schools in Rome, Paris and New York

For details apply to:
Sister Breda Shelly, Principal
Marymount School
George Road, Kingston upon Thames
Surrey, KT2 7PE, ENGLAND
(Tel. 44 1 949 0571)

BUCKSWOOD GRANGE
INDEPENDENT CO-EDUCATIONAL SCHOOL

BUCKSWOOD GRANGE

Uckfield,
East Sussex TN22 3PU
ENGLAND
Tel: (0825) 3544
Tlx: 943763 Crocom G

Buckswood Grange is a coeducational boarding school in Sussex, England, accepting children from the age of 10. We offer a broad-based, balanced curriculum leading to the CE Examinations at 16+.

At Buckswood Grange it is our job to cast the net of opportunity so wide that any talent gets a chance to develop. We believe that the concept of the average pupil must give way to the concept of an infinite variety of youngsters heading for an infinite variety of success. To help achieve this the School remains a close-knit, family-based community, multi-national in make-up and limited, by design, to under 100 students.

A small school puts the emphasis back on individuals both inside the classroom (with an average of 12 students each) and outside: and we build on those traditional values, determination to succeed, self-reliance, independence of thought and straightforward, good manners — in other words those essential qualities associated with a British education.

Buckswood Grange, an elegant Regency house, stands in its own grounds on the outskirts of Uckfield, a quiet Sussex town, and is within easy reach of London and the airports.

ART HISTORY STUDY VISITS

ITALY

This four-week Summer Programme has been designed for juniors and seniors who are interested in indepth art history study stays in Italy's three most important cities — Florence, Rome and Venice.

Although students return with unforgettable memories of happy times spent in the world's most beautiful cities, they will also have immersed themselves in the history and art of the European tradition. After arriving in Rome, students are taken by private coach to *S. Ginesio,* an enchanting medieval hill town near Assisi. It is an ideal place for the course of introductory lectures which initiate them into the main art historical themes of the following weeks. After the introductory three days, the programme continues with a week in Rome, one in Florence and one in Venice. The last three days are again in *S. Ginesio* where the experiences of the preceding three weeks can be considered and discussed with the art historians and where individual projects can be completed.

In Rome, Florence and Venice, students will visit galleries, museums, palaces, churches and other monuments, and they will learn to look at works of art with historical understanding. Students are also provided with free time for recreation and optional excursions out of the cities. Each group will be limited to 30 students that will be accompanied by two professional art historians, a tour administrator and a faculty member from one of the American schools represented as chaperon. Accommodation is in pensioni in the historic centres of the cities. The Summer Programme is based on 21 years of experience of arranging similar courses for English students in the fall and spring sessions.

Further information may be obtained from:

John Hall, *Director*
Academic Study Abroad Inc.
3 Sunset Drive
Armonk, New York 10504
Tel: (914) 273-2250
Telex SWIFT UR ATT ASA

ABC CENTER OF ITALIAN LANGUAGE & CULTURE

Piazza dei Ciompi, 11
50122 Florence, ITALY
Tel. 055/241191
Massimo Pasquinelli, *Director*

The ABC Center is located in the very heart of Florence, in Piazza dei Ciompi (with its typical flea market) in the house of a famous Florentine sculptor of the 15th century, L. Ghiberti. Although the program is operated on a day basis, living accommodations can be arranged.

ABC offers a large variety of Italian language courses. Moreover, it is possible to attend special courses such as History of Italian Art, Architecture in Florence, Italian Literature and History, Commercial Correspondence and Italian Cooking. Opportunities to learn weaving, macrame and vegetable dyeing are also available as well as courses in Italian Tarots and Medicinal Herbs. Films are shown on a monthly basis. Free seminars on topical and cultural subjects are held in the afternoons, and by taking part in them, our students can observe their improvement.

The program is situated in the building which is also the seat of the Cultural Centre 'Michelangelo Buonarroti.' Students may participate in activities sponsored by the Centre which include theatre, photography and folk dancing.

In addition to extensive information on cultural events and shows, ABC periodically conducts guided tours of Florence and Tuscany. ABC aims at facilitating contacts both between students and teachers and among students themselves. Dinners, parties, tours in the country and to the seaside are organized to give students the opportunity to further their knowledge of Italian culture.

ISTITUTO LINGUISTICO MEDITERRANEO

Italian language school for foreigners

Istituto Linguistico Mediterraneo is approaching all those who wish to learn the Italian language or to improve their knowledge. The school organizes its courses in Pisa and Livorno, cities in Tuscany that are far away from mass tourism. *Pisa,* city of great historical and cultural interest in the heart of Tuscany, is considered the ideal place for studying Italian. Istituto Linguistico Mediterraneo of Pisa organizes courses of Italian language from March to December. Livorno shows itself as a "happy" city at the sea with a modern touch and an exceptionally mild climate. Livorno is connected to the Isles of Elba, Capraia, Corsica and Sardegna and it is a center for all lovers of sea and water-sports. Istituto Linguistico Mediterraneo of Livorno organizes courses from April to September.

Istituto Linguistico Mediterraneo organizes the following courses: General course of 80 hours monthly — Intensive course of 30 hours per week — Italian grammar course of 40 hours monthly — Individual intensive course of 10/20/30/40 hours per week — Commercial correspondence of 20 hours monthly. 4 (four) teaching levels. Class max of 10/12 students.

56100 PISA
Via C. Battisti, 3
Italy
Tel: 050/598066-48157

57100 LIVORNO
Via Marradi, 30
Italy
Tel: 0586/804326/810136

JOHN CABOT INTERNATIONAL COLLEGE

Via Massaua, 7
00162 Rome
ITALY
Tel. (06) 8395519

Established in 1972, John Cabot is included in the accreditation of Hiram College, Hiram, Ohio, and all credits are fully transferable to Hiram College. Cabot's elegant location off the Nomentana allows students easy access to all points in Rome. Travelling to countries abroad is facilitated by nearby train and air terminals. The curriculum offers a four-year Bachelor in Business Administration (the only B.B.A. given in Italy), and a two-year Associate of Arts. Students may attend up to their third year at John Cabot for a B.A. degree. Cabot College gives students of every nationality a unique study and living experience which broadens their educational background and encourages the self-reliance necessary to successfully live in a world of rapid change.

For further information write to the Director of Admissions.

THE HANDBOOK OF PRIVATE SCHOOLS

As the most comprehensive reference book of its kind, *The Handbook of Private Schools* contains current facts on over 1800 elementary and secondary boarding and day schools in the nation.

Each annual edition reports on the thousands of changes in the areas of enrollment, curriculum, facilities, administrators, faculty, fees and graduates. Many of the listings include an historical description of the school and the dominant personalities who have influenced it, as well as a critical appraisal of the academic program and activities provided.

The Handbook is an essential guide in selecting schools with appropriate programs to fulfill the aspirations and potentials of students seeking a sound academic foundation.

The Handbook is the definitive, indispensable reference work for any advisor, counselor, or educational administrator truly concerned with meeting the individual needs of each student.

Write for brochure and order form.

PORTER SARGENT PUBLISHERS, INC.
11 Beacon Street, Boston, MA 02108

NOTRE DAME INTERNATIONAL SCHOOL
VIA AURELIA 796, ROME 00165, ITALY

Brother Thomas Dziekan, CSC, *Headmaster*

An American resident and day school in Rome for boys, under the auspices of the Brothers of Holy Cross educators since 1842, divided into upper and lower schools from grades 5 to 12.

In addition to strong college preparatory classes geared to entrance in American universities, Notre Dame offers classes in art, advanced science and math, computers, typing, speech, and creative writing. Additional courses are offered to meet student needs. Every student has a reading program geared to his needs. The program of studies is flexible, insuring maximum efficiency. Tutorial assistance is provided for students with strong academic achievements enabling them to earn college credit through Advanced Placement Examinations. In all grades, guidance and testing programs evaluate progress. Daily activity period provides students with opportunities to participate in enrichment programs including publications, photography, drama, ceramics, etc. Full facilities are available for all sports — gymnasium, courts, and a heated swimming pool. Ski trips scheduled during winter weekends; field trips to historical sites, and visits to museums are integrated with classes.

Boarding accommodations are available for 125 residents on campus in three modern residence wings with recreational facilities. School plant has modern classrooms, laboratories, libraries, lounges, cinema room, and activity rooms. Full counseling program. An activities director plans a full social program.

Accredited by the Middle States Association of Colleges and Secondary Schools.

ST. STEPHEN'S SCHOOL

Via Aventina, 3
00153 Rome, ITALY
Tel: (06) 575.0605
C. Peter Rinaldi,
Headmaster

St. Stephen's School is a nonsectarian, coeducational college preparatory school which serves the American and international communities from Rome. Founded in 1964, the boarding and day program spans grade 9 through 12 and a post graduate year. The curriculum is modeled on American independent school traditions, and is dedicated to the pursuit of knowledge in an atmosphere of trust, fellowship and community.

In the year since its founding, St. Stephen's School has achieved accreditation by the New England Association of Schools and Colleges, and since 1975, has participated in the International Baccalaureate program. The school has won recognition from the United States State Department and from various private foundations, all of whom have awarded St. Stephen's grants in support of its educational program. In addition, the school is a member of the European Council of International Schools.

Small by design, enrollment is kept below 150 students. This is done on the conviction that the school's purpose and those of its students are best served by a concentration of time and resources on a deliberately small student body. In further pursuit of its educational objectives, St. Stephen's maintains a selective admissions procedure. Students are chosen on the basis of personal promise and probable capacity to benefit from the school's curriculum.

St. Stephen's is international in character with over 30 nationalities enrolled. The majority of students are, however, American-born. Although the school has made available the International Baccalaureate diploma (a recognized entrance qualification to universities throughout the world), most students elect the standard American high school diploma. Graduates have entered leading colleges and universities including Brown, Dartmouth, Harvard, Johns Hopkins, M.I.T., Princeton and Vassar.

Field trips and travel are an important part of life and education. Trips and travel maintain the school's ties with the outside world, and, given the school's location in Rome and in Italy, these ties can be extraordinarily valuable. Life at St. Stephen's is intense and enjoyable with a happy blend of rigor and relaxation.

INTERNATIONAL SCHOOL OF AMSTERDAM

P.O. Box 7983
1008 AD Amsterdam
THE NETHERLANDS
Dr. Brian S. Wilks, *Director*

Americans comprise a quarter of the enrollment at this coeducational school located in a quiet suburb of Amsterdam. An American-based curriculum is conducted from pre-kindergarten through grade 12, and the overall teacher-student ratio is 1:12. The elementary school program emphasizes the acquisition of strong reading, language arts and math skills. Dutch is introduced in the third grade and children also participate in art, drama, music and physical education. A comprehensive academic program is offered at the junior high school level which features electives in the creative arts. The college preparatory high school conducts classes in computer science, sociology and U.S. history. The International Baccalaureate is an optional program in the 11th and 12th grades.

Extracurricular activities include sports competitions (athletics, volleyball, basketball and soccer against similar schools in Holland, Belgium, Germany and Luxembourg), field trips, ski week, dramatic productions and choir.

The International School of Amsterdam accommodates approximately 330 students from over 30 countries. It is sponsored by the U.S. State Department Office of Overseas Schools, is accredited by the New England Association of Schools and Colleges and by the European Council of International Schools and has a school-to-school relationship with a Board of Cooperative Educational Services in New York State. For further information on admissions, contact the Admissions Office.

AMERICAN SCHOOL OF MALLORCA

Calle Oratorio, 9 — Portals Nous
MALLORCA, SPAIN
Dr. Stanley Amdurer, *Director*

Dr. Stanley Amdurer founded the American School of Mallorca in 1969 in order to meet the needs of American and international students abroad. Accredited by the Middle States Association of Colleges and Schools and a member of the European Council of International Schools, the school is non-denominational and fully coeducational. The day program operates from kindergarten through grade 12 while the boarding program is for students in grades 7 to 12.

A post high school year is also conducted.

The faculty is comprised of fully-qualified American instructors, and the curriculum offers challenge and diversity. ASM is an approved test center in Mallorca for the College Boards, SAT, PSAT, ACH, ACT, CLEP, SSAT and TOEFL. An English as a Second Language program is conducted and a special center for Learning Disabilities is also operated. After-school tutoring is provided when the need arises.

The school is situated close to North Africa and mainland Spain and students enjoy an enviable climate as well as a wide range of cultural activities. An exacting college preparatory curriculum sends over 90% of its graduates to leading institutions of higher learning throughout Europe and the United States. Creative writing, Journalism, Advanced Placement English and American History, Psychology, Analytical Geometry, and French and Spanish are but a few of the course features. In addition to the college preparatory program, the school offers a technical/academic curriculum leading to Certificates of Pre-Professional Engineering and Business Studies. Included in the program are classes in Drafting, Auto Mechanics, Computer Studies, Engineering, Business English and Math, Typing and Shorthand.

A full range of extra-curricular activities include aquatic sports, school publications and government, camping, sailing, tennis, horseback riding and mountain climbing. Students have opportunities to visit neighboring islands, the mainland and points of interest in Mallorca.

Please contact the Director of Admissions for your personal interview and campus tour.

AIGLON COLLEGE
CH-1885 CHESIERES-VILLARS
Philip Parsons, M.A., *Headmaster*

Aiglon College, founded in 1949, seeks to combine the ideal of Christian teaching practice with the ideas of its Founder, John Corlette, on the education of the whole man. It is a member of the Headmaster's Conference in the UK and is registered as a Charitable Trust in Switzerland, the UK, USA and Canada.

Aiglon is an independent, non-profit, co-educational boarding school situated in the French-speaking Swiss Alps. It has a strong international enrolment of 260 boys and girls (aged 11-18) of some 40 nationalities, mainly British, European and North American. There are three houses for girls and three for boys, each with its own Houseparents. The teaching staff is in a ratio of 1 to 8 students. Facilities include a theatre and gym, four science and language laboratories, three libraries, classrooms and arts centre. The school uses local swimming pools, ice rink and ski slopes as well as its own tennis courts and sports field.

Academically, the School is divided into Lower (ages 11-13), Middle (13-15) and Upper (15-18) Schools, and all courses except foreign languages are taught in English. French, compulsory in most classes, is specially emphasized. The Upper School is divided into Fifth and Sixth forms. Fifth Form students carry six or seven courses leading to British GCE Ordinary level exams. The Sixth Form two year courses lead to the GCE Advanced level exams which may qualify for advanced placement at American college. The school is a centre for the College Board and some International Baccalaureate exams at Subsidiary level. Most graduates (annual average 35 students) go to leading universities and colleges in the United States, Britain, Canada and continental Europe.

Sports include skiing, skating, tennis, soccer, atheltics, gymnastics, swimming and basketball. Character training through adventure is a special feature of life at Aiglon and weekend mountain expeditions take place throughout the year. There is a termly three day Long Expedition; in autumn, to European cultural centres, in spring, on skis and, in summer, on foot.

Admission is through Aiglon's entrance examination, interview and previous school record. A limited number of scholarships and bursaries is awarded to deserving candidates in financial need.

For information, contact the Head of Admissions, Aiglon College, 1885 Chesières-Villars, Switzerland. Tel: 025-35.27.21 Tlx: 456211.

ECOLE D'HUMANITE
6082 Goldern, SWITZERLAND

A non-profit corporation
Armin and Natalie Luethi,
Directors

Noted for the success of its special education system practiced since 1910. Ability groups rather than traditional grades, individually tailored curriculum, extensive extra-curricular program (over 60 different course offerings), emphasis on independent study training, responsible community living, student involvement in all facets of school life from daily work program to curriculum planning.

150 boys and girls aged 6 to 20 and faculty live in small family-style groups. International, inter-racial student body. Main language German, special classes for beginners. Instruction in German and English. 35 English-speakers in college preparatory program. German and English-speakers integrated in living quarters and classes. Faculty-student ratio 1:5. CEEB test center. 20,000 vol. library.

ECOLE NOUVELLE
11, rue Pierre-a-Mazel
2000 Neuchatel
SWITZERLAND
G. Dufaux, *Director*

Ecole Nouvelle is a member of the Swiss Federation of Private Schools and the European Federation of Schools. Although it is operated on a day basis, living accommodations can be arranged upon request. This special French language schools offers:
- Intensive French courses for students (ages 16 and up) of a foreign mother tongue
- Morning, afternoon and evening courses
- Holiday courses in July/August
- Beginner, Intermediate and Advanced Levels
- Preparation for the ALLIANCE FRANCAISES DE PARIS

INTERNATIONAL SCHOOL BRILLANTMONT

12-18, Avenue Secrétan
1005—LAUSANNE
SWITZERLAND

Girls boarding school
from the age of 14
Coeducational day-school.

Teaching program
  International Baccalaureate
  Swiss Federal Maturity Diplomas
  High School Curriculum Grade 8th to 12th
    (US College Boards — SSAT, PSAT, SAT, ACH, AP)
  General Certificate of Education O & A Levels
    (Cambridge Board)
  German, Italian, Spanish
  Official diplomas
  Alliance Francaise I and II (French Proficiency Certificates of
    the University of Nancy)
  Certificat d'Etudes francaises (University of Lausanne)

Classes are small. Students often work in small groups. Everything is done to encourage them to develop their powers of reflection, to broaden contacts with one another, to stimulate their capacity for clear thinking, deepen their awareness of realities, buoy up their confidence and fire their enthusiasm.

Summer and winter sports. Cultural outings. Study trips in Switzerland and Europe.

ECOLE NOUVELLE PREPARATOIRE

Route du Lac 22
CH — 1094 Paudex
SWITZERLAND
Telex 25495 — chmi
Mrs. M. Jomini. Phone: 021/392477
M. Marc De Smet, Prof. *Agrégé Dir.*

Ecole Nouvelle Preparatoire conducts a limited boarding program for boys and a fully coeducational day program for students between the ages of 8 and 18. Located in a lovely area at the shores of Lake Geneva, in the little village of Paudex, the school is about two miles from Lausanne.

ENP employs French and Swiss educational systems and French is the language of instruction. Students receive individual attention in small classroom settings and emphasis is placed on language and mathematics. All students must produce satisfactory work and strict controls are made during each lesson. Frequent visits and study tours in Switzerland, Europe and even overseas help students to increase their knowledge about the world and other cultures. In addition to the pre- and college preparatory programs, Ecole Nouvelle Preparatoire offers commercial and computer science courses.

The school's natural setting is suited for studies and a healthy lifestyle. Since ENP's founding in 1933, it has won many competitions in skiing, rowing, ice hockey and fencing. Students also enjoy basketball, football, golf, horseback riding, judo, karate, swimming and tennis. A summer session is conducted in July and August in which students devote their time to studies and outdoor activities.

For information on admissions contact the Director.

INSTITUT DR. SCHMIDT

International School for Boys
Chateâu De La Rive, CH — 1095 LUTRY
SWITZERLAND

Marc J.F. De Smet, Prof. Agr., *Director*
Phone: 021/39.51.12

TELEX: 25495 — CHMI — CH   TELEGRAMMES: SCHMIDINST. = LUTRY

AIMS OF OUR INSTITUTE
— to provide the young people with an education which will enable them to face life with success.
— to act in such a way as to make the students acquire the sense of responsibility for themselves as well as for the others
— to allow our students to find their place in an everchanging world.
— to develop their character.
— to make well-balanced adolescents out of boys.
— to develop the body as well as the mind.
— to enable the students to spend one or several unforgettable years in a beautiful country.

MEANS TO REACH THESE AIMS
— an individualized teaching.
— classes with a reduced number of students.
— qualified and experienced teachers.
— programs conform to official standards and adapted to general scientific, technological and intellectual progress.

— an education that draws from numerous circumstances and examples in active life.
— the possibility to devote oneself to many creative activities, such as making reduced models, painting, etc.
— a large sport outfit and intensive practice of a number of sport activities.
— family life and leisure time in groups.

THE STUDIES

The studies at the Institute offer the students a double orientation:

1° the compulsory obtention of internationally recognized certificates and diplomas, creating a maximum of possibilities towards higher studies in Switzerland and elsewhere.

2° a very complete general culture.

Yet, these two lines are intimately associated and the teachers establish their own programs accordingly.

Post-graduate for American students

PROGRAMS

— Section of intensive language courses (French or English)
— Commercial section
— Computer Science Section
— French Baccalaureate section
— Swiss Federal Matriculation section
— Primary & Junior College sections

All our programs lead to officially recognized certificates and diplomas.

(For additional details please see our "Study Scheme", obtainable upon request.)

SUMMER SESSION

— in July and August — advised length of stay: 4 weeks
— possibility to enroll: every Monday
— age of students: from 8 to 18.

LEYSIN AMERICAN SCHOOL

for University
Preparatory Studies

CH 1854 Leysin 3
SWITZERLAND
Telephone: 025/34 13 61
Telex: 456 166 TOLE

Founded in 1961, this international, co-educational boarding school offers a comprehensive American high school curriculum, AP courses, electives. Located in a famous resort in the Vaudois Alps at 5,000 ft. above Lake Geneva, LAS has excellent facilities for living and learning: faculty-supervised boys' and girls' dormitories, American-European cuisine, modern classrooms, fully-equipped laboratories, individualized instruction in small classes, personal, academic, and vocational counseling, college entrance and evaluative testing, a new gymnasium and theater, diverse recreation areas. In addition to skiing and ice skating, sports include basketball, volleyball, soccer, tennis, mountain climbing, hiking, horseback riding, and swimming. Leysin's location in the heart of Europe facilitates curriculum-related excursions. An oustanding US/international teaching and counseling staff assures an enviable college acceptance record.

For information write to Director of Admissions, Leysin American School, CH 1854, Leysin 3, Switzerland.

INSTITUTION CHATEAU MONT-CHOISI
SWITZERLAND

Bd. Foret/
Ch. des Ramiers 16
1012 Lausanne - La Rosiaz
Tel. 021/28 87 77

INTERNATIONAL BOARDING SCHOOL FOR GIRLS

- Girls 12 to 20 years. Beautifully situated. Finest facilities for study and residence, tennis courts, heated swimming pool.

- Comprehensive academic program is small classes. Official certificates and diplomas.

- Intensive study of French and English. Language laboratory.

- Full American High School Program, Grades 7-12. CEES (SAT, PSAT, ACH). TOEFL. Post graduate studies. Advanced Placement (AP). College guidance. Excellent university acceptances.

- Secretarial and commercial courses in French or English. Computer Science.

- Diversified activities. Art, music, ballet, cookery, sports. Educational trips. Winter vacations in Crans, Swiss Alps. Summer course.

INSTITUT LE VIEUX CHALET
1837 Chateâu d'Oex near Gstaad, SWITZERLAND

The "Vieux Chalet" accepts young girls of every nationality. In the mountains, in a cultured atmosphere, these young girls study French which is the language spoken in the school.

Our students can take official examinations according to their capabilities (Alliance Française elementary and superior). Lessons in German, Italian and Spanish are available, and a typing course is offered. We also have courses in cooking and dressmaking. Girls interested in music or painting can also have tuition.

At an altitude of 3000 feet, Chateâu d'Oex enjoys a very healthy climate. All summer and winter sports are possible. We have skiing professors from whom the girls receive lessons and training. Ice skating is possible between October and March.

We organise walks and excursions so that our young girls will know everything of interest about our country. During the months of July and August, we have a summer course where French and typing are taught.

For further information write to:

Mr. and Mrs. Jean Bach
Institut Le Vieux Chalet
1837 Chateâu d'Oex
Vaud, Suisse (Switzerland)
Tel. 029- 4 68 79

COLLEGE ALPIN INTERNATIONAL BEAU SOLEIL
1884 Villars-sur-Ollon (Vaud) SWITZERLAND

Pierre de Meyer, *Director*

Situated in the picturesque Swiss Alps near Lake Geneva, Beau-Soleil offers preparation for the U.S. College Boards, British G.C.E. and the French Baccalaureate to boys and girls between the ages of 10 and 18. Beau-Soleil is truly international with over 30 nationalities represented in the enrollment. The Anglo-American section features accelerated language courses in French and a course in computers. Graduates enter leading institutions of higher education such as Barnard, Georgetown and the University of Michigan. Winter and summer activities are carefully coordinated with the academic program. Students enjoy horseback riding, skating, skiing, soccer, swimming and tennis. Excursions to concerts, theatres, museums and cities of cultural interest enrich the curriculum. For information on admissions contact the Director.

MONTE ROSA INTERNATIONAL SCHOOL SWITZERLAND

Founded 1874
Why Monte Rosa?

(1) Beautifully located overlooking Lake Geneva in French-speaking Switzerland.
(2) Coeducational boarding. Local day pupils. Age range 8 to 19 years.
(3) Fully accredited and recognized English-Speaking Schooling.
(4) Intensive university preparatory high school studies.
(5) Preparation for College Boards, Oxford G.C.E., AP, CLEP, etc.
(6) Business, Secretarial and Modern Language studies. Emphasis on French. Summer School.
(7) Low teacher/pupil ratio. Highly qualified faculty.
(8) Counselling. Scholastic and Vocational Guidance.
(9) Integrated sports and recreational program. Excellent skiing.
(10) A FIRST-CLASS EDUCATION!

For further information please write to the Headmaster, Monte Rosa International School and Lycée D'Arvel, CH-1842, Territet-Montreux, Switzerland. Telephone: Montreux Area Code (021) 63 53 41. Telex 453 267.

ROSEHILL INTERNATIONAL SCHOOL

(Swiss American Foundation)
CH-9000 ST. GALLEN,
SWITZERLAND

O. Gademann, *Director*

Founded in 1889.
One of the leading international schools. ECIS member.

An old and well established co-educational boarding school. In the English-speaking Section, students are prepared for British, American and Canadian Universities, for whose examinations the school is a center, and they have individual counseling to advise them in their studies and careers.

Commercial Studies and postgraduate study are also available.

Small classes. Highly qualified staff. Unique facilities for summer and winter sports and regular excursions throughout the year. Holiday language courses in July and August. Prospectus from Director of Admission.

SUMMER CAMPS AND SUMMER SCHOOLS

Over 1100 summer academic, travel, pioneering, camping and recreational programs are described in this comprehensive *Guide to Summer Camps and Summer Schools*. Listings are arranged by type, specialty and individual features. Data includes location, enrollment, director's winter address, fees, length of session and other pertinent data.

Special programs for the handicapped and maladjusted, as well as for those with learning disabilities are included. The geographic range covers recreational programs in the U.S. and Canada, and travel programs throughout the U.S., Canada, Mexico and abroad.

Published biennially, the *Guide* is a comparative reference for all types of summer opportunities. The *Guide* is designed for the counselor or parent concerned with meeting the specific needs of boys and girls.

Write for brochure and order form.

PORTER SARGENT PUBLISHERS, INC.
11 Beacon Street, Boston, MA 02108

THE AMERICAN SCHOOL OF INSTITUT MONTANA

ZUGERBERG, CANTON ZUG, SWITZERLAND

The primary objective of the American School of Institut Montana is to provide the highest standards of a college preparatory program to boys (grades 5-12) who expect to enter United States Colleges. This program is realized under the supervision of devoted masters, in small classes where individual attention is assured, and in a rigorous and challenging curriculum.

What distinguishes Montana from other fine preparatory schools is the opportunity to participate in a community of youth coming from many nations. More than 25 separate nationalities are represented in the Institut's Swiss-German, Italian and American divisions. There is here a unique chance to learn the cultures and languages of the Western world in an immediate and meaningful experience.

The various schools of the Institut are academically independent of one another, but all clubs, sports activities, dormitories, and dining facilities are international. Optional excursions are made frequently during the school year.

Virtually all graduates of the American School attend four-year colleges in the States, and many go with advanced standing as the result of their scores on the College Board Advanced Placement Examinations.

Member National Association of Independent Schools. In addition to College Boards, students are prepared for the American College Test, Secondary School Admission Test, and Preliminary Scholastic Aptitude Test.

For information write the Dean of the American School, Institut Montana, 6316 Zugerberg, Switzerland. Prospective students are urged to apply before June. SSAT scores recommended.

BRENT SCHOOL

Box 35, Baguio
PHILIPPINES

(The Headmaster
Brent School
APO San Francisco
California 96298)

Peter A. Caleb, *Headmaster*

Brent School is an international, coeducational boarding and day school, founded in 1909 by The Rt. Rev. Charles Henry Brent, D.D., first Bishop of the Episcopal Church in the Philippines. The school provides for the educational needs of students from pre-school through 12th grade and accepts students of any nationality and religious persuasion. The high school follows a college preparatory curriculum. The International Baccalaureate program is offered to students in grades 11 and 12 for entrance to universities throughout the world. The faculty is also of an international character, coming from North America, Europe and Asia.

Brent's 20-hectare, pine covered campus is located in the mountains of northern Luzon, 125 miles north of Manila. Its temperate climate (average 60-75 F., 16-24 C.) is ideal for study and sports. A complete athletic program includes basketball, soccer, volleyball, swimming, track and field, tennis and golf. Extracurricular activities include the yearbook, school newspaper, language, mathematics and science clubs, scouting, drama, orchestra, choir, and arts and crafts. An enriched American curriculum is offered with the I.B. in grades 11 and 12.

Faculty and residence assistants are on duty 24 hours in well equipped dormitories to provide a home-like atmosphere for resident students. Leisure activities, beach trips, movies, shopping, hiking and visits to homes of day students are planned regularly by the staff.

Brent is doubly accredited by the Western Association of Schools and Colleges Accrediting Commission for Secondary Schools (U.S.) and the Philippine Accrediting Association of Schools, Colleges and Universities.

GLAMORGAN
of Geelong Grammar School

14 Douglas St.
Toorak, Victoria 3142
AUSTRALIA

I. L. Sutherland, *The Master*

Glamorgan, operated under the Church of England, is a division of Geelong Grammar School. It offers a sound pre-preparatory coeducational day program from the nursery level through grade six (ages three to twelve). Academics are aimed at developing competence in basic literative and numerative skills. Curriculum features include weekly computer sessions, Japanese language instruction, art, music and library skills. Drama, ballet, camping, swimming, soccer and cross country skiing are but a few of the extracurricular opportunities. Glamorgan strives to instill in its students a substantial degree of self-motivation and self-discipline as well as sense of personal integrity and individuality.

THE HANDBOOK OF PRIVATE SCHOOLS

As the most comprehensive reference book of its kind, *The Handbook of Private Schools* contains current facts on over 1800 elementary and secondary boarding and day schools in the nation.

Each annual edition reports on the thousands of changes in the areas of enrollment, curriculum, facilities, administrators, faculty, fees and graduates. Many of the listings include an historical description of the school and the dominant personalities who have influenced it, as well as a critical appraisal of the academic program and activities provided.

The Handbook is an essential guide in selecting schools with appropriate programs to fulfill the aspirations and potentials of students seeking a sound academic foundation.

The Handbook is the definitive, indispensable reference work for any advisor, counselor, or educational administrator truly concerned with meeting the individual needs of each student.

Write for brochure and order form.

PORTER SARGENT PUBLISHERS, INC.
11 Beacon Street, Boston, MA 02108

CANADIAN ACADEMY

Nagaminedai 2-chome,
Nada-ku
Kobe 657, JAPAN

Stuart J. Young, *Headmaster*

Canadian Academy is a coeducational institution founded in 1913. It has an enrollment of 700 students from Pre-School through Grade 12, including 50 students (7-12) who board on campus. Its goal is to blend educational philosophies of Europe, North America and Asia into an international curriculum. College preparatory courses are offered through the International Baccalaureate and American High School Diplomas. There is a summer session for students in the elementary and junior high school grades.

NISHIMACHI INTERNATIONAL SCHOOL

14-7, Moto-Axubu 2-chome,
Minato-ku
Tokyo 106, JAPAN
Tel. 451-5520

Situated on a one-acre campus in central Tokyo, Nishimachi International was founded in 1949 to serve as a coeducational day school for Japanese and foreign children. The kindergarten through grade nine curriculum features a unique dual-language program (English/Japanese). Non-Japanese students are provided with academics that meet their national standards as well as with beginner to advanced level Japanese language instruction. Course work is complemented by activities in arts and crafts, music, school publications and swimming. Nishimachi's educational philosophy is rooted in a spirit of internationalism and humanism which allows children to learn in a caring environment.

AOBA
INTERNATIONAL
SCHOOL

2-10-34, Aobadai, Meguro-ku
Tokyo 153, JAPAN
Tel. 461-1442
Regina Doi, *Principal*

Aoba International School, is a unique bilingual and multi-cultural nursery-kindergarten-pre-first grade for boys and girls ages 1½ to 6. It was founded in 1976 with the aim of preparing children of any nationality for successful entry into a first grade situation at either international or Japanese schools, while at the same time achieving a healthy sense of their own cultural and personal worth. It has a carefully designed curriculum and daily schedule, ideal for children at each of four developmental levels, a program which is as fun as it is educational. A large percentage of the graduates go on to Japan International School with which Aoba is affiliated.

JAPAN
INTERNATIONAL
SCHOOL

4-24-9, Jingumae, Shibuya-ku
Tokyo 150, JAPAN
Tel. 408-4411
Regina Doi, *Principal*

Japan International School is a unique bilingual and cross-cultural elementary and junior high school designed to meet the specific needs of both Japanese and foreign children resident in Japan who come from a wide variety of educational and cultural backgrounds. Class size is kept to a minimum, with extra teachers available for specialized instruction. The curriculum is disciplined and guided to enable students to reach their highest levels of individual potential. It seeks to meet the ever-increasing need for an international education which retains the student's own culture while at the same time preparing him for life in a truly international community. The school is non-parochial and welcomes children of every nationality and religion. It was founded in 1980 out of the successful experience of Aoba International School with which it is affiliated.

For further information, please write to either school.

ST. MARY'S INTERNATIONAL SCHOOL

1-6-19 Seta, Setagaya-Ku
TOKYO 158
Tel.: 709-4311

Br. Andrew, *Headmaster*

Established in 1954, St. Mary's International School's day program is operated by the Brothers of Christian Instruction. Originally founded to provide an education for Catholic boys, today the school welcomes boys of all faiths and nationalities. The 'American style' curriculum is followed in grades 1 through 12 and the option of working towards the International Baccalaureate (IB) is given to students in grades 11 and 12.

Students in grades 1 through 6 are taught the four 'basic' subjects (English, math, science, social studies) in self-contained classrooms. Grades 7 and 8 are departmentalized with all students required to study English, math, science, foreign language (French, Japanese, Latin, ESL), religion (Catholic, Protestant, Ethics), world history and geography. The college preparatory program of the high school features courses in anthropology, psychology, Asian studies, advanced computer science and nine levels of Japanese, five of French and four of Latin. Successful completion of the IB program enables students to gain advanced standing in many U.S. colleges.

Swimming, tennis, ice hockey, soccer, judo, wrestling, baseball, and track and field are but a few of the athletic opportunities available. Boys also participate in a wide range of extracurricular activities including photography, ping-pong, student government and publications, concert and stage bands and debate. The school conducts a multi-national carnival in May which has become famous throughout Tokyo.

St. Mary's International School is located on a seven-acre site in Tokyo's largest residential area. The school aims to have each boy realize his individual importance and sense of responsibility as a member of the world community.

Preparing the women of
the future to meet the
challenges of an ever-
changing world

TOKYO, JAPAN
SEISEN INTERNATIONAL
SCHOOL

12-15 Yoga 1-chome
Setagaya-ku, Tokyo 158

Seisen International School is a Catholic school run by the Handmaids of the Sacred Heart of Jesus operated under the auspices of the Seisen Jogakuin Educational Foundation. It is recognized by the Ministry of Education of Japan and accredited by the Western Association of Schools and Colleges.

As a Catholic school, Seisen is pleased to be of service to the community and believes that students of all races, nationalities and creeds can thrive in its Christian atmosphere.

Seisen provides a college preparatory program which serves the needs of the diplomatic, business, and professional members of the international community. Seisen also provides education for Japanese children who have lived abroad and wish to continue their education in English.

Our Montessori Kindergarten is coeducational, accepting boys and girls from ages 3-5. Grades 1-12 are for girls only. Instruction is in English. Spanish, French and Japanese are offered as second languages. Computer study is offered from grade 6.

Seisen employs 38 full-time and 29 part-time teachers of 11 nationalities. Our student body represents 63 countries, making an international environment which gives each student a glimpse into many worlds. It is our intention that students will learn tolerance, respect, and an appreciation for the beauty and infinite variety in the lives and cultures of people from all countries so that they may leave Seisen with some realization of the oneness of the human race.

Through example, the Seisen student will learn to recognize the importance of honesty and will develop the necessary moral stature to abide by and support personal commitments. She will learn the fundamental skills necessary to function in the academic areas and will also develop scientific attitudes such as open-mindedness, an inquiring mind, and the ability to think critically. Catalogues and information upon request.

SAINT MAUR
INTERNATIONAL SCHOOL

83 Yamate-cho
Yokohama, JAPAN

Sr. Carmel O'Keeffe, *Principal*

Established in 1872 by the Sisters of the Institute of the Infant Jesus, Saint Maur's is the oldest private international day school for boys and girls in Japan. The school offers a complete academic program from the nursery level through grade 12 in a Christian atmosphere.

The coeducational Montessori program is for two-and-a-half to six year olds and is designed to develop a child physically, intellectually, emotionally and socially. An American educational system is utilized in the elementary, junior and senior high schools which allows for easy transition to and from other American, Canadian, British and Australian schools. Basic academic subjects are taught in the elementary and junior programs as well as courses in French, Spanish, Japanese and creative arts. The high school curriculum is primarily college preparatory and features French and Spanish language classes, Japanese history and literature, Latin, Asian and U.S. history and trigonometry and calculus. Intensive English, Japanese and German, advanced speech and drama and art are among elective offerings. Also available are special courses for those students who are not college-bound. Religious studies are an integral part of the overall curriculum.

Students participate in a variety of athletics including basketball, softball, volleyball and tennis. Opportunities in computer programming and dressmaking, music and debate are also provided. Saint Maur is made up of more than 300 students of many nationalities and numerous religious denominations.

For additional information contact the Principal's Office.

SEOUL INTERNATIONAL SCHOOL

Kangdong P. O. Box 61
SEOUL, KOREA, 134
Tel: 445-2119, 445-6091

Edward B. Adams, *Principal*

SIS has a coeducational American curriculum, grades kindergarten through high school, which stresses academic training in preparation for university level. Our teaching staff which is primarily American is fully qualified. In 1973, SIS was officially recognized and licensed by the ROK Ministry of Education and was the first foreign school officially licensed by the Korean government.

The curriculum of SIS is consistent with the philosophy set forth by most American school systems with some adjustments to meet the unique situation of the overseas schools. In the high school a full spectrum of courses is offered for the university-bound students from grades nine through twelve. The low ratio of teachers to students (about 1-8) permits strong individualization. English (ESL) is emphasized at SIS for our students who lack proficiency in English.

The completion in the summer of '84 of a new facility near the present campus will add a gym, special athletic rooms, music rooms, an auditorium, a new cafeteria, and several special function rooms, as well as provide an increase in the numbers and sizes of classrooms.

Sport programs include soccer, softball, volleyball, tennis, tae kwon do and basketball. Numerous extracurricular activities are available including cultural seminars, art, music, photography, drama, dance, climbing, journalism and student clubs.

Though students attending SIS are predominantly American (55%) there are approximately 37 other nationalities represented in the student body. SIS is a member of the East Asia Regional Council of Overseas Schools (EARCOS) and registered with the Educational Testing Services, Princeton, N.J. SIS is accredited with the Western Association of Schools and Colleges with a six year term from 1979. US, SAT, ACT, and PSAT/NMSQT, SLEP as well as the TOEFL are arranged by SIS. A handbook and brochures giving more detailed information are available upon request.

CHAPEL
AMERICAN SCHOOL

C. Postal 21293 — Brooklin
04698 — Sao Paulo, SP, BRAZIL

William O'Hale, *Director*

The Chapel American School (Escola Maria Imaculada) is a private college preparatory day school serving nursery through grade 12. It is located in the Chacara Flora, a beautiful, quiet residential suburb of Sao Paulo. Founded in 1948 for English-speaking Catholics, the school now enrolls approximately 600 students — 34% American, 18% Brazilian, 48% from over 30 other nations, and non-Catholics comprise 50% of the student body.

A sound college preparatory curriculum sends 97% of its graduates to colleges and universities throughout the world. All students take Portuguese through the 10th grade, and the study of religion and ethics is part of the program.

The school emphasizes the development of the "total child." Chapel's expectations are high and are based on the academic achievements of all students (a high majority of the school's students go to colleges and universities), as well as a desire for each student to demonstrate acceptable human values. Compassion, respect, and understanding for the rights and privileges of others, honesty, and integrity are the values that are strongly stressed at Chapel School. In addition the International Baccalaureate is offered to qualified students. Students that successfully complete this program may be granted up to one full year of college credit (sophomore standing) at most U.S. colleges and universities.

The physical education program conducts recreational, instructional and competitive activities. Opportunities are available in interscholastic soccer, tennis, softball, basketball, volleyball and track. Student government, journalism, photography, music, chess, scouting, dance and gymnastics are some of the extracurricular activities offered.

The school's facilities include an auditorium, computer center, language and science labs, infirmary, cafeteria, student union, two libraries, gymnasium and ample athletic fields.

For information on admissions write or call — 247-7455; 7143.

ESCUELA CAMPO ALEGRE

Calle La Cinta — Urbanizacion Las Mercedes —
Telephone: 92-47-31
Mailing Address: S. A. Escuela Campo Alegre
VENEZUELA
APO MIAMI 34037
CABLE: ESCAAL

Roland M. Roth, B.A., M.S., M.Ed., Ed.D., *Superintendent*

Located on Calle La Cinta, Urbanizacion Las Mercedes, Caracas, Venezuela, Campo Alegre offers a central, easily accessible environment which is removed from the daily congestion that makes life in Caracas difficult at times. Thus, the school is able to offer your children a safe, sheltered and quiet environment, conducive to improved learning and better overall development.

The philosophy of Escuela Campo Alegre is: To provide an education equal or superior to that of the best public and private American or international schools.

Escuela Campo Alegre is accredited by the Southern Association of Colleges and Schools, a member of the National Association of Independent Schools, and a member of the Educational Records Bureau, Princeton, New Jersey.

SOME FACTS ABOUT THE SCHOOL:
- Staff of 51 teachers, 14 with masters degrees, 2 doctorates.
- Four teacher aides.
- Three full-time tutors. (E.S.L.)
- Grades: Pre-Kindergarten (4 yrs.) through 9th grade.
- Full-time nurse on duty.
- Bus transportation (for a fee).
- Enrollment now over 630.
- Excellent sports program.
- Strong P.T.A.
- Music and Art Departments.
- Brownies and Girl Scouts, Cub and Boy Scouts.
- Gymnastics and Ballet (for a fee).
- Weekend Little League Program.
- Fifty nationalities.

ST. JOHN'S SCHOOL OF ALBERTA

R. R. 5 Stony Plain
Alberta T0E 2G0
CANADA

Mr. Peter Jackson, B.A., *Headmaster*

St. John's is a boys' boarding school for Gr. 7-12. Founded in 1968 and 70km south-west of Edmonton, it includes 250 acres of parkland, bush and farmland, and borders the North Saskatchewan River. The school's three-fold curriculum incorporates academic, work and outdoor programmes. Literature, history, the sciences and French are integral parts of academic studies with extracurricular options also provided. Students help to maintain and upkeep the school buildings and grounds in the work programme, and also produce honey which is sold to keep tuition fees low. The outdoor programme offers hiking, canoeing, dogsledding and outdoor survival skills.

The School is run by the Company of the Cross, a lay order of the Anglican Church where prayer and service to God are part of a way of life. Boys are encouraged not pressured to participate in this aspect of community life.

LANDMARK EAST

P. O. Box 1270
Wolfville, Nova Scotia
CANADA B0P 1X0

G. Fred Atkinson,
Headmaster

Landmark East is a school for boys and girls with learning disabilities. It accepts applications from both residential and day students ages 8 to 16. Modeled after the Landmark School in Massachusetts, the program is designed to provide help to high-potential, emotionally-sound students with normal to above-average intelligence. Through one-to-one and small group instruction, students can look forward to a return to mainstream education within two to three years. The school's six-acre campus is rich in natural beauty and historical interest. Cultural activities are available as well as opportunities in skiing, hiking, swimming, tennis, horseback riding, woodworking and crafts.

For further information write or call — (902) 542-2237.

ROBINSON SCHOOL
(AND LEARNING CENTER)
Calle Nairn
SANTURCE, PUERTO RICO 00907
Tel: (809) 728-6767
Wayne Ramirez, M.S., M.F.A., *Executive Director*

Robinson School is a college preparatory day school, composed of Kindergarten through Grade 12. Eighty-three years of service to the community is a testimonial of a highly successful educational program. The campus contains four acres of luscious tropical grounds, enhanced by Spanish style buildings (tiled roofs and floors) and open arched courtyards.

We maintain a warm environment, and we realize the importance of friendship. Many of our students and faculty members are bi-cultural and bi-lingual, bringing unique opportunities for cultural exchanges. We understand that for many, these will be their first weeks in a new school. Our atmosphere is an inviting one, as beautiful as our palm tree lined school grounds; this ambience encourages a positive attitude for learning.

Our faculty possesses high academic qualifications, professional preparation, and relevant experience. Ninety-nine percent of our graduates attend the finest colleges and universities in the United States and in Puerto Rico. College credits may be earned through our Advanced Placement Program.

The curriculum includes a wide range of subjects including Advanced Placement English (Grades 9-12), Drama, Speech, Journalism, English as a Second Language and Creative Writing. Among science and math offerings are Physical Science (8th, 9th grades), Advanced Placement Mathematics, SAT Math, Trigonometry, Algebra I & II, Geometry, Computers and Calculus. The Social Science Department offers World and U.S. History, Puerto Rican History, Latin American Affairs and Psychology. Additional courses are Spanish (Levels I through VII), Religion, Home Economics, Typing, Art and Music.

The Elementary School division closely follows standard curriculum offerings, although the curriculum is adapted to the individual needs of each student. The Elementary School includes a computer center. The Junior High School curriculum is flexible in that it allows for changes in course requirements.

A new Learning Center has been established for physically handicapped and learning disabled students. The Learning Center's academic program operates independently from that of the School, however, the facilities and non-academic courses are fully integrated. The Center is completely architecturally accessible to physically handicapped students.

We have numerous adult-education courses; you will find Macrame, Spanish as a Second Language, Art and many more. These classes provide new and exciting educational and social opportunities.

Classrooms are large and fully air-conditioned. Spacious art and music rooms are equipped with modern supplies. Class size remains small to guarantee regular sessions of individualized instruction. The science department has fully equipped laboratories, and the school has photographic dark room facilities. The library contains over 16,000 volumes with a substantial number of audio-visual materials and educational aids. The gymnasium/auditorium is regarded as one of the best in Puerto Rico.

We at Robinson feel that education represents growth and offer numerous athletic and extra-curricular activities.

SPORTS: girls' volley ball, basketball (girls' varsity), baseball, softball (for girls), tennis, track & field, basketball (junior varsity, junior high and varsity), soccer (varsity), swimming and golf.

CLUBS: Political Science, United Nations, Future Scientists of America, Spanish, Drama, Library, Pep, Sailing, Cheerleaders, Scuba Diving, Shalom, Service, Woodshop, Music, Student Government and Math.

SOCIETIES: Senior National Honor, Junior Honor, Mu Alpha Theta Math, Society of Distinguished American High School Students, and Who's Who Among American High School Students.

Robinson School is accredited by The Middle States Association of Colleges and Secondary Schools, The Puerto Rico Department of Instruction, and the National Association of Secondary School Principals. Founded in 1902, the school is related to the Board of Ministries of the United Methodist Church.

We provide scholarship opportunities for students who qualify because of economic need. Personal visitations are welcomed. Please call for enrollment information.

COLEGIO PONCEÑO
PONCE, PUERTO RICO

Tel. (809) 844-2424
Fr. Jose A. Basols, *Director*

Colegio Ponceño is a private Roman Catholic school which offers a comprehensive college preparatory curriculum from kindergarten through grade 12. The school is situated on a 14.8-acre suburban campus in Ponce, Puerto Rico's second largest city with a population of 190,000. Although Colegio Ponceño is run on a day basis, boarding accommodations can be arranged. The campus facilities include four "barrier free" main buildings which are beautifully constructed and connected, science labs, and labs for photography, typing, art and computer studies.

Operated by the Piarist Fathers, the school's faculty is comprised of 85% lay and 15% clergy, 20% of whom hold a masters degree or above. Colegio Ponceño's admissions policy is selective but caring and the enrollment is 60% boys and 40% girls. The student:faculty ratio is 16:1, and daily instruction is required in Spanish, English, Math, Science and Social Science. Religion, physical education and elective courses are conducted three times a week.

The school's guidance services help students to solve their religious, social, emotional and academic problems. A Guidance Center provides useful information on careers, colleges and universities. Individual and group pastoral counseling is also available, and religious activities (i.e., charity drives, retreats) are an important and integral part of student life. A wide variety of activities include intramural and interscholastic sports, scouting and student government.

Each year Colegio Ponceño graduates approximately 75 seniors who have a mean CEEB-PR Verbal score of 589 and Math 666. 62% of these graduates go on to four-year public colleges and 32% enter private programs. Graduates have entered such mainland universities as Assumption College, Columbia, Cornell, Fordham, Georgetown, Harvard and Yale.

Colegio Ponceño's program strives to make its students conscious of their faith so that they may fully live it and to educate the whole person both as an individual and a social being.

TASIS ENGLAND AMERICAN SCHOOL
THORPE, SURREY
M. Crist Fleming, B.A., *Director*
Lyle D. Rigg, A.B., M.A., Ed.M., *Headmaster*

TASIS England is a coeducational boarding and country day school located in Surrey near the historic town of Windsor. The program offers an American college preparatory education for grades Kindergarten through twelve. TASIS England is accredited in grades 7-12 by the European Council of International Schools and the New England Association of Schools and Colleges.

Situated in the picturesque village of Thorpe in two late Georgian mansions with thirty-five acres of grounds, and yet only eighteen miles from the center of London, the campus is an ideal setting for the School. Additional facilities include a library, an art/music complex, a photography lab, a theater, separate Lower School (K-5) facilities and several cottages which serve as student and faculty residences. Offering the highest American academic standards as well as an extensive sports program, diverse extracurricular activities, cultural opportunities, and course-correlated travel, the School is committed to the education of the complete individual.

A brand new gymnasium, three playing fields, and three basketball/tennis courts enable students to participate in a full sports program including basketball, soccer, rugby, tennis, field hockey, aerobics, volleyball, track and baseball. In addition, the school makes use of local athletic facilities for riding, swimming, and boating. Extra-curricular activities are stressed at TASIS England. Students participate in art and music, drama, clubs, dance, hiking, student publications, and student government.

With a highly qualified American and European faculty and a student-faculty ratio of eight to one, the School strives for its ultimate goal: the realization of each student's full potential. In addition to the standard college preparatory curriculum, TASIS England offers Advanced Placement courses, extensive electives in Art, English, History, Music, and Theater.

For catalog, please contact: U.S. Admissions Office, Room 110, 326 E. 69th Street, New York, NY 10021, Tel: (212) 570-1066, Tlx: 971912 or TASIS England, Coldharbour Lane, Thorpe, Surrey, England. Tel: Chertsey (9328) 65252, Tlx: 929712.

TASIS CYPRUS
AMERICAN SCHOOL

11 Kassos St., P. O. Box 2329
NICOSIA, CYPRUS

M. Crist Fleming, B.A., *Director*
L. Ruth Clay, B.A., M.A., Ph.D., *Headmistress*

TASIS Cyprus is located in a residential suburb of Nicosia, the island's capital, and offers an American College Preparatory and General Studies curriculum for boarding students (grades 8-12) and day students (grades 7-12).

The student-faculty ratio is 8:1 and the average class size is 12. The curriculum includes English, History, Mathematics, Science and a choice of French, Spanish, Greek or Arabic. There is a strong emphasis on extra-curricular activities off-campus with course-related and recreational day/weekend trips to the Mediterranean sea, the Troodos mountains, and historical sites throughout the Island. The sports program includes soccer, tennis, volleyball, basketball, track, swimming and skiing.

The school's main campus buildings are former hotel premises, providing complete facilities for boarding and local day students. In addition there are 3 other large dormitories in surrounding terraced garden. There are ten classrooms, a library and two newly constructed laboratories. A tennis court, basketball/volleyball court and swimming pool are adjacent.

The majority of students attending TASIS Cyprus are American, whose parents are on assignment in the Middle East. The school's close proximity to the Kingdom of Saudi Arabia and the Gulf States is advantageous and parents are encouraged to visit frequently. Most students enter colleges and universities in the U.S.A. Travel is an important feature of the program for TASIS students. Participation in inter-scholastic sports competitions in Cairo, or Athens, In-Program travel to Israel or a Greek Island serve to broaden the student's geographic and cultural horizons.

For a catalog, please contact: The TASIS Schools, Room 110, 326 East 69th Street, New York, NY 10021, Tel: (212) 570 1066, Tlx: 971912.

THE AMERICAN SCHOOL IN SWITZERLAND

CH 6926 MONTAGNOLA-LUGANO

M. Crist Fleming, B.A., *Director*
J. Christopher Frost, B.A., M.A., *Headmaster*

The American School in Switzerland (TASIS), founded in 1955, is the oldest American independent boarding school in Europe. Offering a program for grades 7-12 and a Post Graduate year, the School stresses academic training, guidance, and testing in preparation for American colleges. The School's basic aim is to contribute significantly to the growth and development of its students by fostering independent thinking, stimulating an enthusiasm for learning, and encouraging participation as responsible citizens in today's modern society.

To achieve these goals, the School offers diverse curricula, including American College Preparatory and General Studies, and English-as-a-Second Language. Although emphasis is on high academics and thorough learning, the School believes that education is more than acquisition of knowledge, and emphasis is placed on attitudes towards work, study habits, and standards of personal excellence. A dedicated faculty and a 1:8 faculty-student ratio allow for individualized attention to each student.

Based near tri-lingual Lugano, the School takes advantage of its central European location to enrich the student's educational experience by exposure to languages and cultural resources found locally and throughout Europe. An extensive travel program, a diverse student body, and a Humanities video tape lecture series provide an international dimension to a TASIS education.

The sports program includes basketball, cycling, rugby, soccer, swimming, skiing, tennis and volleyball. In January the School reconvenes in St. Moritz for two weeks of study and winter sports. Extra-curricular activities include art, music, theater and dance.

For a catalog please contact: U.S. Admissions Office, Room 110, 326 E. 69th Street, New York, NY 10021, Tel: (212) 570-1066, Tlx: 971912 or CH 6926 Montagnola-Lugano, Switzerland, Tel (091) 54 64 71, Tlx. 79317.

SCHOOL YEAR ABROAD

BARCELONA, SPAIN
RENNES, FRANCE

School Year Abroad (SYA) offers a full academic year living and studying in Rennes, France, or Barcelona, Spain. It is sponsored by Phillips Andover Academy, Phillips Exeter Academy and St. Paul's School (N.H.)

The main purpose of School Year Abroad is to give American students the advantages of living in a foreign culture without sacrificing progress in their schools at home or strong preparation for college.

Students live with host families, join local organizations and clubs, and travel both individually and on school sponsored trips. They select courses from a curriculum designed especially for them, taught by both American (English and math teachers from the sponsoring schools) and carefully selected native instructors (literature, language, history and art all taught in Spanish/French). College Board Examinations are offered. Faculty from the sponsoring schools supervise all aspects of School Year Abroad, and students receive full academic credit for successful completion of the program.

SYA offers the advantages of boarding school...and more: room and board for the full academic year, vacations included; a host family experience; 16-19 days of group travel to important cultural and historical centers within France/Spain; extracurricular activities and sports with host country counterparts; and fluency in a language.

SYA is open to qualified boys and girls from all secondary schools during their 11th or 12th grades. Applicants must have completed the equivalent of two years of study of French or Spanish. Financial aid is available.

Catalogs and information may be obtained by writing: School Year Abroad, Dept. O, Phillips Academy, Andover, MA 01810.

II.

SCHOOLS ABROAD

Brief notes on national history or geography are provided for each country. Within each country schools are arranged alphabetically by city or town.

EUROPE

Austria Belgium Bulgaria
Czechoslovakia Denmark Finland
France Germany Greece Hungary
Iceland Ireland Italy Luxembourg
The Netherlands Norway Poland
Portugal Romania Spain Sweden
Switzerland United Kingdom (England, Northern Ireland, Scotland)
U.S.S.R. Yugoslavia

AUSTRIA

Known for its Alpine beauty and music festivals, the Republic of Austria attracts many tourists to its historical sites. Visitors can see the birthplace of Mozart, the scene of the Napoleonic battles and the home of the Hapsburgs.

Vienna, whose history dates to Roman times and where Europe twice turned back Ottoman armies, is capital of the republic. German is the language of the country. The monetary unit is the schilling (S).

SEA PINES ABROAD
  Bdg Coed Ages 13-18. Gr 9-12 PG.

A-5324 Faistenau bei Salzburg, Austria. Tel. (06228)-253.
Eva-Marie Rowley, Dir.
Col Prep. Tests CEEB TOEFL. Curr—USA. LI—Eng. CF—Greek
  Humanities Earth Sci Hist Econ Bio Ger. SI—Rem Eng & Math.
Enr 56.
Fac 10. Full 8/Part 2.
Tui 149,000 S.
Est 1972. Sem (Sept-May). ECIS ISS.
Bldgs 2. Dorms 5. Lib 2000 vols.

Located in a snowy Austrian ski-resort village, Sea Pines Abroad provides a solid academic program combined with community involvement and a home-like atmosphere. It is the school's philosophy that travel enhances education, motivates the student and makes studies relevant to his/her life. Therefore, as part of its curriculum, the school travels each year to Venice, Munich, Vienna and other cultural centers of Italy or France. Between these excursions basic college preparatory subjects are taught in conventional classrooms by traditional methods, with German a required course of study for all students.

The physical education program offers instruction in mountaineering, gymnastics, softball, swimming, skating, soccer and volleyball. Located in the Alpine village of Faistenau, the school is within walking distance from five ski-lifts.

See also page 57

AUSTRIAN ALPINE INTERNATIONAL ACADEMY
  Bdg Coed Ages 13-18. Gr 8-12.

A-9161 Maria Rain (Carinthia), Austria. Tel. 04227/84449.
Donald Ballentine, MA, Head.

Col Prep Gen Acad. Tests CEEB SSAT. Curr—USA. LI—Eng. CF—Fr
Ger Span Comp Sci Calc.
Enr 40.
Fac 6. Full 4/Part 2. M 3; F 3.
Tui $9400 (+$1000).
Est 1977. ECIS ISS. Sem (Sept-May).
Bldg. Dorms 2. Lib 1500 vols. Gym. Field.

This small coeducational boarding school offers an American
curriculum to children in 8th through 12th grade with an emphasis on
American high school completion. Intensive German is taught at all
levels and French and Spanish are added according to each child's
capability. Drama, art and music are among the curricular activities and
sports include skiing, basketball, tennis and softball. In addition,
cultural trips are made to other cities and countries.

SALZBURG INTERNATIONAL PREPARATORY SCHOOL
Bdg & Day Coed Ages 14-19. Gr 8-PG.

A-5020 Salzburg, Austria. Moosstrasse 106. Tel. (662) 44485. Telex:
633065.
Theodore Worth Rowley, Head.
Col Prep. Tests CEEB TOEFL. Curr—USA. LI—Eng. A—Fr Eng Bio Ger
Math. CF—Russ Lat Music Drama Photog.
Enr 168. Elem 10, Sec 155, PG 3. US—115. Grad '84—45. Col—44.
Fac 35.
Tui Bdg $8750; Day $800 (+$200).
Summer Session. Acad. Tui Bdg $700/mo; Day $500/mo. 4 wks.
Est 1976. Proprietary. Sem (Sept-Je). ECIS ISS.
Bldgs 9. Lib 5000 vols. Labs. Fields.

The broad-based American curriculum at this coeducational boarding
school prepares students for entrance to U.S. colleges and universities.
Classes are small, permitting individualized attention to students' work,
and advanced placement courses may be taken in most subjects.
Culture and history field trips to Paris, Vienna and Munich are an
extension of classroom work. Each year students choose three electives
from offerings in computer programming, business math, oral skills,
astronomy and photography.

Salzburg International Prep is housed in an 18th century palais-style
building with modernized facilities. Students attend dramatic and
musical productions in the town. Nearby mountains and countryside are
opportune for skiing, ice skating, sailing and riding. (See also *Summer
Sessions*).

See also pages 54-5

AMERICAN INTERNATIONAL SCHOOL IN VIENNA
Day Coed Ages 4-17. Gr N-12.

A-1190 Vienna, Austria. 47 Salmannsdorferstrasse. Tel. 44-27 63.
Dexter S. Lewis, Head.

Col Prep Gen Acad. Tests CEEB SSAT IB. Curr—USA. LI—Eng.
Enr 665.
Fac 64.
Tui $1739-3754 (+ $216-650). Schol.
Est 1957. Inc nonprofit. Sem. (Aug-Je). A/OS ECIS ISS. Accred MSA.
Bldgs 3. Lib 7000 vols. Gym. Field. Track.

Located on a 15-acre campus in northwest Vienna, this international
school was founded in 1957 by the American and Canadian Embassies.
Although Americans account for 36 per cent of the enrollment, students
from more than 40 countries attend the school. The basic program is
modelled after the American system, but the International Baccalaureate Diploma is offered to students in the secondary program. The
language of instruction is English, and German is taught at all grade
levels. Full sports and extracurricular programs are also conducted.

VIENNA INTERNATIONAL SCHOOL
  Day Coed Ages 3-18. Gr N-12.

A-1190 Vienna 19, Austria. Peter Jordanstrasse 70. Tel. 37-41-96.
Maurice Pezet, Dir.
Col Prep. Tests GCE IB. Curr—Intl. LI—Eng.
Tui $A12,500-32,000.
Est 1978. Sem (Sept-Je). ECIS.

Formerly the English School of Vienna, this school's primary and
pre-school divisions are located at Grinzingerstrasse 95. The academic
curriculum is designed to meet the unique needs of the international
community and therefore accords special emphasis to the mastery of
languages. The secondary program of study prepares the student for a
general diploma, the International Baccalaureate or the British G.C.E.
Extracurricular activities include team sports and interest clubs.

BELGIUM

Conquered by Julius Caesar, and then ruled by a succession of peoples
following the Romans, the constitutional monarchy of Belgium has been
independent since 1830. The country has universal suffrage and fines
citizens who fail to vote.
A 1964 law attempted to solve Belgium's perennial language dispute
and made Flemish, a form of Dutch, the official language in the north
and French in the south, with the capital, Brussels, designated as
bilingual. The Kingdom of Belgium's monetary unit is the franc (BF).

BRUSSELS ENGLISH PRIMARY SCHOOL
  Day Coed 2$^1/_2$-12. Gr N-7.

1050 Brussels, Belgium. 23 Avenue Franklin Roosevelt. Tel. (02)
  648.43.11.
Mrs. R. H. Matthews, Head.

Pre-Prep. Tests CEEB. Curr—UK. LI—Eng. CF—Eng Math Hist Sci Art.
 SI—Fr EFL Rem & Dev Read & Math.
Enr 220. B 100; G 120. US—14.
Fac 15. Ful 11/Part 4. M 2; F 13. UK.
Tui 13,000 BF; Nursery 9000 BF.
Est 1972. Tri (Sept-July). ISS.
Lib.

This school serves the needs of the British community as well as other English-speaking residents. Education in the fundamentals of reading, writing and mathematics is offered and introduction to French language and culture is emphasized. Extracurricular activities include instruction on musical instruments, dance and athletics.

THE INTERNATIONAL SCHOOL OF BRUSSELS
  Day Coed Ages 3-18. Gr N-PG.

1170 Brussels. Belgium. 19 Kattenberg. Tel. (02) 673-60-50.
Robert L. Ater, BA, Wittenberg, Univ., MEd, Temple Univ., Supt.
Col Prep. Tests CEEB SSAT GCE IB. Curr—USA. LI—Eng. A—Hist Bio
 Fr Eng. Physics Math. CF—Fr Span Ger ESL Land Arts Math Sci.
 SI—Rem & Dev Read & Math.
Enr 1020. B 475; G 545. Elem 365, Sec 650, PG 5. US—530. Grad
 '84—105. Col—95.
Fac 99. M 37; F 62. Full 89/Part 10. US 45.
Tui 55,000-295,000 BF. Schol.
Summer Session. Lang Stud Rec. 4 wks.
Est 1951. Inc nonprofit. Sem (Sept-Je). ECIS ISS NAIS. Accred MSA.
Bldgs 6. 3 Libs 60,000 vols. Gyms 3. Fields.

Americans comprise 50% of the enrollment at this day school where the English-speaking curriculum prepares for entrance to colleges in the United States. Study of the French language is emphasized with no less than three levels offered at each grade level. The high school offers courses leading to the International Baccalaureate program and computer programming is offered as an elective. Extracurricular activities include such clubs as chess, ecology, drama, newspaper, yearbook and creative writing. In addition to a band and chorus, numerous team sports are available.

The school is located on a 40-acre campus with three separate buildings for the elementary, middle and high schools. Students are encouraged to take advantage of the Belgian setting and the community resources in Brussels.

THE ANTWERP INTERNATIONAL SCHOOL, V.Z.W.D.
  Day Coed Ages 4-18. Gr N-PG.

2070 Ekeren/Antwerp, Belgium. 180 Veltwijcklaan. Tel. 32.3.541.60.47.
Robert F. Schaecher, MS, California State Univ., Head.
Col Prep. Tests IB. Curr—USA. LI—Eng. CF—Fr Ger Dutch Sci Math
 Comp. SI—Rem & Dev Read & Math Tut ESL.

Enr 253. B 125; G 128. Elem 127, Sec 126. US—112. Grad '84—27.
Fac 26. Full 24/Part 2. M 9: F 17. US 12.
Tui $5200.
Est 1967. Nonprofit. Sem (Sept-Je). ECIS ISS. Accred NEASC.
Bldgs 4. Lib 10,000 vols. Gym.

This coeducational day school was founded to meet the educational needs of the international community of Antwerp. While approximately 45% of the enrollment is from the United States, many other countries are represented in the student body, most of whom have lived in one or more other countries before coming to Antwerp. French is taught on a daily basis, and German is taught at the secondary levels. Emphasis on the social sciences and languages is strong.

INTERNATIONAL SCHOOL OF LIEGE
Day Coed Ages 4¹/₂-15. Gr K-10.

4000 Liege, Belgium. Blvd. Leon Philippet 7. Tel. (041) 26 84 83.
Halyna Fedyniak, BEd, Univ. of Manchester, Head.
Gen Acad. Tests GCE. Curr—USA UK. LI—Eng. A—Fr Ger Eng Math Hist Chem Biol. CF—Soc Stud Music Crafts. SI—EFL Tut.
Enr 17. B 8; G 9.
Fac 6. M 1; F 5. US UK Nat.
Tui 240,000 BF (+50,000 BF).
Est 1967. Inc nonprofit. Tri (Sept-Je). ECIS ISS.
Bldg. Lib 5000 vols. Gym. Pool. Field.

While predominantly American in enrollment, the school has a large proportion of British children, is international in scope and welcomes students of all nationalities. The curriculum combines elements from American and British systems, preparing students for transfer back into their own national system. French is taught at all grade levels by a Belgian teacher. The school is located in the French-speaking city of Liege, the capital of the Province of Liege, a culturally diverse and geographically interesting area.

THE BRITISH SCHOOL OF BRUSSELS, A.S.B.L.
Day Coed Ages 3-18. Gr N-12.

1980 Tervuren, Belgium. Steenweg op Leuven 19. Tel. Brussels (02) 767-47-00.
John Jackson, MA, PhD, Head.
Col Prep Gen Acad. Tests GCE. Curr—UK. LI—Eng. CF—FR Ger Span. SI—EFL Rem & Dev Math & Read Tut.
Enr 1129. B 519; G 510. Elem 552, Sec 477. US—28. Grad '84—129. Col—118.
Fac 94. Full 79/Part 15. M 33; F 61. US 2. UK.
Tui 51,000-277,000 BF (+3000 BF). Schol.

Summer Session. Rec. Tui 2500 BF. 2 wks.
Est 1970. Nonprofit. Tri (Sept-July). ECIS ISS.
Bldgs 8. Libs 3. Labs. Gym. Field. Sports Center. Aud.

Established to meet the needs of the growing British community in this Common Market center, this school has completed its growth and building program. Students are prepared for the 'O' and 'A' levels of the G.C.E. exams. Class size does not exceed 25 and students are grouped according to ability. While the enrollment is predominantly British, students from 40 nations also attend.

ST. JOHN'S INTERNATIONAL SCHOOL
   Bdg Coed Ages 14-19; Day Coed 3-19. Gr N-PG.

1410 Waterloo, Belgium. 146 Dreve Richelle. Tel. (02) 354.11.38.
Sr. Barbara Hughes, FCJ, MEd, Boston College, Supt.
Col Prep Gen Acad. Tests CEEB SSAT GCE IB. Curr—USA Intl.
   LI—Eng. A—Eng Math Bio Chem Physics Hist Art Hist Fr Ger. CF—Fr
   Ger Stat Physics Am Hist Psych Relig Graphics Photog. SI—Rem &
   Dev Read & Math Tut ESL.
Enr 642. B 21/300; G 11/310. US—355 Grad '84—42. Col—37.
Fac 67. Full 61/Part 6. M 19; F 48. US 38. USA UK Nat.
Tui Bdg 272,000 BF (+ 20,000 BF); Day 52,000-295,000 BF (+15,000
   BF). Schol.
Summer Session. Acad Rec. Tui Day 2500 BF. 2 wks..
Est 1964. Nonprofit. Sem (Sept-Je). ECIS ISS. Accred MSA.
Bldgs 4. Dorms 2. Libs 14,000 vols. Gyms 2. Crts 3. Field.

Situated in a residential area a short distance from the historic battlefields of Waterloo, St. John's offers a basic American course of study which prepares students for the College Boards and a range of G.C.E. examinations. General instruction is in English, with French as a second language. The elementary school emphasizes basic skills in language arts and math in addition to offering daily instruction in French language and culture. Preparation for high school studies through a strong curriculum is provided within the junior high program, while the high school program prepares for college entrance or higher British and European education, with advanced placement and honors courses available in several disciplines. The full International Baccalaureate program is also offered.

A strong intramural program encourages participation in a wide range of sports including baseball, soccer, field hockey, flag football, badminton, basketball and volleyball. During mid-winter vacation, separate ski trips are organized for junior and senior high school students. A two-week ski school in Switzerland is part of the upper elementary program. Local trips are made to places such as Ghent, Bruges, Antwerp and Bastogne.

See also page 58

BULGARIA

Bordered to the north by the Danube and to the east by the Black Sea, Bulgaria was until 1908 a Turkish province. In 1947 it adopted a constitution establishing the People's Republic of Bulgaria. Predominantly an agrarian country, its monetary unit is the lev (LV); the country's language is Bulgarian.

ANGLO-AMERICAN SCHOOL OF SOFIA
Day Coed Ages 4-12. Gr K-8.

Sofia, Bulgaria. 8 Studen Kladenets. Tel. 57 02 67.
Mail to: c/o American Embassy, Sofia, Dept. of State, Washington, DC 20520.
Park D. Kauffman, Dir.
Gen Acad. Curr—USA. LI—Eng.
Enr 88.
Fac 9.
Tui $1900-3800 (+ $250).
Summer Session. Rec. Tui $100. 5 wks..
Est 1967. Inc nonprofit. Sem (Sept-Je). A/OS ECIS ISS.
Bldgs 3. Lib 2000 vols.

This small school was established to provide educational facilities for the children of the diplomatic community in Sofia. Half of the student body is drawn from the United States and Great Britain. The curriculum is American oriented, supplemented with instruction in English as a second language and French as a foreign language. Audio-visual materials are used.

CZECHOSLOVAKIA

Land of the Czechs and the Slovaks, kindred Slavic peoples who have lived in the region for 1400 years, Czechoslovakia historically has occupied a position of great strategic significance in the heart of central Europe. The country's name and boundaries emerged following World War I and the collapse of the Austro-Hungarian Empire. In 1960, the "people's democracy" was converted to the Czechoslovak Socialist Republic.

The capital is Prague, the monetary unit is the koruna (Kc), and the official languages are Czech and Slovak.

INTERNATIONAL SCHOOL OF PRAGUE
Day Coed Ages 4-14. Gr N-9.

125481 Prague, Czechoslovakia. Trziste 15. Tel. 32-67-55.
Mail to: c/o American Embassy (PRG), Dept. of State, Washington, DC 20520.
Don O. Hill, MA, Univ. of Guam, EdS, Univ. of Toledo, Dir.

Gen Acad. Curr—USA. LI—Eng. CF—Fr Ger Read Math Sci Soc Stud.
SI—Tut Math.
Enr 89. B 45; G 44. US—13.
Fac 14. Full 12/Part 2. M 4; F 10. US 11.
Tui $4500.
Est 1948. Inc nonprofit. Sem (Aug-Je). A/OS ECIS ISS.
Bldgs 2. Lib 2500 vols.

Providing elementary education to children of the international
community of Prague, this school occupies quarters in the American
Embassy. A wide range of nationalities is represented in the student
body, including children from the U.S., United Kingdom, Nigeria,
Japan and Sweden.

DENMARK

Descendants of Viking adventurers whose exploits 1000 years ago led
to Scandinavian rule of European waters, Danes today continue in their
innate prowess and love for the sea, a natural concomitant of life in their
peninsular, picturesque country. Copenhagen, or "Merchants' Haven,"
the lovely capital city, has origins as a twelfth century fishing village.
Today about half of Denmark's trade passes through the city, which is
also a center of northern European literature and art.

The Kingdom of Denmark's monetary unit is the krone (DKr) and
Danish is spoken.

RYGAARDS SCHOOL
Day Coed Ages 4-16. Gr K-11.

2900 Copenhagen, Denmark. Bernstorffsvej 54. Tel. 62-1053.
Mathias Jepsen, Head.
Col Prep Gen Acad. Tests GCE CEEB SSAT. Curr—Nat USA. LI—Eng.
CF—Danish Fr Ger Eng Math Soc Stud Relig. SI—Rem & Dev Read &
Math Tut.
Enr 305. B 139; G 166. Elem 198, Sec 107. US—35.
Fac 30. Full 19/Part 11. M 9; F 21. UK US.
Tui 1500-7140 DKr.
Est 1909. Nonprofit. Sem (Aug-Je) ECIS ISS.
Lib. Gym. Crts.

Rygaards was founded by the Sisters of the Assumption and enrolls
students from some 40 countries. The curriculum allows school leavers
to continue their studies in American or British school systems. Danish
instruction is given at all grade levels and special English classes are
provided for non-speakers. Academics are supplemented by arts,
ceramics, woodcraft and photography.

COPENHAGEN INTERNATIONAL JUNIOR SCHOOL
Day Coed Ages 5-14. Gr K-9.

1616 Copenhagen V, Denmark. Stenosgade 4c. Tel. (01) 22 33 03.
Inez Venning, BA, Albion College, MA, Columbia Univ., Prin.
Gen Acad. Curr—USA UK. LI—Eng. CF—Danish Fr Ger Math Sci Soc
   Stud Art Music. SI—ESL.
Enr 315. B 170; G 145. US—50.
Fac 29. Full 26/Part 3. M 6; F 23. US 13.
Tui $1700-2000. Schol.
Est 1973. Inc nonprofit. Tri (Aug-Je). ECIS ISS. Accred NEASC.
Bldgs 2. Lib 4500 vols. Gyms 2.

This junior section of the Copenhagen International School offers a highly individualized curriculum to meet the varied educational needs of children from 44 nations. The school strives for an atmosphere of unity while maintaining a respect for the diversity of the student population. Students are instructed through grade six by their own class teacher and emphasis is placed on the development of basic skills and useful study habits. Special classes are provided for language study, where children are taught Danish each year and French and German for five years. Instruction in all subjects is departmentalized at grade seven. Extracurricular activities include sports, student publications and government.

See also page 59

COPENHAGEN INTERNATIONAL SCHOOL
Day Coed Ages 14-19. Gr 10-PG.

1610 Copenhagen V, Denmark. Gammel Kongevej 15. Tel. (01) 21 46
   33.
James Keson, BA, Michigan, MA, Michigan State, Head.
Col Prep. Tests CEEB IB. Curr—USA. LI—Eng. CF—Danish Fr Ger Art
   Music Soc Stud Sci Math.
Enr 106. B 56; G 50. US—11. Grad '84—35. Col—20.
Fac 18. Full 8/Part 10. US 8.
Tui $4070. Schol.
Est 1963. Inc nonprofit. Sem (Aug-Je). ECIS ISA ISS. Accred NEASC.
Bldgs 2. Lib 5000 vols. Gym.

Copenhagen International School offers a curriculum including advanced and International Baccalaureate courses in all major subject areas preparing students for European and American college entrance. French, German, Danish and English are taught as second languages at all grade levels. A variety of sports and extracurricular activities are offered, while class trips in Denmark and to other parts of Europe are an integral part of the program. A junior division, the Copenhagen International Junior School, was founded in 1973.

ESBJERG INTERNATIONAL SCHOOL
  Day Coed Ages 5-17. Gr K-10.

Esbjerg DK 6700, Denmark. Kronprinsensgade 62. Tel. (05)120289.
Ole Jerg, Head.
Col Prep Gen Acad. Tests GCE. Curr—Intl. LI—Eng. CF—Fr Ger
  Danish Art Music. SI—Rem & Dev Math & Read Tut.
Enr 18. B 10; G 8. Elem 13, Sec 5. US—1. Grad '84—2. Col—1.
Fac 5. Full 3/Part 2. M 2; F 3. UK.
Tui $1650 (+$50). Schol.
Est 1982. Nonprofit. Sem (Aug-Je). ECIS.
Bldg. Lib.

Established in order to provide English-language instruction to
Esbjerg's growing foreign community, this school offers a basic
curriculum of math, science, languages, arts and physical education. The
Scottish Certificate of Education examination is administered in
addition to the G.C.E. Individualized instruction is available for
advanced students. Nine different countries are represented by the
student body. The school has access to science laboratories and athletic
facilities at a nearby public school.

FINLAND

Russia was the dominant force in Finland throughout the 19th
century. Russian was declared the official language, and the military
used Russian battle tactics in times of war. As a result of the Russian
Revolution in 1917, Finland was declared an independent nation.
  The capital, Helsinki, is the center of industry. Finnish and Swedish
are spoken in the Republic of Finland. The unit of currency is the
markka (Fmk).

THE INTERNATIONAL SCHOOL OF HELSINKI
  Day Coed Ages 4-13. Gr N-8.

00550 Helsinki, Finland. Hattulantie 2. Tel. 711-715.
Mark A. Boshko, BA, Muhlenberg College, MA, Univ. of New Mexico,
  Head.
Pre-Prep Gen Acad. Curr—US UK. LI—Eng. CF—Reading Lang Arts Fr
  Finnish Stud.
Enr 70. US—23.
Fac 10. Full 7/Part 3. M 3; F 7. US 3.
Tui $5000. Schol.
Est 1963. Sem (Aug-May). A/OS ECIS ISS.
Bldg. Lib 5000 vols. Gyms 2. Field. Playgrounds 2.

This international elementary school occupies the third floor of a
Swedish language school and is located near the center of Helsinki. The

basic elementary curriculum offers math, music, social studies and arts and crafts. After school activities include pottery, ballet, drama, puppetry, gymnastics, swimming and skating.

FRANCE

One of the dominant forces in world history, France remains the largest country in Europe outside Russia. Geographical location has been a key contributor to the nature of French civilization. Historically, France has been a natural and cultural crossroads between northern and southern Europe.

The political organization of the country by *departements* (departments) has prevailed from the Revolution, although the names of the older provinces (Normandy, Anjou, Burgundy, etc.) continue in frequent, informal usage. The names of the modern departments are nearly all taken from the physical geography of the country, especially from the rivers.

One of the most notable features of France is the great importance of its capital. The number of other very large cities in France is small; Paris is perhaps more nearly an epitome and symbol of a nation than any other of the world's great capitals. The franc (Fr) is the French Republic's monetary unit, and French is the spoken language.

COLLEGE CEVENOL INTERNATIONAL
Bdg & Day Coed Ages 12-19. Gr 9-PG.

43400 Le Chambon/Lignon, France. Tel. 71-59-72-52.
Mail to: c/o Anne W. Burnham, Moses Brown School, 250 Lloyd Ave., Providence, RI 02906.
M. Roger Hollard, Dir.
Col Prep. Tests CEEB. Curr—Nat. LI—Fr. CF—Lang + Ger Greek Philos Hist Arts. Sl—Tut Fr.
Enr 500. US—10.
Tui Bdg $3350 (+$200). Schol.
Summer Session. Fr Lang & Culture. Tui Bdg $600/session. 2 (3 wk) sessions.
Est 1938. Tri (Sept-Je). ISA.
Bldgs 12. Dorms 7. Lib. Gym. Fields. Tennis crts 4.

Offering a program preparing for the French Baccalaureate, College Cevenol provides a special French course to enable foreign students to follow the regular curriculum. Students from the United States, along with students from Great Britain, several other European nations and African countries, account for about 15% of the enrollment, the rest of which is French. Although most of the American youths study here for one year of high school only, they can prepare for the American College Boards through the courses given. The extracurricular program includes a number of sports and activities in music, dramatics and practical arts. Founded by two French Protestant pastors, the school describes itself as an "international center for peace" and welcomes students of all races and creeds. An international workcamp is conducted in July.

The school is located on a 25-acre campus at the edge of the village of Le Chambon, a popular resort area in the rural plateau region of the Cevennes Mountains.

THE BRITISH SCHOOL OF PARIS
Day Coed Ages 4½-18. Gr N-PG.

78290 Croissy-sur-Seine, France. 'Llesna Court', 38 Quai de l'Ecluse. Tel. 976-29-00.
David Cope, Head.
Col Prep. Tests CEEB GCE. Curr—UK. LI—Eng.
Enr 575.
Fac 65.
Tui 4200-6950 Fr/term (+var).
Est 1954. Tri (Sept-Je). ECIS ISA.
Bldgs 2. Lib. Lab.

Situated on the banks of the Seine, about ten miles outside of Paris, The English School serves boys and girls from 38 countries. Emphasizing French in all grades, the program follows a British syllabus and prepares for the G.C.E. examinations, for which the school is the French Center. Two Advanced Level passes on these afford sophomore standing at most American colleges. French-speaking students are provided with special English classes.

COLLEGE FRANCE-AFRIQUE
Bdg Coed Ages 5-18. Gr 1-12.

51700 Dormans (Marne), France. 38, avenue de Paris. Tel. (26) 50-21-12.
Jean Tuaux, Dir.
Pre-Prep Col Prep. Tests GCE SSAT. LI—Span Eng Ger. CF—Math Fr Hist Econ Physics.
Enr 120. B 60; G 60. Grad '84—85.
Fac 17. M 9; F 8.
Tui $4100-4800 (+$800-900). Schol.
Summer Session. Rec. Tui Bdg $27/day.
Est 1959. Tri (Sept-Je).
Bldgs 2. Dorms 20. Lib. Athletic facilities.

Situated at the edge of the Champagne district, College France-Afrique offers a general academic curriculum to an international student body. Sports are an integral part of the program and include swimming, skiing, sailing, judo, karate and fencing. Other activities offered include crafts, stamp collecting, photo clubs and cultural excursions.

INTERNATIONAL EUROPEAN SCHOOL OF PARIS
Bdg Coed Ages 6-18; Day Coed 2¹/₂-18. Gr N-PG.

91210 Draveil, France. Chateau Des Bergeries. Tel. (6) 940-70-03.
Jean Charles Koening, Prin; D. O'Sullivan, Franco-Anglo-Am Section Dir.
Col Prep Pre-Prep Gen Acad. Tests CEEB SSAT GCE IB. Curr—Intl.
LI—Fr Eng. CF—Span Ger Fr Eng World Lit Arts Writing Workshop
Comp Stud. SI—Rem & Dev Read & Math Tut.
Enr 434. B 130/120; G 110/74. US—10.
Fac 37. Full 23/Part 14. M 20; F 17. US 2. Nat.
Tui Bdg $6000; Day $3500 (+$900). Schol.
Summer Session. Acad. Tui Bdg $700. 3 wks..
Est 1957. Inc nonprofit. Tri (Sept-Je). ISA.
Bldgs 5. Dorms 3. Lib 1500 vols. Athletic facilities.

The International European School of Paris, located on the outskirts of the Forest of Senart, conducts an educational program specifically designed for foreign students. An international Montessori method is used in conjunction with bilingualism in the kindergarten. Bilingual instruction is continued within primary classes and adapted into binational sections. Secondary students may follow the French national curriculum or specific studies leading to U.S. college entrance or the International Baccalaureate. Intensive French language courses are arranged for foreign students.

Extracurricular activities include hand crafts, musical instruction, film, dancing and cultural excursions in Paris and the surrounding area. Participation in gymnastics, athletics, football, swimming, horseback riding, sailing and tennis are available.

ANGLO-AMERICAN SCHOOL—MOUGINS
Day Coed Ages 5-19. Gr 1-PG.

06250 Mougins (Alpes-Maritimes), France. 26, route de Valbonne, B.P. 01. Tel. (93) 90.15.47.
David M. Robertson, MA, DipEd Univ. of Edinburgh, Head.
Col Prep Gen Acad. Tests GCE CEEB. Curr—US UK. LI—Eng. CF—Fr
Ger Span Comp Hist (US) Art Drama Geog. SI—Tut.
Enr 100. B 51; G 49. Elem 64, Sec 36. US—25. Grad '84—10. Col—8.
Fac 15. Full 14/Part 1. M 6; F 9. UK.
Tui 25,000-33,000 Fr.
Est 1982. Nonprofit. Tri (Sept-Je).
Bldgs 2. Lib 2000 vols. Pool.

This school's American- and British-based curriculum prepares students for the G.C.E. and U.S. College Board examinations. Small classes and a broad program of math, sciences, social studies, French and electives are emphasized. Physical education is compulsory. Extracurricular activities include computer, drama, yearbook and photography clubs. Students can also participate in tennis, skiing and swimming. Boarding arrangements can be made with local families.

MARYMOUNT SCHOOL
  Day Coed Ages 3½-14. Gr N-8.

92200 Neuilly, France. 72 Blvd. de la Saussaye. Tel. 33-1624-10-51.
Sr. Diane O'Brien, BA, Marymount, MS, Hunter College, Head.
Pre-Prep. Curr—USA. LI—Eng. CF—Relig Fr Comp Music Arts.
  SI—Rem & Dev Read & Math Tut.
Enr 269. B 138; G 131. US—154.
Fac 30. Full 29/Part 1. M 5; F 25. US 13.
Tui $4000 (+2275). Schol.
Est 1923. Inc nonprofit. Roman Catholic. Tri (Sept-Je). ECIS ISS.
  Accred MSA.
Bldgs 4. Lib 10,000 vols. Lab. Gym. Field. Tennis crts. Pool.

Marymount is one of the several Catholic schools established in Paris, London and Rome, having an international character. A non-graded elementary curriculum is offered to English-speaking children. The academic program is enriched by a full range of extracurricular activities. Neuilly, a suburb noted for its elegant residential section, is near the Bois de Boulogne, immediately to the west of Paris. The school is situated on a 1½-acre campus.

ECOLE ACTIVE BILINGUE J.M.
  Day Coed Ages 3-18. Gr N-12.

75015 Paris, France. 70 rue de Theatre. Tel. 575 62 98.
Jacqueline Roubinet, Head.
Col Prep Pre-Prep Gen Acad. Tests CEEB SSAT GCE IB. Curr—USA
  Nat. LI—Eng Fr. CF—Rom Lang Ger Russ Lat Hist (US) Arts Comp
  Stud. SI—Tut.
Enr 2100. Elem 1640, Sec 460.
Fac 150. Full 144/Part 6. US 2. Fr.
Tui 2800 Fr (+150 Fr).
Est 1954. Partnership. Tri (Sept-Je). ECIS ISA ISS.
Bldgs 7. Libs 4. Athletic facilities.

Ecole Active Bilingue J.M. is a bilingual elementary and secondary school that prepares boys and girls for U.S. College Boards, the British G.C.E. 'A' and 'O' exams, the French Baccalaureate and the International Baccalaureate. Pupils from over 25 countries are instructed in French and English from kindergarten, and may elect another language from Spanish, German, Italian or Russian offerings in grade six. Non-French speakers enroll in adaption classes at all levels. Special language courses include Japanese, Arab and Persian studies.
  The school's three locations are within walking distance from the Eiffel Tower. The main building, completed in 1979, houses science labs, word processors, an audio-visual center and other academic and recreational facilities.

INTERNATIONAL SCHOOL OF PARIS
Day Coed Ages 4-18. Gr N-12.

75016 Paris, France. 96, bis, rue du Ranelagh. Tel. 224 43 40.
Patricia Hayot, Prin.
Gen Acad Col Prep. Tests IB GCE CEEB. Curr—UK USA. LI—Eng.
CF—Fr Ger Arts. SI—Tut Rem Read & Math ESL.
Enr 300. B 150; G 150.
Fac 39. Full 26/Part 13. M 18; F 21. US 10.
Tui $4000.
Summer Session. Acad Rec. Tui $600/5 wks..
Est 1964. Nonprofit. Sem (Sept-Je). A/OS ECIS ISS. Accred NEASC.
Bldgs 2. 2 Libs 5000 vols.

In a large townhouse situated in the heart of Paris, this school serves the city's international community. Following an Anglo-American elementary curriculum, the school emphasizes learning French language, culture and history. Primary and intermediate grades work in a self-contained atmosphere with one class teacher supplemented by French, art, music and physical education specialists. The Upper School integrates sixth, seventh and eighth graders, with students working at a pace and depth appropriate to their grade level and ability. A summer program combines a variety of recreational activities with remedial and enrichment classes.

After school sports and activities include ballet, art, pottery, music, karate, jujitsu, soccer, basketball and baseball. Frequent field trips are taken to points of interest in Paris.

UNITED NATIONS NURSERY SCHOOL
Day Coed Ages 3-5. N-K.

Paris, France. 40 Rue Pierre Guerin. Tel. 3315272024.
Brigitte Weill, Dir.
Curr—USA. LI—Eng Fr. CF—Read Drama Arts.
Enr 100.
Fac 6. Denmark Fr UK.
Summer School. Rec Enrich. 4 wks..
Est 1951. Nonprofit. Tri (Sept-Je). ISA ISS.

This international, cooperative, bilingual pre-school, founded by several UNESCO staff members, is under the aegis of the French Ministry of Health and its office for Protection Maternelle et Infantile. Bilingual teachers (English/French) conduct a program based on active methods of instruction. Bilingualism is encouraged though it is not the main objective of the program.

Crafts, music, painting, movement and outings are among the activities offered. Children may grow their own flowers and vegetables in the school garden.

AMERICAN SCHOOL OF PARIS
  Day Coed Ages 5-18. Gr K-12.

92210 Saint-Cloud, France. 41 rue Pasteur. Tel. 602-54-43.
George Cohan, MA, Wesleyan, EdD, Harvard, Head.
Col Prep. Tests IB CEEB. Curr—USA. LI—Eng. CF—Fr Span Ger Relig
  Film-Making Logic Mech Drawing Comp Stud.
Enr 851. B 422; G 429. Elem 452, Sec 399. US—553.
Fac 84. Full 74/Part 10. US 60.
Tui $4800-5500. Schol.
Summer Session. Acad Rec. Tui Day $300-350/wk.
Est 1946. Inc nonprofit. Sem (Sept-Je). A/OS ECIS ISS NAIS. Accred
  MSA.
Bldgs 5. 2 Libs 18,000 vols. Labs. Gyms 2. Aud.

Serving primarily the children of United States nationals living in the
area, this school follows an American college preparatory curriculum.
Americans comprise approximately 65% of the enrollment with 50 other
nationalities represented. French is required of all students and
extensive elective offerings in all subject areas enrich the academic
program. Most graduates enter leading colleges in the U.S. and abroad.

Located 7 miles from the Arc de Triomphe on a 12-acre campus, the
school offers a wide variety of interscholastic and intramural sports such
as soccer, tennis and basketball.

LYCEE INTERNATIONAL—AMERICAN SECTION
  Day Coed Ages 3-19. Gr N-PG.

78100 Saint-Germain-en-Laye, France. 4 Rue du Fer a Cheval. B.P.
  230. Tel. (3) 451-94-11.
Nancy Magaud, Dir.
Col Prep Gen Acad. Tests CEEB IB. Curr—USA Nat. LI—Eng Fr.
  CF—Danish Ger Swed Ital Port Dutch Ger Russ Lat Greek Hist (US)
  Pol Sci Arts. SI—Tut.
Enr 520. Elem 425, Sec 95.
Fac 13. Full 9/Part 4. M 6; F 7.
Tui 6600 Fr.
Est 1954. Inc nonprofit. Tri (Sept-July). ECIS ISS.
Bldgs 9. Lib. Gym. Fields.

Located near the Seine, 13 miles west of Paris, Lycee International
features a strong academic curriculum which centers on mathematics,
natural science and linguistics. Although a French public school, its
faculty and student body are comprised of many nationalities, and are
divided into sections according to country. Within each section,
preparation is offered for the different national university entrance
exams, including the U.S. College Boards, the French Baccalaureate and
the International Baccalaureate.

In the American Section, English and social studies are taught in
English, while science and mathematics courses are conducted in
French. Students whose language ability does not allow them to follow

the French curriculum enter adaptation classes. Recent U.S. graduates have attended Brown, George Washington, M.I.T., Tufts, Yale, Georgetown and Princeton.

The athletic program offers competition in the major sports as well as judo, gymnastics, sailing, golf, theatre and dance. Students are encouraged to take advantage of the many cultural opportunities in nearby Paris and frequent excursions are planned. An adult education program is also offered.

COMPLEXE SCOLAIRE DE SOPHIA ANTIPOLIS—INTERNATIONAL SECTION
Bdg & Day Coed Ages 11-18.

06565 Valbonne, France. Tel. (93) 33-91-91.
Eugene Stevelberg, BA, Univ. of Michigan, MA, Univ. of Minnesota, Dir.
Pre-Prep Col Prep. Tests IB CEEB SSAT. Curr—Intl. LI—Eng Fr.
   CF—Lang Sci Math Hist Art. SI—Tut.
Enr 200. B 45/53; G 45/57. Elem 64, Sec 136. US—35. Grad '84—28.
   Col—25.
Fac 34. Full 30/Part 4. M 15; F 19. US 6. France US UK.
Tui Bdg 31,500-51,000 Fr (+ 1500 Fr); Day 4000-19,500 Fr (+ 1500 Fr).
Est 1979. Nonprofit. Tri (Sept-Je). ECIS ISS.
Bldgs 15. Dorms 8. Libs 2. Gym. Crts. Stadium.

The Complexe Scolaire is a large primary/high school with the International Section composing an integral part of it. A bilingual French and English program is provided in all subjects with special instruction in French if necessary. Other languages offered include German, Spanish, Farsi and Arabic. Students may also elect to take a course of study leading to the International Baccalaureate. Sailing, horseback riding, gymnastics, swimming and team sports are among the recreational activities.

GERMANY

Fragmented for centuries and finally forged into a political state by the King of Prussia in 1871, Germany was divided again by World War II. Today Germany exists as East Germany and West Germany, physically and symbolically divided by the Berlin Wall. The Communist Party presides over East Germany, and West Germany is a parliamentary democracy.

Both countries engage in productive agricultural and industrial pursuits. The Danube, Elbe and Rhine Rivers provide accessibility for ships to travel to other European ports. Shipping is regulated by a commission of international representatives.

Bonn is the capital of the Federal Republic of Germany where the monetary unit is the deutschemark (DM). The German Democratic Republic's capital is East Berlin, and the monetary unit is the ostmark (OM). German is the official language of both countries.

JOHN F. KENNEDY SCHOOL
Day Coed Ages 5-19. Gr K-13.

1000 Berlin 37, Germany. Teltower Damm 87/93. Tel. (030) 807-2713.
Kenneth F. Hadermann, BA, MA, Columbia, Prin.
Col Prep. Tests CEEB. Curr—Nat USA. LI—Eng Ger. CF—Lat
Computer Sci Natural Sci Fr Lat Music Art. SI—Lang Arts Rem & Dev
Read.
Enr 1272. Elem 889, Sec 383. US—666.
Fac 117. Full 104/Part 13. US 57.
Tui Free.
Est 1960. Sem (Aug-Je). A/OS ECIS ISS.
Bldgs 5. Libs 2. Gyms 2. Field.

Situated in a suburb of Zehlendorf in south-west Berlin, this public
school offers a German-American intra-cultural program with bilingual
instruction. The curriculum employs the latest techniques and materials
from both countries, offering a business program preparing for
employment in German and American firms in addition to the college
preparatory program. Students participate in extracurricular activities in
areas such as arts and crafts, cooking, sports, gymnastics, photography,
music and drama.

BRITISH EMBASSY PREPARATORY SCHOOL
Day Coed Ages 4½-13. Gr K-7.

5300 Bonn 2, Germany. Tulpenbaumweg 42. Tel. 0228/32.31.66.
L.J. Middleton-Weaver, Head.
Gen Acad. Tests GCE. Curr—UK. LI—Eng. CF—Ger Fr Geog Hist
Music SI—Rem & Dev Math & Read Tut.
Enr 198. B 99; G 99.
Fac 14. Full 11/Part 3. M 4; F 10. UK.
Tui 7800 DM.
Est 1963. Nonprofit. Tri (Sept-July). ECIS ISS.
Bldgs 3. Lib 1000 vols. Track.

A basic elementary academic program is followed at this school for
children of the British Mission to Bonn. Remedial work is conducted in
English and math. Enrollment priority is given to British children,
however, enrollment is open to English-speaking children of other
countries.

AMERICAN INTERNATIONAL SCHOOL OF DUSSELDORF
Day Coed Ages 4-19. Gr N-PG.

4000 Dusseldorf 31-Kaiserwerth, Germany. Leuchtenberger Kirchweg
2. Tel. 0211/40 70 56.
James M. Cantwell, BA, Univ. of Vermont, MAT, Antioch, MEd, EdD,
Columbia Univ., Dir.

Col Prep Gen Acad. Tests CEEB IB. LI—Eng. A—Chem Biol Physics
Calc Ger Fr Art Eng Hist. CF—Fr Ger Hist Econ Physics Art Music.
SI—Math Rem Read ESL.
Enr 320. Elem 164, Sec 156. US—146. Grad '84—20. Col—18.
Fac 43. Full 39/Part 4. US 30.
Tui $3000-4800 (+ $1500). Schol.
Summer Session. Acad Rec. Tui $150-200/wk. 4 wks..
Est 1968. Nonprofit. Quar (Sept-Je). A/OS ECIS ISS. Accred NEASC.
Bldgs 6. Lib 10,000 vols. Labs 2. Gym. Fields.

Situated on a six-acre campus near the Rhine in the picturesque
suburb of Kaiserwerth, this predominantly American school draws its
enrollment from over 24 countries. Contemporary teaching methods
such as integrated day and team teaching are employed in the
well-rounded curriculum. A wide variety of electives, independent study
and advanced work are also offered, with German taught at all levels.
The extracurricular program features sports, photography, cooking and
crafts.

INTERNATIONAL SCHOOL OF HAMBURG
Day Coed Ages 4-18. Gr N-12.

2000 Hamburg 52, Germany. Holmbrook 20. Tel. (040) 823667.
Allan Wilcox, BSc, BED, Melbourne, Head.
Col Prep. Tests CEEB SSAT GCE IB. Curr—USA UK. LI—Eng. CF—Fr
Ger Hist Sci Soc Stud Art Music Phys Ed. SI—Rem & Dev Math &
Read ESL.
Enr 530. B 270; G 260. Elem 370, Sec 160. US—75. Grad '84—25.
Col—23.
Fac 62. Full 46/Part 16. M 28; F 34. US 15. UK.
Tui 6500-11,055 DM. Schol.
Est 1957. Inc nonprofit. Sem (Sept-Je). A/OS ECIS ISA ISS.
Bldgs 1. 2 Libs 13,000 vols. Gym.

Drawing its enrollment from over 45 different countries, this
international school follows American and British curricular patterns.
Most students come from the U.K., and many from Japan, Iran and the
U.S. Ten years of German and six of French are offered. Elective
courses include computer math, photography, drama and crafts. ESL is
taught by staff specialists. In addition to preparation for the U.S.
College Boards and the British G.C.E. ('O' Level), the International
Baccalaureate was introduced in 1979.

ODENWALDSCHULE
Bdg Coed Ages 9-20; Day 3-20. Gr N-13.

6148 Heppenheim 4, Germany. Odenwaldschule Ober Hambach. Tel.
06252/2061.
Dr. Wolfgang Harder, Dir.
Col Prep Gen Acad. Curr—Nat Intl. A—Arts Lit Psych Sci. CF—Eng Fr
Lat Carpentry Metalwork. SI—Rem & Dev Read & Math Tut.

Enr 330. B 175/32; G 94/29. US—2. Grad '84—34. Col—29.
Fac 51. Full 37/Part 14. M 28; F 23. US 1. Ger.
Tui Bdg 19,000 DM (+1000 DM); Day 5000 DM (+1000 DM).
Est 1910. Nonprofit. Quar (Aug-July).
Bdgs 26. Dorms 14. Lib 26,000 vols. Gym. Field.

Located in a mountainous area north of Heidelberg, Odenwaldschule offers preparation for the German "Abitur" which is recognized as a requirement for university entrance in the U.S. and Europe. The comprehensive curriculum features practical instruction in skills such as metalwork and design. Students have a voice in all major decisions of the school, and the student government is a vital organ in the process. A variety of hobby and interest groups are also available.

See also page 63

MUNICH INTERNATIONAL SCHOOL
Day Coed Ages 5-19. Gr K-12.

Munich, Germany. D-8136 Percha bei Starnberg, Schloss Buchhof. Tel. 3071.
Lista Hanna, Head.
Col Prep Gen Acad. Tests CEEB SSAT. Curr—USA UK. LI—Eng Ger.
Enr 542.
Fac 53.
Tui $1115-3850.
Summer Session. Acad Rec..
Est 1966. Inc nonprofit. Sem (Sept-Je). A/OS ECIS ISS.
Bldgs 4. Gym. Fields. Courts.

Established by a group of business and professional people in the Munich area, this coeducational day school attracts students from many countries. Americans comprise about 40% of the enrollment with France and Britain also numerously represented. The college preparatory curriculum prepares students for the U.S. College Boards and the British G.C.E. exams. Daily instruction is offered in German and there is special tutoring in English as a second language. Special education services are available for learning disabilities, remedial reading, speech therapy and the blind and deaf.

The junior school (Grades K-5) was opened in Munich proper in 1972. The senior school, located 20 miles from Munich, is in the heart of the Bavarian Alps, thereby enabling the students to benefit from the area's ski resources. Trips to Vienna and Paris and use of the wide cultural opportunities of Munich are also encouraged.

THE FRANKFURT INTERNATIONAL SCHOOL E.V.
Day Coed Ages 5-18. Gr K-12.

637 Oberursel/Taunus, Germany. An der Waldlust 5-7. Tel. 06171-2020.
Peter D. Gibbons, PhD, Univ. of Colorado, Head.

Col Prep. Tests CEEB IB. Curr—USA. Ll—Eng. CF—Fr Ger Math Sci Hist Soc Studies Art Music.
Enr 1070. B 535; G 535.
Fac 90. Full 84/Part 6.
Tui 8000-10,800 DM (+ var). Schol.
Est 1961. Inc nonprofit. Tri (Sept-Je). ECIS ISA ISS NAIS. Accred MSA.
Bldgs 5. Lib 25,000 vols. Athletic facilities.

Frankfurt International School was founded to provide a college preparatory education for children of the international community residing in the metropolitan area of Frankfurt/Main, Germany. The curriculum is based primarily on the American model, and the language of instruction is English. German as a second language is obligatory for most students from the first grade. Americans account for the largest number of students, with German and English children next.

Elementary School programs are presented with an emphasis on small group instruction. The Middle School continues to build on the foundation laid in the Elementary School. The school prepares students for the International Baccalaureate Program.

Active intramural and intermural sports are offered at all grade levels. Throughout the school year educational field trips supplement classroom work. The campus is about ten miles from central Frankfurt, surrounded by a natural forest near the Taunus Mountains, and easily accessible by public transportation.

CHEMICAL INSTITUTE DR. FLAD
  Bdg & Day Coed Ages 16-18. Gr 11-12.

D-7000 Stuttgart 1 (Baden-Wuerttemberg), Germany. Breitscheid-strasse 127. Tel. 0711/63 47 60.
Dr. Flad, Head.
Col Prep Voc. Ll—Ger. CF—Eng Span Chem.
Enr 320. B 15/120; G 25/160.
Fac 33. Full 10/Part 23. M 24; F 9. Germany.
Tui Bdg $200/mo (+ $20); Day $90/mo (+ $20). Schol.
Est 1951. Nonprofit. Sem (Aug-July). ISA.
Bldgs 3. Dorms. Lib 8000 vols.

Founded by Dr. Flad, the Chemical Institute provides intensive training in technochemistry. Students receive practical experience in many fields of chemistry and learn to handle equipment in both research and industrial laboratories. Athletic and cultural activities are also available.

GREECE

The historical remnants of later Western civilization are evident in Greece. The Parthenon still stands atop the Acropolis as a testament to the remarkable culture of ancient Greece. Tourists and students also visit the ancient theatre at Epidaurus, Apollonian ruins at Delphi and

Socrates' prison cell. The art and literature of ancient Greece give lasting prominence to the names Aristotle, Plato and Euripides.

The government of early Greece was a city-state ruled by a monarch, and today the Hellenic Republic has a parliamentary structure.

Although Greece is strikingly diverse in geographical composition, a large percentage of Greeks still manage to farm the land. Fruits and vegetables are the main exports.

Athens, the capital city, is a center of political and cultural events of international significance. Greek is the country's language; the drachma (Dr) is the monetary unit.

AMERICAN COMMUNITY SCHOOLS OF ATHENS
Bdg Coed Ages 14-18; Day Coed 4-18. Gr K-12.

Athens, Greece. 129 Aghias Paraskevis St., Ano Halandri. Tel. 6593-200. Telex: 223355 ACS GR.
Mail to: APO New York 09253.
John Dorbis, PhD, Univ. of Paris, Supt.
Col Prep Gen Acad Bus. Tests CEEB SSAT IB. Curr—USA. LI—Eng.
  CF—Greek Fr Ger Span Lat Arabic His (US) Econ Pol Sci Arts Typ.
  SI—Rem & Dev Read & Math Learning Disabilities.
Enr 1647. B 783; G 864. US—948. Grad '84—185. Col—148.
Fac 133. Full 113/Part 20. US 102. Nat.
Tui Bdg $10,850; Day $985-3325. Schol.
Summer Session. Acad Rec. Tui Day $127/Elem level; $45-95/crse
  Sec level. 4 wks..
Est 1950. Inc nonprofit. Sem (Sept-Je). A/OS ECIS ISS NAIS NE/SA.
  Accred MSA.
Bldgs 16. Dorms 2. 3 Libs 28,000 vols. Labs. Gym. Aud. Field.

The American Community Schools of Athens occupy two campuses —in the Athens suburbs of Halandri and Kifissia. English-speaking children of many different nationalities are accepted with about 40% of the enrollment non-American. Each of the schools emphasizes the growth and development of students as individuals, with teachers working with children in groups and separately. Offering a curriculum similar to that of an American school, students are prepared for the U.S. College Boards. The curriculum also includes business education, industrial and applied arts, home economics, advanced placement courses as well as the International Baccalaureate. Modern Greek and French are taught from the first grade, German and Spanish from grade seven and Latin from grade nine. The foreign language program leads to official diplomas. Recent graduates have entered Princeton, UPENN, Johns Hopkins, Tufts and Yale. Activities include language study/travel seminars, model UN, excursion club, forensics and field trips.

ATHENS COLLEGE
Bdg Boys Ages 10-18, Day 6-19; Day Girls 6-12. Gr 1-PG.

Athens, Greece. PO Box 5 Psychico. Tel. 671-4621-8.
Mail to: 380 Madison Avenue, New York, NY 10017.

John Summerskill, Pres.
Col Prep Gen Acad. Tests CEEB GCE. Curr—Nat. LI—Greek.
Enr 2185.
Fac 178.
Tui Bdg 250,000 Dr; Day 100,000 Dr. Schol.
Summer Session. Rec. 9 wks..
Est 1925. Tri (Sept-Je). ECIS ISS.
Bldgs 13. Dorms 5. Lib 45,000 vols. Athletic facilities.

Emphasizing bilinguality in the upper grades, Athens College prepares boys for university entrance in Greece, Europe and the United States. Established by a group of Greek and U.S. citizens, the binational character of the school is reflected in its program and its joint American and Greek sponsorship. While most of the school's students are from Athens and vicinity, others come from other parts of Greece and the world. Approximately 65% of all graduates enter universities in Greece, 17% in the U.S. and 18% in Europe. Those entering college in the U.S. generally receive junior standing if they follow liberal arts programs.

The curriculum, while essentially that of a Greek school, requires boys to study English as a second language in all grades. Some courses in the upper grades are taught in English (i.e. non-Greek history, math and some sciences). All other instruction is in Greek. 20% of the students at Athens College receive scholarship aid. The elementary school is situated on the Kantza campus, six miles out of Athens. The secondary school campus is located in the Athens suburb of Psychico.

THE CAMPION SCHOOL
Bdg Coed Ages 12-19; Day Coed 4-19. Gr K-PG.

154 10 Psychico, Athens, Greece. Box 65009. Tel. 8133883.
A.F. Eggleston, OBE, MA, Oxon, Head.
Col Prep Gen Acad. Tests CEEB GCE SSAT. Curr-UK USA. LI—Eng.
CF—Arabic Fr Ger Greek Lat Span Ital Hist (US) Econ. SI—Tut.
Enr 940. B 20/450; G 20/450. US—150. Grad '84—100. Col—120.
Fac 106. Full 97/Part 9. US 5. UK.
Tui Bdg $10,500 (+ $500); Day $2600-4000 (+ 1500). Schol.
Summer Session. Acad. Rec. 5 wks..
Est 1970. Inc nonprofit. Tri (Sept-Je). ECIS.
Bldgs 3. Dorm. 2 Libs. Athletic facilities.

This school follows a combined British and American curriculum to prepare students for the U.S. College Boards and the British G.C.E. 'O' and 'A' level exams. Instruction is bilingual in English and Greek, and both classical and modern Greek, as well as Arabic are among the language electives. Activities in music and art, team sports and interest clubs are additional curricular features.

See also page 72

ANATOLIA COLLEGE
Bdg & Day Coed Ages 12-18. Gr 7-PG.

Thessaloniki, Greece. P.O. Box 10143. Tel. 301-071(-7).
William W. McGrew, BA, Reed College, MA, PhD, Univ. of Cincinnati, Pres.
Col Prep. Tests CEEB TOEFL. Curr—Nat. LI—Greek Eng. CF—Eng Greek Physics Relig Philos Econ Lit.
Enr 1153. B 42/555; G 30/526. US 15. Grad '84—193. Col—125.
Fac 83. Full 83. M 47; F 36. US 23.
Tui Bdg $2770; Day $1150 (+$160). Schol.
Summer Session. Acad. Tui Bdg $1350. 6 wks..
Est 1886. Inc nonprofit. Sem (Sept-Je). ISS.
Bldgs 19. Dorms 3. Lib 17,000 vols. Gym. Tennis courts. Fields.

Located on 45 acres overlooking the Gulf and old quarter of Thessaloniki, Anatolia is binationally sponsored by American and Greek citizens. Nearly all the students are from Greece, but each year several attend from the U.S. and various countries in the Near East and other parts of the world. Secondary subjects are taught in English and primary subjects in Greek.

PINEWOOD SCHOOLS OF THESSALONIKI
Bdg Coed Ages 13-18; Day Coed 5-18. Gr K-12.

Thessaloniki (Macedonia), Greece. P.O. Box 21001 Pilea. Tel. 301-22155510. Telex: 412634 PHAR GR.
Peter B. Baiter, AB, Princeton, MA, Harvard, Dir.
Col Prep Gen Acad. Tests CEEB SSAT GCE. Curr—USA. LI—Eng. A—Chem Physics Math. CF—Fr Greek Eng Soc Stud Math Sci Comp. SI—ESL.
Enr 132. US—58. Grad '84—15 Col—12.
Fac 17. Full 12/Part 5. US 8.
Tui 157,080-236,900 Drs.
Est 1950. Inc 1961 nonprofit. Sem (Sept-Je). A/OS ISS NE/SA.
Bldg. Lib 15,000 vols. Sci lab. Gym. Fields. Tennis courts.

Pinewood is located in Thessaloniki, the second largest city in Greece. Housed on Anatolia College campus, it was first established as an elementary school in 1950 by a group of British and American parents. All facilities are in one building, constructed with two wings and a multi-purpose room in the center.

Students work in traditional, self-contained classrooms with specialists in music, physical education, foreign languages, ESL and art assisting teachers. Electives at the secondary level include interdisciplinary studies, music, art and consumer math. Students are prepared for the U.S. College Boards.

Activities for older students include chorus, forensics tournaments and school publications. Among sports offerings are soccer, basketball, volleyball, flag football, softball and tennis.

HUNGARY

Strategically located in the fertile Danube Basin of central Europe, Hungary has frequently been a center of unrest, occupied at various points in its history by Austria, Germany and Russia. The historic state was originally formed by the massive migration of the normadic Magyar peoples in 896 A.D. from the steppes of Russia. The population has since been mingled with many other cultures including Turks, Germans, Slavs and Jews. Budapest is the capital of the Hungarian People's Republic. Magyar is the official language, and the forint (Ft) is the monetary unit.

THE AMERICAN SCHOOL OF BUDAPEST
  Day Coed Ages 5-14. Gr K-8.

Budapest, Hungary. Tel. 312-955.
Mail to: American School of Budapest, AMCONGEN (BUD), APO New York, NY 09213.
John R. Lents, BA, George Peabody College, MA, Univ. of Kansas, Dir.
Gen Acad. Curr—USA. LI—Eng. CF—Fr Soc Stud Lab Sci Music Art. SI—ESL.
Enr 97. B 41; G 56. US—9.
Fac 12. Full 8/Part 4. US 7.
Tui $3900 (+ $100).
Est 1973. Nonprofit. Sem (Sept-Je). A/OS ECIS ISS.
Bldgs 1. Lib. Athletic facilities.

A typical American curriculum is offered at this school for American dependent children and children of other English-speaking foreign residents in Budapest. Instruction in French language is given to all students fluent in English. A Hungarian studies program is offered for children in grades 1-8. Facilities at the American Embassy, a five-minute walk away from the school, are used for gym classes.

ICELAND

One of the most volcanic countries in the world, the Republic of Iceland is an Arctic island in the North Atlantic. First settled by the Vikings shortly before 900 A.D., its General Assembly, or Althing, is the oldest democratic governing body in existence. Sheep herding, fishing and farming are the main occupations of the people who are of Scandinavian stock and Lutheran in religion. The language is Icelandic, the capital Reykjavik, and the monetary unit the krona (IKr).

AMERICAN EMBASSY SCHOOL OF REYKJAVIK
  Day Coed Ages 5-10. Gr K-4.

Reykjavik, Iceland. Bergstadastreti 52. Tel. 18209.
Mail to: American Embassy, (Reykjavik), FPO New York 09571.

Mrs. Barbara Sigurbjornsson, BA, Hamline Univ., MS, Mankato State, Head.
Gen Acad. Curr—USA. LI—Eng. CF—Math Sci Soc Stud Lang Arts.
Enr 18. B 8; G 10. US—5.
Fac 3. US 3.
Tui $1300-2350 (+ $10).
Est 1959. Quar (Sept-May). A/OS ISS.

Serving the children of United States Embassy personnel and other foreign residents in the port city of Reykjavik, this small school follows an American curriculum. The children have bi-weekly swimming lessons and access to a small library. Many field trips are taken in the local community.

IRELAND

Separated from England by the Irish Sea and St. George's Channel, Ireland comprises the entire island with the exception of the six northern counties. The Gaelic civilization was cultivated by the Celts in the fourth century B.C. Independence from Britain was established in 1948, and the Republic of Ireland was formed in 1949. Dublin is the country's capital and Irish and English are spoken. The Irish pound (£Ir) is the monetary unit.

ST. ANDREW'S COLLEGE
  Bdg Boys Ages 11-18; Day Coed Ages 6-18. Gr 1-12.

Blackrock, County Dublin, Republic of Ireland. Booterstown Ave. Tel. 88-27-85.
Col Prep. Tests CEEB. LI—Eng. CF—Fr Ger Span Lat.
Enr 784. US—43.
Fac 51. US 1.
Tui $2266; Day $618-824.
Est 1894. Tri (Sept-Je). A/OS ISS.
Lib. Labs 3.

St. Andrew's College provides a liberal education to prepare students for the Intermediate and Leaving Certificate Examinations and college entrance. The wide range of facilities include a computer room, a lecture theatre and a home economics laboratory.

RATHDOWN SCHOOL
  Bdg Girls Ages 10-18; Day Girls 4-18. Gr K-12.

Glenageary (County Dublin), Ireland. Tel. Dublin 853133.
S.G. Mew, MA, DipEd, Dublin Univ., Prin.
Col Prep Gen Acad. Tests GCE. Curr—Nat. LI—Eng. CF—Fr Ger Lat Hist Home Econ. SI—Tut.
Enr 435. B /6; G 96/333. US—3. Grad '84—30. Col—20.
Fac 33. Full 27/Part 6. M 4; F 29. Ireland.

Tui Bdg £3000 (+ £250); Day £1000 (+ £100).
Est 1972. Nonprofit. Tri (Sept-Je).
Bldgs 10. Dorms 17. 2 Libs 10,000 vols. Gym. Fields. Crts.

Rathdown School was founded as the amalgamation of three older Irish schools. Its curriculum includes languages, math, history, physics, chemistry, biology and art. The sports program offers fencing, judo, squash, horseback riding, sailing and canoeing. Students come from Spain, Nigeria, the U.S. and Britain as well as Ireland. Boys ages four to eight are admitted as day students.

ITALY

While having a history more than 2500 years old, making it the oldest nation in Europe after Greece, Italy as a modern state is very young, dating only from 1861 when the establishment of monarchy ended centuries of political disunity. Well known in Italian history is a continual disparity between cultural and political development, the former usually flourishing, the latter generally languishing.

Today Renaissance art and architecture coexist with jet age trappings of the postwar growth that doubled personal income and quadrupled industrial production during Italy's first two decades as a republic. Rome, Eternal City and capital, and Florence, Venice, Pisa and other spots continue to attract millions of visitors, tourists and students yearly. The lira (Lit) is the Republic of Italy's monetary unit and Italian is the official language.

THE AMERICAN SCHOOL OF FLORENCE
  Day Coed Ages 4-19. Gr K-12.

50012 Bagno a Ripoli, Florence, Italy. Villa Le Tavernule, Via del Carota 16. Tel. (066) 640.033.
Anne Dreydel, Prin.
Col Prep Gen Acad. Tests CEEB GCE SSAT. Curr—USA. LI—Eng.
Enr 121.
Fac 24.
Tui $1560-3160 (+ $300). Schol.
Est 1952. Inc nonprofit. Sem (Sept-Je). A/OS ECIS ISS.
Bldg. Lib 10,000 vols. Athletic facilities.

Founded in Rome in 1952, and known until 1973 as St. Michael's Country Day School, this school offers elementary and secondary education to a predominantly American enrollment. An American curriculum is followed with modern mathematics and advanced placement, and students prepare for the U.S. College Boards for which the school is an authorized center.

Conversational Italian is taught at all levels. Emphasis is placed on the historical, artistic and cultural aspects of Rome, Florence and the entire

Mediterranean, and group excursions are arranged to places of interest throughout the city. The school is housed in a 16th century Renaissance villa.

AMERICAN INTERNATIONAL SCHOOL IN GENOA
Day Coed Ages 3-14. Gr N-8.

16147 Genoa, Italy. Via Quarto 13C. Tel. 010/386528.
Kay F. Mongardi, Prin.
Gen Acad. Curr—USA. Ll—Eng. CF—Fr Ital Hist (US) Pol Sci.
Enr 80. B 40; G 40.
Fac 8. M 1; F 7. US 8.
Tui 2,5000,000-5,500,000 Lire.
Est 1966. Nonprofit. Sem (Sept-Je) A/OS ECIS ISS.
Bldgs 1. Lib 3400 vols. Athletic facilities.

Formerly the Overseas School of Liguria, American International School of Genoa enrolls over ten different nationalities. The curriculum is American with all academic subjects taught in English. Grades six through eight are conducted on a departmentalized basis. The study of Italian is compulsory for all students and French is optional in grades five through eight.

CASTELLI INTERNATIONAL SCHOOL
Day Coed Ages 5-14. Gr 3-9.

00046 Grottaferrata, Italy. 13 Via degli Scozzesi. Tel. 06 94 599 77.
Marianne Palladino, BA, Bennington College, MA, Denver Univ., Dir.
Pre-Prep Gen Acad. Tests SSAT. Curr—Nat UK. Ll—Eng Ital. CF—Fr
Russ Ital Art Drama Comp.
Enr 40. B 25; G 15. US—5.
Fac 8. Full 3/Part 5. M 2; F 6. US 2. UK.
Tui 3500 Lit (+900 Lit). Schol.
Est 1977. Nonprofit. Tri (Sept-Je).
Bldgs 3. Lib 1000 vols. Fields.

This school provides bilingual instruction to prepare English and Italian children for the Italian "Licenza Media" and continuation in Anglo-American schools. Individualized research and group projects are incorporated into the curriculum. In addition to academic subjects, participation-oriented classes in organic gardening, wine and olive oil production and bread baking are conducted. Field trips to Rome and vicinity are also arranged. An annual ski trip supplements the sports program of football, volleyball, baseball, basketball, badminton and ping pong. Boarding arrangements can be made with local families.

AMERICAN SCHOOL OF MILAN
Day Coed Ages 3-17. Gr N-12.

Milan, Italy. Villaggio Mirasole. P.O. Box 55. 20090 Noverasco di Opera. Tel. (02) 52-41-546.

Albert A. Chudler, Dir.
Col Prep Gen Acad. Tests CEEB SSAT. Curr—USA. LI—Eng.
Enr 441.
Fac 47.
Tui $2312-4188 (+ var). Schol.
Est 1962. Inc nonprofit. Sem (Sept-Je). A/OS ECIS ISS. Accred MSA.
Bldgs 3. Lib. Athletic facilities.

Growing to its present size from its beginning with 50 students in 1962, this parent owned and operated American community school offers preparation for the U.S. College Boards. Enrollment is predominantly from the United States, with children from countries including Italy, Great Britain, Sweden, Japan and Lebanon. The college preparatory curriculum uses American methods and materials, yet the school is also committed to exploring opportunities for study within the historic city of Milan. Complementing the academic program are field trips, and active student council and interscholastic competition in basketball and soccer.

INTERNATIONAL SCHOOL OF MILAN
Day Coed Ages 3-19. Gr N-PG.

Milano, Italy. Via Bezzola 6. Tel. 40-73-663.
Edward E. Webster, Head.
Col Prep Gen Acad. Tests GCE. Curr—UK. LI—Eng.
Enr 569.
Est 1958. Sem (Sept-Je). ECIS ISA ISS.

This international school draws its enrollment from 38 countries and offers a British-based curriculum preparing students for the 'A' level G.C.E. exams. The study of Italian is compulsory and French begins in the seventh grade. Activities, athletics and cultural trips round out the program.

SIR JAMES HENDERSON SCHOOL
Day Coed Ages 3-19. Gr N-12.

20131 Milano, Italy. Via Lombardia 66. Tel. (02) 289-97-17.
Trevor Wilson, BA, DipEd, Oxford, Head.
Col Prep Gen Acad. Tests GCE. Curr—UK. LI—Eng.
Enr 400.
Fac 32.
Tui 3,000,000-6,000,000 Lit (+ 70 Lit).
Est 1969. Inc nonprofit. Tri (Sept-Je). ECIS.
Bldgs 2. Libs 2. Athletic facilities.

Following the pattern of education found in the majority of English Schools, Sir James Henderson prepares students in lower grades for English Common entrance examinations, with the upper grades geared toward the G.C.E. 'O' and 'A' level exams. Although all instruction is in English the school is open to children of all nationalities. The lower school is housed in monastic buildings dating from 1450 and the senior division is located at Viale Lombardia 66. The school is non-denominational but instruction is available once a week for Roman Catholic and Anglican students.

Activities include after-school ballet classes, stamp collecting and chess clubs. An annual skiing week is available and groups of students participate in field trips throughout the city.

THE AMERICAN CULTURAL ASSOCIATION OF TURIN
Day Coed Ages 4-18. Gr N-12.

10020 Moncalieri (Torinese), Italy. Via Galilei Galileo 1. Tel. 860-9216.
Dr. Douglas Griggs, EdD, Harvard, Head.
Pre-Prep Col Prep. Tests CEEB SSAT. Curr—USA. Ll—Eng. CF—Fr
Ital Lat Eng Soc Stud Math Sci Art Music Comp. Sl—ESL.
Enr 199. B 95; G 104. Elem 174, Sec 25. US—19. Grad '84—6. Col—6.
Fac 23. Full 18/Part 5. M 7; F 16. US 13. UK Nat.
Tui 4,525,000-6,475,000 Lit (+ 600,000 Lit). Schol.
Est 1974. Inc nonprofit. Tri (Sept-Je). A/ OS ECIS ISS.
Bldgs 3. 2 Libs 9000 vols. Field. Crts.

ACAT was established to meet the educational needs of the English-speaking community of Turin. Housed in two villas with extensive grounds, the school is 11 kilometers from Turin. The basic American curriculum emphasizes a balance between group and individual instruction. Drama, yearbook, school magazine and clubs are among the extracurricular activities.

THE INTERNATIONAL SCHOOL OF NAPLES
Day Coed Ages 6-18. Gr 1-12.

80125 Naples, Italy. Mostra D'Oltremare. Tel. 081-635753.
Josephine Sessa, BA, Hunter College, City Univ. of NY, Prin.
Col Prep. Tests GCE SSAT. Curr—US. Ll—Eng. CF—Fr Ital EFL Math
Sci Hist. Sl—Rem & Dev Math & Read.
Enr 70. B 34; G 36. Elem 20, Sec 50. US—21. Grad '84—8. Col—6.
Fac 10. Full 9/Part 1. US 4.
Tui $2000 (+ $100). Schol.
Est 1979. Nonprofit. Tri (Sept-Je). ECIS ISS.
Bldgs 2. Lib 8000 vols. Gym. Field.

The curriculum at the International School of Naples is American but courses are also tailored to prepare students for the British G.C.E. 'O' level examination. Students come from the U.S., England, Turkey, Greece and other countries. Classes are small providing close attention and individual instruction to each pupil. Facilities are available for soccer, gymnastics, basketball and volleyball.

AMERICAN OVERSEAS SCHOOL OF ROME
Day Coed Ages 5-17. Gr K-12.

00189 Rome, Italy. Via Cassia, 811. Tel. 366.4841.
Robert Silvetz, Head.

Col Prep Gen Acad. Tests CEEB. Curr—USA. LI—Eng. A—Fr Ital Art Hist US & Eur Hist Math Chem. CF—Fr Ital Lat Graphics Fine Arts Physics.
Enr 600 US—300. Grad '84—50. Col—40.
Fac 64. Full 54/Part 10. US 40.
Tui 6,000,000-8,700,000 Lit (+ 250,000 Lit). Schol.
Est 1947. Nonprofit. Tri (Sept-Je). A/OS ECIS ISS NAIS. Accred MSA.
Bldgs 3. Lib. Aud. Gym. Field. Tennis crts 2. Amphitheatre.

This school offers an American-based curriculum to English-speaking and international communities in Rome. A comprehensive program of academics features courses in classical Greece, Nazism and World War II, Indians of the U.S., Russian contemporary society, puppetry and computer programming. Graduates have entered Harvard, MIT and Princeton as well as universities in Canada, England and Italy.

School activities include yearbook and newspaper, photography, ballet, scouting, chess and drama. Soccer, track, volleyball, basketball, wrestling and softball are among the sports conducted.

THE JUNIOR ENGLISH SCHOOL
Day Coed Ages 5-13. Gr 1-8.

00178 Rome, Italy. Via Appia Antica 286 (Lower Sch) & Via Erode Attico 52 (Upper Sch). Tel. 799 09 97/799 04 74.
David Black, Head.
Gen Acad. Curr—UK. LI—Eng. CF—Fr Ital Latin Math Hist Sci Art Music Religion Phys Ed.
Enr 250.
Fac 22. UK.
Tui $2500 (+ $300).
Est 1962. Tri (Sept-Je). ECIS ISS.
Bldgs 2. 2 Libs 3000 vols. Athletic facilities.

Serving the English-speaking community in southern Rome, this coeducational day school has considerably expanded since its establishment. A British curriculum is followed, meeting the requirements of the Common Entrance Examinations to British public schools. However, students transfer to high schools in Rome and elsewhere with a minimum of adjustment. Sports and physical education form an integral part of the program.

MARYMOUNT INTERNATIONAL SCHOOL
Bdg Girls Ages 14-18; Day Boys 4-11, Girls 4-18. Gr N-12.

00191 Rome, Italy. Via di Villa Lauchli, 180. Tel. 328.0671.
Sr. Michaeline O'Dwyer, RN, Marymount, MS, Fordham, Prin.
Pre-Prep Col Prep. Tests CEEB SSAT. Curr—USA. LI—Eng. A—Math Ital. CF—Fr Ital Span Theol Art Music. SI—Rem & Dev Read & Math Tut ESL.
Enr 343. B /53; G 90/200. US—170. Grad '84—40. Col—36.
Fac 44. Full 34/Part 10. M 10; F 34. US 35.

**Tui Bdg 8,210,000 Lit; Day 2,860,000-4,010,000 Lit. Schol.
Est 1946. Nonprofit. Tri (Sept-Je). ECIS ISS Accred MSA.
Bldgs 4. Dorms 1. 2 Libs 11,500 vols. Labs 3. Athletic facilities.**

This international school is under the direction of the Religious of the
Sacred Heart of Mary and offers an American-based college preparatory program. Independent study is an integral part of the curriculum
which features electives in anatomy, archaeology and French and Italian
literature. Private lessons are available in piano and ballet. All students
participate in a study and travel program involving other European
countries. Located about three miles from the center of Rome,
Marymount is one of a network of elementary schools, high schools and
colleges around the world.

THE NEW SCHOOL
  Day Coed Ages 5-18. Gr 1-12.

**00135 Rome, Italy. Via Della Camilluccia, 669. Tel. 328 4269.
Armando MacRory, Chrmn.
Gen Acad. Tests GCE. Curr—UK. LI—Eng. CF—Fr Ital.
Enr 125. B 60; G 65. Elem 89, Sec 36. Grad '84—12. Col—11.
Fac 19. Full 12/Part 7. M 9; F 10. US 2. UK.
Tui $3600 (+$700). Schol.
Est 1972. Nonprofit. Tri (Sept-Je). ECIS.
Bldgs 2. 3 Libs 2500 vols. Athletic facilities.**

With an enrollment from 25 different countries, the New School offers
an English curriculum adapted to the needs of international students.
Preparation is provided for 'O' and 'A' level G.C.E. exams and a
majority of graduates go on to British, American or Italian universities.
Italian and French are taught at all levels as well as English as a foreign
language. Activities include cultural trips, drama, skiing, tennis and
swimming.

NOTRE DAME INTERNATIONAL SCHOOL
  Bdg Boys Ages 13-17; Day Boys 10-17, Girls 10-13. Gr 5-12.

**00165 Rome, Italy. Via Aurelia 796. Tel. 621-6051.
Br. Thomas Dziekan, CSC, AB, Stonehill College, MA, Middlebury
  College, Head.
Col Prep. Tests CEEB SSAT. Curr—USA. LI—Eng. CF—Rom Lang Art
  Music Typ Creative Writing Psych Printing Drawing Comp.
Enr 280. B 125/150; G 5. Elem 90, Sec 190. US—250. Grad '84—61.
  Col—51.
Fac 27. Full 27. M 20; F 7. US 26.
Tui Bdg $10,000; Day $4500.
Est 1951. Nonprofit. Quar (Sept-Je). ECIS ISS. Accred MSA.
Bldgs 1. Dorms 6. Lib 9500 vols. Gym. Tennis & handball courts.
  Swimming pool. Fields.**

Operated under the auspices of the Brothers of the Holy Cross, this international boys' school offers a college preparatory curriculum. In addition to the College Boards, students with strong academic achievements are encouraged to earn college credit through advanced placement examinations. Recent graduates have attended Yale, Harvard, Notre Dame, Georgetown and the University of Texas. Notre Dame's sports program includes track, basketball, tennis, wrestling, soccer and swimming. Ski trips to slopes near Rome are scheduled for winter weekends. Field trips are a substantial aspect of the art and history classes.

See also page 77

ST. FRANCIS INTERNATIONAL SCHOOL
Day Boys Ages 6-11; Girls 6-13. Gr 1-8.

00189 Rome, Italy. Via Cassia 645. Tel. 366-0657.
Sr. Helen Marie Schumacher, Prin.
Gen Acad. Curr—USA. Ll—Eng.
Enr 150.
Fac 12.
Tui 1,050,000 Lit (+50,000 Lit).
Est 1960. Roman Catholic. Sem (Sept-Je). ECIS ISS.
Bldgs 1. Lib 1500 vols.

The Sisters of St. Francis of Penance and Charity direct this international elementary school. Italian is taught in all grades and the curriculum is accredited by the Diocese of Buffalo and the State of New York. Gym and dance classes are scheduled twice a week and piano lessons are available.

ST. GEORGE'S ENGLISH SCHOOL
Day Coed Ages 5-18. Gr N-PG.

00123 Rome, Italy. Via Cassia Km 16 (La Storta). Tel. 3790141.
H. J. Deelman, Head.
Col Prep. Tests GCE. Curr—UK. Ll—Eng. CF—Ital Fr Ger Russ Span
  Hist Geog Econ Art Music EFL Rem Read.
Enr 840. B 420; G 420. US—40. Grad'84—60. Col—55.
Fac 75. Full 67/Part 8. M 35; F 40. UK.
Tui 6,200,000-8,000,000 Lit.
Summer Session. Rec. 2 wks.
Est 1958. Inc 1965 nonprofit. ECIS ISA ISS.
Bldgs 2. Lib 20,000 vols. Labs 8. Athletic facilities.

This British-oriented school is located on a 28-acre campus and is divided into an Upper and Lower school. Students follow a college preparatory syllabus directed toward the G.C.E. at the Ordinary and Advanced levels. Graduates have attended colleges and universities in Europe, Australia, Canada, and the U.S. An active sports program includes soccer, hockey, basketball, volleyball, swimming, track and field and tennis.

ST. STEPHEN'S SCHOOL
Bdg & Day Coed Ages 14-20. Gr 9-PG.

00153 Rome, Italy. Via Aventina 3. Tel. 575-0605.
C. Peter Rinaldi, Head.
Col Prep. Tests CEEB SSAT IB. Curr—USA. LI—Eng. A—Fr Ital Eng
Lat Greek Biol Math Architecture Art Hist US Hist.
Enr 130. US—62.
Fac 29. US 19.
Tui Bdg $8200 (+ $500); Day $4200 (+ $350). Schol.
Est 1963. Inc nonprofit. Sem (Sept-Je) A/OS ECIS ISS NAIS. Accred
NEASC.
Bldgs 1. Lib 7000 vols. Courts 2.

Opening its doors in 1964 in the Parioli section of Rome, this
international day school moved to its present location in 1972. Situated
in central Rome, the school is a few minutes walk from the Colosseum
and the Roman Forum. Study of fine arts, history and languages plays a
strong part in the curriculum which prepares students for the U.S.
College Boards. Classical languages are offered and at least one modern
language is required. Additionally, all students are afforded practice in
Italian conversation. Boston University, Sarah Lawrence, Tufts and
University of Pennsylvania are among the colleges entered by recent
U.S. graduates.

A full extracurricular program features debating, arts and crafts,
cooking, modern advances in science and medicine, chorus and various
publications. Soccer, tennis, basketball, dance, fencing and karate are
among the sports offered.

See also page 78

SOUTHLANDS ENGLISH SCHOOL
Day Coed Ages 3-12. Gr N-7.

Rome, Italy 00124. Via Epaminonda 3, Casal Palocco. Tel.
396/60.90.932.
Giulia Bicocchi, Head.
Gen Acad. Curr—UK. LI—Eng.
Enr 100.
Fac 10.
Tui 2,130,000 Lit.
Est 1976. Tri (Sept-Je).
Bldgs 3. Lib. Gym. Field.

Located in a rural setting, Southlands serves the children from the
international community of the surrounding area. The curriculum is
designed according to the British system of education and aims to
facilitate transfer to schools abroad with maximum ease. Instruction in
reading and mathematics is augmented by classes in writing, drama, art
and music which foster self-expression and creativity. Children also
participate in a variety of recreational activities including sports and
gardening.

INTERNATIONAL SCHOOL OF TRIESTE
Bdg Day Coed Ages 3-14. Gr N-8.

34100 Trieste, Italy. Casella Postale 2048. c/o Villagio Conconello 16 (Opicina). Tel. 211-452.
Daniel W. Sheehan, BA, MA, MEd, Dir.
Pre-Prep Gen Acad. Curr—USA. LI—Eng. CF—Ital Ger Fr ESL.
Enr 103. B 53; G 50. US—5.
Fac 16. Full 11/Part 5. US 7.
Tui $2000-3000. (+ $600). Schol.
Est 1964. Tri (Sept-Je). A/OS ECIS ISS.

Originally founded to accommodate children of scientists from the International Centre for Theoretical Physics of Trieste, this school offers an elementary program patterned on the basic American curriculum. Art, music, physical education and Italian are required of all students. English as a second language is taught in nursery and kindergarten.

Chief seaport of the Austrian Empire until World War I, when it passed to Italy, and claimed by Yugoslavia after World War II, Trieste is situated on the gulf of the same name in a setting of great scenic beauty.

LUXEMBOURG

Luxembourg is a landlocked country bordered by Belgium, France and Germany. Spain, France and Austria ruled here between the 15th and 18th centuries. In 1815, the Congress of Vienna declared Luxembourg a Grand Duchy as a gift to the King of the Netherlands. The western part was given to Belgium in 1839. Germany occupied the nation during both world wars.

The principal industries are mining and metallurgy. Luxembourg is the capital and largest city. The monetary unit is the Luxembourg franc (LuxF), and Letzeburgesch, French and German are commonly spoken.

AMERICAN SCHOOL OF LUXEMBOURG
Day Coed Ages 4-19. Gr N-PG.

1511 Luxembourg, Grand Duchy of Luxembourg. 188, avenue de la Faiencerie. Tel. 47-00-20.
Harry C. Barteau, AB, Northeastern Univ., MA, Harvard, PhD, Miami, Prin.
Col Prep. Tests CEEB. Curr—USA. LI—Eng. A—Eng Hist Calc Physics Fr Ger. CF—Soc Stud Sci Art. SI—ESL.
Enr 270. B 135; G 135. Elem 210, Sec 60. US—90. Grad '84—9. Col—5.
Fac 36. Full 30/Part 6. M 6; F 30. US 20. UK.
Tui $1650-3850. Schol.
Est 1963. Inc 1973 nonprofit. Quar (Sept-Je). ECIS ISS.
Bldgs 2. Lib 6500 vols. Field.

This school serves children of the American and international community living in Luxembourg. The American-based curriculum offers instruction in French and German. Cross country, track, soccer and student government are among the activities conducted.

THE NETHERLANDS

Rising to commercial, maritime and artistic eminence as the United Dutch Republic, the seven northern provinces of the Netherlands achieved their independence following Roman, Burgundian and Spanish rule. The country has been a constitutional monarchy since 1814. North and South Holland are the two most populous provinces of the eleven which today comprise the Kingdom of the Netherlands.

Amsterdam is the official capital, but The Hague is the royal residence and seat of government. The guilder (Fls) is the monetary unit and Dutch is the country's language.

BRITISH SCHOOL OF AMSTERDAM
Day Coed Ages 3-11. Gr N-7.

1071 SK Amsterdam, Netherlands. Heinzestraat 9. Tel. 797840.
M. Roberts, Head.
Pre-Prep. Curr—UK. LI—Eng. CF—Dutch Fr Music.
Enr 80. B 40; G 40.
Fac 6. Full 4/Part 2. M 1; F 5. UK Ireland.
Tui 8000 Fls. Schol.
Est 1978. Nonprofit. Tri (Sept-July). ECIS.
Bldg. Lib. Gym.

Founded by the British community in Amsterdam, this school provides a basic primary curriculum supplemented by a program of drama, art and music. Classes are grouped according to ability and individual attention is emphasized. All students learn Dutch. School club activities include ballet, chess, computers, guitar, piano, recorder, folk dancing, handicrafts and football.

THE INTERNATIONAL SCHOOL OF AMSTERDAM
Day Coed Ages 4-18. Gr N-12.

1008 AD Amsterdam, The Netherlands. P.O. Box 7983. Tel. (020) 42 22 27.
Brian S. Wilks, BA, MA, Oxford, EdD, Univ. of Houston, Dir.
Col Prep. Tests IB SSAT. Curr—USA. LI—Eng. A—Eng Math Chem Phys Fr. CF—Fr Dutch.
Enr 325. B 160; G 165. Elem 220, Sec 105. US—65. Grad '84—30.
Fac 35. Full 29/Part 6. M 15; F 20. US 13.
Tui $3400-4600. Schol.
Est 1964. Nonprofit. Quar (Aug-Je). A/OS ECIS ISS. Accred NEASC.
Bldg. Lib 9000 vols. Gym.

Designed to meet the needs of the foreign community in Amsterdam, students from 26 countries attend this school. The curriculum adheres to the American plan and is complemented by art, music, dance and athletics. The school is also a member of the Sports League of the Northwest Council of International Schools.

See also page 79

AFCENT INTERNATIONAL SCHOOL
Day Coed Ages 4-19. Gr N-12.

6445 EE Brunssum, The Netherlands. Ferd. Bolstraat 1. Tel. 045-253076.
D.L. Vinge, Dir.
LI—Eng Ger Fr.
Enr 1500. B 750; G 750.
Est 1967. ECIS.

Afcent provides educational services for the children of four of the nations in the headquarters of the Allied Forces Central Europe (Canada, Germany, England and the United States). Stong emphasis is placed on the learning of languages, including a "partner language" program in English and German at all levels, and French Immersion classes in grades three to six. English language instruction leads to a U.S. high school diploma. Courses are offered in world history, comparative government, international organizations and computer studies. The school has a second location for younger children, the Joseph-Mason-Schule.

REGIONALE INTERNATIONALE SCHOOL
Day Coed Ages 6-13. Gr 1-6.

Eindhoven (Noord-Brabant), The Netherlands. Humperdincklaan 45654 PA. Tel. 040-519437.
J. Voogt, Head.
Pre-Prep. Curr—Intl. LI—Dutch Fr Ger Eng. CF—Dutch Phys Chem.
Enr 225. B 115; G 110. US—23.
Fac 20. M 8; F 12. Holland UK.
Tui 3200 DFL.
Est 1965. Nonprofit. Tri (Aug-Je). ECIS ISS.
Bldgs 1. Lib. Gym. Field.

This school was established to serve the needs of the international community in the Eindhoven area. The curriculum is compatible with those of Holland, England, the U.S., France, Belgium and Germany. Tuition fees are scaled according to income.

VAN DER PUTTLYCEUM (ENGLISH STREAM)
Day Coed Ages 12-18. Gr 6-12.

5622 HA Eindhoven, The Netherlands. Dr. Berlagelaan 13. Tel. 040-436004.

Dr. H. Grielen, Head.
Gen Acad Col Prep. Tests IB GCE. LI—Eng. CF—Dutch Fr Sci Hist Lit Art.
Enr 174. Elem 74, Sec 100. US—16.
Fac 8. Full 3/Part 5. M 6; F 2. Netherlands UK.
Tui 212,50-3000 DFL.
Est 1974. Tri (Aug-Je).

This section provides a bi-cultural education to members of the international community who have an English-speaking background. Students take either a pre-university program or a general course in preparation for technical training. Instruction is also given for the 'O' level of the G.C.E. Dutch is taught to all students in order to facilitate communication with pupils in the other sections. Tuition fees are based on a sliding scale according to income.

THE AMERICAN SCHOOL OF THE HAGUE
Day Coed Ages 3½-17. Gr N-12.

2584 AM The Hague, The Netherlands. Doornstraat 6. Tel. 070-542102.
Gail D. Schoppert, MA, Ohio State, EdD, Univ. of North Carolina, Supt.
Col Prep Gen Acad. Tests CEEB SSAT. Curr—USA. LI—Eng. A—Hist Sci Lang. CF—Fr Span Ger Dutch. SI—Rem & Dev Read & Math Tut.
Enr 900. B 440; G 460. Elem 590, Sec 310. US—460. Grad '84—69. Col—44.
Fac 99. Full 84/Part 15. M 42; F 57. US 77.
Tui Day $3500-4300 (+$1200). Schol.
Est 1953. Inc 1965 nonprofit. Sem (Aug-Je). A/OS ISS ECIS. Accred MSA.
Bldgs 6. 4 Libs 25,000 vols. Athletic facilities.

Providing a full elementary, middle and secondary program to a predominantly American enrollment, this school is comprised of four divisions. Each division is housed separately with its own library and under the supervision of a principal. The buildings are located in one of the loveliest areas of The Hague, near the resort area of Scheveningen on the North Sea.

The Scott Foresman Reading System forms the basis of the primary school's (1-5) nongraded program. In the middle school (6-8) emphasis is placed on the academic program. Team teaching methods are utilized to instruct students in the basic areas of language arts, math, science and social studies. The high school provides an intensive college preparatory program. Counseling and tutoring services are available to all students. The school will accept a limited number of boarding students who live with Dutch families.

RIJNLANDS LYCEUM OEGSTGEEST
Day Coed Ages 12-19. Gr 7-12.

2341 BA Oestgeest, The Netherlands. Apollolaan 1. Tel. 071-155640.
A.J.M. Vaessen, Prin.

Col Prep Gen Acad. Tests IB. Curr—Intl. Ll—Eng Dutch. CF—Fr Ger
Dutch Persian Ital Geog Econ Sci Math. Sl—Tut.
Enr 1319. B 672; G 647. Elem 459, Sec 860. US—9. Grad '84—160.
Col—144.
Fac 90. Full 45/Part 45. M 55; F 35. Nat.
Tui 475-500 DFL (+400 DFL).
Est 1956. Nonprofit. Sem (Aug-July).
Bldg. Lib. Fields 2. Gyms 2.

Sponsored by the national government, Rijnlands Lyceum Oegstgeest
offers the International Baccalaureate to students from 17 countries.
Courses in the IB program are conducted in English, while separate
native college preparatory and general curriculum classes are in Dutch.
The school offers extracurricular activities in botany, glass blowing,
acrobatics, fine arts, archaeology, Russian and Spanish.

INTERNATIONAL SCHOOL EERDE
Bdg Coed Ages 11-19. Gr 7-12.

7731 PJ Ommen, The Netherlands. Kasteellaan 1. Tel. 5291-1452.
Nicholas den Hartog, Head.
Pre-Prep Col Prep. Tests CEEB GCE. Curr—Nat UK. Ll—Dutch Eng Fr.
CF—Dutch Ger Hist Geog Arts Bio Chem Comp.
Enr 93. Elem 10, Sec 83.
Fac 20. Full 11/Part 9. M 14; F 6. US 2.
Tui Bdg 22,000 DFL (+2000 DFL); Day 14,000 DFL (+1000 DFL).
Est 1933. Inc nonprofit. Tri (Aug-July). ECIS ISA ISS.
Bldgs 9. Dorms 3. Gym. Pool. Crts. Field.

Located on a 2,000-acre site, International School Eerde offers
secondary level education, following a dual Dutch-English curriculum
based on a nongraded system. During the first three years, there are
parallel classes taught through Dutch and English. Following the third
year, all instruction is in English. The program prepares for the British
G.C.E. exams 'O' and 'A' levels, but students may take U.S. College
Boards.
Ringed by forest, moat, and spacious lawns, the school's main building
is a chateau in the manner of Louis XIV, raised in 1715 upon a site
occupied by successive castles, ranging back for centuries.

THE AMERICAN INTERNATIONAL SCHOOL OF ROTTERDAM
Day Coed Ages 5-14. Gr K-8.

3051 PA Rotterdam, The Netherlands. Hillegondastraat 21. Tel. 010-22
53 51.
Dos S. Johnson, CAGS, Dir.
Pre-Prep Gen Acad. Curr—USA. Ll—Eng.
Enr 113.
Fac 15.
Tui $1570-3500. Schol.

Est 1959. Inc nonprofit. Sem (Aug-Je). A/OS ECIS ISS. Accred NEASC.
Bldgs 3. Lib 6000 vols. Gym.

A progressive American curriculum is utilized with modifications corresponding to the school's international nature. Extracurricular activities and sports complement the academic program.

INTERNATIONAL SCHOOL VILSTEREN
Bdg & Day Coed Ages 6-12. Gr 1-7.

Vilsteren-Ommen 7734 PD (Overyssel), The Netherlands. Huize Vilsteren. Tel. 05291-8283.
Alfred van Loveren, Prin.
Gen Acad. Curr—Nat US. LI—Eng.
Enr 43.
Fac 3. Holland UK.
Bdg 14,700 DFL; Day 7350 DFL.
Est 1934. Nonprofit. Sem (Aug-Je). ISS.
Bldgs 2. Dorms 1. Lib. Fields.

Situated near the city of Ommen, the International School Vilsteren offers an elementary program to grade seven. Enrollment is predominantly Dutch, but there are some children from England, the U.S. and other countries.

INTERNATIONAL SCHOOL BEVERWEERD
Bdg & Day Coed Ages 12-20. Gr 7-PG.

3985 RE Werkhoven (Utrecht), The Netherlands. Castle Beverweerd. Tel. 03437-341.
Mrs. A.F. Crowe, BS, London Univ., Dir.
Col Prep. Tests CEEB IB. Curr—Nat USA. LI—Eng Dutch. CF—Dutch Fr Ger Sci Hist Math. SI—Tut.
Enr 61. B 30/5; G 24/2. Elem 6, Sec 55. Grad '84—13. Col—13.
Fac 10. Full 2/Part 8. M 4; F 6. US 2.
Tui Bdg 25,500 DFL; Day 13,000 DFL.
Est 1934. Inc nonprofit. Sem (Sept-Je). ECIS ISA ISS.
Bldgs 6. Dorms 4. 2 Libs 1500 vols. Gym. Field. Courts 2.

A coeducational boarding school for secondary students, International School Beverweerd offers preparation in its American Section for U.S. College Boards and the International Baccalaureate. There is also a Dutch curriculum, taught in the native tongue. In addition to an active sports program, students participate in weaving, ceramics, painting and music activities. Excursions to cultural events in nearby towns, as well as field trips throughout Europe are regularly scheduled.

The school originated in 1934, sponsored by the German, English, American and Dutch Societies of Friends to provide teaching for German children whose parents sought an alternative to the educational system developing in early Nazi Germany. Starting with 4 pupils the school grew to 100, and was closed in 1943 by the Nazis. It reopened after the war supported solely by the Dutch Society of Friends. Today, no longer affiliated with the Quakers, it welcomes youngsters of all faiths and nationalities. The school is housed in a renovated medieval castle just outside of the rural village of Werkhoven, ten miles southeast of Utrecht.

NORWAY

Located on the northwest edge of the European continent, the long and narrow Kingdom of Norway is known for its many coastal inlets or fjords. Since the time of the Vikings, the fjords have provided excellent harbors for this seafaring people. The top third of the country, "Land of the Midnight Sun," has sunlight 24 hours a day during certain times of the year. Oslo is the capital city, and the krone (NKr) is the monetary unit. Norwegian is the country's language.

STAVANGER AMERICAN SCHOOL
Day Coed Ages 3-18. Gr N-12.

4040 Madla (Rogaland), Norway. Treskeveien 3. Tel. 47-4-559100. John H. Monson, BA, St. Olaf College, MS, Univ. of Wisconsin, Supt. Col Prep. Tests CEEB SSAT. Curr—US. LI—Eng. CF—Span Fr Nor Math Sci Soc Stud. A—Bio Chem Physics Fr Comp Sci Philos Calc. SI—Rem & Dev Read.

Enr 401. B 200; G 201. Elem 299, Sec 102. US—309. Grad '84—16. Col—14.

Fac 46. Full 44/Part 2. US 45.

Tui 45,000 NKr.

Est 1966. Inc nonprofit. Sem (Aug-Je). ECIS ISS NAIS.

Bldg. 2 Lib 13,700 vols. Gyms 3. Fields. Crts.

Established by representatives of major oil companies operating in the North Sea, the majority of students are from families associated with the oil industry, but enrollment is open to all English-speaking students. The curriculum is American-based, and elementary students work in traditional self-contained classrooms. The secondary school's college preparatory curriculum features advanced courses and independent study. Stavanger administers a number of testing programs in addition to school examinations. Graduates have entered leading universities throughout the U.S.

Stavanger's 15-acre site is a short distance from the city center. The main complex, completed in 1982, contains labs for science, computer study and industrial arts; a theatre/auditorium; classrooms; art and music studios; a library; and cafeteria. Extracurricular activities include varsity team sports, intramural sports for elementary and secondary students, and a wide range of clubs. A pre-school division for three and four year olds is available.

POLAND

A great power in medieval times, Poland was subsequently long coveted and eventually partitioned off the map by its developing neighbors to the east, west and southwest. The country's territory today roughly coincides with the earliest area of the 770-year-long Polish kingdom, which the partition of 1795 dissolved. In 1952, Poland adopted a Consitution making it the Polish People's Republic.

The capital is Warsaw and the monetary unit is the zloty (Zl). Polish is spoken by 90% of the population.

THE AMERICAN SCHOOL OF WARSAW
Day Coed Ages 5-13. Gr K-8.

Warsaw, Poland. ul. Konstancinska, 13. Tel. 42-39-52; 42-56-20.
Mail to: c/o American Embassy Warsaw, Dept. of State, Washington, DC 20520.
Warner A. Hoffman, Dir.
Gen Acad. Curr—USA. LI—Eng.
Enr 174.
Fac 29.
Tui $3700.
Est 1952. Inc 1974 nonprofit. A/OS ECIS ISS.
Bldg. Lib 7500 vols. Gym. Field.

This school offers a complete educational program to the children of the international diplomatic and business community of Warsaw. Situated in the district of Mokotow, the school is a short drive south of the center of the city in the direction of Wilanow. The curriculum emphasizes individualized and small group instruction in order to maximize development of basic communication, computational and thinking skills. In addition to basics, art, music and physical education are offered at all levels. Student activities include intramural sports, ballet, chess and special interest clubs.

PORTUGAL

One of the oldest countries in Europe, Portugal's culture is based on a past that dates from prehistoric times to the Roman and Moorish invasions. Names such as Diaz, Magellan and daGama, leaders in the 15th century explorations of the New World, are symbols of her former status as an imperial power.

Largely agricultural, the Portuguese Republic is one of the world's leading wine-makers. Lisbon, the principal seaport, is also the capital. The monetary unit is the escudo (Esc), and Portuguese is the official language.

PRINCE HENRY INTERNATIONAL COLLEGE
Bdg Coed Ages 7-16; Day Coed 3-16. Gr N-12.

8100 Vale Do Lobo Almansil (Algarve), Portugal. Tel. 089-94145.
Eulalia Duarte, Head.
Gen Acad. Tests CEEB GCE. Curr—UK. LI—Eng.
Enr 70.
Est 1978. Nonprofit. Tri (Sept-Je).
Bldgs 1. Dorms 4. Lib. Athletic facilities.

This school follows a curriculum preparing students for the G.C.E. as
well as entrance into American colleges. The study of both Portuguese
and French is required. Extracurricular activities include football,
swimming, tennis, riding, golf and art and photography.

ST. JULIAN'S SCHOOL
Day Coed Ages 4-16. Gr K-10.

Carcavelos 2775, Portugal. Quinta Nova. Tel. 2470140.
T. A. Bull, Head.
Gen Acad. Curr—UK. LI—Eng.
Enr 307.
Fac 42.
Tui 59,400-119,100 Esc (+20,200 Esc).
Est 1932. Nonprofit. Tri (Sept-July). ECIS ISS.
2 Libs 2000 vols. Gym. Fields. Crts.

A British curriculum is followed at this school which enrolls children
from some 29 countries. The sports program includes soccer, cricket,
tennis, rounders and football.

THE AMERICAN INTERNATIONAL SCHOOL—LISBON
Day Coed Ages 4-19. Gr N-12.

Carnaxide, Portugal. Apartado 10, 2795 Linda-a-Velha. Tel. 218-1266.
Willard L. Smith, MA, PhD, Dir.
Col Prep. Tests SSAT ACT. Curr—USA. LI—Eng. CF—Fr Port Art
Music Photog.
Enr 270. B 145; G 125.
Fac 44. Full 39/Part 5.
Tui $3200-4900 (+var). Schol.
Est 1956. Sem (Sept-Je). ECIS ISS MAIS. Accred NEASC.
Bldgs 11.

Offering an American curriculum, this international school prepares
students for college entrance. Individualized instruction is offered as
well as English as a Second Language. Extracurricular activities include
team sports, drama, yearbook, newspaper and student government. The
middle and upper schools are located in Carnaxide, while the lower
school campus is in Monte Estoril.

ST. DOMINIC'S COLLEGE
Day Coed Ages 3½-16. Gr K-10.

2775 Parede, Portugal. Rua Outeira da Polima, Arneiro. Tel. 2440434.
Sr. Teresa Wade, Prin.
Col Prep. Tests GCE. Curr—UK. LI—Eng.
Enr 301.
Fac 22.
Tui 13,000-31,700 Esc/term (+1000 Esc).
Est 1964. Roman Catholic. Tri (Sept-Je).
Bldgs 1. Lib. Lab. Crt. Gym. Theatre.

St. Dominic's College was established as the international branch of
the Colegio do Bom Sucesso founded over 100 years ago in Belem by the
Irish Dominican Sisters. It is the only Catholic school for English-
speaking children in Portugal and will accept non-Christian students.
The curriculum prepares students for the British 'O' level examinations.

ALGARVE INTERNATIONAL SCHOOL
5-Day Bdg Coed Ages 8-16; Day Coed 4-16. Gr K-10.

Porches-Lagoa 8400 (Algarve), Portugal. Estrada 125. Tel. 52832.
Isobel Hammond, Prin.
Gen Acad. Tests GCE. Curr—UK Nat. LI—Eng.
Enr 383.
Fac 20.
Tui 18,000-35,000 Esc (+var). Bdg 25,000 Esc/term.
Est 1972. Tri (Oct-Je). ECIS.
Dorms 2. Lib. Gym. Field.

A traditional curriculum emphasizes instruction in languages, mathematics, history and the sciences for children who reside in the
international community. In the secondary years, students receive
preparation for the 'O' level of the British G.C.E. Extracurricular
activities are encouraged and include sports, drama and music.

ROMANIA

Primarily an agrarian country, the Socialist Republic of Romania is as
large as the state of Oregon with ten times the population. The oil fields
around Ploesti, about 35 miles north of the capital city, Bucharest,
provide the country's chief export. The official language is Romanian,
loosely classified as one of the Romance Languages. The monetary unit
is the leu (L).

AMERICAN SCHOOL OF BUCHAREST
Day Coed Ages 5-13. Gr K-8.

Bucharest, Romania. Str. Ing. Costinescu #2. Tel. 33-21-20.
Mail to: c/o American Embassy Bucharest, Dept. of State, Washington,
DC 20520.

John K. Johnson, Dir.
Pre-Prep. Curr—USA. LI—Eng.
Enr 106.
Fac 13.
Tui $3750.
Est 1962. Inc 1970 nonprofit. Sem (Sept-Je). A/OS ECIS ISS. Accred
** NEASC.**
Bldgs 1. Lib 2500 vols. Lab.

Conducting an American-based elementary curriculum, this school is located within walking distance of the American Embassy. Emphasis is placed on the individualization of instruction. The American School of Bucharest is paired with the Avon, Connecticut Public Schools through the U.S. Department of State, School-to-School Program.

SPAIN

A major force in the political, cultural and religious history of Europe, Spain's power as a vast empire was due in part to the explorations of Balboa, Cortes and Pizarro. Cultural contributions to the country's heritage are the literary works of Cervantes and the art of Velasquez and Picasso.

Spain's southern neighbor is Africa, separated from Spain by the Strait of Gibraltar. The Pyrenees mountains divide the Spanish State from France. Textiles and minerals are Spain's main exports. About two-thirds of the people speak Castilian, the dominant form of Spanish. Other languages spoken are Basque in the north, Galician in the northwest and Catalan in the east. Madrid is the capital and most populous city. The monetary unit is the peseta (Pts).

THE AMERICAN SCHOOL OF BARCELONA
** Day Coed Ages 3-18. Gr N-12.**

Barcelona-34, Spain. Pasaje Font del Lleo S/N. Tel. 204 47 43.
Michael Schimmel, MA, Univ. of Michigan, Dir.
Col Prep. Tests CEEB SSAT TOEFL. Curr—USA Span. LI—Eng.
** A—Eng Span Math. CF—Span Catalan Fr Arts Sci Music.**
Enr 430. B 215; G 215. Elem 330, Sec 100. US—65. Grad '84—18.
** Col—16.**
Fac 44. M 28; F 16. US 30.
Tui $2500 (+$500). Schol.
Est 1962. Nonprofit. Tri (Sept-Je). A/OS ECIS ISS MAIS.
Bldgs 3. 2 Libs 5000 vols. Athletic facilities. Field. Crts.

The American School of Barcelona provides a U.S. curriculum emphasizing a bilingual-bicultural education, with Spanish as a second language. An American curriculum is followed by all students until sixth grade, after which a Spanish curriculum is pursued or the American curriculum continued. Students whose native language is not English must meet the school's language requirements prior to admission. Extracurricular activities include basketball, soccer, ice skating and swimming.

ANGLO-AMERICAN SCHOOL
Bdg Coed Ages 7-16; Day Coed 5-16. Gr K-10.

Castelldefels-Playa (Barcelona), Spain. Paseo De Garbi, 152. Tel. 365-15-84.
Michael Schimmel, Head.
Col Prep. Curr—UK USA. LI—Eng. CF—Span.
Est 1958. Nonprofit. ISS.

Situated among pine trees one hundred yards from an extensive sandy beach, the Anglo-American School has expanded in plant and enrollment since its establishment. With a predominantly British staff and a student body consisting chiefly of American and English children, the school, nevertheless, enrolls students from other countries and maintains an international outlook. Special emphasis is given toward preparation for the British G.C.E. examination. The school participates in the interscholastic sports program in the Barcelona area.

AMERICAN SCHOOL OF BILBAO
Day Coed Ages 3-13. Gr N-8.

Las Arenas (Vizcaya), Spain. Apartado 38. Tel. 668-08-60.
Teresa de Orueta, Dir.
Gen Acad. Curr—USA. LI—Eng.
Enr 152.
Fac 14.
Tui $1700-3300 (+ $705).
Est 1967. Inc nonprofit. Sem (Sept-Je). A/OS ECIS ISS MAIS.
Bldgs 4. Lib 8000 vols.

Located on six acres in the rolling countryside of Berango, the school's academic program is similar to that found in any progressive U.S. school system. In addition to required course work, all students beginning in first grade take Spanish as part of their program. Athletic facilities are provided for participation in basketball, volleyball, track, baseball and soccer.

AMERICAN SCHOOL OF LAS PALMAS
Day Coed Ages 4-17. Gr K-12.

Las Palmas de Gran Canaria, Spain. Apartado 15, Tafira Alta. Tel. 34 28 350400.
Elsie Hartog Carver, Head.
Col Prep Gen Acad. Tests SSAT. Curr—USA. LI—Eng Span.
Enr 180.
Fac 17.

Est 1967. Inc nonprofit. Sem (Sept-Je). ECIS ISS.
Bldgs 9. Lib. Fields. Courts.

This school conducts an American-based curriculum and features bilingual instruction (English/Spanish) from kindergarten through grade six. Volleyball, basketball and soccer are among the extracurricular activities. The school is situated in the seaport city of Las Palmas, 820 miles southwest of Spain.

AMERICAN SCHOOL OF MADRID
Day Coed Ages 3-18. Gr N-12.

Madrid, Spain. Carretera Humera, Km. 2—Aravaca. Apartado 80. Tel. 207-0641.
Max R. Tudor, BA, MA, PhD, Univ. of Alabama, Supt.
Col Prep Gen Acad. Tests CEEB SSAT. Curr—USA. LI—Eng.
Enr 691.
Fac 72.
Tui $1042-3717.
Est 1961. Inc nonprofit. Sem (Sept-Je). A/OS ECIS ISS MAIS. Accred MSA.
Bldgs 3. Libs 2. Gym.

Located on a site overlooking the city of Madrid, this school enrolls mostly American students. The curriculum is entirely American and all students are required to study Spanish. ESL is conducted for children between the ages of five and eight. Elective courses are offered in art, ballet, drama and music. Swimming, basketball, softball and soccer are included in the after-school sports program.

BRITISH COUNCIL SCHOOL
Day Coed Ages 5-16. Gr K-10.

Madrid 10, Spain. Martinez Campos 31 and Fernandez de la Hoz, 46. Tel. 442-43-00.
John P. Caselaw, MEd, Univ. of Bristol, Head.
Col Prep. Tests GCE. Curr—UK. LI—Eng. CF—Span Soc Sci Music Arts Relig.
Enr 850. Elem 750, Sec 100.
Fac 62. Full 33/Part 29. M 15; F 47. US 1. UK.
Tui £1000/term.
Summer Session. Acad. Tui Day £150. 4 wks.
Est 1940. Nonprofit. Tri (Sept-Je).
Bldgs 3. Lib 5000 vols. Athletic facilities.

The curriculum of the school is similar to that of a British primary-middle school. English studies are taught in the morning, while afternoon classes in Spanish complete the requirements for basic education of the Spanish Ministry of Education.

THE HILL HOUSE MONTESSORI SCHOOL
Day Coed Ages 1-15. Gr N-9.

Madrid 2, Spain. Av. Alfonso XIII, 30-34. Tel. 416-0952.
Judy Amick DeHernandez, BA, MA, Prin.
Pre-Prep. LI—Eng Span.
Enr 250.
Fac 12.
Tui $100-300/mo (+ $200/yr). Schol.
Summer Session. Acad Rec. 4 wks..
Est 1969. Nonprofit. Quar (Sept-Je). ISS. Accred MSA.
Bldgs 3. Lib 2000 vols.

The curriculum at this school is based on the Maria Montessori Theory of education and employs American teaching methods and materials. Children are grouped according to their ability level and are allowed to progress at their own pace. Special education classes are provided for slow learners and hyperactive children between the ages of four and ten. Extracurricular activities include modern dance and competitive swimming.

INTERNATIONAL COLLEGE SPAIN
Bdg Coed Ages 14-18, Day 3-18. Gr N-12.

Madrid, Spain. Calle Vereda Norte 3, La Moraleja. Tel. 6502398.
J.V. Hutchinson, MA, Oxford, DipEd, London, Dir.
Col Prep. Tests IB SSAT. Curr—Intl. LI—Eng. CF—Persian Span Fr
  Dutch Math Bio Physics Hist Geog Chem Comp Stud. SI—ESL.
Enr 103. B 7/45; G 5/46. Elem 48, Sec 55. US—15. Grad '84—6.
  Col—4.
Fac 21. Full 15/Part 6. M 10; F 11. US 4. UK US.
Tui Bdg 654,000 Pts; Day 540,000 Pts. Schol.
Est 1980. Nonprofit. Tri (Sept-Je). ECIS ISS.
Bldgs 2. Dorm. Lib 6000 vols. Courts. Fields. Pool. Gym.

This international College features an academic curriculum based on the International Baccalaureate program. Basic skills are emphasized in the elementary school with music and art supplementing the full course of studies. Students in the secondary school concentrate on math, science and languages in preparation for the IB examination. Athletic facilities are available and numerous activities and excursions are arranged. Founded in Estepona, the College moved to its permanent Madrid facility in 1983.

KING'S COLLEGE
Bdg Boys Ages 8-17, Girls 9-18; Day Coed Ages 3-19. Gr K-PG.

El Goloso Madrid, Spain. Paseo de los Andes s/n, Urb. Soto de
  Vinuelas. Tel. 845-2844.
Peter Stokes, Prin.
Col Prep. Tests GCE. Curr—UK. LI—Eng.

Enr 760.
Fac 57.
Tui Bdg 190,000 Pts (+ var); Day 90,000-175,000 Pts (+ var).
Est 1969. Inc. Tri (Sept-Je). ECIS ISS.
Bldgs 3. Lib 2000 vols. Athletic facilities.

King's College was founded to supply the need for a coeducational boarding and day school in Madrid. The school is divided into two "streams." Students in the English stream follow an entirely British syllabus preparing for the G.C.E. examinations. In the Spanish stream, courses are designed to lead up to the Bachillerato, which provides for entry into Spanish universities. While separate for academic courses, the two streams mix for all other activities. The extracurricular program includes judo, swimming, skiing, riding, drama, music, art and interest clubs.

NUMONT
Day Coed Ages 2-11. Gr N-5.

Madrid 33, Spain. Calle Parma 16. Tel. 200 2431.
Margaret Ann Swanson, Prin.
Gen Acad. Curr—UK. LI—Eng. CF—Fr Span Hist.
Enr 200. B 100; G 100. US—50.
Fac 14. Full 12/Part 2. F 14. UK.
Tui 33,600-64,400 Pts (+ var).
Summer Session. Rem. Tui 14,000 Pts. 4 wks..
Est 1960. Tri (Sept-Je).
Bldgs 2. Lib 1000 vols. Athletic facilities.

While many of the students at this school are from Great Britain, children from the United States and other countries also attend. A British curriculum is followed and activities include tennis, swimming, guitar, ballet and riding.

RUNNYMEDE COLLEGE
Day Coed Ages 11-18. Gr 6-12.

Madrid 2, Spain. Calle del Arga, 9. Tel. 4572327.
Arthur F. Powell, BA, London, Head.
Col Prep. Tests CEEB SSAT GCE. Curr—UK. LI—Eng.
Enr 260.
Fac 18.
Tui 63,600-75,600 Pts.
Est 1967. Inc. Tri (Sept-Je). ECIS ISA ISS.
Bldgs 1. Lib 8000 vols. Athletic facilities.

Runnymede's curriculum prepares students for the College Boards and G.C.E. 'O' and 'A' level exams. Recent graduates have attended Yale, Stanford, Tulane and UCLA. Sports and activities include riding, swimming, skiing and basketball.

ST. MICHAEL'S PREPARATORY SCHOOL
Day Coed Ages 3-11. Gr N-6.

Madrid 16, Spain. Camino Ancho 89, La Moraleja, Alcobendas. Tel.
259.32.58.
Diana B. Linton, Prin.
Pre-Prep Gen Acad. Curr—UK. LI—Eng. CF—Span Fr Eng Hist Math
Sci Relig Music Drama. SI—Tut.
Enr 180. B 90; G 90. US—18.
Fac 14. Full 10/Part 4. M 5; F 9. UK.
Tui 35,000-75,000 Pts (+24,000 Pts).
Est 1968. Tri (Sept-Je).
Bldgs 3. Lib 8000 vols. Gym.

St. Michael's is situated near the outskirts of Madrid and provides a
British education in the basic academic subjects. It aims to serve the
special needs of children away from their home country and therefore
maintains an appropriate teacher/pupil ratio. Extracurricular options
include ballet, judo, swimming and riding.

AMERICAN SCHOOL OF MALLORCA
Bdg Coed Ages 13-18; Day Coed 5-18. Gr K-PG.

Portals Nous Mallorca, Spain. Calle Oratorio, 9. Tel. (71) 67-58-50.
Telex: 69651 AMSC.
Stanley Amdurer, BBA, City Col of New York, BA, New York Univ., PhD,
Univ. of Cape Town, Dir.
Frank Pajares, Head.
Col Prep Gen Acad. Tests CEEB TOEFL. Curr—USA. LI—Eng. A—Eng
Hist Math Sci. CF—Span Fr Writing Drafting Engineering. SI—Rem &
Dev Math & Read Tut.
Enr 190. B 20/80; G 20/70. Elem 90, Sec 100. US—130. Grad '84—25.
Col—21.
Fac 23. Full 20/Part 3. M 10; F 13. US 18.
Tui Bdg $9420 (+$600); Day $2350-5200. Schol.
Est 1969. Sem (Sept-Je). ECIS ISS MAIS. Accred MSA.
Bldgs 10. Dorms 2. 2 Libs 10,000 vols. Labs. Studios. Comp lab. Court.
Field.

The American School of Mallorca is situated on the island of
Mallorca, 125 miles from the Iberian Peninsula and is staffed by a
multi-national faculty. A basic elementary and secondary curriculum is
followed allowing for flexibility through course offerings, achievement
expectations, honors courses and individualized programs. A skills
center is available for the analysis, study and remediation of learning
disabilities.

A trade program offers woodworking, auto body mechanics, basic
electronics, welding and mechanical drawing. Electives are conducted in
typing, shorthand, library skills, journalism and computer programming.

Swimming, tennis and competitive sports are offered in the physical education program.

See also pages 80-1

EDGE HILL COLLEGE
Bdg Coed Ages 8-18; Day 2-18. Gr N-12.

La Nucia (Alicante), Spain. Ctera Benidorm, Km. 53. Tel. (965) 87 35 69.

S.J. Fieldhouse, Prin.

Gen Acad. Tests GCE. Curr—UK. LI—Eng. CF—Fr Span Ger Hist Geog. SI—Rem & Dev Read Tut.

Enr 150. B 25/50; G 25/50.

Fac 12. Full 8/Part 4. M 4; F 8. UK.

Tui Bdg 220,000 Pts (+20,000 Pts); Day 70,000 Pts (+20,000 Pts).

Est l975. Tri (Sept-Je).

Bldgs 3. Dorms 2. Lib Crts.

Located a few minutes from the Mediterranean, Edge Hill College prepares students for the British GCE 'O' and 'A' level exams. Advanced courses are offered in math, biology, art and music. Spanish is taught from kindergarten. The college's enrollment is primarily drawn from the United Kingdom and continental Europe.

BALEARES INTERNATIONAL SCHOOL
Bdg Coed Ages 12-19; Day Coed 4¹/₂-19. Gr N-PG.

San Agustin—Palma de Mallorca 15, Spain. Camino Son Toells y Calle Cabo Mateu Coch 17. Tel. (9) 71-401812. Telex: 68667 PME.

John and Patricia Long, BA, MA, Cambridge Univ., Co-Dirs.

Col Prep Gen Acad. Tests CEEB GCE. Curr—USA UK. LI—Eng. CF—Span Fr Ger Russ Lat Soc Stud Comp Stud Art Drama Lit Journalism. SI—Tut.

Enr 200. B 15/176; G 9. Elem 137, Sec 56, PG 7. US—30. Grad '84—13. Col—10.

Fac 21. Full 17/Part 4. M 10; F 11. UK US.

Tui Bdg $8950 (+$400); Day $3200-4500. Schol.

Est 1957. Quar (Sept-Je). ECIS ISS.

Bldgs 3. Lib 9000 vols. Athletic facilities.

Baleares International School is located in the residential district of San Agustin, five kms. west of Palma de Mallorca. The British-American curriculum prepares students of all nationalities for college entrance through a strong academic program taught principally in English. Baleares also offers a solid general education for pupils not necessarily bound for college but who can benefit from individualized instruction. Recent graduates have entered Arizona State University, Alberta University, University of the Pacific, New England College, Santa Barbara City College of Art and University of Surrey.

A comprehensive sports program includes basketball, volleyball, soccer, swimming and tennis. Activities outside the school include sailing, riding and scuba diving.

THE INTERNATIONAL SCHOOL AT SOTOGRANDE
Bdg Coed Ages 8-16; Day Coed 3-15. Gr N-12.

Sotogrande (Cadiz), Spain. Apartado 15. Tel. (956) 792902.
Rosemary Ridley de Gomez, BA, Sheffield, Prin.
Col Prep Gen Acad. Tests GCE. Curr—UK. LI——Eng. CF—Span Fr
Eng Lit Math Hist Geog Sci. SI—Rem & Dev Math & Read Tut ESL.
Enr 102. B 4/48; G 8/42. Elem 68, Sec 34. US—3.
Fac 12. Full 11/Part 1. M 4; F 8. US 1 UK.
Tui Bdg 418,000-470,000 Pts; Day 150,000-201,000 Pts. Schol.
Summer Session. Acad ESL. Tui Bdg 80,000 Pts; Day 20,000 Pts. 4
wks.
Est 1978. Nonprofit. Tri (Sept-Je).
Bldgs 2. Dorms 5. 2 libs 1000 vols. Athletic Facilities.

The International School at Sotogrande follows a British curriculum, preparing students for the G.C.E. 'O' and 'A' level exams. Classes are conducted in English. A full language program includes Spanish from grade one, ESL for Spanish speakers and optional bilingual classes. Arts and crafts, music, singing, drama, physical education and rhythm and movement are integral to the junior school curriculum. Senior school students in Forms IV to VI choose from eight university prepartory subject options. The school has facilities for golf, tennis, riding, swimming, basketball and volleyball.

SWEDEN

Sweden's history dates to the seventeenth century when Christina, Queen of Sweden, abdicated the throne and left her country forever. She journeyed south to spend her 35 remaining years in sunnier Italy.

Modern statistics suggest how uncommon her move would appear today. In recent years, a substantial percentage of immigrants have become naturalized citizens of the Kingdom of Sweden. The Swedish population of over eight million persons claims the highest per capita income in Europe.

Stockholm, founded in 1260, is the capital, and the krona (SKr) is the monetary unit. Swedish is the official language.

THE ENGLISH JUNIOR SCHOOL
Day Coed Ages 5-12. Gr K-6.

Gothenburg, Sweden 41274. Lilla Danska Vagen 1. Tel. 31 401819.
P. Gabrielsson, Prin.

Gen Acad. Curr—UK. LI—Eng. CF—Fr Swed.
Enr 125.
Fac 9.
Tui 4000 SKr.
Est 1958. Tri (Sept-Je). ISS.

This school is located in Sweden's second most populous city. A British-oriented elementary curriculum is provided to students primarily from England, Sweden, Australia and America.

INTERNATIONAL SCHOOL OF STOCKHOLM
Day Coed Ages 5-14. Gr K-9.

111 38 Stockholm, Sweden. Johannesgatan 18. Tel. (08) 249715.
Gen Acad. Curr—USA. LI—Eng. CF—Fr Swed Soc Stud. SI—Rem Read.
Enr 305. US—37.
Fac 27. Full 24/Part 3. US 13.
Tui $2076-3114.
Est 1951. Sem (Aug-Je). A/OS ECIS ISA ISS.
Bldgs 1. Libs 2. Labs 2. Gym. Aud.

Enrolling students of over 30 nationalities, this day school's curriculum is equal to that of the U.S., with instruction in English. Special classes are conducted in English as a second language. The main emphasis of the program is to facilitate a student's return to his home country's curriculum. Activities include swimming, tennis and ballet.

LUNDSBERG SCHOOL
Bdg Coed Ages 12-19. Gr 6-12.

68800 Storfors (Lundsberg), Sweden. Tel. 0550-70001.
Per Henningsson, PhD, Univ. of Uppsala, Head.
Pre-Prep Col Prep. Curr—Nat. LI—Swed. CF—Eng Fr Ger Span Econ Arts. SI—Tut.
Enr 250. B 145/10; G 85/10. Elem 46, Sec 204. Grad '84—63. Col—63.
Fac 35. Full 21/Part 24. M 25; F 10. Sweden.
Tui Bdg 45,000 SKr (+2000 SKr). Schol.
Est 1896. Sem (Aug-Je).
Bldgs 20. Dorms 6. Lib 10,000 vols. Athletic facilities.

An accredited Swedish high school, Lundsberg offers a college preparatory curriculum to an enrollment that is 75% Swedish. As instruction is in the native tongue, American students must know Swedish or receive special training in the language. A full sports program, including soccer, crew, riflery and skiing, as well as extracurricular activities supplement the academic program.

SWITZERLAND

Switzerland is a mountainous plateau bordered by the Alps on the south and by the Jura Mountains on the northwest. Nearly a fourth of this beautiful country is covered by mountains and glaciers.

Today four different languages and ethnic groups prevail, with international neutrality and individual freedom given the highest priority. Approximately 65% of the people speak German. French is spoken by 18% who live in the west, and the remaining 13% in the southeast speak Italian and Romansch, a language derived from spoken Latin. In German Switzerland are situated Basel, Bern, Interlaken, Lucerne, St. Moritz and Zurich; in French Switzerland are Geneva, Lausanne, Montreux and Vevey; in Italian Switzerland are Lakes Lugano and Maggiore.

The Swiss Confederation is politically organized into 22 cantons, the historical origins of which date to 1291. The cantons are autonomous states and, while joined under a Federal Constitution in 1848, each retains large powers of local control. Many of the cantons have two names, one in German and one in French; some have an additional Italian name.

Bern is the federal capital and the Swiss franc (SwF) is the country's monetary unit.

ECOLE CHANTEMERLE
Bdg Coed Ages 6-14.

1807 Blonay (Vaud), Switzerland. Tel. 021/53 1193.
Jean Wegmuller, Dir.
Lang Stud Gen Acad. Curr—Fr. LI—Fr Eng.
Enr 40.
Rui 12,000 SwF.
Summer Session. (July-Aug).
Est 1966.

Located in a Swiss cottage overlooking Lake Geneva, Ecole Chantemerle offers a program specializing in intensive French language study. A pre-school program is featured in addition to primary and secondary classs which conform to the traditional French "lycee." Classes are kept small and instruction is also provided in English, Arabic, German, Iranian and Italian. Cultural excursions and numerous sports and open air activities supplement the academic program.

INTERNATIONAL SCHOOL OF BASEL
Day Coed Ages 3-14. Gr N-8.

24103 Bottmingen (Baselland), Switzerland. P.O. Box 319. Tel. (061 47 84 83.
Janet L. Galli, BS, Univ. of Nebraska, Dir.
Gen Acad. Curr—Intl. LI—Eng. CF—Ger Math Sci Soc Stud. SI—ESI Tut.

Enr 96. B 50; G 46.
Fac 10. Full 5/Part 5. M 1; F 9. US 3. US UK.
Tui 740-6800 SwF (+50 SwF). Schol.
Est 1979. Nonprofit. Quar (Sept-Je). ECIS ISA ISS.
Bldgs 2. Lib 6000 vols. Gyms 2. Field. Pool.

The International School of Basel has a bilingual curriculum based on the American school system. German is taught to all children in every grade and special classes are given in Swiss history, culture and geography. The curriculum is flexible and classes are small so that students receive much individual attention. Physical education and swimming are integral parts of the program and extracurricular activities include dance, arts and crafts, tennis and various clubs.

ZUG ANGLO-AMERICAN SCHOOL
Day Coed Ages 5-13. Gr K-7.

6330 Cham (Zug), Switzerland. Steinhauserstrasse. Tel. 042 36 78 94.
Gwyn Bevan, DipEd, Univ. of Wales, Head.
Gen Acad Pre-Prep. Curr—USA. LI—Eng. CF—Ger Fr. SI—Rem & Dev Read & Math.
Enr 78. B 40; G 38.
Fac 13. Full 7/Part 6. M 2; F 11. US 28.
Tui $3500 (+$100).
Est 1961. Tri (Sept-Je). ECIS ISS.
Bldg. Field. Gym.

Situated on the edge of Lake Zug, the school offers a curriculum similar to that found in an international American elementary school. While enrollment is not strictly American, all students must speak English. The teaching approach is individual with groups kept as small as possible. Extracurricular activities include skiing, swimming, hiking, skating and field trips to local places of interest.

AIGLON COLLEGE
Bdg Coed Ages 11-18; Day Coed 11-15. Gr 6-PG.

1885 Chesieres-Villars (Vaud), Switzerland. Tel. (025) 3 27 21. Telex: 456 211 alcol ch.
Philip L. Parsons, MA (Cantab), Head.
Mary Newell, Adm.
Col Prep. Tests CEEB SSAT GCE IB. Curr—USA UK. LI—Eng. CF—Fr Ger Ital Span Religion Sci Choir Art Music Carpentry. SI—EFL.
Enr 256. B 140/4; G 108/4. Elem 70, Sec 186. US—53. Grad '84—47. Col—46.
Fac 47. Full 40/Part 7. M 25; F 22. US 3.
Tui Bdg 31,090 SwF (+3500 SwF); Day 21,240 SwF (+3500 SwF). Schol.
Summer Session. Acad. Tui Bdg 2500 SwF. 3 wks.

Est 1949. Inc 1977 nonprofit. Tri (Sept-Je). ECIS ISA ISS. Bldgs 7. Dorms 6. Lib 16,000 vols. Gym. Courts. Fields. Rink. Skiing facilities.

An English coeducational boarding school, Aiglon College stands on a sheltered south slope of the Swiss Alps, at a height of 4250 feet overlooking the Rhone Valley to the Dents du Midi and the Massif du Mont-Blanc. Operated along the lines of an English Public School, over 50% of the students are American, with the remainder largely British and Canadian. The curriculum meets the requirements of the British G.C.E., the American College Boards and the International Baccalaureate, Intermediate Level. French is obligatory, with emphasis on speaking. Recent graduates have entered Princeton, Trinity, Middlebury, Vassar and Skidmore.

As well as skiing, ice hockey, swimming and other sports, the physical education program features expeditions on skis, foot and bicycles and instruction in the techniques of rock climbing, camping and rescue work. Handicrafts and hobbies are encouraged through a system of projects, while other interests may be pursued through clubs and societies.

See also page 82

PRE FLEURI—HOME ECOLE
Bdg & Day Coed Ages 3-11. Gr N-6.

1885 Chesieres-Villars (Vaud), Switzerland. Tel. (025) 35 23 48. Mr. & Mrs. V. Sekaly-Bonzon, Dirs. Gen Acad Pre-Prep. LI—Eng Fr. CF—Ger Fr Eng. Enr 46. Tui Bdg 14,400 SwF (+1000 SwF); Day 3000 SwF. Summer Session. Rec. Tui Bdg 2300 SwF. 4 wks. Est 1948. Quar. Bldg. Dorms 15. Lib. Athletic facilities.

Situated in the French part of the Swiss Alps, Pre Fleuri offers a year-round program of academics and recreational activities. The curriculum is designed to feature small classes, individualized instruction and language study. A wide variety of winter and summer sports include team skiing, ice skating, riding, tennis and judo. Other extracurricular pursuits are activities in art, drama and film.

PREALPINA INTERNATIONAL BOARDING SCHOOL FOR GIRLS
Bdg Girls Ages 11-20. Gr 6-12.

CH-1605 Chexbres (Vaud), Switzerland. Rte de Chardonne. Tel. (021) 56 11 84. Leonard Bettex, Dir. Col Prep Gen Bus Home Ec. Curr—Natl. LI—Fr. CF—Rom Lang + Ger Greek Lat Russ Arabic Econ Hist Math Sci Pol Sci Photog Cooking Steno Arts. Enr 115. US—2.

Fac 30. Full 20/Part 10. M 8; F 22. US 2.
Tui 27,750 SwF (+var).
Summer Session. Acad Rec. Tui 3400 SwF. 4 wks.
Est 1925. Proprietary. Tri (Sept-Je).
Bldgs 2. Lib 5000 vols. Tennis crts. Pool. Fields.

Founded by Professor W.P. Buser, an innovator in the field of private education in Switzerland, Prealpina accepts girls of all nationalities. As the language of instruction is French, non-speakers participate in an intensive French program before commencing other courses. Mathematics, physics, chemistry and the natural sciences are taught in small study groups of eight to ten students allowing teachers to follow each girl's individual progress. In addition to the academic program there are commercial and domestic science sections.

Prealpina's seven-acre campus maintains facilities for tennis, volleyball, basketball, badminton and swimming. The location in the French Alps overlooking Lake Geneva also provides ample opportunity for snow and water skiing. Students may also participate in a cultural program within he school's theatre and movie clubs, attending musical and theatrical events in the Lausanne/Montreux area. (See also *Summer Sessions*).

ST. GEORGE'S SCHOOL
Bdg & Day Girls Ages 9-19. Gr 5-12.

1815 Clarens (Vaud), Switzerland. Tel. (021) 613424.
Rev. Leslie V. Wright, MA, Cambridge, Head.
Col Prep. Tests GCE CEEB SSAT. Curr—UK. LI—Eng Fr. A—Music Art Math Lang. CF—Rom Lang + Arabic Ger Russ.
Enr 108. G 92/16. Elem 21, Sec 72, PG 15. US—8. Grad '84—18. Col—14.
Fac 28. Full 19/Part 9. M 6; F 22. US 1. UK.
Tui Bdg 23,000 SwF; Day 9000 SwF. School.
Est 1927. Nonprofit. Tri (Sept-Je). ECIS ISS.
Bldgs 2. Dorms 2. Lib 12,000 vols. Lab. Gym. Swimming pool. Tennis crts 5. Art studios 2.

Overlooking Lake Geneva and the Savoy Alps, this English girls' school offers a British-oriented curriculum geared towards the British G.C.E. Ordinary and Advanced Level exams and the American College Boards. In addition, students who are fluent in French are prepared for the Diplome of the University of Nancy (France). The study of modern language is strongly emphasized. Instruction is bilingual and the girls are expected to use French in their social encounters every other week to increase fluency. Enriching the academic program are classes in music, art and drama. The extensive athletic facilities permit a wide variety of sports including tennis, swimming, skiing and riding. While most of the girls come from English-speaking countries, students from South America, the Middle East and the rest of Europe are also enrolled.

LE CHAPERON ROUGE
Bdg & Day Coed Ages 5-15. Gr K-9.

CH 3963 Crans-sur-Sierre (Valais), Switzerland. Tel. 027/41.25.00.
Prosper Bagnoud, Dir.
Gen Acad. Curr—Nat. LI—Eng Fr Ger Ital. CF—Span Hist (US) Home Econ. SI—Tut Rem.
Enr 70. B 30/5; G 30/5.
Fac 12. Full 9/Part 3. M 2; F 10. US 2.
Tui 15,150 SwF (+3000 SwF).
Summer Session. Lang Rec. Tui 2100 SwF/mo (+550 SwF/mo). 4-8 wks.
Est 1955. Tri (Sept-Je).
Bldg. Lib. Athletic Facilities.

The enrollment is drawn from all over Europe and the United States at this elementary boarding school. A small number of day students are also accepted. The school is divided into four sections, each with its own language of instruction: Anglo-American, French, German, Italian. In addition to their mother tongues, the children all are required to study another language. A summer holiday program is offered which, while primarily recreational, includes two hours of language study a day.

THE INTERNATIONAL SCHOOL OF GENEVA
Bdg Coed Ages 11-19; Day Coed 5-19. Gr 1-PG.

1208 Geneva, Switzerland. 62 rte de Chene. Tel. 022-36-71-30.
Jan C. ter Weele, Dir.
Col Prep Gen Acad. Tests CEEB IB. Curr—Intl. LI—Eng. CF—Rom Lang Lat GerRuss Hist (US) Econ Philos Geog Drama Arts. SI—Tut Rem Eng.
Enr 2613. B 34/1268; G 34/1277. Grad '84—225. Col—220.
Fac 245. Full 187/Part 58. M 103; F 142. US UK.
Tui Bdg 24,700-27,500 SwF; Day 3570-12,000 SwF (+var). Schol.
Est 1924. Nonprofit. Tri (Sept-Je). ECIS ISA ISS. Accred MSA.
Bldgs 32. Dormis 5. Libs 6. Studios art 7, music 6. Labs 16. Theatre. Athletic facilities.

Started by a group of personalities connected with the League of Nations, this international school became the parent of similar schools later established throughout the world. The International School of Geneva in 1973/74, merged with the College International de la Chataigneraie, the Lycee des Nations and the United Nations School to form the Foundation which now comprises six campuses situated in Geneva and outlying districts, with all campuses offering similar programs.

The school was a co-founder of the International Baccalaureate, now recognized as a valid university entrance examination in most countries. Over 90 nationalities are represented in the student body, the majority of whose parents work for the many international organizations and businesses in Geneva.

Instruction is available in either French or English. Certain subjects such as languages, art, music and physical education are integrated across the Language Programs. In addition to the International Baccalaureate, students may prepare for the U.S. College Boards and the Swiss Maturite. Extracurricular activities include choir, orchestra, cinema, photography and canoe clubs. The athletic department features inter-scholastic competition in soccer, basketball, volleyball, skiing and swimming.

The main campus is situated on a 20-acre estate known as "La Grande Boissiere." The plant includes a few school buildings dating from the 18th century, one an historically famous chateau, as well as modern buildings housing science laboratories, individual music practice rooms, primary schools and sports hall. Three additional schools comprise the Foundation—La Chataigneraie (1297 Founex Vaud) is situatd in the Geneva countryside; Pregny-Rigot (11, Avenue de la Paix, 1202 Geneva) is located near the United Nations; and La Gradelle, annex to La Grande Boissiere, houses young students of pre-school and junior elementary grades and is located just a few minutes from the main campus.

ECOLE D'HUMANITÉ
Bdg Coed Ages 8-18; Day Coed 6-18. Gr 1-PG.

CH 6085 Goldern-Hasliberg (Berner Oberland), Switzerland. Tel. (036) 71 15 15.

Natalie and Armin Luethi, Dirs.

Col Prep Gen Acad. Tests CEEB GCE. Curr—USA Natl. LI—Ger Eng. CF—Fr Ger Lat Ital Esperanto Hist Music Soc. SI—ESL Rem & Dev Read & Math Tut.

Enr 150. B 74/6; G 68/2. Elem 79, Sec 71. US—12. Grad '84—3. Col—3.

Fac 38. Full 35/Part 3. M 18; F 20. US 5. Switz Ger.

Tui 16,300 SwF (+1000 SwF). Schol.

Est 1934. Inc 1946 nonprofit. Tri (Sept-Je). ISS.

Bldgs 20. Dorms 12. 3 Libs 20,000 vols. Fields. Crts.

Children of many nationalities, races and religions study and grow up together in a spirit of cooperation and cultural interchange at this unusual school in the Bernese Oberlands. About half of the students are Swiss nationals, the rest come from the United States and numerous nations in Europe, South America, Asia and Africa.

The educational structures of the school were developed by its founder, Paul Geheeb, who previously directed a school in Germany from 1910 until 1934 when he fled increasing Nazi pressure. Under his course system, only three academic subjects are studied during periods of five or six weeks. Rather than being divided into conventional classes, children are grouped by ability in subjects. They may pursue independent study under a teacher's supervision.

All students are required to learn German, and most classes are taught in this language. U.S. history, math, science, sociology and English courses are taught in English. The program prepares for the U.S. College Boards and the Swiss Maturite. While no longer part of the curriculum, G.C.E. preparation is arranged for any students who desire it. U.S. graduates have entered Antioch, Earlham, Rice, Wellesley, Yale and the University of York in England.

Emphasizing artistic and practical work, the school reserves afternoons for courses in the fine arts and crafts, as well as for athletics, which feature hiking and skiing. Living in small, family-style groups of faculty and students, the children share in the communal self-government of the school and the upkeep of house and grounds.

Near the Brunig pass, an hour's drive from Lucerne or Interlaken, the village of Goldern is situated on the terrace of the Hasliberg at an altitude of 3500 feet.

See also page 83

EDINBURGH COLLEGE—GENEVA
Bdg & Day Coed Ages 16 and up. Gr 9-PG.

1218 Grand Sacconnex (Geneva), Switzerland. 27, Chemin des Crets-de-Pregny. Tel. (202) 91 06 55. Telex: 427 130 READ.
Douglas J.A. Read, MA, Edinburgh Univ., Dir.
Col Prep Gen Acad. Tests CEEB GCE SAT. Curr—US UK. Ll—Eng. A—Eng Math Sci Econ. CF—Fr Span Ger ESL. Comp Stud Sl—TUT Rem & Dev Read & Math.
Enr 150. B 5/60; G 15/70. US—15. Grad '84—15. Col—13.
Fac 26. Full 10/Part 16. M 9; F 17. US UK.
Tui Bdg 22,000 SwF (+1100 SwF); Day 12,000 SwF (+200 SwF).
Summer Session. Acad. Lang Stud. Tui Bdg 1800 SwF (+250 SwF); Day 800 SwF (+250 SwF). 4 wks.
Est 1969. Tri (Sept-Je). ECIS ISS.
Bldgs 3. Lib 5000 vols.

Edinburgh College offers preparation for American and British examinations at both senior high school and junior college level. Language studies is a featured aspect of the curriculum with instruction available in French, German, Spanish and English as a Second Language. Business and secretarial courses are also offered. Instruction is given in small group seminars which are often complemented by individual tutorials. Students come from all over the world and are accommodated in students' residences or with local families. An intensive summer session also offers examination preparation and language study. Recreational facilities are available in nearby Geneva.

GSTAAD INTERNATIONAL SCHOOL
Bdg Boys Ages 11-19.

3780 Gstaad (Berne), Switzerland. Tel. 030-4-20-36.
Marcel M. Mille, Head.
Col Prep. Tests CEEB GCE. Curr—USA UK. Ll—Eng. CF—Fr Ger Math Hist (US) Econ. Sl—Tut.

Enr 18.
Fac 6. Full 4/Part 2. M 6.
Summer Session.
Est 1953. Tri (Sept-Je). ECIS ISS.
Bldgs 1. Lib. Athletic facilities.

This small tutorial school, catering largely to American students, concentrates on the development of good study-habits. In classes that do not exceed four boys, and often on a one-to-one basis, students who have had difficulty in larger schools may benefit from the individualized instruction. Students are prepared for the U.S. College Boards and for the British G.C.E. exams at both the 'O' and 'A' levels. Also accepted are foreign students wishing to improve their written and conversational English to facilitate entrance into a larger international school. In addition to the academic program, the boys are encouraged to utilize the excellent sports facilities in Gstaad; skiing, mountain climbing, tennis, golf and swimming are available.

THE INTERNATIONAL SCHOOL OF BERNE
Day Coed Ages 4-18. Gr N-12.

3073 Gumligen (Berne), Switzerland. Mattenstrasse 3. Tel. (031) 52-23-58.
Keith Costello, PhD, Pacific States Univ., Head.
Col Prep Gen Acad. Tests CEEB SSAT GCE. Curr—USA. LI—Eng. CF—Fr Ger Hist Math Sci Geog Music Art. SI—Rem & Dev Reading Tut ESL.
Enr 160. B 80; G 80. Elem 120, Sec 40. US—40. Grad '84—4. Col—4.
Fac 23. Full 13/Part 10. M 7; F 16. US 8.
Tui $1000-5100. Schol.
Est 1961. Nonprofit. Tri (Sept-Je). A/OS ECIS ISS.
Bldgs 3. Lib 6000 vols. Gym. Fields. Pool. Crts.

Located in the residential community of Gumligen, the school is divided into five academic groupins, which offer a range of programs from morning (kindergarten) to departmental and tutorial sections (high school). The curriculum at all levels emphasizes English language arts and skills, followed by mathematics, science and foreign languages. Music, visual arts and crafts and physical education are part of the program at all levels. Within the academic framework, the school makes full use of the city and surrounding countryside. Alpine summer and winter sports include skiing, skating, hiking and mountain sports.

ZURICH INTERNATIONAL SCHOOL
Day Coed Ages 4-13. Gr N-7.

8802 Kilchberg, Switzerland. Seestrasse 169. Tel. 01-715.35.47.
Mr. S. Mills, Dir.
Gen Acad. Curr—USA UK. LI—Eng. CF—Ger Music Art.
Enr 124. B 61; G 63. US—23.
Fac 14. Full 11/Part 3. M 4; F 10. US 2.

Tui 6400-8750 SwF. Schol.
Est 1970. Nonprofit. Sem (Sept-Je). ECIS ISS.
Bldgs 1. Lib.

Formerly the ELK School, this program prepares students of all nationalities for English-speaking high schools. Small classes facilitate individualized learning in language arts, math, social studies/science, music and art. German is also taught at all grade levels. A local gymnasium and swimming pool are available for the school's sports program.

THE AMERICAN INTERNATIONAL SCHOOL OF ZURICH
Day Coed Ages 13-19. Gr 8-12.

8802 Kilchberg-Zurich, Switzerland. Nidelbadstrasse 49. Tel. 01-715-27-95.
August L. Zemo, BA, Harvard, Dir.
Col Prep. Tests CEEB. Curr—USA. LI—Eng. CF—Fr Ger ESL Sci Math Hist Art Skiing. SI—Tut.
Enr 205. Elem 45, Sec 160. US—100. Grad '84—28. Col—24.
Fac 27. Full 15/Part 12. M 12; F 15. US UK.
Tui 12,600 SwF (+ 600 SwF). Schol.
Summer Session. Acad Rec.
Est 1963. Inc nonprofit. Sem (Sept-Je). ECIS ISS. Accred NEASC.
Bldgs 4. Lib 13,000 vols. Labs 2. Fields.

Offering an American college preparatory curriculum, this coeducational day school enrolls primarily United States nationals, although students from England, Holland and Switzerland also attend. Advanced Placement courses, an independent study program, and numerous electives, particularly in the arts, supplement the standard program of study. The school has sent graduates to Brown, Cornell, Bowdoin, MIT and Stanford as well as universities in the United Kingdom.

The active extracurricular and sports program is similar to that found in American secondary schools, and includes sports activities with students from Swiss schools, excursions to cultural events in Zurich, and vacation study trips to various parts of Europe. Zurich, largest city in Switzerland, is an important manufacturing center and the home of a university. The school's five-acre campus is in Kilchberg, a small community a few miles south of the city, on the western shore of the Lake of Zurich.

INSTITUT VALCREUSE
Bdg & Day Coed Ages 10-20. Gr 5-12.

1010 Lausanne (Vaud), Switzerland. Isabelle-de-Montolieu 26. Tel. 021/32 10 36.
Donato Pian, PhD, LDD, Univ. of Bologna, Dir.
Col Prep Lang Stud. Curr—Swiss French. LI—Fr. CF—Fr Eng Ital Ger Span Lat Philos Hist Econ Physics.

Enr 133. B 27/50; G 10/46. Elem 46, Sec 87. US—8. Grad '84—26. Col—20.
Fac 23. Full 17/Part 6. M 19; F 4. Intl.
Tui Bdg 18,800-24,200 SwF (+ 4500 SwF); Day 6400-9350 SwF (+ 1500 SwF). Schol.
Summer Session. Acad Rec Intensive French. Tui Bdg 2660 SwF (+ 850 SwF). 4-8 wks.
Est 1959. Inc. Tri (Sept-Je).
Bldgs 4. Dorms 2. Crts. Swimming pool.

Institute Valcreuse is set in the university town of Lausanne, 15 minutes from Lake Geneva and at the foot of the Vaudoise Alps. Classes are conducted in French with intensive French courses for non-speakers offered year-round. The curriculum prepares students for the French Baccalaureate and Swiss Maturity and features honors courses in math, economics, physics and languages. The school's unique location provides for a wide range of winter and summer sports and recreations.

Classes at the Institut's associate school, Liceo Pareto, are taught in Italian and prepare students for the Italian Baccalaureate.

INTERNATIONAL SCHOOL BRILLANTMONT
Bdg Girls Ages 12-18; Day Coed 12-18. Gr 7-12.

CH-1005 Lausanne (Vaud), Switzerland. Avenue Secretan 12-18. Tel. (021) 22-47-41.
Francoise Frei-Huguenin, Dipl, Ecole Sociale, Prin.
Pre-Prep Col Prep Lang Sch. Tests IB GCE CEEB SSAT. Curr—USA UK Intl. CF—Fr Ger Ital Span ESL Econ Chem. Sl—Rem & Dev Read Tut.
Enr 160.
Fac 34.
Tui Bdg $10,500; Day $6900. Schol.
Summer Session. Acad Rec. 6 wks.
Est 1882. Tri (Sept-Je). ECIS ISS. Accred NEASC.
Bldgs 6. Dorms 4. Lib. Labs 4. Tennis crts. Gyms 2.

Located on a four-acre site in the university town of Lausanne, Brillantmont comprises three sections—British G.C.E., American high school and language school. The British and American sections are university-oriented with a vast majority of graduates attending four-year colleges in the U.S. and Europe. Diplomas are offered to students who successfully complete courses in modern languages. Lausanne is a mile north of Lake Geneva, facing the Alps, and many outdoor activities are available to students.

See also page 84

INSTITUTION CHATEAU MONT-CHOISI
Bdg Girls 12-20. Gr 7-PG.

1012 Lausanne-La Rosiaz (Vaud), Switzerland. Bd. de la Foret, Ch. des Ramiers 16. Tel. 021 28 87 77.

Jeno Pusztaszeri, Dir.
Col Prep Bus Fr. Tests CEEB SSAT GCE. Curr—Nat USA. LI—Eng Fr.
 CF—Rom Lang + Ger Eng Soc Sci Home Ec Steno Typ.
Enr 125. G 120/5. US—15. Grad '84—7. Col—7.
Fac 28. Full 18/Part 10. M 6; F 22. US 6. Switz.
Tui 25,500 SwF (+ 1500-4500 SwF).
Summer Session. Rec Lang. Tui Bdg 3050 SwF (+ 600 SwF). 4 wks.
Est 1885. Tri (Sept-Je). ECIS ISS.
Bldgs 6. Dorms 4. Lib 4000 vols. Gym. Tennis courts. Swimming pool.

This long-established international girl's school offers a range of study opportunities in academic, commercial and domestic science courses. Students in the American program may prepare for the College Boards. While French instruction is emphasized, a full curriculum is offered in English. Ample opportunities are available for cultural excursions and sports activities. With enrollment drawn from many countries, a strong international atmosphere prevails on the spacious campus in a Lausanne suburb. The school goes to Crans for winter sports and sponsors a trip to another country during the Easter vacation.

See also page 89

LEYSIN AMERICAN SCHOOL
 Bdg Coed Ages 13-19. Gr 8-PG.

1854 Leysin 3 (Vaud), Switzerland. Tel. (025) 34 13 61. Telex: 456 166.
Steven Ott, PhD, Stanford, Dir.
Col Prep. Tests CEEB SSAT. Curr—USA. LI—Eng. A—Fr Math.
 CF—Rom Lang Hist (US) Pol Sci Geog Computer Sci Art. SI—Tut.
Enr 85. B 45; G 40. Elem 3, Sec 75, PG 7. US—20. Grad '84—20.
Fac 17. Full 9/Part 8. M 11; F 6. US 9.
Tui $12,000 (+ $1500).
Summer Session. Acad Theatre Mus. Tui $3000 (+ $300). 8 wks.
Est 1961. Sem (Sept-Je). ECIS ISS.
Bldgs 4. Lib 10,000 vols. Gym.

Students at this American-administered coeducational boarding school are prepared for entrance into United States colleges and universities. Enrollment is predominantly American, as is the faculty except for European language teachers. Leysin does admit non-American students who plan to pursue advanced studies in the United States.
Study of French is required, and language practice is afforded through various activities. Physical education, including a variety of winter and summer sports, publications, clubs, and hobby groups supplement the academic program, which is further enriched by field trips and weekend excursions. Special cultural tours are arranged for students unable to go home during Easter holidays.
The school is located at the edge of the health and ski resort of Leysin, at an altitude of 5000 feet, high above the Rhone Valley and Lake Geneva. The American College of Switzerland is nearby.

See also page 88

INSTITUT DR. SCHMIDT
  Bdg Boys Ages 8-20; Day Coed 8-20. Gr 6-12.

1095 Lutry (Vaud), Switzerland. Chateau de la Rive. Tel. 021/39.51.12.
  Telex: 25495 CHMI-CH.
Marc De Smet, Prin.
Col Prep Gen Acad Bus Lang. Curr—Nat. LI—Fr. CF—Eng Ger Ital
  Span Fr Computer Sci.
Enr 75. B 45/15; G/15.
Fac 19. Full 17/Part 2. M 17; F 2.
Tui Bdg 24,900 SwF (+4000 SwF); Day 10,500 SwF.
Summer Session. Acad Rec. Tui Bdg 3000 SwF (+1000 SwF); Day
  1500 SwF. 4 wks.
Est 1889. Tri (Sept-Je). ECIS ISA ISS.
Bldgs 2. Lib 3000 vols. Gym. Tennis courts. Fields.

While the enrollment at this school is predominantly European, boys
of all nationalities have been represented in the student body. The
school prepares for the Swiss Federal Matriculation, Commercial
Diploma and Baccalaureate, as well as offering special courses geared
toward the U.S. College Boards. The only courses conducted in English
are American History and English composition and literature. However,
preparatory classes in French are provided for English-speaking
students upon their arrival. Training in manual arts and crafts, and visits
to factories and workshops add another dimension to the program. The
school has sent graduates to Yale, Portland and Columbia.

Situated on Lake Geneva, three miles east of Lausanne, the school
occupies a four-acre campus, enlarged and modernized during the 1950s.
The comprehensive athletic facilities abet a broad physical education
program. For a few weeks in January, the school moves to the
mountains to pursue winter sports. Students may remain at the school
during the holidays. (See also *Summer Sesions*).

See also pages 86-7

THE AMERICAN SCHOOL IN SWITZERLAND
  Bdg & Day Coed Ages 12-18. Gr 7-PG.

CH 6926 Montagnola-Lugano (Ticino), Switzerland. Tel. (091) 54 64
  71. Telex: 79317 TASIS CH.
Mail to: US Admission, 326 E. 69th St., Rm. 110, New York, NY 10021.
  Tel. (212) 570-1066.
Mrs. Mary Crist Fleming, BA, Radcliffe, Founder & Dir.
J. Christopher Frost, Head..
Col Prep. Tests CEEB PSAT SAT TOEFL. Curr—USA. LI—Eng. A—Eng
  Fr Math Hist Sci. CF—Rom Lang Ger US Hist Photog Drama Arts.
  SI—Tut ESL.
Enr 255. B 123/10; G 112/10. Elem 16, Sec 221, PG 18. US—191. Grad
  '84—79. Col—68.
Fac 48. Full 40/Part 8. M 29; F 19. US 35.
Tui Bdg $13,900 (+$800); Day $8100 (+$800). Schol.

Summer Session. Acad. Tui Bdg $1500 (+ $200); Day $750 ($200)/4 wks. 8 wks.
Est 1955. Proprietary. Sem (Sept-Je). ECIS ISS NAIS.
Bldgs 12. Dorms 10. Lib 10,000 vols. Labs 3. Theatre. Gym. Field. Indoor & outdoor swimming pools. Crts.

Designed to offer students college preparation within a milieu providing exposure to cultures and languages other than their own, TASIS' enrollment is composed primarily of American boys and girls. Approximately 30% of the enrollment come from 35 foreign countries. The faculty members are primarily American, but European language teachers are employed. Language mastery is furthered by the trilingual atmosphere of Lugano, weekend excursions to various parts of France, Italy and Switzerland, and by the two-week winter stay in the ski resort of St. Moritz.

Offerings such as history, drama, literature, and an extensive art program enrich the basic curriculum which prepares for the American College Boards. Advanced placement courses are available in all disciplines. Graduates have gone on to study at Amherst, Antioch, Boston University, Brown, Cornell, Dartmouth, McGill, Princeton, Radcliffe and Stanford. Interests in the arts are furthered through events and activities on and off campus. The extracurricular program also includes student government, publications, and individual team sports.

The city of Lugano is a medical, financial and trading center, situated in southern Switzerland, close to the lake region and a half-hour from the Italian border. The school is a five-minute drive from the city and a short walk below the village of Montagnola, located on a hill overlooking Lugano. (See also *Summer Sessions*).

See also page 111

LES COCCINELLES INTERNATIONAL SCHOOL
Bdg & Day Coed Ages 3-13.

3962 Montana-Crans (Valais), Switzerland. route de la Moubra. Tel. 027/412423.
Colin Hurst, Dir.
Pre-Prep. Curr—Nat. LI—Eng Ger Fr. CF—Fr Ger Math Hist Skiing.
Enr 57. B 18/15; G 11/13.
Fac 6. Full 6. M 1; F 5. Switz Fr Ger UK.
Tui Bdg $11,500 (+ $500); Day $6000 (+ $500).
Summer Session. Rec. Tui Bdg $1200 (+ $200); Day $500 (+ $200). 4 wks.
Est l950. Tri (Sept-Je).
Bldgs 2. Dorm rooms 40. Crts. Swimming pool. Skating rink. Skiing facilities.

Situated in the heart of the Swiss Alps, this small international school provides secondary school preparation amid a rich variety of local cultural and recreational opportunities. The curriculum follows the Swiss public schools program and instruction is in English, German and

French. A strong activities program includes excursions to nearby lakes and mountains, visits to the town of Montreaux and the castles of Chillon Gruyere and three afternoons of sport each week. Ski instruction is available throughout the season. Children also participate in ice skating, swimmming and riding.

ECOLE NOUVELLE PREPARATOIRE
Bdg Boys Ages 8-18; Day Coed 8-18. Gr 3-12.

CH-1094 Paudex (Vaud), Switzerland. Route du Lac 22. Tel. 021/39. 24.77. Telex: 25495 CHMI-CH.
Marc J.F. De Smet, BSc, Prin.
Pre-Prep Col Prep Gen Acad. Curr—Nat Fr. LI—Fr. CF—Eng Ital Ger Physics Math Comp Stud.
Enr 40. B 25/10; G/5.
Fac 18. Full 17/Part 1. M 16; F 2.
Tui Bdg 24,900 SwF (+4000 SwF); Day 10,500 SwF (+1000 SwF). Summer Session. Acad Rec. Tui Bdg 2000 SwF (+1000 SwF). 2-7 wks.
Est 1933. Tri (Sept-Je). ISS.
Bldgs 1. Dorm. Lib. Athletic facilities.

Located on the shores of Lake Geneva, this school offers a program of individualized instruction with particular attention to languages and mathematics. Each student's progress is closely monitored and small classes are provided in all major subjects. The regular academic curriculum is enriched by many trips and study tours throughout Switzerland and Europe. A wide variety of individual and team sports include football, basketball, skiing, fencing, judo and karate.

See also page 85

COMMONWEALTH-AMERICAN SCHOOL
Day Coed Ages 4-14. Gr K-8.

1009 Pully-Lausanne (Vaud), Switzerland. 73 Ave. C.F. Ramuz. Tel. 021 28 17 33.
John N. Curtis, Jr., BA, Yale, MA, Univ. of Pennsylvania, Head.
Pre-Prep. Curr—USA. LI—Eng. CF—Fr Hist Geog Art Music. SI—Tut Rem & Dev Read.
Enr 100. B 45; G 55.
Fac 14. Full 8/Part 6. M 3; F 11. US 3. UK.
Tui 4050-9620 SwF (+400 SwF). Schol.
Est 1962. Nonprofit. Tri (Sept-Je). ECIS ISS. Accred NEASC.
Bldgs 2. Lib 6000 vols.

Children from the United States, forming nearly one-half of the enrollment at Commonwealth-American, attend school with children from Great Britain, Canada, Holland and Scandinavia. The curriculum is comparable with that of primary schools in Britain and the U.S. and prepares children for secondary education. Instruction is provided in traditional subjects and computer studies, with French studied as a second language. Special courses and individual tutoring are arranged for children whose first language is not English.

The athletic program includes school competition in soccer, skiing, swimming and volleyball. During autumn and spring terms all students participate in swimming and gymnastics or soccer. Older students spend one day a week during the winter term receiving professional skiing instruction in the Alps. Other activities include drama, painting, arts and crafts and music instruction.

INTERNATIONAL SCHOOL LE ROSEY
Bdg Coed Ages 9-18. Gr 4-12.

1180 Rolle (Vaud), Switzerland. Tel. 021-75-15-37.
Philippe Gudin, Gen. Dir.
Col Prep. Tests GCE CEEB. Curr—USA UK. LI—Eng Fr. CF—Rom
  Lang + Arabic Ger Lat Math.
Enr 280.
Fac 47.
Tui 28,500 SwF (+3000 SwF).
Summer Session. Acad Rec. Tui 3900 SwF. 5 wks.
Est 1880. Tri (Sept-July). ECIS ISS.
Bldgs 17. Lib 7000 vols. Athletic facilities.

International from its founding, Le Rosey enrolls boys and girls from more than 35 countries. Among the alumni are counted kings, princes and illustrious persons from the United States. For students older than age nine, entrance exams or SSAT results are required.

While all subjects are taught in both French and English, study of French is compulsory. The program meets the requirements of the American College Boards, as well as the French Baccalaureate, the Swiss Maturite, the British G.C.E. and the Canadian Matriculation. Most United States graduates enter Ivy League colleges. Extracurricular activities in the fine arts, carpentry, daily assemblies, debates, lectures and other cultural and social events round out the program. Placing great stress on physical education, the school offers a full athletic schedule, including track, rowing, skiing, ice-hockey and other sports.

The 13th century Chateau du Rosey with four other buildings and extensive athletic facilities comprise the 50-acre campus in Rolle, a small town on the shore of Lake Geneva, midway between Lausanne and Geneva. For the winter term, the school moves to its Gstaad campus in the Bernese Oberland.

JOHN F. KENNEDY INTERNATIONAL SCHOOL
Bdg Coed Ages 6-13; Day Coed 6-13. Gr 1-8.

3792 Saanen-Gstaad, Switzerland. Tel. (030) 4 13 72.
William M. Lovell, BA, Univ. of Guelph (Canada), Dir.
Pre-Prep. Tests SSAT GCE. Curr—USA UK. LI—Eng. CF—Fr Ger Art
  Math Sci Soc Stud Skiing. SI—ESL Rem & Dev Math & Read Tut.
Enr 32. B 10/6; G 10/6. US—11. Grad '84—7.

Fac 14. Full 9/Part 5. M 2; F 12. US 2. Nat Canada.
Tui Bdg 24,000 SwF (+6000 SwF); Day 13,500 SwF (+3000 SwF).
Summer Session. Acad Rec. Tui Bdg 3200 SwF/3 wks (+300 SwF);
   Day 1800 SwF/3 wks (+150 SwF). 3-6 wks.
Est 1949. Tri (Sept-Je). ECIS ISS.
Bldgs 2. Lib 4000 vols. Playground.

Situated three kilometers from Gstaad, the school is housed in two
chalets surrounded by the Bernese Alps. Combining traditional and
modern teaching methods, students are prepared for enrollment into
Canadian, American or British secondary schools. The program features
small classes with individualized instruction. French is required for all
students and English as a sscond language is also taught.

Sports activities include baseball, football, volleyball, ice-hockey,
swimming and hiking. During the winter students ski every afternoon
with qualified instructors. Professional instruction in tennis, horseback
riding, ballet and music is also available. (See also *Summer Sessions*).

ROSEHILL INTERNATIONAL SCHOOL
(Institut Auf Dem Rosenberg)
   Bdg Coed Ages 8-19; Day Coed 11-18. Gr 3-PG.

9000 St. Gallen, Switzerland. Hohenweg 60. Tel. (071) 27.77.77.
Mr. O. Gademann, Dir.
Mrs. M.A. Zaller, Head, Anglo-American Section.
Col Prep. Tests CEEB GCE. Curr—USA UK. LI—Eng. CF—Ger Fr Soc
   Stud Earth Sci Hist Bus Econ Tech Drawing. SI—ESL.
Enr 59. B 33/2; G 24. Elem 12, Sec 44, PG 3. US—5. Grad '84—14.
   Col—12.
Fac 11. Full 7/Part 4. M 3; F 8. US 3. Ireland.
Tui 24,870-26,820 SwF.
Summer Session. Language Program Rec. Tui Bdg 840 SwF/wk. 7
   wks.
Est 1889. Nonprofit. Tri (Aug-Je). ISS ECIS.
Bldgs 10. Dorms 8. Lib. Athletic facilities.

Overlooking St. Gallen, a town historically famous as a center of
learning, Rosehill's six-acre campus is close to both Lake Constance and
the 8000-foot Santis Mountain. The school's Anglo-American section
provides instruction in English and prepares for the U.S. College Boards
and Oxford G.C.E. exams. Recent graduates have entered Cornell,
Bucknell, Yale, Antioch and the American College of Paris.

German is the official language at Rosehill, which also offers sections
following Swiss, Swiss Commercial, German and Italian curricula. The
Modern Language Studies program leads to diplomas in German,
French and English. Preliminary courses are provided to students who
do not speak German. The athletic program includes field games, tennis,
swimming, winter sports and also offers corrective orthopaedic
gymnastics.

See also page 92

GYMNASIUM HÖRNLIBERG
Bdg & Day Coed Ages 14-20. Gr 9-PG.

CH-8274 Tägerwilen. Nagelshausen (Thurgau), Switzerland. Tel. 0041/72/72.49.12.

Katja Guggenheim-Grob, Prin.

Col Prep Gen Acad. Curr—Nat. LI—Ger. CF—Eng Ger Fr Lat Ital Span Russ Greek Math.

Enr 22. B 8/4; G 6/4.

Fac 13. Full 1/Part 12. M 6; F 7. Nat.

Tui Bdg 12,000 SwF; Day 6000 SwF. Schol.

Summer Session. Acad Rec. Tui Bdg 16,000 SwF. 4 wks.

Est 1955. Inc. Tri (April-Aug).

Bldgs 1. Lib 3000 vols. Swimming pool. Tennis crts.

The enrollment at this school is restricted to 22 students who are primarily from Switzerland, Germany, Venezuela and the U.S. There is no rigid class system and emphasis is placed on intensive independent work. Courses are conducted in art history, chemistry, natural history and drawing. The school prepares students for the Swiss Federal Final Exam and the German Abitur. Swimming, fencing, hiking, skiing, ballet and eurhythmics are offered in the athletic program.

MONTE ROSA INTERNATIONAL SCHOOL AND LYCEE D'ARVEL
Bdg & Day Coed Ages 8-19. Gr 4-PG.

CH-1820 Territet-Montreux (Vaud), Switzerland. 57, Avenue de Chillon. Tel. (021) 63 53 41. Telex: 453 267 rosach.

Bernhard Gademann, Dir.

R.C. Holland, Head.

Col Prep Gen Acad Bus. Tests CEEB GCE. Curr—USA. LI—Eng. A—Fr Ger Span Eng Lit Bio Chem Econ Physics Comp Sci. CF—Rom Lang + Ger Lat Hist (US & Eur) Pol Sci Bus Arts Econ.

Enr 88. B 41/4; G 41/2. Grad '84—10. Col—9.

Fac 24. Full 24. UK Germany Ireland US.

Tui Bdg $11,000 (+$2500); Day $5000 (+$500). Schol.

Summer Session. Languages. Tui Bdg $450 (+$250)/wk; Day $200 (+$25)/wk. 3 wks.

Est 1874. Inc 1954 nonprofit. Tri (Sept-Je). ISS.

Bldgs 3. Dorms 3. 2 Libs 3000 vols. Labs. Gym. Athletic facilities.

The present Monte Rosa was established in 1955 in cooperation with Rosehill International School of St. Gallen. The schools, both founded in the last century, now offer identical curricula, although the study of French is more strongly emphasized at Monte Rosa. The English-speaking section offers a program designed to meet the entrance requirements of the leading American, British, Canadian and European universities. Students may prepare for the U.S. College Boards and the Oxford G.C.E. at 'O', 'A' and scholarship levels. Able seniors are encouraged to take three subjects at advanced levels, preparing for

Advanced Placement exams. French is compulsory at all levels and a second foreign language is required of high school pupils.

The English-speaking section is comprised of students from the United States, the United Kingdom, Canada and 20 other nations. The German-speaking Section offers the official Swiss and German curricula, as well as a Commercial course. A special Language Section prepares for official certificates in English, French, German and Spanish. The vigorous athletic program includes tennis, squash, swimming, skating, cross-country and other team sports with interscholastic competition. Emphasis is placed on skiing and the school employs instructors for the season. Other extracurricular activities include cultural outings and club pursuits.

The village of Territet is on the eastern shore of Lake Geneva, close to Montreux and about 17 miles from Lausanne.

See also page 91

COLLEGE DU LEMAN INTERNATIONAL SCHOOL
Bdg Coed Ages 8-19, Day 5-19. Gr K-PG.

1290 Versoix-Geneva, Switzerland. 74, Route de Sauverny. Tel. 022-55-25-55. Telex: CH 28145.

Francis A. Clivaz, Dir.

Pre-Prep Col Prep. Tests CEEB GCE. Curr—Intl. LI—Eng Fr. CF—Ger Hist (US) Econ Philos Arts.

Enr 796. B 141/291; G 100/264. Elem 428, Sec 364, PG 4. US—132. Grad '84—81. Col—74.

Fac 89. Full 75/Part 14. US 16. Swizt Fr.

Tui Bdg 25,000-28,000 SwF; Day 7250-12,000 SwF.

Summer Session. Acad Rec. Tui Bdg 650 SwF/wk; Day 300-400 SwF/wk. 6 wks.

Est 1960. Proprietary. Quar (Sept-Je). ECIS ISS. Accred MSA.

Bldgs 17. Dorms 8. Lib 19,000 vols. Labs 6. Gyms 3. Aud. Fields. Tennis crts. Swimming pool.

Dual sectioning at this school provides English-language instruction preparing for the U.S. College Boards and the Cambridge G.C.E. and French language instruction preparing for the Baccalaureate and the Swiss Maturite. The English-speaking section, which affords opportunities for advanced work in several subject areas, particularly stresses the study of French. Many countries are represented in the enrollment, giving College du Leman a strongly international flavor. The extracurricular program is organized by an active Student Government and includes a drama club, weekend excursions and a wide variety of sports. During the Easter and Christmas vacations, boarding students may choose to join the various trips organizsd by the school.

Situated in suburban Versoix, seven miles from the center of Geneva, the school has separate residential facilities, including sports grounds, for boys and girls. The campus, formerly occupied for many years by Institut Monnier, was thoroughly modernized by M. and Mme. Clivaz when they started their school.

COLLEGE ALPIN INTERNATIONAL BEAU-SOLEIL
Bdg Coed Ages 10-18. Gr 6-12.

1884 Villars-sur-Ollon (Vaud), Switzerland. Tel. 025-35-21-54. Telex: 456 210 BSVI.
Pierre de Meyer, Dir.
Col Prep Gen Acad. Tests CEEB GCE. Curr—Fr USA. LI—Eng Fr. A—Fr. CF—Fr Ger Sci Hist Geog Lit.
Enr 150. B 60/15; G 60/15. US—35. Grad '84—11. Col—11.
Fac 24. Full 22/Part 2. M 18; F 6. Fr Switz.
Tui Bdg 21,600-27,600 SwF; Day 18,400-22,900 SwF.
Summer Session. Acad Rec. Tui 3300-6000 SwF. 4-6 wks.
Est 1920. Inc. Tri (Sept-Je).
Bldgs 4. Dorms 2. Lib. Athletic facilities.

A coeducational French Lycee and international school, College Beau-Soleil prepares students for the French Baccalaureate. The Anglo-American section provides a curriculum with accelerated language studies designed to prepare students for the U.S. College Boards and coursework leading to the G.C.E. exams.

Situated in the Swiss Alps near Lake Geneva, facilities for skiing and winter sports, year-round ice skating and horseback riding are within walking distance. On-campus sports include soccer, basketball, volleyball, tennis, swimming and bowling.

See also page 91

AMERICAN SCHOOL OF INSTITUT MONTANA
Bdg Boys Ages 10-18; Day Coed. Gr 5-12.

6316 Zugerberg (Zug), Switzerland. Tel. (042) 21 17 22.
Karl Storchenegger, PhD, Univ. of Zurich, Dir; Peter H. Oehrlein, BS, Georgetown, MA, Johns Hopkins, Dean-American Sch.
Col Prep. Tests CEEB SSAT ACT. Curr—USA. LI—Eng. A—Art Eur Hist Calculus Chem Fr Ger. CF—Fr Ger Hist Sci Music.
Enr 51. B 40/7; G /4. US—8. Grad '84—8. Col—8.
Fac 16. Full 9/Part 7. M 13; F 3. US 5. Switz Ital UK.
Tui Bdg 23,700-26,100 SwF (+5000 SwF); Day 13,050 SwF (+1000 SwF). Schol.
Summer Session. Acad Rec. Tui Bdg 565 (+50) SwF/wk. 3-6 wks.
Est 1926. Nonprofit. Tri (Sept-Je). ECIS ISS NAIS.
Bldgs 12. Dorms 4. 3 Libs 8000 vols. Fields 3. Ski lifts 2. Gym. Tennis crts 4.

Located on a 75-acre campus just outside Zug, the cantonal capital, and about 18 miles south of Zurich, this international institute has separate American, Dutch, German-Swiss and Italian divisions with a cumulative enrollment of 190. Each section studies in its own language and prepares for the university requirements of the respective country. The student body represents over 25 different nationalities. Students from countries other than the United States are encouraged to apply to the American division if they are proficient in English.

The demanding academic program includes study of German and/or French every year, commencing in the fifth grade. Honors courses as well as Advanced Placement studies are offered. In addition to College Boards, students may prepare for ACT, PSAT and SSAT exams. United States graduates enter a variety of colleges, including Georgetown, Pomona, Franklin & Marshall, Syracuse, Dartmouth, Colgate and Lafayette.

The international atmosphere is furthered through the dormitories and school teams and organizations. The athletic program offers a wide range of team and individual sports, including obligatory skiing, while other activities include publications, choir, dramatics and hobby clubs. Travel workshops concentrating on specialized interests are organized to visit various countries during the Easter holidays. Shorter trips are also arranged throughout the school year.

See also page 93

THE INTER-COMMUNITY SCHOOL ZURICH
 Day Coed Ages 4-13. Gr N-7.

CH-8126 Zumikon (Zurich), Switzerland. Strubenacher 3. Tel. 01 918 1656.

Robert J. Lilburn, Head.

Gen Acad. Curr—Intl. LI—Eng. CF—Fr Ger Sci Comp Stud Music. Enr 330. B 170; G 160.

Fac 27. UK.

Tui 7500 (+ 600) SwF/term.

Est 1960. Nonprofit. Tri (Sept-Je). ECIS ISA ISS.

Bldgs 2. Lib 12,000 vols. Athletic facilities.

Founded with the cooperation of British, American, Australian and Canadian communities, the enrollment at this school is 40% British and American. Located in a residential area on the outskirts of Zurich, Inter-Community strives to achieve easy transition both to and from the home systems of its students. Instruction is in English, however German is required of all students from grade one. Swimming is a compulsory part of the physical education program from the third grade.

UNITED KINGDOM

The dual elements of Britain's geographic position—insularity yet proximity to continental Europe—are well known as key factors in the development of her history, culture and national character. Britain's role in shaping modern world history has been largely to amalgamate elements of European civilization and to spread European influence to all parts of the world. Yet Britain's geographic insularity has always prevented her permanent attachment to any single center of European culture. School children learn of the significance of the last successful invasion of Britain, 900 years ago, and its lasting effect on England, Europe and the world.

The term, Great Britain, is the popular designation for the United Kingdom of Great Britain and Northern Ireland, which comprises England, Wales, Scotland and Northern Ireland. The Commonwealth, a shortening of the original name of the British Commonwealth of Nations, is a loosely joined association of nations and dependencies once parts of the British Empire. The British monarch is symbolic head of the Commonwealth. The pound (£) is the monetary unit and English, Gaelic and Welsh are spoken.

Today a person living in London, the capital, resides in one of the world's three largest cities yet is a short trip from England's green and pleasant countryside.

ENGLAND

BEDFORD SCHOOL
 Bdg Boys Ages 8-17; Day 7-17. Gr 2-12.

Bedford (Bedfordshire) MK40 2TU, England. Burnaby Rd. Tel. 0234-53431.
C. I. M. Jones, MA, St. John's College-Cambridge, Head.
Col Prep Gen Acad. Tests GCE. Curr—UK. LI—Eng. CF—Fr Ger Greek Lat Russ Span Physics Computer Sci Art Lit. SI—Tut.
Enr 1060. B 360/700. Elem 140, Sec 560. US—16. Grad '84—130. Col—80.
Fac 112. Full 100/Part 12. M 101; F 11. Nat.
Tui Bdg £4020 (+£100); Day £2286 (+£60). Schol.
Summer Session. Acad Rec. Tui Bdg £1340 (+£35); Day £762 (+£20). 10 wks.
Est 1552. Inc nonprofit. Tri (Sept-July).
Bldgs 30. Dorms 6. Lib 7000 vols. Labs 4. Music bldg. Art studios. Shops 3. Gym. Fields. Tennis crts 10. Rifle range. Swimming pool.

With origins as a pre-Norman Conquest monastery school, the present Bedford School's formal founding dates to 1552. The program comprises a preparatory school and a public school, offering primary and secondary education and preparation for the G.C.E., 'O' and 'A' level exams. Specialized advanced courses also prepare for engineering, medical, other professional and special examinations. Latin and French studies are commenced in the primary grades. Greek and German are available in the Upper School. Fine and manual arts are featured in the curriculum and are promoted as extracurricular pursuits.

Rugby, cricket, boating, tennis, fencing, golf and camping are offered in the games program. The Combined Cadet Force, special interest societies and service activities such as the community service unit are also conducted.

The boys in the Preparatory (primary) School have separate buildings and playing fields on the extensive campus, situated on the edge of town. Bedford, on the River Ouse, is about 50 miles north of London.

GREYLANDS INTERNATIONAL COLLEGE
Bdg Coed Ages 16 and up. Gr 10-PG.

Bembridge (Isle of Wight) PO35 5NJ, England. Tel. (0983-87) 2871.
Patrick McKiernan, Head.
Gen Acad Bus ESL. Tests GCE. Curr—Nat. LI—Eng.
Enr 180.
Fac 26.
Tui £1099 (+ £100).
Summer Session. Acad. Lang.
Est 1943. Inc. Tri (Sept-Je). ECIS ISS.
Bldgs 7. Lib 10,000 vols. Athletic facilities.

The program at Greylands is tutorial in nature with students grouped
according to their ability. Courses of instruction are preparatory for the
G.C.E. 'O' and 'A' level exams. Greylands maintains its international
student body by restricting the enrollment of any one nationality. The
sports programs offer tennis, swimming, volleyball, netball, horseback
riding, football, hockey, rugby and cricket.

CHARTERS TOWERS SCHOOL
Bdg Girls Ages 7-18; Day Girls 4½-18. Gr 2-PG.

Bexhill-on-Sea (Sussex) TN40 2NP, England. Hastings Road. Tel.
(0424) 214442.
Miss Dorothy L. Howe, BA, Trinity Col. (Dublin), Head.
Col Prep Gen Acad. Tests GCE. Curr—Nat. LI—Eng. CF—Fr Ger Sci
Math Comp Sci Art Music Phys Ed. A—Lang Hist Math Soc Physics
Chem Bio. SI—Rem & Dev Read & Math Tut Dyslexia EFL.
Enr 279. G 250/29. Grad '84—20. Col—20.
Fac 47. Full 23/Part 24. M 12; F 35. Nat.
Tui Bdg £1205 (+ £60); Day £615 (+ £30). Schol.
Est 1929. Inc nonprofit. Tri (Sept-July).
Bldgs 5. 2 Libs 8000 vols. Art Studio. Gym. Fields. Tennis crts. Pool.

Occupying five connected houses surrounded by extensive playing
fields, Charters Towers stands 150 feet above the English Channel on
the outskirts of town. While predominantly British in enrollment, a
number of girls from all countries are accepted. The normal curriculum
prepares for the Cambridge G.C.E. at 'O' and 'A' levels as well as the
various official music, drama and dance examinations. Girls who are
accepted into the Sixth Form may choose the one-year General Course,
adapted to individual requirements, or a two-year course in preparation
for the Advanced level of the G.C.E. In addition to the basic college
preparatory program including a wide range of foreign languages, the
school offers programs in domestic science and the arts.
Riding and water sports are especially popular features of the athletic
program, as well as hockey, tennis, golf, track, judo and squash. Two
school choirs and clubs for debating, drama, chess and bridge are

available. Weekend outings are arranged to places of historical interest. Each day, the entire school attends a short religious service at the morning assembly.

BADMINTON SCHOOL
Bdg & Day Girls 7-18. Gr 1-12.

Bristol BS9 3BA, England. Westbury-on-Trym. Tel. (0272) 623141.
C.J.T. Gould, MA, Trinity College, Head.
Col Prep. Tests GCE. Curr—UK. LI—Eng. CF—Fr Ger Span Lat Geog Nutrition Relig Arts Music Comp.
Enr 300. G 200/100. Elem 160, Sec 140. US—4. Grad '84—30. Col 28.
Fac 57. Full 27/Part 30. M 10; F 47. Nat.
Tui Bdg £1380 (+£100); Day £700 (+£50). Schol.
Est 1858. Tri (Sept-July).
Bldgs 11. 3 libs. Crts. Pool. Fields. Gym.

This school is located two and one-half miles from Bristol, a university town with many cultural and leisure facilities. The basic academic curriculum is broadened with courses in graphic design, photography, spinning, cookery, dress-making, music and physical education. School musical groups perform locally as well as before their peers. Extra-curricular activities include sports, clubs and social service in the community.

INTERNATIONAL UNIVERSITY HIGH SCHOOL
Bdg & Day Coed Ages 14-19. Gr 9-12.

Bushey (Hertfordshire) WD2 2LN, England. The Avenue. Tel. Watford 49067. Telex: 23869 IVE G.
Robert E. Schaub, MA, Morgan State, MAE, Arizona State Univ., Head.
Col Prep. Tests CEEB. Curr—USA. LI—Eng. CF—Fr Comp Sci Biol.
Enr 44. B 28/6; G 6/4. Grad '84—19. Col—19.
Fac 10. Full 6/Part 4. M 5; F 5. US 6.
Tui Bdg £5870; Day £3270.
Est 1978. Nonprofit. Sem (Sept-Je). ECIS ISS.
Bldgs 25. Dorms 2. Lib 30,000 vols. Gym. Fields. Crts. Pool.

The school's campus is located 16 miles north of London on a 95-acre estate. Mastery in subjects such as English, mathematics, science and social studies is stressed. Study in art and music and a wide range of extracurricular activities complement the academic curriculum. Students who qualify are eligible to take university courses and receive college credit. Affiliated programs are located in Mexico, the United States (10455 Pomerado Rd., San Diego, CA 92131) and Africa.

THE LEYS SCHOOL
Bdg & Day Boys Ages 13-18. Gr 8-12.

Cambridge CB2 2AD, England. Tel. 0223-355327.
B. T. Bellis, MA, St. John's College, Cambridge, Head.

Col Prep. Tests GCE. Curr—UK. LI—Eng.
Enr 415.
Fac 39.
Tui Bdg £1230/term (+£25); Day £925/term (+£25). Schol.
Est 1875. Nonprofit. Methodist. Tri (Sept-July).
Bldgs 13. Dorms 6. Lib 11,000 vols. Fields. Crts. Swimming pool.
  Theatre.

Situated at the south side of Cambridge, The Leys was founded by a group of Methodist laymen. The school's enrollment is comprised mostly of students from Great Britain with a small number of students coming from other European countries, Malaysia, Singapore and the United States. The curriculum prepares pupils for the British 'O' and 'A' level examinations. Rugby, judo, water polo, squash, rowing, weight training and fencing are included in the sports program. Extracurricular activities range from literary clubs to engineering and carpentry.

CASTERTON SCHOOL
  Bdg & Day Girls Ages 8-18. Gr 3-PG.

Carnforth (Lancashire) LA6 2SG, England. Kirkby Lonsdale. Tel. 0468-71202.
G. Vinestock, MA, Cambridge, Head.
Col Prep Gen Acad. Tests GCE. Curr—Nat. LI—Eng. CF—Fr Ger Span
  Lat Hist Geog Chem Biol Physics Art Music Math Riding.
Enr 360. G 328/32. Elem 80, Sec 280. US—1. Grad '84—25. Col—24.
Fac 53. Full 36/Part 17. M 20; F 33. Nat.
Tui Bdg £1053-1176/term; Day £624-710/term. Schol.
Summer Session. Acad.
Est 1823. Inc nonprofit. Tri (Sept-July).
Bldgs 16. Dorms 10. 2 Libs 15,000 vols. Fields.

Situated on 50 acres, the Casterton School's aim is to provide a sound academic and cultural education. Course work is designed to lead to the 'O' and 'A' levels of the G.C.E. or the Certificate of Secondary Education examination. There is a continuous assessment of student progress through staff meetings and small tutorial groups. Recreational activities include hockey and netball, golf, sub-aqua, canoeing, camping and riding.

AMERICAN COMMUNITY SCHOOLS
  Day Coed Ages 4-18. Gr K-12.

Cobham (Surrey) KT11 1BL, England. "Heywood" Portsmouth Rd. Tel. Cobham (09326) 7251.
Gordon E. Speed, BA, MA, Florida State Univ, Head.
Col Prep. Tests CEEB SSAT GCE. Curr—USA. LI—Eng. CF—Span Fr
  Ger Lit Art Music Hist (US). SI—ESL Speech Rem Read.
Enr 1100. B 605; G 495. Elem 755, Sec 345. US—750. Grad '84—81.
  Col—56.
Fac 128. Full 117/Part 11. M 43; F 85. US UK.

Tui £1725.
Summer Session. Acad Rec. 4-6 wks.
Est 1967. Sem (Sept-Je). ECIS ISS. Accred NEASC.
Bldgs 25. 6 Libs 30,000 vols. Tennis crts. Gyms. Fields. Pool. Track.
Golf course.

The American Community Schools serve American, British, Canadian, German, Iranian and Swedish families living in Surrey, Middlesex, Buckinghamshire and Berkshire. In addition to the Surrey campus, a second school is located in Middlesex (Hillingdon Court, Vine Lane, Uxbridge).

Both schools follow an American-based curriculum and have comprehensive educational and athletic facilities. The Surrey campus is located on a 128-acre country estate while the Middlesex school is on an 11-acre site northwest of London. Academic programs are divided into lower, middle and upper schools. Curricula feature advanced placement courses in all major disciplines, and the Middlesex school offers the International Baccalaureate Diploma. Academics are supplemented by extracurricular activities such as soccer, field and track, baseball, drama, arts and crafts and school publications. Field trips are taken to places of interest in and around London. Students in grades five and above have opportunities for holiday trips to European cities as well as Russia and Kenya. Sports clinics, recreational camps and academic summer programs are organized by the schools.

See also page 64

HOLMWOOD HOUSE
Bdg Boys Ages 7-13¹/₂; Day Boys 4¹/₂-13¹/₂. Gr K-8.

Colchester (Essex), England. Chitts Hill, Lexden. Tel. (0206) 74305.
S. E. H. Duggan, MA, Cambridge, Head; J. R. Lucas, MA, Dublin, DipEd, Oxford, Head.
Pre-prep. Curr—Nat. Ll—Eng. CF—Fr Latin Greek Ger Hist Biol Chem Physics Scripture Art Music Drama Photo. Sl—Rem & Dev Read & Math Tut.
Enr 260. B 90/170.
Fac 37. Full 28/Part 9. M 23/4; F 10. Nat.
Tui Bdg £3500 (+ £250); Day £2700 (+ £150). Schol.
Summer Session. Rec. Tui Bdg £100/wk (+ £10); Day £75/wk (+ £10). 2 wks.
Est 1921. Tri (Sept-July).
Bldgs 10. Dorms 1. Lib. Athletic facilities.

Located two miles from the center of Colchester, Holmwood House prepares its students for entrance to Public Schools. Students are grouped according to ability, and individual attention is given to any student with a specific disability or difficulty in a particular subject. Creative activities in writing, art and music are stressed. Students have the opportunity to play several instruments including piano, guitar, violin, trumpet and flute.

Playing fields on the school's 17 acres are used for cricket soccer, rugby and tennis. Other sports include squash, badminton, basketball and swimming.

The summer session, designed for American boys and girls ages 11 to 14, provides first-hand experience in the history, geography and culture of England.

COPFORD COLLEGE
Bdg Coed Ages 12-20.

Copford, Colchester (Essex) CO6 1DQ, England. Tel. (0206) 210341.
Edward Ronca, Head.
Pre-Prep Col Prep. Tests GCE. Curr—UK. Ll—Eng. CF—Fr Business Art. Sl—Tut Rem & Dev Math & Read ESL.
Enr 40. B 36; G 4.
Fac 9. Full 3/Part 6. M 5; F 4. UK.
Tui Bdg £2100-2500/term (+ £850). Schol.
Summer Session. Acad Rec. Tui £190-202/wk. 10 wks.
Est 1958. Inc 1977. Tri (Sept-Je).
Bldgs 7. Lib. Crts. Fields. Pool.

Copford College is an international school preparing students for the G.C.E. 'A' and 'O' level exams. Features of the 'A' level program include math, physics, economics, government and political studies and history. Students are enrolled from Nigeria, Iran, Turkey and the U.S., and intensive English courses are an integral part of the curriculum.

Students participate in football, cricket, tennis, volleyball and swimming on the ample 22-acre campus. Other activities include educational trips, societies and clubs. A summer session is conducted emphasizing English as a Second Language and recreational activities.

REPTON SCHOOL
Bdg & Day Boys Ages 13-18; Girls 16-18. Gr 8-12.

Derby (Derbyshire) DE6 6FH, England. Tel. Burton-on-Trent 702375.
D.J. Jewell, MSc, MA, St. John's Col. (Oxford), Head.
Col Prep Gen Acad. Tests GCE. Curr—UK. CF—Fr Ger Greek Lat Physics Econ Politics.
Enr 551. B 426/61; G 46/18. US—6.
Fac 60. Full 55/Part 5. M 56; F 4. UK.
Tui Bdg £1520 (+ £35)/term; Day £1120 (+ var)/term. Schol.
Est 1557. Tri (Sept-July).
Bldgs 8. Lib. Fields. Swimming pool.

Founded by Sir John Port, Repton is rich in history and houses a school museum as well as libraries of both ancient and modern books. Academics prepare students for the G.C.E. 'O' and 'A' level exams and Careers Masters advise students about their choice of 'A' level courses and future goals. Creative activities include music, art, drama, and wood and metal workshops. A wide range of sports are conducted in addition to social service groups and school societies.

MOIRA HOUSE SCHOOL
  Bdg Girls Ages 8-18, Day 5-18. Gr K-12.

Eastbourne (East Sussex) BN20 7TE, England. Carlisle Rd. Tel. (0323)
  644144.
Adrian R. Underwood, BA, Kent, MA, Dalhousie, Head.
Col Prep Gen Acad. Tests SSAT GCE. Curr—UK. LI—Eng. CF—Fr Ger
  Span Ital. SI—Tut.
Enr 290. G 150/140. Elem 80, Sec 210. US—2. Grad '84—40 Col—25.
Fac 35. Full 28/Part 7. M 9; F 26. Nat.
Tui Bdg £1300; Day £415-895. Schol.
Est 1875. Nonprofit. Tri (Sept-July).
Bldgs 7. Dorms 70. 2 Libs 10,000 vols. Athletic facilities.

The curriculum prepares students for the 'O' and 'A' level G.C.E. tests
and the U.S. SSAT. Courses in art, music, domestic science, drama and
modern dance supplement the academic program. Extracurricular
options include team sports, tennis, riding, sailing and cultural
excursions to London and its environs.

BEDGEBURY SCHOOL
  Bdg & Day Girls Ages 8-18.

Goudhurst (Kent), England. Bedgebury Park. Tel. 0580 211221.
J.H. Delany, MA, Cambridge, Head.
Gen Acad Col Prep. Tests GCE. Curr—UK. LI—Eng. CF—Fr Ger Span
  Lat Hist Geog Art Voc Home Econ. SI—Rem & Dev Read Tut EFL.
Enr 400.
Fac 54. Full 50/Part 4. M 14; F 40. UK.
Tui Bdg £1355 (+£100); Day £803 (+£50). Schol.
Est 1919. Nonprofit. Tri (Sept-July).
Bldgs 3. Dorms 12. 2 libs 5000 vols. Pools. Fields.

Primarily a boarding school, Bedgebury comprises a lower school
located on 35 acres of countryside and an upper school housed in a
17th-century mansion on 200 acres of parkland. The curriculum
prepares students for the GCE 'O' and 'A' levels and for various
vocational and specialty exams. Religious instruction follows the Church
of England's doctrine, but students of all faiths are accommodated.
  Private lessons on musical instruments and drama and art classes are
taught. A variety of clubs, lectures, films and field trips are also
available. The sports program includes gymnastics, lacrosse, tennis,
volleyball, dancing, riding, sailing and ballet.

ORLEY FARM SCHOOL
  Bdg Boys Ages 7-13; Day Coed 4-13. Gr K-6.

Harrow (Middlesex) HA1 3NU, England. South Hill Ave. Tel.
01.422.1525.
C. Justin Davies, MA, King's College, Head.
Pre-Prep Gen Acad. Tests CEE. Curr—Natl. LI—Eng.

Enr 340.
Fac 25.
Tui Bdg £2472; Day £1653.
Est 1850. Nonprofit. Tri.
Bldgs 8. Dorms 10. Lib 2000 vols. Pool. Fields.

The curriculum at Orley Farm School prepares students for the Common Entrance Examination to English public schools. Although 90% of the enrollment is from Britain, overseas students are welcome. Supplementing the academic program are music, drama, art and religion. Extracurricular activities include clubs, societies, soccer, cricket, judo, swimming and other sports.

SPRINGFIELD PARK SCHOOL
Bdg Girls Ages 8-18, Day Girls 3-18; Day Boys 3-9. Gr K-12.

Horsham (West Sussex) RH12 2BQ, England. North Parade. Tel. 0403-52866.
Mr. & Mrs. T. P. Belton, Co-Prins.
Pre-Prep Col Prep Gen Acad. Curr—UK. LI—Eng. CF—Rom Lang & Ger Relig Music Eng Math Sci Hist. SI—Rem & Dev Read & Math Tut.
Enr 173. B /18; G 35/120. Elem 123, Sec 50. Grad '84—12. Col—12.
Fac 24. Full 9/Part 15. M 3; F 21. Nat.
Tui Bdg $5100 (+$840); Day $2400.
Est 1957. Inc 1973 nonprofit. Tri (Sept-July).
Bldgs 5. Dorms 3. Libs 2. Lab. Gym. Tennis crts 4. Swimming pool.

This boarding and day school for girls is divided into three separate departments: the Senior School where girls study for the G.C.E. exams; the Preparatory School, where girls are prepared for the Common Entrance Examination; and the Pre-preparatory School for girls and young boys. Each division has its own school building and its own head. Foreign language study includes French and German with Italian and Spanish instruction provided on request. The curriculum also includes specialized study for students with dyslexia. Athletics include hockey, softball, tennis and swimming. In addition, there are facilities for riding, music, dance, judo, dramatics, volleyball and gymnastics.

The school house is a Queen Anne mansion, located on a 7-acre campus near the center of Horsham, about 40 miles south of London.

MARYMOUNT INTERNATIONAL SCHOOL
Bdg & Day Girls Ages 12-18. Gr 7-12.

(Surrey) KT2 7PE, England. George Rd. Kingston upon Thames. Tel. 01-949-0571.
Sr. Brede Shelly, MA, Columbia Univ., Prin.
Col Prep Gen Acad. Tests CEEB GCE SSAT IB. Curr—USA. LI—Eng. CF—Fr Span Hist (US) Relig Arts Math Art Eng Philos Hist Bio Chem Music. SI—Tut EFL.
Enr 200. G 100/100. Elem 50, Sec 150, US—52.
Fac 20. Full 18/Part 2. M 6; F 14. UK Ireland.

Tui Bdg £5300 (+ £500); Day £2800 (+ £500).
Summer Session. EFL. 4 wks.
Est 1955. Inc nonprofit. Roman Catholic. Tri (Sept-Je). ECIS ISS NAIS. Accred MSA.
Bldgs 7. Dorms 2. Lib 7000 vols. Labs. Gym. Field. Tennis crts.

One of several Marymount schools located throughout the world and conducted by the Religious of the Sacred Heart of Mary, this school enrolls students from England and other northern European countries as well as from the United States. The American curriculum prepares for U.S. College Boards, and many of the graduates enter Marymount College or Manhattanville College, both in New York state.

In the upper grades, courses preparing for the G.C.E. are offered for the British girls and are taken by some Americans as well. An English language course is available for a small number of non-English-speaking students. Student government, drama and music clubs and social activities are included in the extracurricular program. Hockey, tennis, gymnastics, swimming and golf comprise the available sports.

The school is located on a seven and one-half acre campus in a suburb southwest of London.

See also page 70

SUMMERHILL SCHOOL.
  Bdg Coed Ages 7-16.

Leiston (Suffolk) IP16 4HY, England. Westward Ho. Tel. Leiston 830540.
Ena Neill, Dir.
LI—Eng. CF—Fr Ger Ecology Biol Math.
Enr 65.
Fac 8.
Tui £600-800/term (+ £30/term).
Est 1921.

Children from all over the world attend this school founded by A.S. Neill, whose controversial educational philosophies have been published in many books (*Neill, Neill Orange Peel, Summerhill, Talking of Summerhill*). Since his death in 1973, Neill's wife Ena has directed the program and continues the school's policy of self-government and freedom of choice. Summerhill does not indoctrinate in the areas of religion, humanism, politics or morals. Rules concerning day to day living are made by the entire community at the Weekly General Meeting.

Instruction is available in wood and metal work, pottery, art and handwork. Students may prepare for the London University 'O' level exams and the C.S.E. In order to receive a more comprehensive view of the school, individuals are advised to read *Inside Summerhill*, a book written by one of Summerhill's pupils.

THE AMERICAN SCHOOL IN LONDON
Day Coed Ages 5-18. Gr K-13.

London NW8 0NP, England. 2-8 Loudoun Rd. Tel. 01-722-0101. Jack H. Harrison, BA, Univ. of Denver, MA, San Diego State, Stanford, Head.

Col Prep. Tests CEEB SSAT. Curr—USA. LI—Eng. A—Lang Sci Math Hist Eng Comp Sci Art. CF—Fr Span Ger Lit Journalism Soc Stud Hist Econ International Relations Sociol Psych African Stud Math Physiology. SI—Rem & Dev Eng & Math.

Enr 1400. B 762; G 638. Elem 672, Sec 728. US—1183. Grad '84—144. Col—125.

Fac 130. Full 121/Part 9. M 68; F 62. US 108.

Tui £1640-3550 (+ £25). Schol.

Summer Session. Acad Rec. Tui £80-200. 4 wks.

Est 1951. Inc 1964 nonprofit. Sem (Sept-Je). A/OS ECIS ISS NAIS. Accred MSA.

Bldgs 3. 2 Libs 35,000 vols. Studios art 5, music 5. Theatres 2. Gyms 2. Labs 8. Woodworking and Ceramics workshops.

The American School in London was established to provide an American college preparatory program for children of families from the United States residing in London. In addition to the standard College Board preparation, the school offers advanced placement in all major subject areas, and a variety of electives, especially in the fine arts. Extracurricular activities and inter/intramural sports supplement the academic program. While the enrollment is approximately 95% American, students from Canada and other English speaking countries are accepted. Graduates have attended leading colleges throughout the United States, with a smaller number entering foreign universities.

The school is located on a three-acre site in central London. The building complex is designed to promote flexibility and expansion. Bus transportation is provided for children in grades K-6. (See also *Summer Sessions*).

See also page 65

HAMPSTEAD INTERNATIONAL SCHOOL
Day Coed Ages 4-14. Gr N-8.

London NW3, England. 16 Netherhall Gardens. Tel. 01-794-0018/9. Edna M. Murphy, BA, St. John's, MA, George Washington Univ., Prin.

Gen Acad. Curr—USA. LI—Eng. SI—Rem & Dev Read & Math.

Enr 150. B 80; G 70. US—30.

Fac 15. Full 11/Part 4. M 3; F 12. US 8. Nat.

Tui £2850. Schol.

Summer Session. Acad Rec. 4-8 wks.

Est 1981. Sem (Sept-Je). ECIS.

Bldg. Lib 4000 vols.

Hampstead provides a standard American curriculum with Middle School students placed in multi-age groups. French is offered at a variety of levels and the social studies program is international in scope. Students with learning disabilities or for whom English is a second language receive special instruction. Drama, music, arts and team sports are additional curricular features.

See also page 66

INTERNATIONAL COMMUNITY SCHOOL
Day Coed Ages 5-18. Gr K-12.

London NW1 4PT, England. 1, York Terrace East. Tel. 01-935 1206. Telex: 295271 SKOLA G.

Niels Toettcher, Dir.

Pre-Prep Col Prep. Tests GCE. Curr—UK. LI—Eng. CF—Fr Commerce Comp Photog. SI—EFL Tut.

Enr 120. B 65; G 55.

Fac 17. Full 12/Part 5. M 9; F 8. Nat.

Tui £1720-1940 (+ £180).

Summer Session. Acad Rec. Tui £80/wk. 12 wks.

Est 1979. Tri (Sept-July). ECIS.

International Community School in the heart of London offers a British-style curriculum leading to G.C.E. 'O' level exams. The junior, middle and upper schools provide academic instruction to students of 50 nationalities. Junior and middle school curricula develop writing and mathematical skills and introduce students to sciences, history and French. The upper school includes courses in commerce, media and computers. A special English as a Foreign Language program covers all regular course subjects at every level.

Upper school students participate in cultural excursions in London, field trips to Italy and Holland, and an optional six-week summer study sojourn in southwest Spain. The school also operates a boarding division in Old Harlow.

THE INTERNATIONAL SCHOOL OF LONDON
Day Coed Ages 11-18. Gr 6-12.

London NW1 TR, England. Crowndale Rd. Tel. 01-388-9241. Telex: 896691 TLXIRG.

John E. Parkes, MA, DipEd, Oxford, Head.

Richard L.D. Pearce, Admin.

Col Prep. Tests GCE IB. LI—Eng. CF—Arabic Danish Fr Ger Ital Hebrew Japanese Persian Span World Stud Music Chem Physics Math Hist.

Enr 225. Elem 79, Sec 146. US—5. Grad '84—27. Col—25.

Fac 42. Full 33/Part 9. M 19; F 23. Nat.

Tui £3250-3450 (+ £100). Schol.

Est 1972. Inc Tri (Sept-July). ECIS ISS.

Bldg 1. Lib 30,000 vols. Gym.

The curriculum at this school prepares students for the International Baccalaureate and 'O' level examinations. English as a Foreign

Language is taught at all grade levels. Instruction is also given in the native languages of 18 other countries. Electives include computer studies, logic, economics, geography and anthropology. Physical education is compulsory throughout the school and the competitive sports program offers volleyball, swimming, gymnastics, track and field, tennis, soccer and basketball. Other activities include dance, drama, modelmaking and excursions.

SOUTHBANK—THE AMERICAN INTERNATIONAL SCHOOL
Day Coed Ages 11-19. Gr 6-PG.

London SW1V 1PH, England. 55 Eccleston Sq. Tel. 01-834-4684. Milton E. Toubkin, Head.
Col Prep. Tests IB CEEB GCE. Curr—Intl. LI—Eng. A—Eng Math Hist Phys Bio Chem. CF—Fr Ger Span Lat Greek Russ. SI—Tut.
Enr 92. B 53; G 39. Elem 12, Sec 74, PG 6. US—25. Grad '84—22 Col—19.
Fac 15. Full 7/Part 8. M 7; F 8. US 6. US UK.
Tui £2850-3300 (+ £50-200). Schol.
Summer Session. Acad Rec. Tui £75/crse. 3 wks.
Est 1979. Inc nonprofit. Tri (Sept-Je). ECIS ISS.
Bldg 1. Lib.

The American International School provides an individualized college preparatory curriculum for Americans and a variety of other nationalities. Through a cooperative system of tutors and educational institutions, students can choose from a wide range of elective courses. The resources and facilities of London are used extensively and a summer session is offered for just this purpose. Extracurricular activities include school council, yearbook, journalism, photography, chess, drama and a variety of sports.

MALVERN COLLEGE
Bdg & Day Boys Ages 13-18. Gr 7-PG.

Malvern (Worcestershire) WR14 3DF, England. Tel. 3497. R. de C. Chapman, MA, St. Andrews, Head.
Col Prep. Tests GCE. LI—Eng. A—Eng Math Sci Hist Lang Art Econ Span. CF—Fr Ger Greek Lat Span Russ.
Enr 610. B 559/51. Elem 247, Sec 363. US—2. Grad '84—136. Col—115.
Fac 71. Full 66/Part 11. M 66; F 5. UK.
Tui Bdg £1600/term (+ £100); Day £1150/term (+ £75). Schol.
Est 1865. Inc nonprofit. Tri (Sept-July).
Bldgs 35. Dorms 10. 2 Libs 21,000 vols. Swimming pool. Fields. Tennis crts. Rifle range.

Located on a hillside campus overlooking the Severn Valley, Malvern College offers a diverse curriculum preparing boys for the 'O' and 'A' level exams. In addition to the traditional academics, courses and activities are offered in drama, art, woodworking, archaeology, architecture, computers, photography and music. The school also has an active volunteer service organization and a career counseling program. Athletics include squash, soccer, cricket, fencing, tennis, riflery and swimming.

PADWORTH COLLEGE
Bdg & Day Girls Ages 16-20.

Near Reading (Berkshire) RG7 4NP, England. Tel. Burghfield Common 2644. Telex: 847423 COC-RG-G.
Eileen Wake, BA, Head.
Col Prep Gen Acad Bus. Tests CEEB SSAT GCE. Curr—Nat. LI—Eng. A—Eng Fr Ger Hist. CF—Fr Ital Span Ger Hist Art Econ Chem Bio Geog. SI—ESL.
Enr 150. US—6.
Fac 33. Full 10/Part 23. M 12; F 21. UK.
Tui Bdg £1380/term. Schol.
Summer Session. Acad. Rec. 2-12 wks.
Est 1963. Inc 1976 nonprofit. Tri (Sept-Je).
Bldgs 3. Libs 2.

Situated about 30 miles west of London, Padworth occupies a modernized 18th century Georgian country house. While British students form a large percentage of the enrollment, the school is international in character. In classes consisting of seminars, lectures and tutorials, students pursue various academic courses. Programs prepare girls for the G.C.E. 'O' and 'A' level exams as well as the U.S. College Boards. A secretarial program is also provided in addition to language classes for non-English-speaking students.

A coed summer session is conducted for overseas students who wish to learn English. Tennis, swimming, riding and interest clubs complement the academic program and a series of cultural trips are available to overseas girls.

STOVER SCHOOL
Bdg & Day Girls Ages 11-18. Gr 6-12.

Newton Abbot (S. Devon), England. Tel. Newton Abbot 4505.
Mrs. W.E. Lumel, BA, Head.
Col Prep Gen Acad. Tests GCE. Curr—Nat. LI—Eng CF—Fr Ger Latin Span Lit Hist Sci Art Comp Stud Home Econ.
Enr 182. G 123/59.
Tui Bdg £1175-1198/term; Day £615-655/term. Schol.
Est 1930. Nonprofit. Tri (Sept-July).
Bldgs 5. Lib. Gym. Swimming pool. Fields. Tennis crts.

Situated in an 18th century mansion near Newton Abbot overlooking the moors, Stover offers a program of general education preparing students for the G.C.E. 'O' level exams. Students also have a choice between a two-year 'A' level course and a one-year course in general studies. Provisions are made for candidates for Oxford and Cambridge entrance examinations. Student activities include lacrosse, netball, hockey, tennis, rounders, swimming and instruction in pianoforte, string and woodwind instruments, elocution, dancing, drama and riding. Most students are from the British Isles.

See also page 66

ST. CLARE'S HALL
Bdg Coed Ages 16-20. Gr 11-PG. Col.

Oxford OX2 7AL, England. 139 Banbury Rd. Tel. 010-44-865-52031. T.K. Agerbak, Prin.
Col Prep Col. Tests IB GCE. Curr—Intl. LI—Eng. CF—Lang Sci Bus Econ Art Comp. SI—Tut EFL.
Enr 280. B 80; G 200. US—25.
Fac 50. Full 30/Part 20. M 20; F 30. UK.
Tui $8125. Schol.
Summer Session. Acad EFL. Tui Bdg $650 (+ $60). 3 wks.
Est 1953. Nonprofit 1962. Tri Gr 11-PG; Sem Col. (Sept-May). ECIS.
Bldgs 18. Dorms. Lib.

Located in the historic town of Oxford, St. Clare's offers preparatory and college level courses to Americans and students from 36 nations. During the secondary years, candidates prepare for the International Baccalaureate or the 'A' level of the G.C.E. The IB program extends over two academic years and is especially suited for individuals who may be exposed to more than one educational system. Special instruction is also available for students desiring acceptance at Oxford or Cambridge.

American college students may spend their junior year abroad at St. Clare's. This program is designed to provide college instruction in the liberal arts, business and commerce. Small group tutorials are the primary means of instruction. Extracurricular activities for all students include sports, interest clubs, horseback riding and trips to such sites as London, Stonehenge and Stratford-upon-Avon. Summer school is available in Italy for interested students.

BEDALES SCHOOL
Bdg Coed Ages 8-18; Day Coed 3½-18. Gr N-12.

Petersfield (Hampshire) GU32 2DG, England. Tel. Petersfield (0730) 63286.
E. A. M. MacAlpine, MA, MSc, Head.
Col Prep Gen Acad. Tests GCE. Curr—UK. LI—Eng. CF—Fr Ger Lat Span Econ Speech Drama Music Physics Chem Biol.
Enr 565. B 188/86; G 205/86.
Fac 70. Full 45/Part 25. M 38; F 32.
Tui Bdg £1245-1525/term (+ var); Day £455-1010/term (+ var). Schol.
Est 1893. Nonprofit. Tri (Sept-July).
Bldgs 6. Lib 27,000 vols. Labs. Theatre. Fields. Gym. Swimming pool. Tennis crts.

Bedales is situated on a 150-acre site overlooking the Rother Valley about 16 miles from the seashore. The school is divided into four division: Infant School (Dunannie), day only—ages 3½ to 7; Junior School (Dunhurst), ages 7 to 11; Middle School, ages 11 to 13; Senior School, ages 13 to 18.

The curriculum is geared toward 'O' and 'A' level G.C.E. exams. About two-thirds of Bedales graduates go on to universities including Oxford and Cambridge. Emphasis is placed on art, music and craftwork of all kinds. Students also participate in a Voluntary Service program, visiting homes for the aged and handicapped. Volleyball, basketball, squash, judo, cycling, photography and electronics are among school activities.

BATTISBOROUGH SCHOOL
Bdg Coed Ages 13-18. Gr 8-12.

Plymouth (Devon) PL8 1JX, England. Tel. (075 530) 223. Telex: 45639 Comput G.
Simon Gray, BA, MPhil, Cambridge, Head.
Col Prep Gen Acad. Tests GCE CEEB. Curr—Nat. LI—Eng. CF—Fr Ger Art. SI—Rem & Dev Math & Read.
Enr 65. B 55; G 10. US—6. Grad '84—8. Col—8.
Fac 12. Full 7/Part 5. M 8; F 4. Nat.
Tui £1400 (+ £100). Schol.
Summer Session. Rec. Tui Bdg £680 (+ £20). 4 wks.
Est l955. Inc nonprofit. Tri (Sept-Je).
Bldgs 2. Lib. Tennis crts.

Battisborough offers a comprehensive college preparatory curriculum to students from England, Germany, Norway and the U.S. Academic preparation is provided for the G.C.E. 'A' and 'O' level exams as well as the American SAT and TOEFL. Battisborough's average class size numbers 12 pupils. The school's close proximity to the seashore offers opportunities for sailing, windsurfing and canoeing. Conservation and community service projects, climbing, caving, photography and pottery are among the extracurricular offerings.

See also page 68

LEIGHTON PARK SCHOOL
Bdg & Day Boys Ages 11-18, Girls 16-18. Gr 6-12.

Reading (Berkshire) RG2 7DH, England.
J. Hunter, MA, Cambridge, Head.
Col Prep. Tests CEEB GCE. Curr—Nat. LI—Eng. CF—Fr Ger Lat Hist Pol Sci Econ Arts Man Arts. SI—Tut.
Enr 305. US—2.
Fac 30. UK.
Tui Bdg £4356, Day £3051. Schol.
Est 1890. Friends. Tri (Sept-July).

This Boys' Public School, conducted by Quakers, is located 36 miles west of London. Reading, a university city, is the seat of Berkshire County. Leighton Park prepares for U.S. College Boards as well as the British G.C.E.

CRANBORNE CHASE SCHOOL
Bdg & Day Boys Ages 16-18; Girls 12-18. Gr 8-PG.

Salisbury (Wiltshire) SP3 6RH, England. Wardour Castle, Tisbury. Tel. Tisbury 870-464.
Mrs. J. Simmons, Head.
Col Prep Gen Acad. Tests GCE. Curr—Nat. LI—Eng.
Enr 154.
Fac 30.
Tui Bdg £1220 (+ var); Day £810 (+ var). Schol.
Est 1946. Nonprofit. Tri (Sept-July).
Bldgs 1. Dorms 20. Lib. Athletic facilities.

Housed in Wardour Castle, originally the home of the Earls of Arundell, the school occupies 30 acres. The curriculum prepares students for the G.C.E. 'O' and 'A' levels. Student work is supervised throughout the year by a tutor, and an assignment system allows students to organize their own time and research. Participation in school societies is encouraged, and include art, choir, film, photography, history and cookery.

MILLFIELD SCHOOL
Bdg & Day Coed Ages 13-18. Gr 9-PG.

Street (Somerset) BA16 0YD, England. Tel. (0458) 42291.
C.R.M. Atkinson, BA, Durham, BA, Queen's, MEd, DLC, Head.
Col Prep Gen Acad. Tests CEEB SSAT GCE. Curr—UK. LI—Eng. CF—Rom Lang Greek Lat Russ Swed Port Chinese Arabic Persian Swahili Hebrew Japanese Siamese Malay Eng Math Sci Comp Stud Art Music. SI—Rem & Dev Read & Math.
Enr 1144.
Fac 154. Nat.
Tui Bdg £2350-3275/term (+ £60-85). Schol.
Summer Session. Acad EFL Rec. 4 wks.
Est 1935. Inc 1960 nonprofit. Tri (Sept-Je).
Bldgs 100. Dorms 31. Libs. Courts. Stables. Pool. Fields.

Founded by R. J. O. Meyer, Millfield School is still based in its country house, with its Junior School, Edgarley Hall located about two and a half miles away in Glastonbury. In addition to preparing students for the G.C.E. 'O', 'A' and Scholarship levels and the College Boards, students may elect courses geared toward business and artistic careers. Remedial classes in English for foreigners as well as special groups for students with dyslexia are available. An unusually wide range of languages is offered to match the student enrollment from all over the world.

Students participate in the 'game of the term' at both Millfield and Edgarley including cricket, hockey, netball, rugby and soccer. Other activities include archery, karting, orienteering and canoeing. Millfield's Riding School is listed and approved by the British Horse Society and teaches stable management and horsemanship.

See also page 69

TASIS ENGLAND AMERICAN SCHOOL
Bdg Coed Ages 12-18, Day 5-18. Gr K-12.

Thorpe (Surrey) TW20 8TE, England. Coldharbour Lane. Tel. (09328) 65252. Telex: 929172 TASIS G.
Mail to: U.S. Admissions Office, 326 E. 69th St., Rm. 110, New York, NY 10021. Tel. (212) 570-1066.
Mary Crist Fleming, Founder & Dir.
Lyle D. Rigg, Head.
Col Prep. Tests CEEB SSAT TOEFL. Curr—USA. LI—Eng. A—Math Chem US Hist. CF—Fr Ger Lat Span Music Acting Physics.
Enr 500. B 85/185; G 70/160. Elem 244, Sec 256. US—375. Grad '84—54. Col—47.
Fac 65. Full 61/Part 4. M 33; F 32. US.
Tui Bdg $10,500 (+$2100); Day $4125-5250 (+$2100). Schol.
Summer Session. Acad. Tui Bdg $1125 (+$375), Day $570 (+$375).
Est 1976. Inc. Sem (Sept-Je). ECIS ISS NAIS. Accred NEASC.
Bldgs 11. Dorms 10. 2 Libs 10,000 vols. Tennis crts 3. Fields 3. Gym.

TASIS England is a branch of The American School in Switzerland. An American college preparatory curriculum is followed with elective courses available in the Russian revolution, psychology, foreign languages and photography. Located on a 20-acre campus, the school's sports program offers soccer, swimming, tennis, basketball and horseback riding. (See also *Summer Sessions*).

See also page 109

BUCKSWOOD GRANGE
Bdg & Day Coed Ages 10-16. Gr 7-12.

Uckfield (East Sussex) TN22 3PU, England. Tel. (0825) 3544. Telex: 943763 Crocom G.
M.B. Reiser, BS, Prin.
Gen Acad. Tests GCE SSAT. Curr—UK. LI—Eng. CF—Fr Art Comp Stud. SI—ESL.
Enr 76. B 45/10; G 15/6. Elem 20, Sec 56. Grad '84—8.
Fac 14. Full 5/Part 9. M 9; F 7. UK.
Tui Bdg £4875 (+£90); Day £1800 (+£45).
Summer Session. Acad Rec. Tui Bdg £175/wk. 8 wks.
Est 1978. Inc. Tri (Sept-Je).
Bldgs 2. Lib 4000 vols. Fields.

Founded by Mr. Reiser, Buckswood Grange is situated on the outskirts of Uckfield within easy reach of London and Gatwick and

Heathrow airports. The School's international enrollment follows a traditional English curriculum leading to the G.C.E. 'O' and 'A' level exams. Religious education, physics, commerce, computer studies and music are among the academic offerings. The sports program features soccer, rugby and cricket, and the school uses nearby facilities for swimming, tennis, squash, golf and horseback riding.

See also page 71

ABBOTSHOLME SCHOOL
Bdg & Day Coed Ages 11-18. Gr 6-PG.

Uttoxeter (Staffordshire) ST14 5BS, England. Rocester. Tel. (0889) 590217.

D. Farrant, MA, BED, Oxford, Head.

Col Prep Gen Acad. Tests GCE. Curr—Nat. Ll—Eng. CF—Fr Ger Hist Arts Man Arts Bus Eng Math Physics Chem Bio. Sl—Rem & Dev Read Tut.

Enr 261. B 159; G 100/2.

Fac 29. Full 26/Part 3. M 22; F 7. Nat.

Tui Bdg £1520; Day £1014. Schol.

Est 1889. Inc 1941 nonprofit. Tri (Sept-July).

Lib 15,000 vols. Fields. Crts. Labs. Gym.

Abbotsholme draws its enrollment primarily from Britain, with smaller numbers from Canada, America and Asia. The program includes preparation for the G.C.E. 'A' and 'O' levels. The majority of students go on to universities. Others complete preparation for careers in industry and agriculture. Careers advice is available as is special instruction for pupils with dyslexia. The activity program includes canoeing, mountaineering, camping, riding, cross-country skiing, sailing and weekend expeditions to other parts of England as well as the usual games and athletics.

Abbotsholme was founded by Dr. Cecil Reddie, whose innovations in education inspired the foundation of schools in Germany as well as in England and Scotland. The school lies on its own dairy farm of 130 acres, half encircled by hills, half by the River Dove, with woods, streams and meadows nearby. Students have the opportunity to operate the farm in preparation for public examinations in agricultural and horticultural sciences.

FRIENDS' SCHOOL
Bdg & Day Coed Ages 8-18. Gr 4-12.

Wigton (Cumbria), England. Tel. 0965-43131.

J.T. Green, BA, Trinity College, DipEd, Queen's Univ., MA, Head.

Col Prep Gen Acad. Tests GCE. Ll—Eng. A—Eng Hist Math Sci Econ. CF—Fr Ger Span Art Music Tech Drawing. Sl—Rem & Dev Math & Read Tut.

Enr 123. B 53/30; G 20/20. US—1. Grad '84—32. Col—12.

Fac 17. Full 14/Part 3. M 8; F 9. UK.

Tui Bdg $916 (+ $75)/term; Day $490 (+ $23)/term. Schol.
Est 1815. Inc nonprofit. Tri (Sept-July).
Bldg. Lib 4000 vols. Athletic facilities.

Located near the Lake District, Friends' School is run by Quakers but accepts students of all denominations. The curriculum prepares students for 'O' and 'A' levels of the G.C.E. The regular academic program is supplemented by courses in woodworking, languages, domestic science and drama. Sports including swimming, soccer, tennis, hockey and gymnastics are emphasized. Modelmaking, photography, crafts and various interest clubs are also available.

BARROW HILLS SCHOOL
  Bdg & Day Boys Ages 8-13. Gr 4-8.

Witley, Godalming (Surrey) GU8 5NY, England. Roke Lane. Tel. (042-879) 2634.
Rev. A.J. Cadwallader, Head.
Pre-Prep. Tests CEE. Curr—Nat. Ll—Eng. CF—Fr Lat Hist Sci Math Eng. Sl—Rem & Dev Read Tut.
Enr 130. B 102/28. US—3.
Fac 20. Full 15/Part 5. M 13; F 6. Nat.
Tui Bdg £1030 (+ £50); Day £680 (+ £50).
Est 1950. Nonprofit. Tri (Sept-July).
Bldgs 4. Dorms 11. Lib 3000 vols. Athletic facilities.

This school offers a traditional curriculum which prepares boys for entrance to St. George's College and other public schools. It is administered by the Josephite Fathers & Brothers who provide a Roman Catholic setting while accepting boys from other denominations. Particular emphasis is given to the mastery of language and writing skills with remedial help when necessary. All boys receive religious instruction and study art, music and drama.

NORTHERN IRELAND

FRIENDS' SCHOOL, LISBURN
  Bdg Coed Ages 11-19; Day Coed 4-19. Gr K-12.

Lisburn (Antrim) BT28 3BH, Northern Ireland. Magheralave Rd. Tel. Lisburn 2156.
A. G. Chapman, BA, DipEd, Queen's University (Belfast), Head.
Col Prep Gen Acad. Tests GCE. Curr—Natl. Ll—Eng. CF—Fr Ger Lat Relig Home Ec Arts Econ Engineering Drawing.
Enr 1064. B 40/506; G 33/487. US—1. Grad '84—100. Col—80. US—1.
Fac 64. Full 61/Part 3. M 37; F 27. Nat.
Tui Bdg £1330 (+ £100); Day £675 (+ £10).
Est 1774. Society of Friends. Tri (Sept-Je).
Bldgs 9. Dorms 13. Lib 8000 vols. Labs 11. Gym. Pool. Tennis crts. Fields.

Originally established for the children of Quakers, the Friends' School has since 1874 welcomed students of all denominations. The secondary department ("grammar school"), housed separately from the kindergarten and primary grades, provides a seven-year program leading to the Northern Ireland G.C.E. at 'O' and 'A' levels. Music lessons including piano and violin are emphasized at the school. Students are encouraged to join drama, debate, computer and film clubs. The 23-acre campus gives ample space for games and sports which include rugby, hockey, cricket, netball, swimming and tennis.

Lisburn, eight miles southwest of Belfast, is on the river Lagan. The school is situated 200 feet above sea level, overlooking the town.

SCOTLAND

THE AMERICAN SCHOOL IN ABERDEEN
Day Coed Ages 5-18. Gr K-12.

Aberdeen AB1 9QD, Scotland. Craigton Rd., Cults. Tel. 0224-868927/861068.
Everett G. Gould, BA, MA, Supt.
Col Prep Gen Acad. Tests SSAT. Curr—USA. Ll—Eng. CF—Fr Span Hist (US) Scottish Stud Bus Home Econ Comp Mechanical Drawing.
Enr 325. B 155; G 170. US—290. Grad '84—19. Col—18.
Fac 34. Full 32/Part 2. M 13; F 21. US 25.
Tui £3700. Schol.
Est 1972. Inc 1980 nonprofit. Sem (Sept-Je). ECIS ISS. Accred MSA.
Bldgs 6. Libs 15,000 vols. Lab. Gym. Fields.

The American School in Aberdeen has two campuses of lawns and woodlands overlooking the village of Cults and offers an American-based curriculum. Field trips emphasizing Scottish history and traditions are arranged. The school takes part in academic and athletic competition with local schools. Located about 100 miles northeast of Edinburgh, Aberdeen is a port city on the North Sea, lying between the mouths of the Dee and Don Rivers.

THE AMERICAN SCHOOL OF EDINBURGH
Bdg Coed Ages 15-18; Day Coed 13-18. Gr 7-12.

Edinburgh EH3 7EN, Scotland. 29 Chester St. Tel. 031-225-9888.
A. W. Morris, BSc, MInstP, Edinburgh Univ., Prin.
Col Prep Gen Acad. Tests CEEB SSAT GCE. Curr—USA UK. Ll—Eng. A—Math Physics. CF—Fr Span Ger Art Hist Bus Lit Arts Comp Stud. Sl—Rem & Dev Math Tut.
Enr 40. B 10/15; G 5/10. US—20. Grad '84—10. Col—8.
Fac 12. Full 5/Part 7. M 5; F 7. US 3. UK.
Tui Bdg £2500 (+ £50/wk); Day £2500 (+ £50).
Summer Session. Acad.
Est 1976. Sem (Sept-Je).
Bldgs 1. Lib 2500 vols.

The American School of Edinburgh offers an individualized curriculum designed according to the student's needs and interest. Students in grades 7 through 8 follow a mixed curriculum, while those in grades 9 through 12 follow a combination of courses to prepare them for universities or for careers in business or the trades. Student activities and sports include trips to historical buildings, museums and theatres, and instruction in swimming, skiing and ice skating.

FETTES COLLEGE
Bdg & Day Coed Ages 13-18. Gr 7-12.

**Edinburgh EH4 1QX, Scotland. Carrington Rd. Tel. 031-332-2281.
Cameron Cochrane, MA, Oxon, Head.
Col Prep. Tests GCE. Curr—Nat. LI—Eng. CF—Econ Comp Stud Math Lang Sci Hist. CF—Lat Greek Ger Fr Span Russ Tech Stud Music Art. SI—Rem & Dev Read.
Enr 469. B 288/53; G 100/28. US—7. Grad '84—120. Col—65.
Fac 51. Full 44/Part 7. M 42; F 9. Nat.
Tui Bdg £4500 (+£100); Day £3010 (+£70). Schol.
Est 1870. Nonprofit. Tri (Sept-July).
Bldgs 20. Libs 16,000 vols. Gym. Pool. Crts. Fields.**

Fettes College, located on 100 acres near the center of Edinburgh, offers an individualized curriculum designed to prepare students for university entrance. Both the 'O' and 'A' levels of the G.C.E. may be taken. The flexible curriculum also accommodates pupils who wish to pursue careers directly in service or commercial industries. A junior school provides instruction for boarding and day students ages 10 to 13. Coached team sports include rugby, hockey, cricket, tennis and basketball. Swimming, fencing and golf are also available, and students may join drama, film and debating clubs or a community service program. Most students are from Britain and Hong Kong.

GORDONSTOUN
Bdg Coed Ages 13-18. Gr 8-PG.

**Elgin (Moray) IV30 2RF, Scotland. Tel. 0343-830-445.
M. B. Mavor, C.V.O., MA, Cambridge, Head.
Col Prep Gen Acad. Tests SAT GCE. Curr—Nat. LI—Eng. CF—Latin Fr Ger Geol Hist Geog Econ Engineer Tech Metalwork Art Pottery Music.
Enr 467. B 288/14; G 160/15.
Fac 62. Full 49/Part 13. US 1. UK.
Tui Bdg £4980 (+£100). Schol.
Summer Session. Acad Rec. Tui Bdg £1250. 3½ wks.
Est 1934. Nonprofit. Tri (Sept-July).
Lib 8000 vols. Athletic facilities. Pool.**

The school opened in two houses in 1934, Gordonstoun House and the Round Square, a circular seventeenth-century building of historic interest. During the war the school moved to Wales, and when it returned had developed its links with the sea, playing an important part in the founding of the first Outward Bound School at Averdovey, Gordonstoun's curriculum prepares students for the G.C.E. 'O' and 'A' level examinations. Advanced work is encouraged and students prepare for University Scholarship level.

A wide range of games, activities and practical work is available to students. Team sports include rugger, hockey, cricket and tennis. Students may also participate in swimming, athletics, squash and cross country running. During the last two or three years at Gordonstoun, students may elect to join a service, including coastguards, mountain rescue section, fire service, surf rescue, Air Training Corps Squadron and nature conservation. Older students have the opportunity to spend their Christmas and Easter terms at Hopeman Harbour learning the theory and practice of seamanship. Selected students then spend a week during the summer cruising along the coast of Scotland aboard the school's yacht, "The Sea Spirit." Expedition work and field studies are also encouraged, with students participating in surveys in geology, ecology, botany or archeology.

LORETTO SCHOOL
Bdg & Day Boys Ages 8-18; Bdg Girls 16-18. Gr 3-12.

Musselburgh (East Lothian), Scotland. Tel. 031-665-2567.
Rev. N.W. Drummond, MA, Fitzwilliam College (Cantab), Head.
Col Prep. Tests GCE. Curr—Nat. Ll—Eng. CF—Fr Ger Span Hist Econ Arts Lat Chem Bio Physics.
Enr 395. B 340/25; G 30.
Fac 44. Full 31/Part 13. UK.
Tui Bdg £4560 (+ £20): Day £2720 (+ £20). Schol.
Est 1823. Nonprofit. Tri (Sept-July).
Bldgs 20. Dorms 40. 2 Libs. Swimming pool. Gym. Fields.

About 50% of the students at Loretto come from Scotland, 30% from England, and the remainder from families who are based outside of Great Britain. The school is divided into a Junior (ages 8-13) and a Senior (ages 13-18) School. To be admitted to the Upper School, students must normally pass the Common Entrance Examination. However, students from abroad or who have not attended a British preparatory school may not be required to pass all C.E.E. subjects, but should show proficiency in math, English, and one foreign language. Upper School students are prepared for the 'O' and 'A' level G.C.E. examinations.

Loretto is situated in the town of Musselburgh, about six miles southeast of Edinburgh, on the bay of the Firth of Forth.

U.S.S.R.

By far the largest country in the world, the Union of Soviet Socialist Republics covers more than 1/7 of the earth's total land surface. Czarist rule expanded Russian borders prior to World War I. With 15 republics, among them Lithuania, Estonia, Georgia and several Arab states, Soviet Russia is inhabited by an ethnically diverse population. The Communist Party is the only political party in Russia.

Primarily an agricultural and industrial nation, the Soviet Union has vast mineral and timber resources. Fishing is an important industry because of Russia's abundant lakes and rivers. The capital city is Moscow and the rouble (R) is the monetary unit. Russian is spoken by more than 52% of the population.

THE ANGLO-AMERICAN SCHOOL OF MOSCOW
  Day Coed Ages 5-14. Gr K-9.

Moscow, U.S.S.R. 78 Leninsky Prospect. Tel. 131-8755. Telex: 413160
  US650 SU.
Mail to: c/o Amerian Embassy, Moscow, APO, New York 09862.
James E. Buckheit, MA, Univ of Chicago, Dir.
Pre-Prep. Curr—USA UK. LI—Eng. CF—Russian Music Arts. SI—Rem
  Read & Eng.
Enr 270. B 140; G 130. US—75.
Fac 29. Full 26/Part 3. US 17.
Tui $5000.
Est 1949. Nonprofit. Sem (Sept-Je). A/OS ECIS ISS NAIS. Accred
  NEASC.
Bldgs 1. Lib 6000 vols. Aud. Gym.

While most of the enrollment at the Anglo-American School consists of children of the American and British diplomatic missions in Moscow, students of over 20 other nationalities also attend. The school strives to provide an education which will enable a child to return to his/her country with a minimum of difficulty. An American-based curriculum is followed with Russian language instruction from the third grade. Honors courses are offered in math and Russian. The sports program includes soccer, volleyball, ice skating and hockey.

Leased by the British, Canadian and American Embassies, the school building is the former home of the noted Russian geographer and anarchist, Petr A. Kropotkin. The present school supersedes the Moscow Children's Center which opened in 1949.

YUGOSLAVIA

Serbia, Croatia, Bosnia, Macedonia and other names important to the history of eastern Europe today comprise the modern Socialist Republic of Yugoslavia, a country whose present boundaries are essentially those shaped by events immediately preceding and following World War I.

The capital is Belgrade, the monetary unit is the dinar (Din) and the principal languages are Slovene, Macedonian and Serbo-Croatian.

THE INTERNATIONAL SCHOOL OF BELGRADE
Day Coed Ages 5-13. Gr K-8.

Belgrade, Yugoslavia 11040. Temisvarska 19. Tel. 011-651-832.
Mail to: c/o American Embassy, Belgrade, Dept. of State, Washington, DC 20520.
Bernard S. Miller, Dir.
Pre-Prep Gen Acad. Tests SSAT. Curr—USA. LI—Eng.
Enr 61.
Fac 22.
Tui $2200-4100.
Summer Session.
Est 1947. Inc 1972 nonprofit. Sem (Sept-Je). A/OS ECIS ISS. Accred NEASC.
Bldgs 5. 2 Libs 800 vols.

Following a modified American curriculum to meet the needs of students from over 30 different countries, this school serves the diplomatic and business community of Belgrade. While all instruction is in English, about 40% of the pupils take English as a second language. French is taught in grades three through eight. The school facilities consist of a rented villa and adjacent buildings in a residential section of the city.

THE AMERICAN SCHOOL OF ZAGREB
Day Coed Ages 4-14. Gr K-8.

41000 Zagreb (Hrvatska), Yugoslavia. 45 Zelengaj. Tel. (041) 426-594 594.
Mail to: c/o American Consulate General Zagreb, Dept. of State, Washington, DC 20520.
Alan Conkey, BA, MA, Univ. of Oregon, Prin.
Pre-Prep. Tests SSAT. Curr—USA. LI—Eng. CF—Fr Lit Sci Croatian Arts. SI—ESL.
Enr 23. B 16; G 7.
Fac 4. Full 3/Part 1. M 1; F 3. US 3.
Tui $1875-3750.
Est 1966. Inc nonprofit. Quar (Sept-Je). A/OS ECIS ISS.
Bldg. Lib 2000 vols.

Sponsored by the U.S. Consulate General in Zagreb, the enrollment at this school is primarily American with students from many other countries also in attendance. The study of native language and culture is emphasized. School yearbook and newspaper, rocket club and arts and crafts are included in the activities program.

AFRICA

MEDITERRANEAN AFRICA

ALGERIA

Now an independent republic, the Democratic and Popular Republic of Algeria won its freedom from France after a seven-year struggle which ended in 1962. The majority of citizens are of Arab-Berber stock and of Moslem faith. Both French and Arabic are spoken; the unit of currency is the dinar (DA). Algiers is the capital city.

AMERICAN SCHOOL OF ALGIERS
Day Coed Ages 5-14. Gr K-8.

Algiers, Algeria. Tel. 60-37-72.
Mail to: c/o American Embassy, Algiers, Dept. of State, Washington, DC 20520.
Frank Sawyer, Dir.
Gen Acad. Tests SSAT. Curr—USA. LI—Eng.
Enr 135.
Fac 19.
Tui $2400-3900 (+ $400).
Est 1964. Nonprofit. Sem (Aug-Je). AISA A/OS ISS MAIS.
Bldgs 7. Lib 5000 vols.

Open to English-speaking children of all nationalities, The American School of Algiers' enrollment is comprised of 29 nationalities. About 10% of the students are United States nationals. American teaching methods and materials are utilized. Kindergarten through the sixth grade are self-contained with special teachers for French, art, music and physical education. Grades seven and eight are departmentalized.

EGYPT

With archaeological records of ancient empires dating to 4000 B.C., Egypt possesses one of the longest recorded histories of any modern nation. By 100 B.C., native dynasties had collapsed and long periods of foreign influence, especially Byzantine and Islamic, began. Alexandria, founded 332 B.C., still is the chief port and Cairo, established 969 A.D., is the capital.

Egypt has been a republic since 1953. Egypt and Syria, joined at various times in the past, joined again as the United Arab Republic (U.A.R.) from 1958 to 1961. Syria seceded in 1961 and Egypt retained the name of U.A.R. until 1971 when the Arab Republic of Egypt became official. The country's monetary unit is the Egyptian pound (LE) and the official language is Arabic.

SCHUTZ AMERICAN SCHOOL
Bdg Coed Ages 14-18; Day Coed 4-18. Gr N-12.

Alexandria, Egypt. P.O. Box 1000. Tel. 86-22-05.
George W. Meloy, MA, Stanford Univ., Head.
Col Prep Gen Acad. Tests CEEB. Curr—USA. LI—Eng.
Enr 228.
Fac 38. US.
Tui Day $1775-5200.
Est 1924. Inc nonprofit. Tri (Sept-Je). AISA A/OS ECIS ISS NAIS NE/SA.
Bldgs 7. Dorms 3. Lib 12,000 vols. Tennis crts. Swimming pool.

Two diplomas are offered at Schutz, a basic high school diploma and one for students preparing for further study at a higher academic level. The science-math program is traditioal while the English-social studies courses meet two days a week for 12 weeks to study a specific facet of a subject. Electives include music, arts, crafts, sewing, cooking, typing and photography. The curriculum also features Middle Eastern cultural studies.

CAIRO AMERICAN COLLEGE
Day Coed Ages 5-19. Gr K-12.

Maadi (Cairo), Egypt. 1, Midan Digla. Tel. 505-244.
Gunther Brandt, PhD, Supt.
Col Prep Gen Acad. Tests CEEB SSAT. Curr—USA. LI—Eng. CF—Eng Fr Span Arabic Egyptian Hist & Culture.
Enr 1300. B 640; G 660. Elem 650. Sec 650. US—820. Grad '84—84.
Fac 149. Full 138/Part 11. M 48; F 101. US.
Tui $4960 (+ $2000). Schol.
Est 1945. Nonprofit. Sem (Sept-Je). A/OS ISS NAIS NE/SA. Accred MSA.
Bldgs 13. Lib 35,000 vols. Field. Courts 3. Swimming pool.

Originally founded by the business and missionary community in Cairo as an elementary school, Cairo American College has since expanded to include secondary grades. There are 49 different nationalities represented among the students, approximately 63% of whom are American. A United States college preparatory curriculum is followed, and graduates have attended universities in Europe, Asia, Africa and the Americas. Some background in English is required for admission, but

English is offered as a second language to those who lack proficiency. Spanish, French and Arabic are available from the fourth grade.

Sports include intramural and interscholastic competition in soccer, basketball, volleyball, track and judo. In addition, interest clubs, publications, and drama and music groups enrich the academic program.

LIBYA

In 1969 the military seized power in Libya and King Idris I, who had ruled since 1951, was overthrown. The official name became the People's Socialist Libyan Arab Public in 1977, with the Arab Socialist Union Organization installed as the only political party.

In earlier times the country was dominated by European and Near Eastern powers because of its strategic location on the Mediterranean coast of Africa. Independence was granted in 1951 under United Nations auspices. Oil was discovered in 1957, and today the nation ranks among the world's largest producers.

Tripoli is the capital city. The monetary unit is the Libyan dinar (Din), and the Arabic language is used.

OIL COMPANIES SCHOOL
  Day Coed Ages 3-15. Gr N-9.

Tripoli, Libya SPLAJ. P.O. Box 860. Tel. 70094.
Mohamed Badr Elgwel, BA, Univ. of Gar-Younes, Supt.
Gen Acad Pre-Prep. Tests SSAT. Curr—USA. LI—Eng. A—Algebra Geom. CF—Fr Arabic Soc Stud Sci Math Art Comm. SI—ESL Rem Read.
Enr 600.
Fac 60.
Tui 825,000-1,650,000 DL.
Summer Session. Rec. 4 wks.
Est 1958. Nonprofit. Sem (Sept-Je). ISS MAIS.
Bldgs 10. Lib 12,000 vols. Gym. Fields. Tennis crts.

Originally established to meet the educational needs of the major oil companies in the Tripoli area, this large coeducational day school is open to children from the general expatriate and oil communities. In most classes, children are grouped according to ability with accelerated study offered to those whom it would benefit. French and Arabic classes are given, and ninth grade students may choose from a variety of elective offerings. The extracurricular program includes an active student council, publications, drama and glee clubs and intramural sports. The modern well-equipped campus is located three miles to the west of Tripoli, in the Andalous area.

MOROCCO

Founded by the Arabs at the end of the seventh century, the Moroccan Empire once ruled all northwest Africa and most of the Iberian Peninsula. Morocco was a protectorate of France and Spain during the first half of this century, but has been independent since 1956.

The King instituted a new Constitution in 1972 and ruled by decree until 1977. Free elections were held and 176 elected seats were filled in the Chamber of Deputies.

The Kingdom of Morocco's economy depends on agriculture, but since independence there have been efforts to expand industrialization. Rabat-Sale is the capital city; the dirham (DH) is the monetary unit. Arabic, French and Spanish are the languages most often used.

THE AMERICAN SCHOOL OF CASABLANCA
(The Branch School)
Day Coed Ages 3-15. Gr N-10.

Casablanca, Morocco. 9, rue Bartholdi (Quartier Racine). Tel. 27.60.55.
Maurice H. Blum, MEd, Tufts, Dir.
Gen Acad. Curr—USA. LI—Eng. CF—Fr Arabic. SI—ESL Rem Arabic Tut.
Enr 117. B 68; G 49.
Fac 11. M 3; F 8. US.
Tui $1108-2332 (+ $270).
Est 1973. Sem (Sept-Je). A/OS ISS MAIS.
Bldgs 1. Lib 1500 vols.

The Casablanca Branch of the Rabat American School conducts an American-based academic program with French and Arabic offered as foreign languages. Language and fine arts as well as music and drama enrich the curriculum. Activities are available in arts and crafts and soccer. About one-third of the student body is from the United States.

RABAT AMERICAN SCHOOL
Day Coed Ages 5-18. Gr N-12.

Rabat, Morocco. Tel. 714-76; 709-63.
Mail to: c/o American Embassy Rabat, Dept. of State, Washington, DC 20520.
Emmanuel J. Paulos, MA, Western Reserve Univ., Dir.
Col Prep. Tests SSAT. Curr—USA. LI—Eng. CF—Arabic Fr Calc Anthro ESL Reading Math Sci Typ Psych Journalism. SI—Tut.
Enr 225. B 105; G 115. Elem 165, Sec 55. Grad '84— 10. Col—9.
Fac 27. Full 23/Part 4. M 6; F 21. US 20.
Tui $4500. Schol.
Summer Session. Rec. Tui $110. 4 wks.
Est 1962. Inc nonprofit. Sem (Sept-Je). A/OS ISS MAIS.

Serving the international community in Rabat, this elementary school has an enrollment that is one-half American, with children from Europe and Morocco making up the balance. The curriculum is nongraded and follows American guidelines. French is taught throughout the school. Arabic is offered as an elective after school hours. Music, art and physical education are integrated into the academic program. A branch of the school is located in Casablanca.

THE AMERICAN SCHOOL OF TANGIER
Bdg & Day Coed Ages 6-18. Gr K-12.

Tangier, Morocco. 149 Rue Christophe Colomb. Tel. 415.27/8.
Joseph A. McPhillips III, BA, Princeton, Head.
Col Prep. Tests CEEB. Curr—USA. LI—Eng. CF—Arabic Fr Span Hist (US) Arts. SI—Tut.
Enr 210. Grad '84—17. Col—16.
Fac 22. Full 20/Part 2.
Tui Bdg $7760-8360; Day $3800-4560. Schol.
Est 1950. Nonprofit. Tri (Sept-Je). A/OS ISS MAIS NAIS.
Bldgs 1. Dorms 2. Libs 2. Labs 2. Field. Courts.

Located on a 25-acre campus outside of Tangier, this school offers an American college preparatory curriculum to students from Morocco, the U.S. and 20 other countries. Boarding students are drawn primarily from southern Morocco, Algeria, the Middle East and West Africa. Instruction in Arabic begins in the first grade, French in the fifth grade. Spanish is also offered in the high school. Recent graduates have entered Princeton, Bryn Mawr, Oberlin, Yale and Harvard.

Student activities are an integral part of the school program and include an active dramatic society. Basketball and soccer are the chief competitive sports. Tennis, riding and golf are also offered. Situated on the Straits of Gibraltar, the cosmopolitan city of Tangier has had a long history as a commercial and cultural link between Europe and Africa.

TUNISIA

Prominent in Roman times as the site of the Phoenician city of Carthage, and for centuries a Mediterranean pirate state, the independent Republic of Tunisia was formed in 1956. The country divides the Mediterranean Sea into eastern and western sections.

Agriculture is the main industry, although the terrain is varied. The monetary unit is the dinar (D); the capital and chief city is Tunis. Arabic and French are most often used.

AMERICAN COOPERATIVE SCHOOL OF TUNIS
Day Coed Ages 5-15. Gr K-9.

Tunis, Tunisia. Tel. 902-517.
Mail to: c/o U.S. Embassy, 144 Ave. de la Liberte, Tunis, Tunisia.

Richard W. Ryden, EDS, Michigan State Univ., Dir.
Pre-Prep Gen Acad. Tests SSAT. Curr—USA. LI—Eng. CF—Fr Music ESL.
Enr 145. B 75; G 70.
Fac 16. Full 15/Part 1. M 3; F 13. US 14.
Tui $4600 (+$500). Schol.
Summer Session. Rec. Acad. 4 wks.
Est 1957. Nonprofit. Sem (Sept-Je). A/OS ISS MAIS.
Bldgs 1. Lib 10,000 vols. Lab. Field.

Housed in a converted villa, the American Cooperative School follows a curriculum similar to that found in public schools in the United States. Sixty per cent of the enrollment is American, but children from 23 other countries also attend. Instruction is in English, with French offered as a foreign langue.

NORTHERN AFRICA

BURKINA FASO

Formerly the Republic of Upper Volta, Burkina Faso is a nation of rolling hills and high savannas, with a desert region in the north. In 1960, the country became an independent state, ending 63 years of French colonial rule. A period of single-party rule, the product of a 1966 military coup, was followed by the adoption of a republican constitution in 1978. The country was officially named Burkina Faso by presidential decree in 1984. The dominant languages are the African dialects, More and Dioula, and French. Ouagadougou is the capital and the franc (CFAF) is the native currency.

INTERNATIONAL SCHOOL OF OUAGADOUGOU
Day Coed Ages 5-14. Gr K-9.

Ouagadougou, Burkina Faso. B.P. 35, c/o American Embassy. Telex: 335649.
Mail to: c/o American Embassy Ouagadougou, Dept. of State, Washington, DC 20520.
Ron Presswood, MEd,Univ. of Illinois, Dir.
Pre-Prep. Curr—USA. LI—Eng. CF—Fr. SI—Math Read ESL.
Enr 90. B 52; G 38. US—32.
Fac 13. Full 10/Part 3. M 1; F 12. US 5.
Tui $2700-3200 (+$50).
Est 1973. Inc nonprofit. Sem (Sept-Je). AISA A/OS ISS.
Bldgs 3. Lib. Pool. Playground.

Serving the needs of the American community and other students seeking an English language education, the school offers a U.S.

curriculum. The Iowa Test of Basic Skills is administered at the beginning and end of the school year, to test for basic skill improvement. Math and reading are individualized by level. All other subjects are multi-age grouped and include courses in biology, algebra, French and literature. An afternoon program three days a week offers music, art, sports, drama, cooking and culture.

CAMEROON

Situated on the west coast of Africa, the United Republic of Cameroon is surrounded by the countries of Nigeria, Chad, Gabon and the Central African Empire. The only political party is the Cameroon National Union. The country became an independent republic in 1960. Major exports include cocoa, coffee and timber. French and English are the official languages spoken. Yaounde is the capital, and the franc (CFAF) is the monetary unit.

INTERNATIONAL SCHOOL OF YAOUNDE
Day Coed Ages 4-15. Gr K-9.

Yaounde, Cameroon. Tel. 23-40-14. Telex: 8223KN.
Mail to: c/o Admin Officer, ISOY, YAOUNDE, Dept. of State, Washington, DC 20520.
Robert L. Werner, Prin.
Pre-Prep Gen Acad. Curr—USA. LI—Eng. CF—FR Lit SI—ESL Rem & Dev Math & Read.
Enr 170. B 90; G 80. US—90.
Fac 21. Full 14/Part 7. M 3; F 18. US.
Tui $3550. Schol.
Est 1964. Nonprofit. Quar (Sept-Je). AISA A/OS ISS.
Bldgs 3. Lib 9000 vols. Crts. Field.

Founded by U.S. State Department personnel and American Presbyterian missionaries, this small school provides an elementary education to an international student body representative of 28 countries. An American curriculum is followed, with French offered as a foreign language. The social studies program features African history and geography.

ETHIOPIA

A mountainous country on the Red Sea, Ethiopia is one of Africa's oldest nations. Once ruled by emperors, Ethiopia is now a socialist state governed by civilian and military authorities.

Predominantly an agricultural state, the country's crops include wheat, sugar cane and coffee. Gold is mined in the southern and western sections. Amharic is the official spoken language and the capital is Addis Ababa. The birr (Eth$) is the unit of currency.

INTERNATIONAL COMMUNITY SCHOOL OF ADDIS ABABA
   Day Coed Ages 4-18. Gr N-12.

Addis Ababa, Ethiopia. P.O. Box 70282. Old Airport Rd Branch Post
   Office. Tel. 02-08-70. Telex: ILCH 21207.
James R. Bowditch, BA, Stanford, PhD, Harvard, Dir.
Col Prep. Tests SSAT CEEB IB. Curr—USA. LI—Eng. CF—Fr Span
   Amharic ESL Sci Art Music Phys Ed. A—Math Eng Hist Bio Chem
   Physics.
Enr 340. B 150; G 190. Elem 233, Sec 107. US—28. Grad '84—16.
   Col—14.
Fac 34. Full 25/Part 9. M 11; F 23.
Tui $2053-3381 (+$200).
Summer Session. ESL. Tui $200. 5 wks.
Est 1964. Nonprofit. Quar (Sept-Je). AISA A/OS ISS.
Bldgs 6. Lib 11,000 vols. Lab. Gym. Tennis crts. Track.

Students from 42 different countries attend the International
Community School. The American-based curriculum prepares pupils
for U.S. College Boards as well as the International Baccalaureate. In
addition to the academic program, students may participate in student
council, yearbook and newspaper and in interscholastic sports including
soccer, volleyball and baseball.

THE SANDFORD ENGLISH COMMUNITY SCHOOL
   Day Coed Ages 4-18. Gr K-12.

Addis Ababa, Ethiopia. P.O. Box 30056. Tel. 11 22 75.
J. Elson, Head.
Gen Acad. Tests GCE. Curr—UK. LI—Eng Sci. SI—Eng.
Enr 800.
Fac 41.
Tui 999 Eth Birr (+2250 Eth Birr). Schol.
Est 1946. Inc nonprofit. Tri (Sept-July). ISS.
Lib 6000 vols. Athletic facilities.

The Sandford English Community School consists of three divisions:
preparatory, junior and senior preparing students for university
entrance. Curricula for primary children includes English, Amharic and
topics of interest—geography, science and Bible. An intermediate
education through mixed ability classes is offered within the junior
division. Students in the senior division are prepared for the G.C.E. and
Ethiopian National exams. Competitive games and sports include
football, volleyball, basketball, tennis and athletics.

GAMBIA

The Gambia River flows through this nation located on the northwest
coast of Africa. Originally settled in the 17th century by English
merchants, the country declared independence in 1965 and became a
member of the Commonwealth of Nations in 1970. The Republic of

Gambia averages 20 miles in width and its chief industry is peanut farming. Banjul is capital and largest city and the monetary unit is the dalasi (£G). English is the official language.

MARINA INTERNATIONAL SCHOOL
Day Coed Ages 4-13. Gr N-8.

Benjul, The Gambia. Box 717 National Library Approach. Tel. 8471.
R.N.D. Pritchard, Head.
Pre-Prep. Curr—Intl. LI—Eng.
Enr 195.
Fac 12.
Tui $600-650.
Est 1964. Inc. 1972 nonprofit. Tri (Sept-July). A/OS.
Bldgs 5. Lib 3000 vols. Playground.

With a curriculum similar to that of British primary schools, this school aims to prepare students to the Gambian Common Entrance standard. Textbooks and most faculty are British, however, older students may follow the Calvert system if they choose.

GHANA

Ghana, the former British Gold Coast colony, became a republic within the Commonwealth in 1960. Situated in West Africa on the Gulf of Guinea, the country leads the world in the production of cacao. Accra is the capital and the cedi (NC) is the monetary unit. Twi, Fanti and Ga are among the native languages, and English is spoken as well.

GHANA INTERNATIONAL SCHOOL
Day Coed Ages 3-18. Gr N-12.

Accra, Ghana. P.O. Box 2856. 2nd Circular Rd. Tel. 77163.
Leonie Acquah, BA, Canterbury, Prin.
Col Prep. Tests GCE. Curr—UK. LI—Eng. CF—Fr Hist Geog Arts.
 SI—Rem Eng.
Enr 716. Elem 560, Sec 156.
Fac 42. Full 35/Part 7. M 12; F 30.
Tui $200-400 (+250-450). Schol.
Est 1955. Nonprofit. Tri (Sept-Je), ISA ISS.
Bldgs 5. Lib. Athletic facilities.

Opening with only 30 students and one building, Ghana International School has grown considerably. Boys and girls from all over the world have attended, with Americans usually accounting for 7% of the enrollment. Because of the diversity in educational backgrounds, students are grouped according to ability, rather than age. Special classes are provided for pupils who are not fluent in English. Students may prepare at the 'O' level for the British G.C.E., for which the school is the only recognized center in Ghana. Supplementing the academic program are physical education classes, woodworking, swimming, games, dancing and field trips.

LINCOLN COMMUNITY SCHOOL
Day Coed Ages 5-17. Gr K-12.

Accra, Ghana. Abelenke Rd. Achimota Forest. Tel. 74018.
Mail to: c/o American Embassy Accra, Dept. of State, Washington, DC 20520.
John Mapes, MEd, Central Washington Univ., Supt.
Gen Acad. Tests SSAT. Curr—USA. LI—Eng. CF—Fr Biol US Hist Arts. SI—Tut.
Enr 82. B 50; G 32. US 8.
Fac 7. Full 6/Part 1. M 1; F 6. US 4.
Tui Day $1750-3500.
Est 1968. Inc nonprofit. Quar (Sept-Je). AISA A/OS ISS.
Bldgs 2. Lib 5000 vols. Field.

The enrollment of Lincoln Community School is comprised of students from Ghana, the United States and other countries. The curriculum is comparable to that found in elementary and junior high schools in the United States.

GUINEA

Formerly part of French West Africa, this country became the independent Revolutionary People's Republic of Guinea in 1958, but retains French as the official language. The country's bauxite deposits and reserves of hydraulic power have brought prosperity. The capital is Conakry, a port city on the Atlantic Ocean. The monetary unit is the syli (S).

THE INTERNATIONAL SCHOOL OF CONAKRY
Day Coed Ages 5-13. Gr K-8.

Conakry, Guinea. Tel. 44-15-27.
Mail to: c/o American Embassy Conakry, Dept. of State, Washington, DC 20520.
Audrey H. Minot, Dir.
Gen Acad. Curr—USA. LI—Eng.
Enr 50.
Fac 5.
Tui $990-1870.
Est 1964. Nonprofit. Quar (Sept-Je). A/OS ISS.
Bldgs 1. Lib.

Students of nine nationalities attend this small day school which follows an American elementary curriculum. Instruction is in English and French is taught as a foreign language. The capital city, Conakry, is situated on a small island, linked to the mainland by a bridge.

IVORY COAST

One of the most prosperous countries in West Africa, this country became a French territory in 1893 and the independent Republic of Ivory Coast in 1960. The population is composed of several tribes whose animistic religions predominate. Abidjan is the capital and largest city. The franc (CFAF) is the monetary unit, and French is used in addition to various African dialects.

INTERNATIONAL SCHOOL OF ABIDJAN
Day Coed Ages 4-17. Gr N-11.

Abidjan, Ivory Coast. Tel. 41-52-34.
Mail to: c/o Administrative Officer,ISA American Embassy Abidjan, Dept. of State, Washington, DC 20520.
Norrell H. Noble, MA, Columbia, Dir.
Gen Acad Col Prep. Tests CEEB SSAT Curr—USA. LI—Eng. CF—Fr Arts Music Soc Stud Math Sci Comp Stud. SI—ESL.
Enr 280. B 140; G 140.
Fac 29. Full 29. M 3; F 26. US 16.
Tui $1350-3200. Schol.
Summer Session. Acad Rec. Tui $130. 6 wks..
Est 1972. Nonprofit. Quar (Sept-Je). AISA A/OS ISS.
Bldgs 4. Lib 2500 vols. Field.

Serving the international community in Abidjan, this school offers an American educational program from nursery through tenth grade. Secondary school students may participate in a high school correspondence course supervised by the school in conjunction with the University of Nebraska Extension Division. Approximately one-fourth of the students are from the United States. In addition to the academic program, classes are offered in typing, drama and dancing. Students have access to tennis courts, a swimming pool and an ice rink.

IVORY COAST ACADEMY
Bdg & Day Coed Ages 6-18. Gr 1-12.

Bouake 01, Ivory Coast. B.P. 1171.
Russell Ragsdale, BS, Southern Oregon College, MDiv, Western C.B. Seminary, MEd, Portland State Univ., Dir.
Col Prep. Tests CEEB ACT SSAT. Curr—USA. LI—Eng. CF—Fr Journalism Bible Geog Hist Shop.
Enr 161. B 73/4; G 77/7. Elem 55, Sec 10. US—135. Grad '84—29. Col—25.
Fac 20. Full 8/Part 12. M 9; F 11. US.
Tui Bdg $3743 (+$150); Day $1993 (+$50).
Est 1962. Nonprofit. Baptist. Tri (Aug-Je).
Bldgs 19. Dorms 7. Lib 3000 vols. Crts. Fields.

Operated by the Baptist Church, Ivory Coast Academy provides a college preparatory curriculum similar to that found in the United

States. The student body consists of American youngsters whose parents are missionaries on the African continent. French and Bible study are part of the program, and students must attend religious meetings.

LIBERIA

With a government modeled after the United States, Liberia was founded in 1822 for the settlement of freed American slaves in western Africa. In 1847, Liberia became an independent republic, and in 1980 the civilian government was overthrown and replaced by the military People's Redemptive Council.

The country's main industries are rubber and iron ore manufacturing. Monrovia is the capital and largest city. The monetary unit is the Liberian dollar ($L), and English is the country's official language.

FIRESTONE INTERNATIONAL SCHOOL
Day Coed Ages 6-14. Gr 1-9.

Harbel Hills, Liberia. Firestone Plantations Co. Tel. 5-2852.
S.H. Kolison, Prin.
Gen Acad. Curr—USA. LI—Eng. CF—FR. SI—Rem Read.
Summer Session. Acad Rem.
Est 1960. Proprietary. Quar (Sept-Je). ISS.

This school was established by the Firestone Corporation to provide an elementary education for the children of its employees living in Liberia. Tuition is free.

AMERICAN COOPERATIVE SCHOOL
Day Coed Ages 4-21. Gr N-12.

Monrovia, Liberia. c/o US Embassy. Box 98. Tel. 261-860. Telex: 4362 ACS.
Ralph H. Jahr, MA, PhD, Univ. of Wisconsin, Madison, Supt.
Col Prep. Tests CEEB SSAT. Curr—USA. LI—Eng. A—Math Bio Chem Eng. CF—Fr Span Sci Hist Humanities Bus Arts. SI—Rem Read ESL.
Enr 368. Grad'84—28 Col—25.
Fac 34. Full 34. M 14; F 20.
Tui $2250-4936. Schol.
Summer Session. Acad. Tui $150. 4 wks.
Est 1960. Inc nonprofit. Quar (Aug-Je). AISA A/OS ISS. Accred MSA.
Bldg. Lib 14,000 vols. Gym. Field.

Over half of the school's enrollment is comprised of U.S. citizens. The school provides an American curriculum geared toward the College Boards. A variety of electives are offered including photography, college English skills, African culture studies, chess, dramatics and home economics. Students also participate in choir, yearbook and the student newspaper. Sports include soccer, basketball, volleyball and softball.

FARMINGTON COMMUNITY SCHOOL
 Day Coed Ages 4-9. Gr N-4.

Robertsfield, Liberia. P.O. Box 1 Robertsfield International Airport. Tel. 130.
Mrs. F. Hasan, Prin.
Gen Acad. Curr—USA. LI—Eng.
Est 1960. ISS.

Farmington enrolls students from Liberia, England, Canada, Spain, Portugal and the United States.

NIGERIA

The most populous nation in Africa, the Federal Republic of Nigeria is comprised of four self-governing states within a Commonwealth. Full independence was granted in 1963. Situated in West Africa on the Gulf of Guinea, the country is composed of 250 ethnic and linguistic groups. The largest of these groups include the Hausa and Fulani in the north and the Ibo and Yoruba in the south.

Nigeria's natural products are oil and tin, making Nigeria one of the world's largest producers of both. The largest city and capital is Lagos, English is the official language and the niara (N) is the monetary unit.

THE INTERNATIONAL SCHOOL
 Bdg & Day Coed Ages 12-19. Gr 7-PG.

Ibadan, Nigeria. University of Ibadan.
Rev. Canon, J.A., Illuyomade, Prin.
Col Prep. Tests CEEB IB. Curr—UK USA. LI—Eng. CF—Fr Lat Yoruba.
Est 1963. Tri (Sept-Je). ISA ISS.
Bldgs 7. Lib. Labs. Dorms 5. Fields.

Located on the 70-acre campus of the University of Ibadan, this school's enrollment is predominantly Nigerian. The curriculum prepares students for college entrance in Nigeria, Great Britain and the United States.

HILLCREST SCHOOL
 Day Coed Ages 6-18. Gr 1-12.

Jos (Plateau State), Nigeria. Box 652. 13 Bukuru Rd. Tel. 55410.
Kenneth L. Reiner, Prin.
Col Prep Gen Acad. Tests CEEB GCE. Curr—USA. LI—Eng. A—Math.
 CF—Fr US Hist Econ Arts. SI—Rem Read & Math.
Enr 528. Elem 393, Sec 135. US—125. Grad '84—45.
Fac 47. Full 38/Part 9. US 29.
Tui $2200. Schol.
Summer Session. Tut.

Est 1942. Sem (Aug-Je). ISS.
Bldgs 6. Lib. Courts. Fields.

Hillcrest gives admission preference to the children of missionaries, however, other children are welcomed if space permits.

AMERICAN INTERNATIONAL SCHOOL OF LAGOS
Day Coed Ages 5-16. Gr K-9.

Lagos, Nigeria. PO Box 2803. Behind 1004 Federal Estates (Victoria Islands). Tel. 617/793/94.
Robert J. Orlando, Supt.
Gen Acad. Curr—USA. Ll—Eng. CF—Fr Span Comp Stud Lang Arts Nigerian Culture. Sl—Rem Read ESL.
Enr 454. B 244; G 210.
Fac 31. Full 31. US 23.
Tui $5735 (+ $1335).
Est 1964. Inc. Tri (Sept-Je). AISA A/OS ISS.
Bldgs 3. Lib 7500. Crt. Field.

American International School was founded to provide an education for American personnel overseas, however, the school is open to English-speaking students of all nations. The college preparatory curriculum is patterned after public schools in Tacoma, Washington with which A.I.S. is affiliated. Music and art are offered as electives. Extracurricular activities include crafts, cultural studies, basketball, squash, tennis, baseball, football and volleyball.

SENEGAL

A former French possession, the Republic of Senegal became independent in 1960. Largely agrarian, its chief exports are peanuts and peanut products. In addition to French, there are a number of different tribal dialects spoken. 90% of the people are Moslem. Dakar is the capital and the monetary unit is the CFA franc (CFAF).

DAKAR ACADEMY
Day Coed Ages 5-15. Gr K-9.

Dakar, Senegal. B.P. 3189. Rue des Maristes. Tel. 22 06 82.
Ronald G. McCartney, BS, Bowling Green Univ., MEd, Lamar Univ., Prin.
Gen Acad. Tests SSAT. Curr—USA. Ll—Eng. CF—Fr Geog US Hist Art Music Health. Sl—Tut ESL.
Enr 87. B 9; G 38. US—33.
Fac 15. Full 12/Part 3. M 4; F 11. US 13.
Tui $1400 (+ $30).
Est 1961. Inc nonprofit. Missionary. Sem (Sept-Je). AISA ISS.
Bldgs 2. Dorms 1. Lib 6000 vols. Playground.

Sponsored by three missionary boards, United World Mission, Conservative Baptist Foreign Mission Society and the Assemblies of God, Dakar Academy provides educational facilities for the children of missionary personnel in Senegal and nearby countries. Other English-speaking children are welcome to attend on a space available basis. The academic curriculum is supplemented by physical education and activities in yearbook and student council. A limited number of boarding students are accepted.

SIERRA LEONE

The coastal area of Sierra Leone was ceded to Englishmen in 1788 as a home for blacks discharged from the British armed forces and for runaway slaves who had found asylum in London. In 1971 the nation became the Republic of Sierra Leone but remained in the British Commonwealth. The capital is Freetown; English is the official language. The monetary unit is the Leone (Le).

INTERNATIONAL SCHOOL LIMITED
Day Coed Ages 3-12. Gr N-6.

Freetown, Sierra Leone. Mereweather Rd. New England. P.O. Box 85. Tel. 40728.
Mrs. J. Bernard-Jones, Head.
Pre-Prep. Curr—Intl. LI—Eng. CF—Fr Eng Math Soc Studies Art. Enr 370.
Fac 21. Sierra Leone.
Tui $120.
Summer Session. Acad Rec. 4 wks.
Est 1956. Tri (Sept-Je). ISS.
Bldgs 5. Lib 2000 vols. Field.

Founded by a parents' association in 1956, this international school offes an individualized curriculum. Courses include English, social studies, French, music, nature science and physical education.

KABALA RUPP MEMORIAL SCHOOL
Bdg & Day Coed Ages 6-15. Gr 1-9.

Kabala, Sierra Leone. Box 28.
Janet E. Nickel, BS, Fort Wayne Bible College, Prin.
Pre-Prep Gen Acad. Curr—USA. LI—Eng. CF—Bible Health Music.
Enr 26. B 14/2; G 10. Elem 23, Sec 3.
Fac 4. Full 3/Part 1. M 1; F 3. US 4.
Tui Bdg $1810; Day $1770.
Est 1956. Inc nonprofit. Mission. Sem (Aug-May). ISS.
Bldgs 4. Dorm. Lib 4800 vols. Athletic facilities.

This school was established to provide an American education for missionaries' children. Supervised correspondence courses are offered for grades 10 to 12 through the University of Nebraska.

SUDAN

Formerly known as Anglo-Egyptian Sudan, the country was occupied by the Egyptians and the British. In 1956 Sudan was declared independent and the Democratic Republic of the Sudan was formed.

Sudan's chief export is cotton, mainly grown in the south. The Nile River flows through the country from south to north. Khartoum is the capital and largest city. Arabic, English and tribal dialects are spoken, and the pound (Sd£) is the unit of currency.

KHARTOUM AMERICAN SCHOOL
  Day Coed Ages 5-15. Gr K-10.

Khartoum, Sudan. c/o American Embassy. Box 699. Tel. 43909.
Mail to: American Embassy Khartoum, Dept. of State, Washington, DC
  20520.
Richard T. Eng, Admin.
Gen Acad. Curr—USA. LI—Eng.
Enr 227. US—40.
Fac 17. Full 13/Part 4. US 8.
Tui $4850-5150.
Est 1960. Quar (Sept-May). AISA A/OS ISS.
Bldgs 8. Lib. Lab. Field.

Serving the international diplomatic community of Khartoum, this small school offers an American-style curriculum. Instruction is in English. American students have a minimum of difficulty transferring to schools in the U.S.

TOGO

Divided in two after World War I, the British portion of Togo merged with adjacent Ghana, while the French part became independent in 1960. The country retains the French influence with the CFA franc (CFAF) as its monetary unit, and French as the official language. The Republic of Togo's capital is Lome.

THE AMERICAN INTERNATIONAL SCHOOL OF LOME
  Day Coed Ages 5-14. Gr K-8.

Lome, Togo. BP 852. c/o American Embassy, Lome. Tel. 21-3000.
Mail to: c/o American Embassy Lome, Dept. of State, Washington, DC
  20520.

Joseph Durand, Prin.
Gen Acad. Curr—USA. LI—Eng.
Enr 56.
Fac 13.
Tui $2025.
Est 1966. Tri (Sept-Je). AISA A/OS ISS.
Bldg 1. Lib 4000 vols. Crt.

The school was started in 1966 by American missionary parents who wanted an American curriculum to meet the needs of their children in a French-speaking country. Individually Guided Education is stressed, and every child may pursue independent study. One-third of the children are from the United States. Physical education activities include fundamental rhythm, gymnastics and team sports. Among extracurricular activities are macrame, swimming, arts and crafts, cooking, sewing, typing and tennis.

EQUATORIAL & SOUTHERN AFRICA

BOTSWANA

The Republic of Botswana is twice the size of Arizona and is bordered by South and South West Africa, Zambia and Zimbabwe. Gaborone is the capital city and the pula (BP) is the country's monetary unit. English and Setswana are commonly spoken.

NORTHSIDE SCHOOL
  Day Coed Ages 4½-13. Gr K-7.

Gaborone, Botswana. P.O. Box 897. Tel. 52440.
Mrs. M. E. Dixon-Warren, DipEd, London Univ., Head.
Pre-Prep Gen Acad. Curr—UK. LI—Eng. CF—Fr. SI—Rem & Dev Read.
Enr 512. B 258; G 254. US—40.
Fac 23. Full 23. M 2; F 21. UK.
Tui $1200. Schol.
Est 1974. Nonprofit. Tri (Jan-Dec). AISA A/OS ISS.
Bldgs 5. Lib 2500 vols. Crts. Swimming pool.

The curriculum at Northside is British-oriented, however, it does prepare students for American secondary school exams. English history and literature, arts and crafts, social studies, sciences and traditional and modern mathematics are offered. Students participate in a variety of sports and extracurricular activities.

KENYA

Located on the eastern coast of Africa, Kenya became an independent republic in 1963. Since 1969 the President has been popularly elected. North Kenya is arid, but the south is a fertile agricultural area. The principal crops are coffee, tea and sisal. Swahili is the official language, with English, Bantu and Kikuyu also spoken. The capital city is Nairobi, and the shilling (KSh) is the monetary unit.

RIFT VALLEY ACADEMY
Bdg Coed Ages 7-19; Day Coed 5-18. Gr 1-12.

Kijabe, Kenya. African Inland Church Mission. Tel. Kijabe 1.
Roy Entwistle, MA, Seattle Pacific, Prin.
Col Prep. Tests ACT CEEB SSAT. Curr—USA. LI—Eng.
Enr 470.
Fac 38.
Tui Day $264-300 (+ $700-1800); Bdg $1204-1240 (+ $700-1800).
Est 1960. Inc. African Inland Mission. Tri (Sept-July). AISA ISS. Accred MSA.

Sponsored by the African Inland Mission, Rift Valley enrolls students whose parents are missionaries in Africa. The basic American curriculum is supplemented with French, Swahili and advanced studies in biology. Sports activities include basketball, tennis, rugby, hockey, volleyball, softball and soccer.

INTERNATIONAL SCHOOL OF KENYA
Day Coed Ages 4½-18. Gr K-12. PG.

Nairobi, Kenya. P.O. Box 14103. Tel. 582421/2.
Brian McCauley, PhD, Stanford, Supt.
Col Prep. Tests IB CEEB SSAT. Curr—USA. LI—Eng. A—Bio Chem Physics Comp Sci. CF—Fr Span Ger Econ Anthro Comp Relig African Stud Am & African Lit Eur Hist. SI—ESL Read Speech.
Enr 550. B 275; G 275. Elem 400, Sec 150. US—286. Grad '84—40. Col—36.
Fac 49. Full 49. M 15; F 34. US 40.
Tui $5300 (+ $300). Schol.
Summer Session. Acad Rec. Tui $100/4 wks.
Est 1969. Inc nonprofit. Sem (Aug-Je). AISA A/OS ISS. Accred MSA. Bldgs 15. Lib 15,000 vols. Swimming pool. Tennis courts. Fields.

Both the curriculum and school organization of the International School of Kenya reflect that of North American school systems, with students prepared for the College Boards. The International Baccalaureate program is offered. The school's Intercultural Program exposes students to the people, culture and environment of East Africa. Campus activities, reading and research prepare students for a variety of field trips such as visiting various Kenyan tribal societies, a climb of Mt. Kenya, and studying Indian Ocean marine life and the ecosystem of a national park.

Team sports include basketball, soccer, field hockey, netball, rugby, volleyball, softball and handball. Extracurricular activities, modified according to student interest, have included choir, jewelry-making, Swahili, modern dance, ballet, golf and swimming.

LORETO CONVENT MSONGARI
Day Girls Ages 6-18. Gr 2-12.

Nairobi, Kenya. Box 30258. Tel. 60235.
Sr. M. Pauline Boase, Head.
Col Prep. Curr—UK. LI—Eng. CF—Fr Kiswahili Sci Arts Music Cookery Needlework.
Enr 1000. Elem 500, Sec 500. Grad '84—40.
Fac 50. Full 50. M 10; F 40. Nat.
Tui KSh3000.
Est 1921. Nonprofit. Roman Catholic. Tri.
Lib. Courts 9. Pool. Labs 5. Tennis crts 7.

A traditional curriculum emphasizes the basics at the primary level. For the first two years of secondary school a prescribed program is required. In Form III selection of subjects is introduced. Forms V and VI prepare students for the equivalent of the British 'A' and 'O' level examinations.

ROSSLYN ACADEMY
Bdg Coed Ages 7-15; Day Coed 6-15. Gr 1-9.

Nairobi, Kenya. P.O. Box 14146. Tel. 520039.
Gary Sensenig, Prin.
Pre-Prep Gen Acad. Curr—USA. LI—Eng. CF—Fr Swahili Soc Stud Art Music Relig Indus Arts Comp Sci.
Enr 185. B 11/84; G 9/81. Elem 165, Sec 20. US—135.
Fac 18. Full 13/Part 5. M 5/2; F 8/3. US 18.
Tui Bdg $2600 (+$150); Day $2100 (+$150).
Est 1948. Nonprofit. Mennonite. Tri (Aug-Je). AISA.
Bldgs 7. Dorms 1. Lib 4000 vols. Athletic facilities.

Originally located in Tanzania, Rosslyn Academy was established to provide an American education to the children of Mennonite missionaries in East Africa. Today, with an enrollment largely American, the school welcomes students from all backgrounds. The United States-based curriculum is supplemented by the study of African history and culture. Swahili as well as French are offered as electives. The school is situated in the northwest part of Nairobi on a 20-acre campus in the midst of a coffee plantation.

LESOTHO

Lesotho, a mountainous country bordered on the east by the Drakensberg chain, is an autonomous kingdom geographically surrounded by the Republic of South Africa. The nation became independent in 1966 after 80 years of British administration, and is a member of the Commonwealth of Nations. The National Assembly consists of representative political parties and regional tribes. English and Sesotho are the official languages. Maseru is the capital and largest city and the maloti (Ma) is the monetary unit.

MACHABENG HIGH SCHOOL
Day Coed Ages 11-18. Gr 7-12.

Maseru 100, Lesotho. PO Box 1570, Tonokholo Rd. Tel. 323224.
D.A. Kirkwood, BSc, DipEd, Edinburgh, DipPl, Glasgow, Head.
Col Prep. Tests GCE. Curr—UK. LI—Eng. A—Math Physics Chem Biol. CF—Eng Lit Comp Bus Econ Geog Span Ger Nutrition Art. SI—Rem & Dev Read.
Enr 244. B 125; G 119. US—15. Grad '84—27. Col—24.
Fac 25. UK.
Tui $1000-1176. Schol.
Est 1977. Nonprofit. Tri (Aug-July). AISA A/OS.
Bldgs 3. Lib 6000 vols. Field.

Machabeng serves the needs of the local and expatriate communities in Lesotho. The curriculum prepares students for 12 'O' level subjects and four 'A' level exams of the British G.C.E. The student body represents 35 different countries. Students are required to participate in two hours of extracurricular activities each week.

MADAGASCAR

A large island in the Indian Ocean approximately 250 miles off the coast of southeast Africa, the Democratic Republic of Madagascar was an autonomous republic within the French Community from 1958. In 1960 the country became an independent member of the Community. The Betsimisaraka, the Merina (Hova) and the Betsileo are among several of the varied ethnic groups represented in the population. The capital and largest city is Tananarive, and the Malagasy franc (FMG) is the unit of currency. French and Malagasy are the official languages.

AMERICAN SCHOOL OF ANTANANARIVO
Day Coed Ages 3-14. Gr N-8.

Antananarivo, Madagascar. B.P. 1717. Tel. 420 39.
Mail to: c/o American Embassy, Antananarivo, Department of State, Washington, DC 20520.
Susan Rasata, MA, Middlebury, Admin.

Pre-Prep. Curr—USA. LI—Eng. CF—Fr ESL Lang Arts Math Art Music Phys Ed. SI—Rem Read & Math.
Enr 32. B 15; G 17. US—13.
Fac 6. Full 3/Part 3. F 6. UK US.
Tui $2200 (+ $100).
Est 1969. Nonprofit. Quar (Sept-Je). AISA A/OS ISS.
Bldgs 1. Lib 2000 vols. Field.

Serving the international community of Antananarivo, this small school provides American-style elementary education. Instruction is in English, and accelerated courses are available for advanced students.

MALAWI

This nation, once known as Nyasaland, was first explored by Europeans in David Livingstone's expeditions of the 1850s and 1860s. Malawi was made a British protectorate in 1892 after Royal Navy gunboats drove out Arab slave traders who had occupied the territory. Malawi achieved independence in 1964, and two years later became a constitutional republic in the Commonwealth of Nations.

The mountains and plateaus rising out of the great Rift Valley run north to south. Lake Malawi forms the eastern border. The official language is English, though the dialect Chichewa is spoken by many. The capital is Lilongwe and the kwacha (KW) is the currency.

ST. ANDREW'S SECONDARY SCHOOL
Bdg & Day Coed Ages 11-18. Gr 6-12.

Blantyre, Malawi. P.O. Box 211. Tel. 634 432.
W.J. Baker, BA, Head.
Col Prep Gen Acad. Tests GCE CEEB SSAT. Curr—UK. LI—Eng. A—Eng Math Physics Chem Biol Hist Geog Fr Art Music. CF—Music Woodwork Domestic Sci Engineering Drawing. SI—Rem & Dev Read Tut.
Enr 580. B 90/200; G 90/200. Elem 300, Sec 280. US—50 Grad '84—110. Col—50.
Fac 42. Full 40/Part 2. M 28; F 14. UK.
Tui Bdg 3900 KW; Day 2250 KW.
Est 1978. Nonprofit. Tri (Sept-July).
Bldgs 10. Dorms 4. Lib 25,000 vols. 5 Fields. Pool. 6 crts. Gym.

Primarily a school for children of expatriate and diplomatic families living in Malawi, St. Andrew's is located on 35 acres of African countryside overlooked by Mulanje Mountain. Pupils are grouped according to ability. The school has a " basics" curriculum supplemented by handicrafts, music and art. Sixth form students are assisted by tutors in preparation for university examinations. The Royal School of Music and the Pitman's Institute also conduct examinations at the school.

Students are encouraged to join the activities of 25 clubs and societies as well as weekend excursions to nearby forests, rivers and game parks. The sports program includes swimming, cross-country, basketball, squash, water-polo, rugby, golf, football, hockey, tennis and netball.

SOMALIA

The easternmost country in Africa, the Somali Democratic Republic was formed in 1960 with the union of British and Italian Somalilands. Although the country is primarily agrarian, uranium and other minerals are excavated. Islam is the prevailing religion, and the language is Somali. The Somali shilling (SoSh) is the unit of currency; Mogadishu is the capital.

AMERICAN SCHOOL OF MOGADISHU
Day Coed Ages 4-14. Gr N-8.

Mogadishu, Somalia.
Mail to: c/o American Embassy Mogadishu, Dept. of State, Washington, DC 20520.
Ronald Halsey, Prin.
Gen Acad. Curr—USA. LI—Eng.
Enr 188.
Fac 23.
Tui $3500-4300.
Est 1959. Nonprofit. Sem (Aug-Je). AISA A/OS ISS.
Lib. Athletic facilities.

With an enrollment representative of 25 nations, this school provides an elementary education to the children of the diplomatic and business community of Mogadishu. Students who are not fluent in English, the medium of instruction, receive individual tutoring in special groups. Classes are small with each child following an individualized program.

SOUTH AFRICA

Located on the southernmost tip of Africa, the country comprises four provinces: Cape, Transvaal, Orange Free State and Natal. There are three separate capital cities, with Pretoria serving as the administrative seat of government; Cape Town as the legislative center; and Bloemfontein as the judicial capital. The government policy of apartheid has brought international condemnation and has caused much internal unrest.

The country's diverse terrain and climate produce a variety of agricultural products such as sugar and tobacco. South Africa leads the world in the production of gold, with coal, uranium, gypsum and tungsten also mined. Fishing and whaling are also important industries. The rand (R) is the monetary unit. Afrikaans, Bantu and English are spoken.

MICHAELHOUSE
Bdg Boys Ages 12-18. Gr 8-12.

Balgowan (Natal) 3275, South Africa. Tel. 03324-4110.
Neil B. Jardine, BEd, Univ. of South Africa, Rector.
Pre-Prep. Curr—Nat. Ll—Eng. A—Accounting Econ Law Comp Sci.
  CF—Afrikaans Zulu Fr Lat Relig Environmental Ed Health.
Enr 478. Elem 263, Sec 215. Grad '84—100. Col—85.
Fac 40. Full 36/Part 4. M 36; F 4. Nat.
Tui R6700 (+R1500).
Est 1896. Nonprofit. Quar (Feb-Nov).
Dorms 7. Lib. Crts. Gym. Pool. Fields.

The curriculum at this school consists of basic academic subjects and Afrikaans, which is required of all students. Coursework prepares the boys for entrance into South African universities or the G.C.E. 'O' levels. An audio-visual department and music and art classes supplement the academic program. A variety of clubs and a full range of sports stressing outdoor activities are available. Daily chapel attendance is mandatory.

ST. JOHN'S COLLEGE
Bdg Boys Ages 7-18; Day Coed 6-18. Gr K-12.

Johannesburg (Transvaal), South Africa. St. David Rd., Houghton. Tel. 648-1350.
W. W. Malfarlane, BA(Witwatersrand), DipEd (Oxon), Head.
Col Prep Gen Acad. Tests GCE. Curr—Nat. Ll—Eng. A—Math.
  CF—Afrikaans Fr Latin Zulu Hist Geog Computer Sci.
Enr 900. B 180/707; G /13.
Fac 55. Full 51/Part 4. M 39; F 16.
Tui Bdg R2300-3300; Day R1400-1800. Schol.
Est 1898. Inc. Tri (Jan-Dec).
Dorms 30. 3 Libs 10,000 vols. Athletic facilities.

St. John's is one of the Headmasters' Conference Schools in South Africa. Covering primary and secondary levels, it offers preparation for the matriculation examination of the universities of South Africa. At the postmatriculation level, students may prepare for the 'A' level of the British G.C.E. Afrikaans is a compulsory second language.

CLIFTON PREPARATORY SCHOOL
Bdg & Day Boys Ages 7-14.

Natal, South Africa. P.O. Nottingham Road. Tel. 033312-20.
J.H.V. Forbes, Head.
Pre-Prep. Curr—Nat. Ll—Eng. CF—Afrikaans Zulu Lat Relig Art.
  Sl—Rem & Dev Read.
Enr 144. B 143/1.
Fac 12. Full 12. M 8; F 4. Nat.
Tui Bdg R850 (+R200); Day R430 (+R150). Schol.

Est 1942. Quar (Feb-Nov).
Bldgs 12. Dorms 2. Lib. Crts. Gym. Fields.

The Clifton Preparatory School comprises a day school in Durban as well as the boarding school on Nottingham Road. Boys are taught English, math, science, art, music, handicrafts and, in the later grades, a foreign language. Government examinations for entrance to South African secondary and private schools are administered. Outdoor activities including beekeeping, fly-fishing, yachting, natural history clubs and sports are emphasized. Students come primarily from South Africa and Swaziland.

SWAZILAND

Situated between the Republic of South Africa and Mozambique, the tiny Kingdom of Swaziland became an independent country within the British Commonwealth in 1968. Mbabane is the capital and the Lilangeni is the monetary unit (E). English is used, however, Siswati is the country's official language. In 1973 the King renounced the Constitution, assumed total power and suspended all political parties. The Parliament was reconvened in 1979.

WATERFORD KAMHLABA UNITED WORLD COLLEGE OF SOUTHERN AFRICA
Bdg & Day Coed Ages 11-19. Gr 7-PG.

Mbabane, Swaziland. P.O. Box 52. Tel. 42966.
Richard A. Eyeington, MA, DipEd, Durham, Head.
Col Prep. Tests GCE IB. Curr—UK. LI—Eng. CF—Fr Span Afrikaans Zulu Siswati Hist Geog Math Sci.
Enr 350. B 130/55; G 105/60.
Fac 35. Full 30/Part 5.
Tui Bdg $6000; Day $4000.
Est 1963. Inc nonprofit. Tri (Jan-Dec). A/OS ISS.
Dorms 3. Fields. Courts. Pool. Labs 3.

Waterford Kamhlaba offers a five-year course in preparation for 'O' level certificates and the International Baccalaureate. Students come mainly from Swaziland, Botswana, Lesotho, Malawi, Mozambique and South Africa, although 40 different nationalities are represented. Extracurricular activities include a wide variety of athletics, special interest clubs and school publications. This school is one of six United World Colleges.

TANZANIA

The republic of Tanganyika and the island of Zanzibar merged in 1964 and adopted the name United Republic of Tanzania. The port city of Dar es Salaam, located in Tanganyika, is the capital. The monetary unit is the Tanzanian shilling (TSh). Arabic, Bantu, English and Swahili are used.

INTERNATIONAL SCHOOL OF TANGANYIKA, LTD.
Day Coed Ages 5-17. Gr K-11.

Dar es Salaam, Tanzania. United Nations Rd. P.O. Box 2651. Tel. 30076.
T. Michael Maybury, Head.
Col Prep. Tests GCE. Curr—Intl. LI—Eng.
Enr 1045.
Fac 82.
Tui $2235-3330. Schol.
Summer Session. Rec Tui $100/4 wks.
Est 1963. Nonprofit. Tri (Sept-Je). AISA A/OS ISA ISS.
Bldgs 2. Libs 2. Labs 4. Studios art, music, drama. Gym. Fields. Swimming pool. Tennis crts.

With a cosmopolitan enrollment comprising over 45 nationalities, this international school prepares children for secondary and post-secondary school entrance. While many American texts are used, the curriculum is designed to meet the needs of the wide-ranging international community. Sports and extracurricular activities complement the academics.

INTERNATIONAL SCHOOL MOSHI LIMITED
Bdg Coed Ages 12-20; Day Coed 6-20. Gr 1-12.

Moshi, Tanzania. Lema Rd., P.O. Box 733. Tel. 4311/4312.
Brian Garton, Head.
Col Prep. Tests SSAT GCE IB TOEFL. Curr—Intl. LI—Eng. A—Math Sci Soc Sci Humanities. CF—Fr Scan Lang Ger Greek Swahili Ital Econ Soc Stud Music Art. SI—Rem Eng & Math.
Enr 441. B 89/153; G 63/136. US—18. Grad '84—43.
Fac 48. Full 41/Part 7. M 27; F 21. US 16. Intl.
Tui Bdg $8358; Day $4118.
Est 1969. Inc nonprofit. Sem (Aug-Je). AISA A/OS ISA ISS.
Bldgs 12. Dorms 8. Lib 8000 vols. Labs 2. Swimming pool. Fields. Tennis courts. Riding.

Located on a 40-acre campus at the foot of Mt. Kilimanjaro, this school meets the educational needs of all expatriates living in Tanzania, especially those working at the adjacent Kilimanjaro Christian Medical Center. English is the language of instruction in a curriculum offering a wide variety of language electives to a cosmopolitan student body. The school participates in the International Baccalaureate program and students who sit for this exam fulfill requirements for most countries. Religious instruction is given in every class, with boarders attending Sunday worship. Physical education, art and music activities are among the extracurricular offerings.

UGANDA

The Republic of Uganda was first visited by European explorers and Arabian traders in 1844. Under the British sphere of influence from 1890, Uganda became a British protectorate in 1894. Independence was declared in 1962.

General Idi Amin, an erratic former Army sergeant, overthrew President Milton Obote in 1972 and assumed all legislative and executive powers. After a bloody seven year reign, Amin was finally overthrown in 1979 with the help of Tanzanian troops. A Military Commission headed by a civilian was established in 1980 which lifted the ban on opposition political parties and paved the way for a presidential election.

English is the official language, and the capital city is Kampala. The monetary unit is the Uganda shilling (USh).

LINCOLN SCHOOL
  Day Coed Ages 5-14. Gr K-8.

Kampala, Uganda. P.O. Box 4200. 93 Buganda Rd.
Mail to: c/o American Embassy Kampala, Dept. of State, Washington, DC 20520.
Rose Mary Rowland, Dir.
Pre-Prep. Tests SSAT. Curr—USA. LI—Eng. CF—Fr Lang Arts Soc Stud Art.
Enr 98. US—13.
Fac 12. US 4.
Tui $2000-2200.
Est 1966. Inc 1973 nonprofit. Sem (Sept-Je). AISA A/OS ISS.
Bldgs 1. Lib 3000 vols.

Serving the international community of Kampala, this school offers an Anglo-American program. French is taught at all grade levels.

ZAIRE

In the heart of equatorial Africa and entirely inland except for a short stretch on the Atlantic Ocean, the Republic of Zaire was the scene of explorations by Henry M. Stanley in 1877-79. Later, as a colony of Belgium, it was called the Belgian Congo. Independence was proclaimed in 1960. Kinshasa, the capital, is a shipping base on the Zaire River. The unit of currency is the Zaire (Z), and Swahili is most often spoken.

THE AMERICAN SCHOOL OF KINSHASA
 Day Coed Ages 5-18. Gr K-12.

Kinshasa 11, Zaire. B.P. 4702. Tel. 31506.
Mail to: APO 09662, New York, NY.
Dave Holmer, BA, Seattle Pacific, MEd, Univ. of Washington, Supt.
Col Prep. Tests SSAT. Curr—USA. LI—Eng. CF—Fr ESL Bio Sci.
 SI—Rem Read.
Enr 500. B 250; G 250. Elem 260, Sec 240. Grad '84—40.
Fac 43. M 14; F 29. US.
Tui $4415 (+ $700).
Summer Session. Acad.
Est 1961. Nonprofit. Sem (Aug-Je). AISA A/OS ISS. Accred MSA.
Bldgs 16. Lib 10,000 vols. Fields. Swimming pool. Tennis crts. Track.

Enrolling students from 38 countries, over half of whom are Americans, this school provides a United States college preparatory curriculum. Commercial courses and a wide variety of electives including photography, ceramics and journalism are offered. The school's modern complex is situated on a 42-acre tract leased by the American Embassy from the Zairian government. While the school does not provide boarding facilities, three mission-operated hostels located nearby accommodate a limited number of boarders.

ZAMBIA

The former British Protectorate of Northern Rhodesia, the Republic of Zambia became an independent state within the Commonwealth in 1964. Lusaka is the capital and the Kwacha (KW) is the monetary unit. English and a variety of Zambian dialects are spoken.

INTERNATIONAL SCHOOL OF LUSAKA
 Day Coed Ages 5-18. Gr 1-12.

Lusaka, Zambia. Box 50121. Tel. 252291.
James Ambrose, MA, E. Michigan Univ., Supt.
Col Prep. Tests IB CEEB GCE SSAT. Curr—USA UK. LI—Eng. CF—Fr.
 SI—ESL Rem Math.
Enr 1294. US—78.
Fac 73. US 32.
Tui $989-1314. Schol.
Est 1965. Inc nonprofit. Tri (Sept-July). AISA A/OS ISA ISS.
Bldgs 12. Lib 10,500 vols. Courts. Fields. Swimming pool.

The International School of Lusaka provides an Anglo-American curriculum with an international emphasis. College preparatory studies include the International Baccalaureate program. Grades 2 through 12 are housed on one main site, while children in first grade attend classes in the original school building ¾ of a mile away.

ASIA

NEAR & MIDDLE EAST

BAHRAIN

Formerly a British protectorate, the state of Bahrain is composed of several islands in the Persian Gulf. Once known for pearl fishing, it is today a major Middle East oil center. Manama, the capital, is on Bahrain Island, the largest of the group. The unit of currency is the Bahrain dinar (BD), and Arabic is the official language.

BAHRAIN SCHOOL
Day Coed Ages 5-18. Gr K-12.

Manama, Bahrain. P.O. Box 934 Jufair. Tel. 973 727828.
Mail to: Bahrain School SC 5503, FPO, NY 09526.
Frithjof R. Wannebo, PhD, Univ. of Minnesota, Prin.
Col Prep Gen Acad. Tests CEEB SSAT ACT GCE. Curr—USA UK.
  LI—Eng.
Enr 789.
Fac 50.
Tui $4600 (+ $1200).
Est 1968. Sem (Sept-Je). ECIS ISS NE/SA.
Bldgs 20. Lib 14,000 vols. Courts. Fields. Swimming pool.

Beginning as an elementary school for U.S. Defense Department employees, Bahrain School has since undergone phenomenal expansion. Today, the school admits English-speaking children, including Bahraini nationals, through grade 12.

The academic program provides for both American and British curricular requirements, with preparation given for the College Boards and the British G.C.E., 'O' level. There are extensive elective offerings within each department, as well as opportunity for work experience. For students not college-bound courses are provided in business education, home economics and the industrial arts.

CYPRUS

A Mediterranean island off the coasts of Syria and Turkey, the Republic of Cyprus was the site of Greek colonies following the Trojan wars and dominated by a succession of peoples from Phoenicia in the 19th century. A former British crown colony, it became independent in 1960. Greek, Turkish and English are spoken. Nicosia is the capital. The monetary unit is the Cyprus pound (£C).

AMERICAN ACADEMY
Day Coed Ages 5-19. Gr 1-PG.

Larnaca, Cyprus. Gregory Afxentiou Ave. P.O. Box 112. Tel. 52046.
Nicos C. Tjiarris, BA, Hull Univ., Prin.
Gen Acad Col Prep. Tests GCE. Curr—USA UK. LI—Eng. CF—FR
Greek Econ.
Enr 1004. B 603; G 401. Elem 187, Sec 761, PG 56. US—10. Grad '84—56.
Fac 58. Full 55/Part 3. M 29; F 29. Intl.
Tui £C500 (+£C50). Schol.
Est 1908. Nonprofit. Tri (Sept-Je). ISS.
Bldgs 3. Lib 5000 vols. Courts. Fields.

The American Academy (grades 7-PG) and the American Academy Junior School (grades 1-6) were established by the Reformed Presbyterian Church of North America as a Christian Mission school. A general education is offered as well as preparation for university entrance. Advanced level courses are taught in math, physics, chemistry, accounting and economics, and a full range of extracurricular activities include drama, photography and choir. The school's extensive facilities provide many athletic opportunities.

AMERICAN ACADEMY NICOSIA
Day Coed Ages 5-19. Gr 1-12.

Nicosia 162, Cyprus. 3A Michael Parides St. Tel. 021-62886.
Christos Psiloinis, BA, MA, American University-Cairo, Prin.
Col Prep Gen Acad Commercial. Tests GCE SSAT. Curr—USA UK.
LI—Eng. A—Biol Chem Econ Eng Lit Geog Hist Math Greek Physics
Accounting. CF—Child Care Home Econ Office Management Relig
Drawing. SI—Tut.
Enr 746. B 284; G 462. Elem 507, Sec 239. US—5. Grad '84—24.
Col—2.
Fac 41. Full 35/Part 6. M 13; F 28. US 4. Nat UK.
Tui £C300-550 (+£C50). Schol.
Est 1922. Nonprofit. Sem (Sept-Je).
Bldgs 3. Lib 5500 vols. Crts. Field.

This school prepares students for G.C.E. 'O' and 'A' level examinations. Arts and crafts classes, bible instruction and physical education are required. Extracurricular activities include an ambulance brigade which provides first-aid instruction, school newspaper, the Girl Guides, Rotary Club, Bible clubs and UNESCO. The sports program offers volleyball, football, basketball, cycling, gymnastics and folk dancing.

THE JUNIOR SCHOOL
Day Coed Ages 4½-12½. Gr K-7.

Nicosia, Cyprus. Kyriacos Matsis Ave. POB 1940. Tel. 43855.
P. A. J. Bosustow, Head.
Pre-Prep. Curr—UK. LI—Eng. CF—Fr Greek.
Enr 278.
Fac 23. UK.
Tui $718-630 (+ $30).
Est 1944. Inc 1951 nonprofit. Tri (Sept-Je). ISS.
Bldgs 1. Lib 6000 vols. Field.

This British-oriented school enrolls students from Italy, Ireland, Cyprus, the United States and Great Britain. Instruction in modern Greek is only provided to Cypriot students.

THE PRIVATE ENGLISH JUNIOR SCHOOL/
THE GRAMMAR SCHOOL
Day Coed Ages 5-19. Gr 1-12.

Nicosia, Cyprus. Anthoupolis Highway. Tel. 02621744.
Vassos Hajiyerou, BA, Fairleigh Dickinson Univ., Dir.
Col Prep Gen Acad. Tests GCE SSAT TOEFL. Curr—USA UK. LI—Eng. A—Econ Accounting Math Physics Chem Greek Pol Sci. CF—Geog Hist.
Enr 550. B 300; G 250. Elem 150, Sec 400. US—10. Grad '84—50. Col—40.
Fac 25. Full 25. M 17; F 8. US 1. Nat.
Tui $1100 (+ $150). Schol.
Est 1963. Inc nonprofit. Sem (Sept-Je).
Bldgs 5. Lib 10,000 vols. Fields. Crt.

The school's curriculum consists of required courses in math, English, social studies, the sciences, art, religion and physical education. Field trips to the museums and historical landmarks of Cyprus are an integral part of the curriculum. A library, computer terminals and science laboratories are also available. Clubs and sports complete the student activities program. In addition to the Junior School and Grammar School at Nicosia, there is a second branch of the Grammar School at Limassol.

TASIS CYPRUS AMERICAN SCHOOL
Bdg & Day Coed Ages 12-18. Gr 7-12.

Nicosia, Cyprus. P.O. Box 2329, 11 Kassos St. Tel. (021) 43114. Telex: 4601 TASIS CY.

Mail to: U.S. Office, 326 E. 69th St., Rm. 110, New York, NY 10021.
L. Ruth Clay, BA, MA, PhD, Dir.
Col Prep Gen Acad. Tests CEEB SSAT TOEFL. Curr—US. LI—Eng.
  CF—Fr Arabic Greek Span Theatre Computer.
Enr 168. B 70/9; G 81/8. Elem 11, Sec 157. US—151. Grad '84—40.
  Col—31.
Fac 22. Full 22. M 9; F 13. US.
Tui Bdg $8800 (+$720). Schol.
Est 1983. Inc. Sem (Sept-Je). ECIS ISS NE/SA.
Bldgs 7. Dorms 5. 2 Libs 5000 vols. Courts. Pool.

Founded by Mrs. M. Crist Fleming, TASIS Cyprus is a branch of The
American School in Switzerland. Situated in a residential suburb of
Nicosia, the school occupies a former hotel. Americans comprise the
majority of students enrolled in the college preparatory curriculum that
features advanced level study in English, U.S. history, biology and
chemistry. School publications, choir and film are among the extracurricular activities while soccer, tennis, sailing and swimming are part
of the sports offerings.

See also page 110

ANGLO-AMERICAN INTERNATIONAL SCHOOL
  Bdg Coed Ages 11-18; Day Coed 5-18. Gr K-PG.

Paphos, Cyprus. 22-26 Hellas Ave. Tel. (061)32236.
Terry K. Whaling, BCE, Clarkson, MEd, DEd, Univ. of Mass., Amherst,
  Head.
Col Prep. Tests CEEB GCE TOEFL. Curr—UK USA. LI—Eng. A—Sci
  Math Eng. CF—Fr Ger Greek. SI—Tut Greek. SI—Tut.
Enr 78. B 5/40; G 7/36. US—16. Grad '84—2. Col—2.
Fac 8. Full 5/Part 3. M 3; F 5. US 2. UK.
Tui Bdg $3520 (+$350); Day $1425 (+$100).
Est 1980. Inc nonprofit. Sem (Sept-Je). ECIS ISS.
Bldgs 3. Dorm. Lib 2000 vols. Field.

The academic program at the Anglo-American International School
combines features of the American and British systems and prepares
students for the G.C.E. 'O' and 'A' level and Advanced Placement
examinations. Classes are small and the academic program is complemented by offerings in art, music, drama and dance. Extracurricular
activities include hiking the forests and beaches of this Mediterranean
island, cultural excursions, swimming and skiing. The school accepts a
limited number of boarding students.

IRAQ

For centuries called Mesopotamia, "the land between the two rivers,"
Iraq's Tigris-Euphrates valley was the site of the ancient Babylonian and
Assyrian empires. Today, the Republic of Iraq is one of the leading oil
producers in the world. Its capital is the fabled city of Baghdad, and the

monetary unit is the dinar (ID). Arabic and Kurdish are the official languages.

BAGHDAD INTERNATIONAL SCHOOL
Day Coed Ages 4-17 Gr K-10.

Baghdad, Iraq. Airport Rd (Jehad District). Tel. 15569448.
Jacqueline Al Azawi, MA, Georgia State Univ., Prin.
Gen Acad. Curr—USA. LI—Eng.
Enr 273.
Fac 35.
Tui $1215.
Est 1967. Nonprofit. Tri (Sept-May). ISS.
Bldgs 7. Lib 12,000 vols.

This school provides an elementary education for the foreign English-speaking community of Baghdad. Special sessions are arranged for children who are not fluent in English.

ISRAEL

Formerly called Palestine, and birthplace of two major world religions, the modern State of Israel came into being in 1948, after a long history of invasions, conquests and confusing divisions. Today, the country's economy and industry are growing rapidly, despite frequent warring with neighboring Arab states. The holy city of Jerusalem serves as capital; the Israeli pound (I£) is the unit of currency. Hebrew, Arabic and English are the spoken languages.

ANGLICAN SCHOOL JERUSALEM
Day Coed Ages 4-18. Gr K-12.

Jerusalem, Israel. 82, Prophet St., P.O. Box 191. Tel. (02)234874.
J.S.W. Chorlton, BSc, Univ. of Newcastle upon Tyne, Head.
Col Prep Gen Acad. Tests GCE SSAT. Curr—UK USA. LI—Eng.
A—Hebrew Fr Sci Eng Math Hist. CF—Jerusalem Stud Art Ceramics
Office Practice Relig. SI—Rem & Dev Math & Read Tut.
Enr 375. Elem 273, Sec 102. US—75. Grad '84—29. Col—23.
Fac 37. Full 37. M 7; F 30. US 8. UK.
Tui $1950-2950 (+ $50-100). Schol.
Est 1948. Nonprofit. Tri (Sept-Je).
Bldg. Lib. Crt. Field.

The curriculum at Anglican School is based on the British system, but is modified to meet American high school diploma standards. Students in the upper grades take an increasing number of electives including ceramics, computing, typing and advanced courses in basic subjects. Field trips to Jerusalem's many religious, cultural and historical sites are the basis for the Jerusalem studies program. In addition to academics, students take part in musical groups and sports. Pupils are enrolled from

Ghana, the Philippines, England and Ireland as well as the United States.

THE WALWORTH BARBOUR AMERICAN INTERNATIONAL SCHOOL
Day Coed Ages 4-18. Gr N-12.

Kfar Shmaryahu, Israel. Rehov Hazorea. Tel. (052).
Mail to: c/o American Embassy, Tel Aviv, Israel 78225.
Forest A. Broman, AB, Brown, JDL, Harvard Law, Supt.
Col Prep. Tests CEEB SSAT. Curr—USA. LI—Eng. A—Eng Hist Sci.
  CF—Fr Hebrew Sci. SI—ESL.
Enr 369.
Fac 55.
Tui $2150-3950. Schol.
Est 1958. Inc 1967 nonprofit. Sem (Sept-Je). A/OS ISS NE/SA. Accred MSA.
Bldgs 7. Lib 14,000 vols. Gym.

American students comprise 50% of the enrollment at Walworth Barbour, with some 25 other nations represented. A college preparatory, American curriculum is followed, featuring advanced courses in English, history, math and science. Hebrew is taught from the third grade and an individualized E.S.L. is also conducted.

Elective courses include music, sociology, photography, drama, political science, creative writing and archaeology. The school is located in a residential suburb, about 15 kilometers north of Tel Aviv.

JORDAN

Known in the time of Moses as Edom and Moab, the Hashemite Kingdom of Jordan is now a constitutional monarchy. Although largely a desert, the fertile western portion affords much agricultural activity. The monetary unit is the Jordanian dinar (JD), Amman is the capital and Arabic is the official language.

AMERICAN COMMUNITY SCHOOL
Day Coed Ages 5-18. Gr K-12.

Amman, Jordan. c/o American Embassy. Tel. 813946.
Richard Krajczar, MA, Univ. of Wyoming, Supt.
Pre-Prep Col Prep. Tests SSAT. Curr—USA. LI—Eng. CF—Arabic Fr
  Span Music Sci. SI—Rev & Dev Read & Math ESL.
Enr 360. Elem 240, Sec 120. US—160. Grad '84—18. Col—18.
Fac 39. Full 36/Part 3. M 10; F 29. US—19.
Tui $3700-5200.
Est 1957. Nonprofit. Sem (Aug-Je). A/OS ISS NE/SA. Accred MSA.
Bldgs 1. Lib 9000 vols. Fields. Gym. Court.

The school follows an American curriculum supplemented by an elective program offering photography, ballet, band, chorus and team sports. Advanced courses are available in math, physics, chemistry, English and French. Middle East history and culture is taught to promote an understanding of the environment.

KUWAIT

The State of Kuwait, nestled between Iraq and Saudi Arabia at the head of the Persian Gulf, is a leading world exporter of crude oil, an economic activity that provides a national income large enough to guarantee free medical care, education and social security for all citizens. The capital is Kuwait and the dinar (KD) is the monetary unit. Arabic and English are the spoken languages.

AMERICAN SCHOOL OF KUWAIT
Day Coed Ages 5-18. Gr K-12.

Hawalli, Kuwait. P.O. Box 6735. Tel. 31-81-20.
Robert D. Iannuzzelli, Supt.
Col Prep. Tests CEEB. Curr—USA. LI—Eng.
Enr 1061.
Fac 94.
Tui $2500-4172.
Est 1964. Inc nonprofit. Sem (Sept-Je). A/OS ISS NE/SA. Accred MSA.
Bldgs 2. Lib 7000 vols. Labs 4. Swimming pool. Courts.

Located on a 1½-acre campus in a "U" shaped building, The American School of Kuwait attracts students of about 40 different nationalities. At the elementary level, the school features team teaching and individualized instruction in open non-graded classes. Secondary students prepare for the U.S. College Boards, with about 90% entering college.

UNIVERSAL AMERICAN SCHOOL
Day Coed Ages 4-18. Gr N-12.

Khaldiya, Kuwait. P.O. Box 17035. Tel. 615-857. Telex: UNAMS 23752 KT.
Walid Abushakra, BE, American Univ. of Beirut, Supt.
Col Prep. Tests SSAT TOEFL. Curr—USA. LI—Eng. A—Calc. CF—Arabic Fr Eng Math Sci Soc Stud. Rem & Dev Read Tut.
Enr 904. B 529; G 375. Elem 784, Sec 120. US—48. Grad '84—19. Col—18.
Fac 70. Full 69/Part 1. M 12; F 58. US 53.
Tui $2000-3450 (+ $550).
Est 1976. Sem (Sept-Je). NE/SA.
Bldgs 1. Lib 7340 vols. Labs. Comp lab. Gym.

The school serves an international group of children from 44 countries. A diversified curriculum teaches basic skills in the elementary grades and provides college preparation in the secondary years. Additional features include studies of Islamic culture and the Arabic language. The students also enjoy many recreational activities such as ballet, judo, choir, photography and team sports. The school moved to its present facility in 1983.

LEBANON

Settled in earliest times by the Phoenicians, then by Persians, Macedonians and Romans, Lebanon later was long a special part of the Ottoman Empire. It became an independent state in 1920 and achieved complete sovereignty as a republic in 1944.

Historical sites abound, at Siden, Tyre, Baalbeck and in Beirut, the capital, great law and intellectual center of the Roman Empire. Beirut has withstood a recent history of political and religious strife, and today contains a third of the country's population and is the chief seaport. The well known American University of Beirut, one of the largest educational institutions in the Middle East, was founded in the city in 1866 by missionaries from the U.S.

Education reflects the country's diverse historical influences, with Arabic, French and American systems utilized. Many of Lebanon's secondary schools correspond to a year or two after American high school. While Arabic is the official language of the country, and French the official second language, English is used extensively. The Republic of Lebanon's monetary unit is the Lebanese pound (L£).

AMERICAN COMMUNITY SCHOOL AT BEIRUT
  Day Coed Ages 3-18. Gr N-12.

Beirut, Lebanon. P.O. Box 8129. Tel. 366050.
Mail to: American Community School at Beirut, 850 Third Ave., 18th Floor, New York, NY 10022.
Catherine Bashshur, MA, Florida State Univ., Prin.
Col Prep. Tests CEEB. Curr—USA. LI—Eng. A—Eng Calc Fr. CF—Arabic Hist (US) Mideast Stud Art Music Typ. SI—ESL.
Enr 68. B 34; G 34. Elem 49, Sec 19. US—40.
Fac 14. Full 10/Part 4. US 10.
Tui $1800-3000 (+ $200).
Est 1905. Nonprofit. Sem (Sept-Je). A/OS ISS NE/SA.
Bldgs 4. 2 Libs 20,500 vols. Lab. Gym. Field. Tennis crts.

With a secondary division that is entirely college preparatory, ACS offers preparation for American universities. French and Arabic are taught in grades 7 through 12. Athletics, activities and clubs are features of a full extracurricular program which also includes trips in Beirut and Lebanon, as well as one or two yearly excursions to surrounding countries.

A continuation of the Faculty School founded in 1905 to provide day classes for children of the faculty of the American University, then called Syrian Presbyterian College, ACS today is jointly sponsored by A.U.B., the Presbyterian Mission, and the Arabian American Oil Company. The school is situated one block from the Mediterranean.

INTERNATIONAL COLLEGE
Day Coed Ages 4-18. Gr K-PG.

Beirut, Lebanon. P.O. Box 11-0 236.
Mail to: 850 3rd Ave., 18th floor, New York, NY 10022.
Alton L. Reynolds, Pres.
Col Prep. Tests CEEB. Curr—Intl. Ll—Arabic Eng Fr. CF—Near East Stud Philos Arts. Sl—Rem Eng & Fr.
Summer Session.
Est 1981. 1903 Nonprofit. Sem (Oct-Je). ISS NAIS.
Bldgs 13. 2 Libs. Athletic facilities.

This international school utilizes English, French and Arabic as languages of instruction. The program follows American, French and Lebanese curricular lines, preparing students for the French and Lebanese Baccalaureates and the U.S. College Boards.

Founded in 1891 at Izmir, Turkey, International College moved in 1936 to Lebanon where it administered the preparatory section of the American University of Beirut. Affiliation with A.U.B. ended in 1957, however the school continues to occupy part of the campus.

GERARD, THE NATIONAL EVANGELICAL INSTITUTE
Bdg & Day Boys Ages 6-20; Day Girls 16-18. Gr 1-PG.

Sidon, Lebanon. P.O. Box 11 Ein El-Helwi. Tel. 721806.
Bulos B. Butros, BA, American Univ. of Beirut, Prin.
Gen Acad Bus. Curr—Nat. Ll—Eng Arabic. CF—Arabic Math Sci Bus.
Enr 1092. B 30/1022; G/40. US—1. Grad '84—54.
Fac 71. Full 24/Part 47. M 52; F 19. Nat.
Tui Bdg $1500 (+$400); Day $400-900 (+$150). Schol.
Summer Session. Acad. Tui Day $225. 6 wks.
Est 1881. Nonprofit. Presbyterian. Quar (Oct-Je). ISS.
Bldgs 11. Dorms 4. Lib 7394 vols. Athletic facilities.

Gerard follows a high school curriculum based on the Lebanese Baccalaureate, with some adaptations along American lines. English is the language of instruction in all courses except Arabic and social studies. A full entrance examination in Arabic, English, math and the sciences is required for admission and scholarship aid is available to day students only.

Overlooking the Mediterranean, the campus is approximately one kilometer from the historic city of Sidon.

SAUDI ARABIA

By far the largest of the countries of the Arabian peninsula, occupying 80% of its land area, the Kingdom of Saudi Arabia is one of the world's great oil producers. Medina and Mecca, the two holy cities of Islam, are in the province of Hejaz. Medina, site of Mohammed's death, contains the tomb of the Prophet, and Mecca, his birthplace, contains Kaaba, the sacred shrine. The capital is Riyadh and the monetary unit is the riyal (SRl). Arabic is the official language.

ARAMCO SCHOOLS
Day Coed Ages 5-15. Gr K-9.

Dhahran, Saudi Arabia. c/o Arabian American Oil Co. Box 73. Tel. 966-3-875-1676.
Robert B. Gaw, Supt.
Pre-Prep. Curr—USA. LI—Eng. CF—Arabic Fr Span US Hist Arts. SI—Tut Rem & Dev Math & Read.
Enr 3597. B 1835; G 1762. Elem 3204, Sec 393. US—2977.
Fac 323. Full 321/Part 2. M 113; F 210. US 287.
Tui Free.
Est 1947. Nonprofit. Quar (Sept-Aug). ISS NAIS NE/SA.

Established and sponsored by the Arabian American Oil Company for children of its employees, the Aramco school system operates year-round on four campuses throughout Saudi Arabia: Dhahran, Abqaiq, Ras Tanura and Udhailiyah. A U.S. curriculum featuring individualized instruction is offered to an enrollment that is 90 percent American.

DHAHRAN ACADEMY
Day Coed Ages 5-15. Gr K-9.

Dhahran, Saudi Arabia. American Consulate General. Tel. 891-3842. Telex: 601937 YES SJ.
Mail to: c/o American Consulate General, APO, New York 09616.
A. Ernest Weeks, Supt.
Gen Acad. Tests SSAT. Curr—USA. LI—Eng. CF—Arabic Fr Span Hist Arts. SI—Rem Read EFL.
Enr 2000.
Fac 192.
Tui $4500.
Est 1961. Inc nonprofit. Sem (Aug-Je). A/OS ISS NE/SA. Accred MSA.
Bldgs 35. Lib 16,000 vols. Gym.

Approximately 60% of the students at the Dhahran Academy are from the United States, with the remainder coming from 35 other countries. Arabic is taught at all grade levels, while French instruction begins in the upper grades. Emphasis is placed upon preparing students for American and international secondary schools.

The city of Dhahran, on the Persian Gulf, is the site of a large international airport and the headquarters of the Arabian American Oil Company. The academy is the parent organization of Saudi Arabian International Schools, which operates schools in six other locations.

PARENTS' COOPERATIVE SCHOOL
Day Coed Ages 5-15. Gr K-9.

Jeddah, Saudi Arabia. Box 167 c/o Saudi Arabian Airlines, CC 100. Tel. 667-4566.
Mail to: c/o American Embassy, APO, New York 09697.
Stephen N. Twining, BA, Ripon, MA, PhD, Univ. of Michigan, Supt.
Pre-Prep. Tests SSAT. Curr—USA. LI—Eng. CF—Fr Arabic Soc Stud Comp Sci Hist Arts Math. SI—Spec Ed Prgm ESL.
Enr 1750. B 875; G 875. Elem 1650, Sec 100. US—965. Grad '84—100.
Fac 202. Full 202. M 44; F 158. US 175.
Tui $5100.
Summer Session. Acad Rem. Tui $200. 4-8 wks.
Est 1952. Nonprofit. Saudi Arabian Airlines. Sem (Sept-Je). ISS NE/SA. Accred MSA.
Bldgs 14. Lib 30,000 vols. Gyms 2. Fields.

Originally developed by Trans World/Saudi Arabian Airlines and the U.S. Government for employees' children, the school has since evolved to serve a number of companies and American organizations in Jeddah. About 55 percent of the students are United States nationals. The school follows an American curriculum, though a British curriculum track begins at the junior high level. P.C.S. participates in a "school to school" program with the Shawnee Mission Schools. An intramural sports program, vocal and instrumental groups, arts, crafts and Scouts are among the extracurricular activities.

Located on the Red Sea, Jeddah is Saudi Arabia's largest seaport and center for foreign embassies. Site of a major international ariport, it is also the departure point for pilgrimages to the Moslem holy cities of Mecca and Medina.

SAUDI ARABIAN INTERNATIONAL SCHOOL—RIYADH (AMERICAN SECTION)
Day Coed Ages 5-15. Gr K-9.

Riyadh, Saudia Arabia. P.O. Box 990. Tel. 491-5932.
Daryle Russell, EdD, Supt.
Pre-Prep. Tests SSAT. Curr—USA. LI—Eng. CF—Arabic Fr Read.
Enr 2750. Elem 1950, Sec 800. US—1540. Grad '84—120.
Fac 287. US 220.
Tui $4437 (+ $1420).
Est 1963. Nonprofit. Sem (Sept-Je). A/OS ISS NE/SA.
Bldgs 5. Lib 20,000 vols.

This school operates its main campus in Riyadh and a satellite campus at the King Khalid International Airport. The program is open to expatriate children and although 75 percent of the enrollment is from Canada and the U.S., children from 45 other nations are in attendance. SSAT tests are given twice a year and the Stanford Achievement Tests are conducted annually.

An E.S.L. program is conducted as well as electives in typing, economics, speech, drama, German, computer science, photography and psychology.

SYRIA

Greeks, Persians and Phoenicians were among those who conquered ancient Syria. The area remained a Turkish province until World War I. France was granted a mandate over Syria in 1916, and in 1930 recognized the country as an independent republic. During World War II, Syria was an allied base. In 1958 the United Arab Republic annexed the nation, but Syria became independent again in 1961 following a revolution and is now known as the Syrian Arab Republic.

Today agriculture and animal breeding are the major industries, and oil is a chief export. Damascus is the capital city, and the unit of currency is the Syrian pound (S£). Arabic is the official language.

DAMASCUS COMMUNITY SCHOOL
   Day Coed Ages 3-15. Gr N-9.

Damascus, Syria. c/o American Embassy.
Mail to: c/o American Embassy-Damascus, Dept. of State, Washington, DC 20520.
Robert Crawford, PhD, Stanford Univ, Prin.
Pre-Prep Gen Acad. Tests CEEB SSAT. Curr—USA. LI—Eng. CF—Arabic. SI—Rem & Dev Math & Read Tut ESL.
Enr 240. US—17.
Fac 50. Full 50. M 15; F 35. US 4.
Tui $1400-3300.
Summer Session. Acad Rec. Tui $100. 6 wks.
Est 1950. Nonprofit. Tri (Sept-Je). A/OS ISS NE/SA.
Bldgs 7. Lib 12,000 vols. Athletic facilities.

Located on the U.S. government compound in the central city of Damascus, this school stresses individualized instruction and assistance in its program.

TURKEY

The Ottoman Turks first appeared in the early 13th century. At the peak of its power, the Ottoman Empire extended from the Persian Gulf to Poland and from the Caspian Sea to Oran in Algeria. The republic which took the name of Turkey in 1923 for the first time in history remained as the chief successor state.

Ankara is the capital, and Istanbul is the largest city. Turkish is spoken by 90% of the population, and the predominant religion is Moslem. The monetary unit is the Turkish lira (T£).

BRITISH EMBASSY STUDY GROUP
Day Coed Ages 3-12. Gr N-6.

Ankara (Cankaya), Turkey. Sehit Ersan Caddesi 46 A. Tel. Ankara 27-43-10. Telex: 42 320.
David R. Clark, Head.
Prep-Prep Gen Acad. Curr—UK. Ll—Eng. CF—Fr Music Comp Sci.
Enr 103. B 47; G 56. US—20.
Fac 9. Full 8/Part 1. M 2; F 7. US 1. UK.
Tui $500/term (+ $70).
Summer Session. Rec. Tui $25. 2 wks.
Est 1959. Inc nonprofit. Tri (Sept-July).
Bldgs 3. 2 Libs 5000 vols. Gym.

Located on the grounds of the British Embassy, this school was founded to provide a primary education for children of British Embassy staff and the British community in Ankara. Preparing students for British secondary education the curriculum emphasizes language development, mathematics and arts and crafts. English-speaking students from other countries are admitted when vacancies permit.

INTERNATIONAL COMMUNITY SCHOOL
Day Coed Ages 4-15. Gr N-9.

Istanbul, Turkey. Arnavutkoy P.K. I. Tel. 63-57-50.
Carol Fonger, BA, Univ. of Wisconsin, Prin.
Pre-Prep Gen Acad. Tests SSAT. Curr—USA. Ll—Eng. CF—Fr Turkish Latin Sci Comp Sci Hist Music. Sl—EFL.
Enr 185. B 105; G 80. Elem 170, Sec 15. US—50. Grad '84—15.
Fac 24. Full 16/Part 8. M 4; F 20. US 14.
Tui $4500. Schol.
Est 1911. Nonprofit. Sem (Sept-Je). ISS. Accred NEASC.
Bldgs 3. Lib 6000 vols. Gym.

Sponsored by Robert College, the Community School serves both the American residents in Istanbul and students from over 30 nations. With an academic program based on the American system, the school teaches French and Turkish in all grades, offering Latin from grade seven. Numerous field trips are scheduled to heighten students awareness of Istanbul's many historic and cultural sites. The school administers the U.S. Secondary School Admissions Test, for which it is a recognized center.

ROBERT COLLEGE
Bdg & Day Coed Ages 11-19. Gr 7-12.

Istanbul, Turkey. Orta-Lise P.K. 1 Arnavutkoy. Tel. 65-34-30.
A. Donn Kesselheim, Head.

Col Prep. Tests CEEB GCE. Curr—USA Nat. LI—Eng Turk. A—Math Sci Eng. CF—Fr Ger Turkish Lit & Soc Stud.
Enr 907. B 472; G 435. Elem 509, Sec 398. Grad '84—134. Col—132.
Fac 66. Full 63/Part 3. US 24.
Tui Bdg 113,750 LT; Day 60,000 LT (+var). Schol.
Est 1863. Inc nonprofit. Sem (Oct-Je). ECIS ISS NAIS.
Bldgs 7. Dorms 2. Lib 30,000 vols. Gym. Tennis crts. Fields.

The present Robert College is the result of the 1971 merger between Robert Academy for Boys, founded in 1863, and the American College for Girls, established in 1871. The university division of Robert College, the oldest American-sponsored college abroad, was given to the Turkish government and is now the University of the Bosphorus.

The enrollment is predominantly Turkish and the curriculum follows patterns of both the United States and Turkey. English is the language of instruction for science and math while the humanities are conducted in Turkish. All college preparatory courses are conducted on a bilingual basis. Extracurricular activities include computer science, organic chemistry, music, photography and child psychology.

UNITED ARAB EMIRATES

Formed in 1971, the United Arab Emirates is a federation of seven Trucial States—Abu Dhabi, Dubai, Sharjah, Ajman, Fujairah, Ras al Khaimah and Um al-Quwain. These states are situated along the southern coast of the Persian Gulf. Each state has its own ruler and local government.

The country is a major world producer of oil, its chief export. Abu Dhabi is the capital and largest city. The monetary unit is the dirham (Dh) and Arabic is the official language.

AMERICAN COMMUNITY SCHOOL OF ABU DHABI
Day Coed Ages 5-14. Gr K-9.

Abu Dhabi, United Arab Emirates. P.O. Box 4005. Tel. 361461. Telex: 22275EM.
Dr. David Miller, PhD, Miami Univ., Supt.
Pre-Prep Gen Acad. Curr—USA. LI—Eng. CF—Arabic Fr Soc Stud Sci Math. SI—Rem & Dev Reading Tut.
Enr 350. B170; G 180. Elem 325, Sec 25. US—160. Grad '84—25.
Fac 31. Full 31. M 9; F 22. US.
Tui $4200.
Est 1972. Inc nonprofit. Sem (Sept-Je). A/OS ISS NE/SA. Accred MSA.
Bldg. Lib 12,000 vols. Courts. Field. Gym.

This school offers an American curriculum to the children of predominantly American families living in Abu Dhabi. Arabic and French are offered as language electives. Sports, drama, chorus and puppetry are among the extracurricular activities offered.

DUBAI COLLEGE
 Day Coed Ages 12-19. Gr 7-12.

Dubai, United Arab Emirates. P.O. Box 837. Tel. Dubai 481212.
Tom B. Jackson, MA, Cambridge, Head.
Col Prep Gen Acad. Tests GCE. Curr—UK. LI—Eng. A—Math Sci Fr
 Hist Geog Art Music. CF—Ger Arabic. SI—Rem & Dev Math & Read.
Enr 429. B 230; G 199. Elem 173, Sec 256. Grad '84—15. Col—10.
Fac 36. Full 32/Part 4. M 21; F 15. UK.
Tui 15,900 Dh.
Est 1978. Nonprofit. Tri (Sept-Je). ISS.
Bldgs 4. Lib 8000 vols. Field. Pool. Crts.

This school has a student:teacher ration of 11:1 and emphasizes basic
subjects which prepare pupils for the G.C.E. 'O' and 'A' levels. Art
studios, science labs, music rooms and a computer center are among the
facilities. Extracurricular activities include class-associated clubs,
publications, musical groups and outings. Students may also take part in
basketball, volleyball, tennis, gymnastics, swimming, soccer, softball,
sailing, squash and ping-pong.

JUMAIRAH AMERICAN SCHOOL
 Day Coed Ages 5-14. Gr K-9.

Dubai, United Arab Emirates. P.O. Box 2222. Tel. 440824.
Dr. Robert Bell, Head.
Prep-Prep. Tests SSAT. Curr—USA. LI—Eng. A—Lang Arts Math.
 CF—Fr Arabic Middle East Culture Drama Art Photog. SI—Rem
 Read.
Enr 460.
Fac 31.
Tui $1675-5050.
Summer Session. Acad Rec. 3 wks.
Est 1962. Inc nonprofit. Sem (Sept.Je). ISS NE/SA. Accred MSA.
Bldgs 1. Gym. Tennis crts 2. Playground.

Established by the Dubai Petroleum Company, this school offers a
traditional U.S. curriculum. Middle East culture classes are required for
all students. Instruction is semi-departmentalized in grades one through
five. The majority of students graduating from Jumairah enter boarding
schools in the United States.

SHARJAH ENGLISH SCHOOL
 Day Coed Ages 3½-14. Gr N-8.

Sharjah, United Arab Emirates. P.O. Box 1600. Tel. Sharjah 22779.
Michael J. E. Short, Cert Ed, Southampton, DipTh, London, Head.
Pre-Prep Gen Acad. Tests CEE. Curr—UK. LI—Eng. CF—Fr Arabic
 Math Sci Soc Stud. SI—Rem & Dev Read.

Enr 335. B 170; G 165. US—7.
Fac 25. Full 20/ Part 5. M 7; F 18. UK.
Tui $2150-2875.
Est 1974. Inc nonprofit. Tri (Sept-Je). ISS.
Lib 3500 vols. Gym.

Established to provide an education for children of British families living in Sharjah, this school has expanded rapidly and now accepts English-speaking students of all nationalities. The British curriculum features courses in math, science, French, music, art and physical education. Extracurricular activities include soccer, netball, tennis, ballet gymnastics, badminton, history society and clubs in chess, art and drama.

YEMEN

At the southern tip of the Arabian peninsula, the People's Democratic Republic of Yemen is a mountainous country on the Red Sea. Unlike most Arab countries, the soil and climate are well suited to agriculture. Sanaa is capital and largest city. The monetary unit is the riyal (R) and Arabic is the official language.

SANAA INTERNATIONAL SCHOOL
　　Day Coed Ages 5-16. Gr K-11.

Sanaa, Yemen. Box 2002.
James E. Gilson, BS, Seattle Pacific Univ., MS, Oregon State Univ., Dir.
Col Prep Gen Acad. Curr—USA. LI—Eng. CF—Arabic Fr Art Music. SI—ESL.
Enr 228. B 114; G 114. Elem 204, Sec 24. US—48.
Fac 22. Full 20/Part 2. M 8; F 14. US 15.
Tui $6400.
Est 1971. Inc nonprofit. Tri (Aug-Je). A/OS ISS NE/SA.
Bldgs 2. Lib. Fields. Crt.

Employing teaching methods and curriculum organization similar to those found in Europe and America, Sanaa International School enrolls students of several different nationalities. The school's primary purpose is to enable its students to continue schooling in their home countries with a minimum of adjustment problems. The program is individualized, with English also taught as a second language. British studies are available to upper level students.

SOUTH & SOUTHEAST ASIA

BANGLADESH

Formerly East Pakistan, the People's Republic of Bangladesh, with the help of India, won independence from West Pakistan in 1971. Although culturally similar to their Indian neighbors in West Bengal, the Bengalis are predominantly Moslem rather than Hindu. Dhaka is the capital and the taka (T) is the unit of currency. Urdu and English are the principal languages.

AMERICAN INTERNATIONAL SCHOOL OF DHAKA
Day Coed Ages 5-15. Gr K-9.

Dhaka, Bangladesh. Lakeshore Drive, Baridhara. Tel. 602298.
Mail to: c/o American Embassy Dhaka, Dept. of State, Washington, DC 20520.
Stephen Kapner, BA, Univ. of Rochester, MA, New York Univ., Supt Univ., Supt.
Pre-Prep. Curr—USA. LI—Eng. CF—Bangla ESL Fr.
Enr 340. B 172; G 168. Elem 319, Sec 21.
Fac 36. US 25.
Tui $1750-3500 (+ $300).
Summer Session. Rec. Tui $100/6 wks.
Est 1971. Nonprofit. Sem (Aug-Je). A/OS ISS NE/SA.
Bldgs 1. Lib 12,000 vols. Courts. Fields.

Replacing the former Dacca American Society School, founded in l956, this school accepts students of all nationalities. Classes through grade six are self-contained. The curriculum includes art, music and South Asian studies, complemented by diverse extracurricular activities. Typing is offered in the elective program.

BURMA

Annexed to India in 1937, and becoming a Commonwealth country in 1941, Burma gained complete independence in 1948. A major battleground in World War II, the 800-mile Burma Road was the Allies' vital supply route to China. A new Constitution was adopted in 1974, establishing Burma as a Socialist Democratic Republic with a 451-seat unicameral legislature called the People's Congress. Rangoon, on the Gulf of Martaban, is the chief port and capital. The monetary unit is the kyat (K). Burmese is the official language.

THE INTERNATIONAL SCHOOL OF RANGOON
  Day Coed Ages 5-15. Gr K-8.

Rangoon, Burma. 61 Insein Rd. Kamayut P.O. Tel. 30678.
Mail to: c/o American Embassy Rangoon, U.S. Dept. of State,
  Washington, DC 20520.
Ted Grander, Prin.
Gen Acad. Curr—USA. LI—Eng.
Enr 80.
Fac 17.
Tui $1430-2200 (+ $200).
Summer Session. Rec. 4 wks.
Est 1955. Nonprofit. Sem (Aug-Je). A/OS EARCOS ISS. Accred WASC.
Bldgs 2. Lib 5000 vols. Field.

Enrolling students from the United States, Philippines, Korea and
Thailand, this parent-cooperative school is sponsored by the U.S.
government. The basic elementary curriculum is supplemented by
sports, cookery, creative writing, Burmese and embroidery.

INDIA

Birthplace of Hinduism, Buddhism, Jainism and Sikhism, India
possesses one of the oldest civilizations in the world, dating from 3000
B.C. in the Indus Valley. During its long history, the land has had
numerous invaders, Darius of Persia and Alexander the Great among
the earliest. Moguls and Viceroys left their marks during 500 years of
Moslem Empire and 250 years of European and British domination. The
unique climate brings the seasonal monsoon and produces tropical heat
in the south and near Arctic cold in the Himalayan north.

An independent republic since 1950, India today is a union of 22
federated states and 9 territories, and a member of the British
Commonwealth of Nations. There are more than a dozen principal
languages, but nearly half the population speaks Hindi, which became
the official language in 1965. Urdu is the principal Moslem language,
spoken by 10% of the people, and English is used extensively in India's
2000 colleges and universities. The capital city is New Delhi and the
country's monetary unit is the rupee (Rs).

KODAIKANAL INTERNATIONAL SCHOOL
  Bdg Coed Ages 10-18; Day Coed 6-18. Gr N-12.

Kodaikanal (Tamil Nadu) 624101, India. Tel. 278.
Norman C. Habel, BD, PhD, Concordia, Prin.
Col Prep. Tests CEEB IB. Curr—USA. LI—Eng. CF—Fr Ger Hindi Tamil
  Fine Arts. SI—ESL.
Enr 450. B 180/80; G 130/60. Elem 100, Sec 350. US—125. Grad
  '84—55. Col—52.
Fac 65. Full 65. M 30; F 35. Intl.

Tui Bdg Rs 25,000 (+ Rs 5000); Day Rs 18,000. Schol.
Est 1901. Inc nonprofit. Sem (July-May). ISS. Accred MSA.
Bldgs 20. Dorms 11. Lib 20,000 vols. Field. Gym.

United States youths customarily account for 40% of the international enrollment at Kodaikanal School. The curriculum parallels United States lines with adaptations to the Indian environment and to the needs of non-American students. Preparation is offered for the U.S. College Boards and the International Baccalaureate.

The school is located on an extensive plateau in the hill station of Kodaikanal, about 125 miles above the southern tip of India. Surrounded by rolling hills and bordering a lake, the school, with its ten-acre plant, enjoys a natural setting for hiking, camping and other outdoor activities. The 7000-foot elevation insures a temperate climate.

WOODSTOCK SCHOOL
Bdg & Day Coed Ages 6-19. Gr K-12.

Mussoorie (Uttar Pradesh) 248179, India. Tel. 2610.
W.W. Jones, BA, Univ. of Pennsylvania, MDiv, STM, Yale, Prin.
Col Prep. Tests CEEB SSAT GCE. Curr—USA. Ll—Eng. A—Fr Ger Eng Hist Math Sci Art Music. CF—Hindi Soc Stud Relig Typ Bookkeeping Comp Sci Drama Indus Arts. SI—ESL Rem & Dev Math & Read Tut.
Enr 447. B 182/58; G 158/49. Elem 208, Sec 239. US—108. Grad '84—49. Col—45.
Fac 54. Full 48/Part 6. M 22; F 32. US 21.
Tui Bdg $4000 (+ $150); Day $650-4000 (+ $50). Schol.
Est 1854. Nonprofit. Sem (July-Je). ISS NE/SA. Accred MSA.
Bldgs 7. Dorms 5. Lib 30,000 vols. Field. Gym. Pool. Playground.

This long-established international Christian school's enrollment reflects a mix of North American, Indian and other nationalities. The curriculum, which is college preparatory, offers U.S. College Board and British G.C.E. 'A' and 'O' level exam preparation. Electives in industrial arts, commercial subjects and home economics are also available. Emphasis is placed on the intercultural program, with courses in Hindi and special instruction in Indian music and dance. Students have made many field trips to noted cultural, pilgrim and tourist centers in India.

Set on a hillside on the first range of the Himalayas at an altitude of 6500 feet, the school offers ample opportunity for outdoor life. The academic year begins in late July and ends the following June, with the long two and a half-month vacation taken during the Himalayan winter from December to February. An English mission school during its first 20 years, then operated by the American Presbyterian Mission as a girl's school for the next 50 years, Woodstock was until 1976 under cooperative missionary management. Now it is a registered Indian Society, whose members are chosen from the parent body and represent the American, Indian and "other" national interests present in the school.

AMERICAN EMBASSY SCHOOL
  Day Coed Ages 3-18. Gr N-12.

New Delhi 110021, India. Chandragupta Marg, Chanakyapuri. Tel. 605949.
Mail to: c/o American Embassy New Delhi, Dept. of State, Washington, DC 20520.
John M. Nicklas, MSEd, Indiana Univ., EdD, Virinia Tech. Univ., Dir.
Col Prep. Tests IB CEEB SSAT. Curr—USA. LI—Eng. A—Eng Fr His Sci Calc. CF—Span Ger Hindi Soc Stud Humanities Photog Indus Arts Yoga. SI—Rem & Dev Read Tut.
Enr 540. B 257; G 283. US—173. Grad '84—26. Col—22.
Fac 60. Full 46/Part 14. M 18; F 42. US 39.
Tui $900-4050. Schol.
Summer Session. Rec. Tui $95. 5 wks.
Est 1952. Inc nonprofit. Sem (Aug-May). A/OS ISS NAIS NE/SA. Accred MSA.
Bldgs 4. Lib 20,000 vols. Athletic facilities.

Housed in several modified geodesic dome-style buildings near the American Embassy, the school draws students from some 35 nationalities. Within the college preparatory curriculum there are opportunities for seminar study of India and an independent study program. E.S.L. classes are available for non-English speaking students. Students prepare for the U.S. College Boards and the International Baccalaureate with most graduates attending colleges and universities throughout the United States.

HEBRON SCHOOL
  Bdg & Day Coed Ages 5-18. Gr 1-PG.

Ootacamund (Tamil Nadu), India. Lushington Hall. Tel. Ootacamund 2587.
J. C. Ingleby, MA, DipEd, Oxford, Prin.
Col Prep. Tests GCE. Curr—UK. LI—Eng. CF—Fr Ger Sci Soc Stud Relig Art Music Geog.
Enr 221. Elem 140, Sec 62, PG 19. US—2. Grad '84—25. Col—10.
Fac 47. US 3. UK.
Tui Bdg Rs 4800-5430/term; Day Rs 1150-1520.
Est 1899. Inc nonprofit. Sem (Aug-Je).
Bldgs 8. Dorms 6. Lib 10,000 vols. Courts. Fields. Pool.

Located on a 19-acre wooded estate overlooking the Government Botanical Gardens, Hebron prepares students for the G.C.E. 'O' and 'A' level examinations. Basic subjects including English, math and religious studies are required of all students. The athletic program includes hockey, basketball, tennis, gymnastics, cricket, baseball, volleyball and swimming.

LAWRENCE SCHOOL
Bdg Coed Ages 8-18. Gr 4-12.

Sanawar 173202 (Punjab), India. Simla Hills. Tel. Kasauli 9.
S. R. Das, MA, Cantab, Head.
Pre-Prep Col Prep. Curr—Nat. LI—Eng.
Fac 50.
Tui Bdg 5300 Rs (+ 1500 Rs).
Est 1847. Nonprofit. Sem (Feb-Nov). ISS.
Bldgs 200. Dorms 15. Lib 20,000 vols. Athletic facilities.

A coeducational section provides education in the basic subjects to children in grades four through six. Separate divisions for boys and girls are maintained throughout the secondary years. The school has extensive grounds for recreation and co-curricular activities include hiking, camping and social projects. Classical Indian music and dance are taught as well as arts, crafts, dramatics and debating.

INDONESIA

Situated between Indochina and Australia, the 3000 islands of the Republic of Indonesia comprise the world's largest archipelago. A Dutch overseas territory until independence in 1949, Indonesia is one of the world's richest natural areas, with abundant mineral resources and fertile soil. The capital, Jakarta, is on the island of Java. The rupiah (Rp) is the monetary unit and Bahase Indonesia is the official language.

BANDUNG INTERNATIONAL SCHOOL
Day Coed Ages 3-14. Gr N-8.

Bandung, Indonesia. J1. Terusan Pasteur. Kotak Pos 132. Tel. 022 613615. Telex: 28326 AUSPRO BD.
Garry York, Prin.
Gen Acad Pre-Prep. Curr—USA UK. LI—Eng. CF—Indonesian Fr Math Eng Soc Stud Sci. SI—Rem & Dev Read & Math Tut ESL.
Enr 127. US—24.
Fac 17. Full 12/Part 5. M 3; F 14. US 3. Intl.
Tui $3700.
Est 1971. Nonprofit. Tri (Sept-Je). EARCOS.
Bldgs 3. Lib 6000 vols. Gym. Sports field.

The curriculum is designed to integrate children from many different countries who are temporarily residing in Indonesia. A primary aim is to provide the necessary background in the basic subjects to facilitate a student's return to their school at home. Instruction in the Indonesian language and culture is another feature of the program as well as sports, interest clubs, crafts and drama.

JAKARTA INTERNATIONAL SCHOOL
Day Coed Ages 5-18. Gr K-12.

Jakarta (Selatan), Indonesia J1. Terogong Raya 33, Cilandak. P.O. Box 79/KBT. Tel. 762555.

John Magagara, Supt.

Col Prep. Tests IB GCE CEEB SSAT. Curr—UK USA. LI—Eng. CF—Comp Sci Dutch Ger Soc Stud ESL Fr Indonesian Span Sci Eng Math.

Enr 2106. B 1084; G 1022. US—797. Grad'84—33 Col—90.

Fac 170. Full 152/Part 18. M 37; F 133. US 92.

Tui $3000-5000. Schol.

Est 1951. Nonprofit. Sem (Aug-Je). A/OS EARCOS ISS. Accred WASC.

Bldgs 21. Lib 45,000 vols. Gym. Fields. Tennis crts. Swimming pool. Theatre.

Jakarta International School's enrollment represents 51 nationalities, and although the curriculum is American, it reflects the school's international composition. Students are prepared for the CEEB, G.C.E. and SSAT exams, and the two-year International Baccalaureate Program is also featured. Advanced level courses are available in most subjects and a full range of athletic and extracurricular activities includes soccer, swimming, volleyball, cross country, drama, chess, music and debate.

MEDAN INTERNATIONAL SCHOOL
Day Coed Ages 4-15. Gr K-9.

Medan (North Sumatra), Indonesia. P.O. Box 191. Tel. 515-099.

Kay Howdeshell, BS, MS, Univ. of Kentucky, Prin Auburn, Prin.

Gen Acad. Curr—USA. LI—Eng. CF—Fr Indonesian. SI—Rev & Dev Math Read Tut ESL.

Enr 80. US—32.

Fac 14. Full 8/Part 6 US 8.

Tui $4800-7200 (+ $500). Schol.

Est 1969. Inc. Tri (Aug-Je). A/OS ISS EARCOS. Accred WASC.

Bldgs 8. Lib 9000 vols. Field. Gym. Pool.

This school teaches French and Indonesian in kindergarten through grade nine. To meet the diverse interests of the school's international student body, the curriculum incorporates elements of educational programs native to several English-speaking countries. The school occupies a large villa in a residential area of Medan.

BAMBOO RIVER INTERNATIONAL SCHOOL
Bdg Coed Ages 8-14. Day 6-14. Gr K-8.

Serukam (Kalimantan Barat), Indonesia. Kotak Pos 20, Singkawan. Stanley W. Hagberg, AB, Gordon College, BD, Westminster Seminary, Prin.

Pre-Prep. Curr—USA. LI—Eng. CF—Indonesian Read Math. SI—Rem
Read.
Enr 17. B 4/3; G 5/5. US—17.
Fac 5. Full 4/Part 1. M 2; F 3. US.
Tui Bdg $1250; Day $700.
Est 1968. Baptist. Quar (Aug-May). ISS.
Bldgs 3. Dorms 1. Lib 8000 vols. Athletic facilities.

Serving only non-Indonesians, this school provides an American
education for the children of Baptist missionaries stationed in Indonesia.
Indonesian is offered as an elective.

SURABAYA INTERNATIONAL SCHOOL
Day Coed Ages 4-15. Gr N-9.

Surabaya 60225 (East Java), Indonesia. Tromol Pos 2 SBDK, Jalan
Kupang Indah IX/17. Tel. (031) 69324.
William Vodarski, BA, Univ. of Washington, MEd, Central Washington
Univ., Prin.
Gen Acad. Curr—US. LI—Eng. CF—Fr Indonesian World Hist ESL.
SI—Rem & Dev Read.
Enr 152. B 75; G 77. Elem 148, Sec 4.
Fac 20. Full 15/Part 5. M 3; F 17. US 7.
Tui $1800-3650.
Summer Session. Rec. Tui $200. 4 wks.
Est 1972. Inc nonprofit. Tri (Aug-Je). A/OS EARCOS ISS.
Bldgs 5. Lib 5000 vols. Gym. Field.

This school offers an American curriculum adapted to the needs of its
international student body. A strong language arts program aims at
increasing the student's competency and fluency in communication, and
English as a Second Language is available to all who need it. Additional
courses in typing, woodworking, home economics and computer are
offered as after school activities. Extracurricular activities include judo,
volleyball, basketball and baseball.

MALAYSIA

A long strip of land which forms the most southerly part of mainland
Asia, the present-day Federation of Malaysia was created in 1963 when
Malaya, itself an independent federation, joined with Singapore,
Sarawak and Sabah, all former British colonies. Singapore, which
accounted for a fifth of the new Federation's population, withdrew in
1965.

Malay, written in Arabic script, is the national language, but English is
frequently used. The capital is Kuala Lumpur and the monetary unit is
the Malaysian dollar (M$).

INTERNATIONAL SCHOOL OF KUALA LUMPUR
Day Coed Ages 5-18. Gr K-12.

Kuala Lumpur 19-03, Malaysia. Jalan Kerja Ayer Lama. Tel. 460522.
Mail to: P.O. Box 12645, Kuala Lumpur 10-02, Malaysia.
Joseph S. Kennedy, Admin.
Col Prep. Tests CEEB SSAT. Curr—USA. LI—Eng. A—Math Biol
Chem. CF—Span Malay Fr. SI—Rem Read ESL.
Enr 829. US—305.
Fac 82. Full 70/Part 12 US 61.
Tui $2456-4717 (+$1739).
Summer Session. Acad Rec. Tui $174/4 wks.
Est 1965. Nonprofit. Quar (Aug-Je). A/OS EARCOS ISS. Accred
WASC.
Lib 28,000 vols. Pool. Gym. Playing fields. Theatre.

Reflecting the international atmosphere of Malaysia, this school has an enrollment representative of more than 30 nations, almost half of which is American. Courses in French, Spanish, Malay, and Southeast Asia enrich the standard American curriculum which features individualized instruction and extensive use of audio-visual materials. Students prepare for the U.S. College Boards, with graduates attending leading colleges and universities throughout the United States. There is a full extracurricular program of athletics, clubs, student government and publications.

NEPAL

In the Himalayas, bordered by India and Tibet, the Kingdom of Nepal has within its borders the highest mountains in the world, including Mt. Everest. Closed to the outside world for centuries, its capital, Kathmandu, was opened to British residents in 1816. Nepal is ruled under a constitutional monarchy and the country's monetary unit is the Nepalese rupee (NR). Nepali is the official language.

BRITISH PRIMARY SCHOOL, KATHMANDU
Day Coed Ages 5-11. Gr K-6.

Kathmandu, Nepal. P.O. Box 566. Tel. 21794.
Richard Cliff, Head.
Gen Acad. Curr—UK. LI—Eng.
Enr 63.
Fac 4.
Tui 1400/mo NRs.
Est 1966. Nonprofit. Quar (July-Je). ISS.
Lib. Athletic facilities.

This school provides a British primary education for children of the international English-speaking population living in Kathmandu. Children from Britain, Australia, Canada, India, Europe and the United States attend.

LINCOLN SCHOOL
  Day Coed Ages 5-15. Gr K-9.

Kathmandu, Nepal. Tel. 214482.
Mail to: Kathmandu (ID), Dept. of State, Washington, DC 20520.
Frederick L. Thompson, BA, MA, Univ. of Wisconsin, Prin.
Gen Acad. Tests SSAT. Curr—USA. LI—Eng. CF—Fr Ger Span Nepali
  Soc Stud Art Music. SI—Rem Read.
Enr 180. B 107, G 73 US—66.
Fac 21. Full 16/Part 5. M 5; F 16 US 17.
Tui $2420-4170 (+ $950).
Summer Session. Rec. Tui $100/4 wks.
Est 1954. Inc nonprofit. Sem (Aug-Je). A/OS ISS NE/SA.
Bldgs 5. Lib 5000 vols. Field.

The Lincoln School offers a curriculum similar to that of U.S. elementary and intermediate schools. Grades one to five are self contained, emphasizing reading and mathematics while instruction to students in the upper grades is departmentalized. English as a Second Language is offered to children needing special instruction in English and the culture of Nepal is studied in regular subject areas and through a Nepal Field Studies program. Older students participate in an annual trek into mountain villages and India in early March.

PAKISTAN

Deriving its name from the Persian, meaning "Land of the Pure," the Islamic Republic of Pakistan shares the long history of the Indian Subcontinent, its most influential event being the introduction of Islam with the Arab invasion of 711 A.D. For 25 years, Pakistan occupied two zones, East and West Pakistan, 1000 miles apart at opposite ends of India. In 1971, with the aid of Indian troops, East Pakistan changed its name to Bangladesh and proclaimed itself independent.

English is the official language, and the country's monetary unit is the rupee (PR). Islamabad is the capital.

INTERNATIONAL SCHOOL OF ISLAMABAD
  Day Coed Ages 3½-19. Gr N-12.

Islamabad, Pakistan. Sector H-9/1. P.O. Box 1124. Tel. 842401/2.
Mail to: American Embassy Islamabad, Dept. of State, Washington, DC
  20520.
Larry N. Crouch, BA, Univ. of Washington, MA, Univ. of California,
  Supt.
Col Prep. Tests CEEB SSAT. Curr—USA. LI—Eng. A—Fr Span Ger
  Calc Chem Physics. CF—Fine Arts ESL Urdu. SI—Tut.
Enr 434. Elem 314, Sec 120. US—144. Grad '84—20. Col—20.
Fac 47. Full 40/Part 7. M 7; F 40. US 27.
Tui $1300-4500.

Est 1962. Sem (Aug-Je). A/OS ISS NE/SA, Accred MSA.
Bldg. Lib 20,000 vols. Fields 2. Tennis crts 2.

Located on a 20-acre campus between Islamabad and Rawalpindi, this school provides an English-speaking education to an international enrollment comprised mostly of Americans and Pakistanis. The American curriculum is geared toward admission to colleges and universities in the United States.

Electives include shorthand, drama, photography and acting and theatre techniques. The sports program offers football, soccer, volleyball, swimming, field hockey and basketball.

KARACHI AMERICAN SOCIETY SCHOOL
Day Coed Ages 4-18. Gr N-12.

Karachi 8, Pakistan. Amir Khusro Rd. K.D.A. Scheme #1. Tel. 433557.
Mail to: c/o American Consulate General Karachi, Dept. of State, Washington, DC 20520.
Anthony Horton, Supt.
Col Prep. Tests CEEB SSAT. Curr—USA. LI—Eng. CF—Fr Span Urdu ESL Journalism Asian Stud Anthro.
Enr 364. US—75.
Fac 35. US 25.
Tui $1790-3590. Schol.
Summer Session. Rec.
Est 1952. Nonprofit. Sem (Aug-May). A/OS ISS NE/SA. Accred MSA.
Bldgs 7. Lib 12,000 vols. Labs. Fields.

This school is located on a ten-acre campus and follows an American curriculum. E.S.L. is conducted from nursery through grade 12. Americans and Pakistanis comprise the majority of students and faculty. A sports program includes soccer, football, swimming and hockey.

LAHORE AMERICAN SCHOOL
Day Coed Ages 4-18. Gr N-12.

Lahore, Pakistan. Al-Riaze. Canal Bank. Tel. 870-895.
Mail to: AmConGen (Lahore), Dept. of State, Washington, DC 20520.
Andrew Dubin, Supt.
Col Prep. Tests CEEB. Curr—USA. LI—Eng.
Enr 277.
Fac 43.
Tui $935-3000. Schol.
Est 1956. Inc nonprofit. Sem (Aug-May). A/OS ISS NE/SA.
Lib 18,000 vols. Labs. Playground. Swimming pool. Crts.

An international flavor prevails at this American-sponsored school enrolling students from 15 countries. Elementary classes emphasize basic academic skills with the secondary curriculum geared toward the U.S. College Boards. The program is supplemented by offerings in after-school sports, arts, graphics, mechanical drawing, drama and excursions to historical sites.

Three miles from the main business district of Lahore, chief inland city of Pakistan, the school is located on four and one-half acres of wooded land.

MURREE CHRISTIAN SCHOOL
Bdg & Day Coed Ages 6½-18. Gr K-12.

Murree Hills, Pakistan. P.O. Jhika Gali. Tel. 2321.

Charles A. Roub, BA, Mankato State College, MA, Univ. of Minnesota, BD, Bethel Seminary, Prin.

Col Prep Gen Acad. Tests SSAT GCE. Curr—USA UK. LI—Eng. A—Math. CF—Fr Lat Urdu US Hist Man Arts Econ. SI—Rem & Dev Read Tut.

Enr 173. B 56/7; G 43/4. US—41. Grad '84—9. Col—6.

Fac 17. Full 14/Part 3. M 9; F 8. US 4. UK.

Tui Bdg $4000; Day $3700.

Est 1956. Inc 1958 nonprofit. Missionary. Sem (Aug-July). ISS.

Bldgs 4. Dorms 2. Lib 10,000 vols. Athletic facilities.

This interdenominational Christian school follows British and American teaching lines and offers preparation for the U.S. College Boards and the Scottish S.C.E. Ordinary and Highers examinations. The enrollment consists primarily of missionary children from 18 countries. Jhika Gali is about 30 miles from the capital city of Islamabad.

SEYCHELLES

An archipelago in the Indian Ocean northeast of Madagascar, Seychelles became an independent republic of the Commonwealth of Nations in 1974. Britain had seized the country from France in 1810. The capital city is Victoria; the nation's currency is the Seychelles rupee (SRu). English and French are the official languages.

THE INTERNATIONAL SCHOOL
Day Coed Ages 3-13. Gr K-6.

Victoria (Mahe), Seychelles. P.O. Box 315. Tel. 22641.

Mrs. Shirley Hill, Head.

Pre-Prep. Curr—UK. LI—Eng. CF—Fr Math Singing Sci Drama. SI—Eng.

Enr 100. US—16.

Fac 9. US 1. UK.

Tui $900-1685 (+ $35).

Est 1969. Nonprofit. Tri (Sept-July). A/OS ISA.

Bldgs 2. Lib 800 vols. Fields.

This school enrolls students from France, Great Britain, India, Norway, the United States and 10 other nations. Special English classes and individual tuition rates are arranged for non-English speaking students. Remedial classes are conducted in English and reading. An afternoon sports program offers football and rugby.

SINGAPORE

An island off the southern tip of the Malay Peninsula and site of the world's fifth largest port, in 1965 this former British crown colony broke from the two-year-old Federation of Malaysia and became the 117th member of the United Nations. The city of Singapore is capital of the independent island republic and the singapore dollar (S$) is the monetary unit. Malay, Chinese and English are the principal languages.

INTERNATIONAL SCHOOL OF SINGAPORE
Day Coed Ages 5-19. Gr K-12.

Singapore 0410, Singapore. Preston Rd. Tel. 475-4188. Telex: RS34188 INTLSH.
Thomas E. Hart, MA, MEd, Univ. of Oregon, Head.
Col Prep Gen Acad. Tests GCE CEEB. Curr—USA UK. LI—Eng. A—Fr Math Hist Chem Geog Art Econ Physics Biol. CF—Music Asian Stud Bus Journalism Comp Drama Ecology. SI—Tut ESL.
Enr 366. B 192; G 174. Elem 223, Sec 143. US—15. Grad '84—5. Col—4.
Fac 40. Full 37/Part 3. M 10; F 30. UK US.
Tui S$6000-8000 (+ S$1000).
Summer Session. ESL. Tui $150 (+ $50). 4 wks.
Est 1981. Inc nonprofit. Sem (Sept-Je). EARCOS ISS.
Bldgs 7. 2 Libs 20,000 vols. Crts.

This school hosts an international student body and offers the option of study for either an American high school diploma or the G.C.E. 'O' and 'A' levels. During the fourth and fifth grades, a foreign language is added to basic academic subjects. An intensive English as a Second Language program, usually completed within one year, is available to prepare foreign speakers for mainstream classes. Soccer, volleyball, basketball, rugby, squash, badminton, swimming and track and field are included in the sports itinerary.

SINGAPORE AMERICAN SCHOOL
Day Coed Ages 5-18. Gr K-12.

Singapore 1026, Singapore. 60 King's Rd. Tel. 4665-611.
Dr. Melvin H. Kuhbander, Supt.
Col Prep Gen Acad. Tests CEEB. Curr—USA. LI—Eng.
Enr 1881.
Fac 130.
Tui $1643-3756 (+ $479).

Est 1956. Inc nonprofit. Sem (Aug-Je). A/OS ISS NAIS EARCOS.
Accred WASC.
Bldgs 2. Libs 2. Labs. Gyms 2. Theater.

Children of over 40 different nationalities attend Singapore American School, although the majority are United States citizens. The American curriculum offers U.S. College Boards preparation, with most of the graduates entering colleges and universities. Advanced Placement work is available in chemistry, physics, calculus, English, foreign language and U.S. history. Business and industrial education, home economics and music are among elective offerings. A one-week interim semester is featured during which high school students have an opportunity for a variety of educational alternatives.

TANGLIN TRUST SCHOOLS
  Day Coed Ages 3-11. Gr N-6.

Singapore 0513, Singapore. Portsdown Rd. Tel. 7780771.
Gen Acad. Curr—UK. LI—Eng. CF—Art Music Comp.
Enr 1297.
Fac 80. Full 62/Part 18.
Tui S$2700-3750 (+ S$750).
Est 1961. Sem (Sept-July).
Gym. Fields. Crt.

The Tanglin Trust Schools comprise a nursery school for children ages three to four, an infant school for students ages four to seven, and a junior school. In addition to the British-based primary curriculum, students participate in gymnastics, soccer, rugby, cricket, badminton, arts and crafts and school yearbook. The campus is located six miles from the city center, close to the University of Singapore.

SRI LANKA

Known to the Arabs in ancient times as the "Emerald Isle," and later to the British as "The Pearl of the Orient," the Democratic Socialist Republic of Sri Lanka is an independent island nation situated off the southeast coast of India. Famous for its tropical beauty, the country's name was changed from Ceylon to Sri Lanka in 1972. The Sinhalese today comprise over 70% of the population. The capital is Colombo, the principal language is Sinhalese and the monetary unit is the Sri Lanka rupee.

OVERSEAS CHILDREN'S SCHOOL
  Day Coed Ages 3-18. Gr N-12.

Colombo 2, Sri Lanka. 47/51 Muttiah Rd. Tel. 25177.
Al Forster, Head.
Col Prep. Tests IB GCE. Curr—USA UK. LI—Eng. CF—Fr Lang Stud
  US Hist Geog Sci Math Arts. SI—Rem & Dev Math & Read ESL.

Enr 550. B 245; G 305. Elem 441, Sec 109. US—57.
Fac 72. Full 64/Part 8. M 21; F 51. US 5. Nat.
Tui Rs4250-18,000. Schol.
Summer Session. Rec Arts & Crafts. 3-4 wks.
Est 1957. Inc nonprofit. Tri (Sept-Je). A/OS ISS NE/SA.
Bldgs 3. Lib 12,000 vols. Lab. Crt.

A coed international day school, the Overseas Children's School follows an integration of American and British curricula. Students prepare for the British G.C.E. 'O' level exam in grades 9 and 10, and International Baccaluareate diploma and certificate courses are featured in grades 11 and 12. Over 25 nationalities are represented. American history and geography are offered for American children. Facilities are provided for a wide range of extracurricular activities.

THAILAND

Land of the Thai people, whose ancestors migrated from China many centuries ago, this Southeast Asian country is the site of the romantically depicted Kingdom of Siam. Known as Siam until 1939, when the present name was adopted, the Kingdom of Thailand today is a constitutional monarchy. Indian civilization has been the overriding historical influence on the country's tradition and culture, with Buddhism the state religion today.

The language is Thai, a derivation of Pali and Sanskrit, though English is frequently utilized officially. Bangkok is the capital, and the baht (B) is the country's monetary unit.

INTERNATIONAL SCHOOL BANGKOK
Day Coed Ages 5-19. Gr K-12.

Bangkok, Thailand. 36 Soi Ruam Chai Soi 15. Sukhumvit Rd. Tel. 252-8141.
Mail to: P.O. Box 11-1513, Bangkok 10112, Thailand.
Milton D. Jones, Head.
Col Prep. Tests CEEB ACT SSAT. Curr—USA Intl. LI—Eng. A—Bio Physics Eng US & Mod European Hist. CF—Fr Ger Span Latin Thai Hist Geog Music Art Indus Art Earth Sci. SI—ESL.
Enr 1300. Elem 866, Sec 434. US—598.
Fac 100. Full 91/Part 9. US 80.
Tui $3037-3820 (+ $300-450).
Summer Session. Acad Rem. 6 wks.
Est 1951. Inc nonprofit. Sem (Aug-Je). A/OS EARCOS ISS. Accred WASC.
Bldgs 5. Lib. Athletic facilities.

The majority of teachers and students at this large international day school in the capital city are from the United States. The balance off the enrollment is highly multinational, drawing significant numbers from Taiwan, Japan, Britain, India and Australia. An American curriculum and International Baccaluareate program are offered. English as a foreign language is provided for non-speakers.

The school serves as a demonstration center for several Thai teachers' colleges. Most of the U.S. graduates go on to universities in the United States.

RUAMRUDEE INTERNATIONAL
Day Coed Ages 5-20. Gr 1-12.

Bangkok, Thailand. 123/15 Ruamrudee Lane Wireless Rd. Tel. 2517933.
Mrs. Thavida Bijayendrayodhin, Prin.
Col Prep. Tests PSAT. Curr—USA. LI—Eng. A—Math. CF—Fr Span Thai.
Enr 870. B 420; G 450. Elem 430, Sec 440. US—30. Grad '84—56. Col—39.
Tui $1400-2000.
Summer Session. Acad. Tui $150. 6 wks.
Est 1957. Nonprofit. Roman Catholic. Sem (Aug-May). EARCOS. ISS Accred WASC.
Bldgs 3. Lib. Athletic facilities.

Operated by the American Redemptorist Fathers and the Sisters of the Infant Jesus this school admits children of non-Thai parents temporarily living in Thailand. The predominantly Thai faculty follows a curriculum directed towards the U.S. College Boards. Remedial courses are offered in English. English as a Foreign Language classes are offered for students under 16 years of age.

CHIANG MAI INTERNATIONAL SCHOOL
Day Coed Ages 5-13. Gr K-8.

Chiang Mai, Thailand. 13 Chetupon Rd. P.O. Box 38. Tel. 242027.
Clifford Broyles, Supt.
Gen Acad. Curr—USA. LI—Eng. CF—Thai Arts Man Arts. SI—ESL.
Enr 64. US—14.
Fac 15. Full 11/Part 4. US 3. Nat.
Tui $830-1660.
Est 1954. Presbyterian. Sem (Sept-Je). A/OS ISS EARCOS.
Bldgs 3. Lib. Lab. Aud.

Located in northern Thailand, this church-related school enrolls students of all nationalities. The curriculum is based on that of U.S. public schools. Bible is offered as an elective.

FAR EAST & PACIFIC ISLANDS

AUSTRALIA

The country "down under" the equator, the Commonwealth of Australia is both the largest island and the smallest continent in the world. First spotted by European ships in the 17th century, it was later the site of a penal colony to which British convicts were transported for nearly 60 years. Now an independent member of the British Commonwealth, Australia is known for its liberal legislation in health and education.

With sheep ranching as its largest industry, the country produces 30% of the world's wool. Australia is rich in mineral resources and unique animal and vegetable species. The western half of the continent is a desert plateau, a remote and barren region known as the "outback." The country today consists of six states and seven territories, with almost two-thirds of the population confined to the eastern coast. The capital is Canberra, and the unit of currency is the Australian dollar ($A). English is the official language.

NEW ENGLAND GIRLS' SCHOOL
Bdg Girls Ages 9-18; Day 5-18. Gr K-12.

Armidale 2350 (New South Wales), Australia. Uralla Rd. Tel. (067) 72-5922.

Jan Milburn, BA, DipEd, MEd, Sydney, PhD, London, Dir.

Col Prep Gen Acad. Curr—Nat. LI—Eng. A—Eng Math Phys Chem Fr. CF—Fr Ger Jap Lat Computer Stud.

Enr 420. G 350/70. Grad '84—47. Col—30.

Fac 36. Full 31/Part 5. M 6; F 30. US 1. Australia.

Tui Bdg $A3600 (+$A300); Day $A3000 (+$A300). Schol.

Est 1895. Nonprofit. Tri (Feb-Dec).

Bldgs 10. Dorms 4. Lib 9000 vols. Gym.

New England Girls' School, affiliated with the Church of England, is located on a 100-acre estate 350 miles north of Sydney. The academic program is geared to the students' individual needs and stresses the acquisition of basic skills. Remedial instruction is available to children with learning/emotional problems. All children in the primary school receive instruction in a foreign language and have the opportunity to become involved in extracurricular activities. The secondary course leads to the Higher School Certificate Examination.

An extensive language department offers French, German, Japanese and Latin, and conducts student exchanges with a Tokyo girls' school. The Activities Day Program devotes one of every ten days entirely to free-choice activities such as crafts, music, gymnastics, dancing, bush survival, drama, textiles and design, or service groups. Horsemanship is also featured as an extracurricular activity for all girls, and can be taken as an elective course in the 11th and 12th years. John Newcombe and Tony Roche use the school and its tennis courts as part of their summer tennis camp in Armidale.

ALL SAINTS' COLLEGE
Bdg & Day Coed Ages 12-18. Gr 7-12.

Bathurst 2795 (New South Wales), Australia. Ophir Rd. Tel. 063-313911.
D. G. Massey, MA, (Cantab), Head.
Col Prep Gen Acad. Curr—Nat. Ll—Eng.
Enr 267.
Fac 26.
Tui Bdg $A4806 (+ $250); Day $A2556 (+ $A200). Schol.
Est 1874. Nonprofit. Church of England. Tri (Feb-Dec). NAIS.
Bldgs 17. Dorms 5. Lib 20,000 vols. Courts. Fields. Swimming pool.

Set in 60 acres of rolling farmland in the northern suburbs of Bathurst, this school prepares students for Australian universities as well as for agricultural, nursing, commercial and similar careers. Within the varied program students may elect courses ranging from Japanese to computer math to industrial arts. Extracurricular activities include a full range of interest clubs, and among the many sports offered are: rugby, soccer, hockey, netball, cricket, softball, volleyball, swimming, life saving, cross country, squash and golf. American students may take the U.S. College Boards in Sydney.

CANBERRA GRAMMAR SCHOOL
Bdg Boys Ages 12-18; Day Boys 4-18, Girls 4-7. Gr K-12.

Canberra ACT, Australia 2603. Monaro Crescent. Red Hill. Tel. 95-1833.
Paul J. McKeown, DipEd (Oxford), Head.
Gen Acad. Curr—Nat. Ll—Eng. CF—Chinese Fr Ger Lat Tech Drawing.
Enr 921. B 130/714; G /77. Elem 361, Sec 560. Grad '84—116. Col—100.
Fac 107. Full 84/Part 23. M 68; F 39. US 1. Nat.
Tui Bdg $A1122; Day $A525-869. Schol.
Est 1929. Inc nonprofit. Tri (Jan-Dec). NAIS.

This school is affiliated with the Anglican Church. Courses are conducted in industrial arts, music, economics, geography and history. A full sports program includes cricket, tennis, rugby, soccer, squah, rock climbing and swimming.

THE HUTCHINS SCHOOL
Bdg Boys Ages 11-18; Day Boys 3-18, Girls 3-11. Gr N-12.

Hobart (Tasmania) 7005, Australia. 71 Nelson Rd. Sandy Bay. Tel. 002-251626.

The Rev. Dudley B. Clarke, MA, (Cantab), MEd, PhD, Head.
Col Prep Gen Acad. Curr—Nat. Ll—Eng. CF—Fr Ger Indonesian Music Econ Hist Man Arts. Sl—Rem & Dev Read.
Enr 918. B 92/805; G /21. Elem 535, Sec 383.
Fac 64. Full 62/Part 2. M 50; F 14. US 2. Nat.
Tui Bdg $A2190; Day $A510-2355. Schol.
Est 1846. Anglican. Tri (Feb-Dec).
Bldgs 15. Dorms 3. 2 Libs 16,000 vols. Courts. Fields. Gym. Swimming pool.

Located on the lower slopes of Mt. Nelson overlooking the Derwent River, Hutchins offers a comprehensive educational program. The Junior School's curriculum emphasizes the basic skills of literacy and numeracy together with social sciences, and arts and crafts. The two-year Middle School program features English, technical drawing, religious studies and either French or Indonesian. Senior School pupils receive instruction in the sciences, math, languages and arts leading to School Certificate and Higher School Certificate levels.

The study of Indonesian language, culture and history is an integral part of the curriculum in the upper grades. Activities include community service projects, cadet corps, film production and bushwalking. A complete sports program of cricket, soccer, rowing, squash, cross country and lifesaving is also conducted.

SCOTCH OAKBURN COLLEGE
Bdg Coed Ages 10-18; Day Coed 3-18. Gr N-12.

Launceston (Tasmania) 7250, Australia. 85 Penquite Rd. Tel. (003) 44-2501.
B.N. Carter, BA, Sydney, EdM, Harvard, EdD, Toronto, Prin.
Pre Prep Col Prep Gen Acad Bus. Curr—Nat. Ll—Eng. A—Eng Math. CF—Fr Ger Sci Geog Tech Drawing Econ Psych Typ Music Art. Sl—Tut.
Enr 718. B 101/225; G 124/265. Elem 228, Sec 490.
Fac 59. Full 47/Part 12. M 24; F 35. Nat.
Tui Bdg $1665/term (+$20); Day $915/term (+$20). Schol.
Est 1886. Nonprofit. Uniting Church in Australia. Tri (Feb-Dec).
Bldgs 25. Lib 11,074 vols. Fields. Gym. Swimming pool.

Operating under the auspices of the Uniting Church in Australia, Scotch Oakburn offers a program geared toward university entrance as well as careers in agriculture and business. The school emphasizes the fundamentals, in particular English and mathematics, with remedial classes provided in both subjects.

All students are encouraged to participate in one sport each term. These include cricket, rowing, hockey, badminton, swimming, tennis, netball, squash, soccer and fencing. Other activities include chess, drama, music, typing, outdoor education and community service.

SYDNEY CHURCH OF ENGLAND GRAMMAR SCHOOL
Bdg & Day Boys Ages 9-18. Gr 4-12.

North Sydney (New South Wales) 2060, Australia. Blue Street. Tel. 02 929-2263.
R.A.I. Grant, Head.
Col Prep Gen Acad. Curr—Nat. LI—Eng. CF—Fr Ger Lat Hist (US) Econ Divinity.
Enr 1100. B 240/860. Grad '84—166. Col—130.
Fac 77. Full 75/Part 2. M 72; F 5. Nat.
Tui Bdg $A1940-2240/term; Day $A860-1100/term.
Est 1889. Nonprofit. Church of England. Tri (Feb-Dec). NAIS.
Dorms 5. Lib 20,000 vols. Labs. Gym. Fields. Courts. Pool. Chapel.

A liberal education is provided at this school where 70% of the boys matriculate at universities. The program is organized in Preparatory School (grades 4-6) and Senior School (grades 7-12) divisions. Courses are specialized by subject beginning with grade 9, and honors courses are available in all disciplines. Students seeking admission into colleges in the U.S. may take the College Boards.

Religious instruction and chapel attendance are required at all levels. A full program of extracurricular activities includes intramural and inter-scholastic athletic competition in cricket, football, rowing, swimming, tennis, squash, golf and basketball. Boys perform voluntary service once a week and take part in either the Army Cadet or Air Training Corps.

WESLEY COLLEGE MELBOURNE
Bdg Boys Ages 12-18; Day Boys 5-18, Girls 5-9. Gr K-12.

Prahran (Victoria) 3181, Australia. 577 St. Kilda Rd. Tel. 51-8694.
D. H. Prest, BSc, MSc, Adelaide, Prin.
Col Prep Gen Acad Bus. Curr—UK. LI—Eng. CF—Fr Indonesian Greek.
Enr 1636.
Fac 176. Nat.
Tui Bdg $660; Day $170-715 (+ $120). Schol.
Summer Session. Acad.
Est 1866. Tri. NAIS.
Bldgs 5. Dorms 2. Lib. Athletic facilities.

Located on two sites, one in Prahran and one on High Street Road in Glen Waverly, Wesley offers a college preparatory Lower grade students learn fundamental skills and participate in a variety of activities including art, handcraft, social studies, music and a program of religious education. Students in the upper grades are prepared for the universities, Colleges of Advanced Education, public service, and business or agricultural careers. Students also gain experience in community living, environmental studies, the practice of forestry and adventure training.

THE ROCKHAMPTON GRAMMAR SCHOOL
  Bdg & Day Coed Ages 12-19. Gr 8-12.

Rockhampton (Queensland) 4700, Australia. Archer St. Tel. 079-27 1344.
Arthur E. C. Butler, Head.
Col Prep Gen Acad Bus Tech. Curr—Nat. Ll—Eng. CF—Jap Man Arts Speech Econ Agriculture. Sl—Rem Read & Math.
Enr 600.
Fac 34. UK Australia.
Tui Bdg $A1095/term   (+$A100/term);   Day $A395/term (+$A30/term).
Est 1881. Nonprofit. Tri (Jan-Nov).
Bldgs 12. Dorms 10. Lib. Labs. Aud. Swimming pool. Tennis crts. Fields.

Offering preparation for careers in agriculture and business as well as for universities, Rockhampton's curriculum features courses in citizenship, rural bookkeeping, accounting, secretarial studies and technical drawing. Special attention is given to students in the areas of vocational and educational guidance. Extracurricular activities include public speaking, debating, wood and leather work, Cadet Corps and community service projects. Tennis, softball, cricket, rugby, soccer, lifesaving, judo and gymnastics are offered within the athletic program.

THE SOUTHPORT SCHOOL
  Bdg Boys Ages 13-18; Day Boys 5-18. Grades 1-12.

Southport (Queensland) 4215, Australia. Winchester St. Tel. (075) 311. 066.
John H. Day, MEd, Head.
Pre-Prep Col Prep Gen Acad. Curr—Nat. Ll—Eng. CF—Fr Ger. Sl—Rem Eng & Math.
Enr 1100.
Tui Bdg $A2700; Day $A2145-2400.
Est 1901. Church of England. Quar (Jan-Dec).
Fields. Crts. Swimming pool.

Southport is located on 120 acres along the banks of the Nerang River. A comprehensive academic curriculum emphasizes languages, mathematics, the sciences and religion. Manual arts and rural training include courses in technical drawing, woodworking and animal husbandry. Art, music, public speaking, media studies and a wide variety of sports complete the program. While a strong Christian atmosphere is maintained, the school accepts boys from all denominations.

GLAMORGAN
(Geelong Grammar School)
  Day Coed Ages 3-12. Gr N-6.

Toorak (Victoria) 3142, Australia. 14 Douglas Street. Tel. 03-2401527.

I.L. Sutherland, Master.
Gen Acad. Curr—Nat. LI—Eng. CF—Fr Japanese Drama Computer
Stud.
Enr 280. B 187; G 93.
Fac 23.
Tui $A619-1011 (+ $A60).
Est l887. Nonprofit. Tri (Feb-Dec). Church of England.
Bldgs 7. Lib. Field. Tennis crts. Pool.

A division of Geelong Grammar School, Glamorgan offers a comprehensive primary school education. The school's faculty includes specialists in art, music, physical education and Japanese language. Supportive instruction is also available for the slow learner. Academics are complemented by opportunities in drama, gymnastics, jazz ballet, photography, swimming, camping, cross country skiing and sailing. Although Glamorgan's enrollment is mostly Australian, American, French and Japanese students are also enrolled.

See also page 96

TOOWOOMBA GRAMMAR SCHOOL
  Bdg & Day Boys Ages 12-18. Gr 8-12.

Toowoomba (Queensland) 4350, Australia. Margaret St. Tel. (076)
32-4055.
W.M. Dent, BA, FACE, Head.
Col Prep Gen Acad. Curr—Nat. LI—Eng. CF—Ger Fr Latin Math
  Physics Chem Graphics Indonesian Zoology Hist Geog Accounting.
Enr 700. B 400/300.
Fac 45. Australia UK.
Tui Bdg $A2481/term; Day $A900/term Schol.
Est 1875. Nonprofit. Quar (Jan-Nov).
Bldgs 23. Dorms 4. Lib 20,000 vols. Fields. Pool. Rifle range. Tennis
crts.

Toowoomba offers a wide range of subjects preparing boys for entry into all facilities of the universities in Queensland and in other states, as well as institutes of technology, education and agriculture. Located one kilometer from the center of the city, the school's sports program includes cricket, football, rugby, gymnastics, judo and tennis. Orchestra, drama, debating, photography, chess and Cadet Unit are among the extracurricular activities.

THE SCOTS & PGC WARWICK COLLEGES
  Bdg & Day Coed Ages 12-18. Gr 8-12.

Warwick 4370 (Queensland), Australia. Tel. 61-1214.
H.J. Rodger, Head.
Col Prep Gen Acad. Curr—Nat. LI—Eng. A—Eng Math Sci Econ
  Agriculture. CF—Fr Hist Geog Art. SI—Rem & Dev Read & Math.
Enr 401. B 240/30; G 100/31.
Fac 28. Full 26/Part 2. M 20; F 8. Nat.

Tui Bdg $A2800 (+ $A100); Day $A1600.
Est I9I8. Nonprofit. Uniting Church. Quar (Jan-Dec).
Bldgs 22. Dorms 5. Lib.

Since 1970, The Scots College for boys and its sister school,
Presbyterian Girls' College, have been integrated for teaching purposes
on the secondary level. While classroom and library facilities are shared,
separate campuses are maintained and girls are bused to classes.
Students are prepared for matriculation at the University of Queensland.
In addition, boys may pursue a comprehensive agricultural course and
girls are offered commercial courses. Each school has a full program of
sports including golf, swimming, sailing, football, hockey, soccer and
tennis. A few Americans attend yearly.

SLADE SCHOOL
  Bdg Coed Ages 12-18. Gr 8-12.

Warwick (Queensland), Australia. Horsman Rd. Tel. (076) 611922.
Col Prep Bus Tech. Curr—Nat. LI—Eng. A—Math. CF—Agriculture
  Chem Drawing Biol Hist Geog.
Enr 145.
Fac 14. Australia.
Tui Bdg $5000.
Est 1926. Inc. Anglican. Sem (Jan-Nov).
Bldgs 21. Dorms 4. Lib 6000 vols. Swimming pool. Fields. Tennis crts
  4.

One hundred miles west of Brisbane, Slade School has been
coeducational since 1976. Three courses of study are followed
—academic, agricultural and commercial. The school begins each day
with a brief chapel service and all classes have religious instruction
periods. Students are encouraged to participate in competitive sports
which include swimming, rugby, cricket and hockey. Drawing and
painting, lifesaving, photograpy, welding and cookery are among the
activities provided for students.

GUAM

The largest of the Mariana Islands, Guam is an independent
trusteeship assigned to the United States. The island was acquired from
Spain in 1898. The Japanese seized the territory during World War II,
but in 1944 it returned to U.S. hands. The people of Guam are U.S.
citizens with their own government. The capital is Agana.

ST. JOHN'S EPISCOPAL PREPARATORY SCHOOL
  Day Coed Ages 4-16. Gr N-9.

Agana, Guam 96910. Box FB. Tel. 646-5626.
Fr. John T. Moore, Jr., BSc, USMA-West Point, Head.

Pre-Prep. Tests SSAT. Curr—USA. LI—Eng. CF—Span Fr Japanese Lit
  Soc Stud Relig Drama.
Enr 533. US—426.
Fac 38. US 34.
Tui $2260-2266. Schol.
Summer Session. Acad Rec. Tui $110 (+$15). 8 wks.
Est 1962. Nonprofit. Quar (Sept-Je). NAIS.

St. John's offers an American curriculum preparing students for
secondary school entrance. A variety of courses are available, including
the study of Guam and other early American settlements. Chapel is held
once a week and attendance is required, however participation is
optional. School activities include interscholastic sports, student council
and cheerleading.

HONG KONG

Providing one of the finest harbors in the East, the British Crown
Colony of Hong Kong consists of several islands and mainland
territories. Hong Kong Island serves as the nucleus, on which is located
Victoria, the colonial capital. The Hong Kong dollar (HK$) is the
monetary unit.

HONG KONG INTERNATIONAL SCHOOL
  Day Coed Ages 5-18. Gr K-12.

Repulse Bay, Hong Kong. 6 South Bay Close. Tel. 5-92305.
David F. Rittmann, BSEd, Concordia Teachers College, MA, New York
  Univ., Head.
Col Prep. Tests CEEB SSAT. Curr—USA. LI—Eng. A—Math Eng Fr
  Span Soc Sci. CF—Chinese Hist (US) Asian Stud Comp Sci Psych
  Philos Theol Arts. SI—Rem Read ESL.
Enr 1386. B 650; G 736. Elem 977, Sec 409. US—788. Grad '84—89.
  Col—82.
Fac 110. Full 93/Part 17. M 37; F 73. US 86.
Tui $2050-4500 (+$400-500). Schol.
Summer Session. Rec Rem. Tui $50-250/6 wks.
Est 1966. Nonprofit. Lutheran. Sem (Aug-Je). A/OS EARCOS ISS
  NAIS. Accred WASC.
Bldgs 2. 2 Libs 40,000 vols. Gyms 2. Pool. Comp Lab. Theatre.

The only American school in Hong Kong, HKIS is operated under the
auspices of the Missouri Synod of the Lutheran Church. Students of 30
nationalities attend, the vast majority of whom are American. A United
States college preparatory curriculum is offered, supplemented with
courses in Asian studies and languages, including religious studies.
Students pursue independent projects during interim week and may also
elect independent studies during terms. Extensive elective offerings, a
full range of extracurricular activities and sports, and an adult education
program are also provided.

JAPAN

Long a crucible for traditionally nourished and foreign inspired ideas
and innovations, Japan today is a land of contrast and diversity, a
bridge spanning ancient and modern, rural and urban. Consisting
principally of four mountainous islands, the empire abounds with
temples, shrines and pagodas amid contemporary evidence of the
technological skill and material success that have made Japan one of the
leading industrial powers of the world.

Honshu, considered the mainland, contains most of the important
cities, including the capital, Tokyo, the world's second most populous
city. Japan's monetary unit is the yen (Y). Japanese is the spoken
language.

FUKUOKA INTERNATIONAL SCHOOL
Day Coed Ages 6-14. Gr 1-9.

Fukuoka Shi, Japan 812. 4-1-28 Maidashi, Higashi Ku. Tel. 092-
641-0326.
Ellen Sprunger, BS, Bluffton College, Admin.
Gen Acad. Curr—USA. LI—Eng. CF—Japanese Fr. SI—Rem Eng.
Enr 35. B 17; G 18. Elem 34, Sec 1. US—22.
Fac 10. Full 2/Part 8. M 3; F 7. US 7.
Tui 500,000 yen (+30,000 yen). Schol.
Est 1972. Nonprofit. Sem (Sept-Je). A/OS ISS.
Bldgs 1. Lib 5000 vols. Athletic facilities.

Located in the northern part of the island of Kyushu, Fukuoka offers a
curriculum comparable to that in the U.S. The school does not have
facilities or staff to teach non-English speaking students, however,
students of appropriate age of any nationality are enrolled provided they
can do the classroom work in English. Extracurricular interests include
Japanese language instruction, vocal and band music, scouting and a
literature discussion group.

CHRIST THE KING INTERNATIONAL SCHOOL
Day Coed Ages 4-20. Gr N-12.

Ginowan City (Okinawa), Japan 901-22. P.O. Box 14.
Sr. Helen Cannu, OP, Prin.
Col Prep. Curr—USA. LI—Eng. CF—Japanese Span Hist Soc Stud Art
Comp Far East Hist Typ. SI—Rem Eng & Math.
Enr 334. Elem 212, Sec 122. US—94. Grad '84—29. Col—18.
Fac 27. Full 24/Part 3. US 14.
Tui 270,000 yen (+37,000 yen). Schol.
Summer Session. Remedial.
Est 1956. Inc nonprofit. Roman Catholic. Quar (Aug-May). EARCOS
ISS.
Bldg 3. Libs 2. Crts. Fields.

Children of mixed nationalities comprise the largest segment of students at this international and interdenominational school operated by the Catholic Mission of Okinawa. The curriculum is that of an American school with adaptations in Asian studies and languages.

HIROSHIMA INTERNATIONAL SCHOOL
Day Coed Ages 5-14. Gr K-8.

Hiroshima, Japan 730. 2-6,2-chome Ushita Higashi Ku. Tel. 078 221-6202.
Walter Enloe, BA, Eckerd College, PhD, Emory Univ., Prin.
Gen Acad. Curr—USA UK. LI—Eng. CF—Japanese Lang & Cultural Stud. SI—Rem & Dev Read & Math Tut ESL.
Enr 45. B 20; G 17.
Fac 8. Full 4/Part 4. M 4; F 4. US 3.
Tui $4000 (+$1000). Schol.
Summer Session. Acad Rec. Tui $600/6 wks.
Est 1962. Nonprofit. Tri (Sept-Je). A/OS ISS EARCOS.
Bldgs 1. Lib 10,000 vols. Field.

Courses in Japanese language and culture, as well as a variety of electives in the social sciences, art and music enrich the American-oriented curriculum at this small school. Most of the children are American, with smaller numbers from Europe and the Commonwealth countries.

CANADIAN ACADEMY
Bdg Coed Ages 12-18; Day Coed 4-18. Gr N-12.

Kobe 657, Japan. Nagaminedai 2-chome Nada-ku. Tel. (078) 881-5211.
Stuart J. Young, MA, PhD, Univ. of Oregon, Head.
Pre-Prep Col Prep Gen Acad. Tests IB CEEB. Curr—USA. LI—Eng. A—Bio Calc Chem Eng Fr Japanese Physics. CF—Ger Lat Span Kabuki Health. SI—Rem & Dev Read ESL.
Enr 614. Elem 365, Sec 249. US—170. Grad '84—54. Col—52.
Fac 55. Full 51/Part 4. M 22; F 33. US 38.
Tui Bdg 1,361,000-1,537,000 yen (+100,000 yen); Day 871,000-1,047,000 yen (+100,000 yen). Schol.
Summer Session. Acad Rec. 5 wks.
Est 1913. Inc nonprofit. Sem (Sept-Je). EARCOS ISS. Accred WASC.
Bldgs 7. Dorm. 2 Libs 30,000 vols. Field. Gym.

Located on the southern slopes of Mt. Rokko, the school requires proficiency in English for admission. The elementary school follows an American curriculum and includes an emphasis on learning about Japan. Self-contained classrooms provide a base for free-flowing groupings and individualized instruction. In addition to traditional studies, classes are taught by specialists in music, art, physical education and Japanese. The secondary school curriculum is college preparatory with electives in the social sciences, languages and the arts. Canadian

Academy is also a testing center for the Educational Testing Service and the American College Testing Program.

Student activities include drama, choral and concert band, as well as participation in volleyball, soccer, basketball, track and field and baseball.

See also page 97

MARIST BROTHERS INTERNATIONAL SCHOOL
Day Coed Ages 4-19. Gr K-12.

Kobe 654, Japan. 2-1, 1-chome, Chimori-cho, Shuma-ku. Tel. 078-732-6266.
Br. Thomas E. Hart, FMS, BA, Marist College, MA, MEd, Univ. of Oregon, Prin.
Col Prep Gen Acad Bus. Tests CEEB SSAT TOEFL. Curr—USA. LI—Eng.
Enr 327.
Fac 36.
Tui $2800 ($400). Schol.
Summer Session. Acad Rec. Tui $330/7 wks.
Est 1951. Inc nonprofit. Roman Catholic. Sem (Sept-Je). EARCOS ISS. Accred WASC.

This school enrolls students from 23 nations including India, China, Japan, the U.S. and Korea. Preparation is offered for the U.S. College Boards and the TOEFL.

ST. MICHAEL'S INTERNATIONAL SCHOOL
Day Coed Ages 3-12. Gr N-6.

Kobe 650, Japan. 17-2 Nakayamate-dori 3-chome Chuo-ku. Tel. (078) 231-8885.
George E. Gibbons, BEd, London, MA, Reading, Head.
Gen Acad. Curr—UK. LI—Eng. CF—Japanese Fr Soc Stud Bible Music Art. SI—ESL.
Enr 170. B 80; G 90. US—16.
Fac 25. Full 15/Part 10. M 3; F 22. US 4. UK Japan.
Tui 590,000 yen (+60,000 yen). Schol.
Est 1946. Inc 1969 nonprofit.Tri (Sept-Je). EARCOS ISS.

Sponsored by the Anglican Church of Japan, St. Michael's provides an education in English for children of the international community. Curriculum and methods are based on those of schools in Great Britain, with emphasis on individual and small group instruction. Students who do not speak English are divided into groups for English as a Second Language. The faculty also conducts an English language school for adults.

KYOTO INTERNATIONAL SCHOOL
Day Coed Ages 5-14. Gr K-8.

Kyoto, Japan 604. 11-1 Ushinomiya-cho Yoshida, Sakyo-ku. Tel. (075) 771-4022.
Jean P. Stewart, Prin.
Gen Acad. Curr—USA UK. Ll—Eng. CF—Japanese ESL Music.
Enr 37. B 19; G 18. US—19.
Fac 5. Full 3/Part 2. M 1; F 4. US.
Tui $2838.
Est 1957. Inc 1967. Tri (Sept-Je). ISS.
Bldg. Libs 2.

Enrolling many nationalities, this school is supported entirely by a Western community of visiting professors, missionaries, businessmen and artists. An American-British curriculum is followed featuring individualized instruction as well as courses in Japanese language and culture. Graduates enter the Canadian Academy in Kobe, about 40 miles from Kyoto, or return to their home country. Kyoto is a cultural center of Japan, noted for its temples, shrines, palaces and universities.

NAGOYA INTERNATIONAL SCHOOL
Day Coed Ages 3-18. Gr N-12.

Nagoya, Japan 463. 2686 Minamihara Nakashidami, Moriyama-Ku. Tel. (052) 736-2025.
Robert N. Whitaker, MA, Ohio State Univ., Head.
Col Prep. Tests CEEB SSAT. Curr—USA. Ll—Eng. A—Physics Comp Sci Psych. CF—Japanese Fr Soc Stud.Sl—ESL Rem Eng Math Sci & Soc Stud.
Enr 222. Elem 163, Sec 59. US—46. Grad '84—11. Col—8.
Fac 21. Full 21. M 6; F 15. US 14.
Tui 230,000-980,000 yen. Schol.
Summer Session. Rec Intensive Eng. 4-6 wks.
Est 1963. Inc 1965 nonprofit. Sem (Aug-Je). A/OS EARCOS ISS NAIS. Accred WASC.
Bldgs 3. Lib 20,000 vols. Gym. Tennis crts. Field.

Youngsters from Japan comprise over half of the enrollment at this school, with smaller numbers from the United States and other countries. The American curriculum provides College Boards preparation, courses in Japanese language, history and culture. Intensive English and a limited program of adult education are also offered.

One of Japan's principal ports, Nagoya is located at the head of Ise Bay in the southern part of Honshu, about 200 miles west of Tokyo.

HOKKAIDO INTERNATIONAL SCHOOL
Day Coed Ages 6-14. Gr 1-9.

Sapporo (Hokkaido) 062, Japan. 3-jo, 2-chome, 5-35 Fukuzumi, Toyohira-ku. Tel. 011-851-1205.

Cornelia Roghair, BA, Black Hills State, Prin.
Gen Acad. Curr—USA. LI—Eng. A—Speech Arts Typing. CF—Japanese Hist (US).
Enr 32. B 14; G 18. Elem 28, Sec 4. US—19. Grad '84—4.
Fac 6. Full 3/Part 3. M 3; F 3. US 4.
Tui $2500. Schol.
Summer Session. Acad. Tui $300. 5 wks.
Est 1958. Inc nonprofit. Sem (Sept-Je). A/OS EARCOS ISS. Accred WASC.
Bldgs 1. Lib 3000 vols. Gym.

From its beginning in 1958 with five students, this parent founded and operated school has grown apace with its site, the bustling ski resort city of Sapporo. Within the American curriculum, students are prepared for transfer to other English-speaking schools in Japan or high schools in the United States. The school offers English instruction to Japanese children.

THE AMERICAN SCHOOL IN JAPAN
Day Coed Ages 3-20. Gr N-PG.

Tokyo 182, Japan. 1-1-1 Nomizu Chofu-shi. Tel. 0422-31-6351.
Ray F. Downs, BA, Oberlin, MA, Univ. of Michigan, Head.
Col Prep. Tests SSAT. Curr—USA. LI—Eng. A—Calculus Mod Eur Hist Lit Comp Sci Fr Span Biol. CF—Media Fine Arts Outdoor Ed Asian Stud.
Enr 1122. B 574; G 548. Elem 648, Sec 467, PG 7. US—851. Grad '84—123. Col—100.
Fac 110. Full 100/Part 10. M 55; F 55. US 90.
Tui $4800 (+ $200). Schol.
Est 1902. Inc nonprofit. Sem (Sept-Je). A/OS EARCOS ISS NAIS. Accred WASC.
Bldgs 6. 3 Libs 30,000 vols. Gyms 2. Fields 2. Pool. Tennis crts 3.

While the well established American School in Japan primarily serves U.S. citizens, a true international flavor has traditionally prevailed from the more than 30 nationalities represented. The American curriculum includes courses designed to explore the culture and history of Japan and East Asia. In the secondary school, modular scheduling is used to provide a high degree of individualization, enabling students to take an unusually large number of course offerings. An academic support system is available to students needing more guided and structured learning. Japanese language is taught at all grade levels in the elementary school, and as an elective in the secondary school, while Japanese arts and crafts are incorporated into the kindergarten curriculum.

Outdoor education is part of every grade level, and includes the "Miyake Program" for seventh graders, spending a week on a volcanic island in Sagami Bay. The sports program includes football, volleyball, tennis, cross country, gymnastics, soccer, swimming and field hockey.

AOBA INTERNATIONAL SCHOOL
Day Coed Ages 1-6. NK.

Tokyo 150, Japan. 2-10-34, Aoba-dai, Meguro-ku. Tel. 03-461-1442.
Regina Doi, BA, Julliard School of Music, MBA, Univ. of Hawaii, Prin.
Primary Sch Prep. LI—Eng. CF—Japanese Soroban Music.
Enr 167. B 80; G 87. US—25. Grad '84—40.
Fac 20. Full 13/Part 7. M 3; F 17. Nat US.
Tui 600,000 yen.
Summer Session. Acad Rec. Tui Day 50,000 yen. 4 wks.
Est I976. Sem (Sept-Je).

Aoba serves as a feeder school to the Japan International School. The
school's Montessori-based curriculum is tailored to the individual child
from nursery to pre-first grade. Reading, writing, music, math and
science courses comprise the basic academic offerings. Sports are
coordinated to meet various levels of motor development.

See also page 98

CHRISTIAN ACADEMY IN JAPAN
Bdg Coed Ages 12-18; Day Coed 5-18. Gr K-12.

Tokyo 203, Japan. 1-2-14 Shinkawa-cho Higashi-Kurume-shi. Tel.
0424-71-0022.
Claude A. Meyers, MEd, Univ. of Texas, PhD, Univ. of Oregon, Head.
Col Prep. Tests CEEB. Curr—USA. LI—Eng. A—US Hist Calc Lit.
CF—Span Fr Japanese Bible Man Arts Typ. SI—Rem & Dev Read
EFL.
Enr 312. Elem 200, Sec 112. Grad '84—35. Col—28.
Fac 47. Full 28/Part 19. M 15; F 32. US 41.
Tui Bdg $3111; Day $2255.
Est 1950. Inc nonprofit. Missionary. Sem (Sept-Je). EARCOS ISS.
Accred WASC.
Bldgs 7. Dorms 2. Lib 15,000 vols. Gym. Field. Court.

Most of the children at this school are of missionary families from the
United States and northern Europe. The academic program prepares
students for the College Boards and many enter American colleges and
universities. A full range of extracurricular sports rounds out the
program.

INTERNATIONAL SCHOOL OF THE SACRED HEART
Day Girls Ages 3-18. Gr K-12.

Tokyo 150, Japan. 3-1, Hiroo 4-chome Shibuya-ku. Tel. (03) 400-3951.
Sr. Victoria Uy, Head.
Col Prep. Tests IB GCE CEEB SSAT. Curr—USA. LI—Eng. CF—Fr
Japanese Values Prgm. SI—Tut ESL.
Enr 671. Elem 485, Sec 186. US—175. Grad '84—48. Col—48.
Fac 94. Full 70/Part 24. M 12; F 82. US 28. UK.
Tui 1,000,000 yen. Schol.

Summer Session. Acad Rec. Tui 60,000 yen/4 wks.
Est 1908. Inc nonprofit. Society of the Sacred Heart. EARCOS ISS.
  Accred WASC.
Blds 3. 2 Libs 27,000 vols. Gym. Fields 2. Tennis courts.

The Catholic Sisters of the Society of the Sacred Heart conduct a college preparatory program in a Christian setting at this school. Although the school is only open to girls, boys are accepted in the kindergarten. Students prepare for American College Boards and the International Baccalaureate. The educational program strives to develop the whole student and girls have the opportunity to participate in a wide variety of activities.

JAPAN INTERNATIONAL SCHOOL
  Day Coed Ages 6-14. Gr 1-9.

Tokyo 150, Japan. 4-24-9, Jingumae, Shibuya-ku. Tel. 408-4411.
Mail to: Tokyo 150, Japan, J.I.S. Annex, 3-12-2 Jingumae, Shibuya-ku.
Regina Doi, BA, Julliard School of Music, MBA, Univ. of Hawaii, Prin.
Pre-Prep Gen Acad. Curr—USA. LI—Eng. A—Math. CF—Japanese
  ESL Aikido. SI—Rem & Dev Math & Read Tut.
Enr 150. B 75; G 80. US—24. Grad '84—4.
Fac 26. Full 20/Part 6. M 10; F 16. US 14.
Tui 1,000,000 yen.
Summer Session. Acad Rec. Tui Day 80,000 yen. 4 wks.
Est 1980. Sem (Sept-Je).

Japan International School's elementary and junior high school program grew out of the Aoba International School. The school's cross-cultural educational philosophy is reflected in a complete curriculum of English and Japanese language training. Classes are kept small and emphasis is placed on individualized instruction. Curriculum features include Japanese as a Second Language, music and typing. Creative activities are fostered through ceramics, weaving, painting and dyeing. The sports program offers weekly swimming sessions as well as Aikido, one of the traditional Japanese martial arts. J.I.S.'s enrollment is comprised of American and Japanese students.

See also page 98

NISHIMACHI INTERNATIONAL SCHOOL
  Day Coed Ages 5-15. Gr K-9.

Tokyo 106, Japan. 14-7 Moto Azabu 2-chome, Minato-ku. Tel. (03)
  451-5520.
Adair Nagata, BA, Smith, MAT, Harvard, Acting Prin.
Pre-Prep. Curr—USA Nat. LI—Eng Japanese. A—Sci. CF—Lang Arts
  World Hist Music. SI—Rem & Dev Read Math Tut ESL JSL.
Enr 385. B 180. G 205.
Fac 41. Full 40/Part 1. M 15; F 26. US 19.
Tui $3780-4780.
Summer Session. Acad Rec Kindergarten ESL. Tui $313/4 wks.

**Est 1949. Inc nonprofit. Tri (Sept-Je). A/OS EARCOS ISS.
Bldgs 5. Lib 8500 vols. Gym. Courts. Aud.**

Situated in the heart of Tokyo, Nishimachi offers a dual-langauge curriculum (English and Japanese) developed jointly by the faculty and principal that allows students to progress at their own rate. Japanese language studies are required for the entire school with small classes taught by bilingual Japanese. Sports are an integral part of the regular program, including swimming, skiing and traditional team sports. Junior high students twice a year spend weekends in Kazuno for environmental and social science studies while the entire school participates in cultural activities in the surrounding area.

See also page 97

ST. MARY'S INTERNATIONAL SCHOOL
Day Boys Ages 5-18. Gr K-12.

**Tokyo 158, Japan. 1-6-19 Seta, Setagaya-ku. Tel. (03) 709-3411.
Br. Andrew Boisvert, MA, Fordham, Head.
Pre-Prep Col Prep. Tests IB CEEB SSAT. Curr—USA. LI—Eng. A—Eng
Fr Japanese Math Sci. CF—Ethics Art Music Swimming. SI—ESL.
Enr 850. Elem 596, Sec 254. US—195. Grad '84—46. Col—46.
Fac 81. Full 70/Part 11. M 63; F 18. US 28. Can.
Tui $4600. Schol.
Summer Session. Acad Rec. Tui $270. 4 wks.
Est 1954. Inc nonprofit. Roman Catholic. Quar (Sept-Je). EARCOS ISS.
Accred WASC.
Bldgs 4. Lib 25,000 vols. Gym. Field. Swimming pool. Courts.**

St. Mary's is operated by the Brothers of Christian Instruction and accepts boys of all creeds. Although the school follows an "American style" curriculum, the option to work towards the International Baccalaureate is available in grades 11 and 12. Classes in computer science, religion, Japanese, Asian studies and calculus are featured, and a full sports program offers judo, AAU swimming, ice hockey and soccer. Situated in a residential section of Tokyo, the school's enrollment is comprised of students from Great Britain, Japan, Korea, China, the United States and over 50 other nations.

See also page 99

SEISEN INTERNATIONAL SCHOOL
Day Girls Ages 3-18. Gr N-12.

**Tokyo 158, Japan. 12-15 Yoga 1-chome Setagaya-ku. Tel. (03)704-
2661.
Sr. Asuncion Lecubarri, Prin.
Col Prep. Tests CEEB SSAT. Curr—USA. LI—Eng. A—Eng Math
Japanese Hist. CF—Span Fr Japanese Soc Sci Relig. SI—Rem & Dev
Math & Read Tut.
Enr 511. B 75; G 436. US—84. Grad '84—15. Col—15.
Fac 63. Full 43/Part 20. M 5; F 58. US 20.**

Tui 900,000-930,000 yen (+ 100,000 yen). Schol.
Summer Session. Rec Rem. Tui 60,000 yen. 4 wks.
Est 1962. Roman Catholic. Quar (Sept-Je). ISS EARCOS. Accred
WASC.
Bldgs 3. Libs 2. Gym.

One of several schools operated by the Handmaids of the Sacred Heart of Jesus, Seisen International School is the only one which is open to non-Japanese students. Enrolling girls of over 60 nationalities, the school provides a college preparatory curriculum with advanced placement courses in all subjects. A Montessori program admits boys ages three to five. Extracurricular activities include speech, drama, journalism and ballet, and sports such as gymnastics, tennis, cross country and volleyball.

See also page 100

OKINAWA CHRISTIAN SCHOOL
Day Coed Ages 3-18. Gr N-12.

Urasoe (Okinawa), Japan 901-21. P.O. Box 42. Tel. 0988-77-3661.
Joel E. Anderson, BA, Bethel, Supt.
Col Prep Gen Acad. Tests SSAT. Curr—USA. LI—Eng. CF—Japanese
Math Sci Soc Sci Bible. SI—Tut Rem & Dev Read & Math ESL.
Enr 329. B 150; G 179. US—205. Grad '84—15. Col—11.
Fac 31. Full 24/Part 7. M 7; F 24. US 25.
Tui $1009-122/mo (+ $75/yr). Schol.
Summer Session. Acad Rec. Tui $122. 6 wks.
Est 1957. Inc nonprofit. Sem (Sept-Je). EARCOS ISS. Accred WASC.
Bldgs 4. Libs 2. Gym.

This school offers an American curriculum in a Christain atmosphere to an international student enrollment. In addition to the traditional academic courses, students participate in extracurricular activities such as sports, music and drama.

ST. JOSEPH INTERNATIONAL SCHOOL
Bdg & Day Boys Ages 4-19; Day Girls 4-7. Gr K-12.

Yokohama 231, Japan. 85 Yamate-cho, Naka-ku. Tel. (045) 641-0065.
Donald C. McKee, SM, MA, Case-Western Reserve Univ., BSEd,
Dayton, Prin.
Col Prep Bus. Tests CEEB. Curr—USA. LI—Eng. A—Lit Comp Sci
Math. CF—Chinese Fr Japanese Span Hist Asian Stud Relig Arts
Typ.
Enr 265. B 235; G 30. Elem 165, Sec 100. US—20. Grad '84—25.
Col—25.
Fac 30. Full 27/Part 3. M 24; F 6. US 25.
Tui Bdg $7500; Day $4000 (+ $300). Schol.
Summer Session. Acad. Tui $500. 4 wks.

Est 1901. Inc 1948 nonprofit. Roman Catholic. Sem (Sept-Je). ISS EARCOS. Accred WASC.
Bldgs 5. Dorms 2. Lib 16,000 vols. Athletic facilities.

Conducted by the Marianists, this school parallels American curricular patterns, offers U.S. College Board preparation, and also conducts a business program. Students of all religious backgrounds come from the United States, Japan, Korea and China, with smaller numbers from many other countries. Girls are enrolled in kindergarten and the lower elementary grades.

Yokohama, 18 miles southwest of Tokyo, is a principal seaport and the fourth most populous city in Japan. The school will accommodate boarding students on a limited basis.

SAINT MAUR INTERNATIONAL SCHOOL
Day Girls Ages 2½-18. Gr N-12.

Yokohama (Kanagawa Ken) 231, Japan. 83, Yamate-cho, Naka-ku. Tel. (045) 641-5751.
Sr. Carmel O'Keeffe, BEd, Craiglockhart College, BA, Sophia Univ., Prin.
Col Prep. Tests IB CEEB SSAT. Curr—USA. LI—Eng. A—Math Eng Hist. CF—Fr Span Ger Japanese Relig Soc Stud Art Asian Stud Accounting.
Enr 372. Elem 272, Sec 100. US—150. Grad '84—22. Col—17.
Fac 42. Full 27/Part 15. M 7; F 35. US 17.
Tui $2000-4000. Schol.
Summer Session. Acad. Tui $85/crse. 3 wks.
Est 1872. Nonprofit. Sem (Sept-Je). EARCOS ISS. Accred WASC.
Bldgs 3. Lib 10,000 vols. Gym. Tennis crts 2.

St. Maur conducts a coeducational Montessori program for children between the ages of two and one-half to seven, and a college preparatory course of study for girls only. In addition to traditional academics, the school features business-oriented courses. Activities in computer programming, dressmaking, art, kendo, tennis and softball are also enjoyed by students. St. Maur's enrollment is primarily from Japan and the United States.

See also page 101

YOKOHAMA INTERNATIONAL SCHOOL
Day Coed Ages 2½-18. Gr N-12.

Yokohama 231, Japan. 258 Yamate-cho, Naka-ku. Tel. 045-622-0084.
John Tanner, MBE, MA, London, Head.
Col Prep. Tests CEEB GCE. Curr—USA UK. LI—Eng. A—Physics Biol Chem Math Japanese Fr. CF—Ger Dutch Soc Stud Art Music Home Econ Typ. SI—Rem Eng ESL Tut.
Enr 380. B 190; G 190. Elem 300, Sec 80. US—115. Grad '84—15. Col—14.
Fac 36. Full 27/Part 9. M 13; F 23. US 10. UK Canada Australia.

Tui $3000-4300 (+ $350).
Est 1924. Nonprofit. Quar (Sept-Je). EARCOS ISA ISS.
Bldgs 3. Lib 10,000 vols. Gym. Field.

The school combines ideals of American, British and continental European educational systems, preparing students for the U.S. College Boards and British G.C.E. through a traditional curriculum. Remedial English and special classes for students whose native language is not English are also offered. Games include softball, soccer, field hockey, volleyball, badminton, basketball, track and field, and cross country. Students also participate in the interscholastic activities of a sporting, academic or cultural nature. Field trips are an integral part of the school program.

KOREA

Called "Land of the Morning Calm," Korea occupies a mountainous peninsula in northeast Asia, separating the Yellow Sea from the Sea of Japan. The country has been divided into North and South portions since World War II. Seoul is capital of South Korea, where the monetary unit is the won (W). Korean is the official language.

SEOUL FOREIGN SCHOOL
　Day Coed Ages 4-18. Gr N-12.

Seoul 120, Korea. 55 Yunhi Dong. Tel. 323-4786.
Richard F. Underwood, BA, Hamilton, MA,Columbia, MEd, Rutgers, Head.
Col Prep Gen Acad. Tests CEEB IB ACT TOEFL. Curr—USA. Ll—Eng. A—Lang Math. CF—Fr Korean Span Hist (US) Psych Soc Pol Sci Relig Bus Eng & Math Home EC Typ Arts. Sl—Tut Rem & Dev Read & Math.
Enr 662. Elem 357, Sec 305. US—425. Grad '84—29. Col—28.
Fac 59. Full 50/Part 9. M 18; F 41. US 51.
Tui $1700-4650 (+ $865). Schol.
Est 1912. Inc 1922 nonprofit. Sem (Sept-Je). EARCOS ISS NAIS. Accred WASC.
Bldgs 12. Libs 25,000 vols. Gym. Field. Tennis crts 2.

The oldest English language school in Korea, Seoul Foreign School serves a predominantly American enrollment, although about 30 other nations are represented. College Board preparation is given within the full American curriculum, which includes a wide variety of elective offerings, and opportunity for advanced placement. The school also features an academic program leading to the International Baccalaureate.

SEOUL INTERNATIONAL SCHOOL
Day Coed Ages 3¹/₂-20. Gr N-PG.

Seoul, Korea 134. Kangdong P.O. Box 61. Tel. 445-2119.
Edward B. Adams, BA, Whitworth, MEd, E. Washington Univ., Head.
Col Prep Gen Acad. Tests SSAT PSAT TOEFL. Curr—USA. LI—Eng.
 CF—Fr Ger Korean Span Asian Stud Speech Trig Calc. SI—ESL.
Enr 450. B 235; G 215. US—281. Grad '84—18. Col—16.
Fac 45. Full 44/Part 1. M 13; F 32. US 43.
Tui $1500-4600 (+ $650).
Summer Session. Acad ESL. Tui $175 (+ $90). 5 wks.
Est 1973. Nonprofit. Sem (Aug-Je). EARCOS ISS. Accred WASC.
Bldgs 2. Lib 10,000 vols. Tennis crts. Field.

Seoul International School is the only non-religiously affiliated school open to the entire foreign community in Seoul. The enrollment is predominantly American, however over 37 other nationalities are represented. An American curriculum is supplemented by electives in typing, journalism, tae kwon do, modern dance, art and chorus. Emphasis is placed on helping students realize and appreciate the Korean culture as well as their own.

See also page 102

KOREA CHRISTIAN ACADEMY
Bdg Coed Ages 13-18; Day Coed 6-18. Gr 1-12.

Taejon 300 (Choong Chung Namdo), Korea. 210-3 O-Jung Dong. Tel. (042) 72-3663.
James L. Wootton, BS, Southern Illinois Univ., MEd, Univ. of Illinois, Prin.
Col Prep. Tests CEEB SSAT. Curr—USA. LI—Eng. A—Math Chem Physics Writing. CF—Fr Korean Latin Soc Psych Bus Ed. SI—Eng.
Enr 87. B 9/32; G 11/35. Elem 48, Sec 39. US—80. Grad '84—7. Col—7.
Fac 21. Full 11/Part 10. M 5; F 16. US 20.
Tui Bdg $4155-4200; Day $3100-4200.
Est 1958. Inc 1977 nonprofit. Sem (Aug-Je). ISS EARCOS. Accred WASC.
Bldgs 6. Dorms 1. Lib 10,000 vols. Gym. Tennis crts. Fields.

Preparation for U.S. College Boards is available at this mission-sponsored school, whose enrollment and faculty are composed almost entirely of Americans. Recent graduates have attended Baylor, MIT, Wheaton and Duke. Sports, activities and field trips round out the program.

MARSHALL ISLANDS

Placed under United States trusteeship in 1947, the Marshall Islands consist of two parallel chains, about 700 miles in length, in the North Pacific. The majority of the islands are tiny, uninhabitable coral atolls.

KWAJALEIN SCHOOL SYSTEM
  Day Coed Ages 4-18. Gr K-12.

Kwajalein, Marshall Islands.
Mail to: Box 51, APO, San Francisco 96555.
Robert D. Schmitt, Supt.
Col Prep Gen Acad. Tests CEEB. Curr—USA. LI—Eng. A—Math.
  CF—Fr Span Hist (US) Bus. SI—Rem Read.
Summer Session. Acad Rem. May-July.
Est 1963. Nonprofit. Sem (Aug-May). ISS.

Based on Kwajalein, the largest and most populous Marshall Island, this U.S. Army administered school offers an American curriculum. Ninety-nine percent of its students are dependents of Americans employed on the Kwajalein missile range.

PAPUA NEW GUINEA

In 1975 Papua New Guinea gained independence, ending a United Nations' trusteeship administered by Australia. The eastern part of the country was explored by the Spanish and Portuguese, but Europeans did not settle until 1884. Germany then declared a protectorate over the northern coast and Britain over the southern coast. Copper is the chief source of revenue, although the country is heavily dependent on foreign aid. The capital is Port Moresby, and the monetary unit is the kina (K). English and Melanesian pidgin are the principal languages.

GOROKA INTERNATIONAL PRIMARY SCHOOL
  Day Coed Ages 5-13. Gr K-6.

Goroka (Eastern Highlands Province), Papua New Guinea. P.O. Box
  845. Tel. Goroka 721466.
R. T. Denholm, TPTC, DipEd, Coburg (Victoria), Head.
Gen Acad. Curr—Intl. LI—Eng. CF—Soc Stud Sci Art Music. SI—ESL
  Rem & Dev Read & Math.
Enr 246. B 128; G 118. US—12.
Fac 14. Full 10/Part 4. M 3; F 11. US UK Australia New Zealand.
Tui $1300.
Est 1957. Inc 1976 nonprofit. Quar (Feb-Dec). ISS.
Bldgs 10. Lib 15,000 vols. Athletic facilities.

Goroka's program emphasizes basic skill subjects including mathematics, reading and spelling/phonics. This allows the students to develop skills necessary for progress commensurate with the child's performance level. Extracurricular activities include athletics, cooking, badminton, tennis, gymnastics and drama.

BULAE INTERNATIONAL PRIMARY SCHOOL
Day Coed Ages 5-12. Gr K-6.

Lae (Morobe), Papua New Guinea. P.O. Box 1370. Tel. 42-2326.
Alan J. Hooper, Head.
Pre-Prep. Curr—Australia. LI—Eng.
Enr 508. B 269; G 239. US—14.
Fac 22. Full 22. M 4; F 18. UK.
Tui K1104.
Est 1964. Inc. Quar (Jan-Dec). ISS.

Enrolling students from Asia, Australia, New Zealand, Europe and the United States, Bulae offers a full primary school curriculum.

ELA BEACH INTERNATIONAL SCHOOL
Day Coed Ages 4-13. Gr K-6.

Port Moresby, Papua New Guinea. P.O. Box 282. Tel. 21-4720.
R.E. Andrews, Head.
Gen Acad Pre-Prep. Curr—Australian Intl. LI—Eng. SI—Rem & Dev
   Read & Math ESL.
Enr 520. B 273; G 247.
Fac 22. Full 21/Part 1. M 2; F 20. US 1.
Tui $1300.
Est 1946. Inc 1976 nonprofit. Quar (Jan-Dec). ISA ISS.
Bldgs 7. Lib 4000 vols. Athletic facilities.

The Australian-based curriculum at this school incorporates many internatioal features to accommodate a diverse enrollment. A method called "vertical grouping" is employed and places children in classrooms which include more than one age group. A non-graded approach to language arts and mathematics allows the students to progress at an appropriate pace. Extracurricular activities include sports, crafts and music study.

GORDON INTERNATIONAL SCHOOL
Day Coed Ages 5-12. Gr K-6.

Port Moresby (National Capitol District), Papua New Guinea. P.O. Box
   1825 Borako P.N.G. Tel. 255018.
Barrie Dallow, Head.
Pre-Prep. Curr—Nat. LI—Eng. CF—Fr Comp.
Enr 480. B 240; G 240. US—4.
Fac 21. Full 19/Part 2. M 3; F 18. Nat.
Tui K1104 (+K100).
Est I969. Inc I976 nonprofit. Quar (Feb-Dec). ISS.
Bldgs 10. Lib 5000 vols. Fields.

The Gordon School's curriculum meets the requirements of the Australian and New Guinea governments. Elementary French is taught and the math program is of American origin. The social studies course focuses on the history of New Guinea. Both faculty and students hail from several countries. Extracurricular activities include musical and dramatic productions, debate, student council and sports.

KOROBOSEA INTERNATIONAL SCHOOL
Day Coed Ages 5-12. Gr K-6.

Port Moresby, Papua New Guinea. P.O. Box 1319 Boroko P. Tel. 255358.
Ross F. Crilly, BA, TSL, TPTC, Prin.
Gen Acad. Curr—Intl. Ll—Eng. CF—Eng Math Drama Music. Sl—Rem Dev Read & Math.
Enr 450. B 250; G 200.
Fac 26. Full 18/Part 8. M 3; F 23.
Tui $1600 (+ 22150). Schol.
Est 1963. Nonprofit. Quar (Feb-Dec). ISS.
Bldgs 17. Lib 5500 vols. Athletic facilities.

The curriculum at Korobosea is designed to accommodate the educational needs of children from many countries. Mastery of basic academic subjects and the development of communication skills is emphasized. Counseling and remedial help are available when necessary and a full sports program is offered.

PORT MORESBY INTERNATIONAL SCHOOL
Day Coed Ages 11-18. Gr 7-12.

Port Moresby, Papua New Guinea. P.O. Box 276 Boroku. Tel. 675 253166.
T.R. Riles, Prin.
Col Prep. Curr—Natl. Ll—Eng. CF—Fr German Motu Technics Commerce Man Arts Econ Hist Physics. Sl—ESL.
Enr 550.
Fac 34.
Tui K690. Schol.
Est 1959. Inc. Sem (Jan-Dec). ISA ISS.

This school offers a "common curriculum" fulfilling requirements for both the Australian and Papua New Guinea educational systems, preparing students for the New South Wales School Certificate. Foreign nationals obtain qualifactions valid and accepted in their own countries. Various sports are offered including basketball, football, cricket, swimming, tennis and squash.

PHILIPPINES

Discovered by Magellan in 1521, conquered by Spain 21 years later, ceded to the United States in 1899 and conquered by Japan in 1941, the Philippine Islands became an independent republic in 1946. Mountainous and settled chiefly in seacoast areas, the islands' principal industry is agriculture. The capital is Manila and the monetary unit is the peso (P). Filipino, English and Spanish are the principal languages.

BRENT SCHOOL
Bdg Coed Ages 10-18; Day Coed 4-18. Gr N-12.

Baguio City 0201, Philippines. P.O. Box 35. Tel. 40-50. Telex: 442-2260.
Mail to: APO, San Francisco 96298.
Peter A. Caleb, Head.
Col Prep. Tests IB CEEB SSAT. Curr—USA Nat. LI—Eng. CF—Fr Span Filipino Ger Soc Stud Comp Sci Bible. SI—Tut.
Enr 375. B 55/140; G 45/135. US—121. Grad '84—20. Col—20.
Fac 50. Full 41/Part 9. M 20; F 30. US 13.
Tui Bdg $3900; Day $550-2575. Schol.
Est 1909. Inc 1954 nonprofit. Episcopal. Tri (Sept-Je). ISS EARCOS NAIS. Accred WASC.
Bldgs 16. Dorms 4. Lib 22,000 vols. Gym. Tennis courts. Field.

Known originally as the Baguio School and renamed in 1922 in honor of its founder, the Right Rev. Charles Henry Brent, first Bishop of the Episcopal Church in the Philippines, the school accepts students of any religion or nationality. Combining Christian ideals and high standards of scholarship, an enriched American curriculum is offered preparing students for college entrance.

The majority of students are Americans and Filipinos, with students from Australia, Belgium, Canada, Germany, Malaysia and 22 other countries comprising the rest. Recent graduates have entered Texas A&M, Harvard, Northwestern and Cornell.

Located on a 20-hectare campus 5000 feet above sea level, the school enjoys a temperate climate year-round. Outdoor sports include basketball, golf, track and field, tennis, volleyball, badminton, soccer and swimming.

See also page 95

CEBU INTERNATIONAL SCHOOL
Day Coed Ages 4-15. Gr K-10.

Cebu, Philippines 6401. Banilad. P.O. Box 735. Tel. 9-72-68.
Marcia de la Rosa, Prin.
Gen Acad. Curr—USA. LI—Eng. CF—Filipino Cebuano.
Enr 195. US—20.
Fac 20. Full 14/Part 6. US 1. Nat.
Tui $347-631.

**Est 1924. Inc. Sem (July-April). A/OS ISS.
Bldgs 3. Lib. Field.**

The Cebu International School was originally established for
Americans in Cebu. American and Filipino children comprise most of
the enrollment.

INTERNATIONAL SCHOOL
Day Coed Ages 5-19. Gr K-12.

**Makati (Metro Manila), Philippines 3117. Gen Luna St. & Imelda Ave.
Tel. 88-98-91.
Mail to: CCPO Box 323, Makati (Metro Manila), Philippines 3117.
Daryl W. Pelletier, MA, Univ. of Maine, EdD, Harvard, Supt.
Col Prep Gen Acad. Tests CEEB SSAT IB. LI—Eng. A—Eng Math
Span. CF—Chinese Fr Ger Lat Filipino Hist (Philippines US) Econ
Philos Psych. SI—ESL Tut Rem Lang & Math ESL.
Enr 2450. B 1155; G 1295. Elem 1700, Sec 750. US—800. Grad
'84—171. Col—152.
Fac 215. Full 205/Part 10. M 37; F 178. US 30. Nat.
Tui 26,560-44,400 P (+2650-11,750 P).
Summer Session. Acad Rec Enrich. Tui 650-1650 P. 2-8 wks.
Est 1920. Inc nonprofit. Quar (Aug-Je). A/OS EARCOS ISS NAIS
Accred WASC.
Bldgs 16. 3 Libs 44,000 vols. Gyms 3. Swimming pool. Athletic fields.**

Nearly 1000 United States youths yearly attend this international
school founded by American and British residents of Manila. Altogether
more than 50 nationalities are represented, including Filipino, Japanese,
British, German, Australian and Canadian students. The primarily
college preparatory curriculum is broadened with opportunity for
advanced placement, a wide selection of electives, independent study
and work experience programs. Special courses are conducted for 11th
and 12th graders leading to the International Baccalaureate Diploma.
Athletic competition, both intramural and interscholastic, as well as a
full range of activities round out the program. Limited scholarship aid is
available solely to Filipino students.

MARYKNOLL COLLEGE FOUNDATION
Day Boys Ages 4-6; Girls 4-15. Coed 16-22. Gr N-12.

**Quezon City 3004 (Metro Manila), Philippines. Katipunan Rd., Loyola
Heights. Tel. 98.24.21.
Dr. Lourdes R. Quisumbing, PhD, Univ. of Santo Tomas, Pres.
Pre-Prep Col Prep. Curr—Nat. LI—Eng Filipino. A—Span Math Sci.
CF—Span Filipino Hist Relig Advertising.
Enr 5559. Col—892.
Fac 316. Full 255/Part 61. US 2. Nat.
Tui 1265-1472 P (+var). Schol.
Summer Session. Acad. 6 wks.**

Est 1926. Inc nonprofit.
Bldgs 13. 5 Libs 73,939 vols. Field. Crts.

The Maryknoll College Foundation is a Christian Filipino educational institution primarily for women. Academic programs are offered at the elementary, secondary and college levels with instruction in both English and Filipino. Nursery and Kindergarten education is available to both boys and girls in the Child Study Center. Extracuricular activities include art, dancing, dramatics and athletics.

TAIWAN

Portuguese navigators visited this large island off the coast of mainland China during the 16th century and called it "Ihla Formosa" or "beautiful island," giving rise to its popular name in the West. Its official Chinese name through the years has been Taiwan, meaning "Terraced Bay." The island has been site of the government of Nationalist China since 1949.

Taipei, at the northern end, is capital. The monetary unit is the new Taiwan dollar (NT$) and Chinese is the spoken language.

THE AMERICAN SCHOOL OF MAANSHAN
  Day Coed Ages 5-13. Gr K-8.

Hengchun (Pingtung Hsien), Taiwan. P.O. Box 9. Tel. 008 892110-29. Telex: 71386.
T. Patrick Van Kampen, BSc, Western Michigan Univ., MEd, Bridgewater State College, Prin.
Gen Acad. Curr—US. Ll—Eng. CF—Chinese Lang & Stud Music Art.
Enr 45. B 29; G 16. US—45.
Fac 6. Full 4/Part 2. M 2; F 4. US 3.
Est 1978. Nonprofit. Sem (Sept-Je). EARCOS ISS.
Bldg. Lib. Field.

Sponsored by the Bechtel U.S.A. and Taiwan Power companies, this school serves primarily the children of company employees. It features an American curriculum supplemented with studies in Chinese language and culture. Students participate in soccer, basketball, softball, tennis, swimming, school publications and clubs on a regular semi-weekly basis. The school is located near the South China Sea.

MORRISON CHRISTIAN ACADEMY
  Bdg Coed Ages 13-18, Day 6-18. Gr K-12.

Taichung 400, Taiwan. Box 27-24.
Lawrence W. Byous, EdD, Univ. of Northern Colorado, Supt.
Col Prep. Tests CEEB ACT.Curr—USA. Ll— Eng. CF—Chinese Span Fr Bible Soc Stud Hist (US) Typ. SI—ESL.
Enr 472. Elem 362, Sec 110. US—394. Grad '84—29. Col—24.
Fac 40. Full 20/Part 20. M 20; F 20. US 40.

Tui Bdg $4500-6100; Day $2500-3100.
Est 1952. Inc. Sem (Aug-May). EARCOS ISS. Accred WASC.
Bldgs 12. Dorms 2. Libs 2. Gyms 2. Pool. Tennis court. Fields.

Morrison Academy offers a system of six schools with a program from kindergarten to grade 12. The American curiculum is religiously oriented with Bible courses required for every student at all grade levels. Chinese is taught in elementary grades, except kindergarten. The majority of students are Americans, with 58 percent from missionary homes.

The central campus at Taichung also houses an associated Norwegian School for grades one through nine, with dormitories operated by the Norwegian and Finnish Missions located off-campus.

DOMINICAN SCHOOL
Day Coed Ages 4-15. Gr N-9.

Taipei, Taiwan. 76 Tah Chi St. Tel. 02-541-8451.
Sr. Ma. Cristina Castro, Prin.
Gen Acad. Curr—USA. LI—Eng. CF—Fr Span Relig Soc Stud Hist Art Music.
Enr 655.
Fac 28.
Tui $1181 (+ $300).
Summer Session. Acad. Tui $300. 6 wks.
Est 1958. Nonprofit. Roman Catholic. Quar (Aug-May). EARCOS ISS.
Bldgs 3. Lib 6000 vols. Athletic facilities.

Operated by the Dominican Sisters, this school provides an American curriculum to an enrollment that is 50 percent American. Extracurricular activities include baseball, football, soccer, tennis, track and field. A similar school in Kaohsiung, of the same name offers a coeducational program from nursery through the fourth grade.

TAIPEI AMERICAN SCHOOL
Day Coed Ages 5-19. Gr K-PG.

Taipei 111, Taiwan ROC. 731 Wen Lin Rd. Sec 1, Shih Lin District. Tel. 02-831-2111.
Guy Lott, Jr., BS, MS, William Paterson College, EdD, Pacific States Univ., Supt.
Col Prep. Tests IB CEEB SSAT. Curr—USA. LI—Eng. A—Art Biol Calc Eng Hist Art Fr. CF—Chinese Fr Span Ger Japanese ESL. SI—Rem & Dev Math Read Tut.
Enr 1148. B 573; G 575. Elem 548, Sec 600. US—608. Grad '84—74. Col 64.
Fac 90. Full 80/Part 10. M 42, F 48. US 80.
Tui NT$55,350-101,450 (+ NT$36,000).
Summer Session. Acad ESL. Tui NT$1,100 (+ NT$2800). 6 wks.
Est 1949. Inc nonprofit. Sem (Aug-Je). A/OS EARCOS ISS NAIS. Accred WASC.

Bldgs 20. 2 Libs 50,000 vols. Labs. Gym. Fields. Tennis crts. Swimming pool.

Taipei American School has grown from its origin in 1949 to become one of the largest American community-sponsored overseas schools. Located on a 22-acre campus, TAS enrolls students from 45 different nations, with 53 percent coming from the U.S.

Self-contained classes and team teaching situations are conducted at all grade levels. Asian studies are required for elementary students and offered to secondary pupils as an elective. Electives and extracurricular activities include choral and instrumental music, mechanical drawing, ceramics, photography and general business courses.

LATIN AMERICA

CENTRAL AMERICA, MEXICO & CARIBBEAN ISLANDS

BAHAMAS

Located east of Florida and north of Cuba, the Bahamas are a group of over 3000 islands, cays and rocks, of which only 20 are inhabited. The most important of these is New Providence, site of the capital, Nassau.

A crown colony since 1717, self-government was granted in 1964. In 1969, a new constitution was adopted and the colony became the Commonwealth of the Bahama Islands. The country became an independent nation in 1973. The unit of currency is the Bahaman dollar (B$). English is the spoken language.

AQUINAS COLLEGE HIGH SCHOOL
Day Coed Ages 11-17. Gr 7-12.

Nassau, Bahamas. Madeira St. Box N 7540. Tel. (809) 32-28934.
Vincent Ferguson, BA, St. Anselm's College, MEd, Mankato State, Head.
Col Prep Gen Acad Bus. Tests GCE SSAT. Curr—USA UK. LI—Eng.
Enr 639.
Est 1957. Roman Catholic. Sem (Sept-Je). ISS.
Bldgs 2. Field. Track.

Admitting predominantly Bahamian children, and a small number of Americans, this school provides a college preparatory curriculum along American and British guidelines. Students may prepare for either the U.S. College Boards or the British G.C.E. at the 'O' level. School activities include a student council, debating club, choral, oceanography and typing.

KINGSWAY ACADEMY
Day Coed Ages 4-18. Gr K-12.

Nassau, Bahamas. Bernard Rd. P.O. Box N4378. Tel. (809) 324-2158.
Mrs. Carol Harrison, Prin.
Gen Acad. Tests GCE SSAT. Curr—USA. LI—Eng. CF—Span Fr Lang
Arts Soc Stud Art Bible Music Drama. SI—Rem & Dev Read Tut.

Enr 760. Elem 550, Sec 2100. Grad '84—14. Col—12.
Fac 37. Full 35/Part 2. US 8.
Tui B$355-365/term (+ B$130).
Est 1959. Nonprofit. Tri (Sept-Je). ISS.
Bldgs 5. Lib 4000 vols. Athletic facilities.

Kingsway Academy is a Christian day school offering a curriculum
similar to Canadian and American standards, but adapted to meet the
needs of citizens and residents of the Bahamas. Enrollment is basically
Bahamian but other countries are also represented. Instruction is in
English with Spanish offered from grade six.

ST. ANDREW'S SCHOOL
  Day Coed Ages 3-17. Gr N-12.

Nassau, Bahamas. Yamacraw Rd. P.O. Box N-7546. Tel. 809-324-2621.
Philip Cash, MA, Univ. of Wales, Head.
Col Prep Gen Acad. Tests GCE CEEB SSAT. Curr—UK. LI—Eng.
  CF—Fr Span Math. SI—Rem & Dev Read Tut.
Enr 700. B 320; G 380. Elem 400, Sec 300. US—80. Grad '84—41.
  Col—31.
Fac 45. Full 44/Part 1. M 20; F 25. US 4. UK.
Tui B$1335-2985. Schol.
Summer Session. Acad Rec. Tui Day $B240. 4 wks.
Est 1947. Inc 1948 nonprofit. Tri (Sept-Je). NAIS.
Bldgs 5. Lib 12,000 vols. Athletic facilities.

Preparation for the British G.C.E. or the American College Boards is
offered at St. Andrew's. Electives are conducted in art, computer studies
geography, commerce and history.

BERMUDA

A self-governing British dependency, Bermuda consists of approximately 360 islands about 500 miles east of North Carolina. Bermuda
adopted a new constitution in 1968 and gained almost full autonomy,
except for foreign relations and defense. Tourism accounts for a large
percentage of the nation's income. The capital city is Hamilton. The unit
of currency is the Bermuda dollar (Be$) and English is the native
language.

SALTUS GRAMMAR SCHOOL
  Day Coed Ages 5-18. Gr K-12.

Pembroke 5-35, Bermuda. Tel. (809-29)2-6177.
J. Keith McPhee, BA, Durham Univ., MEd, Miami Univ., Head.
Col Prep. Tests SSAT GCE. Curr—UK. LI—Eng. CF—Fr Span Lat
  Physics Music Econ.
Enr 612. B 591; G 21.
Fac 52. Full 38/Part 14. M 22; F 30.

Tui $2700 (+ $67). Schol.
Summer Session. Acad. Tui Day $200. 3 wks.
Est 1880. Inc nonprofit. Tri (Sept-Je). ISS NAIS.
Bldgs 8. Lib 7000 vols. Athletic facilities.

Primarily enrolling Bermudians, students from Great Britain, Canada and the United States are also in attendance. The curriculum prepares students for the British 'O' level examinations.

COSTA RICA

The Republic of Costa Rica is the southernmost Central American state. Columbus discovered and probably named it in 1502. After many years as a Spanish province, it was established as a republic in 1848. Chief exports are bananas and coffee. The capital and largest city is San Jose; the monetary unit is the colon (C). Spanish is the country's language.

ANGLO AMERICAN SCHOOL
   Day Coed Ages 4¹/₂-12. Gr K-6.

San Jose, Costa Rica. Calle 37, Apartado 3188. Tel. 25-17-29.
Antoinette Bourcart de Soto, Prin.
Gen Acad. Curr—USA Nat. Ll—Eng Span.
Enr 715.
Tui $600 (+ $200).
Est 1949. Nonprofit. Sem (Mar-Nov). ISS.
Bldgs 3. Athletic facilities.

Enrolling students from Costa Rica and the rest of South and Central America, Anglo American School combines a native and American curriculum with bilingual instruction in English and Spanish.

COSTA RICA ACADEMY
   Day Coed Ages 4-18. Gr K-12.

San Jose, Costa Rica. Apartado 4941. Tel. 39-09-74.
Paul Orr, Head.
Col Prep. Tests CEEB SSAT. Curr—USA. Ll—Eng.
Enr 187.
Fac 27.
Tui $2090 (+ $400).
Est 1970. Inc nonprofit. Sem (Aug-Je). AASCA A/OS ISS.
Bldg. Lib 8000 vols. Athletic facilities.

Located on an eight-acre site, this school is open to students of all nationalities living in San Jose, and features an American curriculum with bilingual instruction in Spanish and English. Costa Rican history and geography are taught in the elementary grades. Specialized education is available for students with learning disabilities.

COUNTRY DAY SCHOOL
Day Coed Ages 4-18. Gr N-12.

San Jose, Costa Rica. Apartado 86170. Tel. 28-08-73.
Woodson C. Brown, BS, Northeast Missouri State Univ., Dir.
Col Prep. Tests SSAT TOEFL. Curr—USA. Ll—Eng. A—Biol US Hist
Math Span Lang & Lit. CF—Span Sci. Sl—Rem Read & Math Tut ESL.
Enr 501. B 236; G 265. Elem 359, Sec 132. US—178. Grad '84—22.
Col—22.
Fac 48. Full 33/Part 15. M 14; F 34. US 26.
Tui $1744 (+$85).
Summer Session. Tui Day $70. 4 wks.
Est 1963. Inc. Sem (Aug-Je). ISS.
Bldgs 6. Lib 10,000 vols.

This independent school follows a U.S. curriculum featuring bilingual instruction in Spanish and English. Students are predominantly North American, with small numbers from Europe, Asia and Latin America. Preparation is offered for the College Boards and recent graduates have entered Cornell, Oberlin, Duke, Texas Christian University and the University of Florida.

LINCOLN SCHOOL
Day Coed Ages 4-22. Gr N-12 JC 1-2.

San Jose, Costa Rica. Apartado Postal 1919. Tel. 35-77-33.
Dr. Keith Miller, Dir.
Col Prep. Tests CEEB SSAT. Curr—USA Nat. Ll—Eng. A—Bio Math
Span. CF—Fr Ital Span ESL Sociol Hist (Lat Am US World).
Enr 1381. US—156.
Fac 83. US 15. Costa Rica.
Tui $688-1348 (+var).
Summer Session. Acad. Tui $50/crse. 6 wks.
Est 1944. Inc nonprofit. Sem (Feb-Dec). AASCA A/OS ISS. Accred
SACS.
Bldgs 15. 2 Libs 10,000 vols. Labs. Gym. Fields.

Located in a suburban area four miles from San Jose, this school's enrollment is comprised mostly of Costa Ricans. The curriculum prepares students for the U.S. College Boards or the Costa Rican Bachillerato. A program for the learning disabled is also conducted. Sports include intramural and varsity soccer, basketball, volleyball, baseball and gymnastics.

DOMINICAN REPUBLIC

The Dominican Republic shares with Haiti the island of Hispaniola, second largest of the Greater Antilles and situated between Cuba and Puerto Rico. The capital, Santo Domingo, is the oldest white settlement in the Western Hemisphere, founded in 1496. Primarily agricultural, the country exports sugar, coffee, cacao and tobacco. Spanish is the official language; the peso (RD$) is the monetary unti.

CAROL MORGAN SCHOOL OF SANTO DOMINGO
Day Coed Ages 4-18. Gr N-12.

Santo Domingo, Dominican Republic. Apartado 1169. Tel. (809) 532-8551.
Robert D. Zurfluh, BA, MA, Pacific Lutheran Univ., Supt.
Col Prep. Tests CEEB SSAT. Curr—USA. LI—Eng. CF—Span Fr Ger. SI—Rem & Dev Read & Math Speech Eng.
Enr 1465. Elem 1100, Sec 365. US—2660. Grad '84—85. Col—76.
Fac 88. Full 86/Part 2. M 20; F 68. US 72.
Tui RD$2000-3100 (+ RD$130).
Summer Session. Acad Rec. 6 wks.
Est 1933. Sem (Aug-Je). ACCAS A/OS ISS. Accred SACS.
Bldgs 7. Lib 18,000 vols. Athletic facilities.

A North American college preparatory curriculum is offered at Carol Morgan. All instruction is in English, while Spanish, French and German are offered as electives. Students from the Dominican Republic and U.S. comprise most of the enrollment. Proficiency in English and achievement tests are required prior to admission.

EL SALVADOR

Smallest of the Central American republics, the Republic of El Salvador declared independence from Spain in 1821. Numerous revolutions and wars against neighboring countries followed. Today the Constitution calls for a popularly elected President, a unicameral legislature and a National Assembly. San Salvador is the capital city, and the unit of currency is the colon (C). Spanish is the native language.

AMERICAN SCHOOL
(Escuela Americana)
Day Coed Ages 3-18. Gr K-12.

San Salvador, El Salvador. Apartado Postal 01-35. Tel. 23-4353.
Bert Webb, Supt.
Col Prep Gen Acad. Tests SSAT. Curr—USA Nat. LI—Eng.
Enr 1543.
Fac 116.
Tui $600-1000 (+ $555-575). Schol.
Summer Session. Acad. Tui $100. 5 wks.
Est 1946. Nonprofit. Sem (Aug-May). AASCA A/OS ISS. Accred SACS.
Bldgs 4. 2 Lib 27,000 vols. Fields.

Most of the students at this international school come from El Salvador and the United States. For the elementary grades half the day's instruction is in Spanish and half in English. For Grades 7 through 12 an

American curriculum prevails, with one hour's worth of Spanish instruction daily. Preparation is offered for the American College Boards and a large percentage of graduates go on to U.S. colleges and universities.

GUATEMALA

Northernmost state in Central America, the Republic of Guatemala contains famous ruins of the ancient Mayan civilization. Most of the country is mountainous, with many volcanic peaks. The fertile Pacific slope is the most densely populated area. Guatemala City is the capital and largest city, and the quetzal (Q) is the monetary unit. Spanish is the country's language.

THE AMERICAN SCHOOL OF GUATEMALA
  Day Coed Ages 5-19. Gr K-12.

Guatemala, Guatemala. 11 Calle 15-79, zona 15, Vista Hermosa 111. Tel. 690-791.
Jerry D. Hager, PhD, Michigan State Univ., Dir.
Col Prep Gen Acad. Tests CEEB. Curr—USA Nat. LI—Span Eng. CF—Fr Ger Hist (US) Soc Stud Man Arts Typ Home Ec Arts. SI—Rem & Dev Read.
Enr 1390. Elem 1000, Sec 390. US—179.
Fac 114. US Guatemala.
Tui $1590-1945.
Est 1945. Inc nonprofit. Sem (Jan-Oct). AASCA A/OS ISS. Accred SACS.
Lib 40,000 vols. Swimming pool. Fields. Aud.

The program of instruction at this binational school is both English and Spanish. Elementary students divide their school day equally between the two languages. Secondary students may choose between programs predominantly English or Spanish. Recent graduates have entered Texas A&M, University of Florida and North Carolina State.

COLEGIO MAYA
  Day Coed Ages 4-18. Gr N-12.

Guatemala, Guatemala. Apartado 64-C. Tel. 301209.
D. Jeffrey Keller, Dir.
Col Prep Gen Acad. Tests SSAT. Curr—USA. LI—Eng.
Enr 241.
Fac 25.
Tui $630-2300 (+ $600). Schol.
Est 1958. Nonprofit. Sem (Aug-Je). AASCA A/OS ISS. Accred SACS.
Bldgs 4. Lib 5000 vols. Athletic facilities.

This school offers an individualized instruction program from nursery through the sixth grade. Most of the students come from the United States and Guatemala. Spanish is offered as a language elective.

COLEGIO VALLE VERDE
Day Coed Ages 3-17. Gr N-12.

Guatemala, Guatemala. 15 Ave. 3-80, Zone 15. Tel. 690563.
Concha A. de Bianchi, Dir.
Col Prep. Curr—USA Nat. Ll—Eng Span. A—Hist Lit Psych. CF—Soc
Stud Sci Lang. Sl—Tut ESL.
Enr 1000. B 500; G 500. Elem 672, Sec 328. US—20. Grad '84—53.
Col—45.
Fac 60. Full 30/Part 30. M 15; F 45. US 10. Guatemala.
Tui $1060 (+ $250).
Summer Session. Acad. Tui $60. 4 wks.
Est 1966. Inc. Quar (Jan-Oct).
Bldgs 9. Lib 20,000 vols. Athletic facilities.

Valle Verde offers a completely bilingual approach to all subjects from
kindergarten through sixth grade and extensive English instruction from
seventh to twelfth grade. Extracurricular activities include swimming,
choir and interschool sports - volleyball, baseball and basketball.

INTER-AMERICAN SCHOOL
Bdg Coed Ages 15-18; Day Coed 4-19. Gr N-12.

Quezaltenango, Guatemala. Apartado 24, Camino a Chiquilaja Canton
Choqui. Tel. 011-502-61-40-80.
Averill Allen, BA, Pepperdine Univ., Dir.
Col Prep Gen Acad. Tests CEEB. Curr—USA Nat. Ll—Eng. A—Math
Sci Psych. CF—Fr Span Bible Guatemalan Stud. Sl—Tut.
Enr 111. B /62; G 2/47. US—45. Grad '84—5. Col—5.
Fac 19. Full 18/Part 1. M 7; F 12. US 19.
Tui Bdg $250/mo (+ $100); Day $76/mo (+ $100).
Summer Session. Acad. Tui Day $45. 4 wks.
Est 1961. Nonprofit. Sem (Aug-May).
Bldgs 4. Dorm. Lib 8000 vols. Court. Field.

This school was established through the efforts of missionary,
Guatemalan and international families in Quezaltenango. The tri-
cultural atmosphere (Mayan, Spanish, English) fosters the creative arts,
language and social studies in coordination with Guatemalan heritage.
Chapel services are held regularly and individual tutoring sessions are
available. School activities include intramural sports, crafts, chess and
community service projects.

HAITI

The only French-speaking republic in the Americas, the Republic of
Haiti occupies the western third of the island of Hispaniola in the
Greater Antilles and borders the Dominican Republic. The struggle for
independence began in the 1790s and was finally achieved in 1804. A
long period of unrest followed. Francois "Papa Doc" Duvalier was

installed as President in 1956, declared himself President for life in 1964 and served until his death in 1971. An agricultural nation, coffee is the chief export. The capital is Port-au-Prince, and the monetary unit is the gourde (G).

UNION SCHOOL
Day Coed Ages 4-18. Gr N-12.

Port-au-Prince, Haiti. P.O. Box 1175. Tel. 2-2007 10314.
Marie Bogat, BA, Oberlin College, MA, Hofstra Univ., PhD, Univ. of Alabama, Dir.
Col Prep Gen Acad. Tests CEEB SSAT. Curr—USA. Ll—Eng. A—Fr. CF—Fr Soc Stud Art Econ Pol Sci Photog Typ. Sl—ESL.
Enr 345. Elem 197, Sec 148. US—207. Grad '84—77. Col—25.
Fac 31. Full 29/Part 4. M 7; F 24. US 23.
Tui $1800 (+$350). Schol.
Est 1919. Nonprofit. Sem (Aug-May). ACCAS A/OS ISS NAIS. Accred SACS.
Bldgs 4. Lib 11,000 vols. Athletic facilities.

Preparation for the College Boards is offered at this international day school. Most of the students come from the United States and Haiti. French is offered as an elective, with special English-speaking lessons for Haitians.

HONDURAS

A mountainous forested country, the Republic of Honduras was discovered by Columbus in 1502. The nation has a 400-mile Caribbean coastline and a 40-mile Pacific frontage. Since it declared independence from Spain in 1821, the country has been troubled by political unrest. Tegucigalpa is the capital and largest city. The lempira (L) is the national currency and Spanish is the national language.

ESCUELA BILINGUE VALLE DE SULA
Day Coed Ages 4-18. Gr N-12.

San Pedro Sula, Honduras. Apartado 735. Tel. 544494.
Carole A. Black, BA, BS, Admin.
Col Prep Gen Acad. Tests SSAT TOEFL. Curr—USA Natl. Ll—Eng Span.
Enr 450.
Fac 22.
Tui $600 (+$50). Schol.
Summer Session. Acad. Tui $200. 8 wks.
Est 1971. Inc nonprofit. Sem (Sept-Je). ISS.
Bldgs 3. Lib 5,000 vols. Athletic facilities.

Providing a bilingual education in both English and Spanish, this school enrolls primarily students from Honduras with a few from the United States.

THE INTERNATIONAL SCHOOL
  Day Coed Ages 4-18. Gr N-12.

San Pedro Sula, Honduras. Apartado Postal 565. Tel. 54-36-77.
Paul Orr, Jr., PhD, Alabama State Univ., Dir.
Pre-Prep Col Prep. Tests CEEB TOEFL. Curr—USA. LI—Eng.
  CF—Span Math Sci Soc Stud. SI—Rem & Dev Math Tut ESL.
Enr 1020. Elem 800; Sec 220 Grad '84—33.
Fac 51. US 33.
Tui $700-1000.
Est 1953. Inc nonprofit. Sem (Aug-May). AASCA A/OS ISS. Accred
  SACS.
Bldgs 5. Lib 10,000 vols. Gym. Court. Field.

Enrollment at this coeducational day school is primarily Honduran
and North American, with other nations represented in smaller
numbers. Special Spanish language, history and culture programs are
offered. Students may prepare for either the U.S. College Boards or the
Honduran Bachillerato.

THE AMERICAN SCHOOL
  Day Coed Ages 4-18. Gr N-12.

Tegucigalpa, Honduras. Tel. 32-2391.
Mail to: c/o American Embassy Tegucigalpa, Dept. of State, Wash-
  ington, DC 20520.
Clark Brown, EdD, Columbia, Dir.
Col Prep. Tests CEEB SSAT. Curr—USA Nat. LI—Eng Span. CF—Sci
  Psych Soc Stud Econ Sociol Art Hist Man Arts Philos. SI—Rem Read
  Eng & Span.
Enr 1025. Elem 750, Sec 275. Grad '84—50. Col—40 US—116.
Fac 63. Full 61/Part 2. M 26, F 37. US 34.
Tui $1500 (+ $150). Schol.
Est 1946. Inc nonprofit. Sem (Aug-Je). AASCA A/OS ISS. Accred
  SACS.
Bldgs 10. Lib 10,000 vols. Field.

Offering a choice of American or native curriculum in the secondary
division, this school prepares students for either the American College
Boards or the Honduran Bachillerato. Instruction is in English, with
Spanish required of all students. Honduran social studies are taught in
Spanish. Extensive electives are offered in the social sciences.

JAMAICA

Long a mecca for tourists, Jamaica was discovered by Columbus in
1494 and was the center of British pirate activities in the seventeenth
century. It became an independent member of the British Commonwealth in 1962. The country is the world's largest producer of bauxite.

The capital is Kingston and the monetary unit is the Jamaican dollar (J$). English is the native language.

THE PRIORY SCHOOL
Day Coed Ages 3-18. Gr K-13.

Kingston 10, Jamaica. 32 Hope Rd. Tel. 809-926-6636.
Patrick C. Bourke, MA, DipEd, Oxford, Prin.
Col Prep Gen Acad. Tests GCE CEEB SSAT. Curr—USA UK. LI—Eng.
  CF—Span Fr Math Sci Soc Sci. SI—Rem & Dev Read ESL.
Enr 603. Elem 432, Sec 171. US—97. Grad '84—51. Col—25.
Fac 46. Full 41/Part 5. US 9. Jamaica.
Tui $450-857 (+$146). Schol.
Est 1944. Inc 1958 nonprofit. Tri (Sept-Je). ACCAS A/OS ISS. Accred
  SACS.
Bldgs 24. Lib 10,000 vols. Athletic facilities.

Located on a five-acre site with an additional nine acres occupied by playing fields, this school follows an Anglo-American curriculum. Students are enrolled from Canada, England, Jamaica and the U.S. Specialized instruction is offered for students with learning disabilities.

BELAIR SCHOOL
Day Coed Ages 4-18. Gr K-12.

Mandeville, Jamaica. 43 DeCarteret Rd. P.O. Box 156. Tel. 962-3396.
Dudley Stokes, MDiv, D. Theo, Head.
Col Prep Gen Acad. Tests GCE CEEB SSAT. Curr—USA UK. LI—Eng.
  A—Calc. CF—Drama Arts Journalism. SI—Rem & Dev Read & Math
  Tut.
Enr 625. Elem 407, Sec 218. US—16.Grad '84—29. Col—19.
Fac 51. Full 50/Part 1. US 5. Jamaica.
Tui J$800-1800 (+J$60).
Est 1968. Inc nonprofit. Tri (Sept-Je). AACAS ISS. Accred SACS.
Bldgs 4. 2 Libs 11,360 vols. Athletic facilities.

Belair offers both a U.S. college preparatory program and preparation leading to the Common Entrance Examination and G.C.E. 'O' level exams, with most graduates attending colleges and universities in the United States and Europe. Spanish and French are taught from the first grade, and remedial courses in reading and math are conducted in grades one through nine.

The traditional curriculum is supplemented by courses in the fine and practical arts. Belair will accept credits earned through independent study courses offered by approved institutions such as the University of Nebraska. Extracurricular activities include chess, photography, drama, tennis, track and soccer.

MEXICO

With evidence of its advanced aboriginal cultures and customs remaining today, Mexico is one of the most interesting countries of the Western hemisphere to visitor, tourist or student. Nashua, Maya, Toltec, Texcocan and Aztec were most notable among the native Indian tribes during the centuries of pre-Colombian history. Destruction of the Aztec empire by Cortes in 1521 was followed by three centuries of Spanish rule and, finally, revolution. Independence came in 1821.

Its constitution based on that of the United States, the United Mexican States is a federal democratic republic of 31 states and a federal district containing the capital, Mexico City, founded by the Aztecs in 1325. The language is Spanish and the monetary unit is the peso (Mex$).

COLEGIO AMERICANO DE DURANGO, A.C.
Day Coed Ages 4-18. Gr K-12.

Durango (Durango), Mexico. Apartado Postal 15-B. Tel. 1-44-45.
Kenneth Darg, BA, Hamline Univ., Dir.
Col Prep Bus/Tech. Curr—USA Nat. LI—Eng Span. CF—Span Soc Stud Nat Sci Drama Bus. SI—ESL.
Enr 666. B 260; G 406. Elem 550, Sec 116. US—44. Grad '84—33.
Fac 42. Full 25/Part 17. M 12; F 30. US 13. Mexico.
Tui $300-600.
Est 1954. Inc nonprofit. Sem (Sept-Je). A/OS ISS.
Bldgs 6. Lib 6000 vols. Athletic facilities.

Following a bilingual English-Spanish program with half a day's instruction in each language, American School of Durango offers commercial subjects for Mexican students. Most of the enrollment is Mexican, with about 8% North Americans.

AMERICAN SCHOOL OF GUADALAJARA, A.C.
Day Coed Ages 4-18. Gr N-12.

Guadalajara (Jalisco), Mexico. Colomos Apartado Postal 6-1074. Tel. 41-33-00.
Dr. Al Argenziano, Dir.
Col Prep Gen Acad. Tests CEEB. Curr—USA. LI—Eng Span.
Enr 1159.
Fac 77.
Tui $400-720 (+ $166).
Est 1956. Inc nonprofit. Sem (Sept-Je). A/OS ISS. Accred SACS.

A standard U.S. college preparatory curriculum is conducted at this school. The enrollment is largely Mexican.

EL COLEGIO BRITANICO
(The Edron Academy)
  Day Coed Ages 3-18. Gr N-12.

Mexico 01060 D.F., Mexico. Campestre #3 San Angel Inn. Tel. (5) 548
  34 84.
Eric A. Pearse, MA, Cambridge, Head.
Col Prep Gen Acad. Tests GCE. Curr—UK. Ll—Eng. A—Eng Lit Hist Fr
  Span Econ Geog Math Physics Chem Biol Art.
Enr 379. B 176; G 203. Elem 288, Sec 91. Grad '84—14. Col—9.
Fac 40. Full 30/Part 10. M 13; F 27. US 3. UK Nat.
Tui Mex$14,800-27,900/mo (+ Mex$20,000-33,000/yr). Schol.
Est 1968. Nonprofit. Tri (Sept-Je).
Bldgs 2. Lib 2000 vols.

Founded in order to prepare Mexican and British expatriate children
for further education in British universities, this school caters to students
from 20 different countries. Spanish is taught from grade three on.
Pupils sit for both 'O' and 'A' level G.C.E. examinations. Academic
subjects are supplemented by art, music and physical eduation.

AMERICAN SCHOOL FOUNDATION, A.C.
  Day Coed Ages 4-18. Gr K-12.

Mexico City 18, Mexico. Calle Sur 136 #135. Tel. 516-0720.
Robert G. Pickering, Supt.
Col Prep. Tests CEEB SSAT TOEFL. Curr—USA Nat. Ll—Eng Span.
  CF—Fr Ger Hist (US) Econ Pol Sci Philos Psych Sociol Arts Typ.
  Sl—ESL Tut.
Enr 1957. US—705.
Fac 162. US 94.
Tui $1550-2700. Schol.
Summer Session. Acad Rec. 6 wks.
Est 1888. Inc 1921 nonprofit. Sem (Sept-Je). A/OS ISS. Accred SACS.
Bldgs 4. Lib 20,000 vols. Gym. Fields. Swimming pool.

This large coed binational day school, located in Tacubaya overlooking Mexico City, offers a dual program in the elementary grades:
the official Mexican government curriculum in Spanish for half a day, a
typical English-language program the other half. All students are
required to study Spanish through grade six. In high school, the
principal program is a college preparatory course taught in English. For
students who plan to attend the National University of Mexico, there is
a special curriculum starting in grade seven. The school's modern plant
includes an auditorium, a science center, electronic language labs, video
installations, a social studies center, swimming pool and an art salon.

ETON SCHOOL
  Day Coed Ages 1½-17. Gr N-12.

Mexico City 10, D.F., Mexico. Alpes #605-Lomas de Chapultepec. Tel.
  5-20-04-10.

Colleen M. Quinlan de Martinez, BA, MA, Prin.
Pre-Prep Col Prep Gen Acad. Curr—USA Nat. LI—Eng Span. CF—Am Hist. Sl—Rem & Dev Read & Math ESL Span Tut.
Enr 372. B 196; G 176. US—10.
Fac 77. Full 32/Part 45. M 27; F 50. US 74.
Tui 14,500-24,650 pts (+12,000 pts). Schol.
Summer Session. Acad Rec. Tui 9600-16,600 pts. 6 wks.
Est 1971. Inc nonprofit. Sem (Sept-Je).
Bldgs 2. Lib 100,000 vols.

This school offers a bicultural education in English and Spanish for children of many nationalities. In the elementary grades, children acquire basic skills in reading, language and mathematics in an open classroom setting. Students in the secondary years are provided with vocational skills and guidance to augment their academic study. The pre-school program emphasizes reading readiness, familiarity with numerical concepts as well as music and art. A special program is also offered for gifted and talented students. A variety of extracurricular activities such as field trips, sports and swimming are featured throughout all the grades.

PETERSON LOMAS HIGH SCHOOL
Day Coed Ages 14-20. Gr 8-12.

Mexico City 11,000, Mexico. Paseo de la Reforma 1630. Tel. 520-4719.
Marvin A. Peterson, Dir.
Col Prep. Tests CEEB SSAT ACT TOEFL. Curr—USA. LI—Eng. A—Etymology Calc. CF—Span Sci Hist (US). Sl—Rem Eng & Math Tut.
Enr 115. B 65; G 50. US—60. Grad '84—24. Col—22.
Fac 15. Full 3/Part 12. M 4; F 11. US 10.
Tui $1000 (+$150).
Summer Session. Acad. Tui Day $150 (+$15). 6 wks.
Est 1960. Inc l983 nonprofit. Sem (Aug—Je).
Bldgs 1. Lib 5000 vols. Athletic facilities.

An American education is provided for children of American families living in Mexico City, preparing students for college and university entrance.

AMERICAN SCHOOL FOUNDATION OF MONTERREY, A.C.
Day Coed Ages 3-19. Gr N-12.

Monterrey (Neuvo Leon), Mexico. Apartado Postal 1762. Tel. 56-87-71.
William Stockebrand, Supt.
Col Prep Gen Acad. Tests CEEB SSAT. Curr—USA Nat. LI—Eng Span.
Enr 1407.
Fac 96.
Tui $683-1248. Schol.
Est 1928. Inc nonprofit. Sem (Sept-Je). A/OS ISS. Accred SACS.
Bldgs 4. Lib 16,000 vols. Athletic facilities.

Offering a combined Mexican-U.S. curriculum, this school prepares students for the U.S. College Boards and the Mexican Bachillerato. A full range of electives is provided including music, art, the humanities and physical education.

PAN AMERICAN SCHOOL, S.C.
  Day Coed Ages 4-20. Gr N-9.

Monterrey (Nuevo Leon), Mexico 6400. Hidalgo 656 Pte. Tel. 42-07-78.
Mail to: Apartado Postal 474, Monterrey, Mexico.
L. H. Arpee, Dir.
Col Prep Gen Bus. Curr—USA Nat. LI—Eng. CF—Span Hist (US) Arts Home Ec Typ Tech. SI—Tut.
Enr 2098. Elem 1898, Sec 200. Grad '84—90. Col—90.
Fac 69. M 7; F 62. US 18. Mexico.
Tui $1200-1800.
Summer Session. Acad. Tui Day $175. 6 wks.
Est 1952. Inc nonprofit. Quar (Sept-Je). ISS.
Bldgs 3. Lib 5000 vols.

Organized as an elementary and junior high school, the Pan American School also includes a three-year commercial course and a language laboratory that offers instruction in English to Spanish-speaking children. While the official language of instruction is English, the curriculum is national; students who wish to receive the Mexican diploma must take certain courses taught in Spanish.

AMERICAN SCHOOL OF PACHUCA
  Day Coed Ages 3-14. Gr N-9.

Pachuca (Hidalgo 42000), Mexico. Apartado Postal 131. Tel. 3-10-58.
Timothy Gautchier, BA, MA, Univ. of Wisconsin, Dir.
Gen Acad. Curr—USA Nat. LI—Eng Span. SI—ESL.
Enr 525. US—3.
Fac 37. US 12.
Tui $452-573. Schol.
Est 1920. Inc 1948 nonprofit. Sem (Sept-Je). A/OS ISS.
Bldgs 5. Lib 2000 vols.

Originally founded as a company school by the Real del Monte Mining Company, this primary school offers a combined American-Mexican curriculum. The school also features an English-language program for adults and classes for pre-schoolers between the ages of three and five.

AMERICAN SCHOOL OF PUEBLA
  Day Coed Ages 4-18. Gr K-12.

Puebla (Puebla), Mexico. Apartado 665. Tel. 48-01-89.
Arthur W. Chaffee, PhD, Ohio State Univ., Supt.
Col Prep. Curr—USA Natl. LI—Eng Span.

Enr 2643.
Fac 155.
Tui $580-812 (+ var). Schol.
Est 1943. Nonprofit. Sem (Sept-Je). A/OS ISS.

Providing a combined North American-Mexican curriculum from kindergarten through grade 9, and a Mexican Preparatoria and bilingual secretary program for grades 10 to 12, the school has a predominantly Mexican enrollment, with a small percentage of North Americans in attendance. Instruction is bilingual in English and Spanish through primary. Secondary and preparatory students receive instruction in Spanish for all subjects except language arts.

THE JOHN F. KENNEDY SCHOOL
Day Coed Ages 4-16. Gr K-9.

Queretaro, Mexico. Apartado Postal 93. Tel. 2-59-90.
Aleyda G. McKiernan, Dir.
Col Prep. Tests CEEB SAT. Curr—USA Nat. LI—Eng Span. CF—Fr
  Econ Pol Sci Journalism Typ.
Enr 450. US—27.
Fac 42. Full 22/Part 20. US 9. Mexico.
Tui $900 (+ $200).
Est 1964. Inc nonprofit. (Sept-Je). A/OS ISS. Accred SACS.
Bldgs 11. Lib 12,000 vols. Labs 2.

This school was founded by Mexican and North American industrialists residing in the Queretaro area. Mexican culture is taught at all grade levels. The student body is almost equally divided into groups from Mexico and the United States.

THE AMERICAN SCHOOL OF TORREON
Day Coed Ages 3-18. Gr N-12.

Terreon (Coahuila), Mexico. Av. Mayran y Cerrado De Nogal. Col.
  Torreon Jardin. Tel. 3-53-89.
Richard Jacobs, Dir.
Col Prep Gen Acad. Tests CEEB SSAT. Curr—USA Nat. LI—Eng Span.
Enr 1201.
Fac 75.
Tui $431-1019. Schol.
Summer Session. Acad Rec.
Est 1950. Inc nonprofit. Sem (Aug-Je). A/OS ISS. Accred SACS.
Lib 5000 vols. Gym. Field.

Offering bilingual instruction in English and Spanish, this coeducational school provides a college preparatory and commercial program, both of which are accredited. Students may prepare for the College Boards and most go on to colleges in the United States and Mexico.

NETHERLANDS ANTILLES

Part of the Kingdom of the Netherlands, the Netherlands Antilles consist of two groups of islands in the West Indies; one group, including Aruba and Curacao, near the South American coast, the other southeast of Puerto Rico. The area has autonomy in domestic affairs. The chief exports are refined petroleum products, the capital is Willemstad and the monetary unit is the guilder (CFLs).

SEROE COLORADO SCHOOL
Day Coed Ages 5-14. Gr K-9.

Seroe Colorado (Aruba), Netherlands Antilles. Tel. 9-3443.
Mail to: Lago Oil & Transport Co., Ltd., P.O. Box 503, Netherlands Antilles.
Oliver C. Davis, Jr., PhD, Vanderbilt Peabody College, Prin.
Pre-Prep. Curr—USA. LI—Eng. CF—Span Eng Typ.
Enr 97. US—34.
Fac 16. Full 13/Part 3. M 3; F 13. US 13.
Tui $170-400/mo.
Est 1929. Nonprofit. Quar (Sept-Je). ISS. Accred SACS.
Bldgs 1. Lib 6040 vols. Athletic facilities.

Sponsored by the Lago Oil & Transport Company, U.S. students account for 90% of the enrollment. Accelerated courses are arranged on an individual basis and tutoring is available. An elective program offers drama, sports and school yearbook.

NICARAGUA

The largest but most sparsely populated of the Central American states, the Republic of Nicaragua has more than 200 miles of coastline on both the Caribbean Sea and the Pacific. More than half of the country is covered by jungle. Managua is capital, Spanish is the language and the cordoba (C$) is the monetary unit.

AMERICAN NICARAGUAN SCHOOL
Day Coed Ages 4-18. Gr N-12.

Managua, Nicaragua. P.O. Box 2670. Tel. 70111.
Mail to: c/o American Embassy Managua, APO Miami, FL 34021.
Richard Chesley, Dir.
Col Prep. Tests CEEB TOEFL SSAT. Curr—USA Nat. LI—Eng Span. CF—Span Soc Stud Sci Econ Psych Sociol. SI—ESL Tut.
Enr 658. B 298; G 360. Elem 503, Sec 155. US—76. Grad '84—39. Col—36.
Fac 60. M 23; F 37. US 26.
Tui $1000.
Summer Session. Acad. Tui $150. 4 wks.

Est 1944. Inc nonprofit. Sem (Sept-Je). AASCA A/OS ISS. Accred SACS.
Bldgs 12. Lib 15,000 vols. Labs. Crts. Field.

This binational school, based on the American system of education, prepares students for the College Boards and Bachillerato Diploma. While all instruction is in English, Spanish is taught as a required language. Student activities and sports include intramural athletics, Spanish literary club and chess club. Recent graduates have entered Yale, Bowling Green, Denison and Louisiana State University.

PUERTO RICO

Since 1952 Puerto Rico has been a self-governing commonwealth voluntarily associated with the United States. As such, the Puerto Rican government has full jurisdiction over internal affairs, yet inhabitants freely migrate to and trade with the continental U.S. as American citizens. Puerto Ricans elect a Resident Commissioner to the U.S. House of Representatives, who has a voice but non-voting status. The island was originally ceded to the U.S. by Spain as a result of the Spanish-American War.

San Juan, center of Puerto Rico's tourist industry, is capital. Spanish is the official language, but most persons also speak English.

SAN CARLOS/BISHOP MCMANUS HIGH SCHOOL
Day Coed Ages 12-18. Gr 7-12.

Aguadilla, Puerto Rico 00603. Ave. Yumet Carr Parque Colon. Tel. 809-891-1445.
Nydia U. de Nieves, Prin.
Col Prep. Tests CEEB SSAT. Curr—USA Span. LI—Eng Span. A—Math Eng Span. CF—Fr Span Relig.
Enr 950.
Fac 50.
Tui $390-460 (+ var). Schol.
Est 1947. Nonprofit. Roman Catholic. Quar (Aug-May). Accred MSA.
Bldgs 6. Libs 2. Athletic facilities.

Enrolling students from the U.S. mainland, Puerto Rico and Spain, this school conducts grades 7 through 12 on a bilingual basis using English texts. Electives are offered in art and typing.

COLEGIO SAN FELIPE
Day Coed Ages 12-17. Gr 7-12.

Arecibo, Puerto Rico 00612. P.O. Box 673. 566 Ave. San Luis. Tel. 809-878-3532.
Sr. Carmen Gonzalez, Prin.
Col Prep Gen Acad. Tests CEEB. Curr—Nat. LI—Eng Span. A—Math Eng. CF—Fr Hist Soc Stud Relig Man Arts Psych.

Enr 929.
Fac 50.
Tui $615-695 (+ $200). Schol.
Summer Session. Acad. 6 wks.
Est 1932. Inc 1964 nonprofit. Sem (Aug-May). Accred MSA.
Lib 5900 vols. Athletic facilities.

Instruction is bilingual in English and Spanish with students following a native curriculum preparing for the College Boards. Recent graduates have entered Tulane, Duquesne and Alabama Universities, and Assumption and Robert William Colleges.

COLEGIO PUERTORRIQUENO DE NINAS
Day Girls Ages 4-18. Gr K-12.

Caparra Heights, Puerto Rico 00920. Turquesa St. Golden Gate. Tel. 809-782-2618.
Marie Mercedes Serbia de Caro, BA, MEd, Univ. of Puerto Rico, Dir.
Col Prep Gen Acad. Tests CEEB. Curr—USA. LI—Span.
Enr 700.
Fac 53.
Tui $650-1380. Schol.
Est 1913. Sem (Aug-May). Accred MSA.
Bldgs 1. Lib 8100 vols. Labs 4.

All classes at this college preparatory school are conducted in Spanish. English reading and grammar are conducted in grades 1 through 6 with French instruction available in grades 7 to 12. Sociology, physics, humanities and writing courses are among the electives offered.

SOUTHWESTERN EDUCATIONAL SOCIETY
Day Coed Ages 5-18. Gr K-12.

Mayaguez, Puerto Rico 00709. Carr. Tamarindo Box 40. Tel. 834-2150.
Ruth Stover, Head.
Col Prep. Tests CEEB GCE. Curr—USA. LI—Eng. CF—Span Fr Soc Stud Hist (US & Puerto Rico). SI—Eng Span.
Enr 388.
Fac 22. Full 19/Part 3. M 2; F 20.
Tui $80-903. Schol.
Summer Session. Acad Rem. Tui $100. 4 wks.
Est 1973. Nonprofit. Sem (Aug-May).
Bldgs 1. Lib. Athletic facilities.

Through a bilingual and bicultural atmosphere this school provides a strong academic curriculum preparing students for college entrance. English and Spanish are offered as first and second languages at all levels.

ACADEMIA DEL PERPETUO SOCORRO
Day Coed Ages 6-18. Gr 1-12.

Miramar, Santurce (San Juan), Puerto Rico 00907. Jose Marti & Central Streets. Tel. 809-721-4541.
Sr. Armand Marie Ayala, SSND, Prin.
Col Prep Gen Acad. Tests CEEB. Curr—USA. LI—Eng. A—Span Eng Maths Physics Genetics Chem. CF—Theology Soc Stud Arts.
Enr 1200. Grad '84—92. Col—92.
Fac 46. US 4. Nat.
Tui $1122-1456 (+ $1000). Schol.
Est I922. Nonprofit. Catholic. Sem (Aug-May). Accred MSA.
Bldgs 2. Lib. Gyms. Field.

Founded by The School Sisters of Notre Dame, this school is located two miles from Old San Juan. The curriculum of basic subjects and advanced courses prepares students for study in both U.S. and Puerto Rican universities. The variety of clubs and activities available includes art and glee clubs, computer, photography, honor society, needlecraft, student council and yearbook. Former students have attended MIT, Harvard, Tufts, Princeton, Yale, Georgetown and Brown.

THE CARIBBEAN SCHOOL
Day Coed Ages 4-18. Gr N-12.

Ponce, Puerto Rico 00731. Calle 9, La Rambla. Tel. 809-843-2048.
Shirley Pessin, Head.
Col Prep. Tests CEEB. Curr—USA. LI—Eng. CF—Fr Span Hist (US) Arts. SI—ESL.
Tui $860-1970.
Est 1954. Inc nonprofit. Sem (Sept-Je). ISS NAIS. Accred MSA.
Bldgs 3. Lib.

Located on the southern coast of Puerto Rico, the Caribbean School offers a bilingual academic program preparing students for post-secondary training. Recent graduates have entered MIT, Brigham Young University, Baylor College and universities within Puerto Rico.

COLEGIO PONCENO
Day Coed Ages 5-18. Gr K-12.

Ponce, Puerto Rico 00731. CR 00679—Buzon 365-C. Tel. 809-844-2424.
Fr. Jose A. Basols, MA, Villanova, Dir.
Col Prep. Tests CEEB. Curr—USA. LI—Span Eng. A—Math Sci. CF—Eng Art Relig Psych Comp Electronics. SI—Rem & Dev Math & Read Tut.
Enr 891. B 536; G 355. Elem 562, Sec 329. Grad '84—67. Col—67.
Fac 55. M 19; F 36. Nat Spain.
Tui $1400 (+ 200). Schol.
Summer Session. Acad. Tui $75/day (+ $20). 5 wks.

Est 1926. Inc 1967 nonprofit. Roman Catholic. Sem (Aug-May). Accred MSA.
Bldgs 4. Lib 8000 vols. Labs 4. Athletic facilities.

Located on a 14-acre suburban campus, and operated by the Piarist Fathers, Colegio Ponceno offers a curriculum preparing students for the College Entrance Examinations prepared by the College Board of Puerto Rico. The principal language of instruction is Spanish, but all students are required to take daily classes in English and religion. Recent graduates have entered Cornell, Tufts, MIT, Yale and Marquette. Student activities include an intramural and interscholastic sports program and clubs.

See also page 108

COLEGIO SAN JOSE
Day Boys Ages 12-19. Gr 7-12.

Rio Piedras, Puerto Rico 00928. Cap Amezquita Box AA. Tel. 809-751-8177.
Bro. Peter A. Pontolillo, S.M., BS, Univ. of Dayton, MA, Western Reserve Univ., Prin.
Col Prep. Tests CEEB SSAT. Curr—Nat. LI—Eng Span.
Enr 615.
Fac 44.
Tui $1300 (+ $250). Schol.
Summer Session. Acad. Enrich. Tui $100/crse. 6 wks.
Est 1920. Inc 1938 nonprofit. Roman Catholic. Sem (Aug-May). Accred MSA.
Bldgs 2. Lib 8000 vols. Gym. Field. Swimming pool. Tennis crts.

Operated by the Marianist Society, this school provides a North American curriculum, with bilingual instruction in English and Spanish. Extracurricular activities include a full range of sports and athletics.

CARIBBEAN CONSOLIDATED SCHOOLS
Day Coed Ages 4-18. Gr N-12.

San Juan, Puerto Rico 00936. G.P.O. Box 70177. Tel. 765-4426/4411.
Angie Casanas Amador, Head.
Pre-Prep Col Prep. Tests SSAT. Curr—USA. LI—Eng. A—Hist Eng Calc. CF—Span Fr Sci Art. SI—Rem & Dev Math & Read Tut ESL.
Enr 633. Elem 468, Sec 165. Grad '84—43. Col—43.
Fac 53. Full 50/Part 3. M 13; F 40. US 45.
Tui $1300-2923. Schol.
Summer Session. Acad Rec. Tui $180/crse. 6 wks.
Est 1952. Inc 1964. Sem (Aug-Je). NAIS. Accred MSA.
Bldgs 3. Libs 2. Field. Crts.

Caribbean Consolidated Schools was formed by the merger of the Parkville Elementary School (Calle Alabama, Parkville, Guaynabo, P.R.) and the Commonwealth High School (Hato Rey, P.R.). The

Parkville campus includes a lower and middle school and has an international enrollment of 500 students in pre-kindergarten through grade eight. A traditional academic curriculum is offered and all students take music, art and physical education.

Commonwealth High School features a college preparatory curriculum and enrolls 200 students in grades nine through twelve. Electives in computer science, theater, library science, health, music and art are integral parts of the program. Extracurricular activities include band, forensics, photography, sports and school publications.

EPISCOPAL CATHEDRAL SCHOOL
Day Coed Ages 5-19. Gr K-12.

Santurce, Puerto Rico 00908. 209 Canais St. P.O. Box 13305. Tel. 809-723-5478.
Rev. Gary J. DeHope, BS,Wilkes College, MS, State Univ. of New York, MDiv, Episcopal Theological School, Head.
Col Prep. Tests CEEB SSAT. Curr—USA. LI—Eng.
Enr 273.
Tui $1110 (+ $200). Schol.
Est 1946. Nonprofit. Episcopal. Sem (Aug-May). ISS. Accred MSA.
Bldgs 1. Lib.

Growing from a bilingual, bicultural kindergarten begun in 1946 at St. John's Episcopal Cathedral, this English-language school today offers a full elementary and secondary program and preparation for U.S. College Boards.

ROBINSON SCHOOL (AND LEARNING CENTER)
Day Coed Ages 4-18. Gr N-12.

Santurce, Puerto Rico 00907. Nairn St. #5. Tel. 809-728-6767.
Wayne Ramirez, MS, Univ. of Wisconsin, MFA, Univ. of Pennsylvania, Exec Dir.
Pre-Prep Col Prep. Tests SSAT. Curr—USA. LI—Eng. A—Eng Span Math. CF—Psych US & Puerto Rican Hist Relig. SI—ESL.
Enr 525. B 225; G 300. Elem 365, Sec 160. Grad '84—30. Col—30.
Fac 50. Full 50. M 15; F 35. US 48.
Tui $3000 (+ $300). Schol.
Summer Session. Acad. Tui $200.
Est 1902. Inc 1902 nonprofit. Methodist. Quar (Aug-Je). Accred MSA.
Bldgs 8. Lib 16,000 vols. Gym. Aud. Crts.

Affiliated with the Methodist Church, the enrollment at this school is comprised of U.S. mainland and Puerto Rican students. The standard curriculum in the elementary program is adapted to the needs of students and also offers Spanish, music and religion. Academics in grades 9 to 12 are college preparatory, featuring courses in international affairs, drama, science perspectives, journalism and art. Extracurricular activities include soccer, swimming, golf and numerous interest clubs.

The school's Learning Center accommodates learning disabled and physically handicapped children.

See also pages 106-7

SAINT JOHN'S SCHOOL
Day Coed Ages 4-17. Gr N-12.

Santurce, Puerto Rico 00907. 1466 Ashford Ave. Tel. 809-728-5343.
Louis H. Christiansen, BA, Fordham, MEd, Harvard, Head.
Pre-Prep Col Prep. Tests CEEB. Curr—USA. Ll—Eng. A—Eng Span
  Sci Math. CF—Span Fr Lab Sci Soc Stud Psych Comp. Sl—Rem &
  Dev Math & Read Tut.
Enr 681. B 344; G 337. Elem 490, Sec 191. Grad '84—50. Col—50.
Fac 62. M 7; F 55. US Nat.
Tui $2320-2820 (+ $800). Schol.
Est 1915. Inc 1930 nonprofit. Sem (Aug-Je). ISS NAIS. Accred MSA.
Bldgs 3. Lib 12,000 vols. Athletic facilities.

Saint John's School attempts to promote bicultural awareness and bilingual development among students by maintaining a nearly equal ratio of Puerto Rican and continental boys and girls and by requiring all pupils to begin study of Spanish in the first grade. A full U.S. curriculum is offered, including preparation for College Boards. Recent graduates have entered Princeton, Columbia, Georgetown, Brown, Tufts and Tulane.

VIRGIN ISLANDS

Formerly known as the Danish West Indies, the U.S. Virgin Islands comprise about 50 islands east of Puerto Rico. The best known are the three largest and most populous, St. Thomas, St. John and St. Croix. The U.S. purchased the islands from Denmark in 1917 for $25 million. Inhabitants of the islands have been citizens of the U.S. since 1927. The capital is Charlotte Amalie on St. Thomas. Tourism is the principal industry.

ANTILLES SCHOOL
Day Coed Ages 3-18. Gr N-12.

Charlotte Amalie (St. Thomas), Virgin Islands 00801. P.O. Box 7280.
  Tel. 809-774-1966.
Mark C. Marin, BA, Aquinas College, MA, Columbia Univ, Head.
Pre-Prep Col Prep. Tests CEEB SSAT. Curr—USA. Ll—Eng. A—Calc
  Marine Biol Eng Comp Programming Art. CF—Eng Math Soc Sci
  Span Fr Arts. Sl—Tut Rem & Dev Math & Read.
Enr 320. B 168; G 152. Elem 220, Sec 100. Grad '84—26. Col—19.
Fac 33. M 9; F 24. US Nat.
Tui $1900-2500 (+ $100). Schol.
Est 1950. Inc nonprofit. Sem (Aug-Je). ISS NAIS. Accred MSA.
Bldgs 4. 2 Libs 12,000 vols. Athletic facilities.

An academic and college preparatory country day school, Antilles is located on a 27-acre campus in Frenchman Bay Estates. Antilles places equal emphasis on cognitive, social and physical development through its rigorous academic program. An intersession of mini-courses planned jointly by faculty, students and the administration includes special classes, field trips and projects which have included archeological digs and environmental studies. Sports and activities include tennis, soccer, trampoline, gymnastics, baseball, scuba diving, field hockey and volleyball. Recent graduates have entered Case Western Reserve, Simmons, Purdue, Temple, College of William and Mary and Stanford.

ST. CROIX COUNTRY DAY SCHOOL
Day Coed Ages 3-18. Gr N-12.

Christiansted (St. Croix), Virgin Islands 00820. Estate Concordia 00864. Tel. (809) 778-1974.
Margery Boulanger, BA, Univ. of City of NY, MA, College of the Virgin Islands, Head.
Col Prep Gen Acad. Curr—USA. LI—Eng.
Enr 410.
Fac 41.
Tui $1300-2750. Schol.
Summer Session. Acad Rec. Tui $50/wk. 8 wks.
Est 1967. Inc nonprofit. (Sept-Je). ISS. Accred MSA.
Bldgs 10. Lib. Gym. Pool. Field.

The curriculum at St. Croix Country Day prepares students for the College Boards. Recent graduates have entered Trinity College, Georgetown, Harvard, Principia and Louisiana State University.

ST. DUNSTAN'S EPISCOPAL SCHOOL
Day Coed Ages 5-18. Gr K-12.

Christiansted (St. Croix), Virgin Islands 00820. 21 Orange Grove. Tel. 809-773-2650.
Maxine A. Hawkins, BS, Univ. of Tampa, MA, College of the Virgin Islands, Head.
Col Prep. Tests CEEB SSAT. Curr—USA. LI—Eng. A—Span Algebra Calc Sci. CF—Span Carribean & World Hist Marine Biol Studio Art.
Enr 307. B 164; G 143. Elem 205, Sec 102. US—276. Grad '84—23. Col—22.
Fac 24. Full 23/Part 1. M 8; F 16. US 2.
Tui $1475-2200 (+$20). Schol.
Est 1958. Inc 1963 nonprofit. Episcopal. Sem (Sept-Je). ISS. Accred MSA.
Bldgs 7. Lib 9192 vols. Aud. Fields. Crts.

Located on a 13-acre site, St. Dunstan's offers a basic curriculum stressing verbal and communication skills. Teaching is individualized to a great extent in the elementary program while remedial classes are available in reading and Spanish. Complementing the academic program are activities in gourmet cooking, school newspaper and yearbook, career planning and 4-H. Students have the opportunity to participate in an athletic program which offers interscholastic sports, gymnastics, tennis, swimming, hiking and bowling. Recent graduates have entered Harvard, Ohio Wesleyan and Howard.

THE GOOD HOPE SCHOOL
  Day Coed Ages 3¹/₂-18. Gr N-12.

Frederiksted (St. Croix), Virgin Islands 00840. Tel. 809-772-0022.
Harry V. McKay, Head.
Col Prep. Tests CEEB SSAT. Curr—USA. LI—Eng. A—Calculus Biol
  Eng. CF—Span Fr Roman Comedy Caribbean Hist Yoga Photog.
Enr 360. Elem 255, Sec 105. US—324. Grad '84—26. Col—24.
Fac 41. Full 37/Part 4. M 13; F 28. US 34.
Tui $2275-3370 (+ $200). Schol.
Est 1965. Inc nonprofit. Tri (Sept-Je). NAIS. Accred MSA.
Bldgs 11. Lib 12,000 vols. Pool. Fields.

Located on 35 acres on the southwestern coast of St. Croix, the school offers an academic program preparing students for post-secondary education. The lower school program provides instruction through mixed-aged groupings and also offers intensive help in basic skills. Middle school students are exposed to a variety of teaching techniques and taught by teams of teachers. Recent graduates have attended Georgetown, Emerson College, Tampa University and New England College.

SOUTH AMERICA

ARGENTINA

Discovered and explored in the early 16th century by Spanish expeditionary forces en route to thwart growing Portuguese domination in the Far East and the New World, Argentina was subsequently ruled by Spain until the provinces revolted in 1810 to establish an independent republic. Occupying the greatest part of the southern extremity of the continent, the Argentine Republic is South America's second largest in area and population.

Buenos Aires, second largest city on the continent, is capital. The peso ($a) is the monetary unit and Spanish is the national language.

ST. PAUL'S SCHOOL
  Bdg Boys Ages 9-18; Day Coed 9-18. Gr 4-12.

5178 Cruz Grande (Cordoba), Argentina. Tel. Los Cocos 21 & 39.
A.H. Thurn, OBE, Birmingham Univ., Loughborough Univ., Head.

Col Prep Gen Acad. Tests GCE SSAT. Curr—Nat UK. LI—Eng Span.
CF—Span Fr Physics Chem Biol Comp Econ Art Music. SI—Tut.
Enr 107. B 81/19; G 1/6. Elem 35, Sec 72. US—2. Grad '84—10.
Col—10.
Fac 18. Full 11/Part 7. M 9; F 9. Nat UK.
Tui Bdg $2500 (+$300); Day $1000 (+$150). Schol.
Est 1954. Inc. Sem (March-Nov).
Bldgs 10. Dorms 4. 2 libs 3000 vols. Pool. Gym. Fields.

St. Paul's features both English and Spanish curricula. Courses in English prepare students for the G.C.E. 'A' and 'O' level examinations, with Spanish taught as a foreign language. The Spanish curriculum offers basic subjects in the primary grades; secondary students study for the national "Bachillerto" and "Perito Mercantil" at local schools. Industrial classes are also offered.

Outside the classroom, students participate in chess, astronomy, natural history, clubs and publications. Athletics stress outdoor activities such as climbing, hiking, horseback riding and camping as well as interscholastic team sports.

ST. ALBAN'S COLLEGE
Day Coed Ages 3-18. Gr N-12.

1832 Lomas De Zamora (Buenos Aires), Argentina. R. Falcon 250. Tel. 244-0563.
John Ronald Vibart, Head.
Col Prep Gen Acad. Tests GCE. LI—Span Eng. A—Span Math. CF—Fr Span Lit Bible Art Hist Biol Geog Music.
Enr 600. B 390; G 210. Elem 500, Sec 100. US—5. Grad '84—30.
Fac 80. Full 16/Part 64. Nat.
Tui $1200 (+$200). Schol.
Est 1907. Inc 1931 nonprofit. Sem (March-Nov).
Bldgs 7. Lib 10,000 vols. Athletic facilities.

Serving the Buenos Aires community, this school offers a combined bilingual British and Argentinean curriculum. The five-year secondary course leads to the Argentine Baccalaureate and various certificates from the University of Cambridge.

AMERICAN COMMUNITY SCHOOL
Day Coed Ages 4-18. Gr N-12.

1636 La Lucila (Buenos Aires), Argentina. Andres Ferreyra 4073. Tel. 797-5100.
Ralph A. Ruban, Head.
Col Prep Gen Acad. Tests IB CEEB. Curr—USA. LI—Eng Span.
A—Eng Biol. CF—Fr Ger Span Hist (US) Econ Pol Sci Sociol Arts Typ Man Arts Journalism. SI—Tut Rem Read & Span.
Enr 558. Elem 311, Sec 247. US—241.
Fac 67. Full 37/Part 30. US 19. Nat.
Tui $4000-6000.

Summer Session. Acad. 6 wks.
Est 1952. Inc nonprofit. Sem (Aug-Je) AASSA A/OS ISS. Accred SACS.
Bldgs 3. 2 Libs 30,000 vols. Athletic facilities.

This coed school features an American and Argentinean curriculum for grades one through eight with instruction in English and Spanish. Classes are conducted in English only in grades 9 to 12. The academic program is complemented by courses in art, music, communications, computer science, shorthand and typing. Most graduates attend colleges and universities in the United States.

THE INTERNATIONAL SCHOOL
Bdg & Day Coed Ages 8-18.

5879 La Paz (Cordoba), Argentina. Villa Dora, Loma Bola. Tel. La Paz 14.
L. H. Sullivan, BA, MEd, London Univ., Head.
Col Prep Gen Acad. Tests GCE IB SAT. Curr—Intl. LI—Eng. A—Art Chem Eng Geog Math Span. CF—Anthro Soc Studies. SI—Tut Rem & Dev Math.
Enr 41. B 25/2; G 12/2. US—3. Grad '84—5.
Fac 8. Full 6/Part 2. M 5; F 3. US 1. UK.
Tui Bdg $720/mo (+$100); Day $250/mo (+$100). Schol.
Summer Session. Rec. 5 wks.
Est 1977. Inc nonprofit. Sem (Jan-Nov). ISS.
Bldgs 10. Dorms 5. Lib. Pool. Fields. Tennis crts.

The International School offers primary and secondary studies leading to the International Baccalaureate. Staff members are recruited from English-speaking countries. Small enrollment and fully-equipped facilities help provide students with individualized attention. Volleyball, tennis, swimming, cricket, football, riding and golf are included in the sports program, and facilities are also available for camping, hiking and fishing.

ST. GEORGE'S COLLEGE
Bdg Coed Ages 8-18, Day 6-18. Gr 1-12.

1878 Quilmes (Buenos Aires), Argentina. Guido 800, Casilla Correo No. 2. Tel. 253-5091. Telex: 23645 CAMAB AR.
C. T. Gill Leech, MA, Clare Col—Cambridge, Head.
Col Prep. Tests CEEB GCE. Curr—UK Nat. LI—Eng Span. CF—Fr Ger Span Comp Stud Chem Relig Econ. SI—Rem Lang.
Enr 322. B 121/84; G 63/54. Elem 173, Sec 149. Grad '84—30. Col—22.
Fac 57. Full 21/Part 36. M 29; F 28. UK Argentina.
Tui Bdg $5000; Day $3250. Schol.
Est 1898. Nonprofit. Sem (Mar-Dec). ISS.
Bldgs 18. Dorms 11. Lib 6000 vols. Swimming pools 2. Tennis crts 4. Fields 10.

Enrollment at this British-oriented boarding and day school is drawn from England, South America and the United States. The curriculum prepares students for the British G.C.E. 'O' and 'A' level examinations, the U.S. College Boards and the Argentine Bachillerato. A variety of sports and extracurricular activities are available.

BOLIVIA

Cradle of flourishing Andean culture that preceded the Inca civilization conquered by Pizarro in the 1530s, Bolivia was a site of Spanish colonization until revolutionary forces under the famed liberator, Simon Bolivar, achieved independence in 1825. A mining center in both colonial and modern times, the Republic of Bolivia is the larger of South America's two inland countries.

The seat of government is at La Paz, while the legal capital is Sucre. Spanish is the official national language and the peso (Bs) is the monetary unit.

COCHABAMBA COOPERATIVE SCHOOL
Day Coed Ages 4-18. Gr N-12.

Cochabamba, Bolivia. Casilla 1395. Tel. 2-8796.
Clyde D. McKay, MEd, Univ. of Texas, Dir.
Col Prep. Tests CEEB SSAT. Curr—USA. LI—Eng. A—Math Chem Econ Comp Programming Fr Physics. CF—Fr Span Ger Journalism. SI—Rem & Dev Math & Read.
Enr 406. B 205; G 201. Elem 308, Sec 98. US—40. Grad '84—20. Col—20.
Fac 25. Full 23/Part 2. M 9; F 16. US 12. Nat.
Tui $1300 (+$75). Schol.
Est 1958. Nonprofit. Sem (Aug-Je) AASSA A/OS ISS. Accred SACS. Bldgs 7. Lib 5500 vols. Athletic facilities.

With 75% of its enrollment comprised to Bolivians, the Cochabamba Cooperative School offers a combined American-Bolivian program leading to either the College Boards or the Bolivian Bachillerato. Instruction is in English, with French and Spanish offered as foreign languages. An intensive English program is available for students who lack sufficient facility to adjust adequately to the curriculum.

ANGLO-AMERICAN SCHOOL
Day Coed Ages 5-18. Gr N-12.

Oruro, Bolivia. Casilla 524. Tel. 50901.
Hector Beltran, Dir.
Col Prep. Curr—USA Nat. LI—Span Eng.
Enr 714.
Fac 45.
Tui $120-150.

Est 1940. Sem (Feb-Nov). A/OS ISS.
Lib 20,000 vols. Labs 3. Aud. Athletic facilities.

Enrolling predominantly Bolivians, this school offers both a native and U.S. curriculum leading to the Bachillerato. English is taught at all grade levels.

AMERICAN COOPERATIVE SCHOOL
Day Coed Ages 4-18. Gr N-12.

425 La Paz, Bolivia. Tel. 792302.
Mail to: c/o American Embassy-Bolivia, Washington, DC 20520.
Herman J. Penland, MA, California Polytechnic, Supt.
Col Prep. Tests CEEB. Curr—USA. LI—Eng. CF—Fr Span Arts Typing Home Econ.
Enr 549. Elem 278, Sec 271. US—137. Grad '84—52. Col—48.
Fac 50. Full 45/Part 5. US 39.
Tui $2930 (+$1000). Schol.
Summer Session. Acad. Tui $100/6 wks.
Est 1956. Sem (Aug-May). AASSA A/OS ISS. Accred SACS.
Bldgs 5. Lib 12,000 vols. Field. Gym.

An American college preparatory program is offered at this school where 24 nationalities are represented. Instruction is in English and courses in art, music and typing are available. The activities program includes student council, soccer, basketball, ballet, scouting, track, chess and drama.

SANTA CRUZ COOPERATIVE SCHOOL
Day Coed Ages 4-19. Gr N-12.

Santa Cruz, Bolivia. Casilla 753. Tel. 3-2993.
Stephen K. Field, Dir.
Col Prep. Tests CEEB SSAT TOEFL. Curr—USA. LI—Eng. CF—Fr Ger Span Lit Sci Psych Comp.
Enr 371. US—50.
Fac 27. US 15.
Tui $637-1194 (+$20). Schol.
Summer Session. Acad Rec. Tui $50. 6 wks.
Est 1959. Inc nonprofit. Sem (Aug-Je) AASSA A/OS ISS.
Bldgs 6. Lib 8000 vols. Athletic facilities.

With 15 percent of its enrollment coming from families of U.S. citizens in Santa Cruz, this school offers an American curriculum. Spanish is taught at all grade levels. Elective courses include creative writing, art, drama, music and ornithology. Extracurricular activities include typing, languages and photography.

BRAZIL

Discovered by a Spanish companion of Columbus, claimed by a Portuguese commander en route to India, and first explored by a Florentine, Amerigo Vespucci, Brazil subsequently was visited and settled by Portuguese merchants, planters and wealthy adventurers, while long remaining a field of international colonial competition. Independence came in 1822 and a republican government replaced the empire in 1889 with later constitutional changes greatly strengthening the office of President. Today comprising nearly half the land area and population of South America, the Federative Republic of Brazil is the continent's largest nation.

Brasilia has been capital since 1960, superseding Rio de Janeiro. Portuguese is the national language and the cruzeiro (Cr$) is the monetary unit.

AMAZON VALLEY ACADEMY
Bdg & Day Coed Ages 6-18. Gr K-12.

66000 Belem (Para), Brazil. Agencia Independencia. Caixa Postal 3030. Tel. 235-1394.
Larry W. Sharp, BA, Seattle Pacific Univ., MA, Azusa Pacific Univ., Prin.
Col Prep. Tests GCE CEEB SSAT. Curr—USA. LI—Eng Ger.
Enr 120.
Fac 27.
Tui $2200.
Est 1958. Nonprofit Sem (Aug-Je). ISS.
Bldgs 7. Dorms 2. Lib 8000 vols. Gym.

Operating primarily for missionaries' children but admitting others on a space available basis, this school provides an American curriculum for children from the United States, Canada, Germany and Great Britain.

ESCOLA AMERICANA DE BELO HORIZONTE
Day Coed Ages 5-18. Gr K-12.

30.000 Belo Horizonte (Minas Gerais), Brazil. Av. Dom Joao Sexto 3002. Caixa Postal 2501. Tel. (031) 312-2711.
Sid R. Stewart, MA, San Jose State, Dir.
Col Prep. Tests IB GCE CEEB SSAT. Curr—USA. LI—Eng. A—Math Bio Lang. CF—Fr Port Math Soc Stud. SI—Rem & Dev Read & Math Tut ESL.
Enr 55. Elem 34, Sec 21. US—33. Grad '84—5. Col—5.
Fac 10. Full 7/Part 3. M 5; F 5. US 8.
Tui $1595-5860 (+ $300-970). Schol.
Est 1956. Nonprofit Sem (Aug-Je). AASSA A/OS ISS. Accred SACS.
Bldgs 2. Lib 12,000 vols. Gym. Field. Crt.

Enrolling students from the United States, Belgium, Brazil and Germany, this school follows an American curriculum. English as a

Second Language and Portuguese are taught at all grade levels. Extracurricular activities include basketball, soccer and cheerleading.

AMERICAN SCHOOL OF BRASILIA
Day Coed Ages 5-18. Gr N-12.

70200 Brasilia-DF, Brazil. L 2-SUL, Quadra 605-E. Tel. 243-3237.
Mail to: American Embassy—Brasilia, APO, Miami, FL 34030.
Thomas J. Rushcamp, MA, Western Michigan Univ., PhD, Michigan State, Head.
Col Prep. Tests CEEB SSAT. Curr—USA. LI—Eng. CF—FR Port Span SI—Rem & Dev Read & Math ESL.
Enr 528. B 287; G 241. Elem 386, Sec 142. US—119. Grad '84—22. Col—21.
Fac 49. M 18; F 31. US 28.
Tui $4200-5250 (+ $860). Schol.
Summer Session. Acad Rec. 4 wks.
Est 1964. Sem (Aug-Je). AASSA A/OS ISS. Accred SACS.
Bldgs 6. Lib 14,000 vols. Gym. Field.

Serving the capital city's diplomatic community, this school enrolls students from Brazil, Canada, England, Korea, Peru and the United States. Competence in English is an admission requirement. Electives include drama, music and sports.

ESCOLA AMERICANA DE CAMPINAS
(American School of Campinas)
Day Coed Ages 4-18. Gr N-12.

13.100 Campinas (Sao Paulo), Brazil. Caixa Postal 1183. Tel. (0192) 51-7377.
Wesley Boughner, Supt.
Col Prep. Tests CEEB SSAT. Curr—USA. LI— Eng Port. CF—Port Fr Life Sci Indus Arts Typ Hist (US) Soc Stud Engineering Draw Soc Psych Bus Math.
Enr 203. B 102; G 101. Elem 152, Sec 51. US—102. Grad '84—11. Col—11.
Fac 28. Full 23/Part 5. M 8; F 20. US 10. Nat.
Tui $1200-3000.
Est 1957. Inc nonprofit. Sem (Aug-Je). AASSA A/OS ISS. Accred SACS.
Bldgs 8. Lib 13,000 vols. Gym. Crts. Field.

Located on a 12-acre country home site, the school offers a curriculum similar to that found in American schools. Three accredited degree programs are offered: American Diploma, Brazilian Diploma and the International Baccalaureate. Portuguese is a required course of study. School clubs comprise another aspect of the academic program including dramatics, debate, chess club and student council. The athletic program offers participation in soccer, basketball, volleyball, flag football, track, salao and handball.

THE INTERNATIONAL SCHOOL OF CURITIBA
Day Coed Ages 4-18. Gr N-12.

80.000 Curitiba (Parana), Brazil. Rua Des. Hugo Simas, 2530. Caixa Postal 7004. Tel. (041) 223-8266.
Karl M. Lorenz, MA, EdD, Columbia, Dir.
Col Prep. Tests CEEB. Curr—USA. LI—Eng Port. CF—Ger Port Fr ESL.
Enr 75. B 35; G 40. Elem 61, Sec 14. US—25. Grad '84—4. Col—3.
Fac 15. Full 5/Part 10. M 4; F 11. US 6. Nat.
Tui $3500. Schol.
Est 1959. Inc nonprofit. Sem (Aug-Je). AASSA A/OS ISS. Accred SACS.
Bldgs 3. Lib 7000 vols. Athletic facilities.

Enrolling students from Great Britain, Japan, Sweden and the United States, this school is located in the hills of Jardim Schaffer overlooking the city of Curitiba. Basketball, volleyball and soccer are included in the sports program.

PAN AMERICAN SCHOOL OF PORTO ALEGRE
Day Coed Ages 4-15. Gr N-8.

90.000 Porto Alegre (Rio Grande do Sul), Brazil. Rua Joao Paetzel 440. Caixa Postal 64. Tel. 31-5866.
Mail to: AmConGen, Porto Alegre, Brazil.
Ronald McCluskey, Dir.
Pre-Prep. Curr—USA. LI—Eng.
Enr 24.
Fac 6.
Tui $580-2800. Schol.
Est 1966. Nonprofit. Sem (Aug-Je). A/OS ISS.
Bldgs 3. Lib 2000 vols. Field.

This school has an international student body and offers an American elementary program with Portuguese offered as a foreign language. Tutoring is available for dyslexic children and correspondence courses are provided for high school students.

THE AMERICAN SCHOOL OF RECIFE
Day Coed Ages 5-18. Gr N-12.

50.000 Recife (Pernambuco), Brazil. Agencia Boa Viagem. Rua Sa e Souza. Tel. 341-4716.
Helen Vanderbeer Gueiros, Head.
Col Prep Gen Acad. Tests CEEB. Curr—USA. LI—Eng.
Enr 245.
Fac 30.
Tui $1200-3600. Schol.
Est 1957. Nonprofit. Sem (Aug-Je). A/OS ISS. Accred SACS.
Bldgs 6. Lib 12,000 vols.

Enrolling students from Brazil, England, France, Japan, Holland, India and the United States, this school provides an American curriculum. An E.S.L. program is conducted in the elementary grades and electives include photography and journalism. The school is situated on an eight and one-half-acre site in a residential suburb of Recife.

AMERICAN SCHOOL OF RIO DE JANEIRO
(Escola Americana di Rio de Janeiro)
Day Coed Ages 4-18. Gr N-12.

Rio de Janeiro 22451, Brazil. Estrada da Gavea, 132. Tel. 399-0825.
Gilbert C. Brown, PhD, Columbia, Head.
Col Prep Gen Acad. Tests CEEB SSAT. Curr—USA Nat. LI—Eng Port.
Enr 833.
Fac 93.
Tui $2680-3097. Schol.
Summer Session. Acad. Tui $22/crse. 4 wks.
Est 1936. Inc nonprofit. Sem (Aug-Je). AASSA A/OS ISS NAIS. Accred
SACS.
Bldgs 8. 2 Libs 20,000 vols. Gyms 2. Fields 2. Aud. Labs 6.

Providing a combined American-Brazilian curriculum, all students are required to take Portuguese, Brazilian history and geography in addition to standard English requirements. Escola Americana grants two diplomas—the College Entrance and Minimum Course of Study. Recent graduates have entered Brown, Ohio State, Brandeis, Tulane and Brevard.

Extracurricular activities include newspapers in four languages, drama and glee club, and varsity athletics in baseball, soccer, volleyball, track, tennis and golf.

SOCIETY OF OUR LADY OF MERCY
Day Coed Ages 3-18. Gr N-12.

Rio de Janeiro, Brazil. Rua Visconde de Caravelas 48. Botafoga ZC-02.
Tel. 246-8069.
Dr. Charles Richard Lyndaker, Dir.
Col Prep. Tests CEEB. Curr—USA. LI—Eng. CF—Fr Port Hist.
Est 1954. Nonprofit. Roman Catholic. ISS. Accred SACS.

An American college preparatory curriculum is offered at this school. Most graduates attend colleges in the U.S.

PAN AMERICAN SCHOOL OF BAHIA
Day Coed Ages 4-18. Gr N-12.

Salvador (Bahia) 40.000, Brazil. Caixa Postal 231. Tel. 249-9090.
Tomm J. Elliott, MA, EdD, Columbia, Head.
Col Prep. Tests SSAT. Curr—USA. LI—Eng. A—Math Physics.
CF—Port Math Sci Soc Stud. SI—ESL.
Enr 300. B 140; G 160. Elem 270, Sec 30. US—60. Grad '84—6. Col—6.

Fac 30. M 10; F 20. US 15. Nat.
Tui $1584-3818 (+$500). Schol.
Est 1960. Inc nonprofit. Sem (Aug-Je).AASSA A/OS ISS. Accred SACS.
Bldgs 2. Lib 28,000 vols. Crts. Fields.

With a mixed enrollment of Brazilians and Americans, this school provides an American college preparatory program, with instruction in English and Portuguese. Most graduates go on to attend colleges and universities. Extracurricular activites include athletics, drama, music, art and yearbook.

ASSOCIACAO ESCOLA GRADUADA DE SAO PAULO
Day Coed Ages 3-18. Gr K-12.

01000 Sao Paulo, Brazil. Caixa Postal 7432. Tel. 011-240-2499.
Clifford Strommen, PhD, Univ. of Houston, Supt.
Col Prep. Tests SSAT. Curr—USA. LI—Eng. A—Biol Math Eng Chem Physics Comp Hist. CF—Port Span Fr Art Music. SI—Rem & Dev Read & Math.
Enr 883. B 477; G 406. Elem 641. Sec 242. US—454. Grad '84—78. Col—41.
Fac 74. Full 73/Part 1. M 19; F 55. US 36.
Tui $3500 (+$630).
Est 1920. Inc nonprofit. Sem (Aug-Je). AASSA A/OS ISS NAIS. Accred SACS.
Bldgs 15. 2 Libs 45,000 vols. Gyms 3. Fields 2. Courts.

Enrolling students from Brazil, England, Holland, Japan, Sweden and the United States, this school offers an American curriculum. Advanced placement courses are conducted as well as electives in drama, athletics and the school newspaper and yearbook.

CHAPEL AMERICAN SCHOOL
(Escola Maria Imaculada)
Day Coed Ages 3-18. Gr N-12.

Sao Paulo, Brazil. Brooklin 04698. Caixa Postal 21293. Tel. 247-7455; 7143.
Mail to: AMCONGEN Sao Paulo, APO, Miami, FL 34030.
William David O'Hale, BA, Univ. of Arizona, MA, California State Univ., Dir.
Col Prep Bus. Tests IB SSAT. Curr—USA. LI—Eng. CF—Fr Span Portuguese Philos Relig Bus Shorthand Brazilian Studies Math Sci Polit Sci Soc Comp. SI—Rem Read ESL.
Enr 580. Elem 370, Sec 210. US—300. Grad '84—39.
Fac 58. M 11; F 47. US 29.
Tui $2150. Schol.
Est 1942. Inc nonprofit. Roman Catholic. Tri (Aug-Je). AASSA ISS. Accred SACS.
Bldgs 5. Lib 22,000 vols. Gym.

Operated by the Oblate Fathers of Mary Immaculate and staffed by the Felician Sisters, this coeducational Catholic day school provides an American education for English-speaking children in Sao Paulo. There are both college preparatory and commercial programs. Religion and Brazilian studies are salient curriculum features. Preparation is offered for the College Boards and International Baccalaureate Diploma. Extracurricular activities include student council, drama, literary magazine, cheerleading and sports.

See also page 103

PAN AMERICAN CHRISTIAN ACADEMY
  Bdg Coed Ages 14-19; Day Coed 5-19. Gr K-12.

Sao Paulo, Brazil. Rua Queiroz de Araujo 393. Tel. 520-9655.
Henry Thiessen, MA, Seattle Pacific Univ., Prin.
Col Prep. Tests CEEB SSAT. Curr—USA. LI—Eng. CF—Port Ger Bible
  Sci Math.
Enr 300. Elem 180, Sec 120. US—130. Grad '84—21. Col—16.
Fac 30. Full 23/Part 7. M 8; F 22. US.
Tui 200,000 Cr$. Schol.
Est 1960. Nonprofit. Sem (Aug-Je). AASSA ISS.
Bldgs 5. Lib 5000 vols. Field. Gym.

This school gives admission preference to those students with a Protestant Evangelical affiliation. Bible study is required of all students and electives are offered in music, German, business math and typing.

CHILE

For many years considered with Argentina and Brazil as one of the three great "ABC" powers of South America, the Republic of Chile today is an important mining center and one of the world's largest producers of copper.

Capital is Santiago, the monetary unit is the peso ($C) and the language is Spanish.

THE INTERNATIONAL PREPARATORY SCHOOL
  Day Coed Ages 3-13. Gr N-8.

Santiago, Chile. San Damian 450. Tel. 471071.
Barbara Conning, BA, Univ. of Wales, BEd, Univ. of Sheffield, Head.
Pre-Prep Gen Acad. Curr—Intl. LI—Eng. CF—Span Fr Math Sci Soc
  Stud Music Art. SI—Rem & Dev Math & Read Tut.
Enr 106. B 56; G 50. US—30.
Fac 15. Full 12/Part 3. M 4; F 11. US 3. Nat.
Tui $2435 (+$183). Schol.
Summer Session. Acad Rec. Tui $200. 4 wks.
Est 1976. Inc. Sem (March-Dec).
Bldgs 2. Lib. Fields.

The School is located on Santiago's east side. A student:teacher ratio of 10:1 is maintained. The curriculum is supplemented by field trips to area sites and visiting instructors from the community. Progress is not graded, but is regularly evaluated by effort and achievement according to ability. Students come from many countries and an international atmosphere is fostered through world history classes in geography and social studies. Physical education, music and arts and crafts are an integral part of the educational program.

INTERNATIONAL SCHOOL NIDO DE AGUILAS
Coed Day Ages 4-18. Gr N-12.

Santiago, Chile. Casilla 16211-9 (Providencia). Tel. 471007.
Dewey R. Breisch, BS, Univ. of Northern Iowa, MS, Drake Univ., Head.
Col Prep. Tests CEEB SSAT. Curr—USA Nat. LI—Eng. A—Eng Span Math. CF—Fr Ger Span ESL Photog Comp Stud. SI—Rem & Dev Math & Read Tut.
Enr 1057. B 547; G 510. Elem 534, Sec 223. US—153. Grad '84—56. Col—53.
Fac 64. Full 52/Part 12. M 23; F 41. US 21. Nat.
Tui $2000 (+ $500). Schol.
Summer Session. Acad Rec. Tui $330 (+ $75). 6 wks.
Est 1934. Inc 1954 nonprofit. Sem (Mar-Dec).AASSA A/OS ISS. Accred SACS.
Bldgs 8. Lib 18,000 vols. Field. Track. Tennis crts 4. Gym.

Located on a 130-acre site in the foothills of the Andes, this school offers an American curriculum to students predominantly from Chile and the United States. Chilean social studies is taught in Spanish and the curriculum also features an extensive E.S.L. program. Elective courses include writing, world cultures, psychology, music and drama. Special instruction is available for children with learning disabilities. Soccer, tennis, basketball, track and horseback riding are offered in the sports program.

LINCOLN INTERNATIONAL ACADEMY
Day Coed Ages 4-18. Gr N-12.

Santiago, Chile. Casilla 20000, Correo 20. Tel. 471907.
Robert G. Seaquist, BS, Univ. of Wisconsin, MA, PhD, Univ. of Alabama, Head.
Gen Acad Col Prep. Tests SSAT Curr—USA. Nat. LI—Eng. CF—Span Music Art Comp.
Enr 340. B 250, G 150. Elem 310, Sec 40. US—30. Grad '84—10. Col—10.
Fac 50. Full 46/Part 4. M 6; F 44. US 5. Nat.
Tui $3000.
Summer Session. Acad Lang Comp. Tui Day $200. 3 wks.
Est 1976. Inc. Sem (Mar-Dec). ISS.
Bldgs 9. Lib 6000 vols. Fields.

A traditional American curriculum is offered at Lincoln, preparing students for entrance to U.S. and Chilean universities. Students must pass an admissions test prior to enrollment.

SANTIAGO COLLEGE
Day Coed Ages 4-18. Gr N-12.

Santiago, Chile. Casilla 130-D. Tel. 2321813.
Rebeca Donoso Palacios, Dir.
Col Prep Gen Acad Bus. Tests PSAT. Curr—Nat USA. LI—Span Eng.
CF—Fr Hist (US) Arts Typ. SI—Tut Rem & Dev Math & Read.
Enr 2124. Elem 1444, Sec 680.
Fac 158. Full 136/Part 22. M 28; F 130. US 6. Nat.
Tui $1450 (+$150).
Est 1880. Methodist. Sem (Mar-Dec). ISA ISS. Accred SACS.
Bldgs 7. 3 Libs 25,000 vols. Gyms 3. Fields.

The curriculum at Santiago College stresses bilingual development and emphasizes the cultures of both the United States and Chile. Spanish and English are taught from the first grade. After grade ten, students are offered a wide range of electives.

COLOMBIA

Three centuries of domination by Spain ended in 1819 when the great liberator, Simon Bolivar, established the Republic of Gran Colombia. Venezuela, Ecuador and later Panama, eventually withdrew from the federation.

Bogota, founded in 1538 and situated high in the Andes, is capital. The peso (Col$) is the monetary unit and Spanish is the language.

COLEGIO KARL C. PARRISH
Day Coed Ages 4-18. Gr N-12.

Barranquilla, Colombia. Apartado Aereo 52962. Tel. 34-05-74.
W. Cary Anderson, MA, Univ. of Arkansas, EdD, Univ. of Northern Colorado, Dir.
Col Prep. Tests IB TOEFL CEEB SSAT. Curr—USA Nat. LI—Eng Span.
CF—Span Hist Biol Physics Chem Drama Photog Bus Comp Philos ESL.
Enr 866. B 530; G 336. Elem 645, Sec 221. US—233. Grad '84—37. Col—37.
Fac 57. Full 46/Part 1. US 24.
Tui $1275-1862. Schol.
Summer Session. Acad. Tui Day $60. 3 wks.
Est 1938. Inc nonprofit. Sem (Aug-Je). ACCAS A/OS ISS. Accred SACS.
Bldgs 3. Lib 8000 vols. Athletic facilities. Aud. Lab.

Offering a dual American-Colombian curriculum to students from the U.S., Colombia, and several other countries, this school prepares students for the College Boards or the Colombian Bachillerato. Instruction in the American program is in English; that in the Colombian, approximately half English, half Spanish. Spanish is required of all students. Advanced instruction is offered in physics, chemistry, anatomy and geometry. Recent graduates have entered Cornell, Tufts, Columbia and Brandeis.

COLEGIO NUEVA GRANADA
Day Coed Ages 4-19. Gr N-12.

Bogota, Colombia. Apartado Aereo 51339. Tel. 235-5350.
Les Landers, BA, Univ. of Chicago, MA, Harvard, Dir.
Col Prep. Tests CEEB. Curr—USA Nat. Ll—Eng.
Enr 1306.
Fac 121.
Tui $1465-2298 (+ $1500-2500).
Summer Session. Rec. Tui $100 (+ $50). 5 wks.
Est 1938. Inc nonprofit. Sem (Aug-Je). ACCAS A/OS ISS NAIS. Accred SACS.
Bldgs 7. 2 Libs 40,000 vols. Gym. Field. Courts.

This community-sponsored school conducts an individualized curriculum in kindergarten through grade six which includes Spanish classes. A full college preparatory program is provided in the secondary grades. Extracurricular activities include genetics, speech, music, typing and a complete athletic program.

COLEGIO PANAMERICANO
Day Coed Ages 4-19. Gr N-12.

Bucaramanga, Colombia. Apartado Aereo 522. Tel. 86221/13.
Mrs. Lesly Lloyd de Chacon, Dir.
Col Prep Gen Acad. Tests SSAT. Curr—USA Nat. Ll—Eng Span.
Enr 239.
Fac 27.
Tui $536-715 (+ $350). Schol.
Est 1963. Inc nonprofit. Quar (Jan-Nov). ACCAS A/OS ISS.
Bldgs 5. Lib 2000 vols. Field. Courts.

Primarily enrolling Colombian students, this school follows a bilingual curriculum in English and Spanish. The academic program, similar to that in U.S. public schools, is supplemented by recreational activities including basketball, volleyball, tennis and soccer.

COLEGIO BOLIVAR
Day Coed Ages 4-18. Gr N-12.

Cali (Valle), Colombia. Apartado Aereo 4875. Tel. 39 32 01.
Martin Felton, MA, PhD, Miami Univ., Dir.

Pre-Prep Col Prep. Tests CEEB. Curr—USA. LI—Eng. A—Chem Physics Calc Span. CF—Span Comp Philos. SI—ESL.
Enr 776.
Fac 64.
Tui Col$2250-2940.
Summer Session. Rec.
Est 1948. Nonprofit. Sem (Aug-Je). ACCAS A/OS ISS. Accred SACS.
Bldgs 15. Lib 15,000 vols. Gym. Pool. Fields. Crts.

Enrolling students from Colombia, the United States and 25 other countries, this school offers an American curriculum. A teacher for the learning disabled is available for students in the elementary grades. Extracurricular activities include art, music, school newspaper and yearbook, various clubs, soccer, basketball, volleyball, swimming and track and field.

COLEGIO JEFFERSON
Day Coed Ages 4-18. Gr N-12.

Cali (Valle), Colombia. Apartado Aereo 6621. Tel. 68 27 04.
Pola Reydburd, BA, Southern Illinois Univ., Dir.
Col Prep. Tests CEEB SSAT ACT. Curr—USA Nat. LI—Eng Span.
Enr 550.
Fac 45.
Tui $100/mo.
Est 1963. Nonprofit. Quar (Sept-Je). ISS.
Bldgs 15. Lib 5000 vols. Athletic facilities.

Colegio Jefferson offers a bilingual and binational education following prescribed American and Colombian curriculums.

COLEGIO JORGE WASHINGTON
Day Coed Ages 4-19. Gr N-12.

Cartagena (Bolivar), Colombia. Apartado Aereo 2899. Tel. 40848/45220.
Roger Krakusin, Dir.
Col Prep. Tests CEEB SSAT. Curr—USA Nat. LI—Eng Span. CF—Colombian & US Hist Relig Trig.
Enr 435. Elem 345, Sec 90. US—10.
Fac 28. Full 24/Part 4. M 12; F 16. US 13.
Tui $833-1266 (+ $50).
Est 1952. Nonprofit. Sem (Aug-Je). ACCAS A/OS ISS. Accred SACS.
Bldgs 2. Lib 12,000 vols. Field. Crts.

Located on an oceanfront site, Colegio Jorge Washington enrolls students from Colombia, the United States and eight other countries. The curriculum corresponds to a general education in the United States and students are prepared for both the U.S. high school diploma and the Colombian Bachillerato diploma. Extracurricular activities include dance classes, drama and science clubs, baseball, basketball and soccer.

THE COLUMBUS SCHOOL
Day Coed Ages 4-18. Gr N-12.

Medellin (Antioquia), Colombia. Apartado Aereo 5225. Tel. 57-09-62.
John K. Schober, MA, Univ. of Florida, PhD, Univ. of Alabama, Dir.
Col Prep. Tests CEEB SSAT. Curr—USA Nat. LI—Eng Span.
Enr 969.
Fac 69.
Tui $1300-1500. Schol.
Est 1945. Inc nonprofit. Sem (Feb-Nov). ACCAS A/OS ISS. Accred
  SACS.
Lib 10,000 vols. Fields. Crts.

This school offers a bilingual college preparatory program to students
from Colombia, the United States and 12 other countries. The
curriculum prepares students for the U.S. College Boards or the
Colombian National Entrance Exam. Extracurricular activities include
basketball, volleyball, soccer, student council and various clubs.

ECUADOR

Once briefly united with Colombia following nearly 300 years of
Spanish rule, the Republic of Ecuador became independent in 1830. The
manufacture of "Panama hats," made of Toquilla straw, is a leading
industry. Cacao, the chief crop, is grown in the lower river valleys and
coastal areas.
Quito is the capital city, Spanish is the official language, and the sucre
(S) is the monetary unit.

COLEGIO AMERICANO DE GUAYAQUIL
Day Coed Ages 3-18. Gr N-12.

Guayaquil (Guayas), Ecuador. P.O. Box 3304. Tel. 350503.
Albert C. Eyde, MEd, EdD, Rutgers, Dir.
Col Prep Gen Bus. Tests CEEB. Curr—USA Nat. LI—Eng Span.
  CF—Hist (US) Arts Man Arts Home Ec Steno Typ.
Enr 1200. B 600; G 600. Elem 700, Sec 500. US—70. Grad '84—80.
  Col—55.
Fac 65. M 15; F 50. US 5.
Tui $502-626 (+ var).
Est 1942. Inc 1962 nonprofit. Tri (May-Jan). ACCAS A/OS ISS. Accred
  SACS.
Bldgs 10. Lib. Track. Field. Crt.

With an enrollment which is predominantly Ecuadorian and American, this school offers both a native and an American curriculum. The
program meets the requirements for the U.S. College Boards and those
set forth by the Ecuadorian Ministry of Education. A three-year
bilingual secretarial program is offered in grades 10 through 12. Many of
the graduates go on to colleges and universities in the United States and

Ecuador. Students participate in the school newspaper, girl scouts or sports teams.

ALLIANCE ACADEMY
Bdg & Day Coed Ages 5-18. Gr K-12.

Quito, Ecuador. Casilla 6186. Tel. 240-142.
Bennett Schepens, BA, Univ. of Montana, MDiv Bethel Seminary, Dir.
Col Prep. Tests SSAT. Curr—USA. Ll—Eng. A—Math Comp Span Eng.
  CF—Span Hist Pol Sci Home Econ Man Arts. Sl—ESL.
Enr 437. B 40/193; G 38/166. Elem 283, Sec 154. US—347. Grad
  '84—27. Col—25.
Fac 66. Full 59/Part 7. M 22; F 44. US 58.
Tui Bdg $2056-3062 (+$100); Day $645-2850 (+$35). Schol.
Est 1929. Nonprofit. Missionary. Sem (Aug-May). AASSA ISS. Accred
  SACS.
Bldgs 14. Dorms 5. 2 Libs 35,000 vols. Gym. Fields. Courts.

Originally founded to educate missionaries' children, this school accepts non-missionary children in the day division and only missionary-related students in the boarding division. English as a Second Language is offered in the special education department. Extracurricular activities include band, orchestra, school newspaper and yearbook, drama and photography. The interscholastic sports program includes soccer, basketball, track and volleyball.

AMERICAN SCHOOL OF QUITO
Day Coed Ages 4-20. Gr K-PG.

Quito (Pichincha), Ecuador. P.O. Box 157. Tel. 538-847.
Mary Virginia Sanchez, BS, Georgetown, MEd, Univ. of Alabama, Dir
  Gen.
Col Prep Gen Acad Bus. Tests SSAT. Curr—USA Nat. Ll—Eng Span.
  CF—Span Pol Sci Philos Bus Stud Geog. A—Eng. Sl—ESL Rem Eng
  & Math.
Enr 2843. B 1319; G 1524. Elem 2041, Sec 802. US—179. Grad
  '84—169. Col—152.
Fac 194. Full 170/Part 24. M 51; F 143. US 40.
Tui $2000 (+$200). Schol.
Est 1939. Inc nonprofit. Tri (Oct-July). ACCAS A/OS ISS. Accred
  SACS.
Bldgs 20. Labs. 2 Libs 28,000 vols. Gym. Fields. Crts.

Located in Ecuador's capital city, Colegio Americano enrolls students from the international business and diplomatic community. The school's national section follows a basic Ecuadorian curriculum with special emphasis on English, while the international section with a smaller student-teacher ratio to insure individual attention follows a modified U.S. curriculum. Secretarial and business management training programs are offered within the junior college division. Students participate in ecology, theater, oratory and journalism clubs, student council and sports.

COTOPAXI ACADEMY
(American International School)
Day Coed Ages 3-18. Gr N-PG.

Quito, Ecuador. Casilla 199. Tel. 240-074.
Donald A. Fournier, MEd, PhD, Dir.
Col Prep. Tests CEEB IB SSAT. Curr—USA Intl. LI—Eng Span. CF—Eng Span Fr Hist (US) Econ Pol Sci Man Arts. SI—Tut Rem Read ESL.
Enr 662. B 340; G 322. Elem 502, Sec 160. Grad '84—25. Col—22.
Fac 65. Full 65. M 14; F 51. US 59.
Tui $940-3175 (+ $350).
Est 1959. Inc I961 nonprofit. Sem (Aug-Je). AASSA A/OS ISS. Accred SACS.
Bldgs 4. 2 Libs 80,000 vols. Lab. Gym. Fields. Crt.

Curriculum, community involvement, and pupil-teacher relationships similar to those found in contemporary, open-education, United States schools are featured at this school. The program is designed to provide a bi-cultural academic experience while simultaneously utilizing the most innovative educational practices. Team teaching, instructional television and extensive utilization of resources from a number of American universities are used. Extracurricular activities include music, drama, scouting, student council and newspaper and intramural sports.

GUYANA

Formerly known as British Guiana, this small nation now known as the Cooperative Republic of Guyana became an independent member of the British Commonwealth in 1970. Sugar cane and rice are the country's chief crops. The official language is English, but the large Asiatic population speaks Hindi and Urdu. The monetary unit is the Guyana dollar (G$). Capital is Georgetown.

GEORGETOWN AMERICAN SCHOOL
Day Coed Ages 4-13. Gr N-8.

Georgetown, Guyana. Tel. 61595.
Mail to: c/o American Embassy, Georgetown, Dept. of State, Washington, DC 20520.
Carol Franco, Prin.
Gen Acad. Curr—USA. LI—Eng.
Enr 39.
Fac 10.
Tui $1250-2500.
Est 1971. Sem (Sept-Je). A/OS.
Bldg. Lib.

Offering a curriculum compatible with U.S. elementary and junior high schools, Georgetown American School also assists students in the understanding of the history and geography of Guyana and the Caribbean.

PARAGUAY

With Argentina to the south and west, Bolivia and Brazil to the north and east, the Republic of Paraguay is one of the two inland countries of South America. Extensive plains, luxuriant forests and abundant water supply characterize this pastoral and agricultural land.

The capital is Asuncion, the language is Spanish and the monetary unit the guarani (G).

AMERICAN SCHOOL OF ASUNCION
Day Coed Ages 4-18. Gr K-12.

Asuncion, Paraguay. Tel. 60-479/63-518.
Mail to: c/o American Embassy, Asuncion, Dept. of State, Washington, DC 20520.
James Stimson, BEd,Chicago Teachers College, MEd, Loyola Univ., PhD, Univ. of New Mexico, Prin.
Col Prep. Tests CEEB PSAT SSAT. Curr—USA Nat. LI—Eng Span, CF—Fr Latin Ger Soc Stud Music Art Comp.
Enr 423.
Fac 39.
Tui $1800-2200 (+ $2500). Schol.
Est 1955. Sem. AASSA A/OS ISS NAIS. Accred SACS.

Located on an 11-acre site in the capital city of Paraguay, this school follows American and Paraguayan curricula preparing students for college entrance. A variety of intramural sports is conducted as well as gymnastics, weightlifting and tennis. A computer room has been added to the school facilities.

ASUNCION CHRISTIAN ACADEMY
Day Coed Ages 3-18. Gr N-12.

Asuncion, Paraguay. Avenida Santisimo Sacramento 685. Tel. 291-034.
Donald E. Brake, BS, MA, Kansas St. Teachers' College, Dir.
Col Prep. Tests SSAT. Curr—USA Nat. LI—Eng.
Enr 135.
Fac 16.
Tui $700.
Summer Session. Camp. Tui $25/wk. 1 wk.
Est 1965. Nonprofit. Sem (July-Je). ISS.
Bldgs 8. 2 Libs 5000 vols. Athletic facilities.

Enrolling students from America, England, Germany, Korea and Paraguay, this school offers a college preparatory curriculum. Extracurricular activities include Bible, photography, art and music.

PERU

Center of the great native Inca civilization, the Republic of Peru was scene of the decisive expedition under Pizarro which led to Spanish overthrow of the entire Inca Empire. Lima, today the largest and capital city, was founded by Pizarro in 1535 and was seat of Spanish rule of nearly the entire continent until Peruvian independence in 1824.

The Andes Mountains, with some peaks over 20,000 feet, divide the nation into three distinct areas. The country's monetary unit is the sol (S), and the official language is Spanish.

PRESCOTT ANGLO-AMERICAN SCHOOL
Day Coed Ages 4-18. Gr N-11.

Arequipa, Peru. Av. Alfonso Ugarte (Tingo). Apartado 1036. Tel. 23-25-40.
Maria Taboada de Sardon, Dir.
Pre-Prep Col Prep Gen Acad. Tests GCE. Curr—Nat. LI—Eng Span.
Enr 1200.
Fac 63.
Tui S11,000/mo (+ S100,000).
Est 1965. Nonprofit. Quar (April-Dec). ISS.
Bldgs 3. Lib 5000 vols. Athletic facilities.

Prescott Anglo-American School was founded by a group of American, British and Peruvian citizens as a school where children could learn English. In addition to intensive English instruction at all levels, the curriculum includes economics, psychology, philosophy, religion, music, art, architectural drawing and dance. Extracurricular activities include soccer, basketball, volleyball, interest clubs and school magazine.

THE AMERICAN SCHOOL OF LIMA
(Colegio Franklin Delano Roosevelt)
Day Coed Ages 4-18. Gr K-12.

Lima 18 (Miraflores), Peru. Avda. Las Palmeras 325, Urb. Camacho, Ate. Apartado 247. Tel. 350890.
Dale I. Swall, BS, MS, Supt.
Col Prep. Tests CEEB SSAT. Curr—USA. LI—Eng. A—Eng Span Math Bio. CF—Fr Span Soc Stud. SI—Rem & Dev Math & Read.
Enr 1300. B 675; G 525. Elem 720, Sec 580. US—360. Grad '84—90. Col—70.
Fac 113. Full 111/Part 12. M 27; F 98. US 65.
Tui $3956.

Est 1946. Inc 1956 nonprofit. Sem (Aug-Je). AASSA ISS. Accred SACS. Bldgs 7. 2 Libs. Gym. Fields. Courts.

Peruvians accounts for one-half of the enrollment at this school with American students comprising the next largest group. Both American and Peruvian college preparatory curricula are offered, with most instruction in English. Emphasis is placed on Latin American studies in Spanish. Most American students prepare for the U.S. College Boards and go on to colleges and universities in the United States. The school charges a one-time entrance fee upon admission to its program.

URUGUAY

Discovered by Spain in 1516, Uruguay was not settled until the Portuguese arrived in 1680. Spain reclaimed the country in 1778. Uruguay revolted against Spain in 1811, but was conquered by Portuguese from Brazil nine years later. Independence was finally declared in 1836, but nearly fifty years of disorder followed. Today the country is known as the Oriental Republic of Uruguay.

The country has a rolling plain in the south, a low plateau in the north and a 120-mile Atlantic coast. Cattle, sheep and meat are the chief exports. The capital city is Montevideo; the language is Spanish; the new peso (UR$) is the monetary unit.

URUGUAYAN AMERICAN SCHOOL
    Day Coed Ages 3-18. Gr N-12.

Montevideo, Uruguay. Dublin 1785. Tel. 50-63-16 176-81.
Mail to: Administrative Officer, American Embassy, Montevideo (UAS),
    Dept. of State, Washington, DC 20520.
William F. Johnson, Dir.
Col Prep. Curr—USA Nat. LI—Eng Span. CF—Fr Span Hist Pol Sci
    Home Ec Man Arts Steno Typ.
Enr 180. Elem 110, Sec 70.
Fac 34. Full 23/Part 11. US 14. Nat.
Tui $550-3400 (+ $1000).
Est 1958. Inc nonprofit. Sem (Aug-July). AASSA A/OS ISS. Accred
    SACS.
Bldgs 4.

Following American guidelines, the elementary program at the Uruguayan American School follows a grade level organization based on ability. In the secondary school students prepare for the College Boards and subsequent entry into colleges and universities in the United States. Approximately one-half of the enrollment is American, with Uruguayans comprising the second largest number. Approximately one-half of the enrollment is American, with Uruguayans comprising the second largest number.

VENEZUELA

Named Venezuela ("Little Venice") because its European discoverers found native houses constructed on stilts, Columbus first set foot on South American soil here in 1498. Spanish domination ensued, liberation under the leadership of Simon Bolivar came in 1821 and independence as a republic in 1830.

A third larger than the state of Texas, the Republic of Venezuela is the Western Hemisphere's second greatest oil producer. The principal agricultural product is coffee. Caracas, where the ashes of Bolivar are enshrined, is capital. The monetary unit is the bolivar (B) and the language is Spanish.

SAN TOME STAFF SCHOOL
Day Coed Ages 6-14. Gr 1-9.

Barcelona (Puerto La Cruz, Anzoategui), Venezuela. Apartado 4695.
Patrick Hermes, BS, MEd, North Texas State, Dir.
Pre-Prep. Tests SSAT. Curr—USA. Ll—Eng.
Enr 40.
Fac 8.
Tui $280 (+ var).
Est 1939. Nonprofit. Sem (Aug-May). Accred SACS.
Bldgs 3. Lib 5000 vols.

The enrollment at this company-sponsored school is composed almost entirely of Americans who are children of the employees of Mene Grande Oil Company, a subsidiary of Gulf Oil. Instruction is in English, with Spanish offered as a second language.

COLEGIO INTERNACIONAL DE CARACAS
Day Coed Ages 6-18. Gr N-12.

Caracas 106, Venezuela. Apartado 62.170. Tel. 93-04-44.
Richard B. Holzman, MSEd, Hofstra, PhD, Univ. of Massachusetts, Supt.
Col Prep. Tests IB CEEB. Curr—USA Nat. Ll—Eng . A—Ital Fr Span Hist (US) Biol Calc Chem. CF—Comp Bus. SI—ESL Rem & Dev Math & Read Tut.
Enr 550. B 275; G 275. Elem 200, Sec 350. US—220. Grad '84—81. Col—75.
Fac 47. Full 42/Part 5. M 13; F 34. US 35.
Tui $2200 (+ $40).
Summer Session. Acad Rec. Tui $160 (+ $20). 4 wks.
Est 1956. Inc 1958. Nonprofit 1960. Sem (Aug-Je). A/OS ISA ISS. Accred SACS.
Blds 5. Lib 15,000 vols. Crts. Field.

Colegio Internacional de Caracas offers a curriculum which is largely American, with emphasis on Spanish and Latin American history and culture. One course per year in Spanish is required of all students. Students prepare for the College Boards and the International Baccalaureate, and most graduates go on to colleges and universities in the United States, Europe and Venezuela.

ESCUELA CAMPO ALEGRE
  Day Coed Ages 4-15. Gr N-9.

Caracas 106A, Venezuela. Apartado del Este 60382. Tel. 92.47.31.
Roland M. Roth, BA, Lafayette College, MS, State Univ. of New York, MEd, Syracuse Univ., EdD, Temple Univ., Supt.
Pre-Prep. Tests SSAT. Curr—USA. LI—Eng. CF—Span Venezuelan Soc Stud Health Outdoor Ed Drama Music Art Fr. SI—ESL Rem & Dev Math & Read Tut.
Enr 634. B 305; G 329.
Fac 44. Full 44. M 34; F 10. US 24.
Tui $105-211/mo.
Est 1937. Inc nonprofit. Quar (Sept-Je). A/OS ISS NAIS. Accred SACS.
Bldgs 1. Lib 17,000 vols. Gym. Fields.

Sponsored by parents and businessmen of the North American community in Caracas, Escuela Campo Alegre follows a U.S. curriculum but offers Spanish instruction from grades one through nine, plus Venezuelan social studies in Spanish for grades three to six. French is taught in the junior high grades. The daily classes are taught in English. Classes in drama, typing, computers, statecraft, sewing, cooking, gymnastics and mechancial drawing supplement the academic program.

See also page 104

ESCUELA BELLA VISTA
  Day Coed Ages 4-18. Gr N-12.

Maracaibo 4001 (Zulia), Venezuela. Apartado 290. Tel. 911674196.
James E. Holmes, BS, MA, Univ. of Minnesota, Supt.
Col Prep. Tests CEEB. Curr—USA. LI—Eng Span.
Enr 524.
Fac 38.
Tui $765-2245.
Est 1936. Sem (Sept-Je). A/OS ISS. Accred SACS.
Bldgs 6. Lib 10,000 vols. Gym. Tennis crts. Field.

A curriculum based on that used in the United States is offered at Bella Vista, preparing students for the College Boards. Instruction is in English with Spanish offered beginning in kindergarten. Recent graduates have attended Texas A & M, University of Texas and Georgia Tech.

CHRISTIANSEN ACADEMY
  Bdg Coed Ages 10-18; Day Coed 6-18. Gr 1-12.

San Cristobal (Tachira), Venezuela. Apartado 75. Tel. (076) 65581.
David L. Belch, BEd, Eastern Washington Univ., Prin.

Col Prep Gen Acad. Tests CEEB SSAT ACT. Curr—USA. LI—Eng.
CF—Span Comp Bible Soc Stud Art. SI—Rem Reading Tut.
Enr 113. B 49/18; G 35/11. Elem 55, Sec 58. US—82. Grad '84—11.
Col—8.
Fac 19. Full 13/Part 6. M 7; F 12. US 19.
Tui Bdg $1100 (+ $50); Day $600.
Est 1952. Nonprofit. Evangelical Alliance Mission. Quar (Aug-May).
Bldg. Dorms 4. Lib 9000 vols. Athletic facilities.

Enrollment at this church-sponsored school is composed almost
entirely of American and Canadian children of Protestant missionary
families. Other children are accepted when space is available. The
curriculum is American, with instruction in English. Most graduates
enter Bible colleges in the United States.

COLEGIO INTERNACIONAL DE CARABOBO
Day Coed Ages 4-19. Gr N-12.

Valencia, Venezuela. Apartado 103. Tel. (041) 42.1807.
Frank Anderson, BS, Villanova Univ., MEd, Bridgewater State College,
Supt.
Col Prep Gen Acad. Tests CEEB TOEFL. Curr—USA. LI—Eng. CF—Fr
Span Hist (US). SI—Rem & Dev Read.
Enr 265. Elem 190, Sec 75. US—170. Grad '84—23. Col—21.
Fac 24. Full 24. M 10; F 14. US 19.
Tui $2600 (+ $400).
Summer Session. Rem. 5 wks.
Est 1955. Inc 1959 nonprofit. Quar (Aug-Je). ISS. Accred SACS.
Bldgs 6. 2 Libs 12,500 vols. Athletic facilities.

Founded by four North American companies—Celanese, Firestone,
Goodyear, and U.S. Rubber—this school is designed to offer an
American education to the children of employees of those companies
living in Valencia. Instruction is in English, with a daily course in
Spanish required of all students, taught by a Venezuelan teacher. Recent
graduates have attended Boston, Miami and Mississippi Universities.
Over half the enrollment is drawn from the United States, with children
from Canada, Sweden, Japan, Venezuela and Colombia making up the
balance.

CANADA

Alberta   British Columbia
Manitoba   New Brunswick
Nova Scotia   Ontario   Quebec
Saskatchewan

CANADA

The largest country in the Western Hemisphere, Canada is a federation of ten provinces and two territories. Newfoundland, Nova Scotia, New Brunswick and Prince Edward Island are the Maritime or Atlantic Provinces. Occupying most of the northeast is Quebec, former French colony and the oldest and largest province. Bordering Quebec on the west is Ontario, most populous and wealthy of the provinces. Next, from Ontario westward, are Manitoba, Saskatchewan, Alberta and British Columbia. The Yukon and Northwest Territories are to the north. Canada is a self-governing member of the Commonwealth of Nations.

Norseman Leif Ericson was the first to explore Canada's shores. Later, both the French and English established settlements through further explorations. This accounts for the country's bilingualism, a subject of much controversy today.

Primarily an agricultural nation, Canada is one of the world's largest exporters of wheat. Fishing is also a chief industry. Ottawa is the federal capital, and the monetary unit is the Canadian dollar (Can $).

ALBERTA

STRATHCONA-TWEEDSMUIR SCHOOL
  Day Coed Ages 6-18. Gr 1-12.

Calgary, Okotoks (Alberta) T0L 1T0, Canada. RR #2. Tel. 403-938-4431.
Peter B. Ditchburn, BA, MEd, Univ. of Calgary, Head.
Col Prep. Tests CEEB. Curr—Nat. LI—Eng. A—Biol Chem. CF—Fr Lat Soc Stud Art Drama Music Comp Stud.
Enr 520. B 280; G 240. Elem 300, Sec 220. Grad '84—40. Col—36.
Fac 41. Full 39/Part 2. M 24; F 17. Can.
Tui $3010-4050 (+$1000). Schol.
Est 1929. Inc 1969 nonprofit. Tri (Sept-Je). CAIS NAIS.
Bldgs 4. Lib 9500 vols. Labs 4. Athletic facilities. Theatre.

The result of a 1971 merger of Strathcona School for Boys and Tweedsmuir Girls' School, this non-denominational school offers a basic curriculum supplemented with a wide range of electives. The study of French begins in grade one and Latin in grade nine. Recreation clubs and physical education are important aspects of Strathcona-Tweedsmuir's program. These include trap and skeet shooting, white-water canoeing, mountain climbing, cross-country skiing, skating, basketball, gymnastics, track and field, swimming, golf and volleyball.

CAMROSE LUTHERAN COLLEGE
Bdg & Day Coed Ages 16 & up. Gr 12-PG.

Camrose (Alberta) T4V 2R3, Canada. 4901 46 Avenue. Tel. 403-669-1100.
Rev. K. Glen Johnson, Pres.
Erhard Pinno, Adm.
Gen Acad. Tests GCE CEEB SSAT. Curr—Nat. Ll—Eng. CF—Fr Ger Greek Agriculture Bus Engineering Art.
Enr 1101. B 211/311; G 239/340. Sec 70, PG 1031. US—2.
Fac 43. Full 34/Part 9. M 35; F 8. US 2. Nat.
Tui Bdg $4500; Day $2000. Schol.
Summer Session. Acad Rec. Tui Bdg $530-1050. 3 wks.
Est 1910. Inc. Lutheran. Sem (Sept-May).
Bldgs 12. Dorms 8. Lib 30,000 vols. Gym. Field.

Students from Canada, Hong Kong, Iran, Europe and the U.S. attend this junior college which is formally affiliated with the University of Alberta. Courses of study include pre-law, medicine and dentistry, the arts, engineering and nursing. Extracurricular activities are conducted in canoeing, curling, nordic skiing, wrestling, photography, drama and radio. The optional three-week spring session includes an extended camping trip to the Big Horn Mountains during which students can complete one to three environmental studies courses.

ST. JOHN'S SCHOOL OF ALBERTA
Bdg Boys Ages 11-18. Gr 7-12.

Stony Plain (Alberta) TOE 2GO, Canada. R. R. 5. Tel. (403) 429-4140.
Peter Jackson, BA, Univ. of Manitoba, Head.
Col Prep Gen Acad. Tests SSAT. Curr—Nat. Ll—Eng. A—Fr. CF—Physics Relig Comp Stud. Sl—Tut.
Enr 110. Grad '84—7. Col—5.
Fac 27. M 18; F 9. Nat.
Tui $6150 (+$500-900). Schol.
Est l968. Inc nonprofit. Anglican Church. Quar (Sept-Je).
Bldgs 6. Dorms 18. Lib 1500 vols. Fields. Hockey rink. Weight rm.

Located on a 250-acre site, St. John's offers a traditional college preparatory curriculum of literature, grammar, spelling, math, science, history, French and Latin. The school's challenging outdoor education program conducts month-long, 1500-mile canoe trips in June with 50-mile snowshoe hikes and 100-mile dog sled expeditions in the winter. The outdoor program also affords the acquisition of leadership skills. St. John's has no maintenance staff, and students and teachers work together to operate the plant. Students attend nightly chapel and bible study on a voluntary basis.

See also page 105

BRITISH COLUMBIA

QUEEN MARGARET'S SCHOOL
Bdg & Day Girls Ages 10-18. Gr 5-12.

Duncan (British Columbia) V9L 1C2, Canada. 660 Brownsey Ave. Tel. 604-746-4185.

J. Howard Dixon, BS, Univ. of London, Head.

Col Prep Gen Acad. Curr—Nat. LI—Eng. CF—Fr Span Chem Biol Math Word Processing.

Enr 185. G 125/60. Elem 59, Sec 126. US—3. Grad '84—24. Col—19.

Fac 20. Full 16/Part 4. M 6; F 14. Nat UK.

Tui Bdg $10,450 (+ $1000); Day $3825 (+ $400).

Est 1921. Nonprofit. Tri (Sept-Je) CAIS.

Bldgs 9. Dorms 2. 2 Libs 3500 vols. Gym. Stables. Field. Tennis crts. Swimming pool.

Situated on a 26-acre campus, Queen Margaret's enrolls students from Canada, Hong Kong, Mexico and the United States. A traditional college preparatory curriculum is followed with graduates attending universities throughout Canada and the United States. Extracurricular activities feature publications, outings to local events, and music, art and drama clubs. Sports participation in hockey, volleyball, basketball, track, tennis and swimming is encouraged.

SHAWNIGAN LAKE SCHOOL
Bdg & Day Boys Ages 11-19. Gr 8-12.

Shawnigan Lake (British Columbia) V0R 2W0, Canada. Tel. 604-743-5516.

Douglas J. Campbell, DipEd, Head.

Col Prep. Tests CEEB SSAT. Curr—Nat. LI—Eng. A—Fr Math. CF—Rom Lang Ger Hist (US) Man Arts.

Enr 251. B 243/8. Elem 28, Sec 223. US—12. Grad '84—39. Col—35.

Fac 24.

Tui Bdg $10,700 (+ $200); Day $6600 (+ $100). Schol.

Est 1916. Nonprofit 1927. Tri (Sept-Je). CAIS.

Bldgs 15. Dorms 5. Lib 11,500 vols. Gym. Fields. Courts.

Fronting on the north end of Shawnigan Lake, the school is located 12 miles south of Duncan and some 30 miles north of Victoria, the capital of British Columbia. The 160-acre campus affords ample space for all games and outdoor activities with the nearby lake utilized for water sports.

Preparing for university entrance in both Canada and the United States, the school generally enrolls about 15 boys from the U.S. each year. Students from South America and Asia are also in attendance.

CROFTON HOUSE SCHOOL
Bdg Girls Ages 12-17; Day 6-17. Gr 1-12.

Vancouver (British Columbia) V6N 3E1, Canada. 3200 W. 41st Ave. Tel. 604-263-3255.
Rosalind W. Addison, BS, DipEd, St. Andrews, Head.
Col Prep. Tests SSAT. Curr—Nat. Ll—Eng. CF—Fr Ger Russ Span Scripture Arts Comp Stud Typ.
Enr 460. G 50/410. Elem 239, Sec 221. US—4. Grad '84—52. Col—45.
Fac 36. Full 35/Part 1. M 2; F 34. Can.
Tui Bdg $10,000-10,895 (+ $300); Day $3180-4805 (+ $100).
Est 1898. Inc 1937 nonprofit. Tri (Sept-Je). CAIS NAIS.
Bdgs 6. Dorms 1. Lib 15,000 vols. Labs. Tennis crts 3. Field. Gyms.

Located on a ten-acre site, this school offers a curriculum preparing students for entrance into American and Canadian colleges and universities. Activities include choir, orchestra, school paper and magazine, skiing and swimming. Outings to local and regional events are also arranged.

ST. GEORGE'S SCHOOL
Bdg Boys Ages 10-19; Day Boys 7-19. Gr 2-12.

Vancouver (British Columbia) V6S 1V6, Canada. 4175 W. 29th Ave. Tel. 604-224-1304.
Alan C. M. Brown, BASc, Univ. of British Columbia, MAT, Brown, DipEd, Oxon, Head.
Col Prep. Tests CEEB SSAT. Curr—Nat. Ll—Eng.
Enr 625.
Fac 45. Can UK.
Tui Bdg $8425; Day $3700. Schol.
Est 1931. Nonprofit 1955. Tri (Sept-Je). CAIS NAIS.
Bldgs 5. Dorms 20. Lib 40,000 vols. Labs. Fields 5. Gyms 2. Swimming pool. Tennis crts.

St. George's, situated on two proximate but separate locations, comprises a 19-acre campus. Students are prepared for entrance into American and Canadian colleges. Rugby football is the school's major sport, however emphasis is also placed on swimming, cricket, tennis, basketball and ice hockey. Electives include courses in drama, typing, general business and tutorial English.

BRENTWOOD COLLEGE SCHOOL
Bdg & Day Boys Ages 11-18; Bdg & Day Girls 14-17. Gr 8-12.

Vancouver Island, Mill Bay (British Columbia) V0R 2P0, Canada. Mill Bay P.O. Tel. 604-743-5521.
William T. Ross, BA, Univ. of British Columbia, Head.
Col Prep. Tests CEEB. Curr—Nat. Ll—Eng.
Enr 340.
Fac 36. Can UK.

Tui Bdg $6175 (+ $900); Day $2500 (+ $500). Schol.
Est 1923. Nonprofit. Sem (Sept-Je). CAIS.
Bldgs 10. Dorms 6. Lib 4750 vols. Swimming pool. Tennis crts. Gym.
Boats.

Brentwood provides a college-preparatory program for entrance into Canadian and American universities. Extracurricular activities include band, rowing, sailing, swimming, rambling and interscholastic sports teams.

GLENLYON
Day Boys Ages 6-16. Gr 1-10.

Victoria (British Columbia), Canada. 1701 Beach Dr. Tel. (604) 592-2401.
Keith P. Walker, MA, Cambridge, Head.
Pre-Prep Col Prep. Curr—Nat. Ll—Eng. CF—Comp Sci. Sl—Rem & Dev Math & Read Tut.
Enr 230. Elem 170, Sec 60.
Fac 20. Full 16/Part 4. M 12; F 8. Nat UK.
Tui $2800-3900 (+ $250). Schol.
Est 1932. Nonprofit. Tri (Sept-Je).
Bldgs 5. Lib 6000 vols. Gym.

With a waterfront on Oak Bay, Glenlyon stresses academics and outdoor activities. All boys are on a continuous course of studies that will lead to University or Technical College entrance if the same course is maintained at the grade 11 and 12 levels. French is taught from grade one. A full program of art, music, drama, public speaking, computing skills and physical education is also offered.

NORFOLK HOUSE SCHOOL
Day Girls Ages 6-18. Gr 1-12.

Victoria (British Columbia) V8S 4A8, Canada. 801 Bank St. Tel. 598-2621.
Margaret Wilmot, BEd, Univ. of Alberta, MEd, Univ. of Manitoba, Head.
Pre-Prep Col Prep. Tests SSAT. Curr—Nat. Ll—Eng. CF—Latin Ger Span Fr Soc Stud Drama Music Computer Sci Typ. Sl—Rem Eng & Math.
Enr 294. Elem 191, Sec 103.
Fac 36. Full 29/Part 7. M 6; F 30. Can UK.
Tui $3500. Schol.
Est 1913. Nonprofit. Tri (Sept-Je). CAIS.
Bldgs 5. Lib. Gyms 2.

Norfolk combines a broad academic program with training in leadership and athletics. Students primarily from Canada and Hong Kong are prepared for the British Columbia diploma or university entrance. Computer literacy is incorporated into the curriculum at all grades. An enriched course geared to ability is available for French/

English bilingual students. Extracurricular clubs include debating, drama, social service, journalism, photography, sewing and music. Pupils also participate in hockey, soccer, tennis, swimming, cross-country, gymnastics, skating, squash, track and volleyball. A few eleventh and twelfth grade girls are accepted as boarders each year.

ST. MARGARET'S SCHOOL
Bdg Girls Ages 10-18; Day Girls 5-18. Gr K-12.

Victoria (British Columbia) V8X 3P7, Canada. 1080 Lucas Ave. Tel. (604) 479-7171.

Mrs. M. R. Sendall, BA, Univ. of Victoria, Head.

Col Prep Gen Acad. Tests SSAT. Curr—Nat. LI—Eng. CF—Fr Span Lat Ger Soc Stud. SI—Tut ESL.

Enr 350. G 70/280. Elem 208, Sec 142. US—4. Grad '84—27. Col—24.

Fac 32. Full 28/Part 4. M 6; F 22. Nat.

Tui Bdg $10,270 (+$1200); Day $3220 (+$700).

Est 1908. Inc 1947 nonprofit. Tri (Sept-Je). CAIS.

Bldgs 3. Dorms 2. 3 Libs 10,000 vols. Labs. Gym. Courts. Field.

Situated on 20 acres on the outskirts of Victoria, St. Margaret's offers a curriculum preparing students for college entrance. The school emphasizes individual development, with each student encouraged to work according to her own potential. Sports include grass hockey, tennis ,badminton, basketball, track, swimming, gymnastics, horseback riding and volleyball. Private music instruction is available.

ST. MICHAELS UNIVERSITY SCHOOL
Bdg Boys Ages 10-18, Girls 14-18; Day Coed 6-18. Gr 1-12.

Victoria (British Columbia) V8P 4P5, Canada. 3400 Richmond Rd. Tel. 604-592-2411.

John Schaffter, MA (Cantab), Head.

Col Prep. Tests SSAT. Curr—Nat. LI—Eng. A—Lang Physics Bio Chem. CF—Fr Span Ger Comp Sci. SI—Tut.

Enr 590. B 160/330; G 22/78.

Fac 54. Full 44/Part 10. M 40; F 14. Nat UK Fr.

Tui Bdg $8300-9500 (+$550); Day $2900-4100 (+$250).

Est 1906. Inc 1908 nonprofit. Tri (Sept-Je). CAIS.

Bldgs 10. Dorms 3. 2 Libs 3000 vols. Labs. Gyms 2. Swimming pool. Courts. Fields.

The results of a 1971 merger of University School and St. Michaels Preparatory School, this school prepares its students for the U.S. College Boards, with most graduates attending colleges in the United States. Debating, choir, drama, music, an Outward Bound program, scuba diving, camping and skiing are among the extracurricular activities.

MANITOBA

BALMORAL HALL SCHOOL FOR GIRLS
Bdg Girls Ages 13-18; Day Boys 4-5, Girls 4-18. Gr K-12.

Winnipeg (Manitoba) R3C 3S1, Canada. 630 Westminster Ave. Tel. 204-786-8643.
N. Thomas Russell, Head.
Col Prep. Curr—Nat. LI—Eng. CF—Fr Lat Geog Hist Fabric Arts Music Comp Sci Soc Stud. SI—Rem & Dev Math & Read Tut.
Enr 328. B /10; G 28/290. Elem 213, Sec 115. Grad '84—29. Col—29.
Fac 28. Full 20/Part 8. F 28. Nat UK.
Tui Bdg $10,000 (+$500); Day $4450 (+$500). Schol.
Est 1901. Inc 1950 nonprofit. Tri (Sept-Je). CAIS NAIS.
Bldgs 5. Dorms 20. Lib 13,000 vols. Gyms 2. Tennis crts.

Offering boarding facilities to a limited number of older girls and admitting boys to its nursery school, Balmoral Hall enrolls a few American students annually and prepares them for the U.S. College Boards. A variety of clubs and recreational activities are available.

ST. JOHN'S-RAVENSCOURT SCHOOL
Bdg Boys Ages 10-18; Day Boys 6-18, Girls 14-18. Gr 1-12.

Winnipeg (Manitoba) R3T 3K5, Canada. 400 South Dr. Tel. 204-453-3016.
John A. Messenger, BA, Springfield College, MEd, Univ. of Massachusetts, Prin.
Col Prep Gen Acad. Tests SSAT. Curr—Nat. LI—Eng. CF—Fr Lat Comp Sci Hist Arts.
Enr 620. B 100/440; G 80. Elem 350, Sec 270. US—10. Grad '84—66. Col—65.
Fac 47. Full 45/Part 2. M 30; F 17. US 2. Nat.
Tui Bdg $10,100 (+$500); Day $5000 (+$60). Schol.
Est 1820. Inc 1951 nonprofit. Tri (Sept-Je). CAIS.
Bldgs 6. Dorms 3. Lib 20,000 vols. Arena. Gym. Crts. Fields.

A full academic program is offered at this school. The sports program emphasizes hockey. Choir, orchestra, drama and debate are also available as extracurricular activities. A boarding program for girls ages 14-18 is available.

NEW BRUNSWICK

ROTHESAY COLLEGIATE SCHOOL—NETHERWOOD
Bdg & Day Coed Ages 12-18. Gr 7-12.

Rothesay (New Brunswick) E0G 2W0, Canada. College Hill. Tel. 506-847-8224.
Ian C. Rowe, DEd, MEd, Springfield, Head.

Col Prep. Tests CEEB SSAT. Curr—Nat. LI—Eng. CF—Fr Hist Econ
Pol Sci Music Art Divinity Geog Comp. SI—Tut Rem Eng.
Enr 131. B 44/32; G 29/27. Elem 47, Sec 84. US—1. Grad '84—31.
Col—20.
Fac 15. Full 12/Part 3. M 8; F 7. Can UK.
Tui Bdg $7827-8694; Day $3350-3638.
Est 1877. Nonprofit. Tri (Sept-Je). CAIS NAIS.
Bldgs 7. Dorms 3. Lib. Gym. Skating rink. Fields 5.

Enrolling several students from the United States, Hong Kong, Mexico
and other countries, this school offers preparation for entrance into
Canadian and American universities.

NOVA SCOTIA

THE HALIFAX GRAMMAR SCHOOL
Day Coed Ages 5-18. Gr K-12.

Halifax (Nova Scotia) B3H 1G9, Canada. 5750 Atlantic St. Tel.
902-422-6497.
Peter H. Montgomery, BA, Bishop's London, Head.
Col Prep. Tests CEEB. Curr—Nat. LI—Eng. CF—Fr Ger Latin Hist Art.
Enr 297. B 180; G 117. Elem 206, Sec 91. Grad '84—22. Col—22.
Fac 22. Full 20/Part 2. M 6; F 16.
Tui $2135-3015.
Est 1958. Inc nonprofit. Tri (Sept-Je). CAIS.
Bldgs 1. Lib. Gym. Labs. Field.

Open to students of any race, creed or nationality, Halifax Grammar
School prepares students for the U.S. College Boards. Instruction is in
English, with French required of all students from grade one.
Extracurricular activities include fencing, debating, drama, student
council, basketball, soccer, rugby, track and canoeing.

**HALIFAX LADIES COLLEGE—ARMBRAE PREPARATORY
SCHOOL**
Day Boys Ages 5-14; Day Girls 5-18. Gr N-12.

Halifax (Nova Scotia) B3H 3Y8, Canada. 1400 Oxford St. Tel.
902-423-7920.
Bonar A. Gow, PhD, Dalhousie, Prin.
Pre-Prep Col Prep. Tests SSAT. Curr—Nat. LI—Eng. CF—Fr Ger Lat
Hist Music Econ Drama.
Enr 127. B 41; G 86. Elem 96, Sec 31. Grad '84—8. Col—7.
Fac 19. Full 14/Part 5. M 1; F 18. Nat.
Tui $1715-2340 (+ $100). Schol.
Est 1887. Inc 1921 nonprofit. Tri (Sept-Je). CAIS.
Bldg. Lib 6000 vols.

This school emphasizes small group teaching and individual progress plans in both primary grades and college preparatry classes. Sports include gymnastics, basketball, swimming and volleyball. Students may also join drama, debate, computer, typing and crafts clubs.

KING'S-EDGEHILL SCHOOL
Bdg & Day Coed Ages 11-19.

Windsor (Nova Scotia) B0N 2T0, Canada. College Rd. Tel. 902-798-2278.
T. T. Menzies, MA, Cambridge, Head.
Col Prep. Tests IB. Curr—Nat. LI—Eng. CF—Fr Ger Hist Econ Pol Sci Comp Sci.
Enr 170. B 90/15; G 50/15. US—5. Grad '84—47. Col—36.
Fac 20. Full 19/Part 1. M 12; F 8. Can.
Tui Bdg $7800 (+ $400); Day $2500 (+ $200). Schol.
Est 1788. Inc nonprofit. Tri (Sept-Je). CAIS.
Bldgs 8. Dorms 5. Lib. Gym. Rink. Fields Crt.

Located on a 65-acre site, this school is the result of a merger in 1976 between King's College School for boys and Edgehill Church School for Girls. The curriculum prepares students for university entrance and is enhanced by many activities ranging from social service to survival in the wilderness. The school operates a ski patrol and a ground search and rescue team which meet the approval of the local government and authorities.

A brief chapel service is held each morning at which attendance is required. Extracurricular activities include debating, public speaking, dramatics, swimming, skating, curling, riding and skiing.

ONTARIO

ST. ANDREWS' COLLEGE
Bdg & Day Boys Ages 11-19. Gr 7-PG.

Aurora (Ontario) L4G 3H7, Canada. Tel. 416-727-3178.
Robert P. Bedard, BA, BEd, Head.
Pre-Prep Col Prep. Curr—Nat. LI—Eng. CF—Fr Lat Span Geog Math Music Econ Comp Sci. SI—ESL Tut.
Enr 434. B 304/130. US—6. Grad '84—69. Col—67.
Fac 36. Full 34/Part 2. M 34; F 2. US Can.
Tui Bdg $10,950 (+ $500); Day $6250 (+ $400). Schol.
Est 1899. Inc nonprofit. Sem (Sept-Je). CAIS NAIS.
Bldgs 21. Dorms 4. Lib 10,000 vols. Labs. Gyms 2. Tennis crts. Fields. Swimming pool.

Located on a 219-acre site, St. Andrews' educational program places great emphasis on reading, writing and computational skills which prepare boys for universities in Canada, Great Britain and the U.S. The music department offers group instruction in instrumental music and private lessons may be arranged in piano, organ or another instrument.

School activities include cadet corps, dramatics, debating and the school magazine. A wide variety of clubs is organized yearly from aeronautics to gourmet cooking. Students may also take part in gymnastics, skiing, tennis, soccer, ice hockey, cricket and curling. A five month "homestay" exchange program with students in France is optional for eleventh graders.

GREAT LAKES CHRISTIAN COLLEGE
Bdg & Day Coed Ages 13-20. Gr 9-PG.

Beamsville (Ontario) L0R 1B0, Canada. Box 399. King St. Tel. 416-563-5374.

Edwin Broadus, BA, Abilene Christian, MA, Univ. of Wisconsin at Milwaukee, Pres.

Col Prep Gen Acad. Curr—Nat. LI—Eng. CF—Fr Hist Geog Soc Econ Biol Math Sci Phys Ed Bible Ukranian.

Enr 148. Sec 114, PG 34. US—6. Grad '84—57. Col—20.

Fac 13. Full 11/Part 2. M 11; F 2. US 1. Nat.

Tui Bdg $5000 (+$350); Day $2600 (+$350). Schol.

Est 1950. Inc nonprofit. Sem (Sept-Je).

Bldgs 11. Dorms 4. Lib 13,000 vols. Gym. Court. Field.

This Christian college is composed of three divisions—high school, junior college and Bible college—and serves eastern Canada and the northeastern United States. Both general academic and commercial programs are offered. Students are informed of ACT and SSAT testing arrangements. A variety of clubs and intramural and recreational sports including volleyball, basketball, hockey, soccer, track, badminton and swimming are available.

ALBERT COLLEGE
Bdg & Day Coed Ages 13-20. Gr 7-PG.

Belleville (Ontario) K8P 1A6, Canada. Tel. 613-968-5726.

Roy B. Napier, BS, MEd, Head.

Col Prep. Tests CEEB SSAT TOEFL. Curr—Nat. LI—Eng. CF—Eng Fr Math Hist Sci Comp Music Econ Bio Geol Religion Family Stud Phys Ed.

Enr 223. B 112/14; G 88/9. Grad '84—50. Col—47.

Fac 24. Full 21/Part 3. M 14; F 10. US Can.

Tui Bdg $10,450 (+$250); Day $5250 (+$250). Schol.

Est 1857. Inc nonprofit. Tri (Sept-Je). CAIS NAIS.

Bldgs 7. Dorms 4. Lib 7000 vols. Gym. Fields. Pool.

Albert College enrolls students from Canada, the United States and 20 other countries. The academic program prepares students for Canadian and American colleges and is supplemented by athletic, social and cultural activities.

GRENVILLE CHRISTIAN COLLEGE
Bdg Coed Ages 12-19; Day 12-19. Gr 7-PG.

Brockville (Ontario) K6V 5V8, Canada. P.O. Box 610. Tel. 613-345-5521.
Rev. Charles R. Farnsworth, Head.
Col Prep. Tests CEEB SSAT. Curr—Nat. Ll—Eng. CF—Fr Span Lat Hist Music Theatre. Sl—Rem & Dev Read Tut.
Enr 218. B 117/4; G 95/5. US—22. Grad '84—85. Col—53.
Fac 35. Full 25/Part 10. US 19. Nat.
Tui Bdg $9200 (+ $400); Day $4000 (+ $400).
Est 1969. Inc nonprofit. Sem (Sept-Je). NAIS.
Bldgs 6. Dorms 3. Lib 6000 vols. Gym. Fields. Riding stables.

Located on a 250-acre campus one mile north of the St. Lawrence River, Grenville offers an academic curriculum preparing students for college entrance. Emphasis is placed on reading, writing and computation skills in the lower grades while older students are encouraged to maintain a well-balanced course selection. A complete business course as well as a varied program of art, crafts, family studies, music and theatre arts is available. To help maintain high academic standards, the school requires evening study for all students.

Competitive sports activities include cross-country, basketball, volleyball, skiing, badminton, and track and field. Students also have the opportunity to participate in archery, softball, square dancing, hockey, orienteering, soccer and riding. As part of the physical education program students may take at least one weekend trip each year. Grenville's location provides unlimited opportunities for hiking, camping, canoeing and mountain climbing.

NIAGARA CHRISTIAN COLLEGE
Bdg & Day Coed Ages 12-20. Gr 7-PG.

Fort Erie (Ontario) L2A 5M4, Canada. 2619 Niagara Parkway. Tel. 416-871-6980.
Don McNiven, BA, Brock Univ., Pres.
Col Prep. Curr—Nat. Ll—Eng. CF—Fr Hist Geog Relig Bus Ed Music Econ. Sl—ESL.
Enr 176. B 45/40; G 46/45.
Fac 14. Full 11/Part 3. M 8; F 6. Nat.
Tui $9475-9825; Day $1875-2000. Schol.
Est 1932. Nonprofit. Brethren in Christ. Tri (Sept-Je).
Bldgs 8. Dorms 2. Lib 7000 vols. Gym. Fields.

This church-affiliated school offers a five-year secondary program with an evangelical Christian emphasis. The majority of courses are intended to prepare students for university or professional school entrance. In addition, each student must attend regular chapel programs and an appropriate Bible course. A variety of sports activities is offered including badminton, raiderball, basketball, floor hockey, flag football, softball, track and field and volleyball. Choir, band, drama and computer club are also available.

HILLFIELD-STRATHALLAN COLLEGE
Day Coed Ages 3-18. Gr N-PG.

Hamilton (Ontario) L9C 1G3, Canada. 299 Fennell Ave. West. Tel. (416) 389-1367.
M. B. Wansbrough, BA, Bishop's Univ., MEd, Univ. of Western Ontario, Head.
Col Prep. Tests CEEB SSAT. Curr—Nat. Ll—Eng. CF—Fr Ger Lat Sci Music Hist. Sl—Rem & Dev Read Tut.
Enr 878. B 496; G 382. Elem 598, Sec 280.
Fac 62. Full 55/Part 7. M 27; F 35. Nat.
Tui $1765-5200 (+$250). Schol.
Summer Session. Rec. Tui $50/wk. 8 wks.
Est 1901. Inc 1962 nonprofit. Tri (Sept-Je). CAIS NAIS.
Bldgs 10. 4 Libs 15,000 vols. Gyms 2. Fields. Crts.

The 1962 merger between Highfield School for Boys and Strathallan School for Girls made Hillfield- Strathallan the second largest coed day school in Canada. The academic program emphasizes a liberal arts curriculum enhanced by computer literacy and athletics. A Montessori school for three- to nine-year-olds parallels the regular elementary program. Extracurricular activities include drama, music, yearbook and a full range of sports. A summer camp offers tennis, basketball and art lessons.

LAKEFIELD COLLEGE SCHOOL
Bdg & Day Boys Ages 12-18. Gr 7-12.

Lakefield (Ontario), Canada K0L 2H0. Tel. 705-652-3324.
J. T. M. Guest, BA, Bishop's Univ., Head.
Col Prep. Tests CEEB SSAT. Curr—Nat. Ll—Eng. CF—Fr Latin Comp Relig Computer Sci Music Art Econ Typ Outdoor Ed.
Enr 248. B 213/35.
Fac 33. Full 24/Part 9. M 24; F 9. Can.
Tui Bdg $11,000 (+$1200); Day $5500 (+$900). Schol.
Est 1879. Inc 1938. Tri (Sept-Je). CAIS NAIS.
Bldgs 19. Dorms 9. Lib 10,000 vols. Crts. Fields.

This well-established boys' school offers a college preparatory curriculum and a 10:1 student:faculty ratio. The art courses in ceramics, printmaking and etching are particularly strong. The academic program is supplemented by extracurricular activities in drama, choir and debate. A period of volunteer service in the local area is required.

From its inception, Lakefield has emphasized environmental awareness and athletics. In addition to the required "life sports" physical education, boys may participate in baseball, football, soccer, skiing, sailing, hockey, kayaking, tennis, golf, cricket and cycling. Many of these skills are practiced during trips to regional parks and rivers.

A number of American students are enrolled each year and 95 percent of all students are accepted to Canadian and U.S. universities.

UNITED MENNONITE EDUCATIONAL INSTITUTE
Day Coed Ages 13-18. Gr 9-12.

Leamington (Ontario), Canada. R.R. #5. Tel. 519-326-7448.
Erwin Tiessen, Prin.
Gen Acad. Curr—Nat. LI—Eng. CF—Relig Stud Music Fr Ger.
Enr 102. B 53; G 49. Grad '84—23.
Fac 9. Full 5/Part 4. M 4; F 5. Can.
Tui $890-980. Schol.
Est 1946. Inc nonprofit. Mennonite. Sem (Sept-Je).
Bldgs 1. Lib. Athletic facilities.

This Mennonite-sponsored school offers a basic high school curriculum supplemented by activities in music, law, consumer education and sports.

MOUNT ST. JOSEPH ACADEMY
Bdg & Day Girls Ages 14-19. Gr 9-PG.

London (Ontario) N6G 2M3, Canada. 1490 Richmond St. N. Tel. 519-432-1932.
Sr. Monica Marie, BA, Univ. of Windsor, Prin.
Col Prep. Curr—Nat. LI—Eng.
Enr 200.
Fac 30.
Tui Bdg $3000-3600 (+ $500); Day $960 (+ $500).
Est 1953. Nonprofit. Roman Catholic. Tri (Sept-Je).
Bldg 1. Lib. Labs 5.

Conducted by the Sisters of St. Joseph, this girls' boarding and day school prepares students for the Canadian national university entrance examination. Approximately one-fourth of the enrollment is comprised of foreign students.

THE NEWMARKET MONTESSORI SCHOOL
Day Coed Ages 2½-12. Gr N-6.

Newmarket (Ontario), Canada. P.O. Box 1, 337 Queen St. Tel. (416) 895-1921.
Margaret Mair, BA, MA, York Univ., Dir.
Gen Acad. Curr—USA. LI—Eng. CF—Read Math Sci Writing Fr Music Geog.
Enr 80. B 37; G 43.
Fac 4. Full 3/Part 1. F 4. Nat.
Tui $1250-2300 (+ $50).
Est 1973. Inc nonprofit. Tri (Sept-Je).

Using the Montessori method, this school introduces students to a variety of academic subjects as well as the basics of reading, writing and math. Community figures such as policemen, firemen, musicians and librarians visit the classroom. Also, students participate in outings to concerts, plays, museums, conservation areas, farms and picnics.

PICKERING COLLEGE
Bdg & Day Boys Ages 12-19. Gr 7-PG.

Newmarket (Ontario) L3Y 4X2, Canada. 389 Bayview Ave. Tel. 416-895-1700.
Sheldon H. Clark, BA, Hiram, MA, BEd, Univ. of Toronto, Head.
Col Prep. Tests CEEB SSAT IB. Curr—Nat. Ll—Eng. A—Eng Math. CF—Fr Span World Relig Computer Sci Econ Calc Art.
Enr 180. B 160/20. US—10. Grad '84—26. Col—24.
Fac 22. Full 22. M 20; F 2. Can.
Tui $10,700 (+$1000); Day $6500 (+$1000).
Est 1842. Inc 1917 nonprofit. Tri (Sept-Je). CAIS.
Bldgs 6. Dorms 2. Lib 20,000 vols. Gym. Indoor rink. Fields 4.

Founded by the Religious Society of Friends, this interdenominational school enrolls boys from Africa, Canada, Hong Kong, Mexico, the United States and West Indies. The curriculum prepares students for entrance into American and Canadian universities. Extracurricular activities include school publications and student government as well as photography, gardening and wrestling clubs. Football, soccer, basketball, rugby, conditioning, tennis and hockey are among the sports offered.

APPLEBY COLLEGE
Bdg Boys Ages 9-19; Day Boys 8-16. Gr 4-PG.

Oakville (Ontario) L6K 3P1, Canada. Tel. 416-45-4681.
A.S. Troubetzkoy, BA, DipEd, Bishop's, Head.
Col Prep. Tests CEEB SSAT. Curr—Nat. Ll—Eng. CF—Fr Ger Latin Bus Hist Art Music.
Enr 412. B 184/228. Elem 185, Sec 187, PG 40. US—1. Grad '84—40.
Fac 42. Full 39/Part 3. M 33; F 9. Can.
Tui Bdg $9850-10,350; Day $6200-6850. Schol.
Est 1911. Nonprofit. Tri (Sept-Je). CAIS NAIS.
Bldgs 10. Dorms 4. Lib 10,000 vols. Gym. Pool. Crts. Fields.

Offering a college preparatory program for students who wish to study either in the United States or in Canada, Appleby College is a boarding and day school for boys. Students come from Canada, Hong Kong, Jamaica and the United States. Extracurricular activities include drama, music, debate, photography, wilderness survival training and sports.

ST. MILDRED'S-LIGHTBOURN SCHOOL
Day Girls Ages 4-19. Gr K-PG.

Oakville (Ontario) L6J 2L1, Canada. 1080 Linbrook Rd. Tel. 416-845-2386.

Lynda K. Palazzi, MA, Georgetown Univ., Prin.
Col Prep Gen Acad. Tests SSAT. Curr—Nat. LI—Eng. CF—Fr Ger Lat
  World Relig Theatre Arts Music Econ Comp. SI—Rem & Dev Math &
  Read Tut.
Enr 479. Elem 296, Sec 159, PG 24. Grad '84—24. Col—22.
Fac 40. Full 26/Part 14. M 3; F 37. US 2. Nat UK.
Tui $2000-2600 (+ $50-250). Schol.
Summer Session. Rec Rem. Tui $60/wk. 3 wks.
Est 1891. Inc 1969 nonprofit. Sem (Sept-Je). CAIS.
Bldgs 2. Lib 12,000 vols. Gym. Tennis crts. Field.

St. Mildred's College, founded in 1891 by the Community of the
Sisters of the Church, merged with Lightbourn School in 1969. Chapel
services begin each day and attendance at weekly religious instruction is
compulsory. Extracurricular activities include drama, arts and crafts,
French club, publications and music. A sports program offers tennis,
cross country, basketball and swimming. Recent graduates have entered
Vassar, Syracuse and Principia College.

ASHBURY COLLEGE
  Bdg & Day Boys Ages 10-18; Girls 16-18. Gr 5-PG.

Ottawa (Ontario) K1M 0T3, Canada. 362 Mariposa Ave. Tel. 613-
  749-5954.
A. M. Macoun, MA, Oxford, Head.
Col Prep Gen Acad. Tests IB. Curr—Nat. LI—Eng. CF—Fr Span Ger
  Lat Geog Arts Bus Comp Hist. SI—Rem & Dev Read Tut ESL.
Enr 460. B 110/320; G 10/20. Elem 160, Sec 290. Grad '84—356.
  Col—56.
Fac 51. Full 45/Part 6. M 42; F 9. Nat UK.
Tui Bdg $10,950 (+ $500); Day $5850 (+ $300). Schol.
Summer Session. Acad Red. Tui $130-390. 4 wks.
Est 1891. Inc 1952 nonprofit. Tri (Sept-Je). CAIS ISA NAIS.
Lib 8000 vols. Gym. Fields.

Offering a full college preparatory program and a wide range of
extracurricular activities, Ashbury prepares boys and girls for university
entrance and the International Baccalaureate Diploma. Fluency in
French and the liberal arts are emphasized. Daily chapel attendance is
required. The outdoor education program includes skiing, canoeing,
hiking, cycling and orienteering.

ELMWOOD SCHOOL
  Day Boys Ages 6-10; Day Girls 6-18. Gr 1-PG.

Ottawa (Ontario) K1M 0V9, Canada. 261 Buena Vista Rd. Tel.
  613-749-6761.
Margaret White, BA, Univ. of Manchester, Univ. de Montpelier, Head.
Col Prep Gen Acad. Tests IB. Curr—Nat. LI—Eng Fr. CF—Fr Latin
  Span Ger Soc Stud Relig Arts Comp Geog. SI—ESL Rem.

Enr 300. B 30; G 270. Elem 150, Sec 150. US—6. Grad '84—34.
Col—32.
Fac 31. Full 26/Part 5. M 2; F 29. Can.
Tui $4550 (+$500). Schol.
Summer Session. Rec. Tui $120/wk. 3 wks.
Est 1915. Inc 1957 nonprofit. Tri (Sept-Je). CAIS.
Bldgs 1. 2 Libs 10,000 vols. Athletic facilities.

Offering preparation for post-secondary education, Elmwood's curriculum includes study for the International Baccalaureate. A strong French program is offered. Students have the opportunity to take one subject in French in grades five through eight, complemented by instruction in Latin and modern European languages. Grades three and four are coeducational while the rest of the school shares classes and activities with Ashbury College. Participation in drama, choir, debate and computer clubs is encouraged.

TRINITY COLLEGE SCHOOL
Bdg & Day Boys Ages 11-19. Gr 7-PG.

Port Hope (Ontario) L1A 3W2, Canada. Tel. 416-885-4565.
Rodger C.N. Wright, MEd, Univ. of Toronto, Head.
Col Prep. Curr—Nat. Ll—Eng. CF—Fr Ger Lat Span Relig Econ Chem
Politics. Sl—Rem & Dev Read Tut.
Enr 360. B 325/35. US—9. Grad '84—72. Col—70.
Fac 46. Full 42/Part 4. M 40; F 6. Nat UK.
Tui Bdg $10,300 (+$800); Day $5500 (+$800). Schol.
Summer Session. Rec. Tui Bdg $195/wk. 4-8 wks.
Est 1865. Inc nonprofit. Tri (Sept-Je). CAIS NAIS.
Bldgs 15. Dorms 5. Libs 16,000 vols. Gyms 2. Pool. Fields. Crts.

Located on a 100-acre campus overlooking Lake Ontario, this school enrolls boys from Canada, the United States and 16 other countries. The college preparatory curriculum is complemented by activities in drama, music, art, photography, clubs, marksmanship, canoeing and rocketry. Facilities are available for hockey, swimming, squash, tennis, football, soccer, gymnastics, track and skiing. Former students have attended Harvard, MIT, Dartmouth, Princeton, Stanford, Oxford and Cambridge universities.

ROSSEAU LAKE COLLEGE
Bdg Coed Ages 12-18. Gr 8-PG.

Rosseau, Muskoka (Ontario) P0C 1J0, Canada. Tel. 705-732-4307.
D.N. Hodgetts, BA, DipEd, Head.
Col Prep. Curr—Nat. Ll—Eng. CF—Fr Hist Art Music Bus Accounting
Econ Comp. Sl—Tut.
Enr 110. Elem 10, Sec 100. Grad '84—12. Col—12.
Fac 13. M 10; F 3. Nat.
Tui $10,900.

Est 1967. Inc 1968 nonprofit. Tri (Sept-Je). CAIS.
Bldgs 15. Lib 6000 vols. Gym. Fields.

Situated on the lakeshore in Muskoka, Rosseau Lake School's program emphasizes academics combined with outdoor education and activities. Basic academic courses are stressed while tutorials and seminars are used to provide a greater opportunity for discussion and participation in the learning process. Students may learn or further develop their skills in sailing, canoeing, archery, swimming, tennis, snowshoeing and skiing through an extensive outdoors program. Orienteering, rock climbing and survival in the woods under both summer and winter conditions are also taught. Other extracurricular activities include photography, electronics, fishing, dramatics, debating and arts and crafts.

RIDLEY COLLEGE
Bdg & Day Boys Ages 9-19; Bdg & Day Girls 15-19. Gr 5-PG.

St. Catherines (Ontario) L2R 7C3, Canada. Box 3013. Tel. 416-684-8193.
H. Jeremy Packard, BA, Williams College, MA, Columbia, Head.
Col Prep Gen Acad. Tests CEEB SSAT. Curr—Nat. LI—Eng. A—Math Eng. CF—Fr Lat Span Hist. SI—Tut Eng & Math.
Enr 563. B 314/140; G 80/29. Elem 93, Sec 470. US—32. Grad '84—112. Col—105.
Fac 58. Full 45/Part 13. M 46; F 12. Can UK.
Tui Bdg $10,600-11,300; Day $5900-7200 (+$475). Schol.
Summer Session. Rec. 6 wks.
Est 1889. Nonprofit. Quar (Sept-Je). CAIS NAIS.
Bldgs 11. Dorms 5. Lib 16,000 vols. Lang lab. Gym. Fields 10. Rifle range. Sports complex. Swimming pool. Tennis crts 5. Rink.

United States alumni of this school total more than 400. Besides Canada and the U.S., students come from Hong Kong, Mexico, Venezuela and the West Indies. The curriculum prepares students for university entrance with 95 percent of Ridley graduates entering colleges in Canada and the U.S. Debating is encouraged at all levels and the school conducts annual debating tournaments. A full range of athletics and activities is provided. Ridley is situated about 13 miles from Niagara Falls.

ALMA COLLEGE
Bdgs Girls Ages 13 & up. Gr 7-PG.

St. Thomas (Ontario), Canada. 96 Moore St. Tel. (519) 631-3880.
Miss M. E. Bone, BA, Prin.
Col Prep. Curr—Nat. LI—Eng. CF—Fr Math Sci Art Music Relig.
Enr 145. Grad '84—68. Col—45.
Fac 19. Full 12/Part 7. M 4; F 15. Canada.
Tui Bdg $8000 (+$1000); Day $5000 (+$800). Schol.
Summer Session. Rec Music Dance. Tui Bdg $140; Day $60. 4 wks.

Est 1876. Inc. Tri (Sept-Je). CAIS.
Bldgs 3. Dorms 2. Lib. Theatre. Gym. Pool.

Affiliated with the United Church of Canada, Alma College provides a college preparatory curriculum for girls from various countries. Courses are offered under four broad areas: the arts, communications, social and environmental studies, and pure and applied sciences. A nursery school and kindergarten run by the college provide practice teaching opportunities for secondary school students.

An extensive extracurricular program includes swimming, music, ceramics, dance, gymnastics, dramatics and photography. Equestrian studies are available as an elective.

BRANKSOME HALL
  Bdg Girls Ages 12-18; Day 5-18. Gr K-12.

Toronto (Ontario) M4W 1N4, Canada. 10 Elm Ave. Tel. 416-920-9741.
Allison Roach, BA, MEd, Univ. of Toronto, Prin.
Col Prep. Tests CEEB SSAT. Curr—Nat. LI—Eng. CF—Fr Lat Span Physics Comp.
Enr 765.
Tui Bdg $9950 (+ $500); Day $2000-4750 (+ $300). Schol.
Est 1903. Nonprofit. Tri (Sept-Je). CAIS NAIS.
Bldgs 10. Dorms 4. Lib. Tennis crts. Fields. Swimming pool.

This school enrolls students from Canada, Hong Kong, Mexico, the United States and West Indies. Electives are offered in art, drama, music, typing, computer science and economics.

HAVERGAL COLLEGE
  Bdg Girls Ages 12-19; Day Girls 4-19. Gr N-PG.

Toronto (Ontario) M5N 2H9, Canada. 1451 Avenue Rd. Tel. 416-483-3519.
Miss Mary Dennys, BA, Univ. of Toronto, Prin.
Col Prep. Tests CEEB. Curr—Nat. LI—Eng. CF—Fr Ger Greek Lat Russ Span Hist Geog Pol Sci Relig Chem Physics Art.
Enr 738. G 95/643. Elem 330, Sec 409. Grad '84—70. Col—68.
Fac 60. Full 48/Part 12. M 5; F 55. Nat.
Tui Bdg $10,750 (+ $300); Day $2700-5300 (+ $300). Schol.
Summer Session. Rec. 6 wks.
Est 1894. Inc 1917 nonprofit. Tri (Sept-Je). CAIS NAIS.
Bldgs 3. Dorms 1. Lib 9200 vols. Labs. Gym. Tennis crts. Fields. Swimming pool.

Offering the Ontario Curriculum, Havergal enrolls mostly Canadian students, but boarders are drawn from many parts of the world. Elective courses include art, music, theatre and physical education.

LORETTO ABBEY
 Day Girls Ages 7-19. Gr 3-PG.

Toronto (Ontario) M5M 3E2, Canada. 101 Mason Blvd. Tel. (416) 484-9788.
Sr. Evanne Hunter, BA, MEd, Univ. of Toronto, Prin.
Col Prep Gen Acad. Curr—Nat. LI—Eng.
Enr 600.
Fac 36.
Tui $700. Schol.
Est 1847. Roman Catholic. Tri (Sept-Je).
Bldgs 1.Gym. Swimming pool. Tennis crts. Fields.

Religion claims an important part of the daily life of the girls at this Catholic day school. The academic curriculum leads to the Ontario diploma and entrance to universities, nurses' training, and teachers' colleges. A music program is offered which enables girls to earn the Associate Diploma of the Royal Conservatory of Toronto. Festivals, recitals, and retreats are a few of the many extracurricular activities available.

ST. CLEMENT'S SCHOOL
 Day Girls Ages 5-19. Gr 1-13.

Toronto (Ontario) M4R 1G8, Canada. 21 St. Clement's Ave. Tel. (416) 483-4835.
Hazel W. Perkin, BA, Sir George Williams, MA, McGill, Prin.
Col Prep. Tests SSAT. Curr—Nat. LI—Eng. CF—Fr Lat Ger Art Comp Drama.
Enr 396. Elem 217, Sec 179.. Grad '84—30. Col—30.
Fac 34. Full 28/Part 6. M 3; F 31. Can.
Tui $3300-3600 (+$200). Schol.
Summer Session. Acad Arts & Crafts. Tui Day $100. 4 wks.
Est 1901. Inc 1967 nonprofit. Tri (Sept-June). CAIS NAIS.
Bldgs 1. Lib 7500 vols. Gym.

St. Clement's School offers a broad college preparatory program combined with training in the Christian faith. Art, music and handicrafts are integral parts of the curriculum and there is also an active debating club. Athletic activities include basketball, volleyball, baseball, badminton, tennis and archery. Classes are limited to 24 students.

THE TORONTO FRENCH SCHOOL
 Day Coed Ages 3½-18. Gr N-13.

Toronto (Ontario) M4N 1T7, Canada. 296 Lawrence Ave. E. Tel. 416-484-6533.
William Henry Giles, MEd, Univ. of Toronto, Head.
Col Prep Gen Acad. Tests SSAT GCE. Curr—Intl. LI—Eng Fr. CF—Fr Ger Russ Lat Comp Sci. SI—Rem & Dev Math & Read Tut.
Enr 1239. B 609; G 630. Grad '84—60. Col—60.

Fac 106. Full 94/Part 12. M 25; F 81. Fr Belgium UK Nat.
Tui $5700 (+ $250). Schol.
Summer Session. Acad Rec. Tui $500/3 wks. 6 wks.
Est 1962. Inc nonprofit. Tri (Sept-Je). CAIS NAIS.
Bldgs 5. Lib 20,000 vols. Athletic facilities.

This school was founded in response to the need to educate children primarily from English-speaking families in both constitutionally recognized cultures. Classes are conducted in French until the second grade. Thereafter about one-third of the instruction is in English, while the rest is in French. Classes in French are conducted by native French speakers; while classes in English are taught by teachers whose native language is English. There is also an ongoing physical education program including gymnastics, soccer, basketball, volleyball, tennis and track. Clubs and debate are also available. Several private homes accept boarding students. Branches of the school exist in Toronto, Don Mills, Mississauga and North York.

UPPER CANADA COLLEGE
Bdg Boys Ages 13-19; Day 8-19. Gr 3-PG.

Toronto (Ontario) M4V 1W6, Canada. 200 Lonsdale Rd. Tel. 416-488-1125/6.
Richard H. Sadleir, MA (Cantab), Prin.
Col Prep. Tests CEEB SSAT. Curr—Nat. Ll—Eng. CF—Fr Ger Lat Span US Hist Pol Sci Art.
Enr 950. Elem 350, Sec 600. Grad '84—116. Col—116.
Fac 68. Full 68. M 65; F 3. Can UK.
Tui Bdg $10,750 (+ $250); Day $5850 (+ $250). Schol.
Est 1829. Nonprofit. Tri (Sept-Je). CAIS NAIS.
Bldgs 4. Dorms 2. Lib. Gym. Fields. Tennis crts. Swimming pool.

Upper Canada College comprises a Preparatory and a Senior School, grades 3-8, and grades 9-13 respectively. The Preparatory School follows the Ontario Curriculum, and the Senior School follows a 5-year program leading to the grade 13 Matriculation exams. Preparation is also offered for the College Boards. A variety of sports and theatre, debate, photography, art and music activities are available. Situated on a 40-acre site in a residential suburb of Toronto, the school also maintains a 500-acre winter sports facility at Norval, 30 miles outside the city.

ROBERT LAND ACADEMY
Bdg Boys 10-19. Gr 5-12.

Wellandport (Ontario) L0R 2J0, Canada. RR #3. Tel. (416) 386-6203.
Major Scott Bowman, BA, McMaster Univ., Head.
Gen Acad. Curr—Nat. Ll—Eng. CF—French. Sl—Tut Rem & Dev Math & Read.
Enr 110. Elem 35, Sec 75. Grad '84—3. Col—2.
Fac 14. Full 12/Part 2. M 12; F 2. Can.
Tui $9800 (+ $250).

Est 1978. Inc 1973 nonprofit. Tri (Sept-Je).
Bldgs 12. Dorms 3. Lib 5000 vols. Fields.

This military academy, located on 170 acres of farm and woodland, stresses the development of basic academic skills. Classes are small and tutorials are emphasized. A full range of extracurricular activities is offered including compulsory cadet corps membership, track, canoeing, soccer, skiing, swimming and baseball.

QUEBEC

WEST ISLAND COLLEGE
Day Coed Ages 11-17. Gr 7-12.

Dollard des Ormeaux (Quebec) H9B 2L2, Canada. 851 Tecumseh St. Tel. 683-4660.
Jack A. Grant, Head.
Col Prep. Tests IB. Curr—Nat. LI—Fr Eng. A—Fr. CF—Arts Geog Comp Experimental Ed.
Enr 318. B 178; G 140. Grad '84—48. Col—48.
Fac 32. Full 32. M 18; F 14. US 1 Can.
Tui $2600 (+ $350).
Est l974. Nonprofit. Quar (Sept-Je).
Bldgs 3. Lib 5000 vols. Gym. Fields.

West Island College offers a completely bilingual curriculum with math and sciences taught in English and social sciences taught in French. The junior and senior high school program prepares students for the Quebec secondary school diploma. Additionally, an International Baccalaureate program involves advanced studies in the liberal arts with an emphasis on writing and a social service requirement, to prepare students for university study. Finally, a Canadian studies course and a practical program in interpersonal skills and "real life" experiences are available.

Entering students must show some proficiency in both French and English. A strong career guidance program supplements the curriculum and a variety of clubs, associations and sports acitvities are available. The college also maintains campuses in Calgary, Alberta and Ottawa, Ontario.

BISHOP'S COLLEGE SCHOOL
Bdg & Day Coed Ages 12-18. Gr 7-12.

Lennoxville (Quebec) J1M 1Z8, Canada. Tel. 819-562-7683.
David A.G. Crickshank, MA, Queen's, BA, Bishop's, Head.
Col Prep. Tests CEEB. Curr—Nat. LI—Eng. CF—Fr Lat Span Econ. SI—Rem & Dev Math & Read.
Enr 297. B 121/40; G 109/27. Grad '84—74. Col—74.
Fac 41. Full 36/Part 5. M 23; F 18. Can.
Tui Bdg $11,000 (+ $2000); Day $6900 (+ $1000).

Est 1836. Anglican. Tri (Sept-July). CAIS NAIS.
Bldgs 12. Dorms 7. Lib 17,000 vols. Gym. Crts. Fields.

The academic program at Bishop's prepares students for university entrance in Canada and the U.S. The curriculum is complemented by a full range of sports and cultural activities including music, drama, debating and clubs. Recent graduates have entered Dartmouth, Williams, Middlebury and Wellesley.

LOWER CANADA COLLEGE
Day Boys Ages 8-17. Gr 3-12.

Montreal (Quebec) H4A 2M5, Canada. 4090 Royal Ave. Tel. 514-482-9916.
G. H. Merrill, BA, MA, Head.
Col Prep Gen Acad. Tests CEEB. Curr—Nat. LI—Eng. CF—Fr Span Hist Arts.
Enr 600.
Fac 53.
Tui $3550 (+ $344).
Est 1909. Inc 1935 nonprofit. Tri (Sept-Je). CAIS NAIS.

Although affiliated with the Anglican Church of Canada, this school enrolls boys of all faiths and nationalities. The curriculum prepares students for the U.S. College Boards and the Quebec High School Leaving Examinations.

THE PRIORY SCHOOL
Day Coed Ages 5-12. Gr K-6.

Montreal (Quebec) H3Y 1R9, Canada. 3120 The Boulevard. Tel. (514) 935-5966.
Teresa McConnon, BA, Univ. of Montreal, Prin.
Gen Acad. Curr—Nat. LI—Eng. CF—Fr.
Enr 145.
Fac 13.
Tui $1725-2025.
Est 1947.Inc 1948 nonprofit. Roman Catholic. NAIS.

Providing an elementary education for Canadian and other English-speaking children in Montreal, the Priory School attempts to make its students bilingual by offering French from the beginning.

ST. GEORGE'S SCHOOL OF MONTREAL
Day Coed Ages 4-17. Gr N-11.

Montreal (Quebec) H3Y 1R9, Canada. 3100 The Boulevard. Tel. 514-937-9289.
Murray C. Magor, BA, MA, McGill, Prin.
Col Prep Gen Acad. Curr—Nat. LI—Eng. CF—Fr Hist Arts Span Comp.
Enr 474. B 235; G 239. Grad '84—57. Col—57.
Fac 53. Full 45/Part 8. M 20; F 33. Can.

Tui $3500-3750. Schol.
Est 1930. Inc nonprofit. Tri (Sept-Je). CAIS NAIS.
Bldgs 2. 2 Libs 15,000 vols. Gym. Fields.

Instruction in French is required of all students at St. George's. The curriculum provides preparation for the McGill University Matriculation Examination and the U.S. College Boards. Extracurricular activities include debate, chess, ceramics, photography, soccer, basketball, track and publications.

THE STUDY
Day Boys Ages 5-7; Day Girls 5-16. Gr K-11.

Montreal (Quebec) H3Y 1S4, Canada. 3233 The Boulevard. Tel. 514-935-9352.
Eve Marshall, BA, McGill, Head.
Col Prep. Tests CEEB. Curr—Nat. LI—Eng Fr. CF—Fr Ger Lat Hist Arts Music Comp.
Enr 248. B 15; G 233. Elem 130, Sec 118.
Fac 28. Full 20/Part 8. M 4; F 24. US 3. Nat US UK Fr.
Tui $2100-3800 (+$100). Schol.
Est 1915. Inc 1922 nonprofit. Sem (Sept-Je). CAIS NAIS.
Bldgs 3. Lib 8000 vols. Gym.

The Study offers a flexible but comprehensive program with early elementary classes conducted on an ungraded basis. Special emphasis is placed on the study of French which begins in kindergarten and continues at all grade levels. This program is supplemented by courses in drama, geography and history taught in French. Recent graduates have entered Middlebury, Harvard and Brown universities.

TRAFALGAR SCHOOL FOR GIRLS
Day Girls Ages 12-17. Gr 7-11.

Montreal (Quebec) H3G 2J7, Canada. 3495 Simpson St. Tel. 514-935-2644.
Janette Doupe, BEd, Univ. of Manitoba, MEd, McGill, Prin.
Col Prep. Curr—Nat. LI—Eng.
Enr 264.
Fac 22.
Tui $800 (+$200). Schol.
Est 1867. Inc 1887. Tri (Sept-Je). CAIS NAIS.
Bldgs 1. Lib 7000 vols. Labs. Gym. Courts.

Situated on the southern slope of Mount Royal, Trafalgar provides a college preparatory curriculum leading to the U.S. College Boards and to Quebec's Secondary examinations. In addition to the core curriculum, the school offers courses in reading and study skills and accelerated coursework. French is taught at three levels in each class, creating smaller teaching groups with instruction geared to the ability of the students. Field trips and project assignments supplement the regular classroom sessions. Sports and activities include gymnastics, basketball, volleyball, badminton and tennis.

WESTON SCHOOL
Day Coed Ages 6-18. Gr 1-11.

Montreal West (Quebec) H4X 2B3, Canada. 124 Ballantyne Ave. South. Tel. 514-488-9191.
R. Shootey, BS, Sir George Williams Univ., Prin.
Col Prep Gen Acad. Curr—Nat. LI—Eng. CF—Fr Art.
Enr 115. Elem 75, Sec 40. Grad '84—12. Col—10.
Fac 15. Full 13/Part 2. M 7; F 8. US 2. Nat.
Tui $3500 (+$300). Schol.
Est 1917. Inc 1951 nonprofit. Quar (Sept-Je). CAIS NAIS.

The college preparatory program at Weston places special emphasis on the development of bilingual ability in English and French. Small classes allow for individual attention.

STANSTEAD COLLEGE
Bdg & Day Coed Ages 11-17. Gr 7-12.

Stanstead (Quebec) J0B 3E0, Canada. Tel. 819-876-2223.
K.H. Barry Gallant, BA, MA, McGill, Head.
Col Prep. Tests CEEB. Curr—Nat. LI—Eng. CF—Fr Span Hist Arts. SI—ESL.
Enr 154. B 84/10; G 55/5. Elem 30, Sec 124. US—9. Grad '84—20. Col—20.
Fac 22. Full 20/Part 2. M 16; F 6. Nat UK.
Tui Bdg $10,400 (+$1500); Day $3200 (+$500). Schol.
Est 1872. Inc nonprofit. Tri (Sept-Je). CAIS NAIS.
Bldgs 10. Dorms 3. Lib 12,000 vols. Gym. Pool. Tennis crts. Arena. Fields. Weight room.

Situated on a 620-acre site, Stanstead offers courses of study leading to the College Boards, the Quebec Certificate and Stanstead College Leaving Examinations. The curriculum is flexible, based on modules and a course of French study prepares most students for French "mother-tongue" examinations. Students have opportunities to participate in campcraft and wilderness skills as well as in various sports including skiing, tennis, karate, track, soccer, football, hockey, basketball, swimming, archery and fencing. Associated with the United Church of Canada, the school accepts pupils of many religions and nationalities.

ECOLE E.C.S.
(Miss Edgar's and Miss Cramp's)
Day Girls Ages 6-17. Gr 1-11.

Westmount (Quebec) H3Y 3H6, Canada. 525 Mount Pleasant Ave. Tel. 514-935-6357.

Molly Fripp, BA, Head.
Col Prep. Curr—Nat. LI—Eng Fr. A—Fr. CF—Fr Span Hist Geog Drama
  Econ Music Comp.
Enr 320. Elem 208, Sec 112. US—10. Grad '84—36. Col—36.
Fac 30. Nat.
Tui $2900 (+$300). Schol.
Summer Session. Arts Comp Sci. Tui $90. 2 wks.
Est 1909. Inc 1940 nonprofit. Tri (Sept-Je). CAIS NAIS.
Bldgs 2. Lib 5000 vols. Gym. Field.

A strong academic program is offered at this school leading to the
Quebec Secondary diploma as well as university entrance. The school
emphasizes a strong French program aimed at producing graduates who
are functionally bilingual. Individual help is available when needed.
Girls are encouraged to join a variety of clubs including debating,
drama, photography, fencing and choir, and participate in inter-school
sports. An entrance exam is required upon admission.

SELWYN HOUSE SCHOOL
  Day Boys Ages 6-17. Gr 1-11.

Westmount #217 (Quebec) H3Y 2H8, Canada. 95 Cote St. Antoine Rd.
  Tel. 514-931-9481.
Rob Wearing, Dir.
Pre-Prep Gen Acad. Curr—Nat. LI—Eng. A—Fr Math Chem Physics.
  CF—Fr Lat Span Math.
Enr 480. Elem 280, Sec 200. Grad '84—38. Col—38.
Fac 50. Nat.
Tui $3940-4600. Schol.
Summer Session. Acad French. Tui Day $100. 2 wks.
Est 1908. Nonprofit. Sem (Sept-Je). CAIS NAIS.
Bldgs 2. Lib 14,000 vols. Gym.

Boys from this school have attended Princeton, Harvard, MIT,
Williams and universities in Canada.

SASKATCHEWAN

WESTERN CHRISTIAN COLLEGE
  Bdg & Day Coed Ages 14-20. Gr 10-PG.

North Weyburn (Saskatchewan), Canada S0C 1X0. Tel. (306) 842-
  6551.
Max D. Mowrer, MA, Chapman College, LLD, Harding Univ., Pres.
Gen Acad JC. Curr—Nat. LI—Eng. A—Theology. CF—Math Soc Stud
  Art Industrial Art Music.
Enr 147. B 68/10; G 61/8. Sec 121, PG 26. US—12. Grad '84—52.
Fac 12. Full 10/Part 2. M 9; F 3. US 4. Can.
Tui Bdg $4200 (+$200); Day $1900 (+$200).

Est 1945. Inc. Sem (Sept-Je).
Bldgs 11. Dorms 3. Lib. Gym. Fields. Track.

Founded by Church of Christ evangelists, this school offers a
secondary school curriculum and a junior college bible studies program
leading to the Bachelor of Theology degree. Chapel attendance is
required. Soccer, volleyball, basketball, hockey, softball and track
comprise the available sports.

III.
POST-SECONDARY & SPECIALIZED OPPORTUNITIES

POST-SECONDARY SCHOOLS

*Programs are arranged
alphabetically by name*

AMERICAN COLLEGE IN PARIS
Coed Ages 17 and up.

75007 Paris, France. 31 av. Bosquet. Tel. 555.91.73.
Daniel J. Socolow, AMT, Harvard, PhD, Chicago, Pres.
Col. Curr—USA. LI—Eng. CF—Art Hist Comp Fr Stud Intl Affairs Econ
Bus. SI—ESL.
Enr 1000. US—500.
Fac 100. US—50.
Tui $5450 (+$1075). Schol.
Summer Session. Acad. 6 wks.
Est 1961. Inc nonprofit. Sem (Sept-Je). AICU. Accred MSA.
Bldgs 7. Lib 100,000 vols.

A four-year liberal arts college, American College in Paris is the oldest fully accredited and licensed independent American college in Europe. The Bachelor of Arts degree is offered in seven subject areas and the Bachelor of Science is offered in Computer Science. A collaborative program with the Parsons School of Design of New York and Los Angeles offers the Bachelor of Fine Arts degree. An extensive cultural program consists of organized outings and tours to events in Paris and other parts of Europe.

The American College is located in Central Paris and students are housed by the college in the French community. The student body represents 65 different nationalities.

THE AMERICAN COLLEGE OF GREECE—DEREE COLLEGE
Day Coed Ages 17 and up.

Aghia Paraskevi (Attikis), Greece. 6 Gravias St. Tel. 659-3250. Telex:
AGC 22011.
Mail to: Suite 710, 79 Milk St., Boston, MA 02109.
John S. Bailey, BS,Boston Univ., MBA, Northeastern, EdD, Nasson
College, Pres.
Col. Curr—USA. LI—Eng. CF—Fr Ger Ital Greek Span Bus Admin Sec
& Hellenic Stud Eng Hist Drama Arts ESL Dance Psych.
Enr 1618. US—129.
Fac 82. Full 63/Part 19. M 49; F 33.
Tui $1500/sem. Schol.

Summer Session. Acad. Tui $280/2 crse. 5 wks.
Est 1961. Inc nonprofit. Sem (Sept-Je). AICU.
Bldgs 4. Dorms 1. Lib 35,000 vols. Tennis crts. Gym. Track.

Deree College is an independent, international undergraduate institution offering a range of programs leading to a B.A. or B.S. in the areas of liberal arts, fine arts, science and business administration as well as associate degrees in secretarial studies and computer programing.

The liberal arts curriculum follows the traditional structure of divisions in the humanities, social science and sciences. Majors are offered in English, history, dance, economics, psychology, sociology, business administration and a specialized program in Hellenic studies. The latter is an interdisciplinary program designed to give students a comprehensive view of Greek history and civilization. Ten courses or 30 hours is the requirement in each major field and electives satisfy the remainder of the hours needed for the degree.

THE AMERICAN COLLEGE OF SWITZERLAND
  Bdg & Day Coed Ages 17 and up. JC & Col.

CH-1854 Leysin (Vaud), Switzerland. Tel. (025) 342223. Telex: 453227AMCO.
Mail to: Nancy Weaver, Dir. U.S. Operations, P.O. Box 425, Weston, MA 02193.
Daniel Queudot, Pres.
Col. Curr—USA. LI—Eng. CF—Mod Lang Econ Pol Sci Psych Computer Sci Intl Stud Bus Arts. SI—ESL.
Enr 267. B 246; G 121. US—62. Grad '84—80.
Fac 36. Full 27/Part 9. M 9; F 17. US 12.
Tui Bdg $12,760 (+$1500); Day $9940. Schol.
Summer Session. Acad. Tui Bdg 3656 SwF (+$300); Day 3156 SwF. 6 wks.
Est 1963. Inc nonprofit. Sem (Aug-May). AICU ISS. Accred MSA.
Bldgs 3. Dorms 1. Lib 27,000 vols. Athletic facilities.

While established to meet the needs of American families living abroad, the American College of Switzerland enrolls an internationally diverse student body, with instruction leading to the associate and bachelor degrees in the liberal arts and business administration. Students may choose a single or interdisciplinary field of study in the upper division including modern languages and culture, international affairs, international business administration, economics and political science. In addition to students studying for degrees, the college also attracts U.S. and other students electing to take a year or semester abroad.

Leysin, where the College is located, is a small resort village 5000 feet above the Rhone Valley at the east end of Lake Geneva. A complete program of sports, outdoor activities, clubs and publications is available.

AMERICAN UNIVERSITY OF BEIRUT
  Bdg & Day Coed. Univ.

Beirut, Lebanon.
Mail to: 850 3rd. Ave., New York, NY 10022.
Enr 4500.
Fac 500.
Summer Session. Acad & non-credit crses. Enr 950.
Est 1866. Sem (Oct-Je).

Founded more than a century ago by American Protestant missionaries and with many alumni among today's leading figures of government, medicine, education, business and engineering in the Near and Middle East, the American University of Beirut represents a venture in international education that is almost unique in the world. Since its beginnings, AUB has sustained the hope of its first President, Vermont-born and Amherst-educated Dr. Daniel Bliss, that students of all faiths, races and nations attend always. Today AUB enrolls about 4500 young men and women from over 50 nations, extending from Nepal in the Himalayas, to Morocco in North Africa, and to the U.S. in the Western Hemisphere. Nearly two dozen religions are represented among the student ranks. About 90 percent of the students are from the Arab countries of the Middle East and Africa. About 80 percent of the faculty come from the Middle East and the balance from the U.S., Canada and Europe.

The educational philosophy of AUB is similar to that of an American university, but its program is adapted to and built upon the national educational systems of the Middle East. The language of instruction is English. In addition to bachelors degrees in many fields, there are over 50 masters degrees and some selected PhD programs. The well-equipped 75-acre campus overlooks the Mediterranean, and includes a modern medical center complex.

BEIRUT UNIVERSITY COLLEGE
  Bdg Girls Ages 17 and up; Day Coed 17 and up.

Beirut, Lebanon. Box 13-5053. Tel. 811968-70.
Riyad F. Nassar, BS, MS, American Univ. of Beirut, PhD, Georgia Institute of Technology, Pres.
LI—Eng.
Enr 1547. B 710; G 837. US—45.
Fac 114. Full 58/Part 56. Lebanon.
Tui Bdg $2780; Day $1672 (+ $100).
Est 1924. Nonprofit. Sem (Oct-Je). AICU.
Bldgs 8. Dorm. Lib 70,000 vols. Athletic facilities.

An interdisciplinary curriculum is designed to provide a full liberal arts program drawing upon the resources of Middle Eastern culture. Undergraduate study leads to either an associate or bachelors degree. Study in the Arabic language is required of students who have not had previous instruction. The college is chartered by the Board of Regents of the University of the State of New York.

THE CHINESE UNIVERSITY OF HONG KONG
(International Asian Studies Program)
Bdg & Day Coed. Univ.

Shatin, Hong Kong. New Territories. Tel. 0-6352709.
Mail to: The Yale-China Assoc., 905A Yale Station, New Haven, CT 06520.
Thomas Lee, Dir.
East Asian Studies Chinese Lang.
Tui Bdg $4700 ($2100). Schol.
Summer Session. Lang Stud Tui $450. 5 wks.
Est 1963. Sem (Sept-Apr).

This program is conducted at the Chinese University of Hong Kong in cooperation with the Yale-China Association. Situated ten miles from downtown Kowloon, the program is open to undergraduates, graduates and research students. The multi-disciplinary curriculum is taught in English and consists of courses in modern and traditional China and Asia. Intensive language instruction is offered at all levels of Mandarin and Cantonese. Courses in Chinese painting and seal carving, calligraphy, Asian music and religions and international politics are among the many offerings. Students live in Chinese dormitories and are integrated into the University's social and academic life.

COLLEGE OF THE VIRGIN ISLANDS
Bdg & Day Coed Ages 17 and up. Col.

St. Thomas 00802, Virgin Islands. Tel. 809-774-9200.
Dr. Arthur A. Richards, EdD, New York Univ., Pres.
Col. Curr—USA. LI—Eng. CF—Span Fr Bus Ed Math Biol Nursing Music. SI—Rem & Dev Math & Read Tut.
Enr 810. B 76/153; G 158/423. Grad '84—208.
Fac 81. Full 81. M 51; F 30. US.
Tui Bdg $1925 (+$167); Day $792 (+$167). Schol.
Est 1962. Nonprofit. Sem (Sept-May). Accred MSA.
Bldgs 22. Dorms 5. Lib 70,000 vols. Athletic facilities.

The College of the Virgin Islands has campuses in St. Thomas and St. Croix. M.A., B.A. and A.A. degrees are awarded in business administration, humanities, nursing, social sciences, science and mathematics, and teacher education. The college also sponsors ecological research, community resource development and an Upward Bound program of academic enrichment for underachieving high school students. Theatre, drama, band, chorus, student government, clubs and a variety of sports are offered.

COLUMBUS INTERNATIONAL COLLEGE
Day Coed Ages 17 and up.

Sevilla 13, Spain. Avda. de la Victoria, 43. Tel. 61 05 27.
James C. Butler, PhD., Ohio State Univ., Dir.
Col. Curr—US. LI—Eng. CF—Bus Admin Engineering. A—Span Hist
Art Lit.
Enr 450. B 300; G 150. US—50. Grad '84—15.
Fac 22. M 10; F 12. US UK.
Tui $3130 (+ $150).
Summer Session. Acad. Tui $1000. 7 wks.
Est 1972. Inc nonprofit. Sem (Sept-May). AICU.
Bldgs 1. Lib 10,000 vols.

Columbus International College offers the first two years of an American university education in Spain. Two-year programs are conducted in the arts, sciences and business administration, and a one-year course is offered in engineering studies. Accommodations can be arranged in private homes or hostels, or students may rent their own apartments. The many cultural resources of Sevilla are used extensively and a variety of sporting facilities are available, including the college's own riding school.

DENMARK'S INTERNATIONAL STUDY PROGRAM
(University of Copenhagen)
Bdg Coed Ages 18 & up. Col.

1456 Copenhagen K, Denmark. Vestergade 9. Tel. (+ 451) 11 11 00.
Telex: 15834 distud dk.
Col. LI—Eng. CF—Intl Bus Archit & Design.
Enr 474.
Est I959. Nonprofit. Tri.

This school's one semester- or one year-study abroad program is primarily designed for college juniors. Credits are transferable to American universities. Ninety percent of the students choose to live with Danish families. A two- to three-week travel interim is organized each semester.

ECOLE ATHENA
Day Girls Ages 16 and up.

CH 1007 Lausanne (Vaud), Switzerland. Rue de la Caroline 4. Tel.
(021) 23-22-84.
A.T. Hughes, Prin.
Secretarial. LI—Fr. SI—ESL Fr.
Enr 80.
Tui $850/term.
Est 1964.

The school provides a balanced program of study combining secretarial and language courses, including German, Italian, Spanish and French. Instruction in shorthand, typewriting, commercial correspondence, bookkeeping, business math and economy is provided. Emphasis is placed on the role of English in the business world and the training of secretaries for English and American companies with international connections.

FRANKLIN COLLEGE
Day Coed Ages 17-22. JC.

6900 Lugano, Switzerland. Via Tesserete 10. Tel. (091) 228595.
Theodore E. Brenner, Pres.
JC. Curr—USA. LI—Eng. CF—Fr Ger Ital Econ Pol Sci Philos Psych Film Photog.
Enr 150. B 60; G 90. US—90. Grad '84—40. Col—38.
Fac 19. Full 10/Part 9. M 14; F 5. US UK.
Tui $6850 (+ $6000). Schol.
Est 1969. Inc nonprofit. Sem (Sept-Je). AICU ISS. Accred MSA.
Bldgs 7. Lib 20,000 vols.

Franklin College is a junior college with an affiliated post-secondary one-year Institute of European Studies. The academic program features some 100 courses of a general liberal arts orientation. A variety of clubs, publications, student government and sports are offered. In addition, four weeks of academic travel are scheduled yearly in which small groups of students are accompanied by faculty members to destinations relating to their course work. Recent itineraries have included trips to England, Germany, Italy, Greece and France.

Housed in a converted Ticinese patrician home, the school is five minutes from downtown Lugano, in the mountain lake region of Switzerland. Students live in supervised residents' apartments or with Swiss families.

HARLAXTON COLLEGE
Bdg Coed 18 and up.

Grantham (Lincolnshire) NG32 1AG, England. Harlaxton Manor. Tel. 0476-4332/4541.
Graddon Rowlands, MA, Cambridge, PhD, Duke Univ., Prin.
Col. Curr—Nat US. LI—Eng. CF—Arts. SI—Tut.
Enr 150. B 70; G 80. US—120.
Fac 20. Full 10/Part 10. M 10; F 10. UK.
Tui $7650 (+ $1550). Schol.
Summer Session. Col. Tui $995 (+ $200). 4 wks.
Est 1971. Nonprofit. Sem (Sept-May).
Bldgs 2. Dorms 2. Lib 16,500 vols. Atletic facilities.

Housed in a Victorian mansion located in the English midlands, Harlaxton is the British campus of the University of Evansville in Indiana. Its course offerings include art history, archaeology, biology, business studies, computer science, economics, English literature, French, German, history, mathematics, music, philosophy, political science, psychology and sociology, and students may complete an Associate of Arts degree in two years. In addition to the academic schedule, field trips to Italy, France and other parts of Britain are organized. A full range of extracurricular activities is available, including sports, drama, dance and student government. A four- week summer session offers additional graduate and undergraduate coursework and an opportunity for futher cultural enrichment. Credits may be tranferred to United States institutions.

INSTITUTE FOR AMERICAN UNIVERSITIES
Day Coed Ages 18 and up.

13625 Aix-en-Provence, France. 27, Place de l'Universite. Tel. (42) 23.39.35.
Amos Booth, MA, Pres.
Col. Curr—USA. LI—Eng Fr.
Enr 317. B 87; G 230.
Fac 46. Full 2/Part 44. M 38; F 18. Fr.
Tui $3530 (+ $3400). Schol.
Summer Session. Acad. Tui $896 (+ $500). 6 wks.
Est 1957. Inc 1963 nonprofit. Sem (Sept-Je). AICU.
Bldgs 6. 4 libs.

The Institute for American Universities conducts programs in four different cities: Canterbury, Aix-en-Provence, Avignon and Toulon. The British Studies Centre in Canterbury, England offers English literature, theatre, history, politics, sociology and economics. European and Mediterranean studies, advanced French as well as studio art are featured at Aix-en-Provence, while the center at Avignon provides intensive French language instruction. The curriculum at Toulon also includes French studies and offers courses in European business management, economics and law. An art workshop and a European Studies program are conducted in the summer session. Living accommodations are arranged with local families and numerous cultural and sporting facilities are available.

See also page 60

INSTITUTO ALLENDE
Day Coed. Univ.

San Miguel de Allende (Guanajuato), Mexico. Tel. 52 465 201-90.
Stirling Dickinson, Pres.
Col. Curr—USA Span. LI—Eng Span. CF—Span Stud Painting Fine Arts Crafts Photog.
Enr 1500. US—1300.
Fac 35. Full 25/Part 10. M 25; F 10. US Mex.
Tui $95-215/mo.
Summer Session. Acad Arts.
Est 1951. Inc nonprofit. Quar (Jan-Nov).

An incorporated part of the University of Guanajuato, Instituto Allende offers a wide selection of courses in fine arts, crafts, design and Spanish language studies Students may attend the school on a term or year abroad program and earn transferable credits, or enter programs leading to the M.F.A. degree. Furthermore, concentrated "immersion" courses in the Spanish language are given.

The historic town of San Miguel de Allende is located in central Mexico. Boarding facilities are arranged for North American students who comprise about 80% of the enrollment.

INTERNATIONAL SWEDISH UNIVERSITY
Bdg Coed Ages 19-25.

S-223 50 Lund, Sweden. Skomakaregatan 8. Tel. 046/11 77 20.
Ulf Wallin, Dean of Students.
Col. LI—Eng. CF—Swed Archit & Urban Planning Arts Intl Pol Environ Stud.
Enr 32. B 13; G 19. US—32.
Fac 15. Part 15. M 8; F 7. Nat.
Tui $3250.
Summer Session. Acad. Tui $546-886. 4 wks.
Nonprofit. Sem (Feb-May).

The International Swedish University coordinates study programs for foreign students including the Spring Semester which offers a variety of courses taught in English. These include Swedish architecture and urban planning, Scandinavian art history, social welfare policy and communication arts in Sweden, international politics and family sociology. Academics and Swedish language are also available during the summer months. In addition to language instruction, courses include special lectures in English about Swedish society, history and culture.

JOHN CABOT INTERNATIONAL COLLEGE
Day Coed Ages 17 and up. Col.

00162 Rome, Italy. Via Massaua 7. Tel. (06) 8395519.
William D. Cavendish, Pres.
Col. Tests IB GCE SSAT TOEFL. Curr—USA. LI—Eng. CF—Fr Ital Bus Admin.
Enr 150. B 70; G 80. US—20. Grad '84—30.
Fac 29. Full 5/Part 24. M 15; F 14.
Tui $3765 (+$300).
Summer Session. Acad. Tui $375/crse.
Est 1972. Nonprofit. Tri (Sept-Je). AICU ECIS.
Bldg 1. Lib. Field.

Affiliated with Hiram College in Ohio, Cabot confers the Associate of Arts degree as well as the Bachelor of Business Administration. Courses are offered in humanities, social sciences, data processing, finance, accounting, marketing, management, banking, economics and communications. Trimesters begin in September, January and April and run for three months. Two-month courses are offered in November and June.

See also page 76

NEUCHÂTEL JUNIOR COLLEGE
Bdg Coed Ages 16-19. JC.

2000 Neuchatel, Switzerland. Cret-Taconnet 4. Tel. (038) 25-27-00.
J. L. Thayer, BSc, Dip Bus Admin, Univ. of Western Toronto, Prin.
Col. Curr—Can. LI—Eng. CF—Fr Ger Computer Sci Geog Psych Math Biol Chem Physics.
Enr 60. M 25; F 35. US—1. Grad '84—60.
Fac 11. Full 4/Part 7. M 6; F 5. Canada.
Tui Bdg 17,200 SwF (+ 6000 SwF).
Est 1956. Inc 1961 nonprofit. Sem (Sept-Je).
Bldgs 2. Lib 12,000 vols. Labs.

Neuchatel Junior College was founded in order to give North American children a school year aboard. The school is conducted under the cooperation of Canadian and Swiss educational authorities. Neuchatel's year-long program is open to high school graduates and the enrollment is comprised mostly of Canadian and Swiss students.

Boarding arrangements are made with local families and the maitresse de pension maintains close contact with the school. The sports program offers yachting, tennis, soccer, skiing, swimming and basketball. During vacations, tours are organized to different parts of Western Europe. Neuchatel is 20 miles from the French border and thus is a center of French culture in Switzerland.

NEW ENGLAND COLLEGE—BRITISH CAMPUS
Bdg & Day Coed Ages 18 & up.

Arundel (West Sussex) BN18 ODA, England. Tel. 903/88.22.59. Telex: 877450 NECARN G.
Eric C. Nummela, MS, Univ. of Nevada, PhD, Tulane, Dir.
Col. Curr—USA. LI—Eng. CF—Bus Pol Sci Intl Administration.
Enr 200. B 60/60; G 60/20. US—110. Grad '84—27.
Fac 20. Full 13/Part 7. M 15; F 5. US 7. Nat.
Tui Bdg $10,360; Day $6750. Schol.
Summer Session. Acad. 6-8 wks.
Est I971. Nonprofit. Sem (Aug-May). AICU.
Bldgs 6. Dorms 4. Lib 19,000 vols. Pool. Crts. Field.

The British campus of New England College augments the larger New Hampshire campus and has a more international student body. Bachelor of Arts degrees can be earned in business and international administration, English and political science. A full range of courses in the sciences, social sciences, arts and humanities and in communications, computers and British studies are also offered. Degrees in these areas can be completed at the American campus or by tranfer to another university. Outings to other parts of the United Kingdom and a strong internship program are integrated into the curriculum. Sports and social and recreational activities are encouraged.

RICHMOND COLLEGE
Bdg & Day Coed Ages 18-24.

Richmond (Surrey) TW10 6JP, United Kingdom. Queens Road. Tel. 01-940-4487.
William Petrek, BA, St. John's STL, Gregorian, PhD, Louvain, Pres.
Col. Curr—USA. LI—Eng. CF—Fr Span Lit Hist Pol.
Enr 800. US—300.
Fac 68. Full 23/Part 45. US 10. UK.
Tui Day £3790; Bdg £4990. Schol.
Summer Session. Acad. Tui Bdg £580-740. 4-8 wks.
Est 1972. Inc nonprofit. Sem (Aug-May). AICU. Accred MSA.
Bldgs 5. Dorms 6. 2 Libs 30,000 vols.

Located on the banks of the Thames in a London suburb, Richmond offers post-secondary education for students seeking a two- or four-year degree in public administration, fine arts, engineering and computer science. The College has two campuses, the Richmond Hill Campus for freshmen and sophomores, and the Kensington Campus for juniors and seniors.

ST. GODRIC'S COLLEGE
Bdg Girls Ages 16 and up; Day Coed 16 and up.

London, England NW3 6AD. 2 Arkwright Rd. Tel. 01-435 9831. Telex: 25589.
J.W. Loveridge, Esq., MA, Cambridge, Prin.
Gen Bus Tech. Curr—Nat. LI—Eng. CF—Fr Ger Span Secretarial.
Enr 229. US—4.
Fac UK.
Tui Bdg £2189-2289/term; Day £955-1055/term. Schol.
Est 1929. Inc. Tri (Sept-July).
Bldgs 5. Dorms 7. Lib. Tennis crt.

Training students for administrative, secretarial and allied careers, St. Godric's offers courses ranging in length from six months to two years. Programs conducted include advertising, foreign shorthand (French, German, Spanish), management, computer programming, typing, marketing, fashion and accounting. Primarily students from Britain are enrolled, however, students from Colombia, Iran, Nigeria, Norway, Thailand and the United States are also in attendance. The college is situated in the Hampstead part of London, close to Hampstead Heath, yet only 20 minutes from the West End. Limited boarding facilities are available for male students.

SCHILLER INTERNATIONAL UNIVERSITY
  Bdg Coed Ages 18 and up. JC & Col.

51/55 Waterloo Road, London SE1 8TX, England. Tel. (01) 928 1372.
  Telex: 8812438 SCOL G.
Mail to: Sandra Russeff, 1425 LaSalle Ave., Minneapolis, MN 55403.
Walter Leibrecht, PhD, Pres.
JC Univ. Curr—USA. LI—Eng. CF—Rom Lang Ger Hist Pol Sci Philos
  Psych Theatre Fine Arts Bus.
Enr 800.
Fac 98.
Tui Bdg £5600-5800. Schol.
Summer Session. Acad. Tui Bdg £1200. 7 wks.
Est 1964. Nonprofit. Sem (Sept-May).

An international liberal arts college, Schiller maintains study centers at Heidelberg, Strasbourg, Madrid and Paris in addition to the one in London. The enrollment includes students from some 52 countries. The study centers and classes are kept small and emphasis is placed upon acquiring fluency in the host country language. Students board within the community except in London, where residential facilities are provided.

Programs include academic year, and summer courses, as well as a four-year curriculum leading to degrees in language, international relations, business administration, hotel management, psychology, law, public administration, pre-medicine, pre-engineering and computer systems management.

In addition to its university programs, Schiller offers two years of courses at its London campus designed to provide students with the English language skills or the secondary schooling necessary for university entrance.

UNIVERSIDAD DE LAS AMERICAS
  Bdg & Day Coed Ages 16 and up. Univ.

Catarina Martir (Puebla), Mexico 72820. Apartado Postal 100. Tel.
  22047-00-00.
Fernando Macais-Rendon, BS, MS, LLD, Pres.
Col. Tests GCE CEEB SSAT. Curr—Nat. LI—Eng Span.
Enr 3057.
Fac 160.
Tui Bdg 41,100 pesos (+4000 pesos); Day 28,000 pesos (+2000
  pesos).
Summer Session. Acad. Tui Bdg 8000 pesos (+2000 pesos); Day 6000
  pesos (+2000 pesos).
Est 1940. Inc nonprofit. Sem (Aug-May). Accred SACS.
Bldgs 14. Dorms 2. 2 Libs 146,000 vols. Gym. Swimming pool. Courts.

Primarily a liberal arts college, this private school offers undergraduate and graduate degree programs, junior year abroad and a summer session. In addition to the College of Arts and Sciences, the school

operates Engineering and Language Institutes. With the exception of
engineering courses which are chiefly in Spanish, courses may be taken
in English or Spanish.

UNIVERSITY OF GLASGOW
Bdg Coed Ages 18 & up. Univ.

Glasgow G12 8QQ, Scotland. Tel. 041-339-8855. Telex: 778421
GLASUL-G.
Sir Alwyn Williams, Prin.
Univ. Curr—UK. LI—Eng. A—Langs Arts Divinity Engineering Law
Medicine Sci Soc Sci Humanities Veterinary Medicine.
Enr 11,804.
Fac UK.
Tui £4170-8670.
Est 1451. Tri (Oct-Je).
Dorms 16. Lib 1,000,000 vols. Phys Ed Complex.

The University of Glasgow has more than 120 teaching departments
offering a full range of undergraduate and graduate courses in all
disciplines. Overseas students are accepted for three- and four-year
degree programs as well as for a semester or year period. Students have
access to the cultural and recreational facilities of Glasgow, a city of
750,000 people. In addition, the university has a variety of societies and
organizations including an International Students Club. University
housing is reserved for foreign students entering the fall academic term.

WARNBOROUGH COLLEGE
Day Coed Ages 18 and up.

Oxford OX1 5ED, England. Boars Hill. Tel. (0865) 730901. Telex:
83147.
B.D. Tempest-Mogg, BA, MA, Oxford, Pres.
Gen Acad. Tests GCE TOEFL. Curr—Nat. LI—Eng. CF—Fr Ger Span
Ital Russ Econ Bus Stud Music Relig Stud Philos Soc Theatre
Renaissance & Medieval Stud Educ.
Enr 150.
Fac. Nat.
Tui $5500 (+ 1000). Schol.
Summer Session. Acad. Tui $1500. 6 wks.
Est 1973. Inc nonprofit. Sem (Sept-May).
Bldgs 6. Lib 10,000 vols.

Offering a program of teaching based on the Oxford University
tutorial system, Warnborough College admits students who are enrolled
in good standing at American colleges. Students individually choose
from a comprehensive range of subjects, meeting regularly with their
tutors where assignments are presented and discussed. Seminar meetings
and selected lectures at Oxford are also part of the program. Students
are lodged in College houses or private homes. In addition to the fall,
spring, and summer semester programs, there are two six-week summer

sessions and a January Term, all of which may be taken for transferable academic credit. Students have access to local athletic facilities, entertainment and events.

WEBSTER UNIVERSITY—VIENNA
Day Coed Ages 18 & up. Univ.

A-1010 Vienna, Austria. Schubertring 14. Tel. 43-222-52 11 37.
Robert D. Brooks, BA, Washington Univ., MA, PhD, Cornell Univ., Dir.
Univ. Curr—USA. LI—Eng. A—Management Intl Stud Comp Econ
Public Relations. SI—ESL.
Enr 465.
Fac USA.
Tui $3500. Schol.
Summer Session. Acad. 8 wks.
Est 1915. Nonprofit.
Bldgs 1. Lib 5000 vols.

Webster—Vienna is one of three international branches of Webster University in Webster Groves, Missouri. The other two campuses are in Leiden, The Netherlands, and Geneva, Switzerland. Students from 48 different countries attend the university in Vienna and take a variety of courses in international finance, business administration, management and computer studies. The curriculum features five, two-month "bimesters" per year. Ninety percent of the faculty are Americans or have trained or taught at American institutions.

SPECIALIZED OPPORTUNITIES

Travel, study and semester or year abroad programs sponsored by U.S. schools or organizations, or by foreign schools with on-campus programs for American students.

SPECIALIZED OPPORTUNITIES

*Programs are arranged
alphabetically by name*

ABC CENTRO DI LINGUA E CULTURA ITALIANA
  Day Coed All Ages.

50122 Florence, Italy. Piazza dei Ciompi 11. Tel. 055/241191.
Massimo Pasquinelli, Dir.
Ital Lang & Culture.
350.
Tui variable.
Est 1981. Inc 1983.

This center for Italian culture and langauge offers courses in Italian art
history, architecture, literature, cooking, theatre, language and grammar.
Courses also help to prepare students for Italian university entrance. In
addition to academic opportunities, the ABC Centre conducts periodic
guided tours through Florence and Tuscany.

See also page 74

ALLINGTON MANOR SCHOOL
  Bdg Coed Ages 6-20.

Fair Oak (Eastleigh) SO5 7DE, England. Allington Lane. Tel. (703)
  692621.
Ludwig F. Lowenstein, MA, PhD, Univ. of London, Dir.
Pre-Prep Col Prep Gen Acad. Tests CEEB GCE SAT. LI—Eng. CF—Fr
  Ger Span. SI—Tut Rem & Dev Math Read.
Enr 27. B 15; G 2.
Fac 19. Full 9/Part 10. M 9; F 10. US 1. UK.
Tui Bdg $7000/term (+$100). Schol.
Est 1978. Inc. Tri.
Bldgs 5. Dorms 6. Lib 10,000 vols.

Allington Manor is one of two residential and day schools founded
and directed by Dr. Lowenstein. Developed for those children who do
not fit into the normal system of education, the aim of the school is to
provide an individualized program of education and therapy. The
curriculum covers the standard primary and secondary subjects
including arts and crafts, cookery and carpentry. A work training
program is featured as well as vocational assessment and guidance.
  The school is situated on a large estate which includes a lake,

swimming pool, tennis court and a small working farm. Students also have access to a local gym and participate in a variety of sports.

THE AMERICAN COLLEGE IN LONDON
Bdg & Day Coed Ages 17-25.

London W1M 5FP, England. 100 Marylebone Lane. Tel. 01-486-1772. Telex: 884636.
Joseph H. Houghton, BA, SUNY, Diplome des Etudes, Sorbonne, Pres.
Professional Training. LI—Eng.
Enr 345. B /144; G 35/186. US—62.
Fac 38. Full 3/Part 35. M 22; F 16. US 12.
Tui Bdg £3437/quar (+ £200); Day £975/quar (+ £400).
Summer Session. Acad. Tui Bdg £1437/quar; Day £975/quar. 9 wks.
Est 1971. Inc.
Bldg 2. Dorms 3. Lib 4,000 vols.

The American College in London offers two- and four-year programs in fashion merchandising, fashion design, interior design and business administration. A one-year program is also available in general fashion. Students have the option of transferring to the affiliated American College for the Applied Arts in Atlanta, Georgia.

AMERICAN INSTITUTE FOR FOREIGN STUDY (AIFS)
Coed Ages 10 and up.

Greenwich, CT 06830.
Study & Travel.
Tui $800-3000. 1-6 wks.

AIFS conducts educational travel programs in Europe, Asia and Africa. Academic year, term and summer programs are provided. Credits may be earned.

AMERICAN LEADERSHIP STUDY GROUPS
Coed Ages 14-22.

Worcester, MA 01602. Airport Dr. Tel. 617-757-6369.
Dr. Gilbert Scott Markle, Exec. Dir.
Travel Rec Langs.
Fac 230. Full 55/Part 175. M 110; F 120. UK.
Est 1965. Inc 1967.

ALSG sponsors academic, travel and recreational programs during the winter, spring and summer seasons in Europe and Great Britain. High school and college students are accepted and may receive academic credit. Cultural awareness programs are conducted before, during and after excursions.

ANTIOCH INTERNATIONAL SEMINARS
Coed Ages 15 and up.

Yellow Springs, OH 45387. Antioch International, Antioch College.
Tui $4750/grad prgm; $3750/undergrad prgm.
Summer Session. Tui $1350 (+$1000). 8 wks.
Est 1973.

Antioch conducts many writing programs for high school, under-graduate and graduate students in London, England. Credit courses include poetry, publishing, graphic art and design, script writing, children's literature, psychology, small press publishing, the British novel and art history.

ARROWSMITH-COHEN INSTITUTE OF LEARNING
Day Coed Ages 10 & up. Gr 4-12.

Toronto (Ontario), Canada M4W 1L2. 11 Yorkville Ave., Suite 100. Tel. 416-920-3881.
J.M. Cohen, MA, Univ. of Toronto, Dir.
Remedial. LI—Eng. CF—Eng Math Study Skills. SI—Rem & Dev Math & Read Tut.
Enr 25. B 20; G 5. US—1. Grad '84—1. Col—1.
Fac 4. Full 4. M 1; F 3. Nat.
Tui $8500 (+$100).
Summer Session. Remedial. Tut $1000. 6 wks.
Est 1980. Inc 1984. Sem (Sept-Je).

This special education school balances basic math and English skills teaching with exercises in study strategies. Students are required to enroll for two full academic years. Individual attention is emphasized. An after school program allows students with minor learning dysfunctions to supplement their regular schooling with study skills training. Most graduates of the program go on to community colleges or universities.

AVS AUDIOVISUELLES SPRACHINSTITUT
Day Coed Ages 15 & up.

8001 Zurich, Switzerland. Niederdorfstrasse 43. Tel. 01/251.66.25.
Gery Ochsner, Prin.
Ger Stud. CF—Arabic Portugese Ital Fr Span. SI—Tut.
Enr 580. B 180; G 400.
Fac 40. Full 6/Part 34. M 4; F 36. US 2.
Tui 549 SwF/mo.
Summer Session. Ger Stud. Tui 340-549 SwF/mo.
Est 1965. Inc. Quar (Jan-Dec).

This language school employs audio-visual techniques to teach intensive language courses. Each level is completed in four weeks and new courses begin each month. As its primary focus is on German as the language of business and technology, emphasis is placed on spoken

German, but writing and reading are also taught. Though family stays are unusual, the school can provide assistance to students seeking housing in pensions or hotels.

THE BRITISH INSTITUTE OF FLORENCE
Day Coed Ages 16 and up.

50125 Florence, Italy. Lungarno Guicciardini 9. Tel. (055) 28 40 31.
David Rundle, MA, Cambridge, MTEFL, Leeds, Dir.
Ital Stud. LI—Eng Ital. A—Ital Lang & Art Hist. CF—Drawing Painting.
Enr 1510.
Fac UK Italy.
Tui £65-855/crse.
Summer Session. Ital Stud. 3 wks.
Est 1917. Inc 1923 nonprofit.
Bldgs 2. Lib 60,000 vols.

The British Institute, granted a Royal Charter by King George V in 1923, provides English instruction to Italian speakers as well as Italian instruction to English speakers. In addition to the language study program, the school organizes a wide variety of cultural events, outings and exhibitions. Customized courses can be designed for business, professional or academic groups upon request. Students accepted to the program will be advised as to accommodation in Italian hotels or with local families.

BROWN & BROWN AND TUTORS, OXFORD
Day Coed Ages 16 and up.

Oxford (Oxfordshire) OX2 6JA, England. 20 Warnborough Rd. Tel. (0865) 56311. Telex: 83147 BBTO ORG.
Mrs. C. H. Brown, MA, Oxon, Prin.
Col Prep Gen Acad. Tests SSAT GCE CEEB. Curr—Tut. LI—Eng ESL.
SI—Rem & Dev Read & Math Dyslexia.
Enr 120. B 60; G 60. US—8.
Fac 70. Full 15/Part 55. M 43; F 27. US 2. Nat.
Tui £3000 (+ £1900).
Summer Session. Acad ESL. 1-16 wks.
Est 1972. Inc nonprofit. Tri (Sept-Je).
Bldgs 3. Lib 1000 vols. Athletic facilities.

This tutorial system allows students to work under the supervision of one or more tutors at Oxford University preparing for the 'O' and 'A' levels of the G.C.E., Oxford or Cambridge entrance and for advanced placement tests. Students participate in weekly guidance sessions to discuss educational plans and tutorial courses. The school arranges suitable living accommodations for all pupils through approved houses or families in the Oxford area. Tutorials are also conducted for the dyslexic.

See also page 67

BUNKA INSTITUTE OF LANGUAGE
  Bdg Girls Ages 18-22; Day Coed 18 and up.

(Shibuya-ku) Tokyo 151, Japan. 22-1 Yoyogi 3-chome. Tel. 03-379-4027.
Mr. S. Onuma, Pres.
Lang Study.
Enr 310.
Fac 12. M 7; F 5. US 7.
Tui $3000.
Summer Session. Acad Rec. 4 wks.
Est 1980. Inc nonprofit. Sem (April-March).
Bldgs 15. Dorms 4. Lib. Field. Gym. Crts.

The Institute offers intensive language courses in Japanese and English. Classes are conducted five days a week, six hours daily. The language laboratory provides extensive audio-visual instruction to augment classroom and independent study.

CASTERBRIDGE HALL
  Bdg Coed Ages 11-19. Gr 6-12.

Templecombe (Somerset), England BA8 OLB. Bowden Road. Tel. (0963) 70753.
Michael I. Bromfield, MA, Univ. of London, Dir.
Cultural & Historical Tours.
Fac 14. Full 5/Part 9. M 8; F 6.
Tui $200-300/wk.
Est I979. Inc 1980 nonprofit.
Bldg. Lib. Fields. Tennis crts.

Casterbridge Hall is an international holiday program accommodating schools and youth groups that wish to tour England and Europe. Cultural tours of Ireland, London, Oxford, Scotland, Wessex and Wales are featured as well as trips to Amsterdam, Belgium, France and Switzerland. Tours which range from two to six weeks in duration may be arranged year-round.

CENTRE D'ÉTUDES FRANCAISES
  Day Coed Ages 18 and up.

84000 Avignon, France. 5, rue Figuere. Tel. (90) 82.58.50.
Alice Falchetto, MA, Dir.
Fr Lang & Lit Study.
Enr 89. M 11; F 78.
Fac 14. /Part 14. M 9; F 5. Fr.
Tui $3530. Schol.
Summer Session. Acad. Tui $896 (+ $500). 6 wks..
Est 1957. Inc 1964 nonprofit. Sem (Sept-Je).

The Centre offers college level instruction in the French language. Students also may study French literature, poetry and theatre as well as other subjects in the humanities. Recreational activities include participation in French sports and trips to the cinema and theatre. The Centre draws a large portion of its enrollment from the United States, and living arrangements can be made with local French families.

CENTRE D'ETUDES FRANÇAISE POUR L'ETRANGER
(Université de Caen)
  Bdg & Day Coed. Col.

14032 Caen (Cedex), France. Universite de Caen. Tel. (31) 94.63.39.
Fr Stud.
Tui Bdg 4026 Fr (+1200 Fr/mo); Day 1486 Fr (+1800 Fr/mo).
Summer Session. Fr Stud. Tui Bdg 2292-2939 Fr. 3 wks.
Est 1951. Sem (Oct-Je).

Utilizing the resources of the University of Caen, this Center for Foreign Students offers intensive college level courses in French language, civilization and literature. Four 3-week sessions of French studies are also offered in the summer. Various cultural activities and excursions are available to all students.

CENTRE INTERNATIONAL D'ETUDES FRANCAISES
  Coed Ages 16 and up.

49005 Angers Cedex, France. Universite Catholique De L'Ouest 3,
  Place Andre Leroy, B.P. 808. Tel. (41) 88.33.12.
Albert-Paul Carton, Dir.
Col Prep Col. Curr—Nat. LI—Fr.
Tui 790-1700 Fr/sem (+100 Fr/mo).
Summer Session. Acad. Tui 790 Fr. 4 wks.

Affiliated with the Catholic University, this International Centre offers three different programs of French language and culture study. The July Course for 16-year-olds and the Pre-University Course in September for 17-year-olds are both month-long programs which provide intensive instruction in written and spoken French. French music, art, history, economics and theology are features of the University program as well as language comprehension and composition. The University will arrange living accommodations with French families and organize cultural excursions.

CENTRE MÉDITERRANÉEN D'ÉTUDES FRANÇAISES
  Bdg and Day Coed Ages 17 and up.

06320 Cap-d'Ail, France. Chemin des Oliviers. Tel. (93) 78.21.59.
M. Moreau, Dir.
Fr Lang Stud.
Est 1952.

This French language center is intended for those over 17 years of age, however, those under 17 are considered by special application. C.M.E.F. operates intensive (4 to 13 weeks), compact (2 to 3 weeks) and summer courses (4 to 5 weeks). Writing and listening comprehension, and oral and written expression are stressed at all levels. Course work is complemented by conferences, films and cultural excursions. C.M.E.F. is recognized by the French Ministry of Education.

See also page 60

CENTRO DE IDIOMAS, S.A.
Day Coed Ages 16 & up.

Mazatlan (Sinaloa), Mexico. Belisario Dominguez 1908. Tel. 2-20-53.
Dixie Davis, BA, Univ. of Houston, Coord.
Span Stud. LI—Span.
Enr 370. US—20.
Fac 16. Full 12/Part 4. M 4; F 12. US 2. Nat.
Tui $130-400/session.
Est 1973. Inc.

Centro de Idiomas offers two-week sessions of semi-intensive and intensive Spanish instruction to English-speaking students. Classes run from 10 to 20 hours each week. Bicultural activities with Mexican adults studying English at the center and outings to area sites and museums are arranged weekly. Students may select to live with Mexican families for an extra charge. Leisure activities in the popular resort area include swimming, fishing, scuba diving, parasailing, water skiing, mountain climbing and snorkeling.

CENTRO KOINÈ
Day Coed Ages 15 and up.

50122 Florence (Tuscany), Italy. Via Pandolfini No. 27. Tel. 055/265088.
Moradei Andrea, Dir.
Ital Lang & Culture.
Enr 1000. US—80.
Fac 13. Full 7/Part 6. M 5; F 8. Nat.
Tui 280,000 Lit/mo.
Summer Session. Lang Stud. Tui 260,000-330,000 Lit. 3 wks.
Est 1980. Nonprofit.
Bldgs 2. Lib.

Centro Koine, deriving its name from the Greek word for "shared language," offers month-long Italian language and cultural programs. Students in small classes develop their knowledge and use of Italian through dramatizations, readings aloud and interest groups. Beginning in the third week, students strengthen their conversational ability by focusing on one of three subject areas: social and political issues; arts and culture; or travel and folklore. Centro Koine also offers training and refresher courses in language teaching methods. Courses in art history and gastronomy and excursions to local villages enrich language instruction. A booking service arranges boarding accommodations in advance.

Additional summer language and cultural studies are offered in the ancient Tuscan town of Cortona.

CENTRO LINGUISTICO ITALIANO "DANTE ALIGHIERI"
Coed Ages 16 and up.

Florence, Italy. Via dei Bardi 12, P.O. Box 194. Tel. 055/284955.
Dr. Alberto Materassi, Dir.
Ital Study.
Tui $65-1500.
Est 1966.

Housed in a 14th century palazzo near the Ponte Vecchio in Florence, the school offers courses in Italian language and culture to foreign students. Special concentrated programs for individual students are available in addition to normal group classes in language, literature, history and art. The year-round program consists of various levels of instruction of different duration. Excursions, city visits, meetings, dinners and parties are organized for students by the school. Living accommodations are arranged with local families and at boarding houses or hotels.

COLLEGE INTERNATIONAL DE CANNES
Bdg & Day Coed Ages 16 and up.

06400 Cannes, France. 1 avenue du Dr. Pascal. Tel. 47.39.29.
M. Claude Faisant, PhD, Dir.
Lang Stud.
Enr 260. B 80/40; G 60/80.
Fac 25. Full 6/Part 19. M 3; F 22. France.
Tui Bdg 1540-3500 Fr/4 wks; Day 1390 Fr/4 wks.
Summer Session. Acad. 4 wks.
Est 1969. Tri (Oct-Je).
Bldgs. 2. Lib 2000 vols. Athletic facilities.

Located on the Mediterranean Sea, this international college provides intensive French language instruction at all levels. The curriculum features conversation, phonetics, grammar and literature as well as cultural and commercial studies. Students may enroll for 4 to 36 weeks. Extracurricular activities include tennis, swimming, windsurfing, volleyball and cultural excursions.

DEUTSCH IN DEUTSCHLAND
Bdg Coed Ages 10 and up.

8751 Stockstadt/Main, West Germany. Hauptstrasse 26. Tel. (0)6027/1251. Telex: 4188559 euro d.
Madeleine Semidei, Dir.
Ger Stud. LI—Ger.

This German language school offers courses ranging in duration from a weekend to a year at all levels of proficiency and intensity. Many courses are augmented with planned cultural visits and excursions, and holiday stays and educational tours are available without language instruction. Year-round courses can be designed for either individuals or groups. Accommodations for students are arranged with German families.

DEVELOPMENTAL CENTER—CENTER ACADEMY
Bdg Boys Ages 6-16; Day Coed 6-16. Gr K-10.

London SW1P 4NJ, England. Napier Hall, Hide Place, Vincent Square. Tel. 01-821-5760.
Robert E. Detweiler, BA, Lafayette College, JD, Duke Univ., Dir.
Remedial (Ungraded). LI—Eng. SI—Tut Rem & Dev Math & Read.
Enr 62. B 15/35; G 12.
Fac 5. Full 5. M 1; F 4. US.
Tui Bdg $12,000 (+ $1500); Day $5100 (+ $1000). Schol.
Est 1974. Nonprofit. Tri (Sept-July).

The Developmental Center offers an intensive, 11-month remediation program for children with specific learning problems. Each child's curriculum is individually designed with emphasis on perceptual training, motor skills, reading, spelling, language arts and mathematics. The Center's goal is to return the child to a regular school with his peers as soon as possible. Extracurricular activities include art, swimming, movement to music, weightlifting, squash and library. Students are enrolled from the U.S. and Great Britain, and most faculty members are from the U.S.

DIVULGAZIONE LINGUA ITALIANA
(International House)
Coed Ages 16 and up.

00185 Rome, Italy. Via Magenta, 5. Tel. (06)492592/593/602.
Giorgia Piva, Dir.
Lang Study.
Tui 450,000 Lire/mo.
Est 1974. Inc.
Bldgs 2. Lib 300 vols.

This program offers year-round instruction in Italian language study from beginner to advanced levels. Courses are conducted on 4, 8, 12, 16 and 24-week schedules beginning every other week. Those students unable to attend classes may receive private tutoring. Accommodations in nearby hotels and pensions are arranged if requested in advance.

ECOLE DE SECRETARIATE ET DE LANGUES
Bdg & Day Coed Ages 16 and up.

0820 Montreux (Vaud), Switzerland. Territet Avenue de Naye 15. Tel. 021/620880. Telex: 451.030 TXCB CH.
Hermann & Ursula Schusterbauer, Dirs.

Lang Stud. LI—Fr Ger Eng. CF—Fr Ger Eng Span Ital Russ Bus &
Commerce.
Enr 88. B 18/9; G 49/12.
Tui Bdg 16,425 SwF; Day 9450 SwF.
Summer Session. Lang Stud. Bdg 1900 SwF; Day 600 SwF. 3 wks.
Est 1968.

This school offers complete language courses from six months to two
years and intensive and holiday courses lasting only a few weeks.
Courses are available at several levels and intensities and special courses
can be arranged for secretaries, bookkeepers, managers and profes-
sionals in the business community. Swimming, bowling, ice skating,
hiking, golf, table tennis, concerts, films and sight-seeing are among the
activities which students can participate in during their leisure hours.
Half- or whole-day excursions to other Swiss cities and to France are
arranged weekly. The school is housed in a small castle in the
countryside and has its own boarding facilities.

ECOLE NOUVELLE DE FRANÇAIS
　Day Coed Ages 16 and up.

2000 Neuchatel, Switzerland. Piere-a-Mazel 11. Tel. (038) 25.36.46.
Georges Dufaux, Dir.
Fr Lang Stud.
Tui 70-500 Fr/mo.

Ecole Nouvelle offers French language instruction at beginner,
intermediate and advanced levels. Composition, conversation, grammar,
literature, reading and phonetics are emphasized at all levels, and course
work may lead to the Alliance Francaise. The program is operated
year-round on a day basis, and living accommodations may be arranged.

See also page 83

EDWARD GREENE'S TUTORIAL ESTABLISHMENT
　Bdg Coed Ages 16-20; Day Coed 13-20. Gr 8-PG.

Oxford OX1 IBP, England. 45 Pembroke St. Tel. 248308.
E.P.C. Greene, MA, Oxford, Head.
Col Prep Gen Acad. Tests GCE CEEB SSAT. Curr—Tut. LI—Eng.
　CF—Classics Hist Math Sci Langs Econ Pol. SI—Rem & Dev Math &
　Read Tut.
Enr 430. B 193/77; G 99/61. Elem 10, Sec 398, PG 32. US—6. Grad
　'84—350. Col—300.
Fac 200. Full 15/Part 181. M 135; F 61. UK.
Tui Bdg £7350 (+ £700); Day £5600 (+ £700).
Summer Session. Acad. Tui Bdg £210 (+ £20)/wk; Day £160
　(+ £20)/wk.
Est I970. Nonprofit. Tri (Sept-Je).
Bldgs 2.

Edward Greene's tutorial service offers one-to-one instruction in all academic subjects. Most of the 191 tutors available are Oxford University graduates. Mny students prepare to take or retake G.C.E. 'A' level exams or American SAT tests, both of which are administered annually at the school. Text books and other teaching materials are chosen by the student and the instructor, and students are expected to complete several hours of homework for each hour of class. Lodging in rooming houses or apartments is arranged by the school. Students are encouraged to use the library and participate in the social and sporting activities of Oxford.

EUROCENTRES
Bdg & Day Coed Ages 16 and up.

Zurich 8038, Switzerland. Seestrasse 247. Tel. 482.50.40. Telex: 55667.
J.C. Waespi, Dir.
Eng Fr Ger Ital Span Stud.
Tui varies.
Est 1960. Nonprofit.

There are 21 Eurocentres teaching languages in England, Germany, France, Ireland, Italy, Scotland, Spain and the United States. Courses range from two week holiday courses to three-month intensive courses and are offered at beginning as well as advanced levels. Customized courses for teachers, companies or other organizations are available. Studies include morning and afternoon classes supplemented by electives in the culture and customs of the country, lessons on the terminology of professional fields, and individualized study in the multi-media learning center. Students are primarily from Europe and are housed by native families in the host country.

See also page 94

FRENCH AMERICAN STUDY CENTER
Bdg Coed Ages 16-25; Day 16 and up.

14104 Lisieux Cedex (Caluados), France. Boite Postal 176. Tel. (31) 31.22.01.
Phillippe Almeras, PhD, Univ. of California, Dir.
Fr Study. Sl—Tut.
Fac 9. Full 4/Part 5. M 5; F 4. US 2. France.
Tui Bdg $3145 (+ $200); Day $325/wk. Schol.
Summer Session. Acad. Tui $3162 (+ $200). 10 wks.
Est 1974. Inc nonprofit. Tri (March-Dec).
Bldgs 2. Pool. Crts. Farm.

A program of total immersion in the French language and culture is offered by the Center. Intensive oral and audio-visual instruction is combined with life in a French home. Advanced courses are offered in French literature and cinema and a special "A la carte" program is offered for vacationers. Holiday program students are housed in a hundred and fifty-year-old mansion. Lisieux is a country town in the heart of France's apple and cheese producing region.

FRIENDS WORLD COLLEGE
  Bdg Coed Ages 18 and up.

Huntington, NY 11743. Plover Ln. Tel. (516) 549-1102.
Lawrence Weiss, PhD, Columbia Univ., Pres.
Col. LI—Eng.
Enr 150. Grad '84—15.
Fac 18. Full 12/Part 6. M 12; F 6. US 12.
Tui $4700. Schol.
Est 1965. Nonprofit. Sem.

Friends offers an alternative liberal arts program leading to the Baccalaureate degree. The student's freshman year is spent in this country with orientation and field work in preparation for overseas study. With appropriate guidance, students design a course in such diverse fields as anthropology, economics, communications, wildlife studies, community health and education. The college has centers in the Middle East, Africa, Asia, Europe and Latin America.

GRASSROOTS EDUCATIONAL EXPEDITIONS
  Bdg Coed Ages 12-16.

Freedom, ME 04941. RDF 1. Tel. 207-342-5422.
Karl Olson, BA, Earlham College, Dir.
Study & Travel. LI—Eng. CF—Greek Hist Agricultural Perspectives.
Enr 12. B6; G 6. Elem 3, Sec 9.
Fac 2. Full 2. M 1; F 1. US.
Tui $1600 (+ $700).

This unique travel program conducts cart tours of rural Greece. For ten weeks from early February to mid-April, students travel in two horse-drawn carts developing self-sufficiency and outdoor living skills. An hour a day is set aside for modern Greek lessons and students work on individual projects that involve them in the life and history of the Greeks. While exploring ruins, conversing with Greek farmers and families, camping and hiking, students also keep a daily journal of their travels.

INSTITUT LANGUEUROP
  Day Coed Ages 15 and up.

06000 Nice, France. 30 Rue de France. Tel. (93) 88.51.47. Telex: 460.000.
A.G. Pelayo, Dir.
Fr Stud. LI—Fr. CF—Fr Civilization Translation.
450-1030 Fr/wk. Schol.
Est 1965.

Located on the French Riviera, this school combines French language instruction with studies in French literature and culture and visits to local museums and attractions. Class size averages six students and special groups can be accommodated on request. Students are housed either in French hotels or with local families. The Alliance Francaise certificate can be obtained after the four-week intensive course.

INSTITUT LE VIEUX CHALET
Girls Ages 16-20.

1837 Chateau D'Oex (Vaud), Switzerland. La Frasse. Tel. 029-46879.
Telex: CHAX CH 94 0022.
C. Bach, BA, Univ. of Lausanne, Dir.
Lang Stud. Tests GCE. LI—Fr. A—Fr Eng. CF—Art Hist Ger Ital Eng Span Typing.
Tui 15,500 SwF (+ 3500 SwF).
Summer Session. Acad Rec. Tui 1700 SwF (+ 200 SwF). 4 wks.
Est 1955. Tri (Oct-Je).
Bldgs 3. Dorm.

Situated in an Alpine valley, Vieux Chalet provides instruction in French including grammar, spelling, diction, culture and literature. Instruction is also offered in English, German, Italian and Spanish. Students may also take classes in domestic science, music and art. Sports and activities include skiing, ice skating, swimming, tennis, golf, riding and fishing.

See also page 90

INSTITUT MÉDITERRANÉEN D'INITIATION À LA CULTURE FRANÇAISE
Bdg Coed Ages 16 and up.

34690 Fabregues, France. Tel. (67)851355.
Mail to: Dr. Janice Etzkowitz, 303 West 66th St., New York, NY 10023.
Madame Martelliere, Dir.
Fr Stud. LI—Fr. CF—Fr Civilization.
Enr 250. US—45.
Fac 7. Full 7. M 2; F 5. Nat.
Tui $749/mo (+ $100/wk).
Est 1963.

This French language school offers year-round courses ranging in duration from three weeks to nine months. Intensive private courses are available for shorter periods. Accommodations and excursions to local events and attractions are also included in the program.

INSTITUT RICHELIEU
Day Coed Ages 16 and up.

1004 Lausanne (Vaud), Switzerland. 7, rue du Clos-de-Bulle. Tel. (021) 23 27 18.
Philippe Bornand, MA, Univ. of Lausanne, Dir.
Fr Stud. LI—Fr. CF—Fr Culture.
Enr 200. B 80; G 120.
Fac 15. Full 1/Part 14. M 2; F 13. Nat Fr.

Tui 1950 SwF. Schol.
Summer Session. Fr Stud. Tui 1950 SwF. 6 wks.
Est 1962.

Most students attending the Institute Richelieu hope to acquire sufficient proficiency in French to attend French university courses or to master the language in a short period of time. Classes range from 4 to 20 hours per week and employ both verbal and audio-visual instruction. Occasional outings to area attractions are arranged. Information on local housing accommodations is available at the school.

INTERCULTURAL ACTION LEARNING PROGRAM (INTERALP)
  Bdg Coed Ages 16-20.

Peterborough, NH 03458. 7 School St., P.O. Box 464. Tel. 603-924-7535.
Barbara G. Clickenbeard, BA, Mt. Holyoke, MA, Wellesley, Dir.
Col Prep Gen Acad. Tests SSAT. LI—Eng. CF—Anthro Archaeol Hist Lit Arts.
Fac 4. Full 4. M 2; F 2.
Tui $3500 (+ $1000). Schol.
Est 1974. Inc nonprofit. Sem (Sept-May).

INTERALP conducts semester-long programs for high school students in both Greece and Egypt. In Greece, students live and work with the residents of a village while studying the literature, history and art of Greece, while students in Egypt study archaeology and actively participate in digs. The faculty are residents of the host country and emphasis is placed on learning the language and participating in day to day life. Students are primarily from the United States and Canada.

INTERNATIONAL HOUSE
  Day Coed Ages 15 and up.

Barcelona 10, Spain. Trafalgar 14 entlo. Tel. 318 8429. Telex: 97391 IHIH E.
Jordi Bordas, Dir.
Lang Stud.
Tui 57,500-188,000 Pts/mo.
Est 1972.

The International House runs 50 schools in 14 different countries, including this one in northeast Spain. Courses are designed for business and professional groups, individuals, travelers and students. Instruction emphasizes spoken Spanish and class participation exclusively in Spanish, but also covers reading, writing and understanding. Class size is limited to 12 students. Excursions to area attractions are part of the educational program. Students have the option of living in university residences, hotels or hostels or in private homes.

INTERNATIONAL SCHOOLS SERVICES
(Tutorial Service)
  Day Coed Ages 5-12. Gr 1-6.

Puerto Ordaz 8016A (Estado Bolivar), Venezuela. c/o Interalumina, Apartado 289. Tel. 221689.
Margaret Meneses, BA, MA, Univ. of Texas, Prin.
Pre-Prep. Tests SSAT. Curr—USA. LI—Eng. CF—Span Art Music.
Enr 6. B 3; G 3.
Fac 1. USA.
Est 1981. Nonprofit. Sem (Sept-Je).
Bldgs 2. Lib 2500 vols. Crts. Pool.

This tuition free, company-sponsored school enrolls English-speaking children of Interalumina employees. The curriculum is based on and uses texts from standard U.S. public schools. Physically handicapped children and children with learning disabilities cannot be accepted by the school. Extracurricular activities include dancing, stamp collecting, ecology and cooking.

ISTITUTO LINGUISTICO MEDITERRANEO
  Day Coed Ages 18 and up.

56100 Pisa, Italy. Via Cesare Battisti, 3. Tel. 050/598066-48157.
Ital Stud.
Enr 155. US—17.
Fac 25. M 9; F 16. Italy.
400,000 Lit/mo.
Summer Session. Lang Stud. Tui 400,000 Lit/mo.
Est 1981. (March-Dec).

Istituto Linguistico Mediterraneo offers general, 4- to 12-week long Italian language courses in the Tuscany towns of Pisa and Livorno. Beginning through graduate students are assigned to one of four levels of ability based on first day oral and written testing. Students at each level spend 20 hours a week strengthening Italian conversational and reading skills. The Livorno division, which operates from April to September, offers a special, 30-hour-a-week intensive language course and a 20-hour-a-month commercial correspondence course.

Students at both locations spend their free time at Mediterranean beaches, on sailing excursions and visiting local art and cultural centers. The institute in Pisa conducts free afternoon lessons in Italian literature, history, geography and philosophy from October to May. Free assistance is provided in finding lodgings at boarding houses, hotels or with families.

See also page 75

K.I.S.S. DANISH LANGUAGE SCHOOL
  Day Coed Ages 18 and up.

1165 Copenhagen K, Denmark. Norregade 20. Tel. (01) 114477.
Steen Allan Christensen, Head.

LI—Danish Eng.
Enr 250. US—100.
Tui 147 DKr. 2¹/₂ wks.
Est 1971. Nonprofit.

This intensive language school offers individualized instruction in Danish through 11 courses. Pronunciation and speaking ability are emphasized—language labs and machines are not used. All classes meet three times a week for three hours each. An understanding of English is required for admission.

LANDMARK EAST
Bdg & Day Coed Ages 8-16.

Wolfville (Nova Scotia) B0P 1X0, Canada. Box 1270, Main St. Tel. (902) 542-2237.
G. Fred Atkinson, MA, Head.
Lang Remediation. LI—Eng. CF—Auditory Training Motor Skills Lang Arts Math. SI—Rem & Dev Read & Math Tut.
Enr 48. B 38/7; G 3. Elem 42, Sec 6.
Fac 23. Full 23. M 10: F 13. US 1. Canada.
Tui Bdg $17,500 (+ $450); Day $11,500 (+ $200).
Summer Session. Rem. 6 wks.
Est 1978. Inc nonprofit. Sem (Sept-Je).
Bldgs 3. Cabins 8. Lib.

Landmark's intensive program, modelled after the Landmark School in Massachusetts, is designed for children of average or above intelligence who have a language disability but are emotionally stable. The curriculum is ungraded with individual instruction emphasizing reading, writing, spelling and comprehension. Small group classes include such subjects as mathematics, social studies, language arts, computer literacy, arts and crafts, and physical education. Nearby Acadia University provides gym, swimming pool and ice rink facilities. Other available activities include skiing, hiking, tennis, golf and horseback riding.

See also page 105

THE LEARNING PLACE
Day Coed Ages 6-16. Gr 1-8.

Scarborough (Ontario) M1E 2E5, Canada. 20 Waldock St. Tel. (416) 281-3404.
Faye E. Hart, BA, Univ. of Toronto, Dir.
Gen Acad Rem. Curr—Rem. LI—Eng. SI—Rem & Dev Math & Read Tut.
Enr 15.
Fac 25. Full 6/Part 19. M 2; F 23. Nat.
Tui $8900.
Summer Session. Rem. Tui $370. 4 wks.
Est 1978. Inc 1980. Sem (Sept-Je).

The Learning Place is designed for special needs students who have been unsuccessful in traditional schools and for adults who wish to upgrade functional language, math and living skills. A complete elementary day program with a 5:1 student:teacher ratio is supplemented by both day and evening tutorial classes with a 2:1 student:teacher ratio. The evening courses cater especially to adults. The non-graded curriculum emphasizes individual attention and thinking, study and organizational skills.

NEW EXPERIMENTAL COLLEGE
Bdg & Day Coed Ages 18 & up.

Skyum Bjerge (Thy), Denmark. 7752 Snedsted. Tel. 45.7.936234.
Aage Rosendal Nielsen, Rector.
Adult Ed. LI—Eng Danish.
Enr 81. B 18/27; G 9/27.
Tui Bdg 2350 DKr/2 mo; Day 24 DKr/2 mo.
Summer Session. Seminars. Tui Bdg 666 DKr/mo.
Est 1962. Inc nonprofit. Sem (Sept-May).
Bldgs 3. Dorms 2. Lib 5000 vols.

Education at the New Experimental College is both self-designed and self-taught. Students are advised to have some post-secondary schooling or work experience before attending. Participants study subjects of their choice on an individual and communal basis. Interaction in the school's natural environment is considered integral to the experience. Summer seminars discuss subjects like nongovernmental organizations' work, ecology, peace movements, and international political activities.

OEKOS SCHOOL
Bdg & Day Coed Ages 9 & up.

CH-8001 Zurich, Switzerland. Zahringerstrasse 51. Tel. 01/252 49 35.
Telex: 586690 EKO CH.
Fritz Burgi, Dir.
Ger Stud.
Est 1974.

Oekos offers German language study to individuals, groups and holiday travelers. Both day and evening, beginning and advanced programs are available. Outside the classroom, students participate in swimming, golf, table-tennis, tennis, rowing, skating, sailing, horse riding and sight-seeing. Students are housed in the school's hotel.

ÖVAST
Bdg Coed Ages 13 and up.

A-3500 Krems (Lower Austria), Austria. Dr. Gschmeidlerstrasse 10/4.
Tel. 02732/5743.
Dr. Hans Kapitan, Dir.
Ger Stud.

Tui 2000-3800 S/wk.
Est 1964. Nonprofit.

Ovast offers German language study with 15-30 lessons per week. Students are housed with local families. Language study programs supplemented by skiing lessons or holiday excursions are available for children ages six and up. Students who wish to attend Austrian public schools may also be placed by the school in Austrian families.

OXFORD AND COUNTY SECRETARIAL COLLEGE LTD.
   Bdg and Day Girls Ages 16-19.

Oxford OX1 3LH, England. 34 St. Giles. Tel. (0865) 511404.
E. J. Hall, Prin.
Secretarial. Ll—Eng. CF—Fr.
Enr 200. G 180/20. Grad '84—200.
Fac 13. Full 4/Part 9. F 13.
Tui Bdg £715-900 (+ £100); Day £485 (+ £100).
Est 1936. Tri (Sept-Je).
Bldgs 9. Dorm. Courts.

This program offers a straight professional secretarial course of study. Shorthand, typing, accounting, word processing, business English and conversational French are integral to the curriculum, and qualified students may receive private instruction in German, Italian, Russian and Spanish. All girls are required to live together in either the College flats, hostel, or with one of the approved Landladies. Recreational and cultural activities include tennis, squash, riding, drama and orchestral societies.

PARIS AMERICAN ACADEMY
   Bdg & Day Coed Ages 16 and up.

75005 Paris, France. 9, Rue Des Ursulines. Tel. 325-0891/3509.
Richard Roy, Dir.
French Lang & Culture. CF—Art Hist Sculpture Photog Fashion.
   Sl—Tut.
Enr 190.
Fac 80.
Tui Bdg 9300-33,000 Fr (+ 675-5125 Fr).
Summer Session. Acad Rec Fashion Art Lang. Tui Bdg 9200 Fr (+ 625 Fr). 4 wks.
Est 1966. Inc. (Oct-May).

The Paris American Academy conducts intensive French language, culture and fine arts courses. Students design their own program of study from the major disciplines: French, art history, painting, sculpture, ceramics, photography, drawing, serigraphy, engraving and architectural and interior design. The Academy's School of Fashion offers classes in textiles and marketing, and excursions are made to fashion houses. All classes are bilingual (English/French) and university credit may be obtained. A one-month interim program in Florence, Italy is included in the academic year.

See also page 62

PENSIONNAT SURVAL
Bdg Girls Ages 14-22.

1815 Clarens-Montreux (Vaud), Switzerland. Chemin de la Prairie 16.
Tel. 021/64.26.73. Telex: 453162 SURV CH.
Mr. & Mrs. F. Sidler-Andreae, Dirs.
Fr Stud. LI—Fr. CF—Eng Fr Cooking Sewing Typing Arts.
Tui 24,600 SwF (+ 4500 SwF).
Summer Session. Acad Rec. Tui Bdg 2580 SwF (+ 500 SwF). 3 wks.
Est 1961. Tri (Sept-Je).
Bldgs 1. Crt.

Situated in a former hotel on the shore of Lake Geneva, Pensionnat Surval offers intensive language study to girls of all nationalities. In addition to three hours of French study per day, classes are featured in English, German, Italian, Spanish, typing, cooking, etiquette and ceramics. Sports are an integral part of the program and include skiing, swimming, tennis, riding, sailing and bicycling. Cultural excursions are taken throughout the surrounding area of Montreux.

PROGRAMS IN ISRAEL
Coed Ages 15-32.

New York, NY 10022. American Zionist Youth Foundation. 515 Park Ave. Tel. 212-751-6070.
Study & Travel.

The American Zionist Youth Foundation sponsors many varied programs in Israel for high school, college, graduate, post-graduate and professional people. Academic year, six-month, semester and summer programs offer courses in Hebrew language and science, as well as tours of Israel and volunteer work on a kibbutz. Academic credit is available.

ROUDYBUSH FOREIGN SERVICE SCHOOL
Day Boys Ages 16 and up.

12800 Aveyron, France. Sauveterre de Rouergue.
Franklin Roudybush, BA, MA, PhD, Dir.
LI—Eng Fr Span. CF—Diplomatic & Commercial Courses Drawing Lit.
Enr 20. US—5.
Fac 3. Full 3. M 2; F 1. Intl.
Tui $300 (+ $100).
Summer Session. Acad Rec. 3 mos.
Est 1907.
Bldgs 3. Lib 15,000 vols.

Roudybush offers six months of intensive study for a limited number of pre-college boys age 16 and over, with English, Spanish and French utilized as the language of instruction. Men over 20 may prepare for the foreign service and professional exams. The school also has a villa in Portugal where Spanish and Portuguese may be studied in conjunction with diplomatic, international law and commercial courses. Emphasis is placed on drawing and painting. Golf, fishing, sailing and tennis are among the activities. Living accommodations are arranged with local families.

See also page 61

ROYAL COLLEGE OF MUSIC
  Day Coed Ages 16-25.

London SW7 2BS (South Kensington), England. Prince Consort Rd.
  Tel. 01-589-3643.
Michael Gough Matthews, FRCM, Dir.
Col. Curr—UK. LI—Eng. A—Opera Training Orchestral Conducting
  Repetiteurs. CF—Instruments Performance Early Music.
Enr 593. B 304; G 289. US—3.
Tui £3744-4425.
Est 1883. Inc. Tri (Sept-July).

The Royal College of Music offers courses in all orchestral instruments, electronic music, ensemble, conducting, composition and the theory and history of music. Though it is primarily a conservatory for performers, it also offers courses for those intending to teach music. College facilities include two concert halls, two libraries, an opera theatre, an electronics studio, teaching studios, and practice rooms. A Junior Department provides training for musically gifted children ages 10-18. The College was founded by the Prince of Wales and remains under the patronage of the Queen of England.

SCHOOL FOR INTERNATIONAL TRAINING—THE EXPERIMENT
  IN INTERNATIONAL LIVING
  Coed Ages 14 and up.

Brattleboro, VT 05301. Tel. 802-257-7751/0326. Telex: 710-3636774
  EXPER.
Martha J. Bozman, Dir..
Study & Travel.
Tui $1400-6300. Schol.
Est 1932. Sem.

For over 45 years, The Experiment in International Living has offered young Americans the opportunity to live with a family and study in another country. Students may elect to spend time abroad in one of 30 countries, combining homestay with travel, field research, seminars and language study. Groups of 10 to 12 students are accompanied by independently selected and trained adult leaders. This program is available to both high school and college students, and credits earned abroad can often be transferred to United States colleges and universities.

SCHOOL YEAR ABROAD
  Bdg Coed Ages 15-18. Gr 11-PG.

Andover, MA 01810. Phillips Academy. Tel. 617-475-1119.
Harrison F. McCann, BA, Williams, MA, Middlebury, Exec. Dir.
Col Prep Lang. Curr—USA. LI—Eng Span Fr. CF—Lit Hist Art Math.
Enr 108. B 51; G 57. Sec 108. US—108. Grad '84—40. Col—40.
Fac 17. Full 8/Part 9. M 10; F 7. US 5. Spain France.
Tui Bdg $8800 (+ $1500). Schol.
Est 1964. Inc 1974 nonprofit. Sem (Sept-May).
Bldgs 2.

Sponsored by the Phillips Exeter Academy, Phillips Academy, St. Paul's School and associated with 19 others, School Year Abroad provides a fully accredited year of study to high school students in Rennes, France or Barcelona, Spain. The program is open to qualified juniors and seniors from any accredited American secondary school who have completed two years of study in the appropriate language.

Students live with native families and travel during vacation periods. The curriculum includes courses in math and English—taught in English by American teachers, and history, literature, language and art taught by teachers of the host country. All students are prepared for a variety of College Board Achievement Tests and some may sit for the Advanced Placement exams.

See also page 112

SCUOLA LEONARDO DA VINCI
  Bdg & Day Coed.

50123 Florence (Tuscany), Italy. Via de'Pecori. Tel. 055/29 42 47.
Hans-Gedeon Villiger, Dir.
Lang Stud. CF—Ital Eng Italian Culture Pol Econ Music Photog Arts
  Crafts.
Tui Bdg $320-380/mo; Day $240/mo.
Est 1977.

Located in central Italy, this school offers classes in Italian cookery, wines, literature, politics and economics, folk music, cinema and art history, photography, weaving, pottery, leather-craft, silkscreen printing and art as well as Italian language. All of the school's teachers have studied at the University of Florence, but many come from European countries other than Italy. Students are informed of cultural events, leisurely activities and area attractions. Accommodations are available in private homes, boarding houses or student apartments.

SCUOLA PALAZZO MALVISI
  Bdg Coed Ages 18 and up.

47021 Bagno Di Romagna (Forli), Italy. Via Fiorentina 36. Tel.
  0543-917140/911170.
Cesare Portolani, BA, Univ. of Bologna, Dir.

Ital Study. SI—Tut.
Enr 190. B 80; G 110.
Tui 1,300,000-3,800,000 Lire.
Est 1980.

This program provides intensive instruction in the Italian language. Beginner through advanced level courses are offered which stress grammar, conversation, reading and writing. Hotel accommodations are provided and a variety of sporting and cultural activities including tennis and horseback riding are available. Students are primarily from Europe.

SEJOURS INTERNATIONAUX LINGUISTIQUES ET CULTURELS
Bdg Coed Ages 7 and up.

16022 Angouleme Cedex, France. 32, Rampart de L'Est. Tel. (045)
95.83.56. Telex: 791193F.
Pierre Deschamps, Dir.
Lang Study & Travel.
Tui $100-150/wk.
Est 1965. Nonprofit.

SILC organizes language stays of various duration at seven centers throughout Europe, Asia and America. These visits may be in a host home, communal or university setting. One type of visit combines language study with sports instruction and recreational activities.

SOCIETA' DANTE ALIGHIERI
Day Coed.

30122 Venice, Italy. Arsenale-Ponte Del Purgatorio. Tel. (041) 89127.
Rosella Mamoli Zorzi, BA, Univ. of Venice, Dir.
Ital Stud.
Tui 150,000-250,000 Lit/wk.
Est 1978. Nonprofit.

Both beginning and advanced courses in Italian are available at this school. Most courses run for one month with students attending 10 lessons each week, but more intensive classes are also offered. Each class includes guided visits to cultural attractions in Venice and has a maximum of 15 students.

STUDIESKOLEN I KOBENHAVN
Day Coed.

DK-1106 Copenhagen, Denmark. Antonigade 6. Tel. 01-144022.
Jorgen Jorgensen, Prin.
Danish Stud.

Though independent, this school works in collaboration with and uses the facilities of the University of Copenhagen. Danish language instruction is offered at 12 levels which meet from 2 to 10 hours per week. Students may begin the program at any time during the year. Studieskolen also offers courses in basic academic subjects including literature, mathematics and chemistry.

T.I.N.A.
  Bdg and Day Coed Ages 15 and up.

00141 Rome, Italy. Via Dell'Assietta. Tel. 8185678.
Concetta Amato, BA, Univ. of Rome, Dir.
Ital Stud. CF—Ital Culture.
Enr 63. B 10/20; G 15/18. US—3.
Tui Bdg 725,000 Lit; Day 420,000 Lit.
Est 1980.

Courses at T.I.N.A. (Teaching Italian by New Approaches) consist of 60 periods of instruction over 2, 3 or 10 weeks. Students are introduced to Italian literature, art history, music, fashion and tourism in class, and these subjects are followed up with extracurricular activities and excursions. Those who opt for the residential program are housed and take their classes in a local hotel reserved by the school for that purpose. Hotel accommodation or a stay with a local family can be arranged on request. Special programs can be designed for companies or other groups.

TORONTO HIGH SCHOOL FOR THE PERFORMING ARTS
  Bdg & Day Ages 12-20. Gr 7-12.

Toronto (Ontario) M5A 1M8, Canada. 209 Adelaide St. East. Tel. (416) 868-0058.
K.E.L. Livingstone, BA, Wilfred Laurier Univ., Dir.
Col Prep Gen Acad Arts. Tests CEEB SSAT. Curr—Nat. LI—Eng.
CF—Fr Math Sci Hist Geog Comp Children's Lit Music Theatre Dance.
Fac 16. Full 7/Part 9. M 8; F 8. Nat.
Tui Bdg $8000 (+ $500); Day $4600 (+ $300). Schol.
Summer Session. Acad Arts. Tui Bdg $1500 (+ $250); Day $700 (+ $150). 6 wks.
Est 1978. Inc 1979. Tri (Sept-May).

The Toronto High School for the Performing Arts combines a general academic curriculum with intensive study of music, drama or dance. In the mornings students study basic subjects enabling them to earn the Ontario Secondary School Diploma while afternoon sessions concentrate on performance areas. The music program includes instrumental work, voice, music history, composition, theory, conducting and dictation. Theatre students study interpretation, acting, make-up, stage craft, mime, improvisation and music and dance for actors. The dance agenda includes choreography, dance history, modern dance and drama and music for dancers. All three programs are supplemented by visits from professional performers and trips to area presentations.

Most graduates enter university arts programs or join professional performance groups. Admission is contingent on an audition in the student's performance area. Though the school does not have its own boarding facilities, it will arrange for students to live with local families.

UNITED WORLD COLLEGES
Bdg Coed Ages 16-18. Gr 11-12.

New York, NY 10021. 41 E. 72nd St. Tel. 212-734-4990.
Timothy Wright, Admin.
Col Prep Gen Acad. Tests CEEB GCE IB. Curr—Intl. LI—Eng. CF—Fr
Ger Span Russ Chinese Math Sci Econ Relig Art Music. SI—Tut.
Tui $6200-9000. Schol.
Est 1962. Nonprofit. Quar (Sept-Je).

The United World Colleges (UWC) are based on a common educational philosophy and are coordinated by an independent International Council. College preparatory curricula are offered in six locations: United World College of the Atlantic (St. Donat's Castle, Llantwit Major CF69WF, South Wales, United Kingdom); United World College of the Adriatic (Via Trieste, 29, 4013 Duino, Trieste, Italy); Lester B. Pearson College of the Pacific (RR1 Victoria, British Columbia V8X 3W9, Canada); United World College of South East Asia (P.O. Box 14, Pasir Panjang, Singapore 5); The Armand Hammer United World College of the American West (P.O. Box 248, Montezuma, New Mexico 87731); and the Waterford-kaMhlaba United World College of Southern Africa (P.O. Box 52, Mbabane, Swaziland).

Students and faculty are drawn from 60 countries in Europe, North and South America, South East Asia, China and Japan. The majority of students are on merit scholarships raised by UWC National Committees in their own countries. Community service as well as cultural and athletic activities are integral aspects of each program.

UNIVERSITA INTERNAZIONALE DELL'ARTE
Day Coed Ages 18 and up.

Florence, Italy 50133. Villa Il Ventaglio—Via delle Forbici 24/26. Tel. 57.15.03/57.02.15.
Carlo L. Ragghianti, Prof.
Art Criticism Hist Design Museum Sci Restoration. LI—Ital. SI—Ital.
Enr 170.
Tui 300,000-900,000 Lire.
Est 1968. Sem (Sept-Apr).
Bldg 1. 3 Libs 2000 vols.

The International University of Art offers specialized courses promoting the preservation of works of art through scientific and technical research as well as experimental and practical activities. These include instruction in design, theory of restoration and preservation of works of art, an experimental laboratory and a colloquia acquainting students with the international cultural world. An intensive Italian language course is offered to foreign students, while translations into and from English are provided during orientation.

UNIVERSITÉ LAVAL, CELAV
Bdg Coed Ages 18 & up.

Quebec (Quebec), Canada G1K 7P4. Cite Universitaire. Tel. (418) 656-2321.
Jean-Guy LeBel, Dir.
Fr Stud.
Enr 1600. US—500.
Tui $2067 (+ $65). Schol.
Summer Session. Fr Stud. Tui $1064 (+ $50). 6 wks.
Bldgs 20. Dorms 5. Pool.

Students attending this school receive credits in French language study which may be transferred to other institutions. Living accommodations are available on campus or with French-speaking families. Outings to cultural events, workshops and sports are organized.

VIITTAKIVI INTERNATIONAL CENTER
Bdg Coed Ages 19 and up.

SF-14700 Hauho, Finland. Tel. 917-4840.
Eva Launonen, Dir.
Gen Acad. Curr—Nat. LI—Eng Finnish. CF—Russ Finnish Eng Philos Soc Music Psych Relig.
Enr 46. B 14; G 32.
Fac 8. Full 5/Part 3. M 4; F 4. Nat.
Tui $1200. Schol.
Summer Session. Tui Bdg 94 Fmk/day. 1-3 wks.
Est 1951. Nonprofit. Sem (Nov-May).
Bldgs 7. Dorms 4. Lib 10,000 vols. Athletic facilities.

Viittakivi is a study and conference center for young adults and adults offering a variety of courses and seminars dealing with current social problems and examining the alternatives. The winter program is devoted to an international course with both Finnish and English used throughout most of the program, and all foreigners study Finnish. Short courses and seminars including folk dancing, yoga, painting, photography and biodynamic gardening are offered during the summer session. Viittakivi's autumn course is held by the Finnish Settlement Federation and other organizations. Harvesting weekends are also part of the autumn program.

YOUTH VACATIONS
(Vacances-Jeunes)
Bdg Coed Ages 8-19.

75000 Paris, France. 67 Rue de Rome. Tel. 293229. Telex: 650133 VACJEU.

P. De Montbron, Dir.
Lang Stud.
Enr 380. B 280; G 100.
Tui $340-730/2 wks.
Est 1900. Nonprofit.

Youth Vacations offers vacation language study programs from two to seven weeks long in France, Germany, Spain and Ireland. Students take from 10 to 25 hours of language study and participate in at least one organized field trip each week. Sports facilities are accessible in each location, and tennis, judo and riding instructionn is available at the Ecole Des Roches center, France. Participants are accommodated by local families or in supervised student houses.

SUMMER SESSIONS

Summer academic and recreational programs offering study, travel and homestay abroad sponsored by international schools as well as U.S. independent schools and organizations.

SUMMER SESSIONS

*Programs are arranged
alphabetically by name*

AEGEAN INSTITUTE
  Bdg Coed Ages 17 and up.

Port Jefferson, NY 11777. 25 Waterview Dr. Tel. (516) 473-7075.
Niki Stavrolakes, BA, Barnard College, MA, PhD, Yale, Dir.
Study & Travel. LI—Eng. A—Greek.
Enr 30. US.
Fac 5. US.
Tui $1200. 6 wks. Schol.
Est 1966. Inc 1967 nonprofit.

The Aegean Institute offers a six-week summer session on the island of
Poros, Troizen, Greece for college students and graduates. Courses are
offered in art, archaeology, history, drama, anthropology, Greek
language and literature and are supplemented by organized trips to
various sites and museums. Hotel accommodations are provided and
opportunities are available for hiking, swimming and boating.

AMERICAN SCHOOL IN LONDON—SUMMER SCHOOL
  Day Coed Ages 5-17. Gr K-11.

London NW8 0NP, England. 2/8 Loudoun Rd., St. John's Wood. Tel.
  01-722-0101.
Harry Hurtt, BA, Akron Univ., Dir.
Gen Acad & Rec. Curr—USA. LI—Eng.
Enr 200.
Fac 23.
Tui £480-200/crse. 1-4 wks.
Est 1951. Inc 1964 nonprofit. (Je-July). Accred MSA.

The American School in London conducts one- to four-week summer
sessions, which feature courses in math, English, French and computer
studies, as well as dance, art, drama and photography. Remedial
instruction is available and a full recreational program supplements the
academic offerings.

See also page 65

THE AMERICAN SCHOOL IN SWITZERLAND
SUMMER PROGRAM
Bdg Coed Ages 6-18.

CH 6926 Montagnola-Lugano (Ticino), Switzerland. Tel. (091) 54 64 71.
Mail to: U.S. Office, 326 E. 69th St., Rm. 110, New York, NY 10021.
Lang Stud & Arts.

Students between the ages of 12 and 18 are offered two four-week sessions of intensive English, French, German and Italian. An educational summer camp, Le Chateau des Enfants, is conducted for children from 6 to 12 years of age. Sports activities and course-related excursions round out the program.

See also page 111

ART HISTORY STUDY VISITS
Bdg Coed Ages 16-19. Gr 11-PG.

c/o Academic Study Abroad, Inc. 3 Sunset Drive, Armonk, NY 10504. Tel. (914) 273-2250. Telex: SWIFT UR ATT ASA.
John Hall, MA, Oxford, Dir.
Art Hist Stud. Travel in Italy.
Enr 30.
Fac 32. Full 2/Part 30. M 22; F 10. Eng.
Tui $1800 (+ $200)/4 wks.
Est 1965. (July-Aug).

This program offers junior- and senior-year students the opportunity to study art history in Florence, Rome and Venice. Professional art historians conduct structured programs of lectures and visits that deal with the history of Italian art, painting, sculpture and architecture. Academic study is balanced by leisure time recreation and arranged excursions. Students are housed in small hotels in each of the cities visited.

In addition to this summer program, John Hall Tutors conduct pre-university interim courses in France, Italy, Holland and England.

See also page 73

BREITENEICH COURSES
Day Coed All Ages.

A-3580 Horn Schloss Breiteneich, Austria. Tel. (0222) 56 64 822.
Walter H. Sallagar, Dir.
Music Woodwinds.
Tui $275-425/2 wks.
Est 1970. Inc nonprofit.

Breiteneich offers a four-week (July to August) musical and cultural course of study. The program focuses on Viennese wind chamber music, music of the Medieval and Renaissance as well as woodwind making and courtly dancing. Instruction, in English and German, ranges from beginner to advanced levels. Opportunities for swimming, riding, yoga and cultural excursions are also available. Although the program is conducted on a day basis, living accommodations can be arranged.

See also page 56

CHOATE ROSEMARY HALL SUMMER PROGRAMS
Coed Ages 14-19.

Wallingford, CT 06492. Tel. 203-269-7722.
William N. Wingerd, BS, Haverford, MS, Pennsylvania St. Univ., Dir.
Study & Travel. 3-6 wks.
Tui $1525-2660.

Each summer Choate Rosemary Hall sponsors study and travel programs to France, Greece, Italy, Spain and a fifth country which varies from year to year.

EAGLE HOUSE SCHOOL—JUNIOR TOURS IN ENGLAND
Bdg Coed Ages 11-15. Gr 6-9.

Surrey, England. Sandhurst, Camberley. Tel. 0101-03446-2134.
Mail to: c/o K.G. Hagan, 9 Roundabout Lane, Cape Elizabeth, ME 04107. Tel. 207-799-1991.
Richard E. A. Woods, LLB, Dir.
Rec & Touring.
Enr 200. US—200.
Fac 25.
Tui $1400-2200 (+/22100). 2-3 wks.
Est 1981. (July-Aug).

Junior Tours offers students from independent schools in the United States the opportunity to tour England with members of their respective school's faculty. Eagle House, England's third oldest preparatory school, is the program's home base. Situated on 500 acres, Eagle House has extensive facilities and students enjoy rugby, field hockey, soccer, tennis, squash and swimming in addition to their daily itinerary. Trips to Bath, Stratford and London are but a few of the program's highlights, and optional tours are also conducted to Italy, Greece and France.

THE ENGLISH CENTRE
Day Coed Ages 11 and up.

48100 Ravenna, Italy. Via S. Agata 48. Tel. 0544 35088. Telex: 550665 CAREST.
Anna Maria Sartori, Dir.
Ital Lang Stud & Culture.
Tui $550/4 wk crse (+$15).
Est 1971.

From June through August, The English Centre conducts four-week sessions in Italian language study at beginner, intermediate and advanced levels. An elective program offers courses in film, mosiacs and

Romance languages, and guided tours to nearby Florence and Venice are also organized. Living accommodations are arranged with nearby hotels and homestay programs.

GREEK SUMMER
Coed Ages 15-18.

Thessaloniki, Greece. c/o American Farm School, P.O. Box 140. Tel. 411-522.
Mail to: American Farm School, 850 Third Ave., New York, NY 10022. Tel. 12-490-8745.
Katharine Swibold, Dir.
Work-Travel.
Tui $1800. 6 wks.
Est 1904.

At this Peace Corps-type program, high school students work on needy projects in a rural village of northern Greece. Trips to historical sites such as Athens, Delphi, the Aegean Islands and Mount Olympus are scheduled as well as trips to museums and beaches.

INSTITUT DR. SCHMIDT SUMMER SESSION
Bdg Boys Ages 8-20.

CH-1095 Lutry (Vaud), Switzerland. Chateau de la Rive. Tel. 021/39.51.12.
Marc De Smet, Prin.
Acad Rec.
Tui Bdg 3000 SwF (+1000 SwF)/4 wks; Day 1500 SwF/4 wks. 3-7 wks.

This summer session offers intensive English and French language study. Boys also enjoy a variety of sports including wind surfing, sailing, diving and tennis.

See also pages 86-7

INTERNATIONAL CENTER FOR THE STUDY OF MOSAICS
Coed Ages 14 and up.

Ravenna 48100, Italy. c/o Azienda Autonoma Soggiorno e Turismo-Via San Vitale, 2. Tel. 054435755. Telex: 550411 RATUR I.
Giovanni Amadei, Chmn.
Study of Mosaics. LI—Ital Fr.
Tui 120,000-150,000 Lire. Schol.

The Center conducts five two-week courses in the study of mosaics from June until September. Instruction in the beginners' section includes the construction of mosaics copied from antique examples with marbled materials, to encourage the learning of the "tessere" and the construction of a mosaic. Advanced students deal exclusively with mosaics made from personal colored designs. Lessons are combined with tours and visits to mosaic monuments in Ravenna. Instructors of the Center belong to the "Gruppo Mosaicisti" of the Academy of Fine Arts, Ravenna. Students are primarily from Europe.

INTERNATIONALE FERIENKURSE MAYRHOFEN
Bdg & Day Coed Ages 12 & up.

A-6290 Mayrhofen (Tyrol), Austria. Tel. 05285/2562.
Stockl Hugo, Dir.
Ger Lang Stud & Culture.
Tui Bdg AS 5790/crse; Day AS 3390.
Est 1947. Inc nonprofit.

Situated in the Ziller Valley, Mayrhofen's German language study program emphasizes the poetry, landscape, culture and history of Austria. The three-week courses, conducted from July through August, are supplemented by excursions to Salzburg and Vienna.

NORTHFIELD MOUNT HERMON ABROAD
Coed Ages 15-18. Gr 10-PG.

Northfield, MA 01360. Tel. 413-498-5311.
Richard Unsworth, Head.
Study & Travel.
Tui $2600-2900.

The International Programs Office at Northfield Mount Hermon School offers summer programs to England, France, Germany and Spain. Students may also go to India, Morocco or the Dominican Republic. Programs feature homestay, language study and travel. Two years of language study is required for Spain, Germany and France.

OPEN DOOR STUDENT EXCHANGE
Coed Ages 15-18.

Valley Stream, NY 11582. 124 East Merrick Rd., Box 1150. Tel. 516-825-8485.
Anthony J. Lella, Educ. Dir.
Lat Am Eur Middle East Exchange Prgm.
Tui $1000-2800. 2 mos.
Est 1963. Inc nonprofit.

This summer exchange program allows qualified U.S. high school students to live with families and attend school in many parts of Latin America, Europe or the Middle East. During the fall and winter, the students act as hosts to foreign pupils. Progams also exist for a semester or year abroad.

PREALPINA INTERNATIONAL SUMMER COURSE
Girls Ages 10-21.

CH-1605 Chexbres (Vaud), Switzerland. Tel. (021)561184/85. Telex: 452130 PREA CH.

Lang Study Rec Excursions.
Enr 31. US—5.
Fac 30. Full 22/Part 8. M 8; F 22. Fr.
Tui 3750 (+500) SwF. 4 wks.
Est 1925. July.
Bldg 1. Crt. Gym.

Girls from all over the world attend the summer session at Prealpina International Boarding School which combines language studies in Italian, German and Spanish as well as French and English and recreational acitivities. About two-thirds of the students come to learn French, while the remaining third study English. In the morning girls are grouped in language classes according to ability, where integrated, multimedia, audiovisual methods are employed. Afternoons, evenings and weekends are devoted to sports, hobbies and excursions.

Overlooking Lake Geneva and the Alps, Prealpina is 15 minutes from Lausanne, and about one hour from Geneva Airport.

PUTNEY STUDENT TRAVEL
Coed Ages 13-18.

Putney, VT 05346. Tel. 802-387-5885.
Peter J. Shumlin, BA, Wesleyan, Dir.
Jeffrey Shumlin, Co-Dir..
Tui $1680-4640. 4-8 wks.
Est 1952. Inc.

Putney Student Travel offers high school students about ten different summer travel plans throughout Europe, Russia, Australia and Canada. Plans include language-speaking programs, summer skiing, bicycle, sailing and hiking trips, and music and drama festivals.

SAINT MARY'S COLLEGE
Coed Ages 19-22.

Notre Dame, IN 46556. Rome Program Office, 145A Regina Hall.
Peter A. Cheeca, Coord.
Study & Travel.
Est 1970.

Saint Mary's sponsors summer study programs in Rome, Italy and Maynooth, Ireland, primarily designed for college sophomores. However, juniors and seniors who can adapt the program to their own academic sequence are accepted. In cooperation with the University of Notre Dame, Saint Mary's also sends students to France, Austria, Japan, Taiwan and Mexico. All applicants must have at least a 2.5 grade-point average, and language requirements vary with the countries students intend to visit.

SALZBURG INTERNATIONAL LANGUAGE CENTER
Bdg & Day Coed Ages 13 & up. Gr 7 & up.

A-5020 Salzburg, Austria. Moosstrasse 106. Tel. (662) 44485. Telex: 633065.
Jack E. Wenrick, MS, Illinois Institute, Dir.
Lang Stud & Travel. Tests—CEEB TOEFL. Curr—USA. LI—Eng. A—Ger Eng Russ.
Enr 77. US—19.
Fac 13. Full 12/Part 1. M 6; F 7. US Nat.
Tui Bdg $700 (+ $50); Day $600 (+ $50).
Est 1976. Inc 1981 nonprofit.
Bldgs 3. Dorms 2. Lib 5000 vols.

Affiliated with the Salzburg International Preparatory School, this center offers intensive language study in German, English and Russian. American, Asian and European students attend the two four-week sessions that are conducted from July through August. In addition to academic study, there are opportunities for summer skiing, sailing, tennis and horseback riding as well as excursions to cultural and historical points of interest.

See also pages 54-5

SPANISH WORKSHOP OF SALAMANCA
Coed Ages 15-18.

Salamanca, Mexico.
Mail to: c/o St. Stephen's Episcopal School, Box 1868, Austin, TX 78767. Tel. 443-9447.
Hildeyardo Ramirez, MA, Univ. of Texas, Dir.
Span Lang & Culture.
Tui Bdg $2400 (+ $500). 5 wks.

St. Stephen's Episcopal School sponsors this workshop which accepts high school students who have studied at least one year of Spanish. Participants live with Mexican families in Salamanca and study the language, literature, culture and history of Mexico.

STUDENTS ABROAD/CONTINENTAL FRONTIERS
Coed Ages 13-19.

Mt. Vernon, FL 10550. 179 N. Fulton St.
Edward and Ute Finn, Dirs.
Eur Travel.
Tui $1695-4200.

Students Abroad offers summer travel programs throughout Africa, Greece, Russia, Scandinavia and Yugoslavia. Activities include sailing, bicycling, camping, summer skiing and study. Continental Frontiers features domestic camping trips.

TASIS ENGLAND SUMMER SCHOOL
  Bdg & Day Coed Ages 12-18.

TASIS England, Coldharbour Lane, Thorpe, Surrey, England.
US Admissions: Rm. 110, 326 East 69th St., New York 10021. Tel. (212)
  570-1066. Telex: 971912.
Tui $850. 6 wks.

The TASIS England Summer School offers six-week, credit-based courses in a variety of academic subjects, reading and study skills, computer science, and theater. Sports, course-related trips and diverse activities are integral parts of the program.

See also page 109

UNIVERSITY OF OSLO INTERNATIONAL SUMMER SCHOOL
  Bdg Coed Ages 18 and up. PG.

Oslo 3, Norway. P.O. Box 10, Blindern. Tel. 46 48 00. Telex: 72425
  UNIOS N.
Mail to: c/o St. Olaf College, Northfield, MN 55057. Tel. 507-663-3269.
Kjetil Flatin, PhD, Univ. of Chicago, Dir.
Gen Acad. Ll—Eng. CF—Norwegian Stud Peace Research Econ
  Public Health Pol Sci.
Enr 3230. US—151.
Fac 32. M 16; F 16. Norway.
Tui $1200 (+ $250). Schol.
Est 1947. (Je-Aug).
Dorms 1. Lib. Crts. Field. Gym.

This international six-week summer program centers on various aspects of Norwegian and Scandinavian culture. Courses are conducted in Norwegian language, literature, history, art and international relations. Graduate level courses of study are available in education, urban and regional planning, and environmental studies. Applicants should be fluent in English and must have satisfactorily completed two years of college. Recreational activities include hiking, cycling, swimming, sailing and soccer. Field trips to the countryside and towns of Norway are organized.

IV.

ADDITIONAL SCHOOLS

ABROAD

The following section consists of schools for which limited information was available at time of publication. Within each country schools are arranged alphabetically by city or town. Street address or box number follows school name.

EUROPE

BELGIUM

Antwerp — E.E.C. SCHOOL. Amerikalei 131. Tel. 031.39.63.77. Bdg Coed 12-18; Day 5-18. Gr K-12. J. Wells, Head. Col Prep. Tests GCE CEEB SSAT. Ll—Eng. A—Eng Fr Math Econ. CF—Dutch Ger Comp Sci. Sl—Rem & Dev Math & Read Tut. Enr 141. Fac 23. Tui Bdg $4400 (+ $650); Day $2150 (+ $200). Schol. Est 1973. Inc. Tri (Sept-Je). Bldgs 2. Boarding arrangements can be made with French or Dutch-speaking families.

2018 Antwerp — LYCEE D'ANVERS. (College Marie José). Isabellalei 131. Tel. 239 18 89. Day Coed 2½-18. Gr N-12. A.H. Van Frachen, Dir. Col Prep. Tests IB. Ll—Fr. A—Dutch Eng Ger Math. Sl—Intensive Fr. Enr 290. B 140; G 150. Elem 240, Sec 50. Grad '84—6. Col—3. Fac 40. Full 14/Part 26. M 5; F 35. Nat. Tui $500-2500 (+ $50-400). Est 1901. Nonprofit. Bldgs 2. Lib 1500 vols. International Baccalaureate preparation is offered, with immersion French courses for non-speakers.

DENMARK

2880 Bagsvaerd — BAGSVAERD KOSTSKOLE OG GYMNASIUM. Aldershvilevej 138. Bdg & Day Coed Ages 7-20. Gr K-12. Klaus E. Jakobsen, Head. Enr 750. Sem (Aug-Je).

2100 Copenhagen — BJORNS INTERNATIONAL SCHOOL. Gartnerivej 5. Tel. (01) 292937. Day Coed 6-15. Gr 1-8. Leif Kragh, Head. Gen Acad. Curr—UK Nat. Ll—Danish Eng. CF—Ger Arts. Sl—Rem & Dev Math & Read Tut. Enr 120. B 62; G 58. Fac 15. Full 12/Part 3. M 7; F 8. US—1. Nat UK. Tui 6000 DKr. Est 1966. Inc nonprofit. Sem (Aug-Je). ISA.

2900 Hellerup — BERNADOTTESKOLEN. (The International School in Denmark). Hellerupvej 11. Day Coed 6-14. Vang Luttge, Head. Gen Acad. Ll—Danish Eng. Est 1949.

3000 Helsingor — INTERNATIONAL PEOPLE'S COLLEGE. 1, Montebello Alle. Tel. (02) 213361. Bdg Coed Ages 19 and up. Erik Hogsbro Holm, Prin. Ll—Eng. Fac 9. Full 6/Part 3. M 4; F 5. Nat. Est 1921. (Aug-May). Participants from many different countries attend. Courses are offered in humanities, international affairs, languages and the arts.

8410 Rond DK — THE KALOE SCHOOL OF LANGUAGES. Tel. (06) 371286. Bdg Coed 18 and up. Frede Ostergaard, MA, Arhus Univ., Dir. Lang Study. Enr 90. M 41; F 49. US—2. Fac 14. Full 11/Part 3. M 8; F 6. Nat. Tui 750 Dkr/wk (125 DKr/wk). Schol. Est 1952. Instruction is offered for English, German, Spanish, French and Danish.

4780 Stege/Mon — EUROPAHØJSKOLEN. Ulvshale. Tel. 03-815757. Bdg & Day Coed 18 & up. Inglof Knudsen, Prin. Col Curr—Nat. Ll—Danish. CF—Eng Fr Ger. Enr 100. B 30/10; G 50/10. US 2. Grad '84—100. Fac 14. Full 12/Part 2. M 9; F 5. Nat. Tui 775 Dkr/wk. Schol. Est 1976. Nonprofit. This Danish folk high school's philosophy is based on N.F.S. Grundvig's principles of teaching.

FINLAND

00270 Helsinki 27 — THE ENGLISH SCHOOL. Mantytie 14. Tel. 90-480 121. Day Coed 5-16. Gr K-9. Sr. Renee Brinker, Prin. Pre-Prep. Curr—Nat. Ll—Eng Finnish. Enr 403. B 203; G 200. US—8. Fac 21. Full 7/Part 14. M 4; F 17. US 7. Tui 6000 Fmk. Est 1945. Inc nonprofit. Sem (Aug-May). Lib 6779 vols. Gym.

FRANCE

13100 Aix-en-Provence — SACRE COEUR. 20 rue Lacefede. Tel. 421-38-41-32. Day Coed 5-18. Gabriel Meriau, Dir. Col Prep Gen Acad. Tri (Sept-July). Preparation for French Baccalaureate.

92100 Boulogne — COLLEGE PRIVE MIXTE SAINT JOSEPH. 6 rue du Parchamp. Tel. 605-15-40. Day Coed 10-16. Nelle Hyernard, Dir. Curr—Nat. Ll—Fr. Est 1937. Roman Catholic. Tri (Sept-Je). Students are prepared for the French BEPC.

60205 Compiegne (Oise) — INSTITUTION GUYNEMER. 1, Allee des Avenues. Tel. 420-28-02. Bdg & Day Boys Ages 5-19; Day Girls 11-19. Gr N-PG. M. le Chanoine Coulaud, Dir. Pre-Prep Col Prep Gen Acad. Curr—Nat. Ll—Fr. Est 1939. Roman Catholic. Tri (Sept-Je).

Fontainebleau 77300 (Seine & Marne) — LYCEE PRIVÉ SAINT-ASPAIS. 18, Boulevard Maginot. Tel. 6-422-24-89. Bdg Boys 11-18; Day Coed 11-18. Gr 5-12. C. Lavocat, Dir. Col Prep Gen Acad. Curr—Nat. Ll—Fr. CF—Eng Ger Span. Enr 640. B 130/420; G/90. Fac 36. Full 23/Part 13. M 12; F 24. Fr. Tui Bdg 13,000-15,000 Fr (+ 1000 Fr); Day 3000-3500 Fr (+ 500 Fr). Schol. Est 1928. Nonprofit. Tri (Sept-Je). Bldgs 3. Dorms 2. Lib. Gym. Fields.

69002 Lyon — INSTITUT DE LANGUE ET DE CULTURE FRAN-CAISES. 25 rue du Plat. Tel. (7) 842-10-30. Day Coed 18 and up. Ch. Jaquinod, Dir. Lang Study. Enr 500. US—39. Tui 1200 Fr/3 mos. Est l948. Tri (Oct-Je). 2 libs 300,000 vols. Instruction in French at all levels.

78600 Maisons-Lafitte — L'ERMITAGE. 46, Avenue Egle. Tel. 962 0402. Bdg Coed 6-18; Day Coed 3-18. Gr N-PG. Anne Marie Thommeret, Head. Gen Acad. Ll—Fr. CF—Eng Ger Span Lat Math Sci Hist Geog Art. Sl—Tut. Enr 1200. Fac 75. Tui Bdg $2000/term; Day $200/term. Est 1941. Tri (Sept-July). Bldgs 8. Dorms 5. Lib 2000 vols. An extensive extracurricular program includes horseback riding, tennis, squash, photography, ballet, theatre, judo, track, rugby and soccer.

75018 Paris — INSTITUTION SAINTE THERESE. 1 rue Boinod. Tel. 606-98-67. Bdg & Day Coed 3-18. Gen Acad. Curr—Nat. Ll—Fr. CF—Eng Span Ger. Sl—Eng. Tri (Sept-Je).

75116 Paris — LYCEE PRIVES VICTOR HUGO. 8, Rue Benjamin-Godard. Tel. 727-58-04. Day Boys 3-10, Girls 3-17. Gr K-12. Caroline Besson, Dir. Col Prep Gen Acad. Curr—Nat. Ll—Fr. CF—Eng Span Ital Russ Ger Lat Greek Philos Hist Geog Nat Sci Econ. Enr 400. B 20; G 380. Grad '84—50. Tui $250/term. Tri (Sept-July).

06700 St. Laurent-du-Var — AMERICAN INTERNATIONAL SCHOOL ON THE COTE D'AZUR. Quartier de la Tour, La Baronne. Tel. (93) 312097. Day Coed 4-18. Gr K-12. Richard Graham, BS, Princeton, MBA, Berkeley, Head. Pre-Prep Col Prep Gen Acad. Tests GCE CEEB SSAT TOEFL. Curr—US. Ll—Eng. A—Hist Eng Sci Calc. CF—Fr Math Soc Stud Comp. Sl—ESL. Enr 150. B 87; G 63. Elem 91, Sec 59. Grad '84—20. Col—17. Fac 14. M 6; F 8. US 6. Tui 23,000-27,500 Fr. Schol. Est l977. Inc nonprofit. Tri (Sept-Je). ECIS ISS.

24200 Sariat (Dordogne) — ECOLE LIBRE SAINT JOSEPH. Blvd. Eugene Leroy. Tel. 59-15-92. Bdg & Day Coed 11-19. Gr 6-12. Henri Tournier-Lasserve, Dir. Col Prep. Curr—Nat. Ll—Fr. Est 1850. Inc nonprofit. Roman Catholic. Tri (Sept-Je).

92310 Sevres — COLLEGE DE SEVRES. 20 bis, rue du Dr. Ledermann. Tel. 534.75.27. Day Coed 11-15. Gr 6-9. Monique Blampuy, Prin. Pre-Prep. Tests IB. Curr—Nat. LI—Fr. CF—Eng Ger Greek Lat Span Russ. SI—Rem & Dev Math & Read. Tui $500. Est 1960. This program offers preparation for the French and International Baccalaureates.

Strasbourg — COLLEGE LUCIE BERGER. 10 rue St. Marc. Tel. (88) 35.47.15. Bdg Girls 6-18, Day 3-18. Gr N-12. Edith Rouverand, Head. Gen Acad. Curr—Nat. LI—Fr. Est 1872. Tri (Sept-Je).

GERMANY

Dahlenburg (Luneburg) — SCHULE MARIENAU. 2121 Dahlem. Tel. 05851/517. Bdg Coed 10-20. Gunter Fischer, Dir. Gen Acad. Curr—Nat. LI—Ger. CF—Eng Fr Lat Russ. A—Bio Chem Math Physics Hist Soc. SI—Rem & Dev Read. Enr 276. B 77/97; G 33/69. Elem 93, Sec 146, PG 37. Grad '84—37. Col—35. Tui Bdg DM 1920 (+DM 150/mo). Est 1929. Nonprofit. Sem (Aug-July). Bldgs 12. Dorms 9. Lib 6253 vols. Gym. Pool. Crts. Fields.

6417 Hofbieber 6 (Hessen) — HERMANN LIETZ-SCHULE. Schols Bieberstein. Tel. 6657/8072. Bdg Coed Ages 11-19. Gr 5-PG. Ulrich Kindscher, Dir. Gen Acad. Tests GCE. Curr—Natl. LI—Ger. CF—Eng Fr Lat Physics Soc Stud Math Chem Biol Ecology Home Econ. Enr 200. B 130; G 70. Grad '84—35. Col—32. Fac 26. Full 23/Part 3. M 19; F 7. Nat. Tui 1770 DM (+200 DM). Schol. Est 1904. Nonprofit. Sem (Feb-July). Bldgs 5. Lib 8000 vols. Fields. Tennis crts. Swimming pool. A branch campus of this school is located at Schols Hohenwehrda, 6419 Haunetal 1.

7842 Kandern 1 — BLACK FOREST ACADEMY. Postfach 1109. Tel. 07626 7740. Bdg Coed 13-19; Day Coed 6-19. Gr 1-12. Henry J. Toews, BA, BEd, Univ. of Manitoba, Prin. Gen Acad. Tests SSAT. Curr—Can. LI—Eng. CF—Ger Fr Soc Stud. Bible. SI—Rem & Dev Math & Read Tut Music. Enr 300. B 50/90; G 60/100. US—85. Grad '84—29 Col—25. Fac 26. Full 21/Part 5. M 13; F 13. US 8. Can. Tui Bdg $4200 (+$300); Day $2200 (+$400). Est 1970. Inc nonprofit. Quar (Sept-Je). Bldgs 7. Dorms 5. Lib 10,000 vols. Gym. Fields.

4531 Lotte 1 (Kreis Tecklenburg) — KRUGER SCHOOLS. Sennlicher Weg 4-6. Bdg & Day Coed 15-22. Gr 8-PG. Eberhard Mittag, Dir. Col Prep Gen Acad Bus. Tests—IB. LI—Ger. CF—Eng Fr Span Bus Admin Relig. SI—Tut. Enr 200. B 70/50; G 40/40. Elem 120, Sec 80. Grad '84—60. Fac 16. Ger. Est 1945. Inc nonprofit. ISA. Bldgs 3. Lib 3000 vols. Gym. Tennis crt.

8175 Reichersbeueru — MAX-RILL SCHULE. Schlossweg 1. Tel. 08041-6041. Bdg & Day Girls 10-19. Fritz Funk, Dir. Gen Acad. Ll—Ger. Est 1936. Nonprofit. Sem (Sept-July).

GREECE

Thessaloniki — AMERICAN FARM SCHOOL. (Thessaloniki Agricultural and Industrial Institute). P.O. Box 140. Tel. 411-522. Bdg Coed 15-18. Gr 10-12. Bruce M. Lansdale, Dir. Voc Agriculture. Curr—Nat. Ll—Greek. Enr 200. Fac 14. Nat. Tui 500 Dr. Schol. Est 1902. Inc 1904 nonprofit. Sem (Sept-May).

Thessaloniki — THE INSTITUTE FOR BALKAN STUDIES INTERNATIONAL SUMMER SCHOOL. Tsimiski 45. Tel. 225.365. Bdg Coed 18 and up. Prof. K. Mitsakis, Dir. Greek Lang Hist & Culture. 4 wks. (Aug). Tui $600 (+ var). Weekend excursions to various parts of northern Greece are conducted.

HUNGARY

1051 Budapest — BRITISH EMBASSY SCHOOL, BUDAPEST. Harmincad Utca 6. Tel. (1) 182-888. Day Coed 5-11. Gr K-5. Gen Acad. Curr—UK. Ll—Eng. CF—Fr Lat Math Sci. Tui £220. Nonprofit. Tri (Sept-July).

IRELAND

Drogheda County Louth — DROGHEDA GRAMMAR SCHOOL. Tel. (041) 8281. Bdg & Day Coed 11½-18. Gr 7-12. John Siberry, MA, HDE, Head. Col Prep. Gen Acad. Curr—Nat. Ll—Eng. CF—Fr Irish Math Sci Eng. Enr 168. Fac 17. Ireland. Tui Bdg £1200 (+ £150); Day £435 (+ £75). Est 1669. Nonprofit. Tri (Sept-Je). Bldgs 3. Dorm. Lib. Athletic facilities. Located on 22 acres of wooded land, the Drogheda Grammar School prepares students of several nationalities for university entrance.

6 Dublin (Dun Laoghaire) — GLENGARA PARK SCHOOL. Glenageary Rd. Tel. Dublin 801423. Bdg Girls 8-18, Day 4-18. Gr N-12. Mrs. Ann Schofield, Head. Col Prep Gen Acad. Curr—Nat. Ll—Eng. Est 1928. Tri (Jan-Dec).

Dublin 6 — RATHGAR JUNIOR SCHOOL AND KINDERGARTEN. 62/63 Grosvenor Rd. Rathmines. Tel. 972411. Day Coed 4-12. Gr N-6. E. Heather Bewley, Head. Pre-Prep. Curr—Nat. Ll—Eng. CF—Irish Fr Hist Math Bible Art Environ Stud. Enr 135. B 75; G 60. Fac 9. Nat. Tui £600 (£20). Est 1919. Nonprofit. Tri (Sept-Je).

Dublin — SUTTON PARK SCHOOL. Tel. 01-322079. Bdg & Day Coed 5-18. Gr K-12. Laurence Finnegan, MEd, Dublin, Dir. Col Prep. Tests GCE CEEB SSAT. Curr—Nat UK. LI—Eng. CF—Fr Ger Ital Physics. SI—Tut. Enr 331. Elem 245, Sec 86. Grad '84—25. Col—20. Fac 30. Full 25/Part 5. M 15; F 15. US 2. Nat. Tui Bdg $3500 (+ $500); Day $1500 (+ $200). Est 1957. Nonprofit. Tri (Sept-Je). ECIS. Bldgs 10. Dorms 8. Lib. Fields. Tennis crts. Gym. Pool. Sutton Park's curriculum features advanced courses in languages, biology, chemistry and physics.

ITALY

Florence — CULTURAL CENTRE FOR FOREIGNERS. Via Vittorio Emanuele 64. Tel. 055/472139. Day Coed 18 and up. Salvo Mastellone, Dir. 200,000-250,000 Lire/crse. Est 1907. Year-round study of Italian language, culture, literature and history of art.

50126 Florence 34 — AMERICAN ACADEMY OF FLORENCE. Ponte a Ema.Via Di Vacciano 32. Tel. (055) 640016. Day Coed 2½-20. Gr N-12. Michael De Lisio, BS, John Carroll Univ., Dir. Pre-Prep Col Prep. Tests CEEB SSAT. Curr—USA Nat. LI—Eng. A—Math Physics Comp Sci. CF—Eng Ital Fr Span Ger Math Biol Hist Chem. SI—Tut Rem & Dev Read & Math. Enr 20. Fac 9. Est 1978. Inc nonprofit. Sem (Sept-Je). Lib 1000 vols. Crts. The American Academy offers a bilingual kindergarten program as well as middle and upper school courses which prepare students for university entrance.

65013 Marina di Citta' Sant'Angelo (Pescara) — PANTERRA AMERICAN SCHOOL. Contr. S. Martino 35. Tel. 085-27216. Day Coed 5-13. Gr K-8. Virginia Simpson, MEd, Dir. Gen Acad. Curr—USA, LI—Eng. CF—ESL Ital. SI—Rem & Dev Math & Read. Enr 12. B 6; G 6. Fac 4. Full 2/Part 2. Intl. Tui $7700. Est 1981. Inc. (Sept-Je). ECIS ISS. Bldg. Lib 2000 vols. Field. Gym. This school was established to meet the educational needs of foreign children in the Pescara region.

Rome 00189 — THE ACADEMY SCHOOL OF ROME. Via di Grottarossa 295. Tel. (06)366-6071. Bdg & Day Coed 3-13. Gr N-8. Joan Bulgarini, Head. Curr—Intl USA UK. LI—Eng. CF—Ital Lang Arts Math Sci Humanities Art Music. SI—Rem & Dev Read & Math Tut. Enr 56. B 30; G 26. Fac 7. M 1; F 6. US 2. UK. ECIS ISS. Bldgs 4. Libs 3. Gym. Fields 2.

00178 Rome — AMBRIT INTERNATIONAL SCHOOL, S.R.L.. Via Annia Regilla 60. Tel. 06/7992907. Day Coed 3-11. Gr N-6. Valerie Laws, Dir. Gen Acad. Ll—Eng. CF—Ital. Sl—Rem & Dev Math & Read. Enr 120. B 60; G 60. Fac 12. Full 8/Part 4. M 1; F 11. US 3. UK. Tui 3,500,000 Lit. Est 1982. Sem (Sept-Je).

Rome — GREENWOOD GARDEN SCHOOL. Via Vito Sinis 5. Tel. 06-366-6703. Day Coed 2¹/₂-6. Gr N-K. Donna Seibert Ricci, BA, Pennsylvania State Univ., Dir. Pre-School. Curr—USA. Ll—Eng. Enr 35. Fac 7. Full 5/Part 1. M 2; F 5. US 2. Tui 4,000,000 Lire (+250,000 Lire). Est 1974. Tri (Sept-Je). Specific readiness skills are developed at this American-type nursery school and kindergarten, including alphabet recognition, pre-reading exercises, mathematics, writing skills and extended verbal development.

00189 Rome — L'INSTITUT ST. DOMINIQUE. Via Cassia 1173. Tel. 3765117. Bdg Girls 10-18; Day Coed 3-11, Girls 3-18. Gr N-12. Sr. Marie Joannes, Dir. Ll—Fr. CF—Eng Ger Span Ital Lat.

Rome 00123 — INTERNATIONAL SCHOOL OF ROME. Via Della Storta 111. Bdg Coed 7-14; Day 2¹/₂-14 Gr N-8. Mrs. Katherine S. Harris, Dir. Gen Acad. Curr—USA. Ll—Eng. Est 1972. Sem (Sept-Je). ISS.

Rome 00189 — KENDALE PRIMARY INTERNATIONAL SCHOOL. Via Gradoli, 86 - Km. 10,300 Cassia. Tel. 3667608. Day Coed 3-10. Gr N-5. Veronica Tani, Head. Curr—UK USA. Ll—Eng. CF—Math Soc Stud Music Fr Ital Sl—Rem & Dev Read & Math. Enr 49. B 42; G 47. US 20. Fac 13. Full 7/Part 6. M 2; F 11. US—2 UK. Tui $2603 (+$100). Est 1971. Tri (Sept-Je).

Rome 00197 — MONTI PARIOLI ENGLISH SCHOOL. Via Dei Monti Parioli 50. Day Coed 2-10. Gr N-5. Lynette Surtees, Head. Enr 140. B 60; G 80. Fac 12. UK. Tui 3,500,000-6,500,000 Lire.

00134 Rome — SUMMERFIELD SCHOOL. Via Tito Poggi 21. Tel. 6009227. Day Coed 3-8. Gr N-3. Ann Fremantle Morgia, Dir. Gen Acad. Curr—UK. Ll—Eng. CF—Ital. Est 1971. Tri (Sept-Je).

Venice — THE INTERNATIONAL SCHOOL OF VENICE. The British Centre, S. Marco, 4267A. Day Coed 5-11. Gr K-4. John Millerchip, BA, Wales, Dir. Gen Acad. Curr—UK. Ll—Eng. CF—Ital Fr. Enr 30. B 15; G 15. Fac 4. Full 2/Part 2. UK. Tui 4,000,000 lit. Est 1978. Nonprofit. Tri (Sept-Je).

MALTA

Cottonera — **VERDALA INTERNATIONAL SCHOOL.** Tel. 821414. Telex: 1630 REBAT. Day Coed 4-18; Bdg 16-18. Gr K-12. Michael A. Kelly, Head. Pre-Prep Col Prep. Tests GCE SSAT. Curr—USA. LI—Eng. CF—Eng Ital Fr Span Maltese Sci Hist Math Bus. SI—Rem & Dev Read & Math. Enr 60. B /9; G 2/44. Elem 25, Sec 35. US—7. Grad '84—5. Col—3. Fac 16. Full 14/Part 2. M 6; F 10. Tui Bdg $2500 (+ $1000); Day $4300 (+ $150). Schol. Est 1976. Sem (Sept-Je). ECIS. Bldgs 6. Athletic facilities.

THE NETHERLANDS

2252 BG Voorschoten — **BRITISH SCHOOL IN THE NETHER-LANDS.** Jan Van Hooflaan 3. Tel. 01717-4492. Day Coed 5-18. Brian D. Davidson, MA, Oxon, Head. Tests GCE. Curr—UK. LI—Eng. CF—Fr Span Ger Dutch Math Econ Physics. Enr 1116. Fac 68. UK. Nonprofit. Tri (Sept-July). ECIS.

NORWAY

1340 Bekkestua — **OSLO AMERICAN SCHOOL.** Tel. 53 23 03. Day Coed 5-15. Gr K-10. Mail to: APO New York, NY 09085. Harold Haggard, BA, Univ. of Tennessee, MA, Michigan State Univ., Prin. Col Prep Gen Acad. Curr—USA. LI—Eng. CF—Nor Fr. SI—Rem Read. Enr 240. Elem 200, Sec 40. Fac 19. Full 15/Part 4. M 9; F 10. US. Tui $4500. Est 1956. Inc nonprofit. Sem (Aug-Je). Bldgs 1. Lib 8000 vols. Athletic facilities.

Bergen — **BERGEN AMERICAN SCHOOL.** Vilhelm Bjerknesvei 15 5030 Landas. Tel. 5 287716. Day Coed 5-16. Gr K-9. Richard L. Gillogly, Dir. Pre-Prep. Curr—USA. LI—Eng. CF—Fr Nor. Enr 25. Fac 6. Tui $10,000. Schol. Est 1975. Sem (Aug-Je). ECIS ISS. Enrollment is open to all English-speaking children in the Bergen area.

Bergen (Hordaland) — **FANA FOLKEHOGSKOLE.** N-5067 Store Milde. Tel. 05-22 6603. Bdg Coed 18-30. Haakon Smeosvig Hanssen, Prin. Col Prep Gen Acad. Curr—Nat. LI—Nor. CF —Ceramics Textiles Ecol Media Drama. Est 1915. Nonprofit. Sem (Aug-May).

4032 Gausel — **THE STAVANGER BRITISH SCHOOL.** Gausel-bakken 107. Tel. (04)575599. Day Coed $4\frac{1}{2}$-11. Gr N-6. Zelma Roisli, Prin. Gen Acad. Tests CEE. Curr—UK. LI—Eng. CF—Fr Math Hist Sci Art Geog Nature Music SI—Rem & Dev Math & Read. Enr 130. Fac 21. US—3. UK. Tui 35,000 NKr. Est 1977. Inc Nonprofit. Tri (Aug-Je). ECIS. Lib 3000 vols.

3810 Gvarv (Telemark) — SAGAVOLL FOLK HIGH SCHOOL. Tel. 036-64-135. Bdg Coed 18-21. Marton Leine, Rector. Gen Acad. Curr—Nat. Ll—Eng Nor. Enr 125. B 45; G 80. US—5. Fac 22. Full 11/Part 11. M 14; F 8. US 3. Tui $2300 (+ $100). Schol. Est 1893. Inc Nonprofit. Bldgs 2. Dorms 5. Lib 6500 vols. This folk school offers courses in mass media, music and nature and the environment.

1500 Moss (Jeloy) — JELOY FOLKEHOGSKOLE. Tel. (032) 71 211. Bdg Coed 17-25. Fred-Arne Odegaard, Prin. Col Prep Gen Acad. Curr—Nat. Ll—Eng Nor. CF—Music Arts Soc Stud Leadership Trng Computing. Est 1974. Nonprofit. Sem (Aug-May).

1850 Mysen (Ostfold) — BONDELAGETS FOLKEHOGSKOLE. Tel. 02/89 02 44. Bdg Coed 17-25. Johan Hovedalen, Rector. Col Prep. Ll—Nor. CF—Soc Agriculture Econ Psych Journalism. Sl—Nor. Est 1950. Sem (Aug-May).

Os (at Bergen) — KONGSHAUG FOLKEHOGSKOLE. 5220 Hagavik. Tel. 05-305450. Bdg & Day Coed 16-25. Asbjorn Tveiten, Rector. Curr—Nat. Ll—Nor. CF—Arts Theol Music Soc Stud. Est 1964. Nonprofit. Norwegian Lutheran Mission. Sem (Aug-May).

Oslo 2 — BIRKLEA BRITISH SCHOOL. Skovveven 9. Margaret Stark, Head. ECIS.

N-2630 Ringebu — RINGEBU FOLKEHOGSKOLE. Tel. 062-80166. Bdg Coed 17-30. Adne Svendsen, Prin. Gen Acad. Curr—Nat. Ll—Nor. CF—Eng Ger Psych Relig Geog Health Stud Home Econ Ecology. Sl—Skiing Mountaineering. Enr 68. B 20; G 48. US—3. Tui $2000 (+ $1000). Est 1876. Nonprofit. Sem (Aug-May). Bldgs 3. Dorms 3. Lib 4000 vols. Athletic facilities. Foreign students may receive instruction in Norwegian.

7100 Rissa — FOSEN FOLKEHOGSKOLE. Tel. 076-51260. Bdg Coed 18-35. Jon Godal, Rector. Curr—Nat. Ll—Nor. CF—Agriculture Nature Handicrafts. Enr 50. B 15; G 35. Sec 3, PG 47. US—2. Fac 9. Full 7/Part 2. M 7; F 2. Nat. Tui $2000 (+ var). Est 1876. Nonprofit. Sem (Aug-Je). Bldgs 2. Lib 2000 vols. Athletic facilities. Located on the Trondheimsfjord. General education, both theoretical and practical, is offered, as well as outdoor activities.

Trondheim 7000 — BIRRALEE INTERNATIONAL SCHOOL. Bispegate 9c. Tel. (07) 52 16 44. Day Coed 4-13. Gr N-8. Margot Tonseth, Prin. Gen Acad. Curr—Nat. Ll—Eng. CF—Fr Lat Norwegian. Sl—Tut. Enr 66. B 36; G 30. US 20. Fac 9. Full 5/Part 4. F 9. US 3. UK. Tui $2000. Est 1973. Nonprofit. Sem (Aug-Je). ECIS. Birralee is part of a Norwegian primary school and there are many bilingual academic and extracurricular opportunities.

POLAND

Warsaw — AMERICAN SCHOOL OF WARSAW. (Poznan Branch). Tel. 43757. Day Coed. Gr K-6. Mail to: c/o American Consulate General (Warsaw), APO, New York, NY 09757. Gen Acad. Curr—USA. LI—Eng. Sem (Sept-Je).

PORTUGAL

Alvalade (Lisbon) 5 — QUEEN ELIZABETH'S SCHOOL. Rua Filipe Magalhaes 4. Day Coed 4-11. Gr K-8. Gen Acad. Curr—Nat UK. LI—Eng Port. Est 1935. Proprietary. Tri (Sept-Je).

Cascais — ST. GEORGE'S SCHOOL. Villa Goncalves, Quinta das Louieiras. Tel. 28 00 86. Day Coed 3-13. Gr N-9. M. P. B. Hoare, Head. Gen Acad. Curr—UK. LI—Eng. Est 1960. Inc. Tri (Sept-Je).

1200 Lisbon — KINDERGARTEN. Rua Da Arriaga, No. 11-13. Tel. 661841. Day Coed 3-6. Gr N-1. Rita Croft de Moura, Head. LI—Eng. CF—Read Writing Music Painting. Est 1955. Tri (Oct-Je).

SPAIN

Alicante — THE SIERRA BERNIA SCHOOL. La Caneta.San Rafael.Alfaz del Pi. Tel. 889449. Day Coed 3-18. Duncan M. Allan, Dir. Pre-Prep Gen Acad. Tests GCE. Curr—UK. LI—Eng. CF—Fr Span Eng. Enr 160. B 80; G 80. US—5. Grad '84—15. Col—10. Fac 13. Full 11/Part 2. M 3; F 10. US 1. UK. Tui 120,000 pts (+ 20,000 pts). Est 1973. Nonprofit. Tri (Sept-July). Lib. Athletic facilities.

Barcelona — KENSINGTON SCHOOL. Carretera De Esplugas.86 Bis (Pedralbes). Day Coed 5-18. Gr K-12. Edward Paul Giles, Head. Col Prep. Tests CEEB GCE. Curr—USA UK. LI—Eng. CF—Fr Span Hist Sci. Est 1967. Inc. Tri (Sept—Je).

Barcelona 17 — ST. PAUL'S SCHOOL. Martorell y Pena 9. Tel. 2030500. Day Coed 4-14. Gr N-8. Ricardo Pons, Dir. Pre-Prep. Curr—Nat. LI—Eng Span. Tri (Sept-Je).

Gibraltar — LORETO CONVENT. 13 Europa Rd. Tel. 75781. Day Coed 3-12. Gr N-7. Sr. Anne McWilliams, Head. Pre-Prep Gen Acad. Tests CEE. Curr—UK. LI—Eng. CF—Eng Fr Span Math Hist Sci Relig. Sl—Tut Rem & Dev Read & Math. Enr 200. B 50; G 150. Fac 16. Full 9/Part 7. M 1; F 15. UK. Tui £300 (+ £15). Est 1845. Inc 1945 nonprofit. Tri (Sept-July). Bldgs 2. Lib. Crts.

Madrid 23 — THE ENGLISH MONTESSORI SCHOOL. Eduardo Vela, 10. Tel. 457-42-22. Day Coed 2-10. Gr NK-5. Milagros King, Prin. Gen Acad. Curr—UK. LI—Eng. CF—Span. Enr 350. B 175; G 175. Fac 26. Full 25/Part 1. M 4; F 22. US 5 UK. Tui 50,100-57,000 pts. Schol. Est 1975. Inc. Tri (Sept-Je). ECIS ISS. Bldgs 3. Lib 600 vols. Gym.

28022 Madrid — EVANGELICAL CHRISTIAN ACADEMY. Calle Talia, 26. Tel. 741-2900. Day Coed 5-17. Gr K-12. Larry S. Thornburg, MDiv, Los Angeles Baptist Theological Seminary, Prin. Col Prep. Tests CEEB SSAT. Curr—US. LI—Eng. CF—Fr Span Relig. Enr 80. B 40; G 40. Elem 55, Sec 25. US—75. Fac 12. Full 9/Part 3. M 3; F 9. US. Tui 112,000-263,000 Pts (+15,000 Pts). Est 1973. Nonprofit. Sem (Sept-Je). This school was founded to provide a Christian education to children of the evangelical English-speaking missionary community.

Madrid 28002 — INTERNATIONAL PRIMARY SCHOOL. Madre Carmen del Nino Jesus 3. El Viso. Tel. 259 21 21. Day Coed 5-11. Gr N-5. Anne Mazon, Prin. Gen Acad. Curr—USA UK. LI—Eng. SI—Rem & Dev Read EFL. Enr 120. B 55; G 65. Fac 22. Full 12/Part 10. M 7; F 15. US 4. UK. Tui 48,000-84,000 pts (+30,000 pts). Est 1971. Proprietary. Tri (Sept-Je). ECIS. Lib 7500 vols.

Puerto de Santa Maria (Cadiz) — THE ENGLISH CENTRE. Apartado 85. Tel. 956 850560. Day Coed 4-14. Gr N-9. Linda M. Randell, Dir. Pre-Prep. LI—Eng Span. SI—Rem & Dev Math & Read Tut. Enr 400. B 200; G 200. Elem 380, Sec 20. Fac 23. Full 23. M 10; F 13. Nat UK. Tui 8000 Pts/mo. Est 1968. Tri (Sept-Je). The English Centre specializes in English and Spanish language study.

San Carlos (Ibiza, Balearic Islands) — MORNA VALLEY SCHOOL. Apartado 95. Day Coed 3-16. Gr N-12. Mary Blakstad, BA, Univ. of British Columbia, Dir. Col Prep. Tests GCE. Curr—UK. A—Eng Lit Hist Art Span. CF—Span Fr Ger. SI—Rem & Dev Read. Enr 93. B 51; G 42. US—10. Grad '84—5. Fac 13. Full 10/Part 3. M 6; F 7. UK. Tui 150,000 Pts. Est 1974. Nonprofit. Tri (Sept-Je). Bldgs 2. Lib. Crts.

SWITZERLAND

1204 Geneva — ECOLE SCHULZ. Quai de l'Ile, 15. Tel. 022/28. 70.91. Day Coed 16-65. Hartmut Bunde, PhD, Prin. Est 1943. Tri (Sept-Je).

1003 Lausanne — ECOLE DE LANGUE ANGLAIS. Chemin de Mornex 11. Tel. (021) 232330. Day Coed 15 & up. Trevor P. Bent, Dir. Lang Stud. Enr 100. Fac 9. Full 6/Part 3. M 4; F 5. Tui 930-4080 SwF. Est 1964. Tri (Jan-Dec). Private and group lessons are offered in English, French, German, Spanish and Italian.

1001 Lausanne (Vaud) — ECOLE LEMANIA. Chemin de Preville 3. Tel. 20-15-01. Bdg Boys 16-20; Day Coed 10-20. Col Prep. Curr—Nat Fr. Ll—Fr. CF—Eng Rom Lang Ger Hist Pol Sci Econ Bus Typ Tech. Est 1908.

CH-1012 Lausanne (Vaud) — ECOLE NOUVELLE DE LA SUISSE ROMANDE. Rovereaz 20. Tel. 021/32.11.22. Bdg Boys 6-20, Girls 6-14; Day Coed 3-20. Francois Zbinden, Dir. Col Prep. Tests CEEB GCE IB. Ll—Eng Fr. CF—Eng Ger Greek Ital Lat Persian Span Econ Philos Arts. Enr 520. B 53/305; G 17/145. US—10. Fac 53. Full 41/Part 10. M 31; F 22. US 1. Nat. Tui Bdg $7000 (+ $1200); Day $4000 (+ $300). Est 1902. Inc nonprofit. Tri (Sept-Je). Bldgs 8. Dorms 3. 2 Libs 3000 vols. Aud. Gym. Fields. Tennis crts 2. Preparation is offered for the U.S. College Boards, British G.C.E., International Baccalaureate and the Swiss Federal Maturity. Emphasis is placed on the study of French. Coordinate programs are conducted with International School Brillantmont.

1003 Lausanne (Vaud) — WESSEX ACADEMY. Rue de Bourg 43. Tel. (021) 235436/37. Day Coed 14 & up. Jacqueline Fasnacht, Dir. Lang Stud. Tests GCE. CF—Eng Ger Fr Ital Span. Enr 250. B 100; G 150. Fac 15. Full 6/Part 9. M 2; F 13. Nat. Tui Bdg 1000-1650 SwF (+ 300 SwF); Day 500-650 SwF (+ 400 SwF). Est 1976. Tri (Jan-Dec). Year-round language instruction. Living accommodations arranged with local families.

CH 1814 La Tour-de-Peilz (Vaud) — INSTITUT MATIN CALME. Route de Sainte Maurice 130. Tel. (021) 54-01-61. Bdg Girls 14-22. Gr 9-12. Mrs. A. Vaucher, Head. Secretarial & Langs. Tests GCE. Curr—Nat. Ll—Eng Fr. CF—Eng Ger Span Ital Russian Music Art Cookery Dressmaking Typing Shorthand Athletics. Enr 48. Fac 20. Switz Fr. Tui 20,685 SwF (+ 1000 SwF). Est 1960. Tri (Sept-Je). Bldgs 2. Lib. Lab. Students gain a practical knowledge of the French language and Swiss culture.

1222 Vesenaz (Geneva) — GENEVA ENGLISH SCHOOL. 11 Chemin des rayes. Tel. 52 24 02. Day Coed 4-12. Gr N-6. D. Unsworth, MA, Reading Univ., Head. Gen Acad. Curr—UK. Ll—Eng. CF—Fr. Enr 165. B 80; G 85. Fac 11. Full 7/Part 4. M 2; F 9. UK. Tui 7500 SwF. Est 1961. Nonprofit. Tri (Sept-Je). ISA. Bldgs 2. Lib 5000 vols.

UNITED KINGDOM

ENGLAND

Ascot (Berkshire) SL5 9JF — ST. MARY'S CONVENT. Tel. (0990) 23721. Bdg & Day Girls 10-18. Mark Orchard, BA, London Univ., Head. Tests GCE. CF—Ger Fr Ital Span Relig Hist Geog Sci Ballet Fencing. Enr 315. G 300/15. Fac 50. Full 29/Part 21. M 3; F 47. Nat. Tui Bdg £1400 (+£50); Day £840 (+£20). Est 1885. Tri (Sept-Je). Bldgs 10. Dorms 4. Libs 4. Athletic facilities.

Birmingham B29 6LJ — WOODBROOKE COLLEGE. 1046 Bristol Rd., Selly Oak. Tel. 021-472-5171. Roland Ellis, Warden.

Bristol BS8 3JH — CLIFTON COLLEGE. 32, College Rd. Tel. 35945. Bdg & Day Boys 7-18. Gr 1-12. Mr. S. M. Andrews, MA (Cantab), Head. Col Prep. Tests GCE. Curr—Nat. Ll—Eng. A—Lang Hist Art. CF—Fr Span Ger Lat Sci Business. Sl—Rem & Dev Math & Read. Enr 670. Fac 76. M 68; F 8. US 1. UK. Tui Bdg £1710/term (+£100); Day £1175/term (+£75).Schol. Est 1862. Nonprofit. Tri (Sept-July). Dorms 11. Libs. Gym. Pool. Fields.

Buckingham (Buckinghamshire) MK18 5EH — STOWE SCHOOL. Tel. 0280 813164. Bdg & Day Boys 13-18; Girls 16-18. Gr 9-PG. C.G.Turner, Head. Col Prep Gen Acad. Tests GCE. Curr—Nat. Ll—Eng. CF—Fr Lat Greek Ger Span Russ. Sl—Rem Math & Eng Tut. Enr 622. B 565/5; G 40/12. Grad '84—135. Col—80. Fac 86. Full 63/Part 23. M 72; F 14. UK. Tui Bdg £7000 (+£500); Day £4700 (+£900). Est 1923. Tri (Sept-July).

Cambridge CB2 2QF — THE PERSE SCHOOL. Hills Rd. Tel. 248127. Bdg Boys 11-18, Day 7-18. Mr. A. E. Melville, Head. Col Prep. Tests GCE. Ll—Eng. A—Fr Lat Greek Hist Ger Math Chem Bio. Enr 460. B 60/400. US—2. Fac 32. M 29; F 3. UK. Est 1615. Tri (Sept-July).

Canterbury (Kent) CT 1 — THE KING'S SCHOOL, CANTERBURY. Bdg Boys. The Rev. P. Pilkington, Head.

Caterham (Surrey) CR3 6YA — CATERHAM SCHOOL. Harestone Valley. Tel. (0883)43028. Bdg & Day Boys 8-18; Day Girls 16-18. Gr 3-12. S. R. Smith, MA, Emmanuel College, Cantab, Head. Pre-Prep Gen Acad. Tests GCE. Curr—UK. Ll—Eng. CF—Fr Ger Math Sci Hist Relig. Enr 658. B 200/430; G /28. US—5. Grad '84—70. Col—56. Fac 53. Full 52/Part 1. M 49; F 4. UK. Tui Bdg £864-1194 (+£25); Day £420-654 (+£25). Schol. Est 1811. Nonprofit. Tri (Sept-July). Dorms 3. Lib. Gym. Pool. Crts.

Cobham (Kent) — COBHAM HALL. Bdg & Day Girls 11-18. Gr 7-PG. Mr. C. J. Dixon, BA, Cantab, Head. Col Prep Gen Acad. Curr—Nat. Ll—Eng. CF—Fr Ger Span Ital Russ. Est 1962. Nonprofit. Tri (Sept-Je).

County Durham DL2 2AD — HURWORTH HOUSE SCHOOL. The Green, Hurworth on Tees, Darlington. Tel. (0325) 720645. Bdg Boys 8-13, Day 4-13. Gr N-8. Graham N. Burgess, MA, Head. Pre-Prep. Curr—UK. Ll—Eng. CF—Fr Lat Scripture Comp Stud. Sl—Rem & Dev Math & Read. Enr 173. B 35/138. Fac 20. Full 11/Part 9. M 11; F 9. UK. Tui Bdg £820/term; Day £330-545/term. Est 1946. Inc 1970 nonprofit. Tri (Sept-Je). Bldgs 5. Dorms 4. Lib. Field. Tennis crt. Pool. The British-based curriculum at Hurworth prepares boys for the Common Entrance Exam. Academics are complemented by activities in carpentry, cricket, music, rugby, soccer and squash.

Cranbrook (Kent) TN 174AA — BENENDEN SCHOOL. Tel. (0580) 240592. Bdg Girls 11-18. Miss J. R. Allen, Head. Est 1923.

Cranleigh (Surrey) GU6 8QQ — CRANLEIGH SCHOOL. Tel. 3666. Bdg & Day Boys 13-18; Bdg Girls 16-18. Marc van Hasselt, MA, Head. Tests GCE. Ll—Eng. CF—Fr Ger Span Russ Lat Greek Art Music. Est 1863. Tri (Sept-July).

Godalming (Surrey) GU7 2DX — CHARTERHOUSE. Tel. 048684359. Bdg & Day Boys 13-18; Day Girls 16-18. Gr 8-12. P. J. Attenborough, Head. Col Prep. Tests GCE IB CEEB SSAT. Curr—Nat. Ll—Eng. CF—Fr Ger Span Chinese Russ Art Music Sci Math Hist. Enr 700. B 610/20; G 60/10. Fac 63. Full 53/Part 10. M 53; F 10. Nat. Tui Bdg £5400; Day £4500. Est 1611. Tri (Sept-July).

High Wycombe (Buckinghamshire) — LONDON CENTRAL AMERICAN HIGH SCHOOL. Daws Hill Lane. Tel. (0494) 21242. Bdg Coed 13-18; Day 13-18. Gr 7-12. William J. Kilty, BS, MA, EdD, Prin. Col Prep Gen Acad Voc. Tests CEEB. Curr—USA. Ll—Eng. A—Eng Math Comp CF—Electronics Architecture. Sl—Rem & Dev Math Tut. Enr 512. B 257; G 255. Grad '84—109. Col—55. Fac 39. M 18; F 21. US 39. Tui Day $4300. Est 1953. Quar (Aug-Je). Bldgs 30. Dorms 2. Lib 8500 vols. Gyms 2. Fields. Crts 6.

Lancing (Sussex) BN15 0RW — LANCING COLLEGE. Tel. Shoreham-by-Sea 2213. Bdg & Day Boys 13-18, Girls 16-18. Gr 8-12. Col Prep. Curr—Nat. Ll—Eng. Est 1843. Church of England.

Letchworth SG6 3JZ (Hertfordshire) — ST. CHRISTOPHER SCHOOL. Barrington Rd. Bdg Coed 7-18; Day 2½-18. Gr N-PG. Colin Reid, MA, Head. Col Prep. Tests GCE. Curr—UK. Ll—Eng. CF—Fr Span Ital Ger Lat Art Physics. Sl—Rem & Dev Math & Read Tut. Enr 418. B 118/100; G 120/80. Elem 268, Sec 150. US—10. Grad '84—60. Col—45. Fac 60. Full 42/Part 18. M 32; F 28. UK. Tui Bdg £4620 (+ £100); Day £2550 (+ £50). Est 1915. Inc 1954 nonprofit. Tri (Sept-Je). ISA. This school follows a British curriculum supplemented by electives in music, art, drama and pottery. A limited number of dyslexic students are accepted.

London W1Y 3FE — LANGHAM SECRETARIAL COLLEGE. 18 Dunraven St., Park Lane. Tel. 01-629 2904. Telex: 28554 LANG SC G. Day Girls 16-24. Gr 10-PG. C.A.B. Pringle, BS, Dir. Secretarial. Curr—UK. Ll—Eng. CF—Commercial Law Fr Ger Ital Span Public Relations. 125. Fac 20. Full 12/Part 8. M 4; F 16. UK. Tui £2484 (+ £2500). Est 1948. Tri (Sept-Je).

Middlesbrough TS9 6BN — AYTON SCHOOL. High Green, Great Ayton. Tel. 722141. Bdg & Day Coed 11-18. Gr 6-12. Alfred M. Sessa, BA, Colgate Univ., BD, Union Theological Sem, Head. Col Prep. Tests GCE. Ll—Eng. CF—Fr Span Ger Lat Russ Art Sci. Sl—Rem & Dev Math & Read. Enr 200. B 40/60; G 40/60. Grad '84—16. Col—14. Fac 26. Full 18/Part 8. M 14; F 12. US 1. UK. Tui Bdg £3800 (+ £30); Day £1700 (+ £10). Schol. Est 1841. Inc nonprofit. Society of Friends. Tri (Sept-July). Bldgs 10. Dorms 2. Lib 20,000 vols. Crts. Fields.

Middlesex — HARROW SCHOOL. Harrow-on-the-Hill. Bdg Boys. Mr. I. D. S. Beer, Head. Tui £5400. Est 1571.

Near Seven Oaks (Kent) TN14 5SA — ST. MICHAEL'S SCHOOL. Otford Court. Tel. 092 95 2137. Bdg Boys 7-14, Day 4-14. Gr N-9. The Rev. Paul G. Cox, Head. Pre-Prep. Curr—UK. Ll—Eng. CF—Fr Lat. Enr 60. B 42/18. Fac 12. Full 5/Part 7. M 4; F 8. UK. Tui Bdg £800 (+ £20)/term; Day £480 (+ £20)/term. Schol. Tri (Sept-Je). Bldgs 3. Dorms 7. Lib. Field. St. Michael's prepares students for the British Common Entrance Exam.

Oswestry (Shropshire) SY11 2HZ — QUEEN'S PARK SCHOOL. Queen's Rd. Tel. (0691) 652416. Bdg & Day Girls 9-18. P. G. Thomas, Prin. Gen Acad Col Prep. Curr—Nat. Ll—Eng. CF—Fr Ger Hist Geog Sci Relig Music Art Econ. Sl—Tut. Enr 115. G 82/33. Fac 22. Full 8/Part 14. M 2; F 20. UK. Tui Bdg £980 (+ £30); Day £480-600 (£10). Schol. Est 1820. Tri (Sept-July). Bldgs 5. Dorms 12. Lib 1000 vols. Gym. Pool. Crts.

Oxford OX2 7NN — ST. EDWARD'S SCHOOL. Woodstock Rd. Tel. 55241. Bdg & Day Boys 13-18. John C. Phillips, MA, Warden. Col Prep. Tests GCE. Ll—Eng. CF—Fr Ger Span Greek Lat Econ. Est 1863. Tri (Sept-July).

Oxon OX15 5QL — SIBFORD SCHOOL. Sibford Ferris via Banbury. Tel. 0295 78 441. Bdg & Day Coed 11-18. Gr 6-12. Jim Graham, MA (Oxon), Head. Est 1842. Society of Friends.

Pontefract (Yorkshire) WF7 7LT — ACKWORTH SCHOOL. Bdg Coed 11-18; Day Coed 9-18. Gr 7-12. G.R. McKee, BS, DipEd, Head. Col Prep Gen Acad. Curr—Nat. Ll—Eng. Enr 448. B 144/59; G 132/113. Elem 205, Sec 243. Fac 45. Full 41/Part 4. M 30; F 15. Nat. Tui Bdg £3726; Day £2160. Schol. Est 1779. Society of Friends. Tri (Sept-July). Bldgs 7. Libs 3.

Rowledge, Farnham (Surrey) GU10 4EA — FRENSHAM HEIGHTS. Tel. 025 125 2134. Bdg & Day Coed 11-18. Gr 7-PG. A. L. Pattinson, Head. Col Prep Creative Arts. Tests GCE. Curr—Nat. Ll—Eng. CF—Fr Ger Sci Comp Art Drama. Enr 245. B 110.; G 135. Fac 34. M 16; F 18. US 1. Nat. Tui Bdg $5070; Day $3045. Est 1925. Nonprofit. Tri (Sept-July).

Rustington (West Sussex) BN16 3PT — SUMMERLEA SCHOOL. Rustington House, Worthing Rd. Tel. 09062-4009. Bdg & Day Girls 5-18. Gr K-12. Mrs. W.M. Milner, BA, Head. Pre-Prep Col Prep Gen Acad. Tests GCE. Curr—UK. Ll—Eng. CF—Fr Comp Stud Relig. Enr 157. G 106/51. Fac 27. Tui Bdg £938 (+£50); Day £449 (+£20). Tri (Sept-July). Dorms 9. Summerlea offers a complete academic program which prepares girls for the British Common Entrance Exams as well as the G.C.E. 'O' and 'A' levels exams.

Rutland LE 15 9QE — UPPINGHAM SCHOOL. Tel. 0572-822216. Bdg Boys 13-18, Girls 16-18. Gr 8-12. N.R. Bomford, MA, Oxford Univ., Head. Tests—GCE. Enr 650. B 600; G 50. Elem 100, Sec 550. US—2. Grad '84—140. Col—110. Fac 73. M 68; F 5. Nat. Tui £4980 (+£300). Est 1584. Tri (Sept-July).

Saffron Walden (Essex) CB11 3EB — FRIENDS SCHOOL. Tel. 0799-25351. Bdg Coed 11-18. Gr 7-12. J. C. Woods, Head. Col Prep Gen Acad. Tests GCE. Curr—Nat. Ll—Eng. CF—Fr Ger Lat Hist Geog. Enr 330. B 100/60; G 90/80. Grad '84—30. Col—2. Fac 44. Full 31/Part 13. M 21; F 23. US 1. Nat. Tui Bdg $5400 (+$50); Day $3600 (+$40). Est 1702. Society of Friends. Tri (Sept-Je). Bldgs 15. Dorms 4. 2 libs 6000 vols.

St. Peter, Jersey C.I. — **ST. GEORGE'S PREPARATORY SCHOOL.**
La Hague Manor. Tel. 81593. Bdg Coed 7-14; Day 3½-14. J. A. H.
Job, Head. Pre-Prep. Tests CEE. Curr—Nat. Ll—Eng. CF—Fr.
Enr 120. B 15/70; G 5/30. Fac 12. Full 10/Part 2. M 4; F 8. Eng.
Tui Bdg £965 (+£40); Day £465. Schol. Est 1929. Inc nonprofit.
Tri (Sept-July). Students are prepared for Common Entrance and
Scholarship to English public schools.

Sedbergh (Cumbria) LA10 5HG — **SEDBERGH SCHOOL.** Bdg &
Day Boys 11-18. Gr 6-12. R.G. Baxter, PhD, Head. Col Prep. Tests
GCE. Ll—Eng. CF—Fr Ger Span Russ Lat Greek Math Sci. Enr
475. Fac 58. US—3. UK. Tui £4875 (+£250). Schol. Est 1525. Tri
(Sept-July).

Tonbridge (Kent) TN9 1JP — **TONBRIDGE SCHOOL.** High St. Tel.
354946. Bdg & Day Boys 13-18. Mr. C. H. D. Everett, MA, (Oxon),
Head. Tests GCE. Ll—Eng. CF—Lang Music Art Drama. Enr 650.
Fac 65. UK. Tui Bdg £4755 (+£400); Day £3306 (+£300). Schol.
Est 1553 nonprofit. Tri (Sept-July).

Totnes TQ9 6EB (Devon) — **DARTINGTON HALL SCHOOL.** Tel.
Totnes 867567. Bdg Coed 10-18; Day Coed 9-18. Gr N-12. Roger
Tilbury, Eric Adams, Heads. Col Prep Gen Acad. Tests GCE
CEEB. Curr—Nat. Ll—Eng. CF—Fr Ger Hist Sci Art Music.
Sl—Rem & Dev Read. Enr 250. B 85/40; G 85/40. Fac 37. US—1.
UK. Tui Bdg £1635-2025/term; Day £680-1070/term. Est 1926.

Winchester (Hampshire) SO23 9LX — **WINCHESTER COLLEGE.**
Tel. 0962-54328. Bdg & Day Boys 13-18. Gr 9-PG. J.P. Sabben-
Clare, MA, Oxon, Head. Col Prep. Tests GCE CEEB SSAT.
Ll—Eng. CF—Lang Econ Sci Relig Art. Enr 600. US—3. Grad
'84—140. Col—126. Fac 85. Full 77/Part 8. M 78; F 7. Nat. UK.
Tui Bdg £5310 (+£500); Day £3984 (+£500). Schol. Est 1382. Tri
(Sept-July). Bldgs 25. Dorms 11. Lib 50,000 vols.

Winscombe (Avon) BS25 1PD — **SIDCOT SCHOOL.** Tel. 093-
484-3102. Bdg & Day Coed 11-18. Gr 6-12. Thomas C. Leim-
dorfer, BS, Head. Gen Acad Col Prep. Tests GCE. Curr—UK.
Ll—Eng. CF—Lang Math Sci Art Music Drama. Enr 268. B
100/48; G 98/22. Fac 29. Full 24/Part 5. M 17; F 12. UK. Tui Bdg
£4110 (+£250); Day £2160 (£100). Est 1808. Society of Friends.

York YO2 4DD — **THE MOUNT SCHOOL.** Dalton Terrace. Tel.
(0904) 54823. Bdg Girls 11-18. D. June Ellis, BSc, DipEd, Head.
Pre-Prep Col Prep. Test GCE. Curr—Nat. Ll—Eng. CF—Lang
Hist Econ Art Music. Enr 295. Est 1831. Society of Friends.

York YO6 4PR — TERRINGTON HALL. Tel. (065 384) 227. Bdg Boys 7-13, Day 4-13. Gr N-8. D.M.B. Sharpe, BA, Head. Pre-Prep Gen Acad. Curr—UK. LI—Eng. CF—Fr Lat Relig. Enr 92. B 78/14. Fac 15. Full 9/Part 6. M 9; F 6. UK. Tui Bdg £975/term; Day £560/term. Schol. Est 1923. Nonprofit. Tri (Sept-July). Bldgs 6. Fields. Tennis crt. Indoor pool. Firmly founded in Christian ethics, this school prepares boys for the British Common Entrance Exam. Activities in drama, music, cross country, judo and an outward bound program are also available.

SCOTLAND

Edinburgh Douglas 9DNS — HILLSIDE SCHOOL. Tel. 031-225-3340. Day Coed 5-18. Andrew B. Harvey, BA, MA, DipEd, Oxon, Prin. Pre-Prep Col Prep. Tests GCE. LI—Eng. Est 1975. Inc nonprofit. Tri.

Rannoch Perthshire PH17 2QQ — RANNOCH SCHOOL. Tel. 08-822-332. Bdg & Day Coed 11-18. Gr 6-12. Michael Barratt, MA, St. Andrew's Univ., Head. Pre-Prep ColPrep. Tests GCE. CF—Fr Ger Span Comp Geol Technical Drawing. SI—Rem & Dev Math & Read Tut. Enr 270. B 250; G 20. US—2. Fac 26. Full 22/Part 4. M 21; F 5. Tui Bdg £3580 (+£200); Day £2140 (+£50). Schol. Est 1959. Tri (Sept-Je). Bldgs 15. 2 Libs 1000 vols. Mant extracurricular activities are offered, including expeditions to local hills.

U.S.S.R.

Leningrad — ANGLO-AMERICAN SCHOOL. Day Coed. Gr K-12. Mail to: c/o American Consulate, APO, New York 09664. Tel. 274-8235. Col Prep Gen Acad. Curr—USA. LI—Eng. CF—Russ. Enr 3. US—3. Fac 2. Full 1/Part 1. US 1. Tui $1500-4100. Sem (Sept-Je). A/OS.

AFRICA

MEDITERRANEAN AFRICA

ALGERIA

Sidi Amar (El Hadjar, Annaba) BP 376. — ECOLE ATKINS. ISS.

Skikda BP 112. — KELLOGG SCHOOL. ISS.

NORTHERN AFRICA

CAMEROON

Douala — THE INTERNATIONAL SCHOOL OF DOUALA. Rue de Palimer. Day Coed 3-15. Gr N-8. Raymond Richards, Admin. Gen Acad. Curr—USA UK. LI—Eng. CF—Fr Math Soc Stud Lang Arts. SI—Tut Rem. Enr 90. B 47; G 43. Fac 17.Full 11/Part 6. M 4; F 13. Tui $3465 (+ $50). Est 1978. Nonprofit. Tri (Sept-Je). AISA A/OS ISS. Bldgs 4. Lib 2500 vols.

ETHIOPIA

Addis Ababa — BINGHAM ACADEMY. Box 4937. Tel. 137080. Bdg & Day Coed 6-14. Gr 1-8. Col Prep. Curr—USA. LI—Eng. CF—Fr Soc Stud Math Biol Bible. Enr 135. B 65; G 70. Fac 12. Full 10/Part 2. M 3; F 9. US 10. Canada UK. Tui $1100. Est 1946. Sudan Interior Missions. Tri (Sept-Je). Bldgs 9. Lib 8000 vols. Field. Crt.

MALI

Bamako — AMERICAN INTERNATIONAL SCHOOL. Day Coed 5-15. Gr K-8. Mail to: c/o American Embassy Bamako, Dept. of State, Washington, DC 20520. Marien A. Kyzner, Dir. Pre-Prep Gen Acad. Curr—USA. LI—Eng. CF—Fr Math Art Sci Soc Stud. Enr 49. B 24; G 25. Grad '84—3. Fac 7. US—3. Tui $3500. Est 1977. Tri (Sept-Je). A/OS ISS.

MAURITANIA

Nouakchott — AMERICAN INTERNATIONAL SCHOOL OF NOUAKCHOTT. Gr K-8. Mail to: c/o American Embassy Nouakchott, Dept. of State, Washington, DC 20520. Tel. 529-67. Calvin Sloan, Prin. Gen Acad. Curr—USA. LI—Eng. CF—Fr Sci Music. SI—Rem Read ESL. Enr 36. US—21. Fac 8. US 5. Tui $4000. Est 1978. Nonprofit. Sem (Sept-Je). AISA A/OS ISS.

NIGER

Niamey — AMERICAN SCHOOL OF NIAMEY. Day Coed 4-14. Gr N-8. Mail to: c/o American Embassy Niamey, Dept. of State, Washington, DC 20520. Gen Acad. Curr—USA. LI—Eng. CF—Fr Comp Stud. Enr 65. B 35; G 30. US—40. Grad '84—2. Fac 4. US. Tui $3400. Est 1982. Nonprofit. Sem (Sept-Je). AISA A/OS ISS.

NIGERIA

Ibadan — BODIJA INTERNATIONAL SCHOOL. P.O. Box 4086. Dick Hopkins, Supt. ISS.

Kaduna — SACRED HEART INTERNATIONAL PRIMARY SCHOOL. Independence Way, PMB 620. Tel. (062) 212-929. Day Coed. Gr 1-6. Mail to: c/o American Consulate Kaduna, Dept. of State, Washington, DC 20520. Dorothy Ajijola, Head. Curr—UK. LI —Eng. Enr 298. US—6. Fac 14. US 2. Tui $745. Est 1965. Tri (Sept-July). A/OS ISS. Bldgs 3. Lib. Field.

Miango via Jos — KENT ACADEMY. Sudan Interior Mission. Bdg & Day Coed 6-14. Gr 1-9. Gen Acad. Curr—USA Can. LI—Eng. Est 1946.

Samaru (Zaria) — AHMADU BELLO UNIVERSITY STAFF SCHOOL. Gr 1-12. ISS.

SENEGAL

Dakar — THE INTERNATIONAL SCHOOL OF DAKAR. Tel. 23-08-71. Day Coed 6-14. Gr 1-9. Mail to: c/o Administrative Officer-TIS, American Embassy, DAKAR, Dept. of State, Washington, DC 20520. Gen Acad. Curr—USA. LI—Eng. CF—Fr Music Art. Enr 60. US—27. Fac 13. Full 5/Part 8. US 4. Tui $2990. Est 1983. Sem (Sept-Je). AISA A/OS. This school offers correspondence study for students in grades 10 to 12.

SIERRA LEONE

Freetown — SERVICES CHILDRENS SCHOOL. HQ Royal Sierra Leone Military Forces. G. McCavish, Prin. ISS.

Freetown — SERVICES SECONDARY SCHOOL. Juba Barracks. G. C. C. Jarrett, Prin. ISS.

SUDAN

Khartoum — KHARTOUM INTERNATIONAL HIGH SCHOOL. c/o Box 805. Day Coed 10-16. Peter D. G. Smith, BA, Milton Keynet, CertEd, Univ. of Wales, LRICS, London Univ, Head. Tests GCE. Curr—UK. LI—Eng. CF—Arabic Fr Ger Eng Math Sci Art. SI—Rem & Dev Reading Tut. Est 1978. Nonprofit. Sem (Aug-May). ISS.

EQUATORIAL & SOUTHERN AFRICA

BOTSWANA

Francistown — JOHN MACKENZIE SCHOOL. P.O. Box 121.Lobengula St. Tel. 2326. Day Coed 5-14. Gr K-7. M. E. Morley, CertEd, Leeds College, Prin. Pre-Prep Gen Acad. Curr—Nat UK. LI—Eng. CF—Setswana Eng Fr Math Sci Hist Music Drama Ballet. SI—Eng. Est 1899. Nonprofit. Tri (Jan-Dec).

Gaborone — MARU-A-PULA. Private Bag 0045. Tel. 2953. Bdg & Day Coed 12-21. Gr 8-PG. David H. Matthews, BS, DipEd, Head. Col Prep Gen Acad. Tests GCE. Curr—UK. LI—Eng. CF—Fr Lat Setswana. Enr 316. B 55/110; G 44/107. Elem 82, Sec 234. US—21. Fac 26. Full 17/Part 9. M 13; F 13. Tui Bdg 4002-4521 BP; Day 2115-2457 BP. Schol. Est 1972. Inc nonprofit. Tri (Jan-Dec). Bldgs 40. Dorms 2. Lib 7121 vols.

GABON

Libreville — AMERICAN INTERNATIONAL SCHOOL OF LIBRE-VILLE. BP 4000. Day Coed 5-14. Gr K-8. Mail to: Libreville, c/o Dept. of State, Washington, DC 20520. Richard L. Spradling, MA, Indiana Univ., MEd, Alabama Univ., Dir. Gen Acad. Curr—USA. LI—Eng. CF—Fr Lang Arts Soc Stud Music SI—ESL. Enr 42. B 20; G 22. US—10. Fac 8. Full 6/Part 2. M 1; F 7. US 3. Tui $4000 (+ $250). Est 1976. Nonprofit. Sem (Sept-Je). AISA A/OS ISS. Bldgs 1. Lib 1500 vols.

KENYA

Gilgil — PEMBROKE HOUSE. P.O. Box 31. David Opie, Head. ISS.

Malava — MALAVA SECONDARY SCHOOL. P.O. Box 6. Bdg & Day Boys 14-20. Haillam Luvaka Patisi, Head. Col Prep Gen Acad. Curr—Nat. LI—Eng. CF—Kiswahili Relig Lit Sci. Enr 410. B 200/210. Est 1964. ISS. Friends sponsored.

Nairobi — CAVINA SCHOOL. P.O. Box 43090 Nairobi, 119 Argwings-Kohek Rd. Tel. 566011. Day Coed 6-13. Gr K-7. R.A. Massie-Blomfield, Prin. Pre-Prep. Tests CEE. Curr—Nat. LI—Eng. CF—Fr Lat. Enr 160. B 90; G 70. Fac 14. Full 9/Part 5. M 5; F 9. Nat. Tui $1400. Est 1950. Tri (Sept-July).

Nairobi — HILLCREST SECONDARY SCHOOL. P.O. Box 24819. Bdg & Day Coed. Gr 7-12. Richard Stevens, Head. ISS.

Nairobi — KENTON COLLEGE. Box 40580. Tel. 43003. Bdg & Day Boys 6-14. L. N. Usher-Wilson, BA, MA, Head. Gen Acad. Tests CEE. Curr-UK. Ll—Eng. CF—Fr Lat Art. Est 1924. Nonprofit. Tri (Sept-July). ISS.

Nairobi — ST. MARY'S SCHOOL. Msongari, P.O. Box 40580. Tel. 60328. Day Boys 6-18, Girls 15-18. Gr 1-PG. Rev. Fr. E. O'Farrell, Head. Col Prep Gen Acad. Tests IB GCE. Curr—UK USA. Ll—Eng. A—Physics Chem Math Econ Hist Geog. CF—Fr Latin German Swahili Commerce Art Sl—Rem Read. Enr 1237. B 1183; G 54. Grad '84—72. Col—50. Fac 65. M 36; F 29. US 4. Nat. Tui 9000 KSh (+ 2000 KSh). Est 1939. Inc nonprofit. Tri (Jan-Nov). AISA ISS. Bldgs 4. 2 Libs 12,000 vols. Athletic facilities.

Nakuru — GREENSTEDS SCHOOL. Private Bag. R. Albon, Head. ISS.

Thika — IMANI SCHOOL. P.O. Box 750. Tel. 21071. Bdg Coed 8-18; Day 4-18. Gr N-12. Gary D. Jones, BA, ACP, FRSA, MS (Oxon), Head. Col Prep Gen Acad. Tests SSAT GCE. Curr—UK. Ll—Eng. CF—Ger Fr Kiswahili Hist Geog Relig Typ Drama. Est 1969. Nonprofit. Delmonte Corp. School. Tri (Sept-July). ISS.

Turi — ST. ANDREW'S SCHOOL. P.O. Turi. Tel. MOLO 11. Bdg Coed 6-13. Gr 1-7. Kenneth Madden, BA, Durham, PGCE, London, Head. Pre-Prep. Tests CEE. Curr—UK Nat. Ll—Eng. CF—Fr Math Sci Music. Est 1931. Nonprofit. Tri (Sept-July).

LESOTHO

Mafeteng — KINGSGATE PRIMARY/HIGH SCHOOL. P.O. Box 169. Tel. (0506) 312. Day Coed 5 and up. Gr K-10. L.N. Nodder, Dir. Pre-Prep Col Prep. Tests GCE. Ll—Eng. CF—Fr Ger Dutch Sesotho Eng Lang Lit. Est 1978. Nonprofit. Quar (Jan-Dec). ISS.

Maseru 100 — MASERU ENGLISH MEDIUM PREPARATORY. P.O. Box 34, Gauldwell Rd. Tel. 322-2176. Day Coed 5-11. Gr 1-6. Audre Ball, Head. Pre-Prep. Curr—UK. Ll—Eng. CF—Fr Sesotho Afrikaans Gaelic Sl—ESL Rem & Dev Math. Enr 481. B 245; G 236. Fac 22. M 2; F 20. US. Tui 220-550 Ma (+ 100 Ma). Est 1890. Nonprofit. Tri (Sept-July). A/OS ISS. Bldgs 3. Lib.

Roma 180 (Maseru District) — **NATIONAL UNIVERSITY OF LESOTHO. (International Primary School).** National University of Lesotho. Tel. 266 1 218. Day Coed 4-12. Gr N-7. Roshan S. Fitter, Dir. Pre-Prep. Curr—Nat UK. LI—Eng. CF—Fr Sesotho. Enr 185. B 90; G 95. US—1. Fac 9. Full 6/ Part 3. F 9. Intl. Tui R95 (+ R10). Est 1964. Nonprofit. Sem (Aug-Je).

MADAGASCAR

614 Tolagnaro (Tulear) — **AMERICAN SCHOOL.** B.P. 31. Tel. 211-47. Bdg & Day Coed 6-11. Gr 1-8. Elaine G. Perkins, BA, Dakota Wesleyan Univ., Prin. LI—Eng. CF—Fr Malagasy. SI —Tut. Enr 4. B 1/1; G 1/1. US—3. Fac 2. Full 1/Part 1. M 1; F 1. US 2. Tui Bdg $4000 (+ $100); Day $3000 (+ $100). Est 1912. Inc nonprofit. Lutheran. Sem (Aug-May). ISS. Bldgs 2. Dorm. Lib 3000 vols. Play grounds.

MALAWI

Blantyre — **PHOENIX SCHOOL.** P.O. Box 30376. Tel. 635-737. Day Coed 4-11. Gr K-6. David Waite, Head. Pre-Prep. Curr—UK. LI—Eng. CF—Fr. Enr 205. Fac 5. Full 2/Part 3. M 2; F 3. UK. Tui 400KW/term (+ 25 KW/term). Est 1970. Tri (Sept-July). Bldg. Lib. Fields. Crt. Students prepare for entrance to secondary schools in the United Kingdom.

MAURITIUS

Vacoas — **ALEXANDRA HOUSE SCHOOL.** 3 United Nations Rd. Tel. 64108. Day Coed 3-11. Gr N-8. Ida Coombes, Head. Gen Acad. Curr—UK. LI—Eng. CF—Fr. Enr 40. US—8. Fac 8. Full 4/Part 4. Tui $250/term. Tri (Sept-July).

SOUTH AFRICA

Grahamstown (Cape Province) — **KINGSWOOD COLLEGE.** Burton St. Tel. 0461-4351. Bdg Coed 9-19; Day Coed 6-19. Gr 1-PG. G.S., BA, Rhodes Univ., Head. Gen Acad. Curr—Nat. LI—Eng. CF—Afrikaans Fr Ger Hist Geog. SI—Rem Read. Enr 523. Fac 40. Tui Bdg R530-700 (+ R100)/term; Day R60-325 (+ R100)/term. Schol. Est 1894. Nonprofit. Methodist Church of South Africa. Tri (Jan-Dec). Bldgs 19. Dorm rms 22. 4 Libs 10,000 vols. Athletic facilities. This church-sponsored school enrolls most of its students from South Africa and offers preparation for entrance examinations to South African universities.

Hilton (Natal) — HILTON COLLEGE. Tel. 31632. Bdg Boys 13-18. Gr 8-PG. Col Prep. Tests GCE. Curr—UK. Ll—Eng. Est 1872. Inc nonprofit. Quar (Sept-Je).

Johannesburg — ST. BARNABAS COLLEGE. 26 Perth Rd. Bdg & Day Coed 12-18. Mail to: P.O. Box 88188, Newclaire 2112, South Africa. NAIS.

Rosebank 7700 (Cape Town) — AMERICAN INTERNATIONAL SCHOOL OF CAPE TOWN. 1 Alma Rd. Tel. 011 654 895. Day Coed 5-17. Gr K-12. Mail to: c/o Consulate General, Cape Town, Dept. of State, Washington, DC 20520. Mark Adams, EdD, Univ. of Miami, Head. Gen Acad. Tests SSAT. Curr—USA. Ll—Eng. CF—Fr. Enr 30. B 13; G 17. Elem 15, Sec 15. US—23. Fac 8. Full 4/Part 4. M 2; F 6. US 3. Tui $1272-2183. Est 1983. Nonprofit. Quar (Aug-Je). A/OS. This school features a learning disabilities program at all grade levels.

Sandton 2146 — AMERICAN INTERNATIONAL SCHOOL OF JOHANNESBURG. 51 Rivonia Rd., Morningside, P.O. Box 783848. Tel. 783-4007. Day Coed 5-18. Gr K-12. Benna van Vuuren, Dir. Col Prep Gen Acad. Curr—USA. Ll—Eng. CF—Fr Ger Span Comp Stud. Enr 153. US—142. Fac 24. US 18. Tui $1615-2720. Est 1982. Sem (Aug-Je). AISA A/OS. Appreciation instruction in South African history and culture is part of the curriculum at this school.

SWAZILAND

Mbabane — ST. MARK'S HIGH SCHOOL. P.O. Box 31. Tel. 42591. Bdg & Day Coed 12-19. Gr 7-12. L.D. Campbell, BA, Head. Col Prep Gen Acad. Curr—UK. Ll—Eng. CF—Fr Siswati Sci. Enr 440. Fac 28. UK Swaziland. Tui Bdg E295 (+ E150); Day E70 (+ E150). Schol. Est 1909. Nonprofit. Tri. Bldgs 14. Lib 4000 vols. Athletic facilities. St. Mark's is a racially integrated school enrolling students from Swaziland, Mozambique and the United Kingdom.

Mbabane — SIF UNDZANI SCHOOL. P.O. Box A286. Tel. 42465. Day Coed 6-12. Gr 1-7. Gen Acad. Curr—Nat. Ll—Eng Fr. CF—Siswati Music. Enr 207. US—12. Fac 12. Full 10/Part 2. Tui $500. Est 1981. Tri (Jan-Dec). AISA A/OS. A British-based Swazi syllabus is used at Sif Undzani.

TANZANIA

Arusha — ARUSHA INTERNATIONAL SCHOOL. P.O. Box 3042. Tel. 3095. Bdg & Day Coed 5-13. Gr 1-7. Mrs. B. Redding, Head. Gen Acad. LI—Eng. CF—Fr Swahili Art Music. Enr 644. B 87/200; G 90/267. Fac 29. Full 29. M 10; F 19. Nat UK Australia. Tui Bdg 360TSh (+ 120TSh); Day 90TSh (+ 48TSh). Est 1934. Tri (Jan-Nov). ISS. Bldgs 7. Dorms 4. Lib. Crts.

Arusha — ST. CONSTANTINE'S. P.O. Box 221. Tel. 3696. Bdg & Day Coed 5-13. Gr K-6. Pre-Prep Gen Acad. Curr—UK. LI—Eng. Est 1953. Nonprofit. Tri (Sept-Je). ISS. This school is primarily for children of expatriate parents living in Tanzania.

Dar es Salaam — UNIVERSITY COLLEGE. P.O. Box 9184. ISS.

Mwanza — VICTORIA PRIMARY SCHOOL. Africa Island Mission.P.O. Box 1414. Bdg Copd 6½-11. Gr K-5. Don Baker, Prin. Pre-Prep. Curr—USA. LI—Eng. CF—Ger Swahili. Est. 1953. Tri (Sept-July). ISS. Africa Island Mission.

ZIMBABWE

Marondellas — SPRINGVALE SCHOOL. Private Bag 774. Tel. 3598. Bdg Coed 7-14; Day Boys 7-14. Gr K-7. J. I. Stansbury, MA, Cantab, Head. Gen Acad. Curr—UK. LI—Eng. CF—Fr Lat Afrikaans Shona Soc Stud Music Relig. SI—Rem Eng & Math. Est 1952. Inc nonprofit. Tri (Jan-Dec). ISS.

ASIA

NEAR & MIDDLE EAST

BAHRAIN

Awali — AWALI PRIMARY SCHOOL. ISS.

CYPRUS

Limassol — LIMASSOL GRAMMAR & JUNIOR SCHOOL. Homer St. E.W.P. Foley, Head. ISS.

Limassol — LOGOS SCHOOL OF ENGLISH EDUCATION. P.O. Box 1075. Tel. (051) 73650. Bdg & Day Coed 6-18. Gr K-12. Levon Yergatian, BA, Bob Jones Univ., Head. Pre-Prep Col Prep Gen Acad. Tests GCE. Curr—Nat. Tests GCE. Ll—Eng. CF—Greek Fr Eng Math Physics Chem Bio Hist Relig. Sl—Rem & Dev Read & Math Tut. Enr 114. B 18/57; G 10/29. Elem 70, Sec 44. US—3. Grad '84—9. Col—6. Fac 18. Full 16/Part 2. M 4; F 14. US 2. UK. Tui Bdg $2400 (+ $600); Day $1000 (+ $300). Schol. Est 1973. Inc nonprofit. Tri (Sept-Je). ISS. Bldgs 2. Dorm. Lib 3000 vols. Athletic facilities.

Limassol — ST. MARY'S SCHOOL. Griva Digenis Ave. Tel. 051-62481. Bdg Girls 10-20; Day Boys 3-11, Girls 3-20. Sr. Arsene Fantin, Head. Pre-Prep Col Prep. Tests GCE. Ll—Eng. CF—Fr Greek Ital Comm. Est 1923. Inc 1936. Tri (Sept-Je). ISS.

JORDAN

Amman — THE BISHOP'S SCHOOL. P.O. Box 2001. Tel. 24334. Day Boys 5-18. Gr 1-12. J. S. Halaseh, BA, DipEd, Head. Pre-Prep Col Prep. Tests GCE. Ll—Eng Arabic. CF—Arabic Fr Math Sci Hist Relig. Est 1936. Sem (Aug-May). Anglican.

Amman — TERRA SANTA COLLEGE. P.O. Box 9114. Tel. 22366. Day Boys 12-20. Fr. Halim Noujaim, OFM, Dir. Pre-Prep Col Prep. Tests GCE SSAT. Ll—Eng Arabic. CF—Arabic Fr Hist Math Sci. Sl—Tut. Est 1949. Inc nonprofit. Franciscan. Sem (Aug-May).

KUWAIT

Hawalli — NEW ENGLISH SCHOOL. P.O. Box 6156. A. Rodgers, Head. ISS.

LEBANON

Brummana — BRUMMANA HIGH SCHOOL. Tel. 960430. Bdg Coed 8-18; Day Coed 4-18. Gr K-PG. Alan J. Rowland, BSc, Prin. Col Prep Gen Acad. Tests GCE. Curr—UK. Ll—Eng. CF—Arabic Fr Psych Phil Tech Drawing. Sl—Tut. Est 1875. Nonprofit. Society of Friends. Tri (Oct-Je). ISA.

OMAN

Ruwi — MUSCAT ENGLISH SPEAKING SCHOOL. P.O. Box 4907. Tel. 600842. Day Coed 4-11. Gr K-6. D. G. H. Jones, BA, Univ. of London, Head. Gen Acad. Curr—UK. LI—Eng. CF—Fr Oman Stud. SI—Rem Read Tut. Est 1972. Nonprofit. Tri (Sept-Je). ISS.

Seeb — THE SULTAN'S SCHOOL. P.O. Box 9665. Tel. 620-777. Bdg Boys 7½-19, Day Coed 3½-19. John C. Chalfant, BA, Fresno State, MA, Univ. of Pennsylvania, Head. Col Prep. Tests CEEB GCE. Curr—Intl. LI—Arabic Eng. CF—Eng Sci Math Social Stud Relig. SI—Tut Rem & Dev Read. Enr 382. Elem 280, Sec 102. US—7. Grad '84—14. Col—14. Fac 41. Full 39/Part 2. M 16; F 25. US 6. Tui Bdg RO 1200; Day RO 1200 (+ RO 500). Est 1977. Inc. Tri (Sept-Je). ISS NE/SA. Bldgs 17. Dorms 2. Lib 10,000 vols. Crts. Fields.

QATAR

Doha — DOHA COLLEGE. P.O. Box 7506. Tel. 887379. Day Coed 11-18. R.R. MacPherson, BSc, Edinburgh, Prin. Col Prep Gen Acad. Tests GCE. Curr—UK. LI—Eng. CF—Fr. Enr 220. B 110; G 110. Tui QR4700-5100/term. Est 1980. Nonprofit. Tri (Sept-Je). Enrollment is completely British.

SAUDI ARABIA

Jeddah 21442 — THE CONTINENTAL SCHOOL. P.O. Box 6453. Tel. 669-0515. Day Coed 3½-17. Gr N-11. Trevor A. Williams, BA, MA, FRGS, Durham, Princeton, Head. Col Prep Gen Acad. Tests GCE SSAT. Curr—UK. LI—Eng. CF—Fr Comp Stud ESL. SI—Tut. Enr 1250. Elem 1000, Sec 250. US—150. Grad '84—36. Col—24. Fac 90. M 20; F 70. US 10. UK. Tui 9600-16,000 SRI. Schol. Est 1977. Nonprofit. Tri (Sept-July). ISS NE/SA. Lib 5000 vols. Pool. Field.

Tabuk — SAUDI ARABIAN INTERNATIONAL SCHOOL OF TABUK. Gr K-9. Don O. Hill, Prin. NE/SA. Accred MSA.

Taif — PARENTS' COOPERATIVE SCHOOL. c/o Northrop Co. George T. Wright, Prin. Accred MSA.

Taif — SAUDI ARABIAN INTERNATIONAL SCHOOL. Day Coed 5-15. Gr K-9. Mail to: c/o Northrop Corporation, P.O. Box 75, APO, NY 09017. Michael S. Hobbs, BS, Ohio State Univ., MA, Univ. of Guam, Prin. Gen Acad. Tests SSAT. Curr—USA.

LI—Eng. CF—Span Arts Soc Study Music. Quar (Sept-Je). Accred MSA.

Yanbu — INTERNATIONAL SCHOOL OF YANBU. Madinat Yanbu Al-Sinaiyah, P.O. Box 30039. Day Coed 3-15. Gr N-9. William P. Davison, BA, Univ. of Connecticut, MS, West Connecticut State, Supt. Pre-Prep. Curr—US. Tests SSAT. LI—Eng. CF—Fr Span Arab. SI—Rem & Dev Read & Math ESL. Enr 652. B 320; G 332. Fac 40. Full 36/Part 4. M 16; F 24. US 31. Tui 22,900 SRI. Est 1979. Sem (Sept-Je). ISS NE/SA. Bldgs 7. 2 Libs 15,000 vols.

SYRIA

Aleppo — INTERNATIONAL SCHOOL OF ALEPPO. c/o ICARDA, P.O. Box 5466. Tel. 213131. Day Coed 4-13. Gr N-8. Denis Sanderson, Prin. Gen Acad. Curr—USA UK. LI—Eng. CF—Arabic Fr ESL Music Art SI—Tut Rem & Dev Math & Read. Enr 80. B 40; G 40. US—1. Fac 12. Full 7/Part 5. M 2; F 10. US 1. UK. Tui $1700-2300. Est 1977. Nonprofit. Sem (Sept-Je). ISS NE/SA. Bldgs 1. Lib. Crts.

TURKEY

Istanbul Uskudar. — THE AMERICAN GIRLS COLLEGE. Martha Millett, Prin.

Izmir — AMERICAN COLLEGIATE INSTITUTE. Goztepe. Tel. 158608. Telex: 52590 IG TX TR 235. Day Girls 12-18. Gr 6-12. Douglas M. Hill, MEd, Macalester College, Prin. Col Prep. Tests SAT TOEFL. Curr—US Nat. L—Eng Turkish CF—Fr Sci. Enr 773. Elem 470, Sec 303. Grad '84—110. Col—105. Fac 60. Full 49/Part 11. M 14; F 46. US 11. Tui 200,000 TL (+25,000 TL). Schol. Est 1878. Nonprofit. Sem (Sept-Je). ISS. Bldgs 7. Lib 20,000 vols. Gym. Crts. A community social service program is integral to academic offerings. Sports, folk dancing, photography and drama are among the extracurricular activities.

Tarsus (Icel) — TARSUS AMERICAN SCHOOL. P.K. 6. Tel. 11198. Bdg & Day Coed 11-19. Gr 6-12. Wallace M. Robeson, BEd, Wisconsin State College, BD, Oberlin, MA, Univ. of Wisconsin, Prin. Col Prep. Curr—USA Nat. LI—Eng Turk. CF—Eng Turkish Ger Soc Stud. Enr 525. Fac 45. Tui Bdg $1400; Day $680 (+$100). Schol. Est 1888. Inc nonprofit. Sem (Oct-May). ISS. Bldgs 8. Dorms 6. Lib 12,000 vols. Athletic facilities. An interscholastic sports program includes soccer, basketball, volleyball and track.

UNITED ARAB EMIRATES

Abu Dhabi — INTERNATIONAL SCHOOL OF CHOUEIFAT. P.O. Box 7212. Tel. 327700. Day Coed 3½-18. Gr N-12. Ramzi Germanos, BSc, American Univ. of Beirut, Dir. Col Prep. Curr—Nat. Tests IB GCE. Ll—Eng. CF—Arabic Fr Ital Port. Est 1978. Tri (Sept-Je).

Al Ain (Abu Dhabi) — INTERNATIONAL SCHOOL OF CHOUEIFAT, AL AIN. Box 15997, Al Manaseer. Tel. 678444. Telex: 34011EM. Day Coed 3-18. Gr N-PG. S. Mansour, Dir. Col Prep Gen Acad. Tests IB GCE SSAT TOEFL. Curr—Intl. Ll—Eng. A—Physics Chem Biol Econ Comp Sci Hist Art Math Eng. CF—Fr Arabic. Enr 437. B 250; G 187. US—20. Fac 48. Full 48. M 16; F 32. US 3. UK. Tui DH11,700-18,500. Est 1886. Tri (Sept-Je). Bldg. Lib. Swimming pool. Crts. Gym. Choueifat Schools are also located in Sharjah and Abu Dhabi.

Al-Ain (Abu Dhabi) — AL-AIN ENGLISH SPEAKING SCHOOL. P.O. Box 1419. Tel. Al Ain 677444. Day Coed 4-11. Gr K-5. James G. Crawford, Prin. Pre-Prep. Ll—Eng. CF—Arab Fr Soc Stud. Sl—Rem & Dev Read Music. Enr 122. US—23. Fac 13. Full 12/Part 1. M 3; F 10. US 1. UK. Est 1979. Tri (Sept-Je). ISS. Bldgs 5. Lib 8000.

Dubai — ST. MARY'S CATHOLIC HIGH SCHOOL. P.O. Box 1544. Tel. 470252. Day Coed 4-18. Gr K-12. Sr. Fosca Berardi, Head. Col Prep. Tests GCE. Ll—Eng. CF—Arabic Fr. CF—Eng Hist Lit Geog Biol Chem Physics Account Econ Comp. Fac 72. Full 72. M 5; F 67. US 1. Tui 200-350 Dh/mo. Est 1968. Nonprofit. Tri (Sept-Je). Lib 5000 vols.

Ras Al Khaimah — RAS AL KHAIMAH ENGLISH SPEAKING SCHOOL. P.O. Box 975. Tel. 29441. Day Coed 3-11. Irene Finlayson, Head. Pre-Prep. Tests CEE. Curr—UK. Ll—Eng. CF—Fr Arabic Hist Math Music. Sl—Rem & Dev Read Tut. Est 1976. Inc nonprofit. Tri (Sept-June).

Sharjah — INTERNATIONAL SCHOOL OF CHOUEIFAT, SHARJAH. P.O. Box 2077. Tel. 58221/ 8050EM. Day Coed 3-18. Gr N-12. D. Miles, Dir. Gen Acad. Tests IB GCE TOEFL. Curr—intl. Ll—Eng. A—Eng Econ Biol Math Physics Chem. CF—Fr Arabic. Sl—Rem & Dev Math Eng. Enr 965. B 562; G 403. US—17. Grad '84—41. Col—27. Fac 58. Full 58. M 15; F 43. UK. Tui $2900-4700 (+$80). Est 1886. Tri (Sept-Je). Bldg. Lib 2800 vols. Gym.

YEMEN

Taiz — MOHAMED ALI OTHMAN SCHOOL. P.O. Box 4713. Tel. 2996. Day Coed 4-17. Gr K-12. Saleh Zokari, Chrmn. Col Prep Gen Acad. Tests SSAT GCE IB. Curr—Nat. LI—Eng Arabic. CF—Arabic Stud Math. SI—Eng. Est 1972. Nonprofit. Tri (Aug-Je). ISS.

SOUTH & SOUTHEAST ASIA

INDIA

Ajmer — MAYO COLLEGE. 503 001 (Rajasthan). Tel. 21597. Bdg & Day Boys 9-17, Day Girls 9-17. H. L. Dutt, MA, DipEd, Oxon, Prin. Pre-Prep Col Prep Gen Acad. Curr—Nat. LI—Eng. CF—Hindi Sanskrit. Enr 840. B 825; G 15. Elem 427, Sec 413. US—5. Grad '84—87. Fac 72. M 63; F 9. Nat. Tui Bdg 8000 Rs (+ 1500 Rs); Day 5000 Rs (+ 1000 Rs). Schol. Est 1875. Inc. Sem (July-Apr). Bldgs 30. Hostels 10. Lib 40,000 vols. Pools 2. Athletic facilities.

Andhra Pradesh — THE RISHI VALLEY SCHOOL. Rishi Valley PO, PIN517352 Chittoor District. Tel. Madanappalle 37. Bdg Coed 7-17. Gr 3-12. G. Narayan, MA, Prin. Pre-Prep Col Prep. Curr—Nat. LI—Eng. CF—Hindi Telugu Sanskrit Econ Art. Est 1931. Nonprofit. Sem (Je-Mar). ISS.

Bombay — AMERICAN INTERNATIONAL SCHOOL OF BOMBAY. Tel. 823-611. Day Coed 6-12. Gr 1-6. Mail to: c/o American Consulate General, Bombay, Dept. of State, Washington, DC 20520. Gen Acad. Curr—US. LI—Eng. Enr 25. US 5. Fac 5. US Nat. Tui $5500 (+ $1000). Est 1981. Sem (Aug-May). A/OS NE/SA. This school is located across the street from the American Consulate General building.

Bombay 400 001 — THE CATHEDRAL & JOHN CONNON SCHOOL. 6, Purshottamdas Thakurdas Marg. Tel. 261282. Day Coed 5-18. Gr K-12. E. J. Simeon, MA, Allahabad Univ., Dir. Col Prep Gen Acad. Curr—Nat. LI—Eng. CF—Eng Hindi Fr Marathi Hist Geog Arts Crafts. Est 1860. Inc. Tri (Jan-Apr). ISS.

Bombay 7 — BOMBAY INTERNATIONAL SCHOOL. Gilbert Bldg. Babulnath (2nd Cross Road). Tel. 8228206. Day Coed 5-17. Gr K-11. S.N. Srivastava, Prin. Gen Acad. Curr—USA UK. LI—Eng. CF—Fr Ger Hindi Marathi. Est 1962. Inc. Sem (Jan-Dec). ISS. Special emphasis is placed on Indian studies with Hindi required of all students.

Calcutta (West Bengal) — ST. THOMAS BOYS SCHOOL. Diamond Harbour Rd.Kidderpore. Tel. 45-2241. Bdg Boys 4-20, Girls 6-18; Day Coed 3-18. Gr N-12. Curr—Nat. LI—Eng. Est 1727.

Orissa — STEWART SCHOOL. Bhubaneswar 3. ISS.

INDONESIA

Balikpapan (East Kalimantan) — PASIR RIDGE SCHOOL. P.O. Box 76. Day Coed 5-14. Gr K-8. Mail to: Intl address: Unocal Corp., Locked Bag Service #3, Killiney Rd. Post Office, Singapore 9123, Singapore. William Roeder, MA, Univ. of Wisconsin, Prin. Pre-Prep Gen Acad. Tests SSAT. Curr—USA. LI—Eng.CF—Indonesian ESL. SI—Rem & Dev Math & Read Tut. Enr 110. US—60. Fac 12. M 6; F 6. US 11. Tui $9900. Est 1972. Nonprofit. Tri (Sept-Je). ISS. Bldgs 3. Lib 10,000 vols. Athletic facilities.

Bandung 40142 (Java) — BANDUNG ALLIANCE SCHOOL. Jalan Gunung Agung 14. Tel. 81844. Bdg & Day Coed 6-12. Gr 1-6. Alex Valley, Prin. Gen Acad. Curr—USA. LI—Eng. CF—Indonesian. SI—Tut Rem & Dev Read Piano. Enr 39. B 9/12; G 9/9. Fac 17. Full 12/Part 5. M 3; F 14. US 3. Tui Bdg $3135; Day $1385. Est 1956. Sem (Aug-Je). EARCOS. Bldgs 2. Dorm. Lib 3200 vols. Athletic facilities.

Bogor — BOGOR EXPATRIATE SCHOOL. Jalan Papandayan 9.P.O. Box 160. Tel. 24360. Day Coed 4½-12. Gr K-6. Rosemary Allen, Prin. Pre-Prep. Curr—Australian USA UK. LI—Eng. CF —Dutch Indonesian. Est 1974. Nonprofit. Quar (Aug-Je). EARCOS ISS.

Lhokseumawe (Sumatra) — INTERNATIONAL SCHOOL OF LHOKSEUMAWE. c/o Mobil Oil Indonesia.P.T. Arun, Tromol Pos 267 Medan. Day Coed 4-14. Gr N-8. Edwin Burgon, Prin. Gen Acad. Tests—SSAT. Curr—USA. LI—Eng. A—Bio Algebra. CF—Indonesian. SI—Tut. Enr 55. B 28; G 27. US—18. Fac 9. M 3; F 6. US 9. Est 1973. Inc nonprofit. Sem (Sept-July). EARCOS ISS. Bldgs 4. Lib 4000 vols. Swimming pool. Tennis crts. Field.

Malang (East Java) — WESLEY INTERNATIONAL CHRISTIAN SCHOOL. Jalan Raya Dieng 10. Tel. 26684. Day Coed 5-12. Gr K-8. Marilyn Wykes, BA, Michigan State Univ., Prin. Gen Acad. Curr—USA. LI—Eng. CF—Indonesian Sci Art Music. Enr 24. B 12; G 12. Fac 5. Full 1/Part 4. M 1; F 4. US 3. Tui $1450 (+ $50). Est 1971. Inc nonprofit. Sem (Aug-May). ISS. Bldgs 2. 2 Libs 3600 vols. Crts.

Rumbai Pekanbaru (Riau) — CALTEX AMERICAN SCHOOL. Day Coed 5-14. Gr K-8. Paul J. Prester, BS, MS, Wagner College, Supt. Pre-Prep. Curr—USA. Tests SAT. LI—Eng. A—Algebra. CF—Indonesian Math Soc Stud Sci. SI—Rem Read & Math ESL. Enr 80. B 40; G 40. Grad '84—7. Fac 15. Full 13/Part 2. M 8; F 7. US 13. Schol. Est 1953. Caltex Pacific Indonesia. Sem (Sept-Je). EARCOS ISS. Bldgs 3. 2 Libs 10,000 vols. Gym.

Sentani Irian Jaya — SENTANI INTERNATIONAL SCHOOL. Kotak Pos 239. Wayne R. Thompson, MEd, Mansfield, Prin. EARCOS ISS.

Tembagapura — ISS SCHOOL AT TEMBAGAPURA. Day Coed 5-15. Gr K-8. Mail to: P.O. Box 616, Cairns Queensland, Australia 4870. Joseph Barrett, Prin. Pre-Prep. Curr—USA. LI—Eng. Est 1972. Nonprofit. Tri (Sept-July). EARCOS ISS.

MALAYSIA

Kota Kinabalu (Sabah) — KIMABULA INTERNATIONAL SCHOOL. P.O. Box 2080. ISS.

Penang — UPLANDS SCHOOL. Kelawei Rd. Tel. 20788. Bdg & Day Coed 5-16. Gr K-11. John E. Churchman, MA, Dir. Pre-Prep Col Prep. Tests GCE. Curr—UK. LI—Eng. CF—Fr Ger Malay. SI—Rem & Dev Math & Read. Enr 166. B 19/78; G 21/48. Fac 21. Full 16/Part 5. M 7; F 14. Nat. Tui Bdg $M1700; Day $M575-1230 (+$M100). Est 1952. Inc nonprofit. Tri (Jan-Dec). Bldgs 3. Dorms 8. Lib. Field. Uplands' curriculum which leads to the G.C.E. 'O' level exams is supplemented by extracurricular activities in sailing, swimming, music, drama and karate.

Sandycroft (Penang) — DALAT SCHOOL OF THE CHRISTIAN AND MISSIONARY ALLIANCE. Gr 1-12. Elmer Baxter, Dir. Enr 185. EARCOS ISS. Accred WASC.

Tanah Rata (Cameron Highlands Peninsular) — CHEFOO SCHOOL. Gr 1-6. Stuart Melton, Head. Enr 62. EARCOS ISS.

NEPAL

Katmandu — ST. XAVIER'S SCHOOL, JAWALAKHEL. Box 50. Tel. 21050. Day Boys 6-17. Gr 1-10. G. William Robins, SJ, Rector. Pre-Prep Col Prep Gen Acad. Curr—Nat. LI—Nepali. CF—Eng Sci. Est 1954. Inc nonprofit. Tri (Feb-Dec).

SINGAPORE

Singapore 7 — BONTANG INTERNATIONAL SCHOOL. Day Coed 5-13. Gr K-8. Ted Kinnen, BS, MA, Prin. Pre-Prep. Tests SSAT. Curr—USA. LI—Eng. CF—Bahasa. Est 1975.Tri (Sept-July). EARCOS.

Singapore 9123 — CALTEX AMERICAN SCHOOL FOUNDATION. Rumbai Pekanbaru. Day Coed 5-14. Gr K-8. Paul J. Prester, Supt. Curr—USA. LI—Eng. CF—Bahasa Math Soc Stud Sci Comp. SI—Rem & Dev Math & Read Tut. Enr 70. B 35; G 35. US—50. Fac 14. M 7; F 7. Schol. Est 1953. Inc nonprofit. Sem (Sept-Je). EARCOS ISS. Bldgs 3. Lib 5000 vols. Fields. Courts. Swimming pool.

1129 Singapore — FAR EASTERN ACADEMY. 800 Thompson Rd. Tel. 2531155. Bdg & Day Coed 6-18. Gr 1-12. A.W. Robinson, Head. Gen Acad. Curr—USA. LI—Eng. CF—Fr Hist (US). Est 1926. Seventh Day Adventist. Sem (Aug-May). ISS.

Singapore 0513 — INTERNATIONAL PREPARATORY SCHOOLS (PTE.), LTD. Dover Court, Dover Rd. Tel. 2354351. Day Coed 4-13. Gr K-8. E. E. Alliott, Head. Pre-Prep Gen Acad. Tests CEE. Curr—UK. LI—Eng. CF—Fr Span. SI—Rem & Dev Math & Reading Tut EFL. Est 1971. Inc. Tri (Sept-July). ISS.

FAR EAST & PACIFIC ISLANDS

AUSTRALIA

Charter Towers 4820 (Queensland) — BLACKHEATH AND THORNBURGH COLLEGE. P.O. Box 339. Tel. 871644. Bdg & Day Coed 10-18. Gr 5-12. Stanley Mason, Prin. Col Prep. Curr—Nat. LI—Eng. CF—Fr Soc Stud Econ Hist Geog Bus & Indus Stud. SI—Rem. Est 1919. Quar (Jan-Nov).

Indooroopilly 4068 (Queensland) — ST. PETER'S LUTHERAN COLLEGE. 66 Harts Rd.Box 111. Tel. 370 7141. Bdg Coed 11-18; Day Coed 5-18. Gr 1-12. Carson R. Dron, BEd, MEd, Head. Col Prep Gen Acad. Curr—Nat. LI—Eng. CF—Ger Fr Lat Bus. SI—Rem & Dev Read. Enr 1170. B 170/380; G 180/440. Elem 420, Sec 750. Grad '84—144. Col—118. Fac 79. Full 60/Part 19. M 35; F 44. US 2. Nat. Tui Bdg $A2600; Day $A1900. Schol. Est 1945. Inc nonprofit. Quar (Jan-Nov). Bldgs 12. Dorms 2. 2 Libs 35,000 vols. Athletic facilities.

Mowbray Heights 7250 (Tasmania) — BROADLAND HOUSE CHURCH/LAUNCESTON CHURCH GRAMMAR SCHOOL. Button St. Bdg Girls 7-18; Day Boys 3-8, Girls 3-18. Gr K-12. Lillian Powell, BA, Tasmania, BEd, Melbourne, Prin. Gen Acad. Curr —Nat. Ll—Eng. A—Sci Hist Drama Math. CF—Fr Lat Comp Stud. SI—Rem Eng & Math. Est 1845. Church of England. Tri (Feb-Dec).

North Geelong (Victoria) 3215 — THE GEELONG COLLEGE. St. David St. Bdg & Day Coed 5-18. Gr K-12. Enr 997. NAIS.

North Ryde (New South Wales) — THE AUSTRALIAN INTER-NATIONAL INDEPENDENT SCHOOL. 110 Talavera Rd. Tel. 02-8887804. Day Coed 11-18. Gr 7-12. W.J. Eason, Head. Gen Acad. Curr—Nat. Ll—Eng. CF—Indonesian Chinese Fr Ger Intl Stud Art Music. SI—Rem & Dev Math & Read. Enr 190. Elem 50, Sec 140. Grad '84—42. Col—35. Fac 30. Full 11/Part 19. M 14; F 16. Nat. Tui $A2400 (+$A150). Schol. Est 1970. Nonprofit. Tri (Feb-Dec). Bldgs 10. Lib 5000 vols. Field.

Sydney (New South Wales) 2048 — NEWINGTON COLLEGE. Tel. 02-560-5355. Bdg & Day Boys 5-18. Gr K-12. Anthony J. Rae, MEd, Sydney Univ., Head. Col Prep. Ll—Eng. CF—Fr Ger Math Sci. Enr 1500. Elem 850, Sec 650. Fac 115. Full 85/Part 30. M 90; F 25. US 2. Nat. Tui Bdg $7400; Day $3600. Schol. Est 1865. Methodist. Tri (Feb-Dec). NAIS.

CHINA (PEOPLE'S REPUBLIC)

Guangzhou (Canton) — AMERICAN SCHOOL OF GUANGZHOU. Tel. 69- 900. Day Coed 5-12. Gr K-8. Mail to: c/o U.S. Consulate General, Box 100, Dept. of State, Washington, DC 20520. Pamela Maxwell, Head. Gen Acad. Ll—Eng. CF—Chinese Ballet. Enr 20. US 13. Fac 5. Full 4/Part 1. US Nat. Tui $5000. Est 1981. Sem (Sept-Je). A/OS EARCOS. Situated in the Dong Fang Hotel, this school follows the curriculum provided by the Calvert School Home Study Program.

Peking — THE INTERNATIONAL SCHOOL OF BEIJING. Day Coed 5-13. Gr K-8. Mail to: c/o American Embassy 17, Guang Hun Lu, Beijing, China. Tel. 52-38-31. John Ritter, MA, Prin. Pre-Prep Gen Acad. Curr—USA. Ll—Eng. CF—Fr Chinese Math Art Music. Enr 113. US—35. Fac 26. US 14. Tui $3750-4150. Est 1980. Tri (Sept-Je) A/OS EARCOS. Accred WASC. Lib 2000 vols.

Shanghai — SHANGHAI AMERICAN SCHOOL. Day Coed 5-13. Gr K-8. Mail to: c/o U.S. Consulate General Shanghai, U.S. Dept. of State, Washington, DC 20520. Tel. 379880. Bonnie B. Wisnewski, BA, Univ. of Bridgeport, Admin. Pre-Prep. Tests SSAT. LI—Eng. CF—Mandarin Math Lang Hist Sci. Enr 11. B 6; G 5. US—10. Grad '84—2. Fac 5. F 5. US 5. Tui $5000 (+$200). Est 1980. Nonprofit. Sem (Sept-Je). A/OS EARCOS. Bldg 3. Lib 3000 vols.

FIJI

Suva — INTERNATIONAL SECONDARY SCHOOL. Box 2393, Government Bldg. Tel. 393-300. Day Coed 11-18. Gr 7-12. R. Dawson Murray, BS, Dir. Gen Acad. Tests GCE. Curr—UK Nat. LI—Eng. CF—Fr Lat. Sl—Tut. Enr 198. B 90; G 108. Fac 17. Full 16/Part 1. M 7; F 10. Nat. Tui $1200-2100 (+$15). Est 1979. Tri (Jan-Dec). A/OS. Accred WASC. Bldgs 2. Lib 3000 vols. A New Zealand school program is followed at this school, however, preparation for the G.C.E. 'O' and 'A' levels and the International Baccalaureate is available.

Suva — PACIFIC HARBOUR INTERNATIONAL SCHOOL. Pacific Harbor Postal Agency. Day Coed 4-12. Gr N-5. Joyce Chand, Head. Pre-Prep. Curr—Nat. LI—Eng. Est 1976.

Suva — SUVA GRAMMAR SCHOOL. GPO 33. Tel. 313-300. Day Coed 11-20. Gr 7-PG. Dip N. Singh, BA, CertEd, Prin. Col Prep. Curr—Nat. LI—Eng. CF—Fijian Hindi Fr Hist Sci Tech Drawing Geog Accounting. Enr 1140. Fac 60. Tui $84 (+$15). Schol. Est 1960. Tri (Feb-Nov). Lib. Labs. Athletic facilities. This school is primarily for Fijian nationals, with a small portion of the enrollment comprised of children from other Pacific islands, Asia, Britain and the United States.

GUAM

Agana — BISHOP BAUMGARTNER JUNIOR HIGH SCHOOL. Box 394. Tel. 472-6670. Day Coed 12-15. Gr 7-9. Sr. Alice McMullin, FSPA, BS, Viterbo College, MA, Notre Dame Univ., Prin. Pre-Prep. Curr—USA. LI—Eng. CF—Span Fr Eng Theol Math Sci Art Music. Sl—Rem & Dev Read & Math Tut. Enr 280. Elem 210, Sec 70. Grad '84—76. Fac 15. M 4; F 11. US. Tui $1050 (+$100). Est 1955. Nonprofit. (Aug-Je). Accred WASC. Bldgs 5. Lib.

Talofofo 96914 — NOTRE DAME HIGH SCHOOL. San Miguel St. Tel. 789-1676. Day Girls 13-17. Gr 9-12. Sr. Jean Ann Crisostomo, SSND, MA, Univ. of Guam, Prin. Col Prep. LI—Eng. A—Lang Chem Math Lit. CF—Theo Soc Stud Anthro. Est 1968. Nonprofit. Sem (Aug-May). Accred WASC.

HONG KONG

Causeway Bay — CHINESE INTERNATIONAL SCHOOL. 7, Eastern Hospital Rd. Tel. 5- 770557. Day Coed 4-10. Gr N-4. C.A. Stuart-Clark, MA, Prin. Gen Acad. Tests GCE. Curr—UK Nat. LI—Eng. CF—Chinese Mandarin. SI—Rem & Dev Read. Enr 91. B 54; G 37. Fac 15. Full 11/Part 4. M 1; F 14. UK Nat. Tui HK$13,500 (+HK$600). Schol. Est 1983. nonprofit. Tri (Sept-July). Bldg. Lib. Gym. This school offers an international education based on a Chinese cultural heritage. Gymnastics, ballet and Tai Kwon Do are featured in the extracurricular program.

Hong Kong — ISLAND SCHOOL. 20 Borrett Rd. Tel. 5-247135. Day Coed 11-18. Gr 7-PG. C.H.R. Niven, MA, Cantab, DipEd, Oxon, Prin. Col Prep Gen Acad. Tests GCE. Curr—UK Nat. LI—Eng. CF—Ger Ital Lattin Fr Chinese Tech Stud Hist Relig. SI—Rem & Dev Math & Read. Enr 1250. B 570; G 680. US—63. Fac 65. M 40; F 25. UK. Tui $6700 (+$85/term). Schol. Est 1967. Inc nonprofit. Tri (Sept-Je). ISS. Bldgs 5. Lib. Swimming pool. Fields.

Kowloon — SHATIN COLLEGE. 2 Tin Kwong Rd. Tel. 3-7600451. Day Coed 11-14. Gr 6-9. Jennifer Bray, MA, Dir. Gen Acad. Tests GCE. Curr—UK. LI—Eng. CF—Fr Span. SI—Rem & Dev Math & Read. Enr 95. B 45; G 50. US 8. Fac 8. Full 5/Part 3. M 2; F 6. Tui HK$12,700 (+HK$500). Est 1982. Tri (Sept-Je). Bldgs 2. Lib 2500 vols. Gym. Crts 2. Pool. Field. The international enrollment at Shatin is comprised mostly of British students. Technical studies and creative arts are featured in the basic curriculum.

JAPAN

Yokohama 232 — SANCTA MARIA INTERNATIONAL SCHOOL. 41, Karasawa Minami-ku. Tel. 045-251-4963. Day Boys 4-7; Girls 4-13. Gr N-8. Sr. Mary Elizabeth Doll, BA, MA, Prin. Gen Acad. Curr—USA. LI—Eng. CF—Span Jap.

KOREA

Seoul — SEOUL ACADEMY. Young Dong, P.O. Box 85. Tel. 555-2475. Day Coed 4-13. Gr N-8. Thomas P. O'Connor, MA, New York Univ., Dir. Gen Acad. Curr—USA. LI—Eng. CF—Hindi Korean Span. SI—Rem & Dev Math & Read ESL. Enr 110. Fac 7. US. Tui $2600 (+$350). Est 1983. Nonprofit. Sem (Aug-Je). EARCOS. Bldg. Lib 3500 vols. Students from India, South America and the U.S. are enrolled at Seoul Academy.

NEW ZEALAND

Dunedin — JOHN MCGLASHAN COLLEGE. 2 Pilkington St. Tel. 64 24 773335. Bdg & Day Boys 11-18. Gr 6-12. Allan A. Paulin, BS, Head. Col Prep Gen Acad. Curr—Nat. Ll—Eng. CF—Fr Lat. Sl—Tut. Enr 308. B 122/186. Elem 136, Sec 172. US 1. Tui Bdg NZ$2400 (+ NZ$100); Day NZ$2000 (+ NZ$300). Schol. Est 1918. Tri (Jan-Dec). Bldgs 10. Dorms 9. Lib 10,000 vols. Gym. Crts. Track. John McGlashan follows a New Zealand school curriculum. Yachting, cadets and an adventure program are among the extra-curricular offerings.

PAPUA NEW GUINEA

Arawa (NSP) — BOVO INTERNATIONAL PRIMARY SCHOOL. P.O. Box 656. Tel. 95 1486. Day Coed 5-12. Gr K-6. Margaret Bavera, Prin. Gen Acad. Curr—Australia. Ll—Eng. Enr 493. B 233; G 260. Fac 22. M 3; F 19. Australia. Tui K1104. Est 1972. Quar (Feb-Dec). ISS. Bldgs 10. Fields.

Banz (WHP) — BANZ INTERNATIONAL SCHOOL. P.O. Box 66. Tel. 562 216. Day Coed 5-13. Gr K-6. David J. Short, Prin. Gen Acad. Curr—UK. Ll—Eng. CF—Music Math Soc Sci Dramatic Arts. Enr 75. Fac 3. Est 1977. Quar (Feb-Dec). ISS. Bldgs 5. Lib 3000 vols. Athletic facilities.

Boroko (NCP) — BOROKO EAST INTERNATIONAL PRIMARY SCHOOL. P.O. Box 6638. Tel. 255037. Day Coed 5-12. Gr K-6. Leah Dunston, Head. Pre-Prep. Curr—Australian. Ll—Eng. Sl—Rem Read & Math. Est 1961. Inc 1976. Quar (Jan-Dec). ISS.

Boroko — MURRAY INTERNATIONAL SCHOOL. CNR Boroko Dr. and Gabaka St. Gr 1-6. ISS.

Lae Marobe — LAE INTERNATIONAL PRIMARY SCHOOL. P.O. Box 2130. Tel. 42 2394. A. Sadgrove, Prin. ISS.

Madang — MADANG INTERNATIONAL PRIMARY SCHOOL. P.O. Box 306. Day Coed 5-12. Gr K-6. A. Horsefield, BA, Prin. Gen Acad. Ll—Eng. Enr 237. B 105; G 117. Fac 10. Full 9/Part 1. M 2; F 8. Australia. Tui K1104. Nonprofit. Quar (Feb-Dec). ISS.

Mt. Hagen (WHP) — HAGEN INTERNATIONAL PRIMARY SCHOOL. P.O. Box 945. Tel. 521964. Day Coed 5-12. Gr K-6. Miss N. J. Crawford, Head. Gen Acad. Curr—Australian.CF—Math Eng Soc Sci Art. Sl—Rem & Dev Reading & Math ESL. Est 1976. Nonprofit. Quar (Feb-Dec). ISS. Bldgs 5.

Popondetta — BAMBUSI STREET INTERNATIONAL SCHOOL.
P.O. Box 10. Tel. 297180. Day Coed 5-12. Gr K-6. Beverley M.
Flanagan, Head. Gen Acad. Curr—Australian. LI—Eng. SI—Rem
& Dev Read. Enr 45. Fac 3. Tui K1020. Est 1969. Nonprofit. Quar
(Jan-Dec). ISS. Bldgs 2. Lib. Athletic facilities.

Rabaul — RABAUL INTERNATIONAL PRIMARY SCHOOL. Section
31, Court St.P.O. Box 855. Tel. 921485. Day Coed 5-13. Gr K-6.
Bruce Mackinlay, Head. Pre-Prep Gen Acad. Curr—Australian.
LI—Eng. CF—Math Soc Sci Art Music Drama. SI—Rem & Dev
Math & Read. Enr 163. B 79; G 84. Australia. Fac 15. Full
11/Part 4. M 2; F 13. Australia. Tui $1500 (+ $200). Est 1950. Inc
1976 nonprofit. Quar (Feb-Dec). ISS. Bldgs 7. Lib 5000 vols.
Fields.

Ukarumpa — UKARUMPA HIGH SCHOOL. P.O. Box 406. Tel.
77-1059. Telex: NE 77611. Day Coed 11-18. Gr 7-12. Colin D.
Anderson, DipEd, Sydney, Prin. Col Prep Gen Acad. Tests GCE
CEEB. Curr—USA Australian. LI—Eng. CF—Fr Span Ger Indo-
nesian. A—Eng Math Sci Fr Music Art. SI—Rem & Dev Read &
Math Tut. Enr 215. B 103; G 112. Elem 74, Sec 141. US—108.
Grad '84—29. Col—27. Fac 35. Full 24/Part 11. M 22; F 13. US
17. Tui $1130-1180 (+ $15). Est 1962. Sem (Feb-Dec). EARCOS
ISS. Accred WASC. Bldgs 7. Lib 12,000 vols. Field. Crts.

**Wapenamanda (Enga) — HIGHLAND LUTHERAN INTERNA-
TIONAL PRIMARY SCHOOL.** Tel. 574043. Day Coed 5-13. Gr
K-8. Lois Eckert, Prin. Gen Acad. Curr—USA. LI—Eng. CF—Eng
Math Soc Stud Sci Art Music. SI—Rem & Dev Read & Math. Tui
$810. ISS.

Wau Morobe — KATHARINE LEHMANN SCHOOL. P.O. Box 81.
Tel. 44 6228. Bdg Coed 8-12; Day Coed 5-12. Gr K-7. Pre-Prep.
Curr—Australian Ger. LI—Eng Ger. Enr 37. B 11/7; G 11/8. Grad
'84—5. Fac 6. M 2; F 4. US 1. Australia Ger. Tui Bdg K1266
(+ K20); Day K993 (+ K351). Est 1951. Tri (Jan-Dec). Bldgs 20.
Dorms 2. Lib 7500 vols. Pool. Court.

**Wewak (East Sepik) — WEWAK INTERNATIONAL PRIMARY
SCHOOL.** P.O. Box 354. Tel. 862172. Day Coed 5-12. Gr K-6.
Stephen J. Belfrage, DipEd, Prin. Curr—Australian New Zealand.
LI—Eng. CF—Math Soc Stud Health Sci Music Art. SI—Rem &
Dev Read. Enr 160. B 92; G 68. Fac 9. Full 7/Part 2. M 3; F 6.
Australia. Tui K1088. Est 1950. Inc 1976. Quar (Feb-Dec.) ISS.
Bldgs 4. Lib.

PHILIPPINES

Besao (Mountain Province) 0606 — SAINT JAMES' HIGH SCHOOL. Day Coed 13-17. Gr 8-11. John L. Botengan, Prin. Gen Acad. Curr—Nat. LI—Eng. CF—Pilipino. Enr 453. B 196; G 257. Grad '84—109. Col—85. Fac 15. Full 15. M 5; F 10. Nat. Tui P285. Est 1913. Inc 1930 nonprofit. (Je-May). Bldgs 2. Lib 1098 vols. Crts. Fields.

Manila — ST. PAUL COLLEGE OF MANILA. P.O. Box 2061.680 Pedro Gil. Tel. 50-66-26. Day Girls 12-17. Gr 8-Col. Sr. Mary Cyril Corpus, Pres. Col Prep Gen Acad Bus. Curr—Nat. LI—Eng. CF—Filipino Trig Nursing Comm Arts Music. Est 1924. Inc nonprofit. Sem (Je-Mar).

Manila — ST. SCHOLASTICA'S COLLEGE. 2560 Leon Guinto St. Tel. 50-76-86. Day Girls 6-22. Gr K-PG. Sr. Mary Bellarmine Bernas, OSB, MA, PhD, Stanford Univ., Pres. Pre-Prep Col Prep Gen Acad Bus/Tech. Curr—Nat. Tests CEEB SSAT. LI—Eng Filipino. CF—Filipino Span Japanese Comm Arts Soc Stud Relig Bus Theater Arts Mandarin. SI—Rem & Dev Math & Read. Enr 5490. Elem 2128, Sec 1266, PG 2096. US—12. Grad '84—383. Fac 292. Full 163/Part 129. M 65; F 227. Nat. Tui $250. Schol. Est 1906. Nonprofit. Tri (Je-May). Bldgs 12. Dorms 1. 3 Libs 60,000 vols. Gym. Fields.

Manila — ST. STEPHEN'S HIGH SCHOOL. 1267 Guillermo Masangkay St., Sta. Cruz. Tel. 21-86-47. Day Coed 5-18. Gr K-12. Ong To Sieng, BS, Prin. Pre-Prep Col Prep. CF—Chinese Eng Pilipino. Enr 1350. B 642; G 708. Fac 58. Full 54/Part 4. M 47; F 11. Nat. Est 1917. Nonprofit. (Je-March). Bldgs 8. Lib. Gym.

SAMOA (AMERICAN AND WESTERN)

Pago Pago — FA'ASAŌ HIGH SCHOOL. P.O. Box 729. Tel. 688-7331. Day Girls 12-19. Gr 9-12. Sr. Joan Carey, Prin. Gen Acad. Tests SSAT. LI—Eng. CF—Eng Samoan Span SI—Rem & Dev Math & Read. Enr 240. Grad '84—56. Col—32. Fac 14. Full 13/Part 1. F 14. Ireland. Tui /22240. Est 1974. Nonprofit. Sem (Sept-Je). Accred WASC. Roman Catholic. This school's basic curriculum offers advanced level study in chemistry, English and math.

Pago Pago — FAGAITUA HIGH SCHOOL. c/o Dept. of Education.Pago Pago, American Samoa. Tel. 622-7504. Day Coed 13-18. Gr 9-12. Eneliko F. Sofai, BA, State Univ. of NY, MEd, Brigham Young Univ., Prin. Est 1968. Quar (Sept-Je). Accred WASC.

SOLOMON ISLANDS

Honiara (Guadalcanal) — **NEW WOODFORD SCHOOL.** Box 44. Tel. 06-86. Day Coed 4½-12. Gr 1-7. Joseph T. Puia, Head. Pre-Prep. Curr—UK. LI—Eng. CF—Math Hist Geog Sci Art. Est 1959. Nonprofit. Tri (Jan-Dec). ISS.

VANUATU

Port Vila — **CENTRAL PRIMARY SCHOOL.** P.O. Box 988. Tel. 3122. Day Coed 3-12. Gr N-6. John Parsons, Head. Pre-Prep. Curr—UK. LI—Eng. CF—Fr. SI—Tut. Enr 441. B 209; G 232. Fac 15. Full 15. M 1; F 14. Australia. Tui VT30,000. Schol. Est 1946. Nonprofit. Tri (Feb-Dec). Lib. Field. Crt. This multi-cultural school's academic program is designed to meet the needs of expatriate English-speaking students from metropolitan countries. Graduates go on to secondary schools in the United Kingdom, Australia, New Zealand and the U.S.

LATIN AMERICA

CENTRAL AMERICA, MEXICO & CARIBBEAN ISLANDS

BAHAMAS

Freeport (Grand Bahama) — **THE FREEPORT (ANGLICAN) HIGH SCHOOL.** East Sunrise Highway, PO Box F667. Tel. 809-373-3579. Day Coed 11-18. Gr 6-12. Mrs. A.D. Osman, MScEd, Miami Univ., Prin. Col Prep Gen Acad. Tests GCE CEEB. Curr—UK USA. LI—Eng. CF—Fr Span Lat Bus Comp Stud. Enr 450. B 182; G 268. Elem 109, Sec 341. US—9. Grad '84—58. Col—12. Fac 21. Full 20/Part 1. M 10; F 11. US 2. UK West Indies. Tui $1200 (+$150). Est 1965. Inc 1975 nonprofit. Anglican. Tri (Sept-Je). Bldgs 6. Lib 3000 vols. Pool. Crts. Field.

Freeport — **SUNLAND LUTHERAN SCHOOL.** P.O. Box F2469. Tel. 809-373-3700. Day Coed 3-13. Gr N-9. Joycelyn Pinder, Prin. Gen Acad. Curr—Nat USA. LI—Eng. CF—Span Fr Art Music Relig. SI—Rem & Dev Math & Read Tut. Enr 390. US—40. Fac 23. Full 22/Part 1. M 4; F 19. Nat. Tui $1544. Schol. Est 1969. Nonprofit. Lutheran. Tri (Sept-Je). Bldgs 7. Lib 10,550 vols. Field.

Nassau — LYFORD CAY SCHOOL. P.O. Box N7776. Tel. 32 64269. Day Coed 2½-11. Gr N-6. Julian Foulkes, BEd, Newcastle, Head. Gen Acad. Curr—UK. Ll—Eng. CF—Fr Span Drama Music Lang Arts Comp Math. Sl—Rem & Dev Math & Read Tut. Enr 160. B 80; G 80. Fac 12. Full 11/Part 1. M 1; F 11. US 2. UK. Tui $2250. Schol. Tri (Sept-Je). Bldgs 4. Lib 3000 vols. Field. Crt. Three-quarters of the students body are British. The curriculum prepares students for the Common Entrance Exam.

Nassau — QUEEN'S COLLEGE. P.O. Box N 3923.Village Road. Gr 1-12. Curr—UK. Ll—Eng. Tri (Sept-Je). ISS. Students prepare for the British G.C.E.

BARBADOS

St. Michael — ST. URSULA'S URSULINE CONVENT. Collymore Rock. Tel. 65571. Day Girls 11-17. Gr 6-12. Sr. June-Ann Pinkerton, OSU, Head. Gen Acad. Tests GCE. Curr—Nat. Ll—Eng. CF—Span Biol Lit Typing. Enr 302. Fac 18. Tui $B440 (+$B12). Est 1894. Nonprofit. Roman Catholic. Tri (Sept-July). Bldgs 4. Lib 1000 vols. Athletic facilities.

St. Philip — MAPPS COLLEGE. Tel. 4236272. Bdg & Day Boys 9-18. Gr 4-12. A. G. F. Wilkes, DipEd, Head. Gen Acad. Curr—UK. Ll—Eng. CF—Fr Span West Indian Hist. Enr 123.B 38/85. Fac 10. M 7; F 3. UK Nat. Tui Bdg $2250 (+$300); Day $500 (+$200). Est 1960. Proprietary. Tri (Sept-July). Bldgs 7. Dorms 4. Lib 3000 vols. Athletic facilities.

BERMUDA

Hamilton 5-31 — MOUNT SAINT AGNES ACADEMY. Cedar Ave. Tel. 809-292-4134. Day Coed 5-18. Gr K-12. Sr. Judith Marie Rollo, Prin. Col Prep Bus. Tests SSAT Curr—USA. Ll—Eng. CF—Fr Span Econ Man Arts. Roman Catholic. Tri (Sept-Je).

Pembroke 5-34 — BERMUDA HIGH SCHOOL FOR GIRLS. Richmond Rd. Tel. 809-295-6153. Day Girls 5-18. Gr K-12. Ms. J. Myerscough, Prin. Col Prep Gen Acad. Tests GCE SSAT. Curr—UK USA. Ll—Eng. CF—Fr Ger Lat Span. Sl—Rem Eng. Enr 500. Fac 10. M 3; F 7. UK. Tui $2900 (+$100). Schol. Est 1894. Inc 1927 nonprofit. Tri (Sept-July). ISS NAIS.

COSTA RICA

San Jose — COLEGIO METODISTA. Apartado Postal 931. Tel. 25-06-55. Day Boys 5-19, Girls 5-18. Gr K-11. Humberto Perez, P., Dir. Col Prep. Curr—USA. LI—Eng. CF—Fr Ger World Hist Lit. SI—Rem Eng. Est 1921. Inc 1952 nonprofit. Methodist. Sem (Mar-Nov). ISS.

DOMINICAN REPUBLIC

La Romana — ABRAHAM LINCOLN SCHOOL. Central Romana. Tel. 1284-6877787. Telex: 3460511 GWAC. Day Coed 4-18. Gr N-12. David John Tully, Head. Col Prep Gen Acad. Curr—UK USA. LI—Eng Span. Tests GCE SSAT. CF—Fr Math Sci Geog Hist Art Econ Comp Tech Drawing. SI—Rem & Dev Math & Read. Enr 340. B 183; G 157. Elem 278, Sec 62. US—30. Grad '84—9. Col—9. Fac 32. M 12; F 20. US 1. UK. Tui RD$110-150/mo. Est 1920. Quar (Sept-Je). ISS. Bldgs 7. Lib 5000 vols. Athletic facilites.

EL SALVADOR

Santa Tecla (La Libertad) — ACADEMIA BRITÁNICA CUSCATLECA. Km. 10-1¹/₂, Carretera a Santa tecla. Tel. 28-2011. Day Coed 3-18. Gr N-12. Michael W. Cross, MA, Hertford College (Oxford), Head. Col Prep. Tests IB GCE SSAT. LI—Span Eng. Enr 891. B 407; G 484. Elem 713, Sec 178. Grad '84—38. Col—19. Fac 62. Full 44/Part 18. M 19; F 43. US 1. Nat. Tui $1200 (+$100). Est 1970. Nonprofit. Tri (Sept-July). AASCA. Bldgs 6. 2 Libs 80000 vols. Field. Crts. Track. Swimming pool. The International Baccalaureate degree program is offered in addition to preparation for U.S. and U.K. university entrance exams.

GUATEMALA

Vista Hermosa 11 — COLEGIO-INGLES AMERICANO. O Calle 19-70 Zona 15. ISS.

HONDURAS

La Ceiba — MAZAPAN SCHOOL. Standard Fruit Co. Day Coed 6-18. Gr 1-12. Raymond Marshall, Dir. Col Prep. Tests CEEB. Curr—Nat. LI—Eng. CF—Span Soc Stud Art Music Comp. SI—Tut. Enr 250. B 120; G 130. Elem 195, Sec 55. US—28. Grad

'84—7. Col—6. Fac 22. Full 18/Part 4. M 11; F 11. US 16. Tui $1800. Nonprofit. Sem (Sept-Je). AASAC ISS. Accred SACS. Bldgs 6. Lib 6000 vols.

Puerto Cortes (Cortes) — ST. JOHN'S SCHOOL. Apartado 16. Day Coed 4-15. Gr N-9. Marvin L. Ross, BS, Texas Institute of Technology, MA, Stanford Univ., Head. Gen Acad. Curr—USA. LI—Eng Span. CF—Relig Sci Math ESL. SI—Tut. Enr 220. B 132; G 88. Elem 215, Sec 5. Fac 18. Full 13/Part 5. M 7; F 11. US 7. Tui $700. Est 1974. Nonprofit. Roman Catholic. Sem (Sept-Je). Bldgs 4. Lib 3000 vols. This school strives for bilingualism among all its students.

San Pedro Sula — LA LIMA AMERICAN SCHOOL. Apartado 30. Tel. 56-20-66. Day Coed 5-14. Gr K-8. Stephen K. Field, Admin. Pre-Prep. Tests SSAT. Curr—USA. LI—Eng. CF—Read Math Sci Soc Span. Est 1927. Nonprofit. (Aug-May).

Tegucigalpa — ELVEL SCHOOL. P.O. Box 883. Tel. 22-3917. Day Coed 4-18. Gr N-12. Col Prep. Tests CEEB SSAT. Curr—Nat USA. LI—Eng Span. Est 1967. Accred SACS.

Tegucigalpa — THE MAYAN SCHOOL. T-213 Barrio Casamata. Tel. 22-31-77. Day Coed 4-15. Gr N-10. Doris S. Morazan, Dir. Col Prep. Tests CEEB SSAT. LI—Eng. CF—Read Eng Math Span. A—Psych Soc Calc Philos Anthro. Est 1977. Inc. Quar (Sept-Je). ISS.

MEXICO

31280 Chihuahua — INSTITUTO TECNOLOGICO Y DE ESTUDIOS SUPERIORES DE MONTERREY. (Escuela Secundaria Bilingue Isaac Newton). Colegio Militar No. 2011, Nombre de Dios. Tel. /4990. Bdg Coed 11-22. Gr 7-PG. Ricardo Almeida, BA, Monterrey Technical College, Prin. Col Prep Gen Acad. Tests SSAT. Curr—USA. LI—Eng. CF—Span Ed Finance Law Marketing. Enr 786. B 496; G 290. US—20. Grad '84—150. Fac 103. Full 19/Part 84. M 77; F 26. US 4. Tui Mex$139,000 (+Mex$10,000). Schol. Est 1976. Inc nonprofit. Sem (Sept-May). Bldgs 5. 2 Libs 12,000 vols.

Mexico City — COLEGIO VISTA HERMOSA. Loma de Vista Hermosa 221. Tel. 570-36-00. Day Coed 5-17. Gr N-12. Vincente L. Boerboom, Dir. Pre-Prep Col Prep. Tests SSAT. LI—Eng Span. CF—Math Eng Span Bio Hist. A—Philos Sci Math Soc Sci. Est 1954.

Mexico City 11000 D.F. — GREENGATES SCHOOL. Apartado
Postal 41-659 (Balcones de San Mateo). Tel. 373-0088. Day Coed
4-18. Gr K-12. Susan Martinez, BA, London Univ, Prin. Col Prep.
Tests CEEB GCE. Curr—UK. LI—Eng. CF—Span Fr Music Art.
SI—Rem & Dev Math & Read Tut. Enr 450. B 225; G 225. Fac 54.
Full 51/Part 3. M 20; F 34. US 12. UK. Tui 250,000-350,000 pesos.
Est 1951. Tri (Sept-Je). ISS. Bldgs 7. Lib 9000 vols. Gym. Pool.

Mexico City — INSTITUTO MEXICO. Amores 1317. Tel. 5-
75-64-53. Day Boys 7-12. Gr 1-6. Antonio P. Garza, Dir. Pre-Prep.
LI—Eng Span. SI—ESL. Est 1943. Nonprofit. (Sept-Je).

Mexico City — PAN AMERICAN WORKSHOP. Matias Romero
#422. Tel. 575-42-88. Day Coed 3-17. Gr N-12. Frances U.
Cocke, Dir. Gen Acad Col Prep. LI—Eng Span. CF—Fr Ger Ital
Russ Bus. SI—Rem & Dev Read & Math Tut. Est 1948. Inc. Sem
(Sept-Je).

Mexico City 10 D.F. — ESCUELA SIERRA NEVADA. Sierra Madre
155 Lomas de Chapultepec. Tel. 520-39-16. Day Coed 6-12. Gr
1-6. Gen Acad. Tests SSAT. Curr—USA. LI—Eng Span. SI
—Read. Est 1950. A bilingual program is conducted.

04510 Mexico D.F. — SCHOOL FOR FOREIGN STUDENTS. Ave.
Universidad 3002, Ciudad University. Tel. 550-51-72. Day Coed 18
and up. PG. Alvaro Matute, Dir. Gen Acad. LI—Span. Fac 103. Tui
$150-300. Est 1921. Sem (Sept-Je). Bldgs 2. Lib 6000 vols.
Athletic facilities. This program is sponsored by the National
Autonomous University of Mexico. Intensive Spanish language
workshops during the academic year and summer supplement the
college-level curriculum.

**Saltillo Coahuila — INSTITUTO DE ESTUDIOS IBERO-
AMERICANOS.** Apartado Postal 358. Tel. 3-89-99. Coed 14-18.
David Simmons, Dir. Span Lang & Culture. SI—Tut. Tui $170/2
wks, $415/5 wks (+$40). Est 1965. Inc nonprofit. Living
accommodations are arranged with local Spanish-speaking families.

Tampico (Tamaulipas) — ESCUELA AMERICANA DE TAMPICO.
Apartado 407. Tel. 2-32-26. Day Coed 3-14. Gr N-9. Ann S. de
Pumarejo, BS, Univ. of Wisconsin, Dir. Gen Acad. Curr—USA.
LI—Eng. CF—Sci Geog Hist. SI—ESL Tut. Enr 415. Fac 35. Tui
800 Mex$/mo (+500 Mex$). Est 1917. Inc. Tri (Aug-Je). ISS.

NETHERLANDS ANTILLES

Curacao — **INTERNATIONAL SCHOOL OF CURACAO.** Sant Rosastraat A 29.P.O. Box 3090. Tel. 9-2161. Day Coed 5-14. Gr K-9. Frank Lowry, Univ. of Maine, Admin. Gen Acad. Curr—USA. LI—Eng. CF—Fr Sci Math Soc Stud Eng Art. Enr 71. Fac 17. Full 12/Part 5. M 3; F 14. US. Tui $3000-6100 (+ $325). Est 1967. Sem (Aug-Je). ISS.

PANAMA

Balboa — **BALBOA HIGH SCHOOL.** Day Coed 14-19. Gr 10-12. Mail to: Dept. of Defense Dependents Schools, Panama, APO, Miami 34002. Tel. 52 7896. W.Eugene Bondurant, MEd, Duke Univ., PhD, Univ. of North Carolina, Prin. Gen Acad. Tests CEEB SSAT TOEFL. Curr—USA. LI—Eng. CF—Fr Span ESL Bus Comp. SI—Rem & Dev Math & Read. Enr 1006. B 502; G 504. Grad '84—317. Fac 64. M 37; F 27. US 58. Tui $4200 (+ $25). Est 1904. (Aug-Je). Accred MSA. Bldgs 6. Lib 23,000 vols. Gyms 2.

Coco Solo — **CRISTOBAL JUNIOR-SENIOR HIGH SCHOOL.** Day Coed 12-19. Gr 7-12. Mail to: Dept. of Defense Dependents Schools, Panama Region, APO, Miami 34008. Tel. 44-1644. Charles M. Renno, Jr., BA, William Jewel College, MA, Univ. of Redlands, Prin. Tests CEEB SSAT ACT. Curr—USA. LI—Eng. A—Calculus World Lit. CF—Span Fr Latin Hist (US) Soc Stud Drama Music R.O.T.C. SI—Rem Eng Math & Read ESL. Enr 405. Elem 160, Sec 245. Grad '84—57. Col—40. Fac 34. Full 34. M 22; F 12. US 30. Tui $5000. Est 1917. Nonprofit. Sem (Aug-Je). Accred MSA. Bldgs 3. Lib 35,000 vols. Gym. Pool. Fields. Most students are from the U.S.

Panama City 9A — **INSTITUTO PANAMERICANO.** Apartado K. Tel. 24-4667. Day Coed 5-19. Gr K-12. Hugo O. Ortega, Gen Dir. Col Prep. Tests SSAT. Curr—USA Nat. LI—Eng Span. A—Physics Chem Math CF—Shorthand Bookkeeping. Est 1906. Methodist. Sem (Apr-Dec).

Puerto Armuelles — **LAS PALMAS.** Apartado 6-2637. Tel. 70-7283. Day Coed 4-13. Gr N-8. Linda Fitzwalter, BS, Southern Oregon State College, Prin. Gen Acad. Tests SSAT. Curr—USA. LI—Eng Span. Enr 109. Fac 10. Full 8/Part 2. F 10. US 6. Nonprofit. Quar (Aug-May). ISS.

PUERTO RICO

Bayamon 00619 — BALDWIN SCHOOL OF PUERTO RICO. P.O. Box 1827. Tel. 809-790-2421. Day Coed 4-18. Gr N-12. Deborah Richman, MEd, Univ. of Houston, Head. Pre-Prep Col Prep. Tests SSAT. LI—Eng. A—Eng Bio Chem. CF—Span Fr Sci Math Soc Stud Art. SI—Rem & Dev Read. Enr 368. G 196/172. Elem 258, Sec 110. Grad '84—20. Col—20. Fac 35. Full 31/Part 4. M 11; F 24. US. Tui $1900-3300 (+$1000). Schol. Est 1968. Inc nonprofit. (Aug-Je). AASCA. Bldgs 17. Lib 7000 vols. Pool. Crts. Field.

Bayamon 00619 — CARIBBEAN UNIVERSITY COLLEGE. Box 493. Tel. 809-780-0070. Day Coed 16 and up. Col. Angel E. Juan-Ortega, PhD, Walden Univ., Pres. Gen Acad. Tests CEEB. Curr—USA. LI—Span. CF—Eng Fr Math Sci Bus Pre-Legal. SI—Tut Rem & Dev Math & Read & Span. Enr 2700. B 800; G 1900. US—2695. Fac 140. Full 120/Part 20. M 50; F 90. US 138. Schol. Est 1969. Inc nonprofit. Tri (Sept-Aug). Accred MSA. Bldgs 6. 3 Libs 20,000 vols. Crt. The programs of study lead to an associate and/or baccalaureate degree.

Guaynabo — WESLEYAN ACADEMY. Call Box 7890. Tel. (809) 789-3876. Day Coed 5-19. Gr K-12. David A. Wells, Dir. Col Prep. Tests CEEB. Curr—Nat. LI—Eng Span. A—Calc Physics. CF —Hist Bible. Enr 620. B 300; G 320. Elem 470, Sec 150. US—50. Grad '84—30. Col—30. Tui $1100-1200 (+$200). Schol. Est 1954. Inc 1958 nonprofit. Sem (Aug-Je). Bldgs 5. Lib 16,000 vols. Gym. Field. This church sponsored school has a complete bilingual program in Spanish and English with courses in Spanish as a second language.

Rio Piedras 00921 — ACADEMIA MARIA REINA. Avenida Glasgow y Padua College Park. Tel. 809-764-0690. Day Girls 11-18. Gr 7-12. Sr. Maria de Sales, CSJ, Prin. Pre-Prep. Tests CEEB SSAT. Curr—Nat. LI—Eng Span. A—Eng Span Math Physics Physiology Calc. CF—Fr Psych Relig Typing Art Dance. Enr 450. Elem 165, Sec 285. Grad '84—64. Col—64. Fac 43. M 1; F 42. US 40. Tui $1500. Schol. Est 1966. Inc 1967 nonprofit. Sem (Aug-May). Accred MSA. Bldgs 2. Athletic facilities.

Rio Piedras 00928 — COLEGIO SAN ANTONIO. Arzuaga cr. Capuchinos St. Tel. 801-764-0090. Day Coed 5-18. Gr K-12. Father John Schreck, Dir. Gen Acad. Tests SSAT CEEB. Curr—Nat. LI—Eng Span. A—Eng Span Math Biol. CF—Fr Ital US & PR Hist Music Art. SI—Rem & Dev Read Tut. Enr 1089. B 480; G 609. Elem 729, Sec 360. Grad '84—100. Col—100. Fac 65. Full 64/Part 1. M 10; F 55. US 6. Nat. Tui $1250 (+$300). Est 1928. Inc nonprofit. Roman Catholic. (Aug-May). Accred MSA. 2 Libs 15,000 vols. Athletic facilities.

Rio Piedras 00927 — COLEGIO SAN IGNACIO DE LOYOLA. Calle Sauco Final Urbanizacion Santa Maria. Tel. 809-765-3814. Day Boys 11-18. Juan J. Santiago, SJ, STD, Gregorian Univ., Prin. Col Prep. Tests CEEB SAT. LI—Span. CF—Eng Fr Comp Relig. SI—Rem & Dev Read. Enr 814. Elem 308, Sec 506. Grad '84—93. Col—93. Fac 64. Full 55/Part 9. M 30; F 34. US 8. Tui $2000. Schol. Est 1952. Inc I980 nonprofit. Sem (Aug-May). Accred MSA. Roman Catholic. Bldgs 10. Lib 15,000 vols. Crts. Field. Pool.

Rio Piedras 00927 — UNIVERSITY HIGH SCHOOL. University of Puerto Rico. Tel. 809-764-0000. Telex: 3258. Day Coed 13-19. Gr 7-12. Jose M. Alonso, Dir. Col Prep Gen Acad. Tests CEEB SAT. LI—Span. CF—Eng Sci Math. Est 1912. Nonprofit. Sem (Aug-May).

Trujillo Alto 00760 — ANTILLES MILITARY ACADEMY. Ins. Rd., 850 Km 1.0. Tel. 809-761-1710. Bdg Boys 12-18; Day Coed 5-18. Gr K-12. Col Prep. Tests CEEB SSAT. Curr—USA. LI—Eng Span. Est 1959.

VIRGIN ISLANDS

Frederiksted (St. Croix) 00840 — TAMARIND SCHOOL. Box 1078, Estate Beck's Grove. Tel. 809-772-2553. Day Coed 6-14. Gr 1-8. Carla D. Vauthrin, AB, Univ. of California, Head. Pre-Prep. Curr—USA. LI—Eng. CF—Creative Writing Geog Econ. SI—ESL. Enr 24. Fac 4. Tui $2150. Schol. Est 1969. Inc nonprofit. Sem (Sept-Je). Bldgs 11. Lib 2000 vols. Field. Located on an 8-acre site, this school offers a non-graded curriculum designed to meet individual needs as well as programs for the learning disabled.

SOUTH AMERICA

ARGENTINA

Buenos Aires 1428 — BELGRANO DAY SCHOOL. Conesa 2120. Tel. 781-6011. Day Coed 3-18. Gr K-12. Col Prep Gen Acad. Tests GCE TOEFL. LI—Eng Span. Enr 1290. B 650; G 640. Elem 983, Sec 307. Grad '84—88. Col—84. Tui $550-1350 (+ $300-800). Schol. Est 1912. Inc 1915. Proprietary. Sem (Mar-Dec). ISS. Bldgs 5. 2 Libs 2000 vols. Pool. Crts. Fields.

Buenos Aires 1430 — BUENOS AIRES ENGLISH SCHOOL. 1880 Melian. Tel. 552-1533. Day Coed 4-12. Gr K-7. Stella M. A. Rueda, Head. Gen Acad. Curr—Nat. LI—Eng Span. Enr 448. B 279; G 209. Fac 44. M 6; F 38. Nat. Tui $a540,000-1,300,000. Est 1884. Proprietary. Sem (Mar-Nov). Lib 700 vols. Field. Pool.

Cordoba — REYDON SCHOOL FOR GIRLS. 5178 Cruz Chica Sierras De Cordobas. Bdg Girls. Gr 4-12. ISS.

Hurlingham 1686 (Buenos Aires) — ST. HILDA'S COLLEGE. Isabel La Catolica 1710. Tel. 665-0347. Bdg Girls 6-18; Day Coed 2-18. Gr K-12. Martin A. Garvie, Head. Gen Acad. Tests GCE. Curr—Nat. LI—Eng Span. CF—Computer Sci Hist Geog. SI—Tut Rem & Dev Read & Math. Enr 506. B 220; G 286. Elem 433, Sec 73. US—5. Grad '84—8 Col 17. Fac 71. M 14; F 57. Argentina. Tui Bdg $6144; Day $3048 (+$42). Est 1912. Inc nonprofit. Sem (Mar-Dec). ISS. Bldgs 5. Dorms 4. 2 Libs 6000 vols. Gym. Courts. Fields. Pool.

Monte Grande 1842 (Buenos Aires) — ST. MARK'S COLLEGE. Jorge Miles 153. Tel. 290-0215. Day Coed 5-18. Gr K-12. Lorna S. D. de Corley, Dir. Curr—Nat. Tests GCE. LI—Eng Span. CF—Fr Bilingual Instruction. ISS.

Olivos 1636 — ST. ANDREW'S SCOTS SCHOOL. Calle Nogoya 550. Tel. 791-8031. Day Coed 3-18. Gr 1-12. Kevan Prior, EdB, Nottingham Univ., Head. Col Prep Gen Acad. Tests GCE. Curr—UK. LI—Eng Span. CF—Math Sci Bible Drama. Enr 1900. B 1050; G 850. Elem 900, Sec 1000. US—50. Grad '84—85. Col—82. Fac 208. US 8. UK Nat. Est 1838. Nonprofit. Sem (Mar-Nov). ISS.

1704 Ramos Mejia (Buenos Aires) — COLEGIO WARD. Casilla de Correo 35. Tel. 658-0348. Bdg & Day Coed 5-18. Gr K-12. Arthur J. Hand, Dir. Col Prep. Curr—Nat. LI—Span. CF—Eng Fr Hist Pol Sci Arts. SI—Tut. Est 1913. Inc nonprofit. Tri (Mar-Nov). ISS.

BOLIVIA

Cochabamba — INSTITUTO COCHABAMBA. Casilla Correo 175. Tel. 2330. Day Coed 6-18. Gr 1-12. Mario Salazar B., Dir. Col Prep Gen Acad Bus. Curr—Nat. LI—Span. CF—Eng Span Hist (US) Econ Arts. Est 1912. Methodist. Sem (Feb-Nov). ISS. Instruction is in Spanish except for the commercial division which is in English.

BRAZIL

Botafoga (Rio de Janeiro) — THE BRITISH SCHOOL. Rua da Matriz 76. ISS.

San Jose dos Campos — ESCOLA INTERNACIONAL DO VALE DO PARAIBA. Rua Santa Madalena, 36. Tel. (0123) 21-6464. Day Coed 4-14. Gr N-8. Curr—USA. LI—Eng. Est 1950. ISS.

Santos S.P. — AMERICAN SCHOOL OF SANTOS. Caixa Postal 810. Mrs. Isa Thomas, Prin. ISS.

Santos — CENTRO CULTURAL BRASIL-ESTADOS UNIDOS. Jorge Tibirica 5/7. Tel. 34-9965. Day Coed 10 and up. Lilian Numhoz Soares, Coord. Curr—Nat. LI—Eng. SI—ESL Tut. Enr 3000. B 1200; G 1800. Fac 40. Full 29/Part 11. M 10; F 30. US 1. Nat. Tui Cr$80,000/sem. Schol. Est 1943. Nonprofit. Sem (Mar-Aug). ISS. Bldgs 3. Lib 16,000 vols.

Sao Luis — ALCOA AMERICAN SCHOOL. Gr 1-8. Mail to: 1501 Alcoa Bldg, Pittsburgh, PA 15219. Tel. 098-225-0203. Wallace E. McCormick, BS, Univ. of Oregon, MA, California State, Prin. Pre-Prep Gen Acad. Curr—USA. LI—Eng. CF—Port Brazilian Stud. Est 1981. (Sept-Je).

CHILE

Puerto Montt — THE AMERICAN SCHOOL. Vial 486, Casilla 336. Tel. 2170. Day Coed 5-14. Gr K-8. Sergio Wolleter V., Dir. Pre-Prep. LI—Span. CF—Eng Fr. SI—Rem & Dev Read & Math. Est 1960. (Mar-Dec). ISS.

Punta Arenas (Magallanes Region) — THE BRITISH SCHOOL. Waldo Sequell 454, Casilla 379. Tel. 23381. Day Coed 5-18. Gr K-12. Leslie John Pearson, BA, Macquari Univ., Head. Gen Acad. Curr—Nat. LI—Eng Span. CF—Fr. Enr 520. B 260; G 260. Elem 440, Sec 80. Grad '84—14. Col—7. Fac 38. Full 23/Part 15. M 13; F 25. Nat. Tui 8000 pesos/mo (+1000 pesos). Est 1943. Inc nonprofit. Tri (March-Dec). ISS. Bldgs 4. Lib 2000 vols. Crt. Field.

Renaca (Vina del Mar) — THE MCKAY SCHOOL. Vicuna MacKenna s/n. Tel. 803-902676. Day Boys 5-18. Gr K-12. John Harrison, CED, Loughborough Univ., Dir. Gen Acad. Curr—Nat. LI—Eng Span. Enr 650. Elem 450, Sec 200. US—2. Grad '84—54. Col—54. Fac 65. Nat. Est 1857. Nonprofit. Sem (March-Dec).

Santiago — CRAIGHOUSE SCHOOL. Av. Apoquindo 5412. ISS.

Santiago (Las Condes) — REDLAND SCHOOL. Camino El Alba 11357. Tel. 2200481. Day Coed 5-17. Gr K-12. Richard Collingwood-Selby, MA, Oxford, Head. Col Prep. LI—Span. A—Math Sci Art Design Accounting. CF—Eng Fr Span Math. SI—Tut. Enr 514. B 291; G 223. Elem 376, Sec 138. Grad '84—34. Col—24. Fac 51. Full 10/Part 41. M 20; F 31. US 1. Chile UK. Tui $1233 (+$350). Est 1966. Tri (Mar-Dec). Bldgs 5. 2 Libs 4500 vols. Fields.

Vina del Mar — ST. MARGARET'S BRITISH SCHOOL FOR GIRLS.
5 Norte 1351. Tel. 977000. Day Girls 5-18. Gr K-12. Margery Byrne, Head. Gen Acad Pre-Prep. Curr—Nat. LI—Eng Span. CF—Art Fr Music. Enr 850. Fac 62. Full 30/Part 32. F 62. Tui $800. Est 1941. Inc nonprofit. Tri (Mar-Dec). Bldgs 3. Lib 1000 vols. Gym. Courts. Fields.

COLOMBIA

Barranquilla — MARYMOUNT SCHOOL. Apartado Aereo 1912. Bdg Girls 10-18; Day Girls 4-19. Gr N-12. Sr. Johanna Cunniffe, MA, Prin. Col Prep. Tests CEEB. Curr—USA. LI—Eng Span. CF—Fr Hist (US) Sci. Enr 805. Fac 41. Tui Bdg $900; Day $70. Est 1953. Nonprofit. Sem (Sept-Je). ISS. The U.S. curriculum is similar to that offered at other Marymount schools.

Bogota — COLEGIO ABRAHAM LINCOLN. Calle 170 No. 50-25, Apartado Aereo 90339. Tel. 2-54-11-40. Day Coed 4-18. Gr N-12. Donald J. Parker, BS, Miami Univ., MEd, Univ. of Virginia, Prin. Col Prep. Tests CEEB. Curr—USA Nat. LI—Eng Span. A—Calc. CF—Span ESL Lat Am Hist Econ Relig Philos. Enr 630. Fac 53. Tui $700-1000. Schol. Est 1952. Nonprofit. Quar (Sept-Je). ISS. Lib 3000 vols. Athletic facilities. Electives in accounting, horticulture and mechanical drawing, and vocational guidance are offered.

Bogota 2 — COLEGIO ANGLO-COLOMBIANO. Apartado Aereo 21469. Tests IB. ISS.

Bogota — COLEGIO MONTELIBANO. AA 6823. Tel. 66000. Day Coed 3¹/₂-18. Gr N-12. Brian G. Dickson, BA, London, DipEd, San Francisco State Univ., Head. Gen Acad. Tests SSAT. Curr—Nat. LI—Eng Span. CF—Fr Art Music. SI—Tut. Enr 392. B 197; G 195. Elem 324, Sec 68. US—2. Fac 47. M 14; F 33. US 1. Nat. Tui $300 (+$120). Est 1980. Nonprofit. Sem (Aug-Je). Bldg. Lib 60000 vols. Pool. Crts. Field. This school offers a Spanish curriculum in grades 1 through 12, and an English curriculum in grades 1-8. A variety of extracurricular activities are available.

Bogota 2 — THE ENGLISH SCHOOL. Calle 170 No. 31-98 Apartado Aereo 5126-71. Tel. 54-13-18. Day Coed 4¹/₂-18. Gr N-12. Frank O'Reilly, Head. Gen Acad. Tests—IB GCE SSAT. Curr—Nat. LI—Eng Span. Enr 670. B 340; G 330. Fac 54. M 24; F 30. US 2. UK Nat. Tui $80-160/mo. Schol. Est 1962. Quar (Sept-Je). ISS.

Cali — COLEGIO COLOMBO BRITANICO. Apartado Aereo 5774. Tel. 39-30-11. Day Coed 4-18. Gr N-12. Jack P. Cushnan, Head. Col Prep Gen Acad. Tests IB GCE. Curr—Nat. LI—Eng Span. A—Sci Math Philos. SI—Rem & Dev Read. Enr 860. B 420; G 440.

Grad '84—28. Col—26. Fac 70. US 8. Nat UK. Tui Col $1000-1500. Est 1956. Nonprofit. Tri (Sept-Je). Lib 12,000 vols. Athletic facilities.

Valledupar (Cesar) — **FUNDACION COLEGIO BILINGUE.** Apartado Aereo 129. Tel. 20314. Day Coed 4-18. Gr N-12. David J. Barry, MA, Northern Michigan Univ., Dir. Col Prep. Curr—Nat. LI—Eng Span. CF—Fr Relig. Enr 374. Elem 264, Sec 110. US—5. Fac 32. Full 29/Part 3. M 8; F 24. US 9. Nat. Est 1979. Inc 1980 nonprofit. Sem (Aug-Je). ACCAS.

ECUADOR

Guayaquil — **INTER-AMERICAN ACADEMY.** P.O. Box 209 U. Tel. 388072. Day Coed. Gr N-12. Curr—USA. LI—Eng. CF—Span Art Music ESL. Brent Hudson, Dir. Enr 182. Fac 23. US 18. Tui $2250. Est 1979. Sem (Aug-May). AASSA A/OS ISS. Accred SACS.

Quito (Pichincha) — **CARDINAL SPELLMAN GIRLS' SCHOOL.** Mercadillo-442—P.O. Box 125A. Tel. 237-020. Day Girls 5-18. Gr K-12. Sr. Lola Silva, BSc, Central Univ. of Ecuador, Prin. Col Prep Gen Acad Bus. Curr—Nat. LI—Eng Span. Enr 1478. Fac 88. Tui $1000 (+$500). Est 1959. Nonprofit. Roman Catholic. Quar (Oct-July). ISS. College preparatory and secretarial courses are taught.

Quito — **COLEGIO EXPERIMENTAL ALBERTO EINSTEIN.** P.O. Box 5018. Tel. 539-695. Day Coed 4-18. Gr N-12. Benjamin Tobar, MA, Dir. Gen Acad. Tests SSAT. Curr—Nat. LI—Span. CF—Fr Hebrew. Sl—Tut. Enr 409. Elem 300, Sec 109. Grad '84—20. Col—18. Fac 52. Full 23/Part 29. US 12. Nat. Est 1973. Tri (Oct-July). ISS.

PARAGUAY

Asuncion — **COLEGIO INTERNACIONAL.** Rio de Janeiro y Mujer en la Conquista. Tel. 200-575. Day Coed 5-18. Gr N-12. Mail to: Casilla de Correo 241, Asuncion, Paraguay. George E. Wiley Jr., BA, Univ. of Texas, Dir. Col Prep Gen Acad. Curr—Nat. LI—Span. CF—Eng Hist Philos Nat Sci Psych. Enr 1615. Fac 111. Tui $640 (+$60). Schol. Est 1920. Nonprofit. Disciples of Christ. Sem (March-Nov). Bldgs 6. Lib 10,200 vols. Swimming pool. Field.

PERU

Lima 22 San Isidro — **COLEGIO PARTICULAR MIXTO "PERUANO-BRITANICO".** Los Eucaliptos 455-491. ISS.

Lima 100 — COLEGIO SANTA MARIA. La Florests 250; Apartado 4055. Tel. 35-63-43. Day Boys 9-17. Gr 5-11. Br. Fred Fink SM, BS, Univ. of Dayton, Dir. Col Prep. Curr—Nat. Ll—Span. Enr 1266. Elem 540, Sec 726. US—5. Grad '84—160. Col—128. Fac 58. Full 41/Part 17. M 46; F 12. US 4. Nat. Tui $500 (+ $150). Est l939. Nonprofit. Quar (March-Dec). Bldgs 7. Lib 5000 vols. Gym. Crts. Fields. In this school's Peruvian curriculum, some classes are bilingual.

Lima (Miraflores) — MARKHAM COLLEGE. Augusto Angulo 291 San Antonio. Tel. 460039. Day Boys 5-18. Gr K-11. R. C. Pinchbeck, OBE, BS, Durham College, Prin. Pre-Prep Col Prep. Tests GCE. Curr—UK Nat. Ll—Eng Span. F—Fr Sci Math. Sl—Tut. Est 1946. Nonprofit. Sem (Mar-Dec). ISS.

Lima 27 — PERUVIAN NORTH AMERICAN SCHOOL ABRAHAM LINCOLN. Los Libertadores, 490 San Isidro. Tel. 224053. Day Coed 5-18. Gr K-12. Pilar Rodriguez de Hildalgo, Prin. Col Prep Gen Acad. Tests GCE. Curr—USA Nat. Ll—Span. CF—Lit Peruvian Hist & Geog Psych Philos Pol Econ Civics Relig Music Handcrafts. Enr 1138. Fac 78. Est 1950. Inc nonprofit. Sem (April-Dec). ISS. Bldgs 43. Lib 10,500 vols. Fields 4.

SURINAM

Paramaribo — AMERICAN COOPERATIVE SCHOOL. Box 1810. Day Coed 5-14. Gr K-8. Mail to: P.O. Box 560343, Kendall Branch, Miami, FL 33156. Tel. 99806. James F. Holton, MA, Eastern Oregon College, Prin. Pre-Prep. Curr—USA. Ll—Eng. CF—Lang Arts Sci Math Soc Stud. Est 1964. (Aug-May). ISS.

TRINIDAD AND TOBAGO

Maraval (Port of Spain) — ST. ANDREW'S SCHOOL. 16 Valleton Ave. Day Coed 4-14. Gr K-8. Helen Acanne, BA, Univ. of Windsor, Prin. Pre-Prep. Curr—Nat. Ll—Eng. CF—Fr Span Math Sci Soc Stud. Sl—Rem & Dev Read Tut. Enr 325. B 175; G 150. Fac 20. Full 19/Part 1. F 20. Nat. Tui $3200. Est l946. Tri (Sept-Je). ISS. Lib 4000 vols.

Port of Spain — AMOCO GALEOTA SCHOOL. P.O. Box 714. Day Coed 5-15. Gr K-8. Miles M. Mason, BA, Univ. of California, Prin. Curr—USA. Ll—Eng. Est 1972. Nonprofit. Quar (Sept-Je). ISS.

URUGUAY

Montevideo — CRANDON INSTITUTE. Casilla Correo 445. Tel. 4061 21. Day Coed 4-21. Gr N-PG. Maria E. Martorano de Ubillos, Prin. Gen Acad. Curr—Nat. LI—Eng Span. CF—Fr Ital Span ESL. Est 1879. Inc nonprofit. Tri (Mar-Dec). ISS.

VENEZUELA

Anaco — ESCUELA ANACO. Apartado 31. Tel. 082-22683. Day Coed 4-15. Gr N-9. Doris Smith, PhD, Univ. of Southern Mississippi, Dir. Gen Acad. Tests SSAT. Curr—USA. LI—Eng. CF—Span Lang Arts Soc Sci Typ Photog. SI—ESL Rem Reading. Est 1957. Inc 1963 nonprofit. Sem (Aug-May). ISS. Accred SACS.

CANADA

ALBERTA

Edmonton (Alberta) T5J 0S3 — ALBERTA COLLEGE. 10041-101st St. Tel. (403)428-1851. Day Coed 16 and up. Gr 10-12. S.G. McCurdy, Pres. Gen Acad Bus Tech. Curr—Nat. LI—Eng. Enr 1200. Fac 40. Nat. Tui $70/crse. Est 1903.

Fairview (Alberta) — FAIRVIEW COLLEGE. Box 3000. Tel. (403) 835-2213. Coed 16 & Up. Gr 12-PG. Dr. Fred J. Speckeen, Pres. Agricultural Technical Voc. LI—Eng. CF—Agriculture Bus Veterinary Medicine. SI—Rem & Dev Math & Read. Enr 750. Fac 87. Full 65/Part 22. Nat. Tui Bdg $3455 (+ $200); Day $600 (+ $200). Schol. Est 1951. Nonprofit. Sem (Sept-May). Bldgs 15. Dorms 9. Lib 26,000 vols. Gym. Fields.

Three Hills AB (Alberta) — PRAIRIE HIGH SCHOOL. c/o Prairie Bible Institute. Tel. (403) 443-5511. Bdg & Day Coed 14-21. Gr 10-12. Rick Down, BPE, Univ of British Columbia, MA, Simon Frazer Univ., Prin. Col Prep Gen Acad. Tests SSAT. Curr—Nat. LI—Eng. CF—Bible Fr Ger Comp Home Econ Industrial Ed. SI—Rem & Dev Math & Read. Enr 238. B 55/31; G 80/72. US—10. Grad '84—80. Col—62. Fac 20. Full 14/Part 6. M 15; F 5. US 7. Nat. Tui Bdg $2970; Day$1470. Est 1942. Inc 1938 nonprofit. Sem (Sept-Je). Bldgs 2. Dorms 2. Lib 3800 vols. Gym.

BRITISH COLUMBIA

Burnaby (British Columbia) — DORSET COLLEGE. 250 Willingdon Ave. Tel. 291-8686. Day Coed 16 & up. Gr 9-12. S.E. Lawrey, BA, BEd, MA, Univ. of British Columbia, Prin. Col Prep. Tests TOEFL. Curr—UK. Ll—Eng. A—Math. CF—Sci Soc Sci Comp. Sl—Rem & Dev Read Tut ESL. Enr 215. B 120; G 95. Grad '84—75. Col—71. Fac 15. Full 3/Part 12. M 3; F 12. Nat. Tui $3500 (+$6000). Schol. Est 1980. Inc 1981 nonprofit. Tri. Bldg. Lib 3000 vols. Gym. Field. Dorset's English as a Second Language program prepares foreign students for North American universities. Most students come from Hong Kong, Japan, Malaysia and China.

Nelson (British Columbia) — ST. JOSEPH SCHOOL. 523 Mill St. Tel. (604) 352-3041. Day Coed 5-13. Gr K-7. Sr. Emilia Sosnowski, CSJP, BEd, Univ. of Washington, Prin. Gen Acad. Curr—Nat. Ll—Eng. CF—Fr. Sl—Rem Math & Read. Enr 174. B 89; G 85. Fac 12. Full 8/Part 4. M 1; F 11. Nat. Tui $30/mo. Est 1899. Nonprofit. Roman Catholic. Sem (Sept-Je).

Prince Rupert (British Columbia) — ANNUNCIATION SCHOOL. 627 5th Ave. West. Tel. 624-5873. Day Coed 5-13. Gr K-7. Sr. Winnifred, BA, Toronto Univ., Prin. Gen Acad. Ll—Eng. CF—Fr Relig Art Music. Sl—Rem & Dev Math & Read. Tui $36-70/mo (+$100/yr). Roman Catholic. Tri (Sept-Je). Bldgs 2. Lib 5000 vols. Gym.

Vancouver (British Columbia) V6J 2V6 — YORK HOUSE SCHOOL. 1500 West King Edward Ave. Tel. (604) 736-6551. Day Boys 6-12; Girls 6-18. Gr K-12. Rouviere Ritson, Head. Col Prep. Tests IB. Ll—Eng. CF—Fr Ger Span Lat Art Music. Sl—Tut. Enr 575. B 90; G 485. Elem 385, Sec 190. Grad '84—53. Col—45. Fac 53. Full 40/Part 13. M 6; F 47. US 1. Nat. Tui $1575-4050 (+$250). Schol. Est 1932. Nonprofit. Tri (Sept-Je). CAIS NAIS. Bldgs 3. Lib. Gym. Field.

MANITOBA

Winnipeg (Manitoba) R3P 0P8 — ST. PAUL'S HIGH SCHOOL. 2200 Grant Ave. Tel. 204-888-1605. Day Boys 14-18. Gr 9-12. David G. Creamer, S.J., EdD, Univ. of Toronto, Dir. Col Prep. Curr—Nat. Ll—Eng. Enr 452. Fac 28. M 25; F 3. Nat. Tui $1700 (+$150). Schol. Est l926. Nonprofit. Roman Catholic. Sem (Sept-Je).

NOVA SCOTIA

Orangedale (Nova Scotia) — CAPE BRETON SCHOOL. R.R. 1. Bdg Boys 15 and up. John Gardner, BA, Williams, MA, Univ. of Wisconsin, Dir. Col Prep Gen Acad. Ll—Eng. CF—Fr Greek Hist (US) Econ Pol Sci Man Arts. Sl—Rem & Dev Read Tut. Est 1971.

ONTARIO

Agincourt (Ontario) M1T 1C1 — WISHING WELL MONTESSORI SCHOOL. St. John's Campus, 2 Nobert Rd. Tel. (416) 498-0331. Day Coed 3-9. Gr N-6. Sybil Pereira, Dir. Ll—Eng. CF—Fr. Tui $150-250/mo (+ $100). Est 1977. Inc 1979. Tri (Sept-Je). The three Wishing Well schools in Agincourt and Scarborough employ the Montessori method of teaching.

Burlington (Ontario) L7T 1N7 — PARK AVENUE ACADEMY. 924 Park Avenue West. Tel. (416) 637-8266. Day Coed 4-14. Gr N-8. Gen Acad. Curr—Nat. Ll—Eng. CF—Fr. Sl—Rem & Dev Math & Read. Enr 186. B 96; G 90. Fac 11. Full 8/Part 3. M 2; F 9. Nat. Tui $1400. Est 1975. Inc nonprofit. Tri (Sept-Je). Bldg. 2 Libs 2000 vols. Gym.

Hamilton (Ontario) — WENTWORTH MONTESSORI SCHOOLS. 235 Bowman St. Tel. (416) 523-4548. Day Coed 6-9. Gr N-4. D. Crosskill, Dir. Gen Acad. Ll—Eng. CF—Fr. Fac 9. Full 6/Part 3. M 1; F 8. Nat. Tui $1300/half-day program. Est 1979. Inc nonprofit. This Montessori school offers half-day programs for children ages three to five and full-day programs for children ages five to nine.

London (Ontario) N6J 1Y4 — LONDON WALDORF SCHOOL. 303 Commissioners Road West. Tel. (519) 472-4180. Day Coed 3¹/₂-12. Gr N-5. Jane Hadden, Fac Dir. Gen Acad. Ll—Eng. CF—Fr Ger. Enr 63. B 37; G 26. Fac 9. Full 5/Part 4. M 4; F 5. US UK Nat. Tui $2350 (+ $85). Schol. Est 1980. Inc nonprofit. Tri (Sept-Je). Based on the educational principles of Dr. Rudolph Steiner, this school approaches reading, writing, math, science and crafts through the arts.

London (Ontario) N6A 3N1 — ST. PETER SCHOOL. 533 Clarence St. Tel. (519) 439-9771. Day Coed 16-25. Gr 12-PG. J. George Samuelson, BA, BEd, Univ. of Alberta, Prin. Col Prep. Tests TOEFL SAT. Curr—Nat. Ll—Eng. A—Biol Chem Account Econ Eng Geog Hist Math Physics Span Fr. Enr 100. B 60; G 40. Grad '84—60. Col—52. Fac 10. Full 5/Part 5. M 5; F 5. Nat. Tui $3650 (+ $7000). Schol. Est 1981. Inc nonprofit. Tri (Sept-Aug). The curriculum at this school prepares non-English speakers for study in

Canadian universities. School authorities will assist with housing arrangements in private homes or rooming houses.

Meaford (Ontario) N0H 1Y0 — THE MEAFORD INSTITUTE. Box 1912. Tel. (519) 538-4021. Bdg & Day Coed 14-20. Gr 9-PG. S.D. Sharma, Dir. Gen Acad. Ll—Eng. CF—Fr Comp Sci Engineering Math. Sl—Rem & Dev Math & Read Tut. Enr 7. Sec 5, PG 2. Grad '84—3. Col—3. Fac 2. Full 1/Part 1. M 2. Tui Bdg $6000 (+$1200); Day $3180 (+$1200). Est 1983. Inc. Quar. Bldg. Dorm. Lib 500 vols. Crts. Gym.

Oshawa (Ontario) L1H 7MG — KINGSWAY COLLEGE. 1156 King St. Tel. (416) 433-1144. Bdg & Day Coed 14-19. Gr 9-12. Ralph R. Jones, MA, Andrews Univ., Pres. Col Prep. Curr—Nat. Ll—Eng. CF—Relig Arts Sci. Sl—Rem & Dev Read. Enr 290. US—10. Grad '84—120. Col—75. Fac 35. Full 30/Part 5. M 19; F 16. US 8. Tui Bdg $5550 (+$200); Day $3000 (+$170). Est 1903. Seventh Day Adventists. Sem (Aug-Je). Bldgs 9. Dorms 2. Lib 6000 vols. Gym. Crts. Field.

Ottawa (Ontario) — OTTAWA WALDORF SCHOOL. Box 708, R.R. 5. Tel. (613) 822-0772. Day Coed 4-10. Gr N-5. Philip Bowron, Fac Dir. Gen Acad. Ll—Eng. CF—Fr Ger Math Hist Sci Crafts. Sl—Rem & Dev Math & Read Tut. Enr 70. B 40; G 30. Fac 8. Full 4/Part 4. M 2; F 6. Nat. Tui $2200. Schol. Est 1979. Inc nonprofit. Tri (Sept-Je).

Peterborough (Ontario) — ST. PETER'S HIGH SCHOOL. 431 Reid St. Day Coed 14-19. Gr 9-12. C.A. Bruder, MEd, Univ. of Toronto, Prin. Gen Acad. Curr—Nat. Ll—Eng. A—Fr Hist Math Sci. CF—Bus Art. Sl—Rem & Dev Math & Read. Enr 839. B 470; G 369. Grad '84—74. Col—70. Fac 41. Full 40/Part 1. M 26; F 15. US 2. Nat. Tui $750 (+$500). Est 1905. Inc 1913 nonprofit. Sem (Aug-Je). Bldgs 3. Lib 4500 vols. Gym. Field.

South Thorold (Ontario) — THE PENINSULA COLLEGE OF NIAGARA. 47 Morton St. Tel. (461) 227-0864. Day Coed 12-18. Gr 7-12. Douglas M. Swallow, MA, PhD, McMaster, Head. Col Prep. Curr—Nat. Ll—Eng. A—Chem Physics Biol Math Hist Geog Account Econ. CF—Bus Music Fr. Sl—Rem & Dev Math & Read Tut. Enr 60. B 30; G 30. Grad '84—10. Col—10. Fac 7. Full 4/Part 3. M 5; F 2. Nat. Tui $4000. Est 1983. Inc. Sem (Sept-Je). Bldg. Lib 15,000 vols. This school's program accommodates average students as well as academic underachievers by emphasizing basic studies and individual attention.

Stroud (Ontario) L0L 2M0 — INNISFREE VALLEY COLLEGE. R.R. 2. Day Coed 14-19. Gr 9-12. Dieter Urban, Prin. Gen Acad. CF—Fr Ger Span Lat Hist Geog. Enr 30. US—2. Fac 4. Full 4. M 2; F 2. US 2. Est 1978. Bldg. Lib 2000 vols.

Toronto (Ontario) M8Z 4E1 — CAMBRIDGE INTERNATIONAL COLLEGE OF CANADA. 35 Ourland Ave. Tel. 416-252-9195. Day Coed 16-24. Gr 11-PG. Irwin Diamond, BA, Toronto Univ., BEd, York Univ., Prin. Col Prep. Curr—Nat. LI—Eng. A—Eng Math Sci Account Econ Geog Soc. CF—Comp Arts. SI—Rem & Dev Math Tut ESL. Enr 120. B 70; G 50. Grad '84—66. Col—65. Fac 10. Full 10. M 6; F 4. US 1. Nat. Tui $3100 (+ $300). Est 1979. Inc 1980 nonprofit. Sem (Sept-May). Bldg. Lib 10,000 vols. Gym. Crts. Fields. Students who complete this program will be proficient in English and will receive the Ontario Secondary Schools Honours Graduation Diploma.

Toronto (Ontario) M4V 2T5 — CANTAB COLLEGE. 287 Russell Hill Rd. Tel. (416) 922-8318. Day Coed 16 & up. Gr 12-PG. A.T.P. Wong, MSc, PhD, Univ. of Toronto, Prin. Col Prep. Curr—Nat. LI—Eng. A—Math Physics Chem Biol Geog Econ Account Soc. CF—Environmental Sci Comp Film Arts. SI—ESL. Enr 100. B 60; G 40. Grad '84—95. Col—90. Fac 7. Full 5/Part 2. M 4; F 3. Nat. Tui $3000. Est 1934. Tri (Sept-Je). This one to two year program prepares students for entrance into Canadian universities.

Toronto M5R 3B5 Ontario — ST. GEORGE'S COLLEGE. 120 Howland Ave. Tel. 416-533-9481. Day Boys 9-18. Gr 4-13. John D. Allen, Head. Enr 394. Fac 30. Full 25/Part 5. Tui $2650-3000 (+ $55-65). Est 1961.

Whitby L1N 3W9 Ontario — TRAFALGAR CASTLE SCHOOL. 401 Reynolds St. Tel. 416-668-3358. Bdg & Day Girls 12-19. Gr 7-13. Craig Kamcke, Prin. Col Prep. Curr—Nat. LI—Eng. CF—ESL Fr Lat. SI—Tut Rem & Dev Math Reading. Est 1864. Inc nonprofit. Tri (Sept-Je). CAIS.

Willowdale M2L 1A2 Ontario — CRESCENT SCHOOL. 2365 Bayview Ave. Tel. 416-449-2556. Day Boys 9-18. Gr 5-13. Christopher B. Gordon, Head. Col Prep. Tests CEEB SSAT. Curr—Nat. LI—Eng. CF—Fr Lat Sci Math Comp Sci. Est 1913. Inc 1933 nonprofit. Tri (Sept-Je). CAIS NAIS.

Windsor N9C 2K7 Ontario — ASSUMPTION HIGH SCHOOL. 1100 Huron Church Rd. Tel. (519)-256-1813. Bdg Boys 14-19. Gr 9-PG. Lawrence Finke, CSB, BA, Univ. of Windsor, MDiv, St. Michael's College, Dean. Col Prep. Tests CEEB SSAT. Curr—Nat USA. LI—Eng CF—Fr Span Ital Lat Sci Math Hist Music Comp Geog. SI—Tut. Enr 1836. B 136/900; G /800. US—65. Grad '84—36.

Col—30. Fac 94. Full 90/Part 4. M 52; F 42. US 3. Nat. Tui $3300 (+ $400). Est 1856. Inc nonprofit. Sem (Sept-Je). Roman Catholic. Bldgs 5. Dorms 1. Lib 3500 vols. This school, located 15 minutes from Detroit, Michigan, accommodates only Windsor residents in its day program.

QUEBEC

Dorval-Montreal (Quebec) H9P 1X5 — EMMANUEL CHRISTIAN SCHOOL. 1925 Brookdale Ave. Tel. (514) 631-2555. Day Coed 5-17. Gr K-11. C. Neville Bevington, MA, Univ. of Vermont, Head. Gen Acad. Tests SSAT. Curr—Nat. Ll—Eng. A—Chem Math Physics Comp Fr Music. CF—Arts Bible. Enr 240. B 116; G 124. Elem 180, Sec 60. US—3. Grad '84—15. Col—12. Fac 18. Full 12/Part 6. M 5; F 13. US 2. Nat. Tui $2850 (+ $150). est 1975. Inc 1974 nonprofit. Tri (Sept-Je). Bldg. Lib 3000 vols. Gym. Field. This school offers a completely bilingual (English-French) primary program, and some bilingual courses in the upper grades.

Montebello J0V 1L0 Quebec — SEDBERGH SCHOOL. Tel. 819-423-5523. Bdg Boys 8-17. Gr 3-11. Thomas L. Wood, BS, McGill, Head. Col Prep Gen Acad. Curr—Nat. Ll—Eng. CF—Fr Math Hist Art Comp Geog Music. Sl—Rem & Dev Math & Read Tut. Enr 90. Elem 61, Sec 29. US—3. Grad '84—10. Col—10. Fac 15. Full 11/Part 4. M 9; F 6. Nat. Tui $9800 (+ $1000). Est 1939. Inc 1970 nonprofit. Quar (Sept-Je). CAIS. Bldg. Dorms 16. Lib 20,000 vols. Sedbergh's curriculum is complemented by a varied outdoor sports program.

Montreal H4A 3H6 Quebec — CENTENNIAL ACADEMY. 3641 Prudhomme Ave. Tel. 481-7672. Day Coed 12-20. Gr 7-PG. Col Prep Gen Acad. Curr—Nat. Ll—Eng. Est 1966. CAIS.

SASKATCHEWAN

Regina (Saskatchewan) S4T 5A5 — LUTHER COLLEGE. 1500 Royal St. Tel. (306) 352-2101. Bdg & Day Coed 13-19. Gr 9-12. Morris A. Anderson, BA, Univ. of Saskatchewan, MA, Univ. of Oregon, Pres. Gen Acad. Curr—Nat. Ll—Eng. CF—Fr Ger Lat Sci Arts. Sl—Rem & Dev Math & Read Tut. Enr 412. G 125/287. Grad '84—110. Col—80. Fac 20. Full 19/Part 1. M 14; F 6. US 1. Nat. Tui Bdg $4925 (+ $200); Day $1290 (+ $200). Schol. Est 1913. Inc 1926 nonprofit. Sem (Sept-Je). Bldg. Dorms 2. Lib. Gym. Crts. Fields. This church-sponsored school offers a basic high school curriculum and is affiliated with the University of Regina.

Wilcox S0G 5E0 Saskatchewan — ATHOL MURRAY COLLEGE OF NOTRE DAME. Box 220. Tel. 306-732-2080. Bdg & Day Coed 14-19. Gr 9-PG. Enr 278. NAIS.

INDEX OF
SCHOOLS ABROAD

INDEX

Boldface numbers refer to Illustrated Announcement pages

Publisher's Statement:

Since 1914 the Porter Sargent Staff has been compiling and publishing guides for educators, parents, and all concerned with the direction and development of a climate of growth that may lead to man's more hopeful future. **The Handbook Series** provides reference works to guide in the appropriate choice of educational steps for each child's individual needs. **The Special Education** Series presents the definitive directory for special education as well as readings by foremost specialists. **The Extending Horizons Books Series** deals with contemporary concerns, social directions, and perspectives.

GUIDE TO SUMMER CAMPS AND SUMMER SCHOOLS

Over 1100 summer camping, recreational, travel, pioneering, and academic programs are described and compared in this objective, authoritative guide book. Listings are concisely arranged by type, specialty, and individual features. Data includes location and enrollment, director's winter address, fees, length of camping period and other pertinent information.

Special programs for the handicapped and maladjusted, as well as for those with learning disabilities, are included. The geographic range covers recreational programs in the U.S. and Canada, and travel programs throughout the U.S., Canada, Mexico and abroad.

This edition indicates that adventurous mountain climbing and wilderness survival programs as well as specialized sports camps have increased in popularity.

Designed as a comparative reference source for all types of enjoyable and educational Summer opportunities, this guide is for the counselor or parent concerned with meeting the unique needs of young individuals.

464 pp., cloth, $23.00, paper, $18.00

Available directly from

PORTER SARGENT PUBLISHERS, INC.

11 Beacon St., Boston, MA 02108